Rodewald

Bound for Santa Fe

Bound for Santa Fe

The Road to New Mexico and
the American Conquest, 1806–1848

Stephen G. Hyslop

UNIVERSITY OF OKLAHOMA PRESS : NORMAN

Library of Congress Cataloging-in-Publication Data

Hyslop, Stephen G. (Stephen Garrison), 1950–
     Bound for Santa Fe: the road to New Mexico and the American
conquest, 1806–1848 / Stephen G. Hyslop.
          p.   cm.
     Includes bibliographical references and index.
     ISBN 0-8061-3389-9 (hc: alk. paper)
     1. Santa Fe National Historic Trail—History. 2. Southwest, New—
Description and travel.   3. Frontier and pioneer life—Southwest, New.
4. Southwest, New—History—To 1848.   5. Southwest, New—
Commerce—History—19th century.   6. New Mexico—History—
To 1848.   7. United States—Territorial expansion.   8. Pioneers—Santa
Fe National Historic Trail—Biography.   9. Mexicans—Santa Fe National
Historic Trail—Biography.   10. Indians of North America—Santa Fe
National Historic Trail—History—19th century.   I. Title.

F800 .H97 2002
978—dc21

                                                          2001052268

Grateful acknowledgment is made to Yale University Press for permission to
quote from *Down the Santa Fe Trail and into Mexico: The Diary of Susan
Shelby Magoffin, 1846–1847,* edited by Stella M. Drum. Copyright © 1926,
by Yale University Press.

1   2   3   4   5   6   7   8   9   10

Contents

Illustrations

Preface

This book draws on travelers' accounts to follow the course of the Santa Fe Trail geographically, from Missouri to New Mexico, and historically, from the early nineteenth century through the Mexican War, when this avenue of economic and cultural exchange became a path of conquest. Most of the available testimony comes from travelers from the United States, thus giving this book a distinctly American perspective, as reflected in its title, *Bound for Santa Fe*. Mexicans who traveled the trail—and there were many who did so during this period as traders or employees—were more likely to consider the journey east to Missouri as the outgoing portion of their trip and to think of themselves as bound for Independence or St. Louis. To represent their side of the story, I have included entries from several narratives by Mexicans relating to the Santa Fe trade and to conditions in New Mexico as that trade developed. Beyond that, I have paid considerable attention to the ways in which ventures described by American witnesses affected Mexicans and the many tribal peoples encountered along the trail.

The very terms used here to describe the groups involved in the international exchange known as the Santa Fe trade reflect the views of Americans—a title that people from the United States have taken as their own but one to which others have an equally strong claim. Mexicans have long spoken of their northern neighbors as *norteamericanos*, a reminder that those to the south have a distinct American identity. And the various western tribal groups that remained beyond the bounds of the United States during the period covered here also deserve recognition as Americans by virtue of their ancient ties to their homelands on this continent. Such questions of terminology are not new to those writing about the West and its competing cultures. In 1857, Philip St. George Cooke, whose travels along the Santa Fe Trail as an army officer made him keenly aware of how many groups laid claim to some part of the region, described the Pueblo peoples of New Mexico as "native Americans" and asked incisively: " 'Americans.' Can that name continue to distinguish the citizens of the United States?"[1]

Distinctions must be made, however, and my approach here is simply to apply to the parties in question the names by which they were commonly known in English at the time. People from the United States were described then as now as Americans. Those from the colony of New Spain were recognized as Spanish until they achieved independence in 1821 and became Mexicans (albeit with a lasting attachment to their Spanish heritage). Tribes along the trail sometimes formed alliances with Mexicans, Americans, or other tribes but were properly regarded as distinct nations or peoples. Wherever possible, I have identified them by tribe, but early travelers on the trail were not always able to tell one group from another and often resorted, as I must here at times, to that admittedly inadequate generalization "Indian."

Included in this work are hundreds of entries from published accounts, woven together with extensive commentary to form a narrative designed to be accessible both to those familiar with the terrain and to those exploring it for the first time. Altogether, more than eighty travelers are represented here through their writings. Of that number, a dozen or so rank as featured witnesses (introduced in chapter 4), including Josiah Gregg, Matthew C. Field, Susan Shelby Magoffin, Lewis H. Garrard, and others whose perceptive narratives have earned well-deserved recognition in recent times. My aim here is not to summarize or condense those classic accounts but to provide readers with a larger context in which to understand them by supplementing some of their most revealing passages with entries from scores of lesser-known works.

In selecting narratives for inclusion here and in commenting on them, I have taken into consideration not just their value as historical documents but their significance as historical literature, by which I mean all works with any factual basis composed by those who ventured down the trail and interpreted the experience in writing, fairly or otherwise. A number of the entries here might be challenged as historical evidence on the grounds that they were committed to writing long after the events they describe, were distorted by the biases of their narrators, or were refined by writers or editors with the aim of producing a tale that was perhaps more appealing than accurate. But even some accounts containing fanciful elements warrant inclusion here for what they tell us about the attitudes and assumptions of Americans and the ways in which they reckoned imaginatively with competing cultures. To provide historical perspective, I have identified those authors who may have strayed significantly beyond the bounds of what they knew to be true and drawn attention to some of the more conspicuous errors or misconceptions in otherwise dependable accounts. For the most part, however, I have let my sources have their say without putting their every assertion to the test. Most of the testimony here is reliable, and all of it is instructive. Taken together, these narratives form an impressive body of historical literature, with recurring themes bearing on that complex process by which Americans came to terms with the Spanish Southwest and the tribes of the intervening plains. At heart, this is the story of a diverse trade that went far beyond commercial bargaining and involved give-and-take of a personal, cultural, and sometimes combative nature. Over time, those sundry exchanges transformed both the land at the far end of the trail and the expansive nation which assumed that territory and its various assets and obligations.

This book consists of three parts. The first surveys the ground historically up through the Mexican War and explores thematically the many forms of exchange by which competing parties along the trail sought to resolve or exploit their differences. More than an introduction to the subject, these opening chapters serve as a guide for the journey that follows by charting the origins, evolution, and consequences of the Santa Fe trade through the words of those who anticipated, pioneered, and pursued that venture, beginning with Lieutenant Zebulon Montgomery Pike, whose reconnaissance in 1806 and 1807 set the tone for the American encounter with New Mexico. Those who followed in Pike's wake in the decades to come were not just soldiers or merchants. One distinctive aspect of the Santa Fe Trail—often referred to as a road in the early days—was its allure for literary adventurers who sought to capitalize on the growing interest among readers back home in the exotic attractions of New Mexico and the rigors of the journey there. Even travelers who kept their eloquent reflections to themselves and whose accounts were not published until after their deaths made important contributions to this revealing literary exchange, by which Americans came to grips with a region that remained essentially Spanish long after the hostile takeover of 1846.

The second and largest part of this book surveys the ground geographically by drawing on accounts of journeys made over a quarter of a century— between the inauguration of the Santa Fe trade in 1821 and the onset of the Mexican War—to portray the venture as travelers experienced it, including the preparations they made in Missouri, their trek across the plains and their dealings with tribal peoples, and their interactions with Mexicans, principally in Santa Fe and Taos, but also along the road south to Chihuahua, which served merchants as a profitable extension of the Santa Fe Trail. For the most part here, I have organized entries within each chapter in roughly chronological order, but the sequence of events is less important than the setting. In a few places I have included entries describing journeys that occurred in 1846 after the outbreak of the Mexican War but bore little or no relation to that conflict. Lewis Garrard's peaceful interlude in and around Bent's Fort in the fall of 1846, for example, belongs in spirit to the prewar section of this volume, while his description of battle-torn Taos in early 1847 has its rightful place in the history of the ensuing conflict. Susan Shelby Magoffin's enlightening journey in 1846 and 1847, by contrast, followed the path of the army so closely that her diary entries are reserved entirely for the wartime chapters.

This work concludes with the fateful episode that made the Santa Fe Trail a vital conduit for America's larger historical ambitions—the occupation of New Mexico by troops who followed the path from Missouri to Santa Fe in the summer of 1846 and continued on down the road to Chihuahua that winter. As underscored by Jack D. Rittenhouse in the introduction to his indispensable reference work *The Santa Fe Trail: A Historical Bibliography*, this route was a "Trail of Commerce and Conquest."[2] No work that aims as this one does to explore the trail's significance as an avenue of exchange in the broadest sense—including both peaceful and violent transactions—can afford to pass over this confrontation lightly. Furthermore, no other episode in the annals of the road to New Mexico generated such a wealth of testimony from so many gifted observers. Any attempt to survey and interpret the remarkable literature of the trail must deal at some length with this troubling conflict, which served Americans as a kind of baptism in the murky waters of Manifest Destiny.

The volatile exchanges that unfolded along the Santa Fe and Chihuahua Trails during the Mexican War were in many ways an extension of what came before. Despite the bitterness and bloodshed that resulted when American forces embarked on separate campaigns to occupy the city of Chihuahua and put down a revolt by Mexicans and Pueblos at Taos and surrounding communities, the opposing sides continued to bargain fitfully with each other. Far from marking a radical departure from the pattern set earlier, this wartime intercourse simply accentuated the contrasts evident from the start in the relations between Americans and the rival parties they encountered along the road—dealings that ranged from swapping goods and courtesies to exchanging blows.

A work such as this leans heavily on its sources, including not simply the perceptive witnesses who composed the narratives featured here but also the discerning historians and editors who collected their work and prepared it for publication. (The entries on the following pages conform to those sources in all essentials, and no attempt has been made to regularize spelling or punctuation; words that appear within brackets were inserted for clarity by the editors cited.) I would like to thank the following authors, editors, and publishers for allowing me to quote at length from their editions: Mark L. Gardner, Jack B. Tykal, David J. Weber, David A. White, the Arthur H. Clark Company, El Rancho de las Golondrinas, the Missouri Historical Society, the University of New Mexico Press, the University of Oklahoma Press, and Yale University Press. I would also like to thank all those at the following libraries and research centers who helped me obtain the books, images, and insights that went into the making of this book: the Library of Congress in Washington, D.C.; the Library of the Jefferson National Parks Association in the Old Courthouse in St. Louis; the Missouri Historical Society in St. Louis; the State Historical Society of Missouri in Columbia; the Santa Fe Trail Center in Larned, Kansas; the Museum of New Mexico at the Palace of the Governors in Santa Fe; and the New Mexico State Records and Archives in Santa Fe. I am especially grateful to Marc Simmons, Mark Gardner, Leo and Bonita Oliva, acquisitions editor Jean Hurtado, and others within the University of Oklahoma Press and beyond who took an interest in this project, read all or part of this work in manuscript form, and offered suggestions, corrections, and encouragement.

Part of the story of the Santa Fe Trail and other western paths can be read in their surviving traces and monuments. But the adventure can be recaptured in full only through the words of those who followed those roads when they were living arteries that linked the restless heart of America to the farthest extremities of the continent. That vitality endures in the journeys travelers logged, in the passages they undertook at great effort and conveyed to us graciously in writing. This interpretive collection of passages owes much to those who composed and preserved them.

Part 1

The Santa Fe Trail as an Avenue of Exchange (1806–1848)

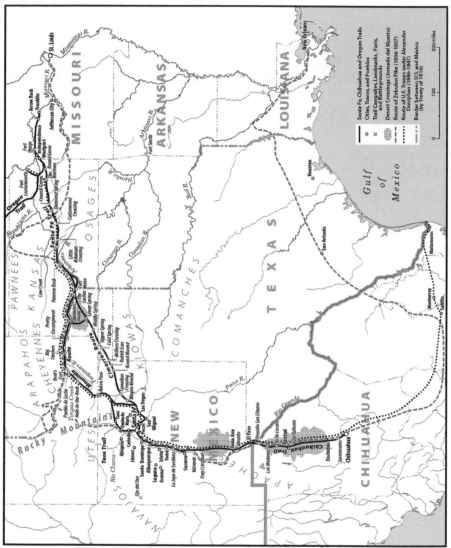

The Santa Fe and Chihuahua Trails. This map shows approximate locations of tribal groups circa 1830 (excluding settled groups such as Pueblos and Shawnees).

1

The Ambiguous Venture of Zebulon Pike (1806–1807)

In early March of 1807, Zebulon Montgomery Pike arrived under Spanish escort in Santa Fe, capital of the province of New Mexico. Unlike some future American visitors to Santa Fe, who would express dismay at the shabbiness of the town and its inhabitants, the twenty-eight-year-old Pike and his ragged contingent of scarcely a half-dozen soldiers were in no condition to complain of their surroundings, having camped in the wild for more than seven months since departing St. Louis on a grueling reconnaissance that traversed part of what would later be known as the Santa Fe Trail. Forced to carry their baggage on their backs after leaving their jaded horses behind, they had dispensed with military finery and clad themselves for survival. By Pike's own account, they looked a bit savage as they entered the plaza and approached the Palace of the Governors, surrounded by a curious throng of onlookers:

> Thus, when we presented ourselves at Santa Fe; I was dressed in a pair of blue trowsers, mockinsons, blanket coat and a cap made of scarlet cloth, lined with fox skins and my poor fellows in leggings, breech cloths and leather coats and not a hat in the whole party. This appearance was extremely mortifying to us all, especially as soldiers, and although some of the officers used frequently to observe to me, that "worth made the man," &c. with a variety of adages to the same amount. Yet the first impression made on the ignorant is hard to eradicate; and a greater proof cannot be given of the ignorance of the common people, than their asking if we lived in houses or camps like the indians,

or if we wore hats in our country; those observations are sufficient to shew the impression our uncouth appearance made amongst them.[1]

Pike's embarrassment was perhaps increased by an awareness that these New Mexicans, however poor they might be, had a sharp eye for the distinctions of dress—a fact that did much to boost the Santa Fe trade in years to come. To make matters worse, Pike was about to meet with the grandest figure in the province, Governor Joaquín del Real Alencaster, who had sent troops to find Pike and his band at their stockade near the upper Rio Grande (also known to New Mexicans as the Río del Norte) and summon them to the capital, an invitation they were not at liberty to refuse. Entering the Palace, or "government house," as Pike put it—an adobe structure that did not strike him as very palatial—he and his men passed through a series of rooms with hard-packed mud floors, covered with "skins of buffalo, bear, or some other animal." At length, the governor confronted Pike and, with a few pointed questions, cut to the core of the matter that set the two men at odds. As Pike detailed the interview in his journal:

> We waited in a chamber for some time, until his excellency appeared, when we rose, and the following conversation took place in French.
>
> *Governor.* Do you speak French?
> *Pike.* Yes sir.
> *Governor.* You come to reconnoitre our country, do you?
> *Pike.* I marched to reconnoitre our own.[2]

The governor had more to ask Pike, but this was the crucial question, and one that left considerable room for disagreement. Both sides here were to some extent correct in their conflicting interpretations of Pike's mission, for the Louisiana Purchase of 1803, by which France ceded to the United States a vast area west of the Mississippi River, had left undefined the limits of that largely uncharted territory and the boundary between Spanish and American holdings. The United States claimed by right of purchase a huge expanse extending from the frontier of British Canada down through Spanish-occupied Texas. Realistically, the Americans had little hope of acquiring Texas without a fight, but they fully intended to press their claim to everything north of the Red River, and exploring that waterway up to its headwaters thus became a priority for the government. Spain, for its part, defined the area covered by the Louisiana Purchase much more narrowly, insisting that it included only a portion of what is now Missouri, Arkansas, and Louisiana and excluded Texas and the country to its north.[3] More to the point, Spain denied the validity of the American purchase, having ceded the region in question to France with the proviso that it not be transferred to a third party. It was this divisive issue that launched Lieutenant Pike—promoted to captain during the journey—on his lengthy reconnaissance. The orders he received from General James Wilkinson before embarking from St. Louis, while instructing him to avoid provoking Spanish forces, nonetheless set him on a path that risked such a confrontation. Specifically, Wilkinson instructed Pike to hold peace parleys with various western tribes, including the Osages, Kansas, Pawnees, and Comanches, an ambitious agenda that Pike could not hope to fulfill without delving deep into territory still claimed by Spain. Furthermore, Wilkinson implicitly invited Pike to explore the unmapped headwaters of two major rivers whose origins lay close to New Mexico, if not actually within that province, raising the possibility that Pike might end up trespassing on territory that lay indisputably under Spanish control:

> As your Interview with the Cammanchees will probably lead you to the Head Branches of the Arkansaw, and Red Rivers you may find yourself approximate to the settlements of New Mexico, and therefore it will be necessary you should move with great circumspection, to keep clear of any Hunting or reconnoitring parties from that province, & to prevent alarm or offence because the affairs of Spain, & the United States appear to be on the point of amicable adjustment, and more over it is the desire of the President, to cultivate the Friendship & Harmonious Intercourse, of all the Nations of the Earth, & particularly our near neighbours the Spaniards.[4]

When Pike set out with a force of fewer than two dozen men to fulfill these difficult and delicate orders—which exposed him to potential opposition but urged him to keep the peace—he inaugurated a complex exchange between the United States and the Spanish Southwest. He was not the first American to travel to the region, but the official nature of his expedition made him a pioneer, testing the limits of the American domain and taking the measure of tribal resistance on the plains and Spanish opposition in the provinces. His reconnaissance would not lead immediately to regular trade between Missouri and New Mexico, but it would establish a pattern for that traffic, which would combine "Friendship & Harmonious Intercourse" with competitive give-and-take that sometimes bordered on hostilities and ultimately crossed that line.

This American bid to stake out the contested Louisiana Territory as far west as the Rocky Mountains did not go unchallenged. As Pike launched his reconnaissance in July 1806, several hundred mounted Spanish troops under Facundo Melgares, a future governor of New Mexico, were heading northeastward from Santa Fe to search for intruding Americans on the plains and to urge Indians of the region to reserve their friendship for Spain. This further

The brave Brigadier General

ZEBULON M. PIKE,

Who gloriously fell in his Countrys cause April 27ᵗʰ 1813.

Brigadier General Zebulon Montgomery Pike, around the time of his death in 1813. Courtesy Library of Congress, Prints and Photographs Division. LC-USZ62-066482.

complicated Pike's mission, tasked as he was with inducing several formidable tribes to keep peace with each other and with the Americans. (The quixotic notion of imposing a Pax Americana on Plains Indians who as yet knew little of Americans and their ways also figured in the instructions given in 1804 by President Thomas Jefferson to Meriwether Lewis and William Clark, who met with many chiefs but failed to achieve that elusive goal.)[5]

In late September of 1806, after visiting among the Osages near the western frontier of what was soon to become the Missouri Territory and persuading some of them to accompany his reconnaissance, Pike and his men entered a Pawnee village along the Republican River near what is now the Kansas-Nebraska border to meet in council with a portion of that tribe.[6] He soon discovered that he had been preceded by a Spanish officer, Melgares, who had left several flags behind, "one of which was unfurled at the chief's door," Pike noted, prompting him to complain heatedly to his Pawnee hosts through an interpreter:

> Amongst various *demands* and *charges* I gave them, was, that the said flag should be delivered to me, and one of the United States' flags be received and hoisted in its place. This probably was carrying the pride of nations a little too far, as there had so lately been a large force of Spanish cavalry at the village, which had made a great impression on the minds of the young men, as to their power, consequence, &c. which my appearance with 20 infantry was by no means calculated to remove. After the chiefs had replied to various parts of my discourse, but were silent as to the flag, I again reiterated the demand for the flag, "adding that it was impossible for the nation to have two fathers; that they must either be the children of the Spaniards or acknowledge their American father."[7]

Considering his presumption in demanding such childlike obedience from the resolute Pawnees, Pike was perhaps fortunate that he was not challenged forcefully, as Lewis and Clark were after they made a similar attempt in 1804 to persuade Lakota Sioux along the upper Missouri that they owed allegiance to their father in Washington. Instead, a Pawnee who was old enough to be Pike's father offered the visiting soldier chief a lesson in diplomacy by sacrificing the "pride of nations" to preserve the peaceful spirit of the council ground. "After a silence of some time," Pike related, "an old man rose, went to the door, and took down the Spanish flag, and brought it and laid it at my feet, and then received the American flag and elevated it on the staff, which had lately borne the standard of his Catholic majesty."[8] This concession must have been painful for the old man and for the Pawnees as a whole, for Pike noticed a sudden darkening of their mood and responded accordingly:

> Perceiving that every face in the council was clouded with sorrow, as if some
> great national calamity was about to befal them, I took up the contested col-
> ors, and told them "that as they had now shewn themselves dutiful children
> in acknowledging their great American father, I did not wish to embarass them
> with the Spaniards, for it was the wish of the Americans that their red brethren
> should remain peaceably round their own fires, and not embroil themselves
> in any disputes between the white people: and that for fear the Spaniards might
> return there in force again, I returned them their flag, but with an injunction
> that it should never be hoisted during our stay." At this there was a general
> shout of applause and the charge particularly attended to.[9]

Thus Pike repaired some, if not all, of the diplomatic damage done by his self-
described "*demands* and *charges.*" But the applause and relief of the Pawnees
did not signal that they had been won over by the Americans in any lasting
way. Indeed, the Pawnee chief Sharitarish made it clear to Pike two days later
that he felt bound by his commitment to the Spanish and had no intention
of acting as a dutiful child of the great American father:

> Paid a visit to town, and had a very long conversation with the chief, who
> urged every thing in his power to induce us to turn back. Finally, he very can-
> didly told us that the Spaniards wished to have gone further into our coun-
> try, but he induced them to give up the idea—that they had listened to him
> and he wished us to do the same—that he had promised the Spaniards to act
> as he now did, and that we must proceed no further, or he must stop us by
> force of arms. My reply was, "that I had been sent out by our *great father* to
> explore the western country, to visit all his red children, to make peace
> between them, and turn them from shedding blood; that he might see how
> I had caused the Osage and Kans to meet to smoke the pipe of peace together,
> and take each other by the hands like brothers; that as yet my road had been
> smooth, and a blue sky over our heads. I had not seen any blood in our paths;
> but he must know that the young warriors of his *great American father were
> not women* to be turned back by *words*, that I should therefore proceed, and
> if he thought proper to stop me, he could attempt it; but we were *men*, well
> armed, and would *sell our lives* at a dear rate to his nation—that we knew our
> *great father* would send our young warriors there to gather our bones and
> revenge our *deaths* on his people—when our spirits would rejoice in hearing
> our exploits sung in the war songs of our chiefs." I then left his lodge and
> returned to camp in considerable perturbation of mind.[10]

Significantly, Pike was making this forceful point to the Pawnees in their own
terms—or at least in what he conceived to be their terms. In a rough approx-

imation of Indian rhetoric, he reminded the chief that American soldiers "*were not women*" (a phrase used by men of various tribes to demonstrate their fighting resolve) and pledged that if he and his troops came to grief, others would hasten to avenge them (an impulse that inspired many tribal raids). Pike may have antagonized the chief with his bravado, but such rhetorical give-and-take was preferable to an exchange of blows. Many Americans who traveled to New Mexico in later years would find themselves adopting the terms of the various groups they dealt with along the way, even when trading defiant words with them or making bids for their territory.

Pike and his men proceeded unhindered, bringing to an end his fitful diplomatic ventures among the Plains Indians. As he told the Pawnee chief, he had "caused the Osage and Kans to meet to smoke the pipe of peace together," a reference to a recent meeting between the Osages who had accompanied Pike and a small party of Kansas who visited the council ground. According to Wilkinson's instructions, Pike was also supposed to seek a "good understanding" with the Comanches, but the path he followed kept him well north of the Comanche heartland and no such meeting ensued. Before leaving the Pawnees, Pike and company learned from French traders that Lewis and Clark had returned safely from the Pacific Northwest with their men to St. Louis, news that "diffused general joy through our party."[11] Like Lewis and Clark, Pike was serving during the expedition as a naturalist as well as an envoy to various Indian tribes, and his journal for the days ahead included fine descriptions of the country and its creatures. Departing the Pawnee village on October 7 with fresh horses obtained in trade, he and his men traveled almost due south and reached the Great Bend of the Arkansas on the eighteenth. It was here that Pike began to follow roughly the route that would later be called the Santa Fe Trail, although the path he took west along the Arkansas had been used by venturesome Indians and Europeans long before Pike or the Santa Fe traders entered the scene.

At the Great Bend, Pike's party built canoes that would carry several men under Lieutenant James B. Wilkinson, the general's son, down the Arkansas River while the remainder prepared to follow Pike up the Arkansas to its headwaters. Before continuing on, he took the opportunity to observe and describe a prairie dog colony, and his was among the first accounts of the species to appear in print:

> Their villages sometimes extend over two and three miles square, in which there must be innumerable hosts of them, as there is generally a burrow every ten steps in which there are two or more, and you see new ones partly excavated on all the borders of the town. We killed great numbers of them with

our rifles and found them excellent meat, after they were exposed a night or two to the frost, by which means the rankness acquired by their subteranneous dwelling is corrected. As you approach their towns, you are saluted on all sides by the cry of Wishtonwish, from which they derive their name with the Indians, uttered in a shrill and piercing manner. You then observe them all retreating to the entrance of their burrows, where they post themselves, and regard every, even the slightest move that you make. It requires a very nice shot with a rifle to kill them, as they must be killed dead, for as long as life exists, they continue to work into their cells. It is extremely dangerous to pass through their towns, as they abound with rattle snakes.[12]

Prairie dogs would long fascinate travelers on the plains, perhaps because the gregarious rodents exemplified the ceaseless vigilance and solidarity that preserved humans as well as lesser animals from ruin in this often-hostile environment. Pike and his men were not targeting the prairie dogs out of spite or sheer curiosity. Part of their mission was to determine what this rugged land had to offer travelers in the way of sustenance, and their culinary experiments thus served a useful purpose. Few who passed this way along the Santa Fe Trail in years to come would have to stoop to eating prairie dogs, however, for the short-grass country along the Arkansas abounded in larger prey, including elk, antelope, and bison in astonishing profusion. On November 4, while traveling up the river to the west of modern-day Dodge City, Pike spotted a prodigious herd:

In the afternoon discovered the north side of the river to be covered with animals; which, when we came to them proved to be buffalo cows and calves. I do not think it an exaggeration to say there were 3,000 in one view. It is worthy of remark, that in all the extent of country yet crossed, we never saw one cow, and that now the face of the earth appeared to be covered with them. Killed one buffalo. Distance 24½ miles.[13]

Many later travelers in the vicinity reported herds comparable in size to this cow band. Such abundance helped make possible the Santa Fe trade, for if merchants had been forced to purchase and carry with them from Missouri all the provisions needed for the long haul to New Mexico, their burdens would have been heavier and their profits lighter.

This splendid hunting ground also attracted Indian hunting bands and brought them in contact—and occasional conflict—with wary traders. Pike and his party, however, passed through the heart of buffalo country undisturbed either by Indians or by the Spanish forces under Melgares, whose trail and abandoned campgrounds the Americans happened upon periodically without ever encountering the troops themselves. On November 11, near what is now the Kansas-Colorado border, Pike reported passing a camp vacated by the Spanish, "where it appeared they remained some days as we conjectured to lay up meat."[14] Buffalo grew scarcer as one moved west along the Arkansas, Pike observed, and the Spanish had evidently decided to stock up on meat before proceeding. In fact, Melgares and company had prudently returned to New Mexico before winter caught them on the open plains. Pike, by contrast, defied the elements and forged ahead, following a route up the Arkansas that was increasingly desolate and devoid of game. He and his men were entering the rain shadow of the Rockies, where grass was scant and horses sometimes went hungry if their riders neglected to carry feed for them. On November 15 the Americans saw lofty peaks in the distance and "gave three *cheers* to the *Mexican mountains*." Those mountains "appear to present a natural boundary between the province of Louisiana and New Mexico," Pike added, an acknowledgment that he and his men were nearing the limits of American territory even by the most generous interpretation of the Louisiana Purchase.[15]

They would find little more to cheer about in the days ahead. On November 22, having recently passed the point where future travelers on the Mountain Route, or Branch, of the Santa Fe Trail would leave the Arkansas and veer off to the southwest up Timpas Creek, Pike's sixteen-man force was approached by a party of sixty Pawnee warriors, who were returning empty-handed from a foray against a rival tribe. "An unsuccessful war party on their return home," Pike commented, "are always ready to embrace an opportunity, of gratifying their disappointed vengeance, on the first persons whom they meet."[16] He tried to satisfy them with presents, including "tobacco, one dozen knives, 60 fire steels and 60 flints," but some of the warriors deemed that insufficient and began pilfering the Americans before Pike ordered his men to wield arms and threatened to kill the first Pawnee who touched their baggage:

> On which they commenced filing off immediately; we marched about the same time and found, they had made out to steal one sword, tomahawk, broad axe, five canteens, and sundry other small articles. After our leaving them; when I reflected on the subject, I felt myself sincerely mortified, that the smallness of my number obliged me thus to submit to the insults of a lawless banditti, it being the first time ever a savage took any thing from me, with the least appearance of force.[17]

Those who traversed this region in years to come would find that strength in numbers indeed helped to reduce such impositions by unfriendly Indians, but wise parties would fortify themselves with plenty of presents as well. For it was not simply "lawless banditti" or frustrated warriors who demanded some sort of tribute or consideration from travelers. Indians of various tribes along the Santa Fe Trail—including groups well disposed to Americans—understood that these passing strangers were engaged in trade and expected to be dealt with in kind. Tribesmen who were duly honored with presents sometimes gave gifts in return, or repaid the favor in other ways, such as tolerating intrusions on their favored hunting grounds. For every hostile exchange between Indians and travelers on the trail, there were numerous bargains struck.

For Pike, as for many who passed this way in later decades, the cost of reckoning with challenges from sometimes-defiant Indians was minor compared to the toll taken by the hostile forces of nature. An excursion by Pike in late November to the base of the mountain later dubbed Pike's Peak in his honor ended when snow and cold forced him back to camp. Winter was tightening its grip, and by the first of December both the men and their horses were feeling the pinch:

> The storm still continuing with violence, we remained encamped; the snow by night one foot deep; our horses being obliged to scrape it away, to obtain their miserable pittance, and to increase their misfortunes, the poor animals were attacked by the magpies, who attracted by the scent of their sore backs, alighted on them, and in defiance of their wincing and kicking, picked many places quite raw; the difficulty of procuring food rendered those birds so bold as to light on our mens arms and eat meat out of their hands. One of our hunter's out but killed nothing.[18]

Pike evidently gave no thought to establishing a winter camp at the base of the Rockies, perhaps because this country seemed barren and exposed or perhaps because he felt that duty required him to forge ahead. In any case, he led his men into higher and snowier elevations. By mid-January he had probed the headwaters of the Arkansas in the frigid heart of the Rockies, and he and his men, suffering sorely from hunger and frostbite, were venturing southward in search of the upper Red River. Several men were crippled by the cold and had to be left behind with provisions and ammunition while Pike and the others moved ahead. Finally, at month's end, they reached what Pike took for the Red River and chose a site for a stockade. Dr. John Robinson, who served as physician to the troops and as Pike's right-hand man, then traveled south on his own with the professed intention of reaching Santa Fe and recovering a debt owed to an American merchant. Pike later confessed in a footnote to his published journal that this was merely an excuse for acquiring intelligence on New Mexico:

When on the frontiers, the idea suggested itself to us of making this claim a pretext for Robinson to visit Santa Fe. We therefore gave it the proper appearance, and he marched for that place. Our views were to gain a knowledge of the country, the prospect of trade, force, &c. whilst, at the same time, our treaties with Spain guaranteed to him, as a citizen of the United States, the right of seeking the recovery of all just debts or demands before the legal and authorised tribunals of the country.[19]

This was as close as Pike would come to admitting any intent to spy on New Mexico, or to "reconnoitre our country," as Governor Alencaster put it. Pike emphasized that Dr. Robinson was acting as a private citizen and in keeping with Spanish law, yet suspicions would arise and persist that Pike had secret orders from General Wilkinson to probe New Mexico and gather intelligence for a possible invasion. Those suspicions were fostered in part by the fact that Wilkinson was a consummate intriguer, and in part by a sense that Pike's actions over the winter—which might charitably be described as bold to the point of recklessness—reflected the urgency of a man on a mission more sensitive than his official orders indicated.[20] Yet no hidden agenda need be assumed to explain Pike's ambiguous position. The ambiguity was there from the start in Wilkinson's written instructions, which led Pike to the brink of an armed confrontation with Spanish forces while admonishing him to keep the peace. Pike himself referred to Dr. Robinson's trip as aimed at gauging "the prospect of trade, force, &c.," suggesting that he saw his mission as a two-sided venture that might indeed lead to what Wilkinson called "Harmonious Intercourse" or perhaps to some form of hostilities. In this as in other respects, his journey offered a preview of things to come, for the history of the American relationship with New Mexico would be one of ambiguous or two-sided exchanges, in which traders cleared the way for conquerors, who in turn had to learn how to deal with this demanding country and bargain with its diverse inhabitants before they could profit from their acquisition.

In late February, the commander of the troops sent out by Governor Alencaster (not to be confused with the force led the previous year by Melgares) approached the stockade and informed Pike to his professed astonishment that he was camped not by the Red River, as he thought, but by the Rio Grande. "I immediately ordered my flag to be taken down and rolled up," he wrote, "feeling how sensibly I had committed myself, in entering their territory, and was conscious that they must have positive orders to take me in."[21] Having recently dispatched two men to retrieve the victims of frostbite whom he left behind in January, Pike was reluctant to leave for Santa Fe before they returned, but the Spanish commander politely insisted, assigning a detachment of his men to await the stragglers at the stockade with two of Pike's soldiers while he and the others were escorted to the capital. Five days later, he was standing before Alencaster in the Palace of the Governors, declaring that he had come to reconnoiter not the governor's country but his own.

Not prepared to take Pike at his word, Alencaster peppered him with more questions about his own role and about the relationship of his party to Dr. Robinson, who had been taken into custody. "The haughty and unfriendly reception of the governor induced me to believe war must have been declared,"[22] wrote Pike, who tried to protect Robinson by claiming that he was unattached to the American reconnaissance. This sharp exchange was followed that evening by a second interview, at which Pike presented his papers, kept in a trunk that had been confiscated by his Spanish guards. Those papers stood Pike in good stead, for they demonstrated that he was acting under orders not to provoke Spanish authorities. As Pike paraphrased his appeal to Alencaster:

> If he would be at the pain of reading my commission from the United States, and my orders from my general, it would be all that I presumed would be necessary to convince his excellency that I came with no hostile intentions towards the Spanish government, on the contrary, that I had express instructions to guard against giving them offence or alarm, and that his excellency would be convinced that myself and party were rather to be considered objects, on which the so-much-celebrated generosity of the Spanish nation might be exercised, than proper subjects to occasion the opposite sentiments.
>
> He then requested to see my commission and orders, which I read to him in French; on which he got up and gave me his hand, for the first time, and said he was happy to be acquainted with me as a man of honor and a gentleman; that I could retire this evening, and take my trunk with me; that on the morrow he would make further arrangements.[23]

It was not the first or last time that Pike was treated generously by Spaniards who had reason to be suspicious of him. Although the governor was not prepared to let Pike off the hook—he informed him the next day that he and his men would have to journey south to the city of Chihuahua "to appear before the commandant-general"—Alencaster sent Pike off with a gift of a shirt and a neck cloth, explaining that they were "made in Spain by his sister and never had been worn by any person," and further honored him with a farewell dinner that featured "a variety of dishes and wines of the southern provinces."[24] The culture of hospitality that Pike and other Americans encountered in New Mexico was one that encouraged hosts to honor guests with conspicuous favors, even in circumstances that bordered on hostilities. The governor knew well that Spain and the United States might yet end up trading blows, but he lavished courtesies on his potential enemy and urged Pike in parting to remember Alencaster, "in peace or war."[25]

Those words served as a fitting epigram for the journey Pike was about to undertake under Spanish escort—a trek down the old Camino Real, or Royal Road, that linked Santa Fe to the Mexican heartland. This path, referred to in later years as the Chihuahua Trail, had long accommodated both traders and conquerors, men of peaceful pursuits and agents of war, and it would continue to do so as Americans infiltrated the region in ever-increasing numbers in the decades to come. For merchants, the Chihuahua Trail would become a lucrative extension of the Santa Fe Trail, linking them to markets in El Paso del Norte, Chihuahua, and points beyond that were larger than the market in Santa Fe and blessed with customers who had more cash in hand. In the process, the enterprise referred to loosely as the Santa Fe trade would expand in scope, involving journeys that were sometimes twice as long as the distance between Missouri and New Mexico. But not all who followed the road to Chihuahua would be engaged in strictly peaceful exchanges. In 1841, a party of Texans who traveled to New Mexico ostensibly to trade—but with the additional aim of promoting an uprising there if the conditions proved ripe— were arrested by Mexican authorities and herded down the Chihuahua Trail. Several died as a result of mistreatment before the survivors were imprisoned in Mexico City, and the plight of the captives became a rallying cry for Americans who later backed Texas in its territorial quarrel with Mexico. In late 1846, American troops would follow that same path south from Santa Fe, defeating Mexican troops in two pitched battles along the way and sealing their not-entirely-bloodless conquest of New Mexico.

For Pike and his men, the journey to Chihuahua was more of a cultural excursion than a march made under duress. By and large, they were well treated. In the little town of Albuquerque, much smaller than Santa Fe in those days, they were feasted in grand fashion by a local priest, who seemed intent not simply on making Pike feel at home but on winning him over, body and soul:

> We were received by father Ambrosio Guerra in a very flattering manner, and led into his hall. From thence, after taking some refreshment, into an inner apartment, where he ordered his adopted children of the female sex, to appear, when they came in by turns, Indians of various nations, Spanish, French, and finally, two young girls, who from their complexion I conceived to be English: on perceiving I noticed them, he ordered the rest to retire, many of whom were beautiful, and directed those to sit down on the sofa beside me; thus situated, he told me that they had been taken to the east by

the Tetaus; passed from one nation to another, until he purchased them, at that time infants, but they could recollect neither their names nor language, but concluding they were my country-women, he ordered them to embrace me as a mark of their friendship, to which they appeared nothing loth; we then sat down to dinner, which consisted of various dishes, excellent wines, and to crown all, we were waited on by half a dozen of those beautiful girls, who like Hebe at the feast of the gods, converted our wine to nectar, and with their ambrosial breath shed incense on our cups. After the cloth was removed some time, the priest beckoned me to follow him, and led me into his "sanctum sanctorum," where he had the rich and majestic images of various saints, and in the midst the crucified Jesus, crowned with thorns, with rich rays of golden glory surrounding his head; in short, the room being hung with black silk curtains, served but to augment the gloom and majesty of the scene. When he conceived my imagination sufficiently wrought up, he put on a black gown and mitre, kneeled before the cross, and took hold of my hand and endeavoured gently to pull me down beside him; on my refusal, he prayed fervently for a few minutes and then rose, laid his hands on my shoulders, and as I conceived, blessed me. He then said to me, "You will not be a Christian; Oh! what a pity! oh! what a pity!" He then threw off his robes, took me by the hand and led me out of the company smiling; but the scene I had gone through had made too serious an impression on my mind to be eradicated, until we took our departure, which was in an hour after, having received great marks of friendship from the father.[26]

In this remarkable entry, articulated with such care and craft that it might pass for an excerpt from a novel, Pike demonstrated his talent for exploring social as well as natural landscapes. Pike was probing a different sort of frontier here, a cultural borderland where the competing claims of Hispanic and Anglo societies were worked out through an intimate exchange that General Wilkinson referred to as "Harmonious Intercourse." In his dealings with New Mexicans, Pike enjoyed no more harmonious an affair than this encounter with Padre Ambrosio Guerra and his "ambrosial" foster daughters and handmaidens, who were evidently old enough to charm Pike in a politely seductive way. And yet this convivial get-together was also a contest, during which Guerra tried to convert his guest and Pike resisted his overtures. As this incident underscored, the claims made by New Mexicans on Americans could be powerful and persuasive. (Indeed, some early American traders in New Mexico would marry local women, convert to Catholicism, and become citizens of their adopted land.) The competition between these two proud and accomplished cultures was closer than the final results might indicate—if, in fact, the Anglo takeover of the Southwest can be considered final even today—and it was conducted through exchanges that covered the spectrum from thrusts and parries of a romantic or spiritual nature to duels in the marketplace to contests on the field of battle.

The remainder of Pike's journey was marked by that same spirit of competition, often congenial but sometimes not. Shortly after leaving Albuquerque, he met with his former nemesis, Facundo Melgares, and noted that this officer possessed "none of the haughty Castillian pride, but much of the urbanity of a Frenchman."[27] Melgares, who took charge of the Americans the rest of the way to Chihuahua, dispatched an order to surrounding villagers to send "six or eight of your handsomest young girls" to a fandango, or ball, that he was sponsoring for the Americans. Pike considered the fact that the villagers obeyed such a command proof of the "degraded state of the common people." But attending a fandango was not an imposition but an honor, and Pike conceded that "there was really a handsome display of beauty."[28] Melgares would not be outdone when it came to obliging his guests and putting them in debt to him. Later, after passing through the flourishing village of El Paso, with its expansive orchards and vineyards, Pike noted that Melgares cultivated the goodwill of the Apaches who were visiting the nearby presidio of San Elizario during one of the occasional truces that punctuated their long-running feud with the Spanish: "With those people Malgares was extremely popular and I believe he sought popularity with them, and all the common people, for there was no man so poor or so humble, under whose roof he would not enter; and when he walked out, I have seen him put a handful of dollars in his pocket give them all to the old men, women and children before he returned to his quarters; but to equals he was haughty and overbearing."[29]

Pike was startled by the change that came over the confident and magnanimous Melgares when they reached Chihuahua—by far the most populous and impressive place Pike had seen since leaving St. Louis—and met there with a higher authority, Nemesio Salcedo, commandant general of the internal provinces. Melgares grew anxious and agitated, and Pike soon discovered that Salcedo was indeed a forbidding overseer. "You have given us and yourself a great deal of trouble," Salcedo observed brusquely in greeting him.[30] In the end, the commandant allowed the intruding Americans to return under escort to the United States by way of Texas, but he confiscated some of Pike's papers.

Pike did not take kindly to being deprived of those papers, for this was very much a "literary expedition"[31]—as Thomas Jefferson wrote in reference to the reporting he required of Lewis and Clark—a mission whose ultimate meaning would be gauged in words more than deeds. Pike's success depended on his ability to account for his journey, to appraise his experience in writing.

Despite the confiscation of documents, he retained enough in writing to sub-stantiate his memories and managed that task admirably, producing a record of his venture that provided both his superiors and the public at large with much useful intelligence about the way to New Mexico and the world he encountered there. Published in 1810, his journal was supplemented by an appendix that offered his general observations on the land and people of New Spain. Based on his brief acquaintance with the Spanish Southwest, those observations, or opinions, were less astute than his journal entries. He claimed, for example, that the Pueblos of New Mexico "may properly be termed the slaves of the state, for they are compelled to do military duty, drive mules, carry loads, or in fact perform any other act of duty or bondage that the will of the commandant of the district, or any passing military tyrant chooses to ordain."[32] This was a serious misreading of the relationship between New Mexican authorities and the Pueblos, who had strenuously resisted subjuga-tion by the Spanish and succeeded in preserving a measure of autonomy. Pueblos in fact served as troops under Spanish commanders, but in no sense did they consider themselves slaves. Still, the notion would persist that Pueblos were seeking deliverance from oppression and would welcome intervention by the United States, a dream tragically dispelled in 1847 when American forces who had recently occupied New Mexico faced an uprising by Pueblos and Mex-icans at Taos and struck back with a vengeance, inflicting far heavier losses on defiant Pueblos there in one day than on New Mexican rebels or troops during the entire campaign.

Pike's portrait of the Pueblos as dupes of Spanish authorities was related to a larger theme that he developed in his observations on New Spain. The people as a whole, he argued, were being exploited by their Spanish overlords and were looking to Americans for relief. Spain had in fact alienated its colonists in the New World by clinging stubbornly to the policy of mercantilism that did much to set colonial Americans against their British masters. That policy discouraged the development of industry in New Spain and kept settlers dependent on the mother country by thwarting trade with other nations. As a result, factory-made goods like fine cotton cloth were so expensive in New Mexico and other remote parts of New Spain that people there had good rea-son to hope that authorities would lower the trade barrier and admit mer-chants from the United States on reasonable terms. Pike praised the people of New Spain for what he called their "heaven-like qualities of hospitality and kindness"[33] and sensed that the cordial treatment he received while in cus-tody implied certain hopes on the part of colonists there in regard to the United States—hopes that might reasonably be interpreted as including a desire for friendship and trade. Yet he indulged in more than a little wishful thinking when he concluded that Spanish colonists regarded the Americans as their potential champions and that under the proper circumstances, such as interference by France in the affairs of New Spain, they would welcome intervention by U.S. troops, provided that those forces came as "friends and protectors" rather than as tyrants: "Should an army of Americans ever march into the country, and be guided and governed by these maxims, they will only have to march from province to province in triumph, and be hailed by the united voices of grateful millions as their deliverers and saviours, whilst our national character would be resounded to the most distant nations of the earth."[34]

Pike was envisioning a war of liberation here, invited by Mexicans and supported by their independent forces. But where did such benign fantasies end and dreams of conquest begin? American notions of enfolding Mexicans in a protective embrace did not dissipate when Mexico rebelled against Spain and went on to win independence. As late as May of 1846, in the opening days of the American war with Mexico, a letter written by Senator Thomas Hart Benton of Missouri described the forthcoming occupation of New Mexico and environs in terms that were not far removed from Pike's rosy picture of benign intervention. "It will be proposed to the people of New Mexico, Chihuahua and the other internal provinces, that they remain quiet and continue trading with us as usual, upon which condition they shall be protected in all their rights and be treated as friends," Benton declared. "This military movement will be to make sure of the main object, to wit: peace and trade, to be secured peaceably if possible, forcibly if necessary."[35]

Even in the act of conquest, Americans tried to sell themselves and people they proposed to conquer on the idea that the transfer of the desert Southwest from Mexican to American hands was merely an extension of the ongoing commercial intercourse between the two sides, a deal that would profit the targets of this proposed takeover as much as it would the successful bidders. For all the posturing this entailed, however, the idea that the campaign to acquire New Mexico was part and parcel of the Santa Fe trade was not as outlandish as it might sound. American forces bound for Santa Fe that summer followed the same route pioneered by the early traders and were preceded and followed by trains of merchants intent on dealing with Mexicans on much the same terms as they had in peacetime. The invasion force itself engaged in delicate negotiations with authorities in Santa Fe in the hope of achieving a bloodless surrender, depended greatly on trade with the populace for food and supplies, incurred heavy obligations as a result of the takeover that included reckoning with Navajos and other resistant tribes, and in the few pitched battles with Mexicans or allied Pueblos during the campaign inflicted losses far out of proportion to any injury the occupiers could claim and left Americans with the task of appeasing their aggrieved antagonists and resuming profitable exchanges.

Much of this was prefigured in the events that unfolded along the Santa Fe Trail in the quarter century between the inception of trade on that route and the outbreak of the Mexican War. From the start, those who set out across the plains for Santa Fe were involved like Zebulon Pike in an ambiguous venture that mingled impulses of friendly give-and-take with forceful expansionism. To be sure, few Americans who straggled wearily into Santa Fe in small parties in the early years had illusions of conquering New Mexico anytime soon. But in the simple act of forming companies for mutual defense as they crossed Indian country, they ceased to be merely traders and became to some extent soldiers (albeit of an irregular and sometimes ill-disciplined sort). The plains served as a kind of training ground, where traders learned that to traffic in this sphere was to engage in exchanges that ranged from harmonious intercourse to hostile intervention. Every encounter with Indians along the way raised those contrary possibilities, aptly symbolized by the pipe tomahawks carried by members of various tribes, with an emblem of peace at one end and an instrument of war at the other. Some tribes conveyed that same duality in their lore by speaking of two paths—the white road of peace and the red road of war (a distinction based not on skin color but on the association of war with blood).[36] In that sense, the Santa Fe Trail was both roads in one, the red and the white, and Americans who ventured down it had to deal not just with Indians or with Mexicans but with the disparity in their own nature that left them poised between peaceful and warlike impulses. Indeed, the very world around them seemed to vacillate between rage and mercy. At the end of a searing day on the shadeless plains, nature released her pent-up fury with lightning, hail, and torrential downpours—then took pity on the helpless victims of her outburst and graced travelers with a dawn so mild and sweet that they felt launched anew across the ocean of grass and cleansed of their own simmering hostilities. The trail encompassed such extremes. Above all, it embraced the many forms of exchange by which travelers tried to resolve the deep and abiding tensions of their ambiguous enterprise and reckon with their surroundings, their competitors, and the contradictions in their own character.

2

Many Nations to Contend With
(1808–1821)

More than a decade elapsed between the time Zebulon Pike returned to the United States with news of the high prices that imported goods fetched in New Mexico—up to twenty-five dollars a yard for fine cloth, he reported—and the first successful efforts by American traders to exploit those opportunities. The main obstacle that stood in the way was the Spanish policy of economic exclusion, reinforced by lingering fears of American military intervention, and that barrier would not be lifted until Mexicans won independence. In the interim, a few bold parties made unsuccessful attempts to penetrate the market at Santa Fe or to canvass for beaver pelts or other prizes amid the mountains and streams of New Mexico. A number of these adventurers became prisoners of the Spanish. In 1812, a small party of traders from St. Louis led by James Baird and Robert McKnight, encouraged by reports of rebellion in New Spain and mistakenly believing that independence was imminent, reached Santa Fe only to be arrested there and dispatched to Chihuahua. They were held captive for eight years. In 1817, Frenchman Jules De Mun and Auguste Pierre Chouteau, a prominent American trader of French ancestry, were apprehended by Spanish troops on the south bank of the upper Arkansas River and hauled off to Santa Fe, where they spent more than six weeks in prison awaiting trial, despite the fact that they had a license from the American government to trap and trade with Indians at the headwaters of the Arkansas. As this incident underscored, the question of where American territory ended and New Spain began remained a matter of hot debate. According to De Mun, Governor Pedro María Allande, who served as president of the court-martial that tried them, not only denied the validity of their license but claimed that the Americans had no territorial rights beyond the Mississippi:

> Many questions were asked, but more particularly why we had staid so long in the Spanish dominions? I answered, that being on the waters of the Arkansaw river, we did not consider ourselves in the domains of Spain, as we had a license to go as far as the head waters of said river. The president denied that our government had a right to grant such a license, and entered in such a rage that it prevented his speaking, contented himself with striking his fist several times on the table, saying, *gentlemen, we must have this man shot*. At such conduct of the president, I did not think much of my life, for all the other members were terrified in his presence and unwilling to resist him, on the contrary do any thing to please him. He, the president, talked much of a big river that was the boundary line between the two countries, but did not know its name. When mention was made of the Mississippi, he jumped up, saying that that was the big river he meant, that Spain had never ceded the west side of it! It may be easy to judge of our feelings to see our lives in the hands of such a man.[1]

In the end, the governor relented and allowed them to depart after confiscating their goods. Their sentence was presented to them in writing, De Mun noted, and they were "forced to kiss the unjust and iniquitous sentence that deprived harmless and inoffensive men of all they possessed of the fruits of two years labor and perils."[2] The governor afterward admitted that the accused were "innocent men," De Mun wrote, although he declined to return their property. Naturally, De Mun resented this and regarded the governor's insistence that Spain had never ceded the west side of the Mississippi as the height of absurdity. In fact, that remained the official position of Spain in 1817, and it was no more outlandish than the enduring American claim to Texas. Wisely, both sides traded in those bargaining chips two years later and arrived at a territorial settlement that fixed the border on a line running up the Red River, then due north along the one hundredth meridian to the Arkansas River and west along that waterway into the Rockies. This compromise was accepted by Mexico when it won independence in 1821, and for a while it quelled the border tensions that would resurface after Texas won independence from Mexico in 1836.

One flaw in the settlement, perhaps, was that it fostered the illusion that Americans actually possessed the open grasslands north of the agreed-upon boundary line. The Louisiana Purchase could not confer that region on the United States because neither Spain nor France had ever held it. Various

European Americans had made economic, military, or diplomatic ventures across the plains, but none had claimed the area north of Texas by right of occupancy, and without occupancy there could be no possession.[3] The land belonged to the Indians who lived and hunted there, and American officials admitted as much by entering into a series of treaties with tribes of the tall-grass prairie west of the Mississippi—land considered suitable for settlement—that recognized them as "nations" and acknowledged their right of possession even while restricting those groups to small portions of the territory they once occupied or to reservations out on the short-grass plains. The land ceded in this fashion went to white settlers or to tribes that were being removed from the East, often under duress. Missouri became a state in 1821, but the unorganized territory to the west of it remained Indian country, and the army erected a string of forts to mark the frontier between that tribal domain and the United States.

All this was of some consequence for the future Santa Fe trade, for it meant that travelers, in gaining access to an independent and newly receptive Mexico, still had to contend with various Indian nations along the way. Travelers may not have regarded those tribes as nations—and American authorities would see to it that their sovereignty was effectively denied in the decades to come—but when traders first crossed into Indian country on their way to Santa Fe, they left behind the protection of American laws and American troops (there were no military escorts on the trail before 1829) and became aliens in a foreign land, subject to the customs and duties of those whose territory they passed through. It did not help matters that the intruding Americans regarded themselves as the rightful owners of the country they traversed, at least until they crossed to the south side of the Arkansas and entered what was nominally Mexican territory.

Among the sovereign tribes that travelers would have to reckon with on their way to New Mexico in years to come were three that Pike encountered on his journey in 1806: the Osages, Kansas, and Pawnees. These groups occupied that well-watered and fertile prairie country between the woodlands bordering the Mississippi and the short-grass plains. (The Pawnees lived farthest north of the three groups, in an area ranging from the Republican River to the Platte, but they made frequent ventures down to the Arkansas.) This was a generous environment, and traditionally these prairie-dwellers lived in sizable permanent villages, where they raised corn and other crops to supplement what they brought back from their hunting trips, including lengthy expeditions out onto the plains to stalk buffalo. As recently as the late 1700s, the Osages had been a formidable power in the region, dominating trade routes between the Mississippi River and the Southwest and courted by both

French and Spanish envoys. In 1808, however, Osage chiefs yielded to American pressure and signed the first in a series of treaties that relegated them to land less suitable for their way of life and made them less of a barrier to the emerging trade route between Missouri and New Mexico that became known as the Santa Fe Trail. The Kansas were similarly diminished by treaties to which Americans subjected them in the early 1800s. Economically and territorially, both tribes lost much that was precious to them. Not surprisingly, they tried to recoup something now and then by raiding travelers on the trail or exacting tribute from them.

While Osages and Kansas were occasionally troublesome to travelers passing to and from New Mexico, Pawnees acquired a reputation for being implacably hostile. That notoriety stemmed from incidents like the one that befell trader Auguste Chouteau in 1816 as he was traveling along the Arkansas River with some twenty men during the toilsome expedition that would later land him in prison in Santa Fe. That summer, his party was attacked by a force of as many as two hundred Indians that consisted largely if not entirely of Pawnees. Chouteau and company sought refuge in mid-river on the spit that would be known thereafter as Chouteau's Island, where by one account they "made a sort of rampart out of their packs, forming three small redoubts, with the horses in the intermediate space."[4] After sharp fighting that left at least five Indians dead and many wounded, the attackers retreated. Chouteau lost one man killed and three injured. Given the intensity of the exchange, this may have been something more than just a raid for horses or other prizes, for Indians of the region seldom risked heavy losses in pitched battle for booty alone. Perhaps these Pawnees, reportedly from the same area visited by Pike in 1806, felt as the chief who confronted Pike did—that Americans were a disturbing new presence on the plains—and preferred dealing with the Spanish. (Pawnees accepted peace offerings from envoys like Melgares while profiting from Spanish colonists by raiding New Mexico occasionally or attacking other tribes that did so and making off with Spanish horses, mules, and other assets.)[5] Some elements of the tribe proved willing to bargain with Americans over the years, but the Pawnees as a whole made a formidable impression on the trail's early travelers, endowing their name to such landmarks as Pawnee Rock and Pawnee Fork. Even after the Pawnees were ravaged by smallpox in the 1830s—an affliction that weakened many western tribes during this period—they retained a fearsome reputation among travelers and were often blamed for violent deeds whose perpetrators were unknown.[6]

Pawnees and other prairie tribes frequently traversed the short-grass buffalo range, but the true masters of that realm on either side of the Arkansas River were the Cheyennes and Arapahos to the north and the Comanches

Pawnee Council.

"Pawnee Council," during the expedition of Major Stephen Long, from Edwin James, *Account of an Expedition from Pittsburgh to the Rocky Mountains* (1823). Courtesy Library of Congress, Prints and Photographs Division, LC-USZ62-7778.

and allied Kiowas and Plains Apaches, or Kiowa Apaches, to the south.[7] These plains-dwellers spoke different languages and came to the grasslands from different places—the Comanches from the valleys of the Rocky Mountains, the Kiowas from up around the headwaters of the Missouri River, the Arapahos from Saskatchewan, and the Cheyennes from east of the Mississippi by way of the Dakotas. But all of them prospered in this boundless and supremely competitive environment by virtue of their mastery of horses and their expert pursuit of buffalo, which provided them with shelter, sustenance, and nearly every tool they required. They were by no means averse to trade or diplomacy, although internal tribal divisions often limited the effectiveness of the peace treaties their various chiefs entered into. Despite such factionalism, the potent and populous Comanches achieved lasting alliances with the Kiowas and other smaller tribes, negotiated a truce with the New Mexicans in the late 1700s that lasted for many years, and allowed Spanish traders called Comancheros to operate in their territory. Cheyennes and Arapahos, for their part, welcomed exchanges with outsiders and ultimately entered into a close trading relationship with Americans in and around Bent's Fort when that outpost was established east of present-day La Junta, Colorado, in the early 1830s.

The talent of the Plains Indians that made the greatest impression on white travelers, however, was their gift for mounted warfare. The term "warlike," often used in reference to tribes encountered along the Santa Fe Trail, scarcely does justice to groups with warrior traditions as rich as any in the European heritage, replete with soldier societies, heraldry, and a body of rituals and beliefs that infused the trials of battle with profound significance. Fighting, like hunting, was for these warriors a quest not just for material advantage but for spirit power. They wrestled with imposing and often hostile forces in the world around them and obtained prizes and blessings that remained with them until they died. Even in death, they communed with something greater than themselves that ennobled their efforts. As men of a Kiowa warrior society chanted when they faced mortal danger:

> I live, but I will not live forever.
> Mysterious moon, you only remain,
> Powerful sun, you alone remain,
> Wonderful earth, you remain forever.[8]

Travelers across the plains had much to learn from these Indians about this mysterious realm and its rules of exchange. This country did not lend itself to large and theoretical claims like the one Americans made to the region before they settled there. On the plains, your territory was no more than what you could defend, and your property was all that you could grasp and hold on to. Given these harsh realities, it was remarkable how many ways the region's tribes had of resolving differences short of violence. Those who were poor could seek help from those who were rich by visiting them and singing begging songs, without incurring the shame often associated with such appeals among Americans. A small party might appease a larger and more dangerous one by offering tobacco or sharing a pipe with their would-be antagonists. Even avid warriors might take less pride in claiming a scalp than in such blood-less coups as touching an enemy with a hand or stick or stealing horses furtively from a rival encampment without firing a shot. Plains Indians were keenly com-petitive and intent on engaging strangers who crossed their path, but that engage-ment could take various forms and sometimes cost intruders no more than a bit of their property or pride.

The sundry exchanges between whites and Indians on the way to New Mexico offered travelers a preview of what awaited them when they reached their destination—a seemingly settled land where Indians retained great lever-age and extracted concessions and trade-offs from Spanish settlers at every turn. It was not the Pueblos who made these insistent demands, for their accom-modation with the New Mexicans had been worked out long ago, after the explosive Pueblo Revolt of 1680. The two groups now found themselves more or less united in their fitful struggles with tribes that remained gladly beyond the pale of European settlement—notably the Navajos to the west and the Apaches to the south and east. (New Mexicans also had trouble occa-sionally with the Utes to their north.) These tribes raided towns and caravans in New Mexico because the opportunity was there and because the rugged land they inhabited offered relatively little in the way of sustenance through such pursuits as hunting, herding, or planting. The Apaches—who like the Comanches were a diverse and far-flung tribal group consisting of several autonomous divisions—had long occupied the southwestern reaches of the plains and lived mainly by stalking buffalo. But in recent times the expansive Comanches had driven all but a few segments of the tribe up into the scrubby mountains and arid valleys of southern New Mexico and northern Chihuahua, where planting or the pursuit of game now brought them fewer rewards than stealing horses, mules, or trade goods. Here among tribes in the desert South-west and neighboring plains—as in many parts of the world down through his-tory—raiding rival groups was considered highly honorable, and war parties that returned laden with stolen goods were touted in much the same fashion as European privateers of recent centuries who sailed home with booty wrested from their enemies.

Apaches, Navajos, and Utes did not just raid New Mexicans, however. They often traded with them, offering the settlers coveted items like Navajo blankets, superbly woven from wool sheared from sheep that Navajos first obtained from the Spanish in early colonial times and herded in the lonely expanses of their desert homeland. Indians of the region—and Comanches visiting for purposes of trade—also sold captives of various tribes and races to the settlers, who freed some of them and kept others as servants or slaves, sometimes intermarrying with them to further the genetic exchange that transformed New Mexican society into what some called a "mulatto" or "Creole" culture. It often seemed to American observers that New Mexicans were hopelessly compromised by this endless round of raiding, trading, and intermingling that left the settlers dealing with Indians on their own terms, rather than imposing terms on them. And yet the path Americans followed to New Mexico was paved with compromises as well—with concessions small and large to the demands of the land and its tribal inhabitants.

The difficult circumstances that impelled Spanish settlers to bargain with their tribal antagonists were aptly summarized in 1812 by a New Mexican official named Pedro Baptista Pino, who traveled to Spain to attend the Cortes, or congress, held at Cádiz that year and submitted an "exposition" on New Mexico to King Ferdinand VII, petitioning him for "relief of the province, so that it may begin to enjoy the prosperity to which it is entitled."[9] Spain was fast losing control of Mexico, and the help Pino sought from the Crown was not forthcoming. His account was published in Spain, however, and offered a rare and revealing insider's portrait of a land whose challenges Americans would soon have to reckon with.

Among the social ills Pino documented was a dearth of doctors or surgeons—he counted only one trained physician in all of New Mexico—and the absence of any place of higher learning to prepare New Mexicans for government or the priesthood. "The governor has no legal adviser nor a secretary (scribe)," he lamented, "because no such persons are available anywhere in the province."[10] Many youngsters received no schooling at all, he added:

> The province does not count, nor has it ever counted upon to date, the kinds of public facilities enjoyed by other Spanish provinces. So backward are things in that regard that some people cannot even put a name to what they lack. The state of primary education, for example, is reduced to this: only those who can contribute to the hiring of a schoolmaster are able to have their children taught. In the capital itself, it has not been possible to fund a teacher for the general instruction of the community.[11]

Contrary to the assertion of some later American visitors that New Mexicans were "priest-ridden," Pino reported that the province did not have nearly enough priests to meet the needs of the people. Most of the priests in

New Mexico resided at the various pueblos, long ministered to by members of the Franciscan order, and the few parish priests serving in towns, or "villas," like Santa Fe and Albuquerque relied for support entirely on offerings and on fees for services like baptisms and funerals, charges that the poor could ill afford. Pino had little hope that these and other concerns of the faithful would be addressed until a bishop was appointed to preside over New Mexico:

> No one born in the last 50 years has been confirmed. And the poor who wish to marry relatives and need a dispensation cannot get it, owing to the high cost of traveling the more than 400 leagues to Durango [where they must apply to the bishop]. Therefore, it happens that many people moved by love, form a family and live in sin. Even though ministers of the church oppose the practice with zeal, it is not enough to avoid this scandal and others which arise as a consequence of the shortage of clergy.[12]

Pino felt that New Mexicans deserved more in the way of pastoral care in return for the tithes they paid. By far the greatest burden shouldered by the populace, however, was the task of defending the province and its isolated settlements against Indian attacks. Pino took pride in the fact that for more than a century New Mexico had "endured continuous warfare with 33 hostile tribes that surround it and to date it has not lost one span of land from its original boundaries."[13] But service in the militia was severely taxing for men who could ill afford to be absent long from their fields or ranches (most New Mexicans subsisted by herding cattle or sheep or by cultivating wheat, corn, fruit, and other crops in fields irrigated from the Rio Grande and its tributaries). Militiamen received no pay and had to furnish their own mounts, weapons, and other supplies for campaigns that sometimes dragged on for two or three months. Even if they came through unscathed, they paid a steep price. "It bears saying that many of those unfortunate militiamen are ruined by a single campaign," Pino noted. "For they have to sell their own clothes and that of their family's to furnish themselves with ammunition and supplies."[14] Some men managed to fulfill their military obligations, he added, only by selling their sons into peonage—debt servitude that for many became an inescapable, lifelong commitment.

New Mexican authorities tried to reduce these burdens by coming to terms with tribes that threatened their communities. At the time Pino wrote, New Mexicans were still benefiting from a pact hammered out with Comanche leaders in the 1780s after fierce fighting. This agreement was reinforced, he observed, by the annual distribution of presents to Comanches that they at first felt obliged to repay: "When they were told that gifts made in the name of the King did not allow for reciprocity, they were much surprised. They have been placed in our gratitude, which grows as has the esteem in which they hold the person and grandeur of the King of Spain whom they call the Great Captain."[15] Despite this pact, there was no true or lasting peace in New Mexico. Troubles with Apaches had mounted for New Mexicans in recent years even as relations with Comanches had improved. "The Apache, who roves from place to place, has no check on his depredations other than his fear of the brave and honorable Comanche," claimed Pino, using terms that few would credit who knew Comanches only as foes. "A nation like the Comanche which instills fear in others, is useful and advantageous for us," he added.[16] Yet coming to terms with Comanches had in fact done little to protect New Mexicans from Apache raids, and settlers who ventured southward from Santa Fe through Apache territory to trade or conduct other business in Chihuahua or points beyond had to see to their own defense. Those heading down the Camino Real with their goods loaded in carts or heaped high atop pack mules found safety in numbers, Pino noted, by forming an annual caravan, one far more impressive in size and organization than most that would later negotiate the hazards of the Santa Fe Trail:

> At the *paraje* [campsite] called Joya de Sevilleta, 43 leagues from the Capital, the interested parties have to be assembled by the end of November with their goods, firearms, ammunition, arrows, bows, horses, etc. Everything is inspected and when the men number 500 or more, the alternating assignments of who will be the vanguard, rear guard and center are made. This includes those who will guard the horse and mule herd and those who will serve as sentries (usually over 100). Also, the scouts who, on dark nights, will have to hold their ear to the ground and listen for footsteps and give the alarm if they hear something in order to avoid the surprises that have often occurred.[17]

Mexicans conditioned to such journeys and the hazards attending them were well prepared for ventures to Missouri and back once the Santa Fe trade got started. And they would bring to that trade not just a talent for handling horses and mules, standing guard, and rationing their resources, but a capacity for cutting deals with potentially hostile Indians. After all, the New Mexico of Pino's day was the product of mutual concessions made by the Spanish settlers and their former Pueblo antagonists, whom he counted as New Mexicans—numbering about sixteen thousand by his estimate, compared to roughly twenty-four thousand Spanish residents—and described as "hardly distinguishable from ourselves."[18] Far from fearing that there were too many Pueblos among the population, he worried that Pueblo women did not want to bear more than four children and were using herbs to induce abortions.

"Mexican Arrieros with an Atajo of Pack-Mules," from Josiah Gregg, *Commerce of the Praries* (1844). Used by permission, State Historical Society of Missouri, Columbia,

He regarded these Indians as an asset to the province and saw little in Cádiz to surpass the charms of their sturdy, multi-story dwellings and their gracious, neatly dressed women.

Alliance with the Pueblos was no cure-all for the troubled province, however. Even after combining strength for their common defense, Spanish colonists and Pueblos found that they were merely one force among many in the area and ill-equipped to dictate to others. Survival in this region was a compromising business, and American traders on the trail who did not absorb that lesson from the Spanish were soon taught as much by the Plains Indians they confronted. Travelers who resorted too quickly to their weapons paid a price in time and energy, if not in blood—a toll that men who weighed profit against loss learned to avoid if they could. American merchants who set out for Santa Fe may have anticipated that they would be bargaining solely with New Mexicans, but they soon discovered that they would have to reckon with many other powers along the way.

3

Foundations of the Trade
(1821–1829)

In February 1821, Mexican nationalists led by Agustín de Iturbide declared independence from Spain. Seven months later, they took power in Mexico City, raised their banner, and proclaimed their homeland a free and sovereign nation. News of the Mexican revolution took some time to reach the United States. Even before Americans were aware of the struggle or its outcome, however, parties of traders or fortune-seekers set out for Santa Fe in the hope that people there would soon be in a position to cast off restraints and bargain with their American neighbors. It was not clear at the time what the best route to Santa Fe might be, and various possibilities were explored. One path that proved ill-suited for purposes of trade was that pursued by a nineteen-year-old adventurer named David Meriwether, a future governor of American-occupied New Mexico. Meriwether returned around March 1, 1821, to an army outpost called Camp Missouri (later Fort Atkinson) at the original Council Bluffs—situated on the west bank of the Missouri some twenty-five miles upriver from present-day Omaha—after a harrowing journey to Santa Fe that he undertook, in his own words, "to ascertain the practicability of a route for wagons and the amount of gold and silver in New Mexico."[1] He was accompanied by one Alfred, whom he described as a "Negro boy that some times acted as our cook."[2] Alfred was thus among the first of sundry African Americans to venture to New Mexico during the nineteenth century as slaves, servants, hired hands, free trappers and traders, or troops.

Meriwether and Alfred had departed Council Bluffs in June 1820 and linked up with a small band of Pawnees from around the Platte River who, unlike those Pike confronted along the Republican River in 1806, were on friendly terms with Americans and hostile to New Mexicans. Troops from that province clashed with Meriwether's party after it crossed the Arkansas and reached the vicinity of the upper Canadian River. Most of the Pawnees were killed, and Meriwether and Alfred were captured and imprisoned for a while in Santa Fe. They had reached New Mexico a bit too early—a year before the change in power—and in the wrong company. Facundo Melgares, who had earlier conducted Zebulon Pike through Mexican territory, was serving as governor in Santa Fe, and Meriwether had a pointed exchange with that official, whose position he would one day occupy:

> The Governor then told me that if I would promise never to return he would set me at liberty, which promise I readily made him. He then asked what guarantee I had to give for my compliance with this promise. I replied that the only guarantee I could give was to repeat an old saying in my country, "A stray dog always lives longest where he was treated best," and that I had been much better treated in my own country than in his. This caused a laugh among the whole party, and the Governor then said, "You must leave tomorrow, and if ever you return, I'll have you shot." To this I replied, "I will take it as a favor if your Excellency will take me out on the plaza and have me shot today." He then asked me why I desired to be shot, and I told him that when his people had taken me prisoner, I was well mounted, armed, and equipped for the trip, and that everything had been taken from me, and, if I started across the plains without a proper outfit, I would perish in a week, and I would rather be shot at once than to die a lingering death from cold and starvation. He then asked me to give to the priest a memorandum of what had been taken from me. The priest proceeded to write down the articles from my dictation, after which we returned to the priest's house, the Governor telling me to come again in the morning.[3]

For all the complaints voiced over the years by Americans about New Mexican officials, they often proved willing to negotiate and grant visitors better terms. In this case, Meriwether talked Melgares into restoring his weapons and providing him and Alfred with mules to ride, a third mule to carry supplies, and two Mexican soldiers to escort them part of the way home. It was a still a rough and perilous journey, but they might not have made it back alive without the governor's concessions. In years to come, some trappers would follow the route to New Mexico traced by Meriwether, but the Council Bluffs area was simply too remote to serve traders as a profitable jumping-off point—steamboats were just beginning to navigate the treacherous Missouri, and none ventured up that far on a regular basis. For now, at least, any serious commercial venture to Santa Fe would have to originate from a spot more accessible to the Mississippi and the big market in St. Louis.

Another route that seemed worth trying was the one followed to New Mexico in the summer of 1821 by traders Thomas James and John McKnight, who was hoping to find his brother Robert, recently released from his long confinement in Mexico. Carrying at least $10,000 worth of trade goods, James and company traveled down the Mississippi by boat from St. Louis to the mouth of the Arkansas, then up that river past Fort Smith to the Cimarron, whose waters proved too low to be navigable. After purchasing horses from some Osages and caching the heavier goods, the party continued up along the Cimarron for a while and then cut across to the Canadian—a route that took them through the heart of Comanche country. In his account of the journey, narrated a quarter century later, James told of being confronted by Comanches who noticed that he and his men had Osage horses and accused them of being in league with that rival tribe. Other Comanches they met with seemed friendlier, but on more than one occasion they were not allowed to proceed without offering sizable tribute:

> The Indians then demanded presents and about a thousand chiefs and warriors surrounded us. I laid out for them tobacco, powder, lead, vermillion, calico and other articles, amounting to about $1,000 in value. This did not satisfy them, and they began to break open my bales of cloth and divide my finest woolens designed for the Spanish market, among them. After losing about $1,000 more in this way, I induced them to desist from further robbery. The principal chief, named Big Star, now appeared and said they had enough. They divided the spoil among two or three thousand, of whom all got some. They tore up the cloth into garments for the middle and blankets. They tied the silk handkerchiefs to their hair as ornaments, which streamed in the wind.
>
> This robbery over, I smoked with them and prepared to go on my journey. This they forbade and we were compelled to stay over that day.[4]

James was not the most reliable of witnesses. He probably overstated the size of the Comanche bands he confronted and almost certainly exaggerated his losses in "presents."[5] Yet he and his small party were undoubtedly in a tight spot. In Comanche country, Americans as yet lacked recognition of the sort Spanish envoys had achieved among large elements of the tribe by confronting them in sufficient strength to command their respect and offering them presents and promises of trade if they refrained from hostilities. Indeed, James discovered that the same Comanches who were hostile to him and his party— and who nearly attacked them at one point—were on cordial terms with the

Spanish and promptly ceased their threats when a Spanish officer kindly inter-vened on their behalf:

> The Spaniards asked the Indians why they were going to kill us. They answered that the Spanish governor at Santa Fe had commanded them not to let any Americans pass, but that we were determined to go in spite of them, so that to stop us and keep their promise to the Spanish governor, they thought they were compelled to take our lives. The Spaniards told them that this was under the government of Spain, but that they were now independent and free, and brothers to the Americans. This was the first news I had heard of the Mexi-can revolution.[6]

Not all the Comanches James met with were partial to the Spanish or sus-picious of Americans. One chief called Cordero (or Cordaro, in James's account) carried a certificate from a U.S. Indian agent certifying him and his followers as "true friends of the United States." He took James under his wing and advised him not to proceed to Santa Fe. "You will meet the fate of all your countrymen before you," he warned.[7] But James, having invested too much in the venture to turn back, continued on to Santa Fe, arriving there by his own account on December 1, 1821. The newly independent authorities allowed him to offer his remaining wares in trade, with results that were less rewarding than he had hoped. His chief importance to the emerging Santa Fe trade was to demonstrate the difficulties of any route to New Mexico that passed through the Comanche heartland. Comanches were not averse to trad-ing or treating with Americans. James himself later wrote that they were "anx-ious to have traders from the United States and form an alliance with the Americans."[8] But they would not tolerate intruders who reserved the bulk of their favors for others. Such interlopers were considered fair game and might have to pay with their livestock, if not their lives. This Comanche barrier helped determine the path that traders would follow to Santa Fe, a route that brushed the northern and western edge of the territory dominated by the Comanches and their Kiowa allies.

During his westward journey, while purchasing horses from the Osages along the Verdigris River in present-day Oklahoma, James met with an Amer-ican adventurer named Hugh Glenn, who was heading for "the Spanish coun-try" with a party of some twenty men. James invited Glenn and company to join him, but they declined. Their expedition began in September of 1821 and took the men and their packhorses up the Arkansas River. Along the way they encountered Indians of various tribes, including Arapahos who were eager to trade with them. Glenn and his companions had some goods to offer those plains-dwellers but were more interested in trapping for pelts in the mountains to the west and would not long be detained. One Arapaho chief took their leaving particularly hard. "I never parted with a man who showed as much sorrow as the chief of the arrapoho," wrote Glenn. That chief, he added, tried to persuade the Americans "to stay with him one moon longer—stating to us the danger of having our horses stolen &c &c but finding in the morning we determined to start he made no objection." Glenn gave the chief a medal as a going-away present, and the Arapaho appeared satisfied, but "when I shook hands with him to start he threw himself on his bed in tears."[9]

Continuing on up the Arkansas, Glenn and company met with Mexican troops, who "all dismounted and embraced us with affection and friendship,"[10] signaling that Americans were now welcome in their newly independent country. In early January 1822, Glenn's partner, Jacob Fowler, and others in the party dug in for a few months in the vicinity of modern-day Pueblo, Colorado, while Glenn went ahead to Santa Fe with the Mexicans and received official permission for his party to trap beaver. In years to come, many rugged trappers would follow their lead. They came and went not by one trail but by various paths, but they had a significant impact on the Santa Fe trade and the development of Taos, their principal rendezvous in New Mexico.[11] Some of these so-called mountain men were not just trappers or hunters but also enterprising merchants, guides, and leaders who figured prominently in the Americanization of New Mexico, notably Christopher "Kit" Carson, who first reached Taos in 1826 and eventually settled there (to the extent that the restless Carson settled anywhere).

The distinction of inaugurating trade on the Santa Fe Trail fell to William Becknell, who reached the New Mexican capital with a small party from Missouri in mid-November of 1821, two weeks before Thomas James and two months or so before Hugh Glenn. That in itself mattered little, since the various parties were not engaged in a race. Becoming the first American visitor to receive permission to trade in Santa Fe after Mexico achieved independence guaranteed neither the success nor the long-term significance of Becknell's venture. His accomplishment lay in establishing a viable route—and in making enough money in the process to encourage a larger party to accompany him back to Santa Fe in 1822, this time with wagons. It was that decisive follow-up that truly launched the Santa Fe trade and made Becknell, a man haunted by debts and disappointments, the father of an enterprise that bridged the plains and linked America inexorably to the Spanish Southwest.

Born in Virginia around 1787, Becknell immigrated as a young man to Missouri, where he enlisted during the War of 1812 with a company of mounted rangers led by Daniel Morgan Boone, the pioneer's son, and campaigned against Indians allied with the British. Afterward, he bought property in the budding

"The American Trapper," by John Filmers, from *Appleton's Journal*, April 1871. Courtesy Library of Congress, Prints and Photographs Division, LC-USZ61-063405.

town of Franklin, situated on the Missouri River roughly midway across the territory and soon to become the cradle of the Santa Fe trade. Many there hailed as he did from Virginia, or from Tennessee or Kentucky like the Boones, and had some experience dealing with Indians. And many brought with them from the border South a tolerance for slavery that harmonized with prevailing opinion in Missouri, which entered the Union as a slave state as a result of the Missouri Compromise of 1820. Becknell was far from being one of the Franklin area's more prosperous residents, but he arranged to hire the services of four blacks from their white owner for business purposes before he went west in 1821. And shortly after he departed for New Mexico that September, leaving his tangled affairs in the hands of his wife, his creditors went to court and claimed by writ of attachment "one Negro Girl Slave named Sally," among other items of property.[12] For Becknell and others, the Santa Fe Trail was an avenue to freedom and financial redemption, but that liberty and opportunity ran at variance with the various forms of servitude that persisted at either end of the road and helped make such ventures profitable by keeping labor cheap. Such contradictions would not soon be abolished. In 1846, when volunteers from Missouri took up arms and marched for Santa Fe in what some portrayed as a campaign to shed the blessings of freedom and democracy on New Mexico, several of the officers were accompanied by their slaves.[13]

Becknell's account of his two expeditions to Santa Fe, which appeared in 1823 in the *Missouri Intelligencer*, published in Franklin, clearly underwent some polishing by a hand more literate than his own. Perhaps his brother Thomas helped out, or the newspaper's editor, Nathaniel Patten. The narrative of his first journey, for example, contains this improbable literary flourish:

A continual and almost uninterrupted scene of prairie meets the view as we advance, bringing to mind the lines of Goldsmith,

"Or onward where Campania's plain, forsaken, lies
A weary waste extending to the skies."

The immense number of animals, however, which roam undisturbed, and feed bountifully upon its fertility, gives some interest and variety to the scenery. The wolves sometimes attack the buffaloe; and whenever an attack is contemplated, a company of from ten to twenty divide into two parties, one of which separates a buffaloe from his herd, and pursues him, while the others head him. I counted twenty-one wolves one morning in a chase of this kind.[14]

Becknell likely knew little of Oliver Goldsmith, or the weary waste of Campania, but he was better versed in the behavior of wolves, which abounded on the plains in those days, and the gritty details here on their hunting methods, along with many other specifics in the report, most likely represent his genuine contributions. This edited account was the first of many instances in the annals of the Santa Fe Trail in which the raw material of memory or observation was processed for good or ill by the travelers themselves or by those to whom they entrusted their tales. From the beginning, stories of the Santa Fe trade were themselves items of speculation and exchange, articles to be dusted off, spiffed up, and offered to advantage in the journalistic marketplace. The editor of the *Intelligencer* claimed in his preface that Becknell's account was an "unvarnished relation of circumstances, and perhaps may not present the reader with that entertainment and gratification of his curiosity which his fancy may anticipate."[15] In truth, it was varnished considerably for the reading public, but not to the extent that Becknell's testimony was unrecognizable beneath the sheen.

Claiming that he was heading westward "for the purpose of trading for Horses & Mules, and catching Wild Animals of every description"[16]—a vague agenda that veiled his apparent intention to visit New Mexico, where the attitude of authorities toward American visitors remained uncertain—Becknell launched his pioneering venture from Franklin on September 1, 1821, with a company of five men, equipped with packhorses. After a journey of several days, they stopped at Fort Osage, a government trading post some ten miles east of the future site of Independence. At the fort, Becknell noted, "we wrote letters, purchased some medicines, and arranged such affairs as we thought necessary previous to leaving the confines of civilization."[17] Then they headed out across the "high prairie," where, like many who followed in their path, they found the prospects lovely and the going rough. Rain swelled the streams and soaked their baggage, and by September 20 they were "nearly all sick and much discouraged." Illness haunted the party for some time to come—a warning for those who cared to heed it that a journey across the plains was not necessarily the tonic many assumed it to be. On the twenty-fourth they reached the Arkansas and entered the realm of the prairie dog, "strong and unpalatable" to Becknell's taste; the rattlesnake, "of which there are vast numbers here," he noted; and the buffalo, whose dried droppings served this and many later parties for fuel in a region largely destitute of timber.[18] They also saw wild horses, but made no effort to catch them, as Becknell had indicated they might. If they really meant to bargain for horses, Plains Indians would have been their logical trading partners, but they met with no Indians and were glad of it. By all signs, they had their sights set on New Mexico.

Becknell and company spent the better part of a month traveling westward up the Arkansas until on October 21 they "arrived at the forks of the

river, and took the course of the left hand one." This was probably the Purgatoire River in present-day Colorado, which led them southwestward up into
craggy terrain, haunted by "mountain sheep," or bighorns. There they negotiated a perilous pass to reach the high plateau of New Mexico:

> We had now some cliffs to ascend, which presented difficulties almost unsur-
> mountable, and we were laboriously engaged nearly two days in rolling away
> large rocks, before we attempted to get our horses up, and even then one fell
> and was bruised to death. At length we had the gratification of finding our-
> selves on the open plain; and two days' travel brought us to the Canadian fork,
> whose rugged cliffs again threatened to interrupt our passage, which we finally
> effected with considerable difficulty.[19]

Judging by this account, Becknell's party did not go through Raton Pass—a
steep and demanding defile, to be sure, but not as treacherous as what Becknell described. Even if he had found that better passage to New Mexico, however, he might still have looked for another route home, for he may already
have been thinking of bringing wagons with him on his next trip, and the way
through Raton Pass—which became the Mountain Route of the Santa Fe
Trail—was not well suited for heavy vehicles laden with trade goods (although
that did not stop wagon trains from later making the attempt). After reaching
Santa Fe in mid-November, conferring amicably with Governor Melgares, and
disposing of his goods, Becknell returned to Missouri with a few companions
by a quicker route in mid-December, making it home in about fifty days compared to seventy-five or so on the way out. He said little about this path (perhaps he regarded it as something of a trade secret). But he most likely traveled
on or near to what became known as the Cimarron Route of the Santa Fe Trail.
This route avoided the rigors of Raton Pass and reduced the length of the trip
considerably by cutting across what is now the panhandle of Oklahoma along
the course of the upper Cimarron River and rejoining the main course of the
trail roughly in the vicinity of modern-day Dodge City, Kansas.

Neither the Cimarron Route nor the Mountain Route was discovered by
the Santa Fe traders. Indians and Spaniards had followed those paths, or ones
close to them, for centuries. Becknell's contribution lay in recognizing the
potential of the shorter and flatter Cimarron Route as a wagon trail. On his
winter's journey back to Missouri, he did not experience either of the travails
later associated with the Cimarron Route—dehydration (long stretches of the
route were waterless, and parties sometimes had to travel at night to avoid
withering) and opposition from Comanches and Kiowas (the trail grazed the
northwestern fringe of their territory and brought travelers into competition
for their hunting grounds and precious watering spots). The only hardships

he complained of were the cold and wind. "We had provisions in plenty," he wrote in a passage that betrayed some editorial polishing, "but Boreas was sometimes rude, whose unwelcome visits we could not avoid, and whose dis-agreeable effects our situation often precluded us from guarding against."[20]

Becknell made enough from this first journey to settle with his creditors in Franklin. An account of his return there with his small party, related long afterward by a descendant of one of the town's early residents, offers some idea of the glittering visions of profit evoked by Becknell's successful venture: "My father saw them unload when they returned, and when their rawhide packages of silver dollars were dumped on the sidewalk one of the men cut the thongs and the money spilled out and clinking on the stone pavement rolled into the gutter. Everyone was excited and the next spring another expedition was sent out."[21] This story may have been invented or inflated, but Becknell's coup yielded enough genuine interest to prompt others to join him when he returned to New Mexico in 1822 or to compete with him by forming their own trading parties that year. In early May, a few weeks before Becknell left Franklin with twenty men and three wagons, Benjamin Cooper—an accom-plished veteran of the War of 1812, commonly referred to as Colonel Cooper—started for New Mexico with fourteen men and pack animals carrying up to $5,000 worth of goods. Their journey took them roughly along the Moun-tain Route to Taos.[22] Late that same summer, the ill-fated James Baird and Samuel Chambers, both of whom had been held captive in Mexico along with Robert McKnight, led a sizable party of men and pack animals west from St. Louis out along the emerging Santa Fe Trail. This time, nature was against them. They made slow progress and were caught along the Arkansas in a fall snowstorm that claimed many of their animals and forced them to take shel-ter in mid-river on an island for the winter. Come spring, they excavated large pits on the north side of the Arkansas and cached their goods there for later retrieval before continuing on to New Mexico with their few remaining ani-mals. In years to come, those empty pits became monuments to the adversi-ties traders faced on the trail and learned to deal with. As the journey to Santa Fe took on aspects of a pilgrimage, the Caches became a kind of shrine, where travelers could admire the depths to which their hardy precursors went to sal-vage something from this perilous and taxing enterprise.

By the time Baird and Chambers settled in uncomfortably for the win-ter, Becknell had returned from his second journey to New Mexico, follow-ing a modified route back along the Cimarron that was even shorter than the one he took out. His party had met with some adversity on the way west when their horses were stampeded by buffalo and two men were stripped of their clothes, guns, and mounts in an attack attributed to "rascally Osages."[23] But this venture was evidently even more profitable than Becknell's first, for the wagons he took with him allowed him to deliver more goods to his receptive customers. "A very great advance is obtained on goods, and the trade is very profitable," he wrote of his dealings with New Mexicans; "money and mules are plentiful, and they do not hesitate to pay the price demanded for an article if it suits their purpose, or their fancy."[24]

Becknell's career on the trail was brief. He made only one more journey to New Mexico, but he deserved his reputation as the father of the trade by virtue of his keen entrepreneurial instincts. His concern from the start was to lessen the toll that distance, time, and the sheer weight of goods placed on traders. By shortening the length of the journey and shifting the burden from pack animals to wagons, he made the exchange more rewarding for merchants and opened New Mexico to regular intercourse with the United States. That intercourse seemed harmonious and soon attracted Mexicans to the trade as well as Americans. But whatever the nationality of those involved, this enterprise grew and flourished through profits reaped in Mexican markets with goods that came from America or from Europe through America—profits large enough to offset the cost of journeys that lasted months and involved occasional losses of livestock and other assets to accidents or Indian raids. In sum, the trade was imbalanced, and that imbalance was expressed not just in financial but in cultural terms, as American goods and the men who conveyed them acquired currency and clout in New Mexico and environs. Becknell and the traders who followed in his path set the terms for an exchange with Mexico that took sundry forms—including, ultimately, settlements in blood—and that tended in the long run to enhance America's fortunes, economically and territorially.

This did not mean that traders who ventured to New Mexico always profited by their efforts or harbored a sense of manifest destiny (a term that was not coined until the 1840s). The annals of the trade were filled with mishaps that would have cured all but the most arrogant men of the notion that they were destined by Providence to be lords of the plains and inheritors of the Southwest. On June 1, 1823, for example, a party from Missouri led by Benjamin Cooper, bound for Santa Fe with their goods loaded on pack animals, lost most of their horses and mules while encamped along the Little Arkansas River in a dawn raid attributed variously to Osages and Comanches. As was often the case on the trail, this well-coordinated attack was aimed not at claiming lives but at enlarging the herds of the Indians who pulled off the coup. According to a report that appeared in the *Missouri Intelligencer* a few weeks later:

On the morning of the first instant, at about dawn, while all the company were asleep except two, who, not apprehending danger, had retired from an advanced position to the campfires, they were alarmed by the discharge of guns, and the yells of the savages. Although the guns were discharged towards the encampment, it is not the belief of those from whom we had our information that they designed personal injury. Their object was to frighten away the horses, in which they completely succeeded. Being on horseback they took advantage of the alarm and momentary confusion occasioned by such an unexpected attack, and evident appearance of assault, to drive off the horses unmolested, whose speed was increased by shouting and other exertions. Four men pursued them about ten miles, when their horses failing they were obliged to desist.[25]

Such expert raids—for which the warriors involved no doubt received well-deserved credit back in their villages—left a lasting impression on the travelers targeted. A half century or so later, an elderly Joel P. Walker, one of the traders who experienced that attack in 1823, recalled the incident in vivid terms that matched the report in the *Intelligencer* almost to the letter:

Two men who were guarding the Animals came in and said they thought there were Indians near by. I told them to drive in the Animals immediately. I had hardly given the order before bang! bang!! bang!!! went the guns of the Indians who also stampeded our horses. . . . I was bareheaded, barefooted and without Clothes, but I ran about a quarter of a mile thinking some of the horses would stop. I then heard someone halloaing, and saw the Indians driving horses; we yelled and broke for camp. They caught four of the horses. I then with four of the Company mounted our horses and started in pursuit of the Indians which we continued until 10 o'clock that night. The Indians discovered the pursuit and took to the sand hills and got away with fifty head of our horses and mules, leaving us only *nine* with which to continue our journey.[26]

The troubles of Walker and his fellow traders were far from over. After waiting three weeks for several members of their party to return to Missouri and fetch more horses, they continued along the poorly defined trail and lost their way in arid country below the Arkansas. As Walker recalled: "The men suffered so much from want of water that they killed Buffalo and drank the blood, and cralled into the dead animals for it."[27] Walker and others rescued one man in their party who had strayed off on his own and was drinking blood in this desperate manner when they found him: "He had crawled into the dead Buffalo and came out a spectacle horrid to behold. He was covered with blood. We got him to camp that night, and next day he was taken to the creek, soaped and washed; had his hair cut, and made him look more like a human being."[28]

Some traders may have been put off by reports of such mishaps, but others drew lessons from them and tried to avoid the same pitfalls on their own journeys. Parties who became lost or ran short of water on the trail, for example, often exposed themselves to even greater peril if they split up. And guards who abandoned their posts to warm themselves at the campfire or warn others belatedly that there might be Indians nearby were all but inviting raiders to make off with the company's herd. Overall, large parties had a better chance of fending off raids than small ones, and it became customary for independent traders to rendezvous at the edge of what was deemed hostile Indian country (a line that advanced westward over the years) and assemble there into sizable companies for defensive purposes, with elected leaders. Fort Osage was among the first of these rendezvous points. By the 1830s, traders were gathering regularly at Council Grove in what is now Kansas to form companies and cross the plains in caravan.

The prototype of these caravans formed on May 24, 1824, near Fort Osage. The company elected as captain Alexander Le Grand. Other prominent figures involved in the venture were Meredith M. Marmaduke, a future governor of Missouri, and Augustus Storrs, an early authority on the trade who was later appointed American consul in Santa Fe. Marmaduke, in his journal, detailed the roster of the caravan: "We this evening ascertained the whole strength of our company to be 81 persons and 2 servants; we also had 2 road waggons, 20 dearborns, 2 carts and one small piece of cannon about 3 lbr. We could not ascertain with certainty the amount of goods with us but estimated them at between 25 + 30,000 dollars—we have with us about 200 horses and mules."[29] The presence here of so many Dearborn carriages, which served better for carrying a few passengers than for hauling large amounts of goods, indicated that the big Conestoga-type wagons had not yet come to dominate the Santa Fe caravans. When they did, they would serve almost entirely as freight carriers rather than as homes on wheels. Travelers would ride horses or mules, or walk alongside the wagons, which sheltered them only at night, assuming that they could find enough room among the crates and bales to stretch out (if not, men sometimes slept under the wagons). Wagons stuffed with trade goods made serviceable bulwarks against attack when arrayed at night in a circle or square, with the animals corralled inside. That men who joined the 1824 caravan were concerned about such attacks was evidenced by preparations they made for the journey in Franklin, as described by Alphonso Wetmore, an army paymaster who had lost his right arm in battle during the War of 1812 and was not much impressed with these merchants-in-arms:

> These "Santa Fee boys" as they denominate themselves, are armed at all points. A long backwoods rifle is thrown in real vagabond style over the shoulder; a tomahawk, or as it is here termed a "Tommy hatchet" and knife graces the waist belt—and these not being sufficiently indicative of Banditti, they add to them a pair of horse pistols. Taking their arms and habiliments into view, and I am constrained [to] cry out in the language of honest Jack Falstaff "Who ever saw such scare crows!—I'll not march Through country with them, that's flat!" Most of these gentlemen cut throats are mounted [upon] worthy members of the Jackass family, who might claim kindred with some few of their riders. Their merchandize consists of every species of wares from a sheet anchor up & down to a Jewsharp.[30]

As often happened on the trail, the greatest challenge awaiting these "Santa Fee boys" came not from restive tribesmen but from hostile terrain. Marmaduke, whose journal entries seldom ran on at any length, was moved to eloquence by the ordeal his party faced when they crossed the Arkansas in late June, encamped amid the scrubby sand hills on the south bank, and set out early the next morning across the bleak and waterless expanse between the Arkansas and the Cimarron that became known as the Jornada—a desert crossing akin to the forbidding *Jornada del Muerto* (Journey of the Dead) between Albuquerque and El Paso:

> Tuesday 29th. Travelled about 30 miles, left our encampment at 4 o'Clock A.M. and travelled without making any halt until about 4 o'Clock P.M. without one drop of water for our horses or mules—by which time many of them were nearly exhausted for want of water, heat and fatigue—and many of the men whose water had all been drank early in the day, were also very nearly suffocated for want of water—a dog which had travelled with us during our rout, fell this day in the Prairie and expired in a few minutes, such was the extreme heat and suffering of the animals—fortunately, for us all at about 4 o'Clock P.M. a small ravine was discovered, and pursued for a few miles, and after digging in the sand in the bottom of it, water was procured in sufficient quantity to satisfy both man & horses but not until after 5 or 6 wells were sunk—and such was the extreme suffering of the animals, that it was with the utmost difficulty that the horses Could be kept out of the holes until buckets could be filled for them—I have never in all my life experienced a time when such general alarm and Consternation pervaded every person on account of the want of water.[31]

Was anything worth such deprivation, which could reduce men and beasts to fighting over the same filthy puddles? Apparently so, for Augustus Storrs estimated a return on trade with New Mexico in 1824 of no less than $180,000, much of which came from this caravan with its combined investment of some $30,000. Storrs, in answers to queries submitted to him by Senator Thomas Hart Benton of Missouri, summed up the venture and its rewards:

> *Query 5.* What time was occupied in going, accomplishing the object of the expedition, and returning?
>
> *Answer.* Four months and ten days.
>
> *Query 6.* What kinds of merchandise are principally carried out to the internal provinces?
>
> *Answer.* Cotton goods, consisting of coarse and fine cambrics, calicoes, domestic, shawls, handkerchiefs, steam-loom shirtings, and cotton hose. A few woollen goods, consisting of super blues, stroudings, pelisse cloths, and shawls, crapes, bombazettes, some light articles of cutlery, silk shawls, and looking glasses. In addition to these, many other articles, necessary for the purposes of an assortment.
>
> *Query 7.* What is received, and brought back, in exchange for merchandise carried out?
>
> *Answer.* Spanish milled dollars, a small amount of gold and silver, in bullion, beaver fur, and some mules.[32]

Most of the traders' profits, in other words, came in the form of currency, with the exception of beaver fur (prized as a kind of "soft gold") and mules, which were herded to Missouri in such quantities that they came to be identified with the state. A number of those mules were plowed right back into the Santa Fe trade, for they withstood the strain of hauling wagons better than horses and made good mounts, swift enough in some cases to chase down buffalo. (Not until the 1830s would oxen begin to supplant mules as draft animals on the trail.) The Santa Fe trade would have been a much chancier proposition in the early years without Mexican mules and Mexican muleteers, who kept many a caravan moving with their expertise and their stinging oaths.

Of all the assets Mexico brought to the exchange, however, it was the silver and gold that mattered most to cash-poor Missouri, where the influx of coins and bullion provided a boost to existing towns like St. Louis and helped build new ones like Independence, which supplanted Franklin as the jumping-off point for the Santa Fe trade around 1830. The trade meant prosperity not just for merchants but for wagonmakers, saddlers, dry goods dealers, and others who supplied the caravans. "The circulating medium of Missouri now consists principally of Mexican dollars," wrote Alphonso Wetmore a decade after the Santa Fe trade began. "Many of our citizens are profitably engaged in the trade; horses, mules, and oxen, are employed in carrying it on; the farmers and mechanics derive advantage from the outfits, and our whole community is benefited by this interesting traffic."[33]

Mindful of such potential benefits, Senator Benton used testimony he solicited from Augustus Storrs and others about the profitability of the trade to support a bill he pushed through Congress in early 1825 that provided $10,000 for surveying and marking out a road from the Missouri frontier to the boundary of Mexico (a road that would follow the ill-defined route traders were already using) and another $20,000 for treating with Indians along the way and securing their goodwill. Whether the survey would continue across the Arkansas through Mexican territory to Santa Fe remained to be seen. Benton remarked grandly in Congress that "I had always been opposed to the boundary line of 1819; and I liked it less when I found it a stumbling block in my road to Mexico."[34] Benton's bill made Benton's road the responsibility of the United States, however, and those conducting the survey could not mark a road through Mexico without permission from Mexico City to that effect.

The leading member of the three-man commission that conducted the survey was forty-three-year-old George Champlin Sibley, who had served for many years as the factor, or government trader, at Fort Osage and was well acquainted both with the Santa Fe trade and with the Osage and Kansas tribes, whose cooperation he would be seeking. Sibley understood that the road to New Mexico might serve not just to promote trade but to project American power. (In 1808, when tensions between the United States and Spain were running high, he had written that Fort Osage could serve as "a rallying post from whence to attack Santa Fee; we could march there and seize their rich mines in less than 20 days.")[35] But Sibley was no hotheaded expansionist. As factor, he had served as a kind of intermediary between Indians and the government, and he brought to his assignment as chief commissioner of the survey a patience and persistence that served him well in dealing both with tribal chiefs and with Mexican officials. He was also a gifted observer who documented the journey in fine detail. On August 5, 1825, when he and others of the surveying party reached the shady banks of the Neosho River in present-day Kansas and stopped at the spot he dubbed Council Grove for a meeting he held there a few days later with members of the Osage tribe, Sibley apologized in his journal for not describing the country he had traversed in greater detail:

> The manner that I was obliged to travel from Fort Osage to this place, fighting the flies, if I rode in the day time, without a moment's cessation, or else

feeling my way in the dark as I traveled by Night, made it impossible for me to notice the Country as particularly as I wished and intended if I had been able. I may remark generally that the far greater part of the way is Prairie, & that tolerably level & smooth, affording good Road, and with two exceptions, plenty of Water at convenient intervals. As we return, I shall be particular to Note everything worth notice that has been now omitted.[36]

Such dutifulness was characteristic of Sibley. Upon reaching the Arkansas, he went ahead to New Mexico with surveyor Joseph C. Brown and other members of the expedition after his two fellow commissioners elected to return to Missouri, having failed to receive permission to proceed through Mexican territory. Sibley's aim in continuing was not to provoke Mexican authorities (he refrained from marking the road in any way and simply measured the distance from point to point) but to seek permission to complete the project once he reached Santa Fe, thus saving the United States the trouble of reorganizing the costly expedition at some later date. He had been given a job to do, and he intended to finish it. As it turned out, he was received politely in Santa Fe by Governor Antonio Narbona and lavished with hospitality by the locals during the winter he spent there awaiting permission from Mexico City to mark the road on the way back. Mexican authorities did not want Americans marking their territory, however, and he was allowed only to examine, or survey, the road on his return journey that fall. It mattered little in the long run, for those mounds of sod that Sibley and company managed to erect on the American side of the boundary did not last very long or serve much of a purpose. "The Road as traveled is already well enough Marked by the Waggons," Sibley concluded, "any Mounds put up would be Soon thrown down by the Buffalo and Indians."[37] The official report he submitted was shelved in Congress, and he and his fellow commissioners spent years seeking reimbursement for extra expenses they paid out of their own pockets while surveying what Sibley, in a rare moment of pique, called "Benton's d——d Santa Fe road."[38]

The real significance of the survey was that it involved the federal government in what Benton envisioned hopefully as a "protected trade" on a protected route.[39] As yet, that protection consisted only of providing funds for settlements with Indians, but soon it would take the form of dispatching troops to safeguard travelers on the trail. Little by little, Washington was committing itself to a course of expansion that would lead ultimately to the taking of New Mexico and the displacement of the intervening tribes.

Few observers other than the irrepressible Benton could have foreseen consequences of that magnitude sprouting from the humble seeds of the Santa Fe trade. In 1823, according to the estimate of trader and trail historian Josiah

Gregg, only about fifty men—of whom thirty were traders and twenty were helpers or hired hands—set out from Missouri to New Mexico, carrying merchandise totaling scarcely $12,000 in value, roughly three-quarters of which was sold in Santa Fe with the rest destined for markets in Chihuahua and points beyond. Twenty years later, by contrast, thirty merchants employing more than three hundred men would transport $450,000 worth of merchandise to New Mexico, fully $300,000 of which would find its way to Chihuahua and beyond.[40] As attested by those figures, an enterprise that began with traders of limited means hauling small amounts of goods to Santa Fe with little or no help would increasingly become a concern for American and Mexican businessmen of extensive resources who sometimes traveled to New York and Philadelphia to purchase goods in bulk for shipment to Missouri, hired crews of up to a dozen or more men to escort their wagonloads across the plains, and sold their goods at markets deep inside Mexico. Santa Fe, once the prime destination for traders, would become for many a way station on the road to Chihuahua—a place of such well-advertised rewards for adventurers by the time of the Mexican War that American forces who claimed New Mexico in 1846 would readily abandon occupied Santa Fe in hazardous pursuit of that larger and wealthier objective to the south.

Benton helped foster such far-reaching developments not just through deft political maneuvering in Congress but through artful rhetoric. In arguing for the survey in 1825, for example, he managed to make a trade that as yet involved fewer merchants than did business in a single good-sized town sound like an undertaking of epic proportions and limitless possibilities. As he remarked in Congress of the report by Augustus Storrs:

> His account was full of interest and novelty. It sounded like romance to hear of caravans of men, horses, and wagons traversing with their merchandise the vast plain which lies between the Mississippi and the Rio del Norte. The story seemed better adapted to Asia than to North America. But, romantic as it might seem, the reality had already exceeded the visions of the wildest imagination. The journey to New Mexico, but lately deemed a chimerical project, had become an affair of ordinary occurrence. Santa Fe, but lately the *Ultima Thule* of American enterprise, was now considered as a stage only in the progress, or, rather, a new point of departure to our invincible citizens. Instead of turning back from that point, the caravans broke up there, and the sub-divisions branched off in different directions, in search of new theatres for their enterprise.[41]

Such rhetorical flights did as much as any marker or signpost to point the way to New Mexico for others to follow. From the beginning, the Santa Fe Trail was surveyed in imaginative terms and paved with legends, and that lore helped enhance the glamour of the trade and coax fresh legions of adventurers down the path. Although success was by no means assured, Americans came to think of New Mexico as a country where hopes were renewed and fortunes redeemed. It was "the land of promise—and the land of payment," in the words of Alphonso Wetmore, whose mock-epic send-up of the Santa Fe trade, "The Book of the Muleteers," appeared anonymously in the *Missouri Intelligencer* in August of 1825. As the author elaborated in biblical fashion, the gold and silver carried home from New Mexico seemed to ease doubts, erase debts, and restore vitality:

> 23. And the music thereof is like the music of running waters in a great desert when the horse and rider thirsteth with a parched tongue.
> 24. It maketh the feeble strong, the lame leap, and the aged forget their grey hairs, yea it turneth the hair of the head like the plumage of the raven.
> 25. It inclineth the maiden to listen unto the word of him that wooeth, even the old men and the maidens are made glad thereat.
> 26. It buildeth up kingdoms and layeth the city and high palaces low.
> 27. It breaketh the bolts of the prison door—it causeth disease to flee away.[42]

This might be the first piece of outright fiction concerning the trade, but the literature of the Santa Fe Trail already had a fair start in the journals of Becknell, Sibley, and others. Whether jotted down on the spot, reconstructed in retrospect, or refashioned by scribes or editors for the printed page, these accounts were all earnest attempts to appraise in English a strange and challenging world that honored other currencies and could not easily be captured in any language. This effort to evaluate foreign experiences in familiar words— to offer the right terms for prospects that often seemed to defy calculation— was among the most important exchanges travelers on the road to New Mexico engaged in, for that process transformed what might otherwise have been mere annals or ledgers into an alluring body of literature that drew many others down the trail in person or in spirit and involved Americans imaginatively in this complex and fateful encounter with Indian country and the Spanish Southwest. In the quarter century between Becknell's first journey and the Mexican War, scores of travelers left written records of their journeys to Santa Fe and back, some of which reached large audiences in the author's lifetime and others of which appeared posthumously. Of these chroniclers, a dozen or so produced narratives of unusual merit—discriminating accounts that weighed profit against loss, promise against reality, and summed up this ambiguous venture in all its rich variety.

4

Authors on the Trail
(1829–1848)

In 1829, Lieutenant Philip St. George Cooke embarked on the first of
several trips down the Santa Fe Trail that would make him a vital witness
to America's westward expansion. Assigned to an expedition led by Major
Bennet Riley that escorted traders as far as the Arkansas River in July and
accompanied them back to Missouri in the fall, the twenty-year-old Cooke
was part of the first such effort to protect travelers on the trail from raids by
Indians. This pioneering escort was not a great success. The U.S. Army as yet
had no cavalry, and Riley's foot soldiers had difficulty coping with mounted
Indians of considerable skill and determination—most likely Comanches and
perhaps their Kiowa allies—who harried the troops and the traders on either
side of the Arkansas, leaving Cooke and others with the impression that the
presence of ill-equipped troops had perhaps done more to incite trouble here
than to repress it. The expedition was far from being a lost cause for Cooke,
however, who found ample material for diary entries that he transformed
many years later into a memoir, *Scenes and Adventures in the Army: Or
Romance of Military Life* (1857). In one characteristic passage, Cooke
described his Indian opponents in words that conveyed both resentment and
respect:

> It was a humiliating condition to be surrounded by these rascally Indians,
> who, by means of their horses, could tantalize us with the hopes of battle,
> and elude our efforts; who could annoy us by preventing all individual excur-
> sions for hunting, &c., and who could insult us with impunity. Much did we

regret that we were not mounted too; and I believe nearly all prayed that the enemy would become bolder, and enliven us with frequent attacks; but this was their last, though they were frequently seen hovering around; and the running of buffalo was a sign of their vicinity, frequently observed on our hunts. It is known that they crawl to the tops of commanding hills, and using the head and skin of a wolf as a mask, spy out the motions of an enemy, with little or no risk of discovery; but despising us—wholly on the defensive—they now took not this trouble, but appeared openly on the hills.[1]

Cooke might call these warriors enemies and "savages," but in such passages he paid due tribute to their powers. He shared their conception of battle as noble and enlivening and dreaded their contempt no less than that of his peers. It required a man of some complexity to honor the virtues of foes others derided and despised, and Cooke was a study in contradictions. Born in Virginia to slaveholders, he later sided with the Union in the Civil War. Educated at West Point, he cared as much for poetic feats as for military exploits, referring to the prairie in Shakespearean fashion at one point as "stale and unprofitable"[2] and faulting his messmates for lack of literary enthusiasm. "Strange, indeed, that of ten young officers, not one brought a Don Juan into the wilderness," he complained. "Is it possible that already the torrent of *steam literature* has cast Byron into the drift?"[3] From literature, Cooke derived a keen sense of irony and an appreciation for the fine line separating heroism from villainy, or callousness from compassion. He himself was capable of both in roughly equal measure. He once fired a cannon at a distant herd of buffalo simply to study the effect, and went chasing after a wolf that meant no harm and emptied his pistol at the animal (such vengeance on dumb brutes was by no means uncommon on the trail). Yet he also had a rare appreciation for the plains and its oft maligned creatures, remarking of the howling of wolves and coyotes (often referred to as prairie wolves)—a nocturnal serenade that prompted some weary travelers to take potshots at the animals—that "I *never* heard without pleasure this voice of the Night."[4]

Cooke's capacity to take the part of the downtrodden was not limited to the animal kingdom. In 1843 he led an expedition down the Santa Fe Trail to guard Mexican traders against marauders acting in the name of Texas. He characterized those he was assigned to protect crudely at one point as "ragged-rascal greasers,"[5] but such language belied his determination to defend them against attacks like the one that claimed the life of Mexican trader Antonio José Chávez earlier in 1843. "Here, without a tear, a word, a look of human sympathy, was poor Charvis deliberately murdered," Cooke lamented at the site of the crime. "The famished howling wolves do not tear their kind!"[6] So

Brigadier General Philip St. George Cooke. Used by permission, State Historical Society of Missouri, Columbia, all rights reserved.

conscientiously did he carry out his orders to defend Mexicans on the trail that summer that he was selected by his commander, Stephen Watts Kearny, to travel ahead of the army of conquest in 1846 with a delegation that may have helped induce Governor Manuel Armijo of New Mexico to yield without a fight, an experience Cooke chronicled in another book drawn from his diaries, *The Conquest of New Mexico and California, an Historical and Per-*

sonal Narrative (1878). He did not relish the idea of entering Santa Fe under a white flag—military glory in the form of "stirring war scenes"[7] seemed to elude him—but he carried out that delicate assignment to the letter and went on to lead the Mormon Battalion across the desert to California that fall. Like the army he cherished and long served, Cooke often found himself in an ambiguous position, caught between war-making and peacekeeping, between exploring the West and exploiting it. As luck would have it, he was ideally suited by temperament to appreciate and elucidate the contradictions of his own task—and of the larger mission that began in 1806, when Lieutenant Pike headed west on the journey that brought him to the Palace of Governors as a prisoner, and culminated forty years later when General Kearny claimed that same palace as his headquarters.

Cooke may have witnessed more of the history of the trail than any other chronicler up through the Mexican War, but no traveler knew the Santa Fe trade better or described it more eloquently than Josiah Gregg, who came of age in Missouri not far from Franklin. In his youth he tried his hand at surveying and schoolteaching, read law for a while, and considered studying medicine (an interest to which he later returned) before heading west to cure an obscure illness in 1831 at the age of twenty-four and finding both his health and his calling on the road to New Mexico. In 1844, after several trips to Santa Fe and beyond as a trader, he published his classic account, *Commerce of the Prairies*, edited lightly by John Bigelow, who later described the author as he appeared at the time: "He had fine blue eyes and an honest although not a cheerful expression, due, as I afterward learned, to chronic dyspepsia. He was withal very shy and as modest as a school-girl."[8] Gregg's book was immediately recognized as definitive by readers who had traveled the Santa Fe Trail, and it became a guidebook for others who aspired to the journey. A review that appeared in the *Independence Journal* on September 19, 1844, offered an assessment that few readers in later years would quarrel with:

> It possesses great merit, and we cannot speak too highly of it as a literary production: the style is easy and flowing—the contents rich in incident, and highly graphic of prairie life; besides, it contains a vast amount of information not to be found in any other work. . . . Perhaps the highest encomium which could be passed upon it, is the universal commendation which it receives from all who have visited Santa Fe, and who have had opportunities of becoming acquainted with Mexican manners, prairie life and the Indians of the plains; and there are many such here.[9]

The reviewer went on to note that "the work comprises two volumes, and may be had at the store of Mr. S. C. Owens, in this place," a reference to Samuel

C. Owens, a prominent Independence merchant who traveled to New Mexico as a trader more than once and died in battle in 1847 as part of a merchant battalion enlisted to bolster American troops as they were marching from Santa Fe to Chihuahua.

The war that occasioned Owens's death was not particularly welcome to Gregg, even though he volunteered to accompany American troops in the conflict as a sort of guide and interpreter. "When the subject was first agitated," he noted, "I had my misgivings as to the consequences and policy, and also thought the rights of Mexico should be to some degree respected."[10] Those initial misgivings were more characteristic of Gregg than his subsequent decision to join the war effort. It was not that he felt Mexico was necessarily in the right. (His book contains sharp criticisms of Mexicans and their rulers.) But Gregg was a trader at heart, who believed in negotiating differences to mutual advantage when possible. While devoting considerable attention in his book to the warlike propensities of those he called "wild Indians" or "savages," for example, he argued forcefully that conflict could be avoided on the trail through a combination of vigilance and a willingness to engage Indians in peaceful exchanges:

> The Santa Fé caravans have generally avoided every manner of trade with the wild Indians, for fear of being treacherously dealt with during the familiar intercourse which necessarily ensues. This I am convinced is an erroneous impression; for I have always found, that savages are much less hostile to those with whom they trade, than to any other people. They are emphatically fond of traffic, and, being anxious to encourage the whites to come among them, instead of committing depredations upon those with whom they trade, they are generally ready to defend them against every enemy.[11]

As late as 1844, Gregg hoped that trade and the "familiar intercourse" it entailed would have a similar effect of diverting the United States and Mexico from hostile exchanges. He was soon to return to the study of medicine, and throughout his book one can detect the musings of an intellect concerned with the causes of social as well as physical ills. He believed that life on the trail and immersion in the trade had cured him, and he sensed that free and vigorous trade was therapeutic for societies as a whole, that it channeled toward constructive ends competitive energies that might otherwise lead to bitterness and bloodshed. After a tour with the army in Mexico during the war that brought him little satisfaction, it was fitting that he returned to Mexico and practiced as a doctor in Saltillo for a while. "If I could make myself as easy in American society," he wrote his brother John, "I would be willing to live in the United States."[12] America was fortunate that this restless son never

Josiah Gregg. Courtesy Museum of New Mexico, negative no. 9896.

felt quite at ease in his native land and ventured out repeatedly to treat with cultures rich and strange and come to grips with them in writing.

A few months after Josiah Gregg embarked on his first journey to New Mexico in 1831, another young man of literary disposition started down the Santa Fe Trail. Born in Boston in 1809, Albert Pike showed early promise as a scholar, poet, and schoolmaster in New England but went west at twenty-one in search of fortune and inspiration. Unlike Gregg, who composed his account more than a decade after he began his travels, Pike was quick to trade on his travels in print. He evidently saw this as a literary adventure from the start and soon fulfilled its promise in a remarkable volume, *Prose Sketches and Poems, Written in the Western Country* (1834). In several newspaper articles he wrote around the same time, he dealt succinctly with his journey to New Mexico with a caravan captained by Charles Bent, a trader of exceptional energy and ambition who was soon to establish Bent's Fort. Bent's company left Independence in September 1831 with ox-drawn wagons and endured drought, cold, and snow along the way. Pike did not much care for the rigors of the trail or the duties he had to perform, but his imagination was stirred by the sheer desolation of the country and the harsh terms it imposed on intruders, as when his party crossed the Arkansas in mid-October and set out across the desert to the bone-dry Cimarron: "Our oxen, from hunger and drought, began to fail, and we were, every day or two, obliged to leave one behind us. The hungry jaws of the white wolves soon caused them to disappear from the face of the earth, and by thus affording these voracious animals food, we had a continual train of lean, lank and gaunt followers, resembling Hunger-demons, following us stealthily by day, and howling around us by night."[13] For Pike as for Cooke and other impressionable witnesses, it was the wolf more than the buffalo that seemed to capture the spirit of the plains, where the quick and the keen triumphed over the stubborn and plodding.

Not until Pike reached the end of the trail, however, did he truly find grist for his literary mill. His fruitful encounter with New Mexico yielded not only poetry but also "prose sketches" after the fashion of Washington Irving. These stories ventured beyond the limits of Pike's experience into the realm of fiction and conveyed the wondrous sensation of coming into a country at once younger and infinitely older than the world the author left behind. He was welcomed there in isolated settlements with a hospitality that astonished him, as it did many other early visitors. As the narrator remarked in one of his tales: "I have never, at a single door, requested food and lodging, by the untranslatable expression, *tengo posada?* (literally, have I a tavern?) without being promptly answered in the affirmative."[14] The privilege of being received thus was not lost on Pike, who was graced both with a knowledge of Spanish and with a sharp eye for the landscape and interiors of New Mexico, as in this fine view of a home where the narrator spent the night:

> Passing through the sala, or long hall, which was garnished with vast quantities of buffalo meat, in thin, dry fleeces, as well as with huge strings of onions, and of red and green pepper, besides numberless saddle-trees, heavy bridles, and not a few buffalo robes, we entered the small square room which was the winter residence. In one corner of it stood the little fireplace, like a square stove, open on two sides, and filled with small sticks of pine set upright and

burning, filling the room with all heat and comfort. Round the whole room, except the part occupied by two mattrasses, was a pile of blankets, striped red and white, answering the purpose of sofas. High up on the walls were various small looking-glasses, pictures of saints, wooden images of the Saviour, and wooden crucifixes, interspersed with divers roses of red and white cambric. These, with two or three wooden benches which served for both chairs and tables, completed the furniture of the room. . . . Contrary to our fears, supper came in a reasonable space of time, and we did good justice to the pounded dry buffalo meat, the beans and the blood-red dish of meat and pepper, all of them inseparable from a New Mexican table, and forthwith consigned ourselves to the blankets and mattrasses of our landlady.[15]

For all his precision, Pike was not always faithful to New Mexico in spirit. He was intrigued by the idea that Americans were destined to inherit this country and personified that possibility in characters such as Lem, "a Kentuckian and a blacksmith, who, from the spirit of curiosity, had come to New Mexico, and from the spirit of gain, had remained there." Brave as a lion, Lem was "ready to follow his feelings in any enterprise" and acted with a freedom and firmness that seemed to elude the New Mexicans Pike described.[16] Pike himself later overcame some initial qualms and served as an officer in the Mexican War, taking part in the Battle of Buena Vista. A longtime resident of Arkansas, he went on to side with the South in 1861 and serve as Confederate commissioner to the Indians, luring factions of the Cherokees and several other tribes into alliances with the Confederacy that embroiled those Indians in ruinous conflict with their fellow tribesmen and brought Pike himself grief from critics on both sides of the conflict. Nothing in his military career proved quite as rewarding as that first foray down the trail as a young man, when he was captured by New Mexico and claimed the place imaginatively in return.

The opening of Bent's Fort around 1833 provided a haven for travelers following the Mountain Route of the Santa Fe Trail and an alluring new setting for travelers to weave tales around. Some of those who traveled to Bent's Fort early on were either unable or unwilling to write but offered their engaging stories to readers in later years through literate intermediaries. One such teller of tales was Richens Lacy Wootton, born in Virginia in 1816 and known in later years as Uncle Dick. In 1836 he inaugurated an eventful career as a mountain man—engaged variously as a trapper, trader, wagon driver, hunter, and guide—by enlisting with Charles Bent and company and joining an outfit in Independence bound for Bent's Fort. By his own account, young Wootton could handle a mule team and "use a gun as well as anybody,"[17] but like many other greenhorns on the trail, he was inclined to see hostile Indians everywhere. One night on guard duty, he related, he blazed away prematurely at a seemingly threatening figure in the distance:

> I wasn't a coward, if I was a boy, and my hair didn't stand on end, although it may have raised up a little. Of course, the first thing I thought of was Indians, and the more I looked at the dark object creeping along toward the camp, the more it looked to me like a blood-thirsty savage. I didn't get excited, although they tried to make me believe I was afterward, but thought the matter over and made up my mind that whatever the thing was, it had no business out there. So I blazed away at it and down it dropped. The shot roused everybody in camp, and they all came running out with their guns in their hands to see what was up.
>
> I told them I had seen what I supposed was an Indian trying to slip into camp and I had killed him. Very cautiously several of the men crept down to where the supposed dead Indian was lying. I stood at my post and listened for their report, and by and by I heard one of the men say "I'll be cussed if he haint killed Old Jack." "Old Jack" was one of our lead mules. He had gotten loose and strayed outside the lines, and the result was that he met his death. I felt sorry about it, but the mule had disobeyed orders you know, and I wasn't to blame for killing him.[18]

How much of this artfully constructed tale was Wootton's work, one wonders, and how much of it was shaped and varnished by Howard Louis Conard, who set the story in print in 1890 after interviewing the elderly Wootton? Conard admitted in his preface to knocking some rough edges off Wootton's speech and rounding out some sentences, but he challenged the notion that Wootton and others of his ilk were incapable of expressing themselves in plain English. "I shall not try to make it appear that the mountaineers were a lot of highly educated, polished gentlemen," Wootton remarked by Conard's account, "nor shall I make them talk like a pack of savages, as they generally do in frontier stories, because that would be doing all of them a rank injustice."[19]

This could be a reference to the frontier tales of Englishman George Frederick Ruxton, who traveled widely in the West in the 1840s and visited New Mexico soon after it was occupied by American troops. Ruxton's writings did much to popularize the mountain men and their vernacular, which he presented as a goulash of English, French, and Spanish, with a few Indian terms thrown in for good measure. ("Voyez-vous dat I vas nevare tan pauvre as dis time," one such mountaineer complained to Ruxton; "mais before I vas siempre avec plenty café, plenty sucre; mais now, God dam, I not go à Santa Fé, God dam, and mountain-men dey come aqui from autre côté, drink all my café.")[20] Other accounts confirm that mountain men of French extraction used a lingo much like this to communicate with those of other tongues. But that did not mean they were necessarily inarticulate in their native tongue, any more than Wootton was according to Conard. Some mountain men were indeed crude in speech and rough in manner, frittering away their earnings by drinking and gambling and never amounting to much. But the evidence of Wootton's career suggests that he was one of the more polished members of his trade, who knew how to craft a good story, cultivate the trust of shrewd men like Charles Bent, and explore his own profitable avenues, including building and operating a toll road through Raton Pass in his later years.

In one respect, Wootton lived up to the image of the mountain man purveyed by Ruxton—his low regard for Indians and Mexicans. Although he traded peacefully with various plains tribes for Bent (who sought buffalo furs from Indians to compensate for the dwindling number of beaver pelts that trappers brought in) and described himself as being "in high favor among the Arapahoes,"[21] Wootton was living proof that trade did not always breed tolerance. He laced his account with some of the baldest expressions of Indian-hating in the literature of the Santa Fe Trail, remarking of a run-in with Comanches in 1836 that "when they finally retreated they left three good Indians where they had fallen from their horses. You understand, when I say good Indians, that I mean dead ones."[22] During the Mexican War, by his own account, he joined enthusiastically in the retribution against Mexicans and Pueblos who rose up against American rule and killed Charles Bent, appointed governor of the occupied territory by General Kearny. Not all mountain men were intolerant or truculent, but more than any other group on the trail they embraced the full spectrum of dealings with Indians and Mexicans, ranging from the most intimate forms of exchange (many mountain men married Indians or Mexicans and adopted some of their customs or costume) to guarded commercial intercourse to savage give-and-take on the battlefield.

The year 1839 was a busy one for literate travelers on the Mountain Route of the Santa Fe Trail. In late May, an adventurous writer and lawyer from New England in his mid-thirties named Thomas Jefferson Farnham led a party of eighteen men with pack mules west from Independence. Known as the Peoria party for the town in Illinois where they first banded together, they were headed for Oregon but traveled on the Santa Fe Trail as far as Bent's Fort before continuing on to the Pacific Northwest in smaller groups, having quarreled and lost cohesion on their way to the fort. Farnham's account of his journey, *Travels in the Great Western Prairies* (1841), was lively and impressionistic. Compared to Gregg, his knowledge of the country and its inhabitants was superficial, and he was prone to error and exaggeration. But he offered readers the fresh perspective of a greenhorn, not yet hardened to the rigors of the trail and willing admit to fears and fancies that more experienced travelers might suppress. A proud veteran might make no greater admission to hunger than tightening his belt a notch and jotting down a few spare words in his diary to the effect that another day had passed without sight of game. But Farnham made a verbal feast of the famine he and his ill-provisioned men endured briefly in June on their way to the Arkansas, until one of their number made a fortunate kill:

> Two of the advance platoon took the liberty in the absence of their commander to give chase to an antelope that seemed to tantalize their forbearance by exhibiting his fine sirloins to their view. Never did men better earn forgiveness for disobedience of orders. One of them crept as I learned half a mile upon his hands and knees to get within rifle shot of his game;—shot at three hundred yards distance and brought him down! And now, who, in the tameness of an enough-and-to-spare state of existence, in which every emotion of the mind is surfeited and gouty, can estimate our pleasure at seeing these men gallop into our ranks with this antelope? You may "guess" reader, you may "reckon," you may "calculate" or if learned in the demisemi-quavers of modern exquisiteness, you may thrust rudely aside all these wholesome and fat old words of the heart and "shrewdly imagine" and still you cannot comprehend the feelings of that moment! Did we shout? were we silent? no, neither. Did we gather quickly around the horse stained with the blood of the suspended animal? No nor this. An involuntary murmur of relief from the most fearful forebodings, and the sudden halt of the riding animals in their tracks were the only movements, the only acts that indicated our grateful joy at this deliverance.[23]

Farnham's literary effusiveness stood in stark contrast to the lean observations of another traveler, German-born physician and naturalist Frederick A. Wislizenus, who stopped at Bent's Fort that September and journeyed back to Missouri along the Santa Fe Trail on the last leg of a western tour. Wislizenus, in the book he published describing this 1839 journey and a later account covering his trip west along the Santa Fe Trail and down into Mexico in 1846, confined himself to brief, precise journal entries that revealed more about the country and its characteristics than about the author and his traveling companions.[24]

If Wislizenus was a bit sparing and Farnham at times overgenerous with his reflections, a third traveler who reached Bent's Fort between the two that summer on his way to Santa Fe came as close as any chronicler of the trail to achieving a perfect balance between astute observation and imaginative interpretation. Actor Matthew C. Field, born in England to Irish parents and raised largely in New York City, left the stage in St. Louis in his late twenties and headed west to recover his health and gather material for a new career as a writer. He had schooled himself in Shakespeare and performed in supporting roles with some of the finest actors of his day. His literary instincts were high-flown and feverishly romantic, but he harnessed his talents to the task at hand and translated his impressions of the journey into a prodigious series of more than eighty articles, written for the *New Orleans Picayune* over the course of two years after he returned from New Mexico in November 1839. Those pieces were not collected in book form during his lifetime, but they were widely reprinted in other newspapers, often without crediting him as the author. Like Albert Pike, Matt Field ruminated on his travels in poetry as well as prose and sometimes ventured into the realm of legend or fancy, but his best work was rooted in the prosaic details of life on the trail. From those common threads of experience he wove a tapestry that spanned the physical and cultural distance between Missouri and New Mexico.

"The tenants of the fort were merry fellows," Field wrote of his stay at Bent's establishment, adding that "we were a set of youths well worthy to shake hands with them, and as such meetings, to the lonely sojourners in the desert, were indeed much like 'angels' visits,' the time was mutually appreciated, and by no means suffered to pass unimproved."[25] He and his companions improved their time by telling stories—and improved those stories by grinding and polishing them to bring out new facets for the enjoyment of their audience, an operation at which Field was expert. More than Albert Pike, however, he was concerned with offering readers enlightenment as well as entertainment. Few Americans who traveled to New Mexico in the early years wrote with more sympathy or understanding of its culture or customs. His story "A Wedding," for instance, paid generous tribute to the decision of a roving American to settle down with the Mexican woman who had borne him several children out of wedlock. "We found our young countryman in a situation which we were far more inclined to envy than to commiserate," Field wrote. "The Mexican girl, it was evident, stored up the whole treasure of her young affections in her American husband, and he seemed to love his children the more for possessing the dark eyes of their mother."[26] Field showed a rare appreciation in such sketches for the ways in which New Mexico and its people could lay claim to Americans and draw them into a world richer in some ways than their own.

In a sense, "A Wedding" and other hopeful sketches by Field of fruitful exchanges between New Mexicans and Americans marked the end of an era. In the near future, relations between the two sides would be severely strained by a gathering conflict that received its impetus not so much from Missouri—although there were more than a few Missourians who would be glad to see

Matthew C. Field. Courtesy Missouri Historical Society, St. Louis.

their nation seize New Mexico—but from Texas. When the Union embraced Texas as a state in 1845, Americans inherited troublesome claims by Texans to territory that Mexico regarded as its own, including everything east of the Rio Grande (an area that included Santa Fe and most other New Mexican settlements). One party of adventurers had already attempted to stake that claim, or at least explore the possibility of doing so—the ill-fated members of the

Texan Santa Fe expedition of 1841, whose plight was chronicled by another gifted writer connected with the *New Orleans Picayune*, George Wilkins Kendall, editor and cofounder of that newspaper. Although the expedition Kendall joined as an observer followed a route well south of the Santa Fe Trail—one through northern Texas that brought the Pioneers, as they called themselves, up against defiant Kiowas—this ambiguous undertaking was a crucial link in the chain of events that began with Zebulon Pike's reconnaissance early in the century and culminated in an American invasion. Inspired in part by reports of the lucrative Santa Fe trade, a force of several hundred Pioneers ventured to New Mexico with merchandise in train to peddle those goods—and if the conditions proved ripe, to sell the populace on the idea of overthrowing their rulers and uniting with Texas, which had achieved independence from Mexico just five years earlier. Kendall scoffed at the notion that the Pioneers were "but a company of marauders, sent to burn, slay and destroy,"[27] and indeed their orders specified that they were not to attempt an uprising if Mexican authorities offered armed resistance with the support of "the mass of the people."[28] But this two-sided expedition demonstrated how seemingly harmonious intercourse could lead under certain conditions to a takeover bid. Like Lieutenant Pike, the Texans claimed to be merely reconnoitering their own country and exploring the possibilities for peaceful exchanges, but Mexican officials had good reason to view their venture otherwise.

As it turned out, the Pioneers reaped neither profit nor glory. Disorganized and depleted by the rigors of the journey, those who made it to New Mexico did so in tattered groups and soon became prisoners. This was a costly victory for Mexican authorities, however, for the taking of captives and the harsh treatment they received from their overseers, who herded them southward along the Chihuahua Trail to confinement in Mexico City, stirred up fiery resentments in Texas and parts of the United States and brought Mexico a step closer to war with a powerful and expansive neighbor who would soon assume the quarrels of Texas along with its territory.

Kendall's vivid account of the ordeal, *Narrative of the Texan Santa Fé Expedition* (1844), may have contributed to the war fever, but the author was no mere propagandist. He was sympathetic to the New Mexicans in some respects and gratefully acknowledged the kind treatment he and his fellow captives received from the women of the country in particular. "That the women all pitied us was evident," he wrote, "for the commiserating exclamation of *pobrecitos!* as they gave us bread, cheese, and such food as they had at hand, fell from their tongues in softest and most feeling tones."[29] Kendall looked far less kindly on the men of the country, however, and he sometimes tinged his assaults on New Mexican governor Manuel Armijo and others whom he held responsible for mistreatment of the captives with racial venom. "He is afraid of Anglo-Saxon blood," the author wrote of Armijo, "and he seeks to spill it by protecting the knife of the secret assassin, or by influencing, to most outrageous decisions, his farcical courts of law."[30] Kendall ran the gamut in his responses to Mexico and her people, praising the "dark-eyed *señoras* of the northern departments" for their uncorseted charms ("the forms of the gentler sex obtain a roundness, a fulness, which the divinity of tight lacing never allows her votaries"),[31] sparring rhetorically with Armijo and his minions, and coming to terms with nobler representatives of the Mexican cause, including his considerate host in El Paso, Padre Ramón Ortiz, a devout patriot who seemed to recognize the risks for his country of mistreating the Pioneers and did his best to remind Kendall that most Mexicans preferred accommodation and gracious give-and-take with their neighbors to the alternatives of entangling intimacy or ruinous conflict.

As demonstrated by Kendall's harmonious interlude with Ortiz, the peaceful aspects of the American exchange with Mexico were not entirely obscured by the gathering storm clouds. The year 1843 was indeed a tempestuous one along the trail, marked by attacks on Mexicans by marauders from Texas and elsewhere that prompted Philip St. George Cooke's peacekeeping mission that summer. But between that flurry of violence and the outbreak of war in 1846, a number of chroniclers made journeys to New Mexico and back that were devoted to commerce and other inoffensive pursuits. Perhaps the best spokesman for those who took to the trail during this period and pursued trade while others contemplated war was James Josiah Webb, a storekeeper from Connecticut who left the dry goods business in St. Louis in the summer of 1844 at the age of twenty-six to join a caravan to Santa Fe. Graced with patience, persistence, and a lively sense of humor, he valued what he gained in terms of experience and amusement along the way as much as any material rewards, which were not always substantial. While other travelers prided themselves on the fine horses they rode, Webb settled gladly for his mule Dolly—a steady mount and swift enough to chase down buffalo—and was not ashamed to confess himself indebted to her:

> This is a long story about a mule, but Dolly with all her naughtiness was an animal I loved. She never failed me from weariness, carried me as fast as it ever became necessary to ride, and as easy as the rocking of a cradle, through many long and weary journeys, and under the protection of a kind Providence through dangers seen and unseen. And I cannot do less in giving this account of my journeyings than pay this affectionate and merited tribute to her memory.[32]

Webb penned this memoir late in life, and here as elsewhere he seemed intent on settling accounts and giving his companions and partners their due while he still had the chance. Unlike other traders who railed against the tariffs they had to pay in Santa Fe and the corruption that sometimes attended the collection of duties there, Webb accepted those and other customs of the country as he found them. He understood that trade with another culture required certain adjustments in one's material and moral evaluations. He was even inclined to extend some credit to Governor Armijo, regarded by Kendall and others as beyond redemption:

> From a long acquaintance with him, and from the representations of other traders who had a more intimate acquaintance with him, I am satisfied the American opinion of him, derived from the manner of his obtaining the position of governor and [from] the account of him given by Kendall in his *Expedition*, is unjust. He was naturally irritable and sometimes overbearing, but allowance should be made for his early opportunities. He was emphatically a self-made man, and rose from the position of pastor, or sheep herder, to that of governor by his own energies, without aid, counsel, or even sympathy from those in higher position.[33]

Armijo was not in fact of humble origins, but Webb was correct in stating that the governor labored under a handicap, for his department and his administration were impoverished, even if he himself was not, and he received little help from higher authorities in Mexico City.[34]

Although Webb dabbled in politics in later years, serving for a term in the New Mexico Assembly in the 1850s and later as a state senator in Connecticut, he remained a trader to the core and often expressed himself in financial terms, making due "allowance" for Armijo's difficulties and paying Dolly her "merited tribute." While other Missourians prepared for war in 1846, he went about his business, traveling to Santa Fe with a caravan in early May ahead of the occupation forces. The war caught up with him eventually, and he was detained by Mexican troops in Chihuahua for a while. But unlike trader Samuel Owens, who helped Webb get started on the trail in 1844 and later became embroiled in the fighting, Webb stayed resolutely on the sidelines, awaiting the opportunity to reengage Mexicans on his own terms.

He was not the only trader who looked forward to a peaceful and profitable foray in 1846 and had to reckon with the complications of war. Trader Edward James Glasgow, the son of a prominent St. Louis merchant, was preparing with his brother William for a venture deep into Mexico. He described the hubbub that May in Independence, where traders bound for Santa Fe and points beyond jostled with emigrants heading for the Oregon Trail and volunteers destined for nearby Fort Leavenworth, the training ground for Kearny's Army of the West:

> In this good town everything is now alive with excitement. All the traders are busy, hurrying to get off, and the balance of the lords of creation are drumming up their courage and enlisting to go west and carry destruction and all sorts of balls and bowie knives into the humble village of Santa Fe. The Emigrants to Oregon and California are passing through daily in numbers, and it appears that very soon there will hardly be enough people left to take care of the town.[35]

Aside from the sundry merchants, soldiers, and emigrants heading west, several talented artists and writers traveled that year to Independence and the budding new town of Westport (the future Kansas City) to immerse themselves in the spring flood of humanity that surged through the area and branched out along the Oregon and Santa Fe Trails. Young Francis Parkman reached the area by steamboat in early May to pursue the journey that would form the basis for his celebrated account, *The Oregon Trail* (1849), a work concluding with a brief description of his return trip along the Santa Fe Trail in the fall of 1846.[36] Others who passed through Independence that spring included Josiah Gregg, looking for a way to make himself useful in the forthcoming conflict; and artists John Mix Stanley and Alfred S. Waugh, an Irish immigrant who composed an irreverent account of his stay in Independence during one of the most exciting seasons ever experienced in the so-called prairie ports that embraced travelers and their cash and disgorged them well equipped onto the western trails. (Waugh reached Santa Fe in June, in advance of American troops, and penned a dispatch that testified to the influence of Josiah Gregg and George Kendall on travelers to New Mexico around this time. "I have Gregg's 'Commerce of the Prairies,' and Kendall's Texan 'Santa Fé Expedition' with me," he wrote, "but do not intend reading either book until I have made my own observations; at the same time, I would recommend both to your perusal, for I am told they are interesting and graphic.")[37]

The army mustered more than a few gifted chroniclers of its own in this spring of high suspense and lofty expectations. Although the volunteers for Kearny's force were recruited in Missouri, many had come to the state in recent years from other places. Frank S. Edwards, for example, who enlisted with an artillery company in St. Louis at the age of nineteen, was a native of England, but he readily identified with his fellow Missourians and saw the campaign as a quarrel between his adopted state and New Mexico. The Santa Fe trade was "principally managed by citizens of Missouri," he wrote, and those enterprising Missourians had been subjected by Governor Armijo to "numerous extortions."[38] Edwards conceded that there was a bit more to the conflict than this—the complaints he cited were minor irritants in Mexican-American relations compared to the long-running dispute between Mexico and Texas that sparked the war—but he aptly described the mixed impulses of resentment, excitement, patriotism, and opportunism that led more than a thousand Missourians to join several hundred Regular Army troops for the grueling campaign. The lucrative trade with New Mexico, Edwards noted, inspired in those who had not yet made the journey visions of "vast mines of gold and silver at Santa Fé; and the young men of all classes were eager to go."[39]

What Edwards and his comrades encountered in New Mexico—after a march that exposed them to brutal heat, bad water, and plagues of mosquitoes and other pests—was not a place of glittering opportunities but a poor country that could barely meet its own needs, let alone those of the occupiers. For many of the volunteers, New Mexico was a land of disenchantment. As one officer complained in a letter home: "You have always heard that this was an El dorado of a country abounding in beautiful hills and valleys . . . and teeming with a happy cheerful population, it is all a humbug. the country is a sandy barren country covered with a sickly vegitation, and inhabited by a race of people but little superior to our negroes living in low mud houses, in a word the whole of Mexico that I have seen as yet is not worth the devils Fetching."[40]

The sense of having gained at great effort a prize that seemed scarcely worth fighting for left some of the troops feeling slighted and resentful toward the populace. Frank Edwards served as quartermaster for his company and proved less than tactful in securing provisions from locals who had little to spare—or little desire to share what they had with the enemy. At one point, he accused a priest of cheating him in a deal for corn, and the priest responded by calling him a liar. "On which, I caught him by the neckcloth," Edwards related, "drew out my butcher's knife, told him that, in my opinion, he was a rascal, and that if he dared to repeat such words, I should use my cold steel."[41] Underlying the frustrations of brash young recruits like Edwards was the discovery that their seeming victory in no way exempted them from having to bargain with New Mexicans. Kearny's army was woefully undersupplied, and while some quartermasters requisitioned what they needed from the locals, pilfering was discouraged as a matter of principle and policy, for fear of provoking a popular uprising against the troops. Victory had come without expense in blood because Armijo chose not to resist, but maintaining control of New Mexico was a costly and delicate proposition that required soldiers to function partly as traders or middlemen and make compromises that did not come easily to fighting men.

Reckoning with this strange brand of warfare required some perspective and maturity, and two of the most insightful and fair-minded chroniclers of the New Mexico campaign were journalists and lawyers accustomed to weighing competing claims and balancing accounts—Richard Smith Elliott and George Rutledge Gibson. Elliott, born in Pennsylvania in 1817, worked as a newspaper editor in Harrisburg in the late 1830s and served subsequently as an Indian agent at Council Bluffs in the Iowa Territory before moving to St. Louis to practice law. He had little success in that line, and the coming of war in 1846 gave him a chance to see action and pursue his preferred trade by composing dispatches for the *St. Louis Reveille*. Many who participated in the campaign described the taking of Santa Fe that August in their diaries or memoirs, but Elliott's account was distinctive for considering the triumphant parade of arms from the Mexican point of view:

> Our march into the city, I have already told you, was extremely warlike, with drawn sabres and daggers in every look. From around corners, men, with surly countenances and downcast looks, regarded us with watchfulness, if not terror; and black eyes looked through latticed windows at our column of cavaliers, some gleaming with pleasure, and others filled with tears. Strange, indeed, must have been the feelings of the citizens, when an invading army was thus entering their home—themselves used only to look upon soldiers as plagues, sent to eat out their substance, burn, ravage and destroy—all the future of their destiny vague and uncertain—their new rulers strangers to their manners, language and habits, and, as they had been taught to believe, enemies to the only religion they had ever known. It was humiliating, too, to find their city thus entered, without a gun having been fired in its defence; and we thought that humbled, mortified pride, was indicated in the expression of more than one swarthy face.[42]

Elliott overstated the case here when he implied that New Mexicans dreaded the sight of their own soldiers no less than enemy forces. (In fact, it was the neglect of New Mexico by the central government and the shortage of trained troops to deal with Indian raids and other threats that did most to weaken Mexico's grip on the region.) But he could be just as sharp in challenging American authorities and their assumptions. "The army of the west was too hastily fitted out, and have marched too great a distance from home, to have everything in first rate order," he wrote in early November after General Kearny continued on to California with a detachment of regulars. "It is now without an experienced head, and in a country which does not afford supplies sufficient for the sustenance of either man or beast."[43] Well before the uprising that claimed the life of Governor Charles Bent and others in January 1847, Elliott reported that "there prevails, among many of the New Mexicans, a very bitter feeling towards our Government and people."[44] And he riled readers back home by questioning the utility of the venture that many Missourians regarded as their greatest coup during the war—the march from Santa Fe to Chihuahua by volunteers under Colonel Alexander Doniphan that resulted in American victories in two battles along the way and the occupation of Chihuahua in March 1847. Arguing that Doniphan's force was too small to hold Chihuahua and that his success would have no impact on the war's outcome, Elliott concluded that Doniphan's "unprofitable march" was nothing to celebrate: "I regret that his bravery, and the sagacity manifested on the field, should have been so uselessly expended."[45]

Here, as in other probing passages written by those who ventured down the Santa Fe Trail in wartime or peacetime, the issue of profit and loss was foremost. Did the rewards justify the expenditure? One participant in Doniphan's campaign who pondered the same question was George Gibson. Born in Virginia around 1810, Gibson practiced law for a while in Indiana in the 1830s before moving to Missouri and founding the short-lived *Independence Journal* in 1844. He endorsed the candidacy that year of the Whig nominee for president, Henry Clay, that great compromiser, and Gibson himself had a knack for compromise, as revealed in the splendid journal he kept during the Mexican War. Having backed Clay in his provisional support for the annexation of Texas, an objective Clay hoped to achieve without war, Gibson volunteered to fight in the conflict that ensued. But he regarded Mexicans with curiosity and compassion rather than with hostility and managed to fulfill his duties as company quartermaster more judiciously than Frank Edwards. Gibson even succeeded in befriending some of the locals he dealt with, particularly in El Paso. "On all occasions I have been well treated by the people," he wrote of his sojourn there on the way to Chihuahua, "and find them ready to return civilities or good treatment."[46] He was sobered by the steep Mexican losses at the Battle of Sacramento in February 1847—the fight that cleared Doniphan's way to Chihuahua—and wondered afterward if any objective or gain could justify such carnage: "Many of the prisoners died, and the spectacle next morning was such that no man could help but feel that war was an evil of the worst kind and one which should be avoided if possible."[47]

In the end, however, Gibson concluded that the battle and the campaign had been worthwhile, depriving those opposed to American rule in New Mexico of any hope of relief from the south and thus securing "peace in our newly acquired possessions."[48] Gibson was confident that New Mexico would thrive under American rule, and he returned to Santa Fe after the Chihuahua campaign to edit the *Santa Fe Republican*, the town's first English-language newspaper, which also included pages in Spanish. In a declaration of principle in the inaugural issue that September, the editor predicted over-optimistically that American forces would swiftly subdue the Apaches, Navajos, and other defiant tribes of the region and that "all the benefit of a lasting and permanent peace will soon be felt." He expressed his hope that the occupied territory would progress rapidly with the help of American institutions, including his own newspaper, "intended to be of equal interest and benefit to the old and new citizens."[49]

The occupation of New Mexico was as much a cultural confrontation as a military one, and one of the finest accounts to emerge from this tumultuous period was produced by a young visitor who was neither a soldier nor eligible to become one—Susan Shelby Magoffin, the wife of Samuel Magoffin, a trader with strong and deep ties to Mexico. Born to a wealthy family in Kentucky, Susan wed Samuel in November 1845 when she was eighteen and he was past forty. She chose not to stay behind when he set out to do business in Mexico shortly after war was declared in May, and she thus became a pioneer of sorts on the trail, describing herself as the "first American lady" to enter American-occupied Santa Fe. (Mexican women had traveled the Santa Fe Trail as early as 1829; a Missourian named Mary Donoho ventured to Santa Fe in 1833 with her husband, William, and infant daughter to work as innkeepers there; and a servant or slave named Jane accompanied Susan Magoffin, whose caravan was made up of "Americans, Mexicans, and negroes" and was not the first such company on the trail to include a black woman.)[50]

Whatever her claims to priority, this was undiscovered country to Susan Magoffin, and she produced a diary brimming with revelations and insights. Unlike other journals of the trail reworked for publication, her account was private and spontaneous. Like many a greenhorn on the trail, she sometimes felt, amid the heat, rain, and pestilence, that she was being scourged by an angry God. "Millions upon millions were swarming around me," she wrote of the mosquitoes near the Little Arkansas River, "and their knocking against the carriage *reminded me of a hard rain*. It was equal to any of the plagues of Egypt."[51] Yet she never failed to count her blessings—including her attentive husband, her faithful hound Ring, and the rare privilege of having a carriage to ride in and tent to sleep in—and she looked forward to emerging from this wilderness into a promised land, one whose exotic terms she was already beginning to master and weave into her diary as she struggled to keep dry in her tent: "I have books, writing implements, sewing, kniting, somebody to talk with, a house that does not leak and I am satisfied, although this is a juicy day *en el campo*!"[52]

Susan Magoffin underwent one of the most severe trials of her journey when she and her husband stopped at Bent's Fort, where the traders had to wait for Kearny's troops to proceed to Santa Fe and follow in their wake. On the

Susan Shelby Magoffin. Courtesy Missouri Historical Society, St. Louis.

night of July 30, her nineteenth birthday, she suffered a miscarriage. "The mysteries of a new world have been shown to me,"[53] she wrote afterward. And indeed the experience, combined with the travails of entering a strange country in wartime, seemed to equip her with a deeper sense of what it meant to cross over into a new life in a far land. At first blush, she found the New Mexicans rather more than she had bargained for, mothers with babies sucking at their breasts and "cigarittas" dangling from their lips, buzzing around her to get a look at this strange young white woman, until she could no longer wait to be back in her "little tent, unmolested by the constant stare of these wild looking strangers!"[54] But she grew into her role as a trader's wife, sometimes handling the sale of goods when her husband was otherwise occupied and reassuring his well-to-do Mexican acquaintances that Americans could still be trusted as friends and partners. In the process, her appreciation for the country and its people matured. Late in the year, the Magoffins left Santa Fe and followed behind Doniphan's troops on their slow advance to Chihuahua. Reaching El Paso in February, they were hosted by the sisters of Padre Ramón Ortiz— the same priest who had befriended Kendall in 1841 when he and his fellow captives were being driven to Chihuahua. The patriotic Ortiz had recently been arrested by Colonel Doniphan on suspicion of spying for Mexican forces, but his plight in no way lessened the hospitality shown the Magoffins. She returned the favor by accompanying her hostesses to Mass and offering one of the more charitable reflections by a Protestant about the faith that sustained Mexicans through this crisis. "It is not for me to judge; whether it be right or wrong; judgement alone belongs to God," she wrote. "One thing among them they are sincere in what they do."[55] Susan Shelby Magoffin showed at such moments that she was a trader in her own right, in the best sense of that word—one who sought the middle ground between her own values and those of her hosts and learned to honor their terms as they honored hers.

The last word on the Santa Fe Trail during the Mexican War period belongs to a young traveler from Cincinnati christened Hector Lewis Garrard, who started west belatedly in the fall of 1846 as the furor was beginning to subside, saw more at the tender age of seventeen than most men see in a lifetime, and transformed his impressions into a strange and often stirring book entitled *Wah-to-yah, and the Taos Trail* (1850), which served as an elegy for a world that died—or entered a new phase of existence—when America claimed New Mexico, thus setting the stage for the conquest of the intervening plains. Garrard reached Taos in the spring of 1847 in the aftermath of the uprising there, witnessed the trial and execution of several of the rebels charged with the murder of Governor Bent and others, and walked amid the ruins of the church at Taos Pueblo, where some 150 men died resisting American forces—and where today crosses mark the site of a hallowed battleground transformed into a burial place. If Garrard wrote nothing else of interest or importance, his book would still be valuable for his haunting and sympathetic portrait of that ravaged native community, whose grievous and disproportionate loss was then considered by many to be fitting punishment:

A few half-scared Pueblos walked listlessly about, vacantly staring in a state of dejected, gloomy abstraction. And they might well be so. Their alcalde dead, their grain and cattle gone, their church in ruins, the flower of the nation slain, or under sentence of death, and the rest—with the exception of those in prison—refugees, starving in the mountains. It was truly a scene of desolation.[56]

For all the significance of Garrard's portrait of Taos after the uprising, however, his main subject was the life and prospects of Plains Indians at this turning point in their history, when the long columns of troops marching down the trail foreshadowed unprecedented intrusions on tribal territory in the years ahead by soldiers, emigrants, prospectors, and wagon drivers carrying freight to American forts and settlements. (In 1846 alone, the quartermaster's department purchased for Kearny's Army of the West 1,106 wagons, 10,000 oxen, 400 mules, and 300 horses.)[57] On his way west, Garrard signed up with a company wagon train bound for Bent's Fort and spent an absorbing few months in and around that outpost trading with and living among Cheyennes who were becoming increasingly dependent on trade goods they received from the company in exchange for furs. Like many young romantics of the day, he had an idealized image of the unfettered life of Plains Indians, and his first impressions seemed to bear that vision out:

> In the morning, at ten o'clock, we were at the camp of the Indian braves. Many of the younger and more ardent met us; as they dashed by, on their handsome horses, I thought, with envy, of the free and happy life they were leading on the untamed plains, with fat buffalo for food, fine horses to ride, living and dying in a state of blissful ignorance.[58]

As he spent more time among the Cheyennes, however, Garrard discovered that all was not so blissful. Even as tribespeople welcomed trade with whites and benefited materially, they were feeling the disruptive effects of that traffic on their culture and environment. And this was still an age of peace and plenty compared to what the Cheyennes and other tribes along the trail would experience in the near future. Although the American troops who crossed the plains in the summer of 1846 met with little opposition from Indians, the import of their presence was not lost on tribal leaders. The Mexican War would soon be over, but the contest for control of the plains was just beginning. By 1847, troops and supply trains heading out to relieve the weary forces in New Mexico were coming under fierce attack by Indians. The army responded by building its first outpost on the trail—Fort Mann, near present-day Dodge City—soon to be followed by Fort Union in New Mexico and other fortified points of supply and defense in the army's escalating Indian campaigns.

Lewis H. Garrard. Courtesy Missouri Historical Society, St. Louis.

Garrard, on his way back east, stopped at Fort Mann—little more than a depot for government wagons—and worked there for a month or so, helping to finish the buildings. Shortly before his arrival, he noted, a small party of Comanches let the occupants of the fort know what they thought of their incursion by shooting and lancing a man who was fishing in the river, "not three hundred yards from the fort, in sight of the forty armed men," and making off with his scalp. This and a subsequent raid on the fort's horses and mules so intimidated those manning Fort Mann, he added, that they "ventured not to show their uncomfortable countenances outside the gate."[59] For Garrard, it was a somber but fitting conclusion to a journey that carried him from a camp circle near Bent's Fort where white traders were still welcomed into tepees at night, to a battered Pueblo in New Mexico where Anglos could enter at will only because walls had been leveled by troops and the occupants subjugated, to this desolate outpost near the Arkansas where Americans toiled in lonely isolation, hemmed in by fears of what lurked beyond.

The Mexican War and the Indian conflicts that ensued had such a dramatic—and in some ways tragic—impact that it can be hard to keep the events that preceded those upheavals in perspective. Were the traders who ventured down the Santa Fe Trail in the early decades forerunners of the troops who marched in 1846—advance agents of American expansion, infiltrating a foreign camp in peaceful guise, seducing Mexicans with alluring goods, and easing the way for conquest? In certain respects, perhaps, they were. By 1846, some New Mexicans, including Governor Armijo, had become so used to bargaining with Americans and conditioned to their presence and their offerings that they were probably less inclined to resist the American takeover than they would have been a quarter century earlier before regular trade was established between the two countries. And yet Mexican resistance to the occupiers still ran deep in 1846 and boiled up more than once, indicating that the traders, if they were indeed part of some subtle cultural infiltration, did not exactly sell the populace on all things American. Certainly, the trail itself and the knowledge and lore that accumulated around it over the years were indispensable to Kearny's campaign and provided him with a well-trod path to follow, reliable intelligence on the country he was out to claim, and a ready supply of recruits. The road to New Mexico belonged to them, the volunteers reasoned, so why not New Mexico itself?

History affords numerous examples in which merchant adventurers served as willing accomplices in imperialistic schemes. Europeans of various nationalities used trade as a means of gaining access to the resources of the New World and planting colonies there that exploited or displaced native peoples who at first welcomed the opportunity to exchange goods with the newcomers. And long before the first Europeans arrived, expansive Indian states had arisen in Mesoamerica that used trading ties with distant tribes to render them subservient. The Aztecs, for example, forged a mighty empire with the help of long-distance traders called *pochteca*, some of whom disguised their identity and loyalty and collected intelligence that could be used against tribal trading partners who became targets of Aztec aggression.[60]

There were, in fact, some American merchants who played a similarly subversive role in New Mexico before and during the American takeover in 1846. But overall, the exchange between the two sides was far too complex and ambiguous to be characterized simply as the exploitation of a weak partner by a stronger one. For one thing, Americans were not alone in harboring an urge to exploit the opportunities they encountered in the Southwest. Mexicans had their own tradition of empire building, rooted in the deeds of the Aztecs and the Spanish conquistadores who subdued and then intermingled with those aboriginal imperialists to forge an assertive Neo-Aztec culture that continued to seek outlets for its energies on distant frontiers.[61] This convergence of Spanish and native adventurism reached its high point in the late seventeenth and eighteenth centuries with the reconquest of New Mexico after the Pueblo Revolt and the colonization of Alta California. By the nineteenth century, however, the tide of New Spanish colonialism was fast receding, leaving the northern provinces vulnerable to American incursions. Yet for all the disadvantages New Mexicans labored under, they proved resourceful enough to compete with the intruders from the States at their own game and to shape the outcome of the contest. Ostensibly, the tumultuous events of 1846 cleared the way for the Americanization of the Spanish Southwest. But like earlier, peaceful dealings between the two sides, this combative exchange worked both ways, endowing the United States in 1848 with vast new possessions of an indelibly Hispanic character and altering the nation's course and complexion in ways unforeseen by the prophets of Manifest Destiny.

That this fateful confrontation between the United States and Mexico might prove as unsettling for Americans as it would for Mexicans was signaled beforehand by the anxious reactions of traders to news that hostilities were imminent. Some American merchants, like Charles Bent, welcomed and abetted the conquest of New Mexico, but others were far less enthusiastic about that prospect. A dispatch from Independence that ran in a St. Louis newspaper on June 1, 1846, summed up the reaction there to the mustering of troops for an invasion:

> The opinion of those here who know best, is, that such a thing would be exceedingly impolitic, and that it would ruin our trade with that country. Every business man in St. Louis knows, or ought to know, that a very large amount of goods are annually bought there for New Mexico, and if we send a military force against them without cause or provocation (for they are with us in part,) it would intercept this trade entirely, and thereby cut off a trade that has reached to nearly two millions of dollars per annum.[62]

Such objections receded as the campaign gained momentum and it appeared that Kearny's venture might succeed without disrupting business seriously or for long. But traders with close ties to Mexico, like Edward James Glasgow, who seemingly harbored little admiration for those "lords of creation" who were itching for a fight, were inclined to disapprove of settling differences through battle that might yet be resolved through bargaining.

As a group, those who engaged in the Santa Fe trade—and in the related enterprise of chronicling the trade and the trail for the press and public— tended to be mediators, negotiating the middle ground between submission and aggression, between the impulse that leads some travelers to yield to alien cultures and go native and the imperative that drives others to confront rival powers and conquer them. This mediating tendency did not prevent more than a few men in the trade from going to either extreme, for the lines between one way of dealing with competing forces and another were narrow and easily crossed. The various forms of exchange engaged in by these Santa Fe adventurers—a term embracing those who set out along the trail in pursuit of profit, honor, renown, or sheer diversion—were all attempts to resolve or exploit differences between rival parties, whether in romantic, cultural, economic, or military terms. A single venture often involved all those forms of exchange and revealed ways in which they were interchangeable. George Kendall, for example, in the course of accompanying the Texan Santa Fe expedition and reflecting on it in writing, engaged in an affectionate and mildly erotic flirtation with Mexican women; in an enlightening cultural give-and-take with Padre Ortiz; in sundry economic trade-offs with Mexicans; and in verbal duels with Armijo and his cruel underlings, with whom Kendall might gladly have traded shots if given the chance. None of these forms of exchange was utterly distinct from the others. When Kendall praised Mexican women for their generosity, for instance, he was in some ways taunting the men. Making verbal advances of this kind could be a hostile act, a prelude to battle. And a complex takeover bid like the American occupation of New Mexico could be everything in one— a bald act of aggressive prowess, a variation on the existing trading relationship, an exercise in cultural accommodation, and an attempt to seduce the locals and draw them into America's tight embrace.

On balance, however, the early history of the Santa Fe Trail and the literature produced by its most discerning travelers taught the virtues of moderation and mediation and warned against the extremes of heedless hostility or encroaching intimacy. This was the middle way favored by the likes of Josiah Gregg, Matt Field, and Susan Shelby Magoffin. They served as guides for those who followed them down the trail in how to confront powers beyond one's sphere without either subduing or surrendering to them. The powers to be reckoned with on this journey resided not only in other cultures but in the land beyond and the heavens above. From the start the trip was a pilgrimage, a search not just for earthly profit but for intangible rewards that came from bargaining with something greater than oneself. Gregg, Field, Magoffin, and Garrard were among many such pilgrims who set out on their journeys seeking redemption in the form of a cure. And while the physical ills they hoped to banish sometimes persisted or recurred, they felt stronger in spirit for having wrestled with the challenges of the road.

Few early travelers had the reverence of Susan Magoffin, and they did not often speak of God. But even cynics like Cooke were known to thank Providence for deliverance from the perils of passage. The initial sense of freedom and impending good fortune that many adventurers experienced when they embarked on the journey often gave way to a deep sense of vulnerability and indebtedness. To be destined thus for a new land—to be bound for another world—was to find oneself at the mercy of superior forces, powers that tried the soul and exacted due tribute. At times, travelers on their pilgrimage did not know whether to laugh or cry, whether to curse their fate or thank heaven for the chance to follow this road and bid for a better place. The idea that New Mexico was a promised land for Americans was in some ways a cruel joke. It was also a deep and abiding hope, an enduring dream, a rainbow that drew weary wayfarers on to a golden place they might never find.

That those heading west across Missouri to pick up the Santa Fe Trail had to cross a small river named the Jordan was a fact that some perhaps regarded as portentous and others found merely curious. But one traveler made something of it in verse and achieved a kind of immortality when his words were set down in print by William Watts Hart Davis, author of *El Gringo* (1857), among the finest postwar memoirs of the road to New Mexico. One of Davis's traveling companions in 1853 on the recently inaugurated stagecoach line to Santa Fe was Captain Alexander W. Reynolds, who had been delayed reaching Independence from the east and was in danger of missing the once-monthly run. So Reynolds sent a cable on the telegraph lines that now spanned the state, imploring the stagecoach operator in terms none could resist to delay the departure—and allow yet another eager traveler to join in that fabled pilgrimage to the land beyond:

> Then hold your horses, Billy,
>   Just hold them for a day;
> I've crossed the River Jordan,
>   And am bound for Santa Fé.[63]

Part 2

The Road to New Mexico
(1821–1846)

5

Embarking from St. Louis

In June of 1839, Matt Field, actor turned adventurer, boarded a steamboat in St. Louis and headed up the Missouri River to Independence, the starting point for his overland journey to Santa Fe. Among his fellow passengers on the paddle wheeler was an "oddity of the first water," Field noted in one of many articles he wrote for the *New Orleans Picayune* after his return from New Mexico, a Frenchman "who had, for seventeen years, been domesticated among the Indians."[1] Field had a fine ear for the nuances of language and chose his words carefully. He used the term "domesticated" here not only to indicate that this man had lived at length among Indians (to domesticate with others meaning to lodge with them) but also to suggest in a deeper sense that he had been transformed by his tribal keepers. The result, Field noted, was a man caught between two worlds:

> He had that free and lordly tread so characteristic of the Indians, but it was most strangely amalgamated with a dancing-master trip, which he was in the habit of assuming, and he would cock his hat over the right eye, and run his fingers through his hair in the most approved and accepted fashion of a modern beau. He had been a Frenchman—I say *had been*, for really I feel a hesitation in saying that he is one—and these symptoms plainly told that he has been a youth of some fashion—noticed by the fair—a wild boy, and a rake. His language he had forgotten. English he spoke about as well as a border Indian, who catches enough to trade his skins, &c. True, he may never have spoken it, but his French was about as bad as his English, and he evidently

had no relish for either. I drew him into conversation, and questioned him freely about his life. After many years residence among a tribe where he had his family, his dignity, his wigwam, and his home, he had visited St. Louis with $3,000 dollars, and was now returning to his forsaken squaw without a dollar.[2]

This forlorn "Frenchman," perhaps one of the many venturesome French Canadians who lived among Indians as trappers or traders along the Missouri River frontier, was hardly the first visitor ever to squander a small fortune in St. Louis. The city teemed with grogshops and gambling dens that deprived frontiersmen of their earnings in short order and sent them back upriver to their labors with scarcely a penny. (One lively French district near town, Carondelet, was known evocatively as Vide Poche, or "empty pocket.")

Some who went on sprees in St. Louis ended up in jail like Abraham Bogard, a French Canadian trapper who accompanied artist George Catlin on a journey down the Missouri River from Fort Union in 1832. Catlin described St. Louis at that time as a bustling city of fifteen thousand inhabitants that served as "the great depôt of all the Fur Trading Companies to the Upper Missouri and Rocky Mountains, and their starting-place; and also for the Santa Fe, and other Trading Companies, who reach the Mexican borders overland, to trade for silver bullion, from the extensive mines of that rich country."[3] Some of the wealth gleaned through such trade was expended wisely in St. Louis by shrewd merchants seeking goods and equipment for future ventures. But other visitors like Catlin's companion and helper Bogard were freer and looser with their cash. Bogard had profited in a small way as a trapper and "made show of a few hundred dollars" in St. Louis, Catlin noted. "He came down with a liberal heart, which he had learned in an Indian life of ten years, with a strong taste, which he had acquired, for whiskey, in a country where it was sold for twenty dollars per gallon; and with an independent feeling, which illy harmonized with rules and regulations of a country of laws." Predictably, Bogard took to the bottle in St. Louis and ended up in the jug, "where he could deliberately dream of beavers, and the free and cooling breezes of the mountain air, without the pleasure of setting his trap for the one, or even indulging the hope of ever again having the pleasure of breathing the other."[4]

Although Catlin did his best to console "poor Bogard," he did not seem to regard the trapper's plight as a tragedy. By contrast, Matt Field saw something deeply pathetic in the situation of that Frenchman-gone-native he met aboard the steamboat—a frontiersman who had lost not only his fortune but his identity. Like Bogard, this wayfarer had a weakness for liquor and reverted under the influence of alcohol to what Field called "his savage manner." Encouraged by his fellow passengers, the man danced that night in a drunken frenzy to the strains of a violin in the steamboat's social hall, exhibiting the "wild contortions of the Indian," Field reported, and losing all self-control:

> In this state he pounced upon me, his acquaintance of the morning, and it required my utmost address to shake him off and take refuge in my state room, from whence I heard him half the night yelling and whooping, and now and then mingling a French or English oath with his Indian lingo.
>
> What a most novel, yet most melancholy subject for reflection was this man! There can be no doubt but in the excited state in which I saw him he actually fancied himself an Indian. His habits, even his tastes, his very nature had become *savage*, and I saw before me the degrading spectacle of a Christian being wandering forever like a thing accursed, an outcast from his kin, his people and his God.[5]

Field, like most of his American contemporaries, took it for granted that Indians were intrinsically wild or savage (he sometimes referred to them as "red devils") and assumed that whites who lived at length among them and adhered to their customs risked becoming savages themselves. Yet by Field's own account, this Frenchman had achieved a measure of prosperity and "dignity" among his tribal hosts. Was it they who degraded him, or was it rather his contacts with whites and their intoxicating wares that brought him to this sorry pass? Was it his years among the Indians that reduced him to a "thing accursed," or his trip to St. Louis?

This episode is one of many in the literature of the Santa Fe Trail inviting varying interpretations. Matt Field himself, in other articles he wrote about his journey to Santa Fe and back, demonstrated a keen awareness of the competing claims made by civilization and the wilderness on those who crossed frontiers. Every party that ventured down the Santa Fe Trail was in some sense weighing the values of one world against another and exploring the uncharted ground that divided Anglo-American society from the rival cultures of the West, whether Indian, Spanish, or French—cultures often presumed by Anglos to be inferior to their own and yet so durable, distinctive, and well suited to the frontier environment that few English-speaking travelers escaped their influence. That influence was felt not just in tribal territory or in New Mexico but in that great depot of western travelers, St. Louis, a city steeped in the traditions of its French settlers, its former Spanish governors, and its many Indian visitors.

Strictly speaking, St. Louis was not the "starting-place" for the Santa Fe trade, as Catlin suggested. The traders who pioneered commerce with New Mexico set out in the early 1820s from the vicinity of Franklin, situated on the Missouri River roughly midway across the state. Later the jumping-off point shifted westward, first to Independence and then to nearby Westport, within what is now Kansas City. Each of those so-called prairie ports had stores and shops that met the basic needs of merchants gearing up for their expeditions. But many traveling the Santa Fe Trail for the first time reached Franklin or Independence by road or by river from St. Louis, as Matt Field did. And veteran traders often returned to St. Louis to take advantage of its larger market, where they could purchase wagons, weapons, or trade goods that might be cheaper or of higher quality than that available at the prairie ports.

James A. Shirley, a storekeeper in the town of Fayette, near Franklin, placed a notice in a local newspaper in 1829 that tacitly acknowledged the bargains to be had at St. Louis: "We are determined to sell Goods as low as they can be purchased in any retail house west of St. Louis, without any exception."[6] Shirley may well have been miffed to see this recurring advertisement in the same newspaper that year, placed by Henry Reily, who kept a store in St. Louis: "The subscriber has just returned from New York, with a fresh and Extensive stock of Seasonable and Fashionable Goods, which he is enabled (from having purchased most of them at auctions) to dispose of at prices much less than what has usually been obtained in this market, for similar Goods. Country merchants, and those engaged in the SANTA FE TRADE, are particularly invited to call and examine the goods."[7] The phrase "Seasonable and Fashionable Goods" was well calculated to appeal to Santa Fe traders, whose New Mexican customers relished fine fabrics and apparel. To meet that demand, some enterprising merchants went as far afield as Philadelphia or New York, where they secured better deals on choice articles produced in eastern factories or imported from Europe and shipped their wares back to Missouri. All this ensured that St. Louis would remain a conduit for the Santa Fe trade even as the prairie ports grew and prospered.

Those heading west with their wares from St. Louis generally boarded steamboats for Franklin, Independence, or Westport by early May. This allowed them to assemble their wagon trains and cross the plains while the grass their animals depended on was still fresh and green. It also got them out of St. Louis before summer arrived with its oppressive heat and humidity, which tried visitors' nerves and left them pining for fresher and healthier climes. One foreign visitor in that vexing season, Captain Frederick Marryat, an English novelist and veteran of the Royal Navy, remarked after stopping in St. Louis in 1838:

> In point of heat, St. Louis certainly approaches the nearest to the Black Hole of Calcutta of any city that I have sojourned in. The lower part of town is badly drained, and very filthy. The flies, on a moderate calculation, are in many parts fifty to the square inch. . . . I found sleep almost impossible from the

sultriness of the air, and used to remain at the open window for the greater part of the night. I did not expect that the muddy Mississippi would be able to reflect the silver light of the moon; yet it did, and the effect was very beautiful. Truly it may be said of this river, as it is of many ladies, that it is a candle-light beauty. There is another serious evil to which strangers who sojourn here are subject—the violent effects of the waters of the Mississippi upon those who are not used to them.[8]

Some residents touted the city's notoriously murky water for its purgative effects, remarking that it "scours out the bowels."[9] But visitors remained understandably leery of water the color of coffee and other apparent health hazards.

Humidity, pestilence, and poor water were not unique to St. Louis, of course. Residents of many eastern and midwestern towns faced similar conditions, particularly in the summer, and some who fell ill were inclined to blame their surroundings and seek a more invigorating setting. A number of them looked to the West for a cure, hoping that arduous exposure to its clear, dry air and purportedly pure waters would restore their health. The West and its native inhabitants might be savage, such venturesome invalids reasoned, but there was strength in the wild, and many who embarked down the road to New Mexico and other western trails hoped to tap into that presumably restorative power. Benjamin Taylor, an editor who refashioned a traveler's account of his journey to New Mexico for publication, touted the venture as a tonic for the soul as well as the body:

> No monotony, no life on a sea becalmed, is the tour to Santa Fe, but a moving diorama of stirring and unexpected incidents, that quicken the pulse like an electric thrill, promote a brisk and healthful circulation, develop courage, endurance, presence of mind, generosity and patience, of which the new possessor never before dreamed—in a sentence, it brings out the whole man, physical, mental and moral.[10]

Those who knew more about the Santa Fe trade than Taylor did might question whether it transformed men into paragons of virtue, but many people shared the belief that a pilgrimage to New Mexico could work wonders for those frail in constitution and sick at heart. Matt Field set out for Santa Fe in the hope of curing a stomach ailment that he saw as symptomatic of deeper disturbances in his life. As he wrote in his diary in April 1839, a few months before he left St. Louis and his career on the stage: "My sickness still continues—worse—worse! Doctors do me no good. I am very miserable, and I am lonely—very lonely. But how shall I marry? Where shall I marry? Why should I marry when *Death* seems to be at work within me?"[11] For heartsore invalids

like Field, taking to the trail offered not only the hope of a cure but the welcome prospect of an absorbing engagement abroad, free of romantic complications and disappointments. (Like those Frenchmen who signed on with trading and trapping outfits that embarked from St. Louis, Field was happily *engagé*,
or pledged to the company for the duration of the expedition.) A year or so
after returning from New Mexico, bolstered by his success in trading on that
invigorating journey in print, he married Cornelia Burke Ludlow, daughter of
Noah Ludlow, his former theatrical producer.[12] Field lived only a few more years,
leaving behind his wife and two children, but his stint as a Santa Fe adventurer
defined him as no other role had and infused his remaining days with purpose.

Another Missouri bachelor—in this case, a lifelong one—who took to the
Santa Fe Trail in his twenties to improve his health and lift his lagging spirits
was Josiah Gregg, who felt restored by the experience and recommended the
regimen to others:

> The Prairies have, in fact, become very celebrated for their sanative effects—
> more justly so, no doubt, than the most fashionable watering-places of the
> North. Most chronic diseases, particularly liver complaints, dyspepsias, and
> similar affections, are often radically cured; owing, no doubt, to the peculi-
> arities of diet, and the regular exercise incident to prairie life, as well as to the
> purity of the atmosphere of those elevated unembarrassed regions. An invalid
> myself, I can answer for the efficacy of the remedy, at least in my own case.
> Though, like other valetudinarians, I was disposed to provide an ample sup-
> ply of such commodities as I deemed necessary for my comfort and health,
> I was not long upon the prairies before I discovered that most of such extra
> preparations were unnecessary, or at least quite dispensable. A few knickknacks,
> as a little tea, rice, fruits, crackers, etc., suffice very well for the first fortnight,
> after which the invalid is generally able to take the fare of the hunter and team-
> ster. Though I set out myself in a carriage, before the close of the first week I
> saddled my pony; and when we reached the buffalo range, I was not only as
> eager for the chase as the sturdiest of my companions, but I enjoyed far more
> exquisitely my share of the buffalo, than all the delicacies which were ever
> devised to provoke the most fastidious appetite.[13]

Many shared Gregg's hope of finding a cure on the trail, but experience
taught travelers that a trip west could just as easily ruin one's health as restore
it. Among the serious ailments that sometimes afflicted those embarking from
St. Louis was malaria, often described as "fever and ague." One traveler laid
low by fever and ague was Alexander Barclay, an Englishman raised in genteel
poverty who crossed the Atlantic in the hope of making his fortune. Barclay
spent two years working as a clerk in St. Louis before setting out on the Santa

Fe Trail in the summer of 1838 to serve as bookkeeper and superintendent of stores at Bent's Fort. One of his motives for leaving St. Louis was to escape the suffocating humidity and swarms of mosquitoes. As others had before him, however, he soon discovered that those same pestiferous conditions prevailed in summertime clear across Missouri and into the eastern reaches of Indian country. On the way to Bent's Fort, he came down with a severe case of fever and ague that sapped his strength for months to come. "I am so reduced every movement is an exertion and cannot walk 60 yards without resting," he wrote home from the fort that October.[14]

A similar fate befell William Fairholme, a British officer who stopped in St. Louis briefly in 1840 before taking to the Santa Fe Trail for a hunting expedition with some comrades serving with him in Canada. Fairholme was delighted with the flora and fauna he met with on his journey, but he was less enthusiastic about the society he encountered. Much like Missourians visiting New Mexico, he found Americans on the frontier rather boorish and backward. A run-in with a high-handed magistrate in Illinois left him fuming. "So much for the administration of Justice in the United States," he wrote.[15] And when he fell sick on his way across Missouri after sweltering in St. Louis—the heat there "in summer is quite overpowering,"[16] he complained—a physician of doubtful qualifications in Jefferson City offered him a cure that was perhaps worse than the disease: "In the evening I was obliged to take to my bed, and sent for a doctor who, giving me mercury in quantities that would have astonished an English M.D., told me that I had a severe attack of fever & ague. He had the prudent kindness to inform me at the same time that 3 men had died of it within the last week at that house."[17] Had it not been for the attentions of a fellow traveler and a "dear little Englishwoman" who was boarding at the same hotel, Fairholme added, "I do not think I should have lived, for the people of the house took scarcely any trouble about me and little groups of the townspeople used to assemble in my room at all hours of the day to stare at me." Whether because of the disease he contracted or the harsh cure his doctor administered, he was debilitated for some time and had to leave much of the hunting to his companions. He would have been better off taking the quinine pills devised by Dr. John Sappington, who settled in the town of Arrow Rock, where travelers heading to and from Santa Fe crossed the Missouri River by ferry, and purveyed his worthy medicine to those suffering from malarial fever.

Travelers bound for Santa Fe were less likely to come down with "fever and ague" once they reached drier country with fewer mosquitoes, but they remained at risk of contracting dysentery and other disorders caused by poor sanitation or foul drinking water (streams on the plains could be as muddy as

the Mississippi). In this as in other respects, St. Louis offered less of a contrast
to conditions at the far end of the trail than it did a preview of what lay ahead.
The city's rough, frontier aspects were neatly summarized by Philip St. George
Cooke, who was stationed at Jefferson Barracks, near St. Louis, before embarking on the first of several eventful journeys on the Santa Fe Trail:

> The characteristics of St. Louis, in 1827, which first struck me, were the mud-
> diness of the streets—the badness of the hotels—the numbers of the Creole-
> French, speaking the French language—working on the Sabbath—a floating
> population of trappers, traders, boatmen, and Indians—and finally, an absence
> of paper currency. These were all very distinctive; and in truth, St. Louis had
> very little of the Anglo-American character. *Rowdyism* was the order of the
> day—the predominating influence of the street population of Indian traders
> and other northwestern adventurers. These men, in *outre* dresses, and well
> armed, were as characteristic in their deportment as sailors; exhibiting the inde-
> pendence, confidence, and recklessness of their wild and lawless way of life.[18]

Cooke would find conditions much the same when he later reached New
Mexico, where trappers and other rowdies mingled with Indians and settlers
who might be described in Cooke's terms as Creole-Spanish (in the sense that
their Hispanic heritage had been modified by native influences). In both St.
Louis and Santa Fe, the populace seemed to defy Protestant scruples in ways
that went beyond the custom of trading on the Sabbath. One young east-
erner who arrived in St. Louis in 1829 complained that its French inhabitants
were "Generally absolute Strangers to the Social virtues and remarkable for
Laziness & Debauchery,"[19] a complaint of the sort often directed at New
Mexicans.

Over time St. Louis took on more of an Anglo-American flavor, but up
until the 1840s it embodied the polyglot nature of the frontier West. Hundreds, perhaps thousands, of Indians lived in and around the town, and many
more visited there on such occasions as the treaty councils convened by William
Clark, the celebrated explorer and longtime superintendent of Indian Affairs.
Clark's nephew, William Clark Kennerly, witnessed several of those councils
while growing up in St. Louis in the late 1820s and 1830s:

> We were, of course, fascinated with the pirogues (sort of dugout canoes)
> which kept arriving at the water front. We would tag along with the Indians
> to their camp sites and watch them make their domestic preparations and
> would later help distribute the presents which Uncle Clark had brought out
> to them. . . . After the real business was concluded, they would relax their
> dignity and, to the rhythm of their drums, sing and dance through the streets.

They would call on their white friends and partake of much refreshment; and, as much of the entertainment was of an alcoholic nature, things got pretty lively toward the end. I have sometimes wondered if there were not many aching heads and bad tempers in the departing canoes.[20]

Many Indians living along the upper Missouri found it more convenient to travel to and from councils in St. Louis by steamboat once paddle wheelers began venturing farther up that river on a regular basis in the 1830s. Santa Fe traders who boarded steamboats in St. Louis packed with Indians and other exotic figures got a taste of what they might encounter later at Bent's Fort on the Mountain Route, where Cheyennes and other tribal trading partners of the fort's proprietors camped outside the gates and made themselves at home. And few stretches of the trail's notorious Cimarron Route were as hazardous for wayfarers as Battle Row and other mean streets down by the levee in St. Louis. William Fairholme described the shock of disembarking there in 1840 after a tranquil journey down the Mississippi:

> The stunning, never ceasing roar of the steam of boats coming in & departing, the hum of the bustling throng of people on the shore, the rattling of numerous drays & carts, and the loud vociferations and strange appearance of the crowds of black porters, touters of hotels, &c. who make a rush at each steamer as she takes up her berth, formed a disagreeable contrast to the silence and solitude of the prairies & forests we had for some days past been traversing.[21]

Among those lurking amid the crowds on the levee were more than a few thieves and cutthroats. Kennerly, who got to know George Catlin during the artist's frequent visits to the home of William Clark, which included a museum of Indian artifacts, recalled that Catlin "used to complain that he could leave no baggage on the levee or he would never see it again."[22] One wary merchant disembarked from a steamboat there to make purchases for the Santa Fe trade with two strongboxes, watched over by six Mexican guards toting carbines and wearing "formidable sombreros."[23]

Those strongboxes most likely contained bullion or specie—money in coin form—both of which were heartily welcomed in St. Louis and in the prairie ports upriver. Missouri was chronically short of cash, and trade with Mexico, which abounded in silver, did much to reduce the reliance of Missourians on barter or on suspect banknotes. In May 1841, a newspaper in St. Louis announced the imminent arrival in Independence of a wagon train returning from Santa Fe with as much as "200,000 dollars in specie." Around the same time, the same issue related, a group of merchants including citizens of Mexico arrived from that country in St. Louis by boat: "It is reported that

View of Front Street, St. Louis, by J. C. Wild, 1840. Courtesy Missouri Historical Society, St. Louis.

this party bring with them about $120,000 in specie. An acceptable commodity here just now."[24] Mexican and Spanish coins mingled in the cashboxes of St. Louis with American dollars, French crowns, and English shillings, Kennerly noted, and merchants had to be "alert to compute the circulating coin of so many realms."[25]

Infusions of cash from the Santa Fe trade helped to transform rough-and-ready St. Louis into a city of some refinement by the 1840s, with paved streets, public schools, and at least one hotel of distinction, the Planter's House. Frenchman Victor Tixier, who stopped in St. Louis in 1840 during an expedition that carried him up the Missouri River into Osage country, observed that the frontier had advanced far beyond the city in recent decades, leaving its inhabitants relatively safe and secure:

> We took lodging at the house of a M. Viguier, a countryman of ours who keeps a boarding house on Main Street. One can see on this street, across the Market Place, an old house, built like the old Louisiana houses; it is shielded on one side by a wall with loopholes, which protected it twenty-five years ago from the attacks of the Osage who lived close to Saint Louis. At that time people went to New Orleans on sailboats. It was a six months trip that one never undertook without writing his will. But times have changed; Saint Louis has become an American city; one can travel in five or six days the 1,221 miles which separate it from New Orleans, and the Osage have been driven beyond the borders of the State of Missouri.[26]

St. Louis may have lost its raw frontier character by the 1840s, but it still derived much of its wealth and vitality from dealings with people who were making plans to set out across frontiers at considerable risk and expense. Wagonmakers like Joseph Murphy prospered in St. Louis, for example, by successfully competing for the business of Santa Fe traders, who used their vehicles both as freight carriers and as bulwarks against attack and often had need of new ones. (Many sold their battered wagons for a tidy sum once they reached Mexico and bought a fresh set of wheels for their next venture after returning to Missouri.) Some traders ordered wagons from Pittsburgh, renowned for its sturdy Conestogas, and others purchased their vehicles in Independence or one of the other prairie ports. Murphy and his fellow wagonmakers in St. Louis knew the needs of their customers, however, and adapted to their changing requirements. When Governor Manuel Armijo of New Mexico altered the tariff on American goods imported to Santa Fe in 1839 by charging a flat $500 fee for each wagonload, Murphy reportedly came up with a bigger vehicle that entered legend and grew to fabulous proportions—his son later described that behemoth as having a fifty-foot-long tongue and wheels that were eight inches wide at the rim and stood seven feet high.[27] A monster of those dimensions never stalked the trail, but local wagon-makers like Murphy indeed built larger vehicles in response to Armijo's new tariff. Traders made the most of such oversized wagons, Josiah Gregg noted, loading them with the costliest articles and forcing Governor Armijo to "return to an *ad valorem* system."[28]

Those who catered to the Santa Fe trade and other frontier ventures in St. Louis were by no means assured of success. Traders seldom paid cash in full for goods they purchased to be sold in Mexico or offered to Indians along the way. Often, they bought on credit and settled their accounts when they returned from their ventures, as much as a year or two later. When traders Charles Bent and Ceran St. Vrain formed the partnership in 1832 that led to the establishment of Bent's Fort, for example, they purchased goods on credit from merchants James and Robert Aull of Missouri and left the brothers this note: "Ten months after date we promise to pay James & Robert Aull or order—at St. Louis, Eight hundred and forty Two dollars and Sixteen cents for Value recd."[29] This was a favorable arrangement for the Aulls, for the note specified the date of payment and the borrowers were men of their word. Not all accounts were settled promptly or in full, however, and merchants await-ing payment from Santa Fe traders sometimes had trouble meeting their own obligations.

James J. Webb, before embarking for New Mexico in 1844, operated a dry goods store near the levee in St. Louis that featured such items as muslins, calicoes, and linens—popular offerings in the Santa Fe trade as well as in the local market. That store turned out to be a losing proposition, and Webb con-cluded that he would be better off trying to sell such wares directly to the New Mexicans. In July 1844, he related, "I found myself with six hundred dollars left from a borrowed capital of one thousand dollars, and out of business and ready for any adventure that offered employment and a reasonable prospect of future profit." Eugene Leitensdorfer and other veterans of the Santa Fe trade offered Webb advice and helped him obtain credit. "I bought about twelve hundred dollars' worth of goods," Webb wrote, "and left St. Louis about the fifteenth for Independence, with money enough to pay my freight and passage up the river and hotel bill at Independence."[30] There he received further credit from one of the town's leading merchants and outfitters, Sam Owens, an asso-ciate of the Aulls' who helped many get started in the trade and ventured to New Mexico himself more than once.

As illustrated by Webb's story, failure or adversity often had much to do with propelling men down the road to New Mexico. Merchants who faltered in St. Louis or Independence could always try to recoup their fortunes in Santa

Fe or Chihuahua. And mountain men who drank or gambled away their savings in town could always enlist with a westbound caravan as wagon drivers or hunters and regain a measure of solvency and self-respect. Like the hope of a cure that drew invalids westward, the dream of financial redemption on the trail had spiritual overtones. Every journey was indeed an "adventure," as Webb put it, a commercial outing that took on aspects of a pilgrimage, replete with trials that tested a man body and soul and held out the promise, for those who prevailed, of rewards that transcended financial calculation.

Such were the dreams that drew the aspiring young writer and historian Francis Parkman to St. Louis in the spring of 1846 on a journey that would carry him up the Missouri to Westport, out along the Oregon Trail to Fort Laramie, and back east along the Santa Fe Trail. Born in Boston to a prominent family, Parkman did not seek fortune in the West, but he did hope to restore his faltering health and enhance his prospects as an author. He reached St. Louis in mid-April, less than a month before the United States declared war on Mexico. Santa Fe traders were racing to get started before hostilities interfered with their business, while land-hungry emigrants, largely oblivious to border tensions, were hectically outfitting for long journeys west that could prove disastrous if launched too late in the year. The burst of activity provided Parkman with a compelling lead for his classic, *The Oregon Trail:*

> Last spring, 1846, was a busy season in the city of St. Louis. Not only were emigrants from every part of the country preparing for the journey to Oregon and California, but an unusual number of traders were making ready their wagons and outfits for Santa Fé. The hotels were crowded, and the gunsmiths and saddlers were kept constantly at work in providing arms and equipments for the different parties of travellers. Steamboats were leaving the levee and passing up the Missouri, crowded with passengers on their way to the frontier.[31]

These were exciting times, but the crush of goods and humanity in St. Louis—and on the steamboat *Radnor*, which Parkman boarded with a friend and relative in late April—forced the young Bostonian to confront realities that defied any romantic notions he may have harbored about the frontier. In his book he described the scene dispassionately, but in the journal he kept during his travels he made it clear that he found these first encounters with the West somewhat disillusioning. Such were his considered impressions of the *Radnor* and its diverse cargo in *The Oregon Trail:*

> The boat was loaded until the water broke alternately over her guards. Her upper-deck was covered with large wagons of a peculiar form, for the Santa Fé trade, and her hold was crammed with goods for the same destination. There

were also the equipments and provisions of a party of Oregon emigrants, a band of mules and horses, piles of saddles and harness, and a multitude of nondescript articles, indispensable on the prairies. . . .

The passengers on board the "Radnor" corresponded with her freight. In her cabin were Santa Fé traders, gamblers, speculators, and adventurers of various descriptions, and her steerage was crowded with Oregon emigrants, "mountain men," negroes, and a party of Kanzas Indians, who had been on a visit to St. Louis.[32]

In his journal, Parkman had more to say about these passengers, and little of it was complimentary. He offered these tart observations on the Kansas, or Caw, Indians, in his entry for the last day of April, which brought the *Radnor* to Jefferson City:

The wretched Caw Indians on board were hired, for a pint of whiskey, to sing. The chief, a mean-looking old fellow, expecting a friend at Jefferson, painted, took his sword, and wrapped his blanket about him. In this attire he went ashore, and saluted his acquaintance—a white man—with great cordiality. One of the others indulged in a little fooling with a fat Negro, who danced while the Indian sang.[33]

On the following day, Parkman noted that the Indians were "playing cards about the deck. They have a paper for begging, and one of them sat on the deck collecting contributions yesterday."[34] Parkman was not the only observer who found something "wretched" or unseemly in the way members of the Kansas tribe sought favors from strangers. Many traveling up the Missouri River and out along the Santa Fe Trail complained of their penchant for "collecting contributions" or otherwise imposing on wayfarers they encountered. These Kansas seemingly resembled that Frenchman-gone-native lamented by Matt Field, only in reverse. They had been transformed in tragic ways by too-close contact with whites—deprived of their ancestral lands by treaty, relegated to meager reservations that offered them little in the way of subsistence, fobbed off with annuity payments that sometimes ended up in the hands of unscrupulous traders in exchange for whiskey, and reduced on occasion to begging or stealing. Knowing little of their history, Parkman and others could only deplore their dismal and dependent condition.

Perhaps what most disturbed travelers about the Kansas, however, was that their plight was not really that exceptional. They were vivid embodiments of the dangers that faced all those who crossed cultural frontiers and exchanged one way of life for another. Anyone who abandoned his native ground and lost his moorings—whether willingly or reluctantly, whether in pursuit of mere

"Snags on the Missouri River," after Karl Bodmer. Courtesy Library of Congress, Prints and Photographs Division, LC-USZ62-7740.

subsistence or conspicuous profit—might end up "wandering forever like a thing accursed," as Matt Field put it. Indeed, the *Radnor* had among its wealthier passengers a merchant who was as much an outcast in his way as Field's fellow traveler. As Parkman observed in his journal on May 1: "Speyer, the Santa Fe trader, has an immense number of goods on board."[35] This was Albert Speyer, a man of many countries and no fixed loyalties who held passports from his native Prussia and from England. He gained lasting notoriety in the months following his voyage up the Missouri on the *Radnor* by eluding pursuing American troops and carrying a shipment of arms and ammunition to Mexico, which by then was at war with the United States. Speyer was not an American citizen, and he had contracted to deliver the goods before hostilities erupted. But those facts did not keep him from being regarded as suspect.

Parkman and his companions on board did not have to know much about Speyer or the nature of his business to sense that there was something about the Santa Fe trade that defied custom and lured risk takers. The journey up the Missouri by steamboat, for all its excitements and diversions, was fraught with warnings of the dangers that lay ahead for those who ventured too far afield and crossed boundaries. Passengers could hear those warnings in the drunken cries of whites who like Field's traveling companion had seemingly lived too long among Indians or in the begging songs of Indians who had perhaps come to depend too much on whites. And they could sense those warnings as well in the angry antics of the river itself, described with poetic precision by Parkman in his book:

> Thus laden the boat struggled upward for seven or eight days against the rapid current of the Missouri, grating upon snags, and hanging for two or three hours at a time upon sand-bars. We entered the mouth of the Missouri in a drizzling rain, but the weather soon became clear, and showed distinctly the broad and turbid river, with its eddies, its sand-bars, its ragged islands, and forest-covered shores. The Missouri is constantly changing its course,— wearing away its banks on one side, while it forms new ones on the other. Its channel is continually shifting. Islands are formed, and then washed away; and while the old forests on one side are undermined and swept off, a young growth springs up from the new soil upon the other.[36]

It must have seemed at times to those who struggled upward against the current in pursuit of profit that the fitful Missouri was dead-set against them. What could adventurers hope to gain in a race for riches or redemption that began at a snail's pace on a course that was constantly shifting? Perhaps their dreams would be undermined as thoroughly as those old trees on the crumbling banks of the Missouri, leaving only pointed tales of their folly to alert future travelers. Or perhaps they would persist in defiance of all warnings and forebodings, negotiate the hazards in their path, and profit handsomely in the end by those fresh opportunities that seemed to sprout up eternally on one side of the abyss even as ambitions tottered and collapsed on the other.

6

Franklin: Cradle of the Trade

Josiah Gregg dubbed Franklin, Missouri, the "cradle of our trade."[1] Franklin indeed fostered the Santa Fe trade, but the town itself was nurtured by the Missouri River, which fertilized the surrounding bottomlands with its rich silt and offered passage to the keelboats and occasional steamboats that linked Franklin with St. Louis and provided an alternative to the laborious overland route. In the summer of 1819, Edwin James, a naturalist exploring the West with an expedition commanded by Major Stephen Long, traveled with other scientists in Long's party up the Missouri by steamboat and stopped at Franklin, founded in 1816. James later offered one of the first detailed descriptions of that blossoming community:

> This town, at present increasing more rapidly than any other on the Missouri, had been commenced but two years and an half before the time of our journey. It then contained about one hundred and twenty log houses of one story, several framed dwellings of two stories, and two of brick, thirteen shops for the sale of merchandise, four taverns, two smiths' shops, two large team mills, two billiard rooms, a court house, a log prison of two stories, a post office, and a printing press issuing a weekly paper. . . .
>
> The Missouri bottoms about Franklin are wide, and have the same prolific, and inexhaustible soil as those below. The labor of one slave is here reckoned sufficient, for the culture of twenty acres of Indian corn, and produces ordinarily about sixty bushels per acre, at a single crop. In the most fertile parts of Kentucky, fifteen acres of corn are thought to require the labour of one slave,

and the crop being less abundant, we may reckon the products of agriculture there, at about one third part less than in the best lands on the Missouri.[2]

This was an apt comparison on the author's part. The area around Franklin was settled largely by emigrants from Kentucky and other slave states of the border South. Of Franklin's one thousand or so inhabitants in the early 1820s, about two hundred were slaves. Few whites here owned more than three or four slaves, but slave labor was nonetheless important to the success of farms and businesses.[3] One of the attractions of the Santa Fe trade for men of limited means may have been that they could pursue it profitably without investing in slaves (although some well-to-do merchants traveled with slaves, often referred to as servants in the annals of the trade).

Franklin and environs derived more from Kentucky than a tolerance for slavery. Among the first to settle here were sons of that celebrated Kentuckian, Daniel Boone, who made their living by extracting salt from natural springs of brine at Boone's Lick (or Boon's Lick). Franklin grew up on the north bank of the Missouri a short distance east of Boone's Lick and directly across the river from Boonville, another town bearing the name of that pioneering family. The restless opportunism of Daniel Boone and kin seemed to permeate the atmosphere.

The "weekly paper" that Edwin James referred to in his roster of Franklin's civic accomplishments was the *Missouri Intelligencer*, established in 1819. Like most newspapers then and later, the *Intelligencer* devoted much of its space by necessity to paid notices, and those advertisements often revealed more about the community than the articles, many of which the editor picked up from other journals. The formative years of Franklin and surrounding settlements in Howard County were shadowed by the lingering effects of the financial panic of 1819, which caused banks to fail and left many settlers short of cash. Here as elsewhere in Missouri, people had some difficulty holding on to their assets and meeting obligations. There were notices in the *Intelligencer* from men whose wives had left them and who renounced debts incurred by their absent spouses, from businessmen threatening legal action against those with overdue accounts, from farmers seeking to retrieve horses or oxen that had strayed or perhaps been stolen, and from masters offering rewards for the return of fugitive slaves or indentured servants. A notice placed in the *Intelligencer* in August 1821 sought the return of "A NEGRO MAN" who had run off from a saltworks in Howard County: "Any person delivering said negro to the subscriber, in Franklin, shall be liberally rewarded for their trouble."[4] The subscriber seemed unconscious of the cruel irony of rewarding someone "liberally" for depriving a man of liberty.

Franklin's position at the frontier made it easier for those who felt abused, hampered, or financially embarrassed to slip away and try for something better. Servants weary of their tasks or taskmasters, debtors hounded by their creditors, youngsters oppressed by their elders or slighted by their sweethearts—none had too far to run before they were free, particularly if they headed west. Yet those who crossed that frontier on their own did so at considerable risk. Adventurers needed company on the way west, and the process of forming a company placed them under certain restraints. When William Becknell, laboring under heavy debts in Franklin, conceived of the expedition that inaugurated trade on the Santa Fe Trail, he recruited a company by placing a notice in the *Missouri Intelligencer* on June 25, 1821, an "article" whose opening paragraphs resembled the official charter of an association or business:

> An article for the government of a company of men destined to the westward for the purpose of trading for Horses & Mules, and catching Wild Animals of every description, that we may think advantageous to the company.
>
> Sec. 1 Every man will fit himself for the trip, with a horse, a good rifle, and as much ammunition as the company may think necessary for a tour or 3 months trip, & sufficient cloathing to keep him warm and comfortable. Every man will furnish his equal part of the fitting out for our trade and receive an equal part of the product. If the company consist of 30 or more men, 10 dollars a man will answer to purchase the quantity of merchandise required to trade on.
>
> No man shall receive more than another for his services, unless he furnishes more, and is pointedly agreed on by the company before we start. If any young man wishes to go the trip, and is not in a situation to equip himself, if he chooses to go for any person that may think proper to employ and equip him with every necessary required by this article, the employer shall receive an equal dividend of the benefits arising from our trade. There will be no dividend until we return to the north side of the Missouri river, where all persons concerned shall have timely notice to attend and receive their share of the profits.[5]

Becknell was envisioning a company here in the corporate sense, with shares and dividends. Although his plan seemed well thought out, it was perhaps too formal and elaborate to excite the enthusiasm he hoped for. Although he specified in his notice that "signers to the amount of 70 will be received until the 4th of August," only seventeen men gathered on that date to form a company, and of that number only five accompanied Becknell to New Mexico. Some potential recruits may have been put off by the vague objectives of the expedition. With whom, precisely, were they to trade for horses and mules?

Perhaps with the Plains Indians, but the New Mexicans had plenty of mules and horses to offer as well, and Becknell may well have set his sights on Santa Fe from the start, concealing that objective because he was not yet sure that American traders would be welcomed by authorities there. Others in and around Franklin who knew Becknell may have been reluctant to invest money and effort in an enterprise conceived by a man whose own finances were in disarray. In the spring of 1821, he was more than $1,000 in debt and barely escaped imprisonment when his creditors took action against him.[6] Some in Franklin may have recoiled when they read in his notice for the expedition that a penalty of fifty dollars would be assessed any man who "signs and does not perform the trip, unless some unavoidable accident occurs." (Others may have wondered about the organizational skills of a man who headed the first paragraph of his charter "Sec. 1" and neglected to enumerate any further sections.)

Yet in other respects, Becknell proved to be just the leader this risky venture required. A veteran of the War of 1812 and other campaigns against Indians who were allied to the rival British or simply hostile to white settlers, he was well qualified to command a company in the military sense—the sense that mattered most to those crossing the perilous plains. Becknell emphasized that aspect of the expedition belatedly in the final paragraph of his notice: "I think it necessary for the good order and regulation of the company that every man shall be bound by an oath to submit to such orders and rules as the company when assembled shall think proper to enforce." He added that those who joined the company would choose their own officers, as volunteers for armed service commonly did in those days. The recruits who convened on August 4 expressed their faith in Becknell's leadership by unanimously electing him captain.

In the end, Becknell's venture proved profitable, but leaders of later expeditions dispensed with his plan for shares and dividends and allowed the members of each caravan to act as free agents once they reached New Mexico, risking as much as they pleased and reaping their own rewards. By contrast, Becknell's provisions for the election of officers and the drawing up of rules and regulations set an enduring standard for the Santa Fe trade. Those elected to command these companies in the early years were often men of some military experience like Becknell and Benjamin Cooper, who led a small company from the Franklin area to Taos in 1822 and conducted a larger group of about thirty traders to Santa Fe the following year, as reported in the *Missouri Intelligencer*:

> Each of them is provided with one or two pack-horses, and takes, on average, about two hundred dollars worth of goods. We are gratified to learn that

they have selected Col. *Cooper*, one of our most respected citizens, (who visited that place last summer,) to command them. His knowledge of the route, and his experience of Indian warfare, admirably qualify him for the task, and render him a very valuable acquisition to the company. The whole party is well armed, and will no doubt be able to resist successfully an attack from any of the wandering tribes of savages which it may encounter on the way.[7]

The same article referred to this expedition as a "commercial adventure to Santa Fe," but it was clear that Cooper and company foresaw the possibility of military adventures as well. This became the pattern on the trail. With the exception of sizable firms like Bent, St. Vrain & Co. that sometimes formed their own caravans, a company on the Santa Fe Trail was a temporary association organized not for business purposes but for defensive reasons, and its members were bound for the length of the journey by rules and requirements similar to those governing a volunteer militia. The hardy individualists who came together to form these caravans did not always obey their officers or heed regulations, but the organization of such companies nonetheless had the effect of militarizing these otherwise commercial ventures and contributing to that volatile blend of accommodation and aggression that would long characterize exchanges on the Santa Fe Trail.

To those who stayed behind in Franklin, minding the shops and fields, these ventures must have seemed fabulous, if not incredible. A debtor on the brink of ruin like William Becknell went off with a few pack mules loaded with trade goods and returned five months later a man of means. Perhaps his satchels were not overbrimming with silver coins, as one account suggested, but he had enough in hand to stave off his creditors and launch a second expedition to New Mexico in 1822, during which he inaugurated the use of wagons on the trail. Soon whole caravans of vehicles—including hulking Conestogas drawn by Mexican mules and light Dearborns or "pleasure carriages, with elegant horses"[8]—were embarking from Franklin for Santa Fe, a name that conjured up thoughts of exotic rites and riches, accessible to those bold enough to confront the "wandering tribes of savages" along the way. There was something biblical about these errands into the wilderness, and in 1825 Alphonso Wetmore deftly satirized that aspect of the trade for the *Missouri Intelligencer* in his "Book of the Muleteers," chronicling in scriptural language a trek to the land of the Montezumians (Mexicans) by the "men and brethren of the tribe of Benjamin" (perhaps an allusion to Benjamin Cooper):

CHAPTER I

1. And it came to pass in the reign of Ellick the fat, that the dwellers round about Boon's Lick marvelled with one another.

2. And said, verily we have corn and oil, and milk and honey, and cattle and horses, and he goats in abundance, but nevertheless we have few pieces of silver.

3. And one of the judges, a father of preemptioners, rose up and said, men and brethren, hearken unto me.

4. And they did hearken.

5. And he said, there lieth over against us a province wherein dwelleth a people called Montezumians.

6. And they go in and out of tabernacles of clay and they be miners and shepherds.

7. And they have among them gold and silver and precious furs and ass colts in abundance and they be moreover a barbarous people and heathen idolators.

8. And he said, men and brethren of the tribe of Benjamin, hearken unto me—and they answered, and said, we do hearken.

9. And he said go ye unto your several places of abode and tarry three days; and on the fourth day rise up early in the morning while it is yet dark, and saddle your asses.

10. And on the fourth day they gathered themselves together as they were wont, every one on his own ass, and came, and stood still over against the habitation of Benjamin, and they said lo! we are come unto thee as thou has bidden.

11. And Benjamin combed his locks, rose up, and came forth to where his ass was tethered by the way side.

12. And he said, men of Boon's Lick, let your loins be girt about & your hearts filled with the oil of gladness, for you are going into a far country.

13. And they answered with one voice, yea, verily, we rejoice exceedingly and marvel not.

14. And moreover they cried out as one man, be ye our centurian & we will do thy bidding; and say unto each of us singly, go, and we will go, come, and we will come.

15. And they were armed every one with weapons of war according to his fashion, and they were valiant men and true, and well skilled in all stratagems and divers cunning devices.[9]

Benjamin and his brethren made their way across the plains, standing watch against "the *Arapehoes*, the *Camanchies*, and the ungodly *Paducas*," or Apaches, and subsisting in the wilderness by drinking brackish water and feasting on "certain wild oxen," or bison, that seemed to fall into their hands like manna from heaven. ("And they slew of the wild oxen half a score and the humps upon their backs were as sweet morsels under their tongues.") Arriving at last in Santa Fe, the seekers were richly rewarded for their pains:

CHAPTER II . . .

8. And the dwellers of Santa Fe looked up and beheld the men of Benjamin, and they were sore afraid because of their habiliments and their harness of war.

9. And they marvelled with one another, and said, what manner of men are these whose skin is like unto the whiteness of a leper?

10. And the elders and the chief men of Santa Fe spake in a strange language, and said whence came ye?

11. And Benjamin answered and said, we be from a far country, from the land of corn and swine's flesh.

12. Now they of the Ethiope skin spake again unto the strangers and said, what seek ye?

13. Then Benjamin the caravan bachi stood forth and said, we come from afar with our asses laden with merchandize and we seek gold and silver, the ox and the ass and all that is within thy gates.

14. Then the men of Santa Fe cried out with one voice, saying, tarry ye, come in and sojourn, and our maidens shall wash your feet and anoint your beards.

15. And they tarried, and did eat of the flesh of the lamb, and of goat's milk, and of barley water.

16. And they spake with one another and said, it is good for us to be here, for we are weary and our lot is cast in pleasant places.

17. Now it came to pass when they had sojourned awhile that there came among them certain money changers and set before them strange coins and said

18. These we will give unto you, yea more for your purple raiment and fine linens and sandels.

19. And the men of Benjamin said, add thereunto from the flocks and herds of your hills four score of ass colts, and mules and jennets a great many.

20. And those of swarthy skin answered them according to all they had spoken and thus did as the men of Benjamin had commanded and rose up and departed.

21. Then they of Benjamin shouted with one accord and cried aloud saying, this is the land of promise—and the land of payment—for we are laden with the gold of Ophir.

22. And it is moreover of greater value than Loan Office, and the sound thereof is like unto sounding brass and a tinkling cymbal.

23. And the music thereof is like the music of running waters in a great desert when the horse and rider thirsteth with a parched tongue. . . .

27. It breaketh the bolts of the prison door—it causeth disease to flee away.

28. Now therefore all the men of Benjamin rose up and set their faces toward the land wherein their kin folk dwelt, every one his saddle upon his own ass.

29. And they rejoiced with exceeding joy that their sojourning in the land of idolators was at an end.[10]

After the brethren had "wandered in the wilderness for the space of forty days," they reached the great Missouri and crossed over, returning home laden with "shekels of silver, and mules and ass colts" and basking in the admiration of the "old men and maidens."

For all its frivolity, this piece said much about the emerging legend of the Santa Fe trade. New Mexico might be a verminous "land of idolators," but it was also "the land of promise," a place of redemption and regeneration for those daring enough to take up the "weapons of war" and fight their way through the wilderness to lay claim to its bounties. For men who felt thwarted or slighted in small towns on the Missouri frontier, the challenges of the open plains and the glittering prospects of New Mexico were like a tonic. Such a journey, they believed, could truly break the "bolts of the prison door" (as in Becknell's case) and cause "disease to flee away" (as in the case of Josiah Gregg, who grew up in Howard County near Cooper's Fort—established by Benjamin Cooper—and may well have read of the exploits of the pioneering Santa Fe traders in the *Missouri Intelligencer* while he was studying as a surveyor there in the early 1820s). Another restless young man in the Franklin area, Christopher "Kit" Carson, unhappily indentured to saddler David Workman, broke the bonds of his apprenticeship in 1826, at the age of sixteen, by running off to join a wagon train bound for New Mexico. That October, the disgruntled Workman placed this infamous item in the *Intelligencer*:

NOTICE IS HEREBY GIVEN TO ALL PERSONS
That Christopher Carson, a boy about 16 years old, small of his age but thick-set, light hair, ran away from the subscriber, living in Franklin, Howard County, Missouri, to whom he had been bound to learn the saddler's trade, on or about the first of September. He is supposed to have made his way toward the upper part of the state. All persons are notified not to harbor, support or assist said boy under the penalty of the law. One cent reward will be given to any person who will bring back the said boy.[11]

Workman thus earned for himself an unenviable place in history by putting so little value on the services of a youngster whose later deeds on the Santa Fe Trail and other western paths would earn him such renown. Yet Workman's pique was understandable. By Carson's own account, the saddler had treated him well. But how could confinement to such a trade compete with the lure of adventure and profit beyond the frontier?

Residents of Franklin got an enticing glimpse of the wealth to be had at the far end of the trail in June 1826 when a Mexican trader and envoy named Manuel Simón Escudero passed through town on his way back to his homeland, as reported in the *Intelligencer*:

> Six or seven new and substantial built wagons arrived in this place on Tuesday last, heavily laden with merchandise, on their way to New Mexico, owned exclusively, we believe, by Mr. *Escudero*, a native of that country, and who accompanies his valuable adventure. This gentleman has expended a very large sum in the purchase of goods, wagons and equipments. This may be considered as a new era in the commerce between Mexico and this country, and it is probable the example of Mr. E. will be followed by others of his rich countrymen, who will bring hither large portions of their surplus wealth, for the same purpose.[12]

There was not in fact much "surplus wealth" in New Mexico, but Missourians who judged the prosperity of the place by the value of the caravans traveling to and from Santa Fe might easily conclude otherwise. David Workman, fretting over Kit Carson's abrupt departure from his premises, may well have felt he was missing out on something by remaining in Franklin while others were seeking fortune at the far end of the trail. His brother, William Workman, with whom he had emigrated from England and established the saddlery, had recently traveled to Taos and settled there. In 1826, William wrote David a letter that detailed some of the problems of life in New Mexico, including the scarcity of doctors and medicine ("it is one of the meenest Country to be sick in the world") and the periodic shortages of cash in the settlements that led some American merchants to travel south to Chihuahua, where the residents had more to spend ("it is not in the power of man to sell goods where their is no money").[13] But William did not seem at all discouraged. He was laying plans to build a whiskey still in Taos with confederates from the States, including Samuel Chambers, formerly a prisoner in Chihuahua who had since converted to Catholicism and ingratiated himself with New Mexico's governor, Antonio Narbona. Writing in a breathless style that seldom paused for punctuation, William asked David to purchase the necessary equipment from Franklin merchant Abraham Barnes and have it delivered discreetly to New Mexico, where Mexicans operated their own stills and the importation of such equipment by foreigners was forbidden:

> My chance was never more flattering than it is at present Chambers has been to St ta Fee and got the holy water put on his head and the Governor is a great friend of his he will assist us in any thing that we under take so we have want you to get of Aberham Barns eighty gallon stills and some other articles which I will give you a list of, if you could do me the favour I shall be very glad for we are not on any uncertinty about it for we have got the stuf that will bring the money in the spring so that you and Mr Barns need not be the least affraid to get those articles but be shoor never to name it to any person for they are contraband Articles.[14]

Judging by this letter, New Mexico was a land of opportunity for adventurers prepared to adapt to their surroundings. Samuel Chambers did not mind having holy water sprinkled on his head if that would serve his interests (embracing Catholicism enabled him to become a Mexican citizen, which in turn had economic advantages). And other Americans underwent similarly convenient conversions. William Workman, for one, accepted Catholicism and Mexican citizenship while remaining at heart a foreigner whose interests sometimes conflicted with those of his adopted country. David Workman, back in Franklin, soon wearied of minding his shop in Missouri while others were severing bonds to family, employers, or creditors and heading for New Mexico. In 1827, he made the first of many ventures to Santa Fe and beyond.[15] He ended up with his brother in California, where William settled in the early 1840s after fleeing Taos under suspicion of plotting with Texans to foment an uprising in Santa Fe.

One did not have to be a visionary to recognize the advantages of abandoning Franklin for points west. As early as 1819, Edwin James had wondered how long the low-lying town would withstand the intrusions of the Missouri and its periodic floods: "It is even doubtful, whether the present site of Franklin, will not at some future day be occupied by the river, which appears to be at this time encroaching on its bank."[16] In the spring of 1826, not long before Kit Carson left town, the surging Missouri inundated the area, and other floods of equal or greater severity followed in succeeding years, impelling much of the population to remove two miles inland, where they founded New Franklin (what remained of the original settlement was known thereafter as Old Franklin).

Even without those disastrous floods, the Franklin area was destined to lose its status as a jumping-off point for westbound travelers in the 1830s when steamboats began carrying passengers and freight farther upriver on a regular basis to the budding prairie port of Independence, safely located on high ground a few miles south of Independence Landing. Up until then, men driving wagons consumed a week or more traveling overland from the vicinity of Franklin to Fort Osage, which served as the first of several gathering places along the trail for traders who reached the designated rendezvous in small groups at their own pace and then formed into a sizable company for the journey across potentially hostile Indian country. (Any spot along the trail where travelers convened in significant numbers to make plans or do business might be classified as a rendezvous. Long after Council Grove achieved the status of the main rendezvous or staging ground for Santa Fe traders in the 1830s, travelers continued to refer to Independence and other gathering places as rendezvous.)

To reach Fort Osage from Franklin, travelers crossed by ferry to Arrow Rock on the south bank of the Missouri and proceeded westward along a path called the Osage Trace, a route requiring them to ford several tributaries of the Missouri that were often swollen in springtime when the wagons headed out. As Josiah Gregg observed, this journey involved "upwards of a hundred miles of troublesome land-carriage, over unimproved and often miry roads."[17] One trader bound for Santa Fe in May of 1825 filed a report for the *Missouri Intelligencer* from his camp near Fort Osage that tried to cast the journey there in an optimistic light but made painfully clear the various frustrations encountered along the way: "We arrived here last evening, after a pleasant journey in every respect, except the rains.—We have been detained several days by different circumstances, mostly by the loss of some horses, which we recovered, by the badness of the roads, and by the necessity of building bridges over the mire on each bank of the Big Sniabar."[18]

After reaching Fort Osage, the 105 men who convened as a company with thirty-four wagons that May and elected as their captain veteran Santa Fe trader Augustus Storrs could look forward to traversing another two hundred miles or so of similarly demanding terrain—prairie interspersed with stands of trees and laced with creeks and bogs—followed by more than five hundred miles of open plains, country so dry and desolate that it could make men nostalgic for the morasses they left behind. (It often seemed to travelers on the trail that there was either too much water in their way or too little.) Few who undertook that long trek with heavy loads would willingly add to their exertions by traveling overland from Franklin once they had the option of journeying by steamboat to Independence Landing. Operations on the Santa Fe Trail were governed by ruthless laws of economy. Mules, horses, wagons, wells, pastures, springs, groves, and settlements—all were consumed by the voracious demands of this urgent enterprise and abandoned with little ceremony when they no longer served their purpose. Scarcely a decade after Becknell formed his infant company, the cradle of the trade he inaugurated, Old Franklin, found itself among the castoffs, all but forgotten in the rush to Independence and fresh opportunity.

7

The Lure of Independence

U nlike Franklin, which had a special bond to the Santa Fe trade, Independence shared its favors indiscriminately with travelers bound for sundry parts of the West, including the Oregon country, which by 1840 was attracting significant numbers of land-hungry emigrants from the East. Josiah Gregg, writing in 1843, underscored the broad appeal of Independence to adventurers of various descriptions and destinations:

> It is to this beautiful spot, already grown up to be a thriving town, that the prairie adventurer, whether in search of wealth, health, or amusement, is latterly in the habit of repairing, about the first of May, as the caravans usually set out some time during that month. Here they purchase their provisions for the road, and many of their mules, oxen, and even some of their wagons—in short, load all their vehicles, and make their final preparations for a long journey across the prairie wilderness.
>
> As Independence is a point of convenient access (the Missouri river being navigable at all times from March till November), it has become the general 'port of embarkation' for every part of the great western and northern 'prairie ocean.' Besides the Santa Fé caravans, most of the Rocky Mountain traders and trappers, as well as emigrants to Oregon, take this town in their route. During the season of departure, therefore, it is a place of much bustle and active business.[1]

Even before the trickle of immigrants to Oregon swelled to a flood, those passing through Independence on their way to Santa Fe had to compete for supplies, livestock, and lodging or camping space with travelers heading south toward Texas or trappers moving out along the emerging Oregon Trail, which could be reached by a spur diverging from the Santa Fe Trail in what is now eastern Kansas. All of this spelled profits for the merchants of Independence. English author Charles Joseph Latrobe, who visited Independence with Washington Irving in 1832 on a literary expedition to Texas, testified to the rich commercial possibilities of a town that was still taking shape:

> The town of Independence was full of promise, like most of the innumerable towns springing up in midst of the forests in the West, many of which, though dignified by high-sounding epithets, consist of nothing but a ragged congeries of five or six rough log-huts, two or three clap-board houses, two or three so-called hotels, alias grogshops; a few stores, a bank, printing office, and barn-looking church. It lacked, at the time I commemorate, the last three edifices, but was nevertheless a thriving and aspiring place, in its way; and the fortune made here already in the course of its brief existence, by a bold Yankee shop-keeper who had sold sixty thousand dollars' worth of goods here in three years,—was a matter of equal notoriety, surprise, and envy. It is situated about twenty miles east of the Kansas River, and three south of the Missouri, and was consequently very near the western frontier of the state. A little beyond this point, all carriage roads ceased, and one deep black trail alone, which might be seen tending to the southwest, was that of the Santa Fe trappers and traders.[2]

As illustrated by the tale of the Yankee shopkeeper, Independence was a sellers' market, and customers who arrived there belatedly often found that the best offerings had already been snapped up. Naturalist John Kirk Townsend, accompanying a trading expedition to the Northwest in 1834, reached Independence by steamboat with others of his party, including botanist Thomas Nuttall (referred to here as "Mr. N."), in mid-April only to discover that merchants bound for New Mexico had already cleaned out the local supply of mules:

> On the morning of the 14th, we arrived at Independence landing, and shortly afterwards, Mr. N. and myself walked to the town, three miles distant. The country here is very hilly and rocky, thickly covered with timber, and no prairie within several miles.
>
> The site of the town is beautiful, and very well selected, standing on a high point of land, and overlooking the surrounding country, but the town itself is very indifferent; the houses, (about fifty,) are very much scattered, composed of logs and clay, and are low and inconvenient. There are six or eight

stores here, two taverns, and a few tipling houses. As we did not fancy the town, nor the society that we saw there, we concluded to take up our residence at the house on the landing until the time of starting on our journey. We were very much disappointed in not being able to purchase any mules here, all the salable ones having been bought by the Santa Fee traders, several weeks since. Horses, also, are rather scarce, and are sold at higher prices than we had been taught to expect, the demand for them at this time being greater than usual. Mr. N. and myself have, however, been so fortunate as to find five excellent animals amongst the hundreds of wretched ones offered for sale, and have also engaged a man to attend to packing our loads, and perform the various duties of our camp.[3]

As was customary, the caravan to Santa Fe did not form that year until May, so the traders must have purchased the mules well in advance and grazed them in the vicinity for a month or two before departing.[4] One of the great advantages of Independence as a jumping-off point was the abundant pasturage near town. Local artisans produced and repaired wagons, and storekeepers offered a wide assortment of provisions and trade goods, but the stock that mattered most to travelers heading west was of the four-footed kind. Horses and mules predominated in the early days, but by the 1830s traders and emigrants were coming to recognize the advantages of oxen for pulling their wagons. The breakthrough on the Santa Fe Trail had come in 1829, when Major Bennet Riley, assigned to protect traders on the trail, used oxen to draw his supply wagons and found them superior to mules for that purpose, as attested by this newspaper report from Council Grove by an unnamed officer in Riley's command: "Since we have travelled upon the prairie, we have made very good progress for ox teams—some days twenty five miles. . . . Many officers of the command thought the ox teams could not perform the trip: but I had great confidence in them; and we now find that some days, it troubles the traders with their mule teams to keep up with us."[5]

Oxen were not without their drawbacks. They were tender-footed and fared poorly on the short, coarse grass of the open plains. But they had greater strength than mules or horses and less appeal to Indian raiders, who did not relish beef and saw little honor in stealing an animal that was useless for hunting or fighting. American traders and emigrants, by contrast, much preferred the idea of slaughtering an ox when faced with starvation on the trail than of feeding on mule or horse flesh. Nonetheless, many travelers continued to use mules as draft animals, and all who could afford mounts sought horses or mules for that purpose. (Since wagons bound for Santa Fe were generally filled to the brim with trade goods, leaving no room for passengers, most members of the company made the journey on horseback or muleback—with the notable exception of bullwhackers, who walked alongside the teams with whip in hand, and those unfortunate hangers-on who lacked the funds to purchase mounts or lost theirs along the way.)

Such was the importance of animals to the trade that almost any man who knew how to handle them—and fire a gun—could find a place in the caravan. Those twin talents enabled young Richens Lacy Wootton, celebrated in his later years as Uncle Dick Wootton, to catch on with a wagon train bound for Bent's Fort, thus launching his eventful career on the Santa Fe Trail:

> When I left Independence, in the summer of 1836 I was a little under nineteen years of age, but I was pretty near full grown and had been away from home long enough to know how to take care of myself.
>
> I could use a gun as well as anybody, knew how to handle a team, and while I was never particularly in love with hard work, I wasn't afraid of it and when there was anything to be done I was always ready to do my share. That was all that was required of me as a "wagon man," and I got along first-rate from the start.[6]

Among the best at handling mules and horses were Mexicans. After all, their Spanish ancestors had introduced horses to the plains, and Mexico had bequeathed mules to Missouri. Albert Pike, one of the first to head down the Santa Fe Trail in search of literary inspiration, recalled vividly the wild mules his party wrestled with on their overland journey from St. Louis to Independence in 1831—and the man who mastered those animals, a "New Mexican Spaniard" whom Pike considered the best rider he had ever seen:

> After he joined us we soon had all our mules broken, but before, we had some amusing scenes, and one or two broken heads. A number of mules were purchased, after we had been three or four days from St. Louis, and such of the men as had no horses, undertook to ride them. They were perfectly unbroken, and for two or three mornings we had a most ridiculous scene. None of the men knew how to manage the animals, and they were generally no sooner on than off. One poor fellow was no sooner on his mule's back, than he was seen describing a somerset—pitching probably in his fall plump upon his head. Another would go up into the air as straight as an arrow, and a light on his feet. Others would stick on, and the mules taking the bit in their teeth, would run with them a mile or two like incarnate fiends. It is very little use to try riding a mule with an American saddle and bridle. You want a deep Spanish saddle, a heavy double cast bridle with which you can break your animal's jaw—and then you can ride.[7]

Breaking mules was a tough business at which Mexicans excelled, as confirmed by Thomas Jefferson Farnham, who traveled the Santa Fe Trail with his Peoria party as far as Bent's Fort in 1839 before heading northwestward to Oregon. Farnham stopped at Independence that May with his company of greenhorns to gear up for the lengthy expedition. He later described in lavish detail how they prepared for their first trip down the trail—and how the green mules were broken to harness, an operation even more grueling than conditioning those same animals to bear riders:

> Pack mules and horses, and pack-saddles were purchased, and prepared for service. Bacon and flour, salt and pepper, sufficient for 400 miles were secured in sacks; our powder-casks were wrapt in painted canvass; and large oil cloths were purchased to protect these and our sacks of clothing from the rains; our arms were thoroughly repaired; bullets were run; powder-horns and cap-boxes filled; and all else done that was deemed needful, before we struck our tent for the Indian territory. But before leaving this little woodland town, it will be interesting to remember that it is the usual place of rendezvous and "outfit" for the overland traders to Santa Fee and other northern Mexican States. In the month of May of each year, those traders congregate here, and buy large Pennsylvania wagons, and teams of mules to convey their calicoes, cottons, cloths, boots, shoes, &c., &c., over the plains to that distant and haz-ardous market. And it is quite amusing to a "green horn," as those are called who have never been engaged in the trade, to see the mules make their first attempt at practical pulling. They are harnessed in a team two upon the shaft, and the remainder two abreast in long swinging iron traces. And then by way of initiatory intimation that they have passed from a life of monotonous con-templation, in the seclusion of their nursery pastures, to the bustling duties of the "Santa Fe trade," a hot iron is applied to the thigh or shoulder of each with an embrace so cordially warm, as to leave there, in blistered perfection the initials of their last owners name. This done, a Mexican Spaniard, as chief muleteer, mounts the right-hand wheel mule, and another the left hand one of the span next the leaders, while four or five others, as a foot-guard, stand on either side, armed with whips and thongs. The team is straightened; and now comes the trial of passive obedience. The chief muleteer gives the shout of march, and drives his long spurs into the sides of the animal that bears him; his companion before follows his example; but there is no movement. A leer—an unearthly bray, is the only response of these martyrs to human supremacy. Again the team is straightened; again the bloody rowel is applied; the body-guard on foot raise the shout; and all as one apply the lash. The untutored animals kick and leap, rear and plunge, and fall in their harness.

In fine, they act the mule; and generally succeed in breaking neck or limb of some one of their number, and in raising a tumult that would do credit to any order of animals accustomed to long ears.

After a few trainings, however, of this description, they move off in fine style. And although some luckless one may, at intervals, brace himself up to an uncompromising resistance of such encroachment upon his freedom, still, the majority preferring passive obedience to active pelting, drag him onward, till, like themselves, he submits to the discipline of the traces.[8]

Lewis Garrard, traveling west in 1846 on his way to Bent's Fort, witnessed another deft Mexican mule handler who achieved the same end through a different but no less demanding technique:

The way the mules were broken to wagon harness, would have astonished the "full-blooded" animals of Kentucky and other horse-raising states exceedingly. It is a treatment none but hardy Mexican or scrub mules could survive. They first had to be lassoed by our expert Mexican, Blas, their heads drawn up to a wagon wheel, with scarce two inches of spare rope to relax the tight noose on their necks, and starved for twenty-four hours to subdue their fiery tempers; then harnessed to a heavy wagon, lashed unmercifully when they did not pull, whipped still harder when they ran into still faster speed, until, after an hour's bewilderment, and plunging, and kicking, they became tractable and broken down—a labor-saving operation, with the unflinching motto of "kill or cure."[9]

Josiah Gregg chided his fellow writers for "giving an air of romance"[10] to such mundane activities as breaking animals to harness (Gregg may have had in mind Farnham's account, which appeared three years before *Commerce of the Prairies*). But such scenes clearly branded themselves on the imagination of travelers, and with good reason. Men could identify with the mule or the horse as it resisted harsh discipline, for they too had to be broken to the trail. After wagon trains departed Independence, animals that were left free to graze at night sometimes ran off and headed back to what Farnham termed their "nursery pastures" near town. Greenhorns in camp who had not yet become inured to torrential downpours, wagon-miring bogs, and relentless swarms of flies and mosquitoes sometimes wished they could do the same. If they needed a lesson in endurance, they could look to tough Mexican hands like Blas who shared such travails with well-bred gringos like Garrard. Raised in harsh circumstances, they submitted to the "discipline of the traces," in Farnham's words, and more than pulled their weight. Without them, the Santa Fe trade might have stalled in its tracks.

Hired hands for the wagon trains, whether Anglos, Mexicans, or French Canadians, occasionally saved enough of their earnings to set themselves up as traders, trappers, or ranchers. But the towns at either end of the trail had many ways to part men from their money. If the Frenchman Matt Field encountered heading up the Missouri by steamboat managed to lose $3,000 in St. Louis, it was no great matter for wagon drivers to expend their modest earnings carousing in Independence, which by Field's reckoning had swelled to a population of some five thousand by the time he disembarked there in 1839 to begin his journey to Santa Fe. On the day his small wagon train headed out from Independence, he could hardly help noticing that more than a few of the drivers on the road had indulged in farewell binges:

> In the square you observe a number of enormous wagons into which men are packing bales and boxes. Presently the mules are driven in from pasture, and a busy time commences in the square, catching the fractious animals with halters and introducing them to harness for their long journey. Full half a day is thus employed before the expedition finally gets into motion and winds slowly out of town. This is an exciting moment. Every window sash is raised, and anxious faces appear watching with interest the departure. The drivers snap their long whips and swear at their unruly mules, bidding goodby in parentheses between the oaths, to old friends on each side of the street as they move along. Accidents are very apt to occur on the occasion of a setting out. Sometimes the unmanageable mules will not stir at all, and then they are just as likely to take the opposite notion and run off with the enormous weight of merchandise behind them. This occurred on the day of our departure. A drunken driver lashed his mules into a fright and then tumbled into the road, while the team dashed aside, and dragged the loaded vehicle down a steep lane over stumps and stones and other inequalities with most dangerous velocity, until they were brought up against a log house in the middle of the way. Nothing could have appeared more alarming than the huge wagon loaded heavily with new goods, jumping over the tree stumps and seeming every moment on the point of being dashed to atoms. Another accident happened before the wagons got well out of town. The fact was the drivers had all made the most of their last day in *Independence*, and were in condition better adapted to anything else than the performance of their duty. The whole road from the town, four miles, to where the prairie opened was at that time in very bad order, and at one place a wagon tipped over in a gully, the body of the vehicle with all the merchandise being cast entirely clear of the wheels, which fell back into their proper position. On account of these disasters it was midnight when we reached and camped for the first time upon the prairie.[11]

The drivers' "last day in *Independence*," as Field underscored, was their farewell to freedom for a while, and like sailors about to ship out, they went on sprees before submitting once more to discipline. The prairie port resembled the seaport not only in its proximity to the ocean (in this case, a sea of grass) and its opportunities for hell-raising but also in its diverse assemblage of races and languages. Many who passed through Independence in its heyday described it as a place of ceaseless bustle and babble, echoing with greetings and oaths uttered in assorted languages. Editor Benjamin Taylor described the motley crowds in the streets as "jabbering in Dutch, higgling in Spanish, swearing in bad French, anathematizing some refractory mule, in good long-drawn Yankee—shouts and execrations—laughing and singing in tones unknown till Babel cleft the tongue of humanity so marvelously."[12]

The mountain men who frequented Independence garbled English with other languages in their curious lingo, as memorialized by George Ruxton. In his fictional account *Life in the Far West*, Ruxton offered this sample of mountain-man pidgin spoken by a French trapper named Maurice, who, when asked on one occasion how many Indians he had seen on his way to camp, replied: "Enfant de Gârce, me see bout honderd, when I pass Squirrel Creek, one dam war-party, parce-que, they no hosses, and have de lariats for steal des animaux."[13] Ruxton portrayed Independence as a place where such loose-tongued and free-spirited characters found ready companionship in the grogshops and joined in wild sprees before returning empty-handed to their labors:

> Independence may be termed the "prairie port" of the western country. Here the caravans destined for Santa Fé and the interior of Mexico, assemble to complete their necessary equipment. Mules and oxen are purchased, teamsters hired, and all stores and outfit laid in here for the long journey over the wide expanse of prairie ocean. Here, too, the Indian traders and the Rocky Mountain trappers rendezvous, collecting in sufficient force to ensure their safe passage through the Indian country. At the seasons of departure and arrival of these bands, the little town presents a lively scene of bustle and confusion. The wild and dissipated mountaineers get rid of their last dollars in furious orgies, treating all comers to galore of drink, and pledging each other, in horns of potent whisky, to successful hunts and "heaps of beaver." When every cent has disappeared from their pouches, the free trapper often makes away with rifle, traps, and animals, to gratify his "dry" (for your mountaineer is never "thirsty"); and then, "hos and beaver" gone, is necessitated to hire himself to one of the leaders of big bands, and hypothecate his services for an equipment of traps and animals.[14]

Revelers in Independence were most likely encouraged in their spendthrift ways by dancing girls or "soiled doves" of the sort who frequented the "Rocky Mountain House" in St. Louis, where in Ruxton's words "bear-like mountaineers" cavorted wildly with "coquettish belles from 'Vide Poche' ['Empty Pocket'], as the French portion of a suburb is nicknamed."[15] Ruxton contrasted the dress and deportment of one such contingent of free-wheeling mountain men, still laboring under the effects of their celebration, to that of other members of a caravan assembling just outside Independence:

> Upwards of forty huge waggons, of Conestoga and Pittsburg build, and covered with snow-white tilts, were ranged in a semicircle, or rather a horse-shoe form, on the flat open prairie, their long "tongues" (poles) pointing outwards; with the necessary harness for four pairs of mules, or eight yoke of oxen, lying on the ground beside them, spread in ready order for "hitching up." Round the waggons groups of teamsters, tall stalwart young Missourians, were engaged in busy preparations for the start, greasing the wheels, fitting or repairing harness, smoothing ox-bows, or overhauling their own moderate kits or "possibles." They were all dressed in the same fashion: a pair of "homespun" pantaloons, tucked into thick boots reaching nearly to the knee, and confined round the waist by a broad leathern belt, which supported a strong butcher knife in a sheath. A coarse checked shirt was their only other covering, with a fur cap on the head.
>
> Numerous camp-fires surrounded the waggons, and by them lounged wild-looking mountaineers, easily distinguished from the "greenhorn" teamsters by their dresses of buckskin, and their weather-beaten faces. Without an exception, these were under the influence of the rosy god; and one, who sat, the picture of misery, at a fire by himself—staring into the blaze with vacant countenance, his long matted hair hanging in unkempt masses over his face, begrimed with the dirt of a week, and pallid with the effects of ardent drink—was suffering from the usual consequences of having "kept it up" beyond the usual point, and was now paying the penalty in a fit of "horrors"—as *delirium tremens* is most aptly termed by sailors and the unprofessional.
>
> In another part, the merchants of the caravan and Indian traders were superintending the lading of the waggons, or mule packs. These were dressed in civilised attire, and some bedizened in St. Louis or Eastern City dandyism, to the infinite disgust of the mountain men, who look upon a bourge-way (bourgeois) with the most undisguised contempt, despising the very simplest forms of civilisation.[16]

Ruxton was dealing here with the mountain man as a type, and he felt free to ignore such notable exceptions as the sober and supremely accomplished Jedediah Strong Smith and the enterprising Uncle Dick Wootton.

In truth, mountain men did not always wear buckskin or spend their money exclusively on liquor and other diversions. According to one storekeeper in Independence: "Such is their situation when they come here they are about ragged and destitute of every necessary article either of comfort or convenience and they are hence compelled to purchase their clothing and such articles of the merchants here. A little soap and clothing of a decent order soon changes their appearance and renders them once more similar to those around them."[17] Mountain men visiting Independence were not too particular about where they slept, but other visitors were more fastidious and found fault with the local lodging. "We stopped at the best hotel in Independence," Frenchman Victor Tixier wrote ruefully of his stay there in May 1840. "We were led to a poorly enclosed dormitory where eight large beds were strewn about so as to accommodate sixteen travelers."[18] Tixier also echoed the complaint about Santa Fe merchants' monopolizing all the good mounts: "It was, we were told, a season when horses were scarce and expensive, for the traders of the Santa Fe trail had just left."[19] A local newspaper later took Independence to task for neglecting the needs of travelers: "Why do not men who are able to build, erect a hotel sufficiently large to accommodate the great numbers of visitors which often flood the town in the summer season? . . . There are places not half so advantageously situated, which may beat Independence in securing the advantages she at present enjoys, as one of the toll-gates of the country."[20] Many travelers used to life on the trail found it cheaper and more congenial simply to camp amid their wagons and livestock on the outskirts of Independence and visit the town for business or diversion.

The rougher element that frequented the taverns of Independence to drink and gamble had at least one thing in common with the calculating merchants, or "bourgeois," who set up shop there and sometimes took to the trail themselves—a willingness to risk their cash in the hope of greater returns. One mountain man portrayed by Ruxton, having lost his last penny gambling, was forced to seek "credit for a couple of pounds of powder at Owin's store,"[21] a reference to merchant Samuel Owens of Independence, who gave James Webb his start in the Santa Fe trade and extended credit to many others. In the summer of 1844, Owens furnished Webb with "an outfit on credit" that included a wagon costing $100, four yoke of oxen at $28 per yoke, and other advances to the "amount of about $100."[22] That in itself was something of a risk on the lender's part, considering that Webb was new to the Santa Fe trade, but Owens took a bigger gamble that summer by closing his

"Independence—Courthouse," from Charles A. Dana, *The United States Illustrated* (1853). Courtesy Library of Congress, Prints and Photographs Division, LC-USZ62-3667.

store and venturing to Santa Fe himself. Widely respected by men on the trail, he was elected captain of a company that formed in August at Council Grove, with Webb as one of its members. It was late in the year for a caravan to head west—a delay occasioned by hostilities between Texas and Mexico that closed Santa Fe to commerce for a while—and when the traders reached New Mexico they found business slow. Owens salvaged something from the expedition, however, thanks to a misfortune that befell one of the biggest risk takers in the trader, Albert Speyer, who left Independence with a wagon train in September and was caught in a snowstorm on the Cimarron Route that killed most of the one hundred or so mules hauling his merchandise.[23] Speyer went ahead to Santa Fe to purchase a fresh supply of mules and ended up buying out Owens, who unloaded his wagons and goods along with his eight mule teams and counted himself fortunate.[24]

While he was away, Owens signaled his intention to close his store in Independence by placing this announcement in a local paper there:

FINAL NOTICE

All those indebted to the late firm of SAMUEL C. OWENS & CO., either by note or open account, are requested to come forward and pay the same by the 15th of October next. Don't wait for another invitation, as this is positively the LAST. I am determined to close up the business of the old firm; and to do it, I MUST HAVE MONEY. On the above date all unpaid claims will be put in suit, *without fail.* Further indulgence will not be given.[25]

Now in his mid-forties, Owens had decided that it was time for a change and that he would do better by financing his own trading ventures than by extending credit to others and waiting months or years for them to pay up.

Owens entered the Santa Fe trade at a difficult juncture, for recent years had not been as rewarding as many in Independence had hoped. Nearby Westport, situated some ten miles west of Independence near the confluence of the Kansas and Missouri Rivers, had emerged as a serious rival for the business of traders and emigrants. Of further concern were the lingering effects of a recession that hit Missouri in the late 1830s and the unsettling possibility that the border tensions that interrupted the trade in 1843–44 might flare up anew. Rufus B. Sage, an eloquent adventurer from New England who traveled widely across the West and passed though Independence on more than one occasion, found the town in the summer of 1842 "in a rather confused state. Times were hard and all kinds of business at their lowest ebb."[26] Those who lived by the trade, however, seldom let economic problems or international disputes keep them off the trail for long. Throughout the early 1840s, Mexican merchants and their employees braved hardship and hostility and ventured to and from Missouri in large numbers. Sage encountered one such Mexican caravan bound for Independence as he was he heading west from that town in 1841 with a party of mountain men. His account of that meeting offers some idea of what Mexicans were up against in their dealings with disdainful Americans:

> Thus appearing, these creatures, some mounted upon mules, with heavy spurs attached to their heels, (bearing gaffs an inch and a half in length, jingling in response to the rolling motions of the wearer,) ensconced in bungling Spanish saddles, (finished with such ample leather skirts as almost hid the diminutive animal that bore them, and large wooden stirrups, some three inches broad,) were riding at their ease; while others, half naked, were trudging along on foot, driving their teams, or following the erratic mules of the caravan, to heap upon them the ready maledictions of their prolific vocabulary. Passing on, we were accosted:
> "Como lo pasa, caballeros?"
> The salutation was returned by a simple nod.
> "Habla la lengua Espanola, senors?"
> A shake of the head was the only response.
> "Es esta el camino de Independenca?"
> No reply.
> "Carraho! Que quantos jornadas tenemos en la camina de Independenca?"
> Still no one answered.
> "Scha! Maldijo tualmas! Los Americanos esta dijabelo!"[27]

Companies like the one Sage joined were seldom without someone who could interpret Spanish, at least to the extent or replying "Si" or "No" to a few simple questions. These Mexicans seemed to have little doubt that the silence which met their inquiries was a gesture of contempt. They entered into this fruitless exchange with all due courtesy, addressing the Americans as gentlemen ("caballeros" and "senors") and asking them how they were doing, whether they spoke Spanish, and whether this was indeed the road to Independence. But the stony silence on the American side reduced them to curses ("Carraho!") and a summary judgment on these ill-mannered travelers: "Americans are devils!" Sage, for all his prejudices, let these Mexicans have their say in his account, leaving their remarks untranslated as if to signify that no translation was necessary. The import of their questions was clear enough to the men who chose to ignore them.

Fortunately, not all Americans who met with Mexicans on the trail or in the prairie ports responded to them in this curt fashion. Matt Field, who returned to Missouri in late 1839 with a party of Mexican traders, told of a similar incident in which a company made up largely of Americans passed them by with barely a word.[28] But other meetings between the two sides were more cordial. Storekeepers in Independence who equipped Santa Fe traders of various origins resented hostile acts that discouraged Mexicans from traveling to Missouri and stocking up there. And American merchants who ventured to Santa Fe often developed close ties with Mexicans and blamed their own government as well as Mexican authorities for trade barriers between the two countries. One sore point was that Americans who sold foreign-made goods in Santa Fe or Chihuahua had to pay duties twice, once for importing those goods and again for exporting them to Mexico. This made it hard for them to compete in some parts of Mexico with British merchants, who were taxed only once, when they brought their wares into Mexican ports. Missourians repeatedly pressed Congress for drawbacks, or relief from duties on goods imported from abroad for the Mexican market, and finally received that break in 1845. Given such drawbacks, the *Independence Journal* declared, "our traders will supply the whole of the Provinces of Santa Fe, Chihuahua, Sonora, California, and others, now supplied with British goods through Matamoras, Vera Cruz, and other ports, and our trade from half a million will become four or five millions."[29] This may have been overstating the case, but traders whose profits had been lagging recently were indeed eager to take advantage of the Drawback Act of 1845, and the following year promised to be one of the busiest ever on the Santa Fe Trail.

Adding to the excitement in town were the crowds of emigrants passing through on their way to Oregon. Many artists, writers, and curiosity-seekers flocked to Independence in early 1846 to immerse themselves in this rising tide of westward expansion. (That American troops might soon be heading west from Fort Leavenworth, upriver from Independence, to seize Mexican territory in the Southwest was something few people in the area anticipated long before the fact. It was not war fever that gripped them but the hunger for fresh profits or fertile land at the end of one trail or another.) One of those who experienced Independence in this heady season of promise was artist Alfred Waugh, who arrived there in March and found much to occupy him:

> As soon as it was known that I was in town many citizens commissioned [me] to paint pictures for them and this occupied so long a time that the season came round for the Santa Fe trader[s] to assemble here, previous to their start across the plains. Emigrants to California and Oregon this year were numerous, indeed to a greater extent than was ever known before, which [gave] to this flourishing little town an exceedingly bustling appearance. Almost every

nation on the face of the globe had sent its representatives to this starting point. The streets were alive with quadrupeds and bipeds. The neighing of horses, the braying of mules, the lowing of oxen, the cracking of whips, with the systematic swearing of teamsters, made its otherwise quiet thoroughfares, most inharmoniously musical, if one can call anything musical which lacks harmony. The rich and the poor; the mechanic and the farmer; the trader, the speculator and gambler; the pious christian and profane unbeliever whose every other word is an oath; the visionary who sees in the distance whole cities growing up under his superior guidance, the artist, the naturalist, and man of letters; and though last, the gentleman of leisure who was amply provided with ellegantly constructed weapons for the chase, with a plentiful supply of the luxuries of life to render the trip agreable.[30]

Among the artists in Independence that spring were Waugh himself and John Mix Stanley, who would travel to Santa Fe and on to California in the company of American troops before the year was out. Among the naturalists on hand was German-born Frederick Wislizenus, who would join the wagon train of Albert Speyer, laden with contraband weaponry, and delve deep into Mexico. Among the men of letters were Francis Parkman, Josiah Gregg—characterized by Waugh as a "gentleman of great truth, but of no poetry in his writings"[31]—and journalist Edwin Bryant, bound for California, where he would end up serving as alcalde, or chief magistrate, of American-occupied San Francisco. (Before Bryant left town, he and Waugh attended a Masonic ceremony in honor of those heading down the Oregon and Santa Fe Trails, during which the grand master riled Bryant with an overwrought farewell that "consigned us all to the grave, or to perpetual exile.")[32]

None of the luminaries encountered by Waugh gained more notoriety that spring than a gentleman of leisure from Baltimore named William Wirt Meredith, who arrived from St. Louis on the same steamboat as Parkman, reportedly with the intention of curing himself of consumption by visiting Santa Fe in the company of Sam Owens.[33] Meredith—denounced by Parkman as "flash genteel"[34]—came to grief in Independence after flirting with the wife of lawyer John Henry Harper, who shot his rival dead and blamed the deed on a quarrel over cards (an excuse that fooled no one). Compounding the resulting furor was the fact that Harper's wife, Fanny, was Sam Owens's daughter. Fanny had married Harper as a teenager without the permission of her father, who had then tried unsuccessfully to break her attachment to the lawyer by enrolling her in school in New York. According to a local history written many years later, Harper, "said to be a bright fellow without character," threatened rash action before father and daughter left for the East:

He told Mr. Owens, if he took Fannie away from him he would commit sui-
cide and suiting the action to the words, drew a small pocket pistol, placed
the muzzle to his head and drew the trigger. It snapped; Mr. Owens coolly
walked to his desk and pulled out a pair of Colts dragoon revolvers and handed
them to Harper, remarking, "Try one of these, I have killed buffalo with them
on the plains, and have never known either one of them to snap yet. I think
which one of either you take, will answer your purpose." Needless to say, Mr.
Harper did not accept the offer. When Mr. Owens got back home, he sent for
Harper and told him, "Here, take her, if you can do anything with her, it is a
great deal more than I can, and you are perfectly welcome to her."[35]

Whatever the truth of this anecdote, Owens must have been badly shaken by
the scandal surrounding Fanny, who after offering Meredith more than a little encouragement tried to make things up to her husband by helping him to
escape from jail. He slowly carved a hole through the wall, Waugh reported,
and Fanny dutifully carried out the debris under her cloak after each visit,
"thus concealing the work that was being done from day to day."[36] She lost
all sympathy for her husband, however, when he was later recaptured. "Woman
as I am," she told him by Waugh's account, "if I once got out they could not
catch me again. You deserve to be hanged."[37] Others in town may well have
felt the same, but Harper twice obtained a change of venue for his trial, Waugh
reported, and after much delay won acquittal with the help of one of Missouri's
most popular lawyers and officers, Colonel Alexander Doniphan, a hero of
the army's New Mexico campaign.

Everything seemed to be coming together in Independence in the spring
of 1846—impulses of trade, expansion, conquest, and sheer curiosity—and
Waugh, for one, marveled at the scene in all its variety. He admired the mountain men in buckskin: "From the length of time these men spend in those far
off wilds among wild animals and wilder Indians they have assumed some of
the dress and manners of their savage neighbors."[38] Waugh relished the contrast they presented to the nattily attired pleasure-seekers and convalescents:

Here stood a tall weather beaten fellow with long, dark elflocks reaching to
his shoulders, dressed in a suit of buckskin, fancifully ornamented with needle-
work, looking with perfect contempt upon the city-bred amateur hunter
whose travelling coat displayed a row of enormous bronze buttons, and an
endless variety of pockets. There lounged the pale valetudinarian who is going
to seek in "change of scene" that relief which cannot be granted him by his
physicians. But who have we here? Why! he looks out of place in that superb
morning gown, and yellow slippers, but what am I talking about, never mind
the dress, the tailor made hat,—look at the creature's face, that was the work

of madam nature, and certainly we must give her credit for her handywork. She has given a pretty face, a fine complexion and an abundance of superbly flowing hair, but, in the bestowal her kindness was displayed on the externals only, and what few brain she may have given him at first, have long since been expended in the nourishment of his darling, lady killing tresses.[39]

Waugh identified this dandy as a "young fellow from New York or Philadelphia" who was placed by his father under the charge of Albert Speyer but who proved to be "so great a ninny" that Speyer sent him home. Speyer, for his part, impressed Waugh as everything that callow youth was not, a man possessed of few external charms but graced with deep reserves of cunning and determination:

> There, do you see that small, spare man, with a wirey figure and thin, sharp visage, him with the sallow complexion and dark moustache you percieve what a keen deep set eye he has got, and a nose so aquiline he might pass for a roman. The firm compression of his thin lips, indicate a strong determination of purpose. He is a man of great energy of character—nothing daunts his courageous spirit. That man lost in one night, during a snow storm, on the prairies, last November upwards of three hundred mules, they were killed by the cold. Which misfortune led to a loss of thirty eight thousand dollars. Every person believed him to be a ruined man; they thought he could not possibly recover himself, but he did, however and now is master of twenty two waggon loaded with merchantdize for the Chihuahua market, and is likely to realize one hundred thousand dollars by the trade this year.[40]

Waugh exaggerated Speyer's losses to the storm, in mules if not in dollars, and mistakenly denied the well-founded allegation that Speyer was carrying "arms and ammunition to the Mexicans."[41] But Waugh was correct in surmising that the trader hoped to profit handsomely by his investment.

For Speyer as for many others in this year of destiny, however, events failed to unfold according to expectations. Speyer would encounter resistance and frustration in embattled Mexico. Sam Owens would join forces with American troops and meet with death there in an act of reckless daring that some felt was prompted by his family misfortunes. Alfred Waugh would embark for Santa Fe and reach that goal but would find the town and its inhabitants less than enchanting. ("They are, almost with an exception, a set of very depraved, unprincipled wretches, from the *ruler* to the *ruled*," he wrote haughtily, "and it would be rendering them a signal service to take them under our mild and wholesome government.")[42] Francis Parkman would confront the harsh realities of life in the West and conclude that it could be as trying for one's health and ideals as it was exhilarating. By the time he arrived in Independence in early May, on the same steamboat as Speyer and the doomed Meredith, he had already glimpsed the seamier side of frontier life, but he retained hope that better things awaited pioneers in the direction of the setting sun and that the journey west would refine and strengthen the American character. He expressed that hope in his flattering portrait of an emigrant he witnessed at the landing as he approached Independence, a pioneer whose free and easy manner contrasted sharply to the subservient look of some Mexicans who waited nearby:

> Parties of emigrants, with their tents and wagons, were encamped on open spots near the bank, on their way to the common rendezvous at Independence. On a rainy day, near sunset, we reached the landing of this place, which is some miles from the river, on the extreme frontier of Missouri. The scene was characteristic, for here were represented at one view the most remarkable features of this wild and enterprising region. On the muddy shore stood some thirty or forty dark, slavish-looking Spaniards, gazing stupidly out from beneath their broad hats. They were attached to one of the Santa Fé companies, whose wagons were crowded together on the banks above. In the midst of these, crouching over a smouldering fire, was a group of Indians, belonging to a remote Mexican tribe. One or two French hunters from the mountains, with their long hair and buckskin dresses, were looking at the boat; and seated on a log close at hand were three men, with rifles lying across their knees. The foremost of these, a tall, strong figure, with a clear blue eye and an open, intelligent face, might very well represent that race of restless and intrepid pioneers whose axes and rifles have opened a path from the Alleghanies to the western prairies. He was on his way to Oregon, probably a more congenial field to him than any that now remained on this side of the great plains.[43]

In the original journal entry from which Parkman derived this passage for *The Oregon Trail*, he referred to the foreigners at the landing as "piratical-looking Mexicans,"[44] a description that made them sound menacing but impressive. By altering the phrase to "slavish-looking Spaniards" and portraying them as "gazing stupidly out" from under their sombreros, the author heightened the contrast between these lowly foreigners and the "intelligent" and "intrepid" American pioneer. Parkman did not expand on this dubious theme. To the contrary, he wrote critically of the American emigrants he later encountered along the trail, few of whom seemed to live up to that noble ideal he glimpsed from a distance at the landing. The West that Parkman encountered beyond the frontier and described with austere eloquence was a place where neither conquerors nor conquered, neither settlers nor "savages," seemed to have any special claim to nobility.

Observers of a different temperament, however, found much to celebrate in the prairie ports and out along the trails. For them, the promiscuous mingling in places like Independence of various races, types, and temperaments, each with its conspicuous strengths and weaknesses, was diverting and invigorating. Naturalist Frederick Wislizenus found the raucous town of Independence that he passed through in May of 1846 much more to his liking than the sleepy village he had encountered seven years before on his earlier western tour: "I now find it very much improved, and the great throng of emigrants to the 'far west,' and of Santa Fe traders, at present there collected, gives it quite a lively appearance. This varied crowd of strangers was composed of the most different materials—all united in one object; that is, to launch themselves upon the waste ocean of the prairie, and to steer through it in some western direction."[45] Perhaps it took a foreigner to feel at ease in this crowd of strangers—and a naturalist to appreciate the way in which different materials or elements, some of them seemingly humble or coarse, could combine to accomplish something grand. This risky venture required human material whose virtues were not always readily apparent to those heedless of the challenges that lay ahead, including ruthless entrepreneurs like Speyer, whom Wislizenus praised for his "energy, perseverance, and fearlessness,"[46] and including those oft-maligned Mexicans, whose retiring manner sometimes disguised the fact that they kept the caravans running. All the diverse elements that came together at the prairie ports—Mexicans, mountain men, merchants, and mules, among other creatures—united ultimately for one great object and launched themselves across the sea of grass.

8

Rendezvous at Council Grove

Travelers heading west over the grasslands had not truly embarked on that voyage until they splashed across the Big Blue River at a ford situated a day's journey or so southwest of Independence and left Missouri and its ample forests behind. That crossing was a tricky one for wagon trains, and some travelers circumvented it by starting out at Westport, on the far side of the Big Blue. Those who made it across the river from Independence in one day were doing well, given the sorts of mishaps reported by Matt Field and others on their way out of town. Even if the wagon drivers were sober and the animals were conditioned to their task, bad weather or poor footing often forced travelers to spend their first night amid the sparsely settled outskirts of Independence. The experience of Thomas Farnham, who left Independence with his party by pack train on May 30, 1839, was not unusual:

> Our pack-saddles being, therefore, girded upon the animals, our sacks of provision, &c., snugly lashed upon them, and protected from the rain that had begun to fall, and ourselves well mounted and armed, we took the road that leads off southwest from Independence in the direction of Santa Fe. But the rains that had accompanied us daily since we left Peoria, seemed determined to escort us still, our illnatured scowls to the contrary notwithstanding. We had travelled only three miles when it fell in such torrents that we found it necessary to take shelter in a neighbouring school-house for the night. It was a dismal one; but a blazing fire within, and a merry song from a jovial number of our company imparted as much consolation as our circumstances

seemed to demand, till we responded to the howling of the storm—the sonorous evidences of sweet and quiet slumber. The following morning was clear and pleasant, and we were early on our route. We crossed the stream called Bigblue, a tributary of the Missouri, about 12 o'clock, and approached the border of the Indian domains. All were anxious now to see and linger over every object that reminded us that we were still on the confines of that civilization which we had inherited from a thousand generations; a vast and imperishable legacy of civil and social happiness. It was, therefore, painful to approach the last frontier enclosure—the last habitation of the white man— the last semblance of home. The last cabin at length was approached. We drank at the well and travelled on. It was now behind us. All was behind us with which the sympathies of our young days had mingled their holy memories. Before us were the treeless plains of green, as they had been since the flood—beautiful, unbroken by bush or rock; unsoiled by plough or spade; sweetly scented with the first blossomings of the spring. They had been, since time commenced, the theatre of the Indians prowess—of their hopes, joys and sorrows. . . . A lovely landscape this, for an Indian's meditations! He could almost behold in the dim distance where the plain and sky met the holy portals of his after state—so mazy and beautiful was the scene![1]

If Josiah Gregg found Farnham's description of mule-breaking too fanciful, one can only imagine his reaction to this heated passage. Yet Farnham was not the only traveler to view the prospect west of the Big Blue, where the woodlands receded and the tall-grass prairie opened up, as a stirring overture to a new world that seemed ages apart from the settled country he and his companions were leaving behind. California-bound Edwin Bryant, who traveled the Santa Fe Trail briefly in early May of 1846 before turning off on the Oregon Trail, expressed a similar sense of awe as the prairie loomed before him:

The view of the illimitable succession of green undulations and flowery slopes, of every gentle and graceful configuration, stretching away and away, until they fade from the sight in the dim distance, creates a wild and scarcely controllable ecstasy of admiration. I felt, I doubt not, some of the emotions natural to the aboriginal inhabitants of these boundless and picturesque plains, when roving with unrestrained freedom over them; and careless alike of the past and the future, luxuriating in the blooming wilderness of sweets which the Great Spirit had created for their enjoyment, and placed at their disposal.[2]

Standing at what he called "the line which divides savage life and civilization,"[3] Bryant felt possessed by the spirit of that beckoning Indian country and its "aboriginal inhabitants" (who were not in fact as careless of the past and future

as romantics like Bryant imagined). Frederick Wislizenus expressed much the
same idea more prosaically in his journal entry from Big Blue Camp on May
15, 1846:

> A charming spot is this first camp in the prairie. It lies just on the western
> boundary line of the State of Missouri, the military road from Fort Towson
> to Fort Leavenworth passing by it. This road forms the dividing line between
> the last settlements and the Indian country. Situated thus at the very junction
> of civilization and wilderness, we could overlook them both with a single
> glance. Towards the east we perceived the blessings of civilization—fine farms,
> with corn-fields, orchards, dwelling-houses, and all the sweet comforts of home:
> towards the west, the lonesome, far stretching prairie, without house or cul-
> tivation—the abode of the restless Indian, the highway of the adventurous
> white man.[4]

This dividing line between civilization and wilderness was not quite as sharp
or as well defined as such idyllic passages implied, however. Before Kansas was
organized as a territory in 1854, the federal government indeed recognized
the land west of Missouri as Indian country and guarded the frontier with a
string of outposts that included Forts Leavenworth and Towson. But that did
not prevent land-hungry whites from crossing the boundary and squatting
on Indian territory. Furthermore, the Indians who held title to that land by
treaty were not entirely strangers to what Wislizenus called the "blessings of
civilization." They included tribes removed from the East such as the Shawnees
and the Delawares, who had waged hard battles against encroaching whites
in the past but had come to terms with American might and adopted American practices. Some welcomed preachers and teachers like those who founded
the Shawnee Methodist Mission just west of the Missouri border in the early
1830s. Many lived in cabins and raised crops and livestock (although men
from these Indian settlements continued to venture afar to trade, hunt, or
make war, as did their white counterparts on the frontier). These were the
first legitimate settlers of the Kansas prairie under American law—and they
were by no means the first Indians to live in villages there and cultivate the
land. Nonetheless, even some observant and astute travelers on the Santa Fe
Trail lent credence to the idea that the grasslands were exclusively the domain
of the "restless Indian," as Wislizenus put it, or the "theater of the Indians
prowess," in the words of Farnham—thus reinforcing the misconception that
only whites could cultivate, or civilize, this promising wilderness.

Aside from such native settlers as the Shawnees and Delawares, other
Indians encountered by travelers west of the Missouri border included the
Osages and Kaws, or Kansas, prairie-dwellers who had been pressured by

treaty makers into surrendering much of their territory, which had then been allotted to tribes removed from the East. The Osages and Kansas suffered as a result, and members of both groups sometimes stole livestock from wagon trains or pressed wayfarers for "presents." Edwin Bryant heard a rumor before leaving Independence that "Kansas Indians had collected in large numbers on the trail, for the purpose of robbery and murder."[5] Wisely, he put little stock in the report, recognizing that plying greenhorns with dire warnings was something of a sport along the trail. (Shortly after leaving town, he met with a weary assemblage of Santa Fe traders returning east, one of whom assured Bryant that his life would be shortened ten years by the trip to California and that if he was fortunate enough to return, his hair "would be white, not with the frosts of age, but from the effects of exposure and extreme hardships.")[6] In truth, neither the Kansas nor the Osages constituted a major threat to traffic on the trail. The verdant prairie beyond the Missouri border was no longer the theater of the Indian's prowess, and that fact made it possible for travelers to postpone the regrettable necessity of forming into large companies for defensive purposes—regrettable because large parties were harder to manage and sustain. Many travelers felt secure enough to proceed in small groups to Council Grove, 150 miles or so from Independence, before organizing there into a company large enough to cope with the more formidable tribes of the plains (or short-grass buffalo country).

Most parties reached the rendezvous at Council Grove within ten or twelve days after traversing rolling country laced with creeks—an appealing landscape whose chief hazards consisted of quagmires that sucked at the wheels of wagons and swarms of flies so maddening that mules or oxen sometimes ran amok, forcing parties to travel by night to avoid the pests. Although there was little danger of Indian attack between the Missouri border and Council Grove, wise travelers always welcomed company. Josiah Gregg, who embarked from Independence on his first trading venture to Santa Fe on May 15, 1831, was grateful that he made that opening stretch of the journey with other wagons, for it often took the combined efforts of men and their teams to free vehicles that became bogged down amid the frequent storms that drenched the prairie in springtime.

Those difficulties began in earnest for Gregg's party shortly after they left Round Grove, a popular camping spot on the trail some thirty-five miles from Independence. (In 1831 Round Grove was still worthy of the name, but by 1846 it had been reduced by travelers seeking firewood to a single tree, Lone Elm, and Wislizenus had good reason to be concerned for the future of that surviving specimen: "How long the venerable elm-tree, that must have seen many ages, will yet be respected by the traveller, I am unable to say; but I fear

that its days are numbered, and that the little valley will look then more desolate than ever.")[7] West of Round Grove, Gregg and his companions were
beset by a rainstorm that continued "without let or hindrance for forty-eight
hours."[8] The ailing Gregg had been riding in a Dearborn carriage, but he found
that "berth not exactly waterproof" and took shelter in one of the wagons,
where he lay bundled in a blanket atop the tightly packed trade goods, protected from the rain by the "stout Osnaburg sheets" that covered the vehicle's
wooden frame. Far less fortunate under similar circumstances was Lewis
Garrard, who spent a stormy night on the prairie en route to Bent's Fort in
1846 with a train whose wagons were filled to the brim, leaving the men no
choice but to sleep on the ground: "As the water penetrated, successively, my
blankets, coat, and shirt, and made its way down my back, a cold shudder
came over me; in the gray, foggy morning a more pitiable set of hungry, shaking wretches were never seen."[9] Gregg, for his part, may have succeeded in
keeping dry, but that was the least of his party's problems:

> The loose animals sought shelter in the groves at a considerable distance from
> the encampment, and the wagoners being loth to turn out in search of them
> during the rain, not a few of course, when applied for, were missing. This,
> however, is no uncommon occurrence. Travellers generally experience far
> more annoyance from the straying of cattle during the first hundred miles, than
> at any time afterwards; because, apprehending no danger from the wild Indi-
> ans (who rarely approach within two hundred miles of the border), they sel-
> dom keep any watch, although that is the very time when a cattle-guard is
> most needed. It is only after some weeks' travel that the animals begin to feel
> attached to the caravan, which they then consider about as much their home
> as the stock-yard of a dairy farm.[10]

Mules as well as oxen exhibited this tendency to stray or bolt for home in the
early stages of the journey. As Wislizenus wrote in his journal when his party
was still a few days short of Council Grove: "A severe thunder storm came on
in the night, during which some of our mules took it into their heads to run
back to cultivated life; but our Mexican mule boys (the best set of men for that
purpose) brought the prisoners to camp in the morning."[11] Osages, Kansas,
and other Indians in the vicinity sometimes exploited the loose bonds between
these four-legged "prisoners" and their careless keepers by rounding up "an
occasional stray animal," Gregg noted, "which they frequently do with the
view alone of obtaining a reward for returning it to its owner."[12]

Parties on the trail were well advised to retrieve their animals by whatever
means necessary if they hoped to haul their heavy wagons through the treacherous Narrows. Located some thirty miles west of Round Grove, this was a

slightly elevated corridor of seemingly dry ground between river basins that concealed surprising depths of muck. Gregg described the ordeal: "On such occasions it is quite common for a wagon to sink to the hubs in mud, while the surface of the soil all around would appear perfectly dry and smooth. To extricate each other's wagons we had frequently to employ double and triple teams, with 'all hands to the wheels' in addition—often led by the proprietors themselves up to the waist in mud and water."[13]

After several days of such exertions, the proprietors were glad for a chance to rest and refit, and they found it at Council Grove, the finest campground along the Santa Fe Trail, fed by the Neosho River and graced with abundant pastures for the horses, mules, and oxen and handsome stands of hardwood timber for repairing battered wagons and wheels. As Gregg related:

> Early on the 26th of May we reached the long looked-for rendezvous of Council Grove, where we joined the main body of the caravan. Lest this imposing title suggest to the reader a snug and thriving village, it should be observed, that, on the day of our departure from Independence, we passed the last human abode upon our route; therefore, from the borders of Missouri to those of New Mexico not even an Indian settlement greeted our eyes.
>
> This point is nearly a hundred and fifty miles from Independence, and consists of a continuous stripe of timber nearly half a mile in width, comprising the richest varieties of trees; such as oak, walnut, ash, elm, hickory, etc., and extending all along the valleys of a small stream known as 'Council Grove creek,' the principal branch of the Neosho river. This stream is bordered by the most fertile bottoms and beautiful upland prairies, well adapted to cultivation: such indeed is the general character of the country from thence to Independence. All who have traversed these delightful regions, look forward with anxiety to the day when the Indian title to the land shall be extinguished, and flourishing 'white' settlements dispel the gloom which at present prevails over this uninhabited region.[14]

Of course, Indians had been traversing these "delightful regions" far longer than whites, and the "anxiety" they felt about losing title to the land was no doubt sharper and more unsettling than the restless anticipation Gregg implied by that word. From the start, this enviable meeting place was shadowed by the rival claims of whites and Indians, and those claims would not be happily reconciled.

Council Grove took its name from a parley in August 1825 between leaders of the Osages—who once dominated much of Missouri and environs—and U.S. commissioners led by George Champlin Sibley, sent to survey the road to New Mexico and placate tribes along the way, tasks for which they were allotted $30,000. After leaving Fort Osage in mid-July and working their way meticulously across the prairie, measuring each leg of the journey and fighting plagues of flies as they went, Sibley and company—including Stephen Cooper, the well-traveled nephew of pioneering Santa Fe trader Benjamin Cooper—arrived on August 5 at the inviting place Sibley dubbed Council Grove. As he related in his journal:

> Fine morning. Started early. Drove 6 64/80 miles and arrived to Breakfast at a Main Branch of the Nee Ozho River; and here we find most excellent pasturage, and a Large & beautiful Grove of fine Timber; and we determine to wait here for the Osages, who are expected in two or three days. Our Camp is arranged with the view of receiving our expected Visitors in a suitable manner. Very few flies Here. . . .
>
> As we propose to Meet the Osage Chiefs in council Here, to negotiate a Treaty with them for the Road & c. I suggested the propriety of naming the place "Council Grove" which was agreed to, & Capt. Cooper directed to Select a Suitable Tree, & to record this name in Strong and durable characters—which was done.[15]

The tree selected for the purpose was a "venerable White Oak,"[16] Sibley later remarked, and the anticipated meeting with the Osages occurred nearby on August 9. This parley, as described in his journal, was remarkably brisk and businesslike, without the lengthy speeches and deliberations that often marked such gatherings:

> Council today with the Osages. The Commissioners explained to them fully & clearly what they desire respecting the Road; and proposed to give them $800 as compensation for the privilege of Marking it through their Land, & the free use of it forever. After a few Minutes conversation among themselves, the chiefs declared their Assent to the proposition, & expressed their Readiness to execute a Treaty to that effect. And they were told that The Commissioners would meet them again tomorrow, prepared to conclude & sign the Treaty as now agreed on. And then the Council Rose, to meet again tomorrow.[17]

Perhaps one reason the chiefs assented so readily was that the thorny issue of the tribe's claim to the land through which the road passed had seemingly been settled two months earlier at a big council in St. Louis, presided over by William Clark. There, a larger and more representative group of Osage leaders than the sixteen chiefs and warriors who signed the agreement at Council Grove had agreed to a sweeping treaty by which they relinquished "right, title, interest, and claim"[18] to all their remaining lands within the state of Missouri and the Arkansas Territory and to any lands west of Missouri and Arkansas, with the exception of a reservation set aside for the tribe along what is now the Kansas-Oklahoma border. That treaty effectively extinguished Osage claims to the area traversed by the Santa Fe Trail, but it had yet to be ratified by Congress when Sibley met with the Osages at Council Grove in August. And in any case, not all members of the tribe felt bound by the St. Louis agreement.

Sibley and company thus deemed it prudent to draw up a treaty that offered the "Chiefs and Head Men of the Great and Little Osages" (the southern and northern branches of the tribe) $800 in cash or goods for the use of any part of the trail they might still claim, if only to buy peace for the surveying party from the Osages in their vicinity. The first two articles of the Council Grove treaty entitled the commissioners to "survey and mark out a road, in such manner as they may think proper, through any of the territory owned or claimed by the said Great and Little Osage Nations" and declared that the road "shall, when marked, be forever free for the use of the citizens of the United States and of the Mexican Republic, who shall at all times pass and repass thereon, without any hindrance or molestation on the part of the said Great and Little Osages."[19] The third article went even further in attempting to guarantee the safety of travelers on the trail: "The Chiefs and Head Men as aforesaid, in consideration of the friendly relations existing between them and the United States, do further promise, for themselves and their people, that they will, on all fit occasions, render such friendly aid and assistance as may be in their power, to any of the citizens of the United States, or of the Mexican Republic, as they may at any time happen to meet or fall in with on the road aforesaid."[20]

This treaty, like many that agents of the United States negotiated with Indians over the years, operated on the dubious assumption that a select group of tribal leaders had the power to make broad and lasting commitments on behalf of entire "nations" (a status effectively denied to tribes once they moved to reservations and came under federal authority). Some who signed the Council Grove treaty for the Osages were in fact important chiefs, including White Hair, or Pahu-sha (Pahusca), one of several signatories who had earlier attended the council at St. Louis and put their marks to that accord as well. But the names of other notable Osage chiefs were missing from the Council Grove treaty. Realistically, the best Sibley could hope for was that the Osages he dealt with would use what influence they possessed to protect from "hindrance or molestation" the surveyors themselves and others who traveled the road in the near future. Some Osages would indeed be friendly toward whites, but the notion of wayfarers on the trail receiving "aid and assistance" from members of the tribe as a permanent treaty right was a mere pipe dream. The enormous obstacles facing the once-mighty Osages—who had little hope of subsisting as farmers on the reservation assigned to them and would have to compete for hunting grounds with powerful plains tribes like the Comanches and Kiowas—meant that few Osages would be willing or able to serve as Good Samaritans on the road. Instead, some would try to make up for lost ground by raiding travelers on the trail or seeking tribute from them.

Whatever the practical limitations of the treaty, Sibley appeared pleased with it, as did the Osages in attendance, with a few exceptions, as he noted in his journal on August 11:

> Three or four individuals of but inferior note seemed a little dissatisfied because they had not Shared as largely as they expected in the distribution of the Goods; for this they blamed their chiefs however, under whose direction the Goods were divided.
>
> The Chiefs & principal Men all went away perfectly satisfied, as well they might, for The Commissioners allowed them very liberally, as I think, for the Right of Way through the country claimed by them, as *their* right, is at best a doubtful one, if the Treaty lately Signed by them at St. Louis, with General Clark, is ratified and confirmed by Congress.[21]

Five days later, Sibley and his fellow commissioners reached an identical accord with chiefs of the Kansas. Like the Osages, the Kansas had ceded much of their territory to the United States at St. Louis in June in exchange for a reservation (in their case, one located north of the Santa Fe Trail). An Indian agent later conceded that the St. Louis treaty was a "bad bargain"[22] for the tribe, but even worse deals would follow for the Kansas. In 1846, having been substantially reduced in population by disease and other travails, they yielded to pressure from federal authorities and agreed to sell for a pittance the land set aside for them in 1825 and move to another, much smaller reservation—one encompassing Council Grove. That unfortunate move would bring the beleaguered Kansas into conflict with whites who were just beginning to transform the place from a campground into a town. Missionaries would attempt with little success to convert the Kansas into sedentary farmers, traders would ply them with liquor in violation of federal law, and settlers and travelers would clash with them periodically and agitate for their removal. After the Civil War, the Kansas would be ousted from the vicinity of Council Grove—their last refuge in the state that bears their name—and relegated to the Indian Territory (present-day Oklahoma), there to join Osages, Shawnees, Delawares, and others whose title to land coveted by encroaching whites had been summarily extinguished.

Such bleak historical realities belied the soothing images evoked by the name Council Grove. According to legend, this had been a place of peace and reconciliation for Indians long before Sibley sat down with the Osages. Benjamin Taylor, in his edited account of a journey to Santa Fe that perpetuated more than a few myths about the trail and its sites, offered this fanciful tribute to Council Grove as an aboriginal Eden, untouched by conflicts that tainted the surrounding territory:

> The Indian tribes whose eyes . . . are quick to catch the beautiful in nature with whom they are constantly communing, selected this spot and consecrated it, as the name indicates, to national councils, the wampum belt, the festive sports and "green corn dances." There is a beauty, almost a sublimity in the thought, that while wars have raged around it, and the streams that circle it, have blushed with the blood of kindred, no cry of vengeance or shout of defiance, rising to Heaven, has ever quivered *those* forest tops.[23]

Such musings irritated the ever-skeptical Josiah Gregg, who tried his best to set the record straight:

> Frequent attempts have been made by travellers to invest the Council Grove with a romantic sort of interest, of which the following fabulous vagary, which I find in a letter that went the rounds of our journals, is an amusing sample: "Here the Pawnee, Arapaho, Comanche, Loup and Eutaw Indians, all of whom were at war with each other, meet and smoke the pipe once a year." Now it is more than probable that not a soul of most of the tribes mentioned above ever saw the Council Grove. Whatever may be the interest attached to this place, however, on account of its historical or fanciful associations, one thing is very certain,—that the novice, even here, is sure to imagine himself in the midst of lurking savages.[24]

Veterans of the trail, Gregg added, knew that the real dangers for travelers lay to the west and made sport of such naive fears. Yet newcomers might be forgiven for their ambivalent responses to Council Grove, whose dense growth made travelers feel both sheltered from the hostile elements and exposed to the enemies they imagined lurking behind the bushes. Such was the reaction of Thomas Farnham when he arrived there in 1839 after spending the night with his party amid the remains of an encampment vacated some years before by Kansas Indians:

> In the morning we moved down the hill. Our way lay directly through the little grove already referred to; and however we might have admired its freshness and beauty, we were deterred from entering into the full enjoyment of

the scene by the necessity which we thought existed of keeping a sharp look out among its green recesses for the lurking savage. This grove is the northern limit of the wanderings of the Camanches, a tribe of Indians who make their home on the rich plains along the western borders of the Republic of Texas. Their ten thousand warriors, however, their incomparable horsemanship, their terrible charge that can scarcely be resisted by the troops of the Saxon race . . . did not arrest our march. And merrily did we cross the Savannah between the woodland, from which we emerged, and Council Grove—a beautiful lawn of the wilderness.[25]

Here as elsewhere, Farnham was prone to fancies of the sort that irritated Gregg, who knew well that Council Grove lay safely beyond the range of Comanches (and that Comanches, while certainly formidable warriors, were not always the implacable foes greenhorns like Farnham imagined them to be). Yet Farnham and his party were not the only ones to be afflicted by fears of the "lurking savage" in this otherwise idyllic setting.[26] Those imagined enemies were like serpents in the garden, inspiring a dread that was all the greater for the lushness of the surroundings. Long before the Kansas were allotted a reservation in the area, wary travelers often encountered members of that tribe around Council Grove and feared the worst—only to discover that these Indians were more interested in swapping goods or favors than trading blows. They sought tobacco, coffee, gunpowder, flint, or something strong to drink, if not in trade then as presents (which they no doubt felt entitled to for leaving these intrusive strangers in peace). Farnham, while departing Council Grove, had a bloodless exchange of this sort with a Kansas "brave" who seemed the very model of a warrior:

> His head was shaven entirely bare, with the exception of a tuft of hair about two inches in width, extending from the centre of the occiput over the middle of the head to the forehead. It was short and coarse, and stood erect, like the comb of a cock. His figure was the perfection of physical beauty. He was five feet nine inches or ten inches in height, and looked the Indian in every thing. He stood by the roadside, apparently perfectly at ease; and seemed to regard all surrounding objects with as much interest as he did us. This, every body knows, is the distinguishing characteristic of the Indian. If a bolt of thunder could be embodied and put in living form before their eyes, it would not startle them from their gravity. So stood our savage friend, to all appearances unaware of our approach. Not a muscle of his body or face moved, until we rode up and proffered him a friendly hand. He seized it eagerly, and continued to shake it very warmly, uttering, meanwhile, with great emphasis and rapidity, the words "How de," "how," "how," "how." As soon as one individual had

withdrawn his hand from his grasp, he passed to another, repeating the same process and the same words. From the careful watch we had kept upon his movements since he took his station, we had noticed that a very delicate operation had been performed upon the lock of his gun. Something had been warily removed therefrom, and slipped into the leathern pouch worn at his side. We expected, therefore, that the never-failing appeal to our charities would be made for something; and in this we were not disappointed. As soon as the greetings were over, he showed us with the most solicitous gestures, that his piece had no flint. We furnished him with one; and he then signified to us that he would like something to put in the pan: and having given him something of all, he departed at the rapid swinging gait so peculiar to his race.[27]

Whites called this begging or extortion and resented it, but the man who exacted these offerings from Farnham and company did so without any apparent animosity or embarrassment. In effect, he took his toll and let the travelers proceed (much as the chiefs who accepted gifts from Sibley had done). He handled the transaction neatly, as did Farnham, who found that reckoning with Indians here was a more complex, and less violent, exchange than the one he had imagined with trepidation as he entered Council Grove. This was neither a place of lurking savagery nor a peaceable kingdom, where lions lay down with lambs beneath the council oak. It was simply a spot blessed by nature whose attractions made it the site of frequent encounters between whites and Indians—exchanges that were not always easy or amicable but which remained roughly equitable until the pressures of settlement tipped the scale.

To traders arriving here on their way west, the only council that really mattered was the one they held with their fellow travelers to form a company, elect officers, and draw up rules of the road. Not all parties participated in this process. Some had already organized themselves into a caravan that they deemed large enough for defensive purposes by the time they reached Council Grove and simply paused here to "recruit," or refresh, their animals and to repair their wagons, if necessary. Such was the case with the train of twenty-two large wagons and several smaller vehicles that Speyer organized in 1846 and which spent just one night in Council Grove in late May, leaving Wislizenus little time to study this charming watershed, which he recognized as a "dividing point in the character of the country," a transitional zone between prairie and plains, "where the horizon extends further, the soil becomes dryer and more sandy, the vegetation scantier, timber and water more rare."[28] For other parties, however, the stopover in Council Grove was longer and more significant. At least once a year, and sometimes more often than that, various independent traders here formed into a caravan ranging in size from a few dozen wagons to as many as one hundred or more. In true frontier fashion, Gregg observed, those who coalesced into such companies chose their leaders democratically, while reserving the right to ignore their commands:

> The designation of 'Council Grove,' after all, is perhaps the most appropriate that could be given to this place; for *we* there held a 'grand council,' at which the respective claims of the different 'aspirants to office' were considered, leaders selected, and a system of government agreed upon,—as is the standing custom of these promiscuous caravans. One would have supposed that electioneering and 'party spirit' would hardly have penetrated so far into the wilderness: but so it was. Even in our little community we had our 'office-seekers' and their 'political adherents,' as earnest and as devoted as any of the modern school of politicians in the midst of civilization. After a great deal of bickering and wordy warfare, however, all the 'candidates' found it expedient to decline, and a gentleman by the name of Stanley, without seeking, or even desiring the 'office,' was unanimously proclaimed 'Captain of the Caravan.' The powers of this officer were undefined by any 'constitutional provision,' and consequently vague and uncertain: orders being only viewed as mere requests, they are often obeyed or neglected at the caprice of the subordinates. It is necessary to observe, however, that the captain is expected to direct the order of travel during the day, and to designate the camping-ground at night; with many other functions of a general character, in the exercise of which the company find it convenient to acquiesce.[29]

This company, captained by Elisha Stanley, consisted of some two hundred men and a few Mexican women, returning to their homeland after being exiled in 1829 because they were of Spanish birth.[30] The members of the company and their vehicles—one hundred or so wagons and more than a dozen carriages—were then organized into four divisions, each under the guidance of a lieutenant who oversaw the progress of his column and made sure that none of the men shirked such essential tasks as guard duty. (Out on the trail, the four columns of a company often formed a square at night, with the livestock in the middle, and they sometimes adopted a similar formation for defensive purposes when under attack.) Once organized, Gregg and his companions made provision for future mishaps by stocking up on hardwood, available in such abundance here that years of harvesting failed to exhaust the supply:

> During our delay at the Council Grove, the laborers were employed in procuring timber for axle-trees and other wagon repairs, of which a supply is

always laid in before leaving this region of substantial growths; for henceforth there is no wood on the route for these purposes; not even in the mountains of Santa Fé do we meet with any serviceable timber. The supply procured here is generally lashed under the wagons, in which way a log is not unfrequently carried to Santa Fé, and even sometimes back again.[31]

This rendezvous routine remained much the same over the years. When Matt Field arrived here in 1839, he and others in his party who had no wagons to worry about had an easier time of it than those with vehicles to care for:

In Council Grove (a most beautiful and fairy like place, an *oasis* in reality) we had rested two days, fishing, fowling, and hunting, while the traders were securing strong sticks of timber to repair their wagons in case of accident. Here also council was held, a commander appointed, the plan and all necessary arrangements of the travel adopted, balls were cast, rifles and pistols cleaned, and every preparation made for the long journey that lay before us.[32]

Field found this layover refreshing, as did William Fairholme when he stopped here in September 1840 with other British officers on their hunting expedition. Fairholme described Council Grove in his journal as "a lovely wooded valley, surrounded with an amphitheatre of low hills," and he made a fine sketch of the site that offered posterity a rare glimpse of this lush spot in the days before settlement.[33] Fairholme and a companion were still recuperating from the illnesses they had contracted on their way across Missouri, and they rested up in Council Grove while others in their party stalked game in the dense woods along the Neosho River. "There were plenty of turkeys brought in today and rumours of deer having been seen were flying about the camp," he noted appreciatively, "so arrangements were made for a grand chasse for tomorrow."[34]

Other travelers who stopped here over the years had to wait longer than they cared to for the various elements of their companies to arrive and coalesce. At times, Council Grove became overcrowded and lost some of its charm. Such was the case in 1843, when Philip St. George Cooke, now a captain in the army, passed this way with troops to protect from marauders the increasing numbers of Mexicans involved in the trade both as merchants and as employees. The acerbic Cooke deemed the grove itself delightful but found more company here than he cared for:

What a collection of wagons! there are hundreds, and nearly all have Mexican owners; look at their men! they show ivories as white as negroes; they are Indians, but New Mexicans as well, and speak Spanish. There are herds of mules in every valley, on every hill, and hundreds of oxen too. It is unhealthy

here; many who have stayed a week are sick; the dragoon company has been waiting three days, and they are already suffering.[35]

A year later, in August 1844, James Webb spent a week at Council Grove, waiting for others of his prospective company to arrive and passing the time by domesticating with a few of his fellow traders in "bark lodges left by the Kaw Indians on their return from their spring buffalo hunt."[36] (The Kansas and other Indians of the region refurbished and reoccupied such lodges on occasion and may have regarded the use of these shelters by white travelers as one of the impositions for which they had a right to exact tolls or tribute.) Webb's wait came to an end when Sam Owens—referred to here loosely as Colonel—reached Council Grove with other traders and was duly chosen by Webb and the others to lead a company of twenty-three wagons and forty men:

> The next day we held an election, by ballot, for captain. Colonel Owens was elected, and he appointed four sergeants of the guard, who drew lots for choice of men; and the guard organized, leaving a cook for each mess free from guard duty. This being the last place where we could procure hard wood for repairs of wagons, one day was spent in cutting and slinging timber under the wagons and preparing for an early start the next morning. As soon as possible after daylight we "catched up" and drove out, every person in camp in good health and spirits, and we greenhorns hoping we should see the Indians.[37]

The Indians that such greenhorns most hoped to see (with an anxiousness that perhaps contained a larger element of fear than they cared to admit) were not the Kansas, the Osages, the Shawnees, or other inhabitants of the prairie. These adventurers were "out to see the Elephant," and that meant confronting something beyond their ken, beyond the sheltering woodlands and the tall-grass prairie that was already yielding to the plow. That meant reckoning with the hard-fighting Indians of the boundless buffalo country and confronting the buffalo itself, the creature that brought those Indians strength and prosperity. As Matt Field wrote of his bright days of expectancy at Council Grove:

> We fished, bathed, read, sang, talked of home, of the strange country we were about to visit, of the wild travel we had yet to encounter, and with burning curiosity we discoursed about the buffalo, the lordly brute now sole master of the vast wilderness we were to cross. Through unnumbered myriads of a creature of which we had never seen one, even exhibited as a curiosity, we were to pass, and strange as wanderers in the moon were we to feel while treading the yet unexplored territory inherited by the buffalo.[38]

That keen sense of anticipation would endure even as Council Grove evolved from a campground into a settlement. Lewis Garrard, who arrived here on the last day of September 1846, after American troops bound for New Mexico had passed through, witnessed the first sign of civilization in Council Grove: "On the west skirt of the belt of timber, under the wide-spreading protection of a huge oak, was a diminutive blacksmith's shop, sustained by government, for the purpose of repairing wagons *en route* to the army at Santa Fé."[39] Yet for all the changes wrought by soldiers and settlers here in Council Grove and in distant New Mexico in years to come, it would be decades before Americans altered the essential character of the intervening plains. As late as 1865, when a young recruit named Frank Doster went west with the Eleventh Indiana Cavalry, Council Grove remained for him and for others "the jumping-off place of civilization, into the great mysterious land of legend and adventure. Beyond was distance and sunset only."[40]

It was not only white Americans who harbored such feelings as they approached buffalo country. The same frontier was crossed expectantly by Mexicans, and by Indians from woodland or prairie tribes such as the Delawares that furnished hunters to westbound wagon trains, and in later years by those venturesome black recruits known as buffalo soldiers. Men and women of all descriptions who ventured onto the open plains sensed that they were entering a land of power and peril that demanded more than a little from them in the way of courage and persistence. Many found that challenge invigorating and regarded their advance onto the plains—which for travelers on the Santa Fe Trail came as they headed west from Council Grove—as one of life's defining passages. As Josiah Gregg observed in a stirring passage that defined that moment for posterity, not until he and his companions left Council Grove were they truly "under way." The cry sounded by the captain and his lieutenants on that occasion—"Catch up! Catch up!"—was more than just a summons for the drivers to put their animals in harness. It was a call for the entire company to take heart, form ranks, and advance, a call that thrilled trail-hardened veterans no less than it did fresh recruits like Gregg:

> The woods and dales resound with the gleeful yells of the light-hearted wagoners, who, weary of inaction, and filled with joy at the prospect of getting under way, become clamorous in the extreme. Scarcely does the jockey on the race-course ply his whip more promptly at that magic word 'Go,' than do these emulous wagoners fly to harnessing their mules at the spirit-stirring sound of 'Catch up.' Each teamster vies with his fellows who shall be soonest ready; and it is a matter of boastful pride to be the first to cry out—"All's set!" . . .

"All's set!" is finally heard from some teamster—"All's set," is directly responded from every quarter. "Stretch out!" immediately vociferates the captain. Then the 'heps!' of drivers—the cracking of whips—the trampling of feet—the occasional creak of wheels—the rumbling of wagons—form a new scene of exquisite confusion, which I shall not attempt further to describe. "Fall in!" is heard from head-quarters, and the wagons are forthwith strung out upon the long inclined plain, which stretches to the heights beyond Council Grove.[41]

Into Buffalo Country

Beyond Council Grove, travelers found themselves in increasingly arid country and made the most of the occasional springs and creeks they met with along the trail, often camping by those precious water sources. They sometimes likened those spots to oases in the desert—although the worst of the desert in fact lay farther on, south of the Arkansas. The first and finest of these watering holes was Diamond Spring, which lay roughly fifteen miles from Council Grove, or a long day's journey for wagon trains, which could travel no faster than their heavily burdened draft animals. George Sibley credited Benjamin Jones, one of those employed by the surveying party in 1825, with discovering this spring and described it as "uncommonly large and beautiful, and the Water very pure & cold."[1] Philip Cooke sang the praises of the place in 1843, calling it "a true 'Diamond of the Desert,' a Pearl of the Prairie—were pearls but as transparent as its cold and crystal waters!"[2] And James Webb stopped here with Sam Owens and company on their way west in 1844 to partake of mint juleps and offer "a vote of thanks to the public benefactors who some years before had transported and set out some mint roots at the spring which by this time had increased to a bountiful supply for all trains passing."[3]

The watering spots and campsites reached farther along the trail in the days ahead—among them Cottonwood Creek, the Little Arkansas, and Cow Creek—were less idyllic, for each stream had to be forded at considerable effort, including leveling banks that were too steep, cutting and laying down carpets of grass and brush to prevent the wheels from sinking irretrievably into the mire, and doubling or tripling up the teams to ease the heavy wagons down one side and haul them back up the other (in the worst cases, wagons had to be emptied of their goods and reloaded on the far bank). All this toil often had to be performed at the end of the day, when men were weary and hungry, for as Gregg explained, companies reaching a stream in the evening tried to cross it before they camped, knowing that rain in the night might render it impassable and that teams in "cold collars" (just starting out in the morning) seldom pulled as well as they did in the heat of prolonged exertion.[4] As greenhorns on the trail discovered, this portion of the Great American Desert, as Major Stephen Long termed the plains, was wetter in places than they might wish, particularly in late spring, when evening thunderstorms were common. Alphonso Wetmore, captain of a caravan bound for Santa Fe in June of 1828, told in his diary of downpours and swollen streams that slowed his wagon train to a crawl west of Council Grove and left the men in a rebellious mood:

> 13th. Made a bridge to the water edge and crossed the wagons in season to encamp before the storm; rain in the evening, and at midnight a thunder gust.
>
> 14th. Rain continues, which detains us until the middle of the day. Made only six miles, and encamped in time to reef wagon cover before a Noah-like tempest descended.
>
> 15th. Under way at 8 o'clock; made eight grievous miles, and encamped early at [Otter Creek] Diamond spring; a mutinous disposition repressed by bandit logic.
>
> 16th. With infinite labor, through mud, we reach 8 miles, and slept in the prairie at a spring; no fuel.
>
> 17th. In four hours march made only 8 miles; found weeds and brush sufficient to boil coffee.[5]

Before the day was out, Wetmore added, men who had been awash in water a few days earlier were suffering "extreme thirst." Such were the trials that greeted travelers as they edged out onto the plains. It was here that they began to appreciate just how taxing this journey could be—and to wonder if their resources were equal to the demands. What took the heaviest toll on body and spirit at this point was not thirst (which was usually slaked by evening when travelers reached the next stream or spring that served as their campsite) but fatigue and hunger, for the buffalo that companies largely relied on for sustenance were seldom encountered in great numbers before wagon trains reached the vicinity of the Arkansas. Thomas Farnham was not burdened with wagons—he and his party traveled on horseback with pack mules in tow—but the rains pelted them mercilessly, and within a few days of leaving Council Grove the provisions that they had hoped would last them as far as Bent's Fort were nearly exhausted. After crossing the rain-swollen Little Arkansas in mid-June, Farnham and company were themselves near exhaustion:

> The 14th, 15th and 16th were days of more than ordinary hardships. With barely food enough to support life—drenched daily by thunder-storms—and by swimming and fording the numerous drains of this alluvial region, and wearied by the continual packing and unpacking of our animals; and enfeebled by the dampness of my couch at night, I was so much reduced when I dismounted from my horse on the evening of the 16th, that I was unable to loosen the girth of my saddle or spread my blanket for repose.[6]

Amid such exertions, travelers watched warily for Indians and eagerly for game. Before entering prime buffalo country, they sometimes spotted elk or antelope, but the former were too wary and the latter too few and fleet to provide companies with more than an occasional treat. Beyond Diamond Spring, Sibley reported that his surveying party chased some elk and saw "plenty of Game, but got only one Goat," or antelope, "which was rejected as not fit to eat."[7] Farnham recalled his party's first tantalizing glimpse of an elk herd "tugging lustily through the mud," a short distance west of Council Grove, upon which "the advance guard shouted 'Elk! Elk' . . . and 'steaks broiled' and 'ribs boiled.'"[8] But the hunters never got close to their alert quarry and shot at them in vain. Later, in an episode Farnham exploited to humorous effect, two famished men from his party went chasing after the ill-fated antelope that made the mistake of "exhibiting his fine sirloins to their view"[9] and brought the animal down at three hundred yards—a deliverance Farnham made much of in his account. One surprising source of sustenance for this Peoria party and for others who expected to subsist solely on game here were the catfish that lurked in the rivers and streams. Obadiah Oakley of Farnham's party told in his journal of catching a dozen catfish in the Little Arkansas: "'fat yellow fellows,' which proved to be of excellent flavor."[10]

Matt Field and his companions evidently carried more in the way of provisions with them from Missouri. Otherwise, they might not have been so forbearing when they spotted a "noble deer" with two fawns in the shade of the trees lining Cottonwood Creek:

> Our rifles were loaded in our hands, and with leisurely aim we might have planted a ball in the creature's heart as it stood with its nose in the water, while another might have pierced both fawn as they rolled together on the grass. But we were young travellers, and as yet the love of Nature had not given place

to the hunter's fiercer passion. The idea never occurred to us of what a treasure of game was there almost inviting our powder and shot. We never thought of firing, but paused in utter forgetfulness of aught save the rare beauty of the scene before us.[11]

Field the nature lover would not long remain innocent of the hunter's "fiercer passion." Several days later, as he and his companions gathered fruit at a mound he called "Plum Point" (perhaps one of the Plum Buttes, situated near the Great Bend of the Arkansas), they at last spotted their first buffalo and rode off in hasty pursuit:

> Our horses were saddled and we were mounted in a space of time that surprised ourselves; but the poor animals were tired, and after descending from the hill, we soon lost sight of the buffalo. After an hours wandering, we again discovered him; we approached as near as we could without his perceiving us, and there, dismounting, left one to guard the horses, while the other three started on foot for the slaughter. One of the three was a former traveller who understood the sport, and this method of killing buffalo he called "crawling." We approached slowly, bending our bodies and taking off our hats while on the high ground, to conceal ourselves from the beast, but when in a hollow where he could not see us, we ran with our best speed to shorten the distance between us as quickly as possible, for the day was growing late and a dark storm was thundering in the distance.[12]

Like many others on the trail who dashed after buffalo, whether on horseback or on foot, Field and his two companions got carried away, traversing "roll after roll of the prairie" in pursuit of that one elusive animal. In such cases the reward might seem small compared to the effort expended and the risks incurred, but even prudent traders, given to weighing likely profits against potential losses, were known to abandon such calculations in the passion of the chase. Field and friends paid little heed to those gathering storm clouds or to the possibility of encountering hostile Indians and went scrambling after their quarry:

> Abandoning our hats we approached on our hands and knees, till our distance from the buffalo could not have been more than 120 yards. We were now prostrate upon the grass, with our heads raised to scan the curious monster. Our rifles were cocked, and our aim taken, but still we paused, for our aim was not good; we could distinguish only a dark mass, and it is necessary to hit the buffalo in a certain spot. Suddenly the animal rose—he had heard our whispering, and now looked directly at us. Click! bang! Three balls pierced his liver, and the huge brute fled; at 20 yards he turned to look at us,

and then disappeared over another roll in the prairie. We followed at leisure, for we had seen the blood streaming from his mouth—a sure sign that the work was done. . . .

In a few moments we stood beside the bleeding carcase of the beast we had slaughtered. Its dark, fiendish eye was rolling in agony, and it struck at the ground with it's short horns, exhibiting in it's dying moments the instinctive principle of revenge. But one of us had ever seen a buffalo before. He was instantly at work with his large knife, stripping the animal of it's skin in order to get at its flesh.[13]

Field was not alone in characterizing buffalo as monstrous and fiendish. ("The head of no other creature that the writer ever saw," he asserted, "resembles so clearly the idea that we are apt to conceive of the devil.")[14] William Fairholme, who had recovered enough from his fever to go chasing after buffalo when he reached their grazing grounds near the Arkansas in late September 1840, described them in similar terms, noting that their "savage looking bloodshot eyes" and "polished black horns" gave them "a most demoniacal appearance."[15] And James Webb, on one of his first buffalo hunts, retreated without firing a shot after finding himself flanked by two bands that stood "so near I could see their glaring eyes, sharp horns, and vicious appearance. I dropped in the grass and crawled away as carefully as I had formerly approached them."[16]

These beasts could seem menacing even in their death throes. They did not succumb easily, and their stubborn defiance often inspired more fear than pity. As Lewis Garrard wrote of one wounded buffalo that he chased down and killed: "With long, shaggy, dirt-matted, and tangled locks falling over his glaring, diabolical eyes, blood streaming from nose and mouth, he made the most ferocious looking object it is possible to conceive."[17] Indians honored that unyielding spirit in the creature—and sometimes invoked it by wearing buffalo horns in battle—but few white buffalo hunters shared that sense of kinship with their prey. To them, the animal was part of a largely hostile environment that had to be overcome if they hoped to reach their goal. Obadiah Oakley recalled how he and another member of Farnham's party, Robert Shortess, confronted an immense herd of buffalo that blocked their way and emitted a "muttered thunder" so deafening that the two men could not "hear each other speak at the distance of a few yards." Whether to get the herd moving or simply to vent his spleen, Shortess crept up on one buffalo that was "quietly ruminating, and suddenly cut off his tail, when the affrighted creature bounded and bellowed as if under the influence of a galvanic battery."[18]

For Matt Field on his first hunt, the menace in the eye of that wounded buffalo he and his companions brought down was accentuated by the gloom of the surroundings. Lightning was flashing overhead, and he had lost his hat and his bearings in the chase. Only by following the sound of a distant gun, fired by another member of their party, did he and his companions manage to find their way back in the pouring rain that night to camp, where they roasted their fresh cuts of meat over smoldering buffalo dung.

Field's fledgling buffalo hunt was well considered compared to the wild scrambles that ensued when some hungry parties lit out after a herd. While venturing west to protect traders on the trail in 1829, young Lieutenant Cooke first sighted buffalo near Cow Creek and joined with other soldiers in the mad chase:

> Many pleaded for permission to pursue; our few horses, about a dozen, were in great demand, and several went on foot. We dashed over the hills, and beheld with a thrill of pleasure, the first stragglers of these much-talked-of animals; pell-mell we charged the huge monsters, and poured in a brisk fire, which sounded like an opening battle; our horses were wild with excitement and fright;—the balls flew at random—the flying animals, frantic with pain and rage, seemed endued with many lives. One was brought to bay with whole volleys of shots; his eyeballs glared; he bore his tufted tail aloft like a black flag; then shaking his vast head and shaggy mane in impotent defiance, he sank majestically to the earth, under twenty bleeding wounds.[19]

Hunting buffalo on horseback in this fashion was laden with risks. Men firing carbines or pistols with reckless abandon sometimes wounded their mates, their mounts, or themselves. And skittish horses often threw their riders. Even a mount with steady nerves might catch its foot in a prairie-dog hole—a common hazard given the fondness of those burrowing rodents for terrain browsed and trampled by buffalo. Nonetheless, hunters could greatly increase their chances of avoiding falls and hitting their targets if they entrusted themselves to a horse—or a mule—that had the composure to chase down angry buffalo without flinching. That a mule could indeed stand up to that challenge was confirmed by James Webb and his beloved Dolly, a "tricky and headstrong" animal he purchased at Bent's Fort on the assurance that she could run down a "fat bull." Later, he spotted a lone buffalo along the trail and put Dolly to the test:

> After riding cautiously, sufficiently near as I thought to commence the run, I called Dolly to the gallop and found she knew her business better than I did. She did not spend her strength at the first dash, but gradually increasing her speed until she came within a dozen or twenty rods, when she let out and was soon alongside and sufficiently near for me to shoot, yet carefully

"Travelling," with buffalo hunters in background, by William Fairholme, 1840. This item is reproduced by permission of The Huntington Library, San Marino, California, HM 40696.

and persistently refusing to approach near enough to be in danger of getting horned if he should turn upon her.[20]

A mount like Dolly that combined courage with a healthy dose of caution was a godsend for a greenhorn like Webb. As he admitted, Dolly was "looking out for the danger which I was too much excited to comprehend." She kept Webb at a safe distance, and his last shot hit home.

Such adventures reinforced the bonds between man and mount. If the buffalo represented much that was harsh and inimical in the enveloping plains, the faithful horse or mule evoked fond thoughts of the world the travelers left behind, where breeding and training prevailed over the raw forces of nature. These domesticated animals made men feel at home in the wild and were addressed by them with nearly as much affection as their absent wives, sweethearts, or sisters. "Dolly with all her naughtiness was an animal I loved," declared Webb.[21] And trader William Henry Glasgow was no less effusive in a letter he wrote to his sister in 1846 as he headed west from Independence: "My Mare Lucretia is as fat as a seal & quite saucy, she will follow me like a dog any where & when I sit down come up & poke out her head for me to *scratch it* just like your ugly polk stalk of a husband. My *Mule Mary Jane* is a beauty & can out pace any horse or animal in our camp. They both, send their respects to you."[22] Not all travelers on the trail were so devoted to their mounts. Poor riders had a way of choosing poor animals that drove them to exasperation. William Glasgow told of one man who grew so angry when his mule took fright during a buffalo hunt and ran bucking back to camp that "he tried to get a pistol out of his holster to shoot her in the head but she kept jumping so that he could not get it out."[23]

Such blind rage stood in stark contrast to the perfect communion between a skilled rider and an expert mount in the heat of a chase. Few who experienced that thrill described it with greater relish than Cooke in this account of an elk hunt he and his horse Brown engaged in as he was returning east along the Santa Fe Trail in 1843:

> Exquisite the excitement of race-horse speed, and the near approach to these grand animals, straining every muscle, in *powerful* motion, their cloven hoofs sharply rattling!—and for the first time! What novelty of sensation!—what astonished curiosity!—my horse snorts, and shares my joy! Thunder we on! Now, my noble Brown, take the spur. Wildly excited he dashes into the herd, and I am rushing in ecstasy in their very midst, their large eyes flashing fire, their antlers sweeping the air above my head. But Brown reminds me he brought me not there for fun alone; and so I fire my pistol into the nearest

buck, and take a pull on the willing horse. My elk—poor fellow—seconds my
intent, and soon we are motionless on a profoundly silent plain.

Now, my fierce excitement subsides. I observe curiously—almost timidly—
a magnificent animal, large as my horse, but of a loftier crest. Ah! what beauty
and what suffering! What majesty in all his bearing, he violently grits his teeth
in pain or defiance; but in his beautiful eyes I imagine that rage is yielding to
a mournful reproach.

And now I suffer a reaction. We are alone with Death, which my hand
has summoned to this peaceful solitude. The still erect but dying animal faces
me at six feet, and painfully heaves. I stare dreamily into those fascinating eyes:
his dignity of suffering seems to demand of me an explanation, or, a conclusion
to the fatal scene.

At length, with a sigh, I finish my work; and with another ball end his
pains forever![24]

Seldom did travelers on the trail accord the buffalo they preyed on as much
respect as Cooke paid to this majestic elk. As he pointed out, confronting the
dignity of that animal's suffering in no way detracted from the pleasure of
feasting on it. He ate "heartily of the elk-steak" and suffered no pangs of
remorse. In the words of his "Friend," a fictitious companion with whom he
conversed in his journal: "Kill your meat with a good conscience . . . solid
indeed is the hunter's comfort!"[25]

Plains Indians pursued their prey in much the same spirit, honoring the
animal—or the power behind the animal that bestowed its blessings on
humans—while savoring its flesh to the full and making exhaustive use of its
hide, bone, and sinew. Those who intruded on the Indian domain rarely con-
formed to that worthy example. To be sure, white buffalo hunters along the
trail emulated certain Indian practices, including the habit of savoring choice
parts of the slaughtered buffalo on the spot, as Lewis Garrard observed: "The
men ate the liver raw, with a slight dash of *gall* by way of zest, which served
a la Indian, was not very tempting to cloyed appetites; but to hungry men,
not at all squeamish, raw, warm liver, with raw marrow, was quite palatable.
Before the buffalo range was half traversed, I liked the novel dish pretty
well."[26] Many parties also adopted Indian methods for preserving buffalo
meat by drying strips over fire or in the sun or mixing it with fat and berries
to form that durable blend known as pemmican. Some travelers even carved
buffalo bone into needles or spoons or fashioned the hide into various articles, including slippers for their oxen, whose feet grew sore treading the short,
coarse grass. All too often, however, white buffalo hunters simply removed
the slaughtered animal's tongue, hump, or other tasty and easily excised morsels

"The Herd on the Move," by W. J. Hays, 1861. Courtesy Library of Congress: Prints and Photographs Division, LC9USZ62-738.

and left the bulk of the carcass to rot—a sight that must have been galling indeed to Indians who depended mightily on these bountiful creatures and seldom let much of their offerings go to waste.[27]

Even worse, from the Indian point of view, was the wanton slaughter of animals by wayfarers who had no pressing need for food. Buffalo often grazed in such abundance near the Arkansas River that travelers regarded them as pests (they could in fact cause harm if they charged into wagon trains or over-ran encampments) and took potshots at them. On one grim occasion in 1843, Cooke aimed howitzers at a large herd for target practice. That exchange, described here in his journal—less polished in its prose than the book he later wrote—had none of the glory of his elk hunt:

For *six miles* we marched through one "village" of the "prairie dogs," whose shrill barkings were incessantly sounding in our ears, but their strange anticks scarcely attracted attention, when 10,000 of buffalo dotting the visable world far and near were the whole day seen around us; each moment a shifting scene, of chases, by officer or trader, fixing the attention with a new interest. In the afternoon, from the brow of a small hill overlooking a ravine and the rise beyond, we saw hundreds of the huge terrible looking animals grazing and lying about in a state of undisturbed nature 300 yards from us: I instantly determined to give the artillerists more practical skill, and to obtain more experience of the range and effects of the howitzers. I directed one at a group: the shell overshot the mark, but in ricochêt, upset an animal; still they did not fly: another was discharged which passed in their midst, in three or four rebounds, and then exploded, creating a wonderful confusion; still another was directed at a dense group, full 500 paces off, and on higher ground; it struck rather beyond, exploding beautifully at the same instant; but none were prostrated (the cartridges are marked to range 300 yards.) I then marched, and in ten minutes the bull which had been struck down, raised up on his chest: the command was halted; and, riding a very wild horse, I dis-mounted and approached afoot with a carbine to 25 paces; when the piece snapped, and the bull rose and dashed at me; after passing the spot I had stood on, his attention was drawn off by the discharge of a horseman's pis-tol; and at another essay I struck him as he ran at speed, full in the side; when, again he rushed at me; again his course was changed; and threatening con-tinually to break through the column, and to frighten the wagon teams he was assailed by many horsemen whom I did not wish to restrain; pistols and carbine shots increased every moment, and the frightened horses rendered them dangerous; it seemed a confused action; a doubtful battle: after falling with a great shock, the beast arose and attacked a mounted corporal: tossed his horse like a plaything, goring him in two places: the corporal fell headlong on the bull's horns, his pistol discharged at the same instant, the ball passed through his horse's neck, which then ran off frantically: the man was borne, hanging by his clothes on the horns, for several leaps: a bull dog seized the monster by the lip, and all fell into a confused heap; we next through the dust saw the corporal scrambling desperately from the mêlee, having wonderfully escaped from injury; the deathless animal again rose, and shook his black and shaggy front, in defiance: then many deliberate carbine shots were fired at him: and he fell and rose repeatedly—while lying down carbine balls were fired with deliberate aim at 10 paces, seemingly without effect: when finally I sent one through the eye into his brain—the shell had broken the shoulder blade. The animal died, and has been eaten: the horse is doing well.[28]

Cooke did not reflect on the significance of this strange and doubtful battle. After all, he was writing an official account, not a treatise on the struggle between man and nature. And in any case, it would have taken a writer on the order of Herman Melville to do full justice to this harrowing episode, where the "deathless animal" seemed intent on avenging wrongs done to him and his kind by these men and their monstrous weapons. Crossing the plains, like crossing the sea, exposed travelers to much that they found "huge" or "terrible looking" (as Cooke described the buffalo) and which drove them to measures that were sometimes far out of proportion to any real threats they faced. They had reason to shoot at rattlesnakes, which represented a mortal danger, but they did the same to the wolves and coyotes that hunted and scavenged buffalo and other animals at no risk to humans. Many travelers hated those lurking canines and the howling they kept up at night. Most companies had rules that no one could fire a gun in or around camp unless his own life or the safety of the group depended on it. But wolves were targeted nonetheless, and the results were sometimes disastrous. Kit Carson, in an edited version of his dictated reminiscences, recalled the fate of one man attached to the caravan bound for New Mexico that Carson joined as a runaway apprentice in 1826:

> On the road, one of the party, Andrew Broadus, met with a serious accident. He was taking his rifle out of a wagon for the purpose of shooting a wolf and, in drawing it out, accidentally discharged it, receiving the contents in the right arm. We had no medical man with us, and he suffered greatly from the effects of the wound. His arm began to mortify and we were all aware that amputation was necessary. One of the party stated that he could do it. Broadus was prepared for any experiment that was considered of service to him. The doctor set to work and cut the flesh with a razor and sawed the bone with an

old saw. The arteries being cut, to stop the bleeding, he heated a kingbolt from one of the wagons and burned the affected parts, and then applied a plaster of tar taken off the wheel of the wagon. The patient became perfectly well before our arrival in New Mexico.[29]

By one account, Carson himself performed this operation, but it likely required more poise and know-how than even a precocious sixteen-year-old would have possessed. Such was the hatred inspired by wolves that even trail-hardened veterans remained bitterly contemptuous of them. Over the years, Uncle Dick Wootton spent so much time hunting buffalo for his own consumption and for the occupants of Bent's Fort, where he was employed, that he grew familiar with the animal and fond of it. He was among the first on the plains to try his hand at domesticating buffalo, taking advantage of the fact that calves separated from their mothers willingly attached themselves to caravans. But the more time Wootton spent among bison, the more he came to detest their enemy the wolf:

> When hunting buffalo, I have sat many a time all night by a blazing fire, throwing the red-hot brands every now and then at a pack of wolves, to keep them from stealing the game which I had slaughtered.
>
> One night I remember, when I was alone, there must have been hundreds of the vicious brutes in the pack that kept me company all night. They would come so close that I could see their eyes shining like balls of fire in the darkness, and all the time they kept up a snapping and snarling which would have set a man crazy who did not know what cowardly brutes they were.
>
> I didn't care to waste much ammunition on them, but I killed three or four during the night and the dead wolves were at once torn to pieces and devoured by the balance of the dirty gang of cannibals. They sneaked away just before daylight came in the morning, but they had given me a mighty lively all-night serenade.[30]

Plains Indians surely had similar problems keeping wolves away from the buffalo they killed, yet they honored the wolf for its craft and cunning. Pawnees and members of other tribes who served as scouts proudly called themselves wolves, wore wolf hides in disguise as they crept through the grass, and yelped like wolves to send signals to their fellow warriors. A traveler standing guard at his campsite at night could not always be sure if the howls he heard in the distance came from real wolves or from scouts posing as such. It was not surprising, then, that some whites used the same terms to disparage Indians as they did to condemn wolves. Wootton, for example, referred to Pawnees as "sneaking, murderous scoundrels"[31] and noted elsewhere that when Indians did not have white men to kill, they turned on each other, like the wolves around the campfire. He admired the way buffalo banded together to repulse wolves, using a defensive formation much like the one used by wagon trains to fend off Indians and protect their livestock:

> The buffalo were intelligent enough to know that in union there was strength, in a fight with wolves. When a band of them lay down at night, it was usually in a circle, inside of which were the calves.
>
> Then if they were attacked by wolves, standing side by side, with their heads down, they presented a solid fighting front, and could take care of themselves.[32]

Wootton and his traveling companions once used similar tactics to beat back an attack by Comanches at Pawnee Fork, who charged the camp several times in the hope of triggering a stampede by the mules corralled within the cordon of wagons and making off with the animals after they broke loose. Wootton gave the Comanches credit for persistence but was no sorrier to see them pay with their lives than he was to see wolves killed:

> We made it too hot for them though, and when they finally retreated, they left three good Indians, where they had fallen from their horses. You understand, when I say good Indians, that I mean dead ones. Some people may not agree with me on this point, but I think I know what I'm talking about. If I don't I ought to, because I've been among 'em long enough.[33]

Wootton seemed to feel that this murderous antagonism between whites and Indians was a natural state of affairs, as inevitable as the struggle between buffalo and wolves. But whites and Indians were not unduly hostile to each other when they first met on the plains. The hatred that Wootton voiced without apology—and which some Plains Indians came to harbor in return for whites—was a product of historical circumstances. Among those circumstances was the burgeoning traffic on the Santa Fe Trail, and in particular on that stretch of the trail that approached the Arkansas River at the Great Bend, carrying travelers into the heart of one of the richest and most hotly contested buffalo-hunting grounds in all of Indian country.

10

Conflict at the Crossing

Accrding to Josiah Gregg, early trading parties on the Santa Fe Trail "but seldom experienced any molestations from the Indians."[1] A few companies came under attack while crossing the plains in the first several years of the trade, but other groups either escaped the attention of Indians or, if spotted by them, were considered too insignificant or innocuous to bother with. William Becknell and his little company, on their inaugural journey to Santa Fe in 1821, watched in vain for Indians when they entered the heart of buffalo country that September:

> Late in the evening of Monday the 24th, we reached the Arkansas, having traveled during the day in sight of buffaloe, which are here innumerable. The Arkansas at this place is about three hundred yards wide, very shallow, interrupted by bars, and confined by banks of white sand—the water has every appearance of being as muddy as that of the Missouri; we, however, crossed one of its branches whose waters were limpid and beautiful, and which was one hundred yards wide a mile from its mouth. We gave this the name of Hope Creek. These streams afford no timber except a few scattered cottonwoods. It is a circumstance of surprise to us that we have seen no Indians, or fresh signs of them, although we have traversed their most frequented hunting grounds; but considering their furtive habits, and predatory disposition, the absence of their company during our journey, will not be a matter of regret.[2]

Such were the talents of Indian scouts that they could easily have observed Becknell's party without being seen in return, but if so, they must have judged these few white men and their pack mules to be neither a serious threat nor a worthwhile target.

What Becknell called the "predatory disposition" of the Plains Indians was in fact a calculated approach on the part of tribal warriors, who might better be described as hunter-warriors since hunting was their principal occupation. Far from attacking impulsively, these men and their chiefs carefully weighed rewards against risks in choosing their targets. The buffalo that congregated in great numbers here periodically to drink from the Arkansas and its tributaries, graze along the grassy riverbanks, and cross from one side to the other were their main target. Buffalo hunting brought Plains Indians tremendous benefits at relatively little risk, and they devoted far more energy to that pursuit than they did to warfare. Men did the hunting, and women processed the meat, tanned the hides, and worked the bone and sinew. Like many other observers, Josiah Gregg thought that men among the buffalo-hunting tribes had it easy compared to the women: "Besides war, *hunting* seems the only creditable employment in which a warrior can engage. Every other labor is put upon the squaws; and even when a party of hunters set out, they generally provide themselves with enough of these 'menials' to take charge of the meat: the Indian only deigns to shoot down the game; the squaws not only have it to cure and pack, but to skin and dress."[3]

The labors of Indian women on the plains may not have been much heavier than the many hard tasks performed by American farmwives of the day in and around the home, but Indian women worked in the open and often toiled hardest at the very time when their men were relaxing after the exertions of the hunt, fostering an impression among white observers that their status was menial. Whatever travelers thought of the treatment of "squaws," they welcomed the sight of women and children among a party of Indians, for it indicated that this was a hunting band rather than a war party. The same areas that lured hunting bands, however, also attracted dedicated war parties, made up almost exclusively of males (although some tribes allowed a few exceptional women to take to the warpath in one capacity or another). These warriors asserted their rights to contested territory by clashing with rival parties in open battle or swooping down on enemy bands in their encampments to steal horses, claim lives, seize captives, and take scalps, which figured prominently in stirring ceremonies that restored tribal morale and consoled those who had lost loved ones in past battles.

These war parties often fought for reasons that were emotional or spiritual, including a hunger for vengeance and a longing for the prestige that came with counting coup, which meant performing actions that were tallied as brave deeds and became part of a man's legend. But success in war also benefited the tribe materially by protecting or expanding its territory and by enriching it with captured horses and other spoils. Conversely, losses in battle cost the tribe dearly by depriving it of prized warriors who were also valued hunters. The bands that made up a tribe were small and could ill afford to lose more than a few men in their prime, on whom so much depended. Among the Kiowas, for example, a war party that lost a single man in battle, regardless of the outcome of the fight, returned home quietly and without celebration.[4] Gregg, who shared the opinion that plains warriors were lacking in courage, nonetheless observed astutely that they acted cautiously in battle because the tribe as a whole abhorred casualties and discouraged fighting men and their chiefs from taking undue risks:

> They rarely attack an enemy except with a decided advantage; for the prospect of losing even a single warrior will often deter them from undertaking the most flattering adventure. It is true that, in addition to their timidity, they are restrained by the fact that the loss of a man often casts a gloom upon the most brilliant victory, and throws a whole clan into mourning. On this account they generally attack by surprise, and in the night, when all are presumed to be asleep; having care, if against a formidable enemy, that it be long enough before the morning dawn to allow them to retire beyond reach of pursuit before daylight.[5]

What made these adventurous warriors so troublesome for travelers, in sum, was that they operated on much the same principles as the traders themselves, always seeking to minimize their losses and maximize their gains. In the process, they forced travelers to take elaborate precautionary measures that made the hard journey across the plains all the more taxing. To guard against the occasional night attack, companies camped along the trail had to post guards each evening from dusk until dawn—an unenviable duty that few able-bodied men could avoid. Matt Field described the lonely nighttime vigil of a guard outside camp:

> There he stands in the dark, leaning upon his rifle in utter silence, by the side of the farthest mule staked outside of the camp. What can the eye distinguish in the darkness? Knowing the wagons are there, you can discover their white tops, but otherwise you might fancy the faint light came from some clearing away of the clouds in that direction. In addition to this, you recognize a man's form and a few of the nearest horses and mules, all else is black. What is heard? The mules munching the grass; if it is near a water course, the ripple or rush of the wave; if buffalo are near, you hear their low bellowing, like a distant ocean surge, or like wind moaning through hollow caverns; perhaps an opposite

sentinel whistles or sings a merry air, but this might serve to guide an enemy and is not often indulged in; these sounds you *may* hear, but at times death itself is not more solemn or more still.[6]

Although the main purpose of standing vigil was to protect mules and horses against Indian raiders—who coveted those animals and cared little whether the men themselves lived or died—anxious guards sometimes fired at anything moving in the distance and harmed the very creatures they were out to protect. Young Dick Wootton suffered such an embarrassment on that first night he stood guard duty in buffalo country, taking aim at what he thought was an Indian and killing a mule that had gotten loose "and strayed outside the lines."[7] Men could laugh about such mishaps, but the strain of keeping watch through the night took a toll on them and did nothing to soften their feelings toward Indians. The need for vigilance increased over the years as the Santa Fe trade grew and the number of horses and mules attached to caravans increased, particularly on return journeys from New Mexico, where traders often acquired animals in payment for their goods.

A further provocation to attack was the route most companies followed to New Mexico—the so-called Cimarron Route, which took them south across the Arkansas at one of several crossings and down to the Cimarron River, whose course they followed in a southwesterly direction for a while before continuing on across the desert to the Mexican settlements. This path was shorter by roughly a hundred miles than the Mountain Route of the Santa Fe Trail via Bent's Fort and Raton Pass and was much more suitable for heavy wagons, which ascended Raton Pass only at great effort by man and animal. But the Cimarron Route was also more dangerous than the alternative, not only because it was devoid of water for much of the way but because it brushed the territory of the determined Comanches and their Kiowa allies, whose warriors were not at all shy about challenging whites who competed for hunting grounds they favored, camped at precious springs along the often-dry Cimarron River, or otherwise made themselves obnoxious to members of one of the strongest tribal alliances in North America, unsurpassed at mounted warfare. Even before companies crossed to the south side of the Arkansas, they ran some risk of encountering venturesome Comanches and Kiowas—or far-ranging Pawnees, who often rode down from their villages along the Platte and Republican Rivers to the vicinity of the Great Bend to hunt and to raid. As early as 1823, reported trader Augustus Storrs to Missouri senator Thomas Hart Benton, the caravan bound for Santa Fe was challenged twice by Indians, once on the way out by Comanche or Osage raiders who made off with most of the company's horses and mules, as described by Joel Walker, and

again on the way back by Pawnees: "The same company, thirty two in number, on their return, encountered a war party of eighty Pawnees. The war-whop
was sounded, and both parties ranged themselves for battle. But the enemy
agreed to a compromise, when they found that they could not rob without
losing the lives of their warriors, which they hardly ever risk, unless for revenge,
or in open warfare."[8]

This was a telling incident, for aside from the Comanches, no tribe
encountered on the Santa Fe Trail was more dreaded than the Pawnees. Landmarks like Pawnee Rock—an impressive outcropping just north of the
Arkansas on which many travelers incised their names—testified to the extent
to which the Pawnees and their warlike reputation loomed over this contested
stretch of the trail. And yet the Pawnees were no more eager than any other
tribal group to expend the lives of their men in dubious battle. Like the Osages
and Kansas, their homeland lay near the frontier of white settlement and they
suffered the consequences, succumbing to diseases communicated by whites
and coming under intense pressure from American authorities to yield ground.
Even before smallpox ravaged the Pawnee population in the early 1830s and
sapped their fighting strength, they were engaged in a complex interchange
with whites that mingled aggression with accommodation. Companies like
the one described by Storrs sometimes found these supposedly implacable
foes open to compromises that typically involved appeasing warriors and their
chiefs with gifts such as blankets, bundles of tobacco, and other items that
prudent travelers carried with them for such purposes.

That the Pawnees and other assertive tribes sometimes cut deals with travelers and even sat down with them now and then and smoked peace pipes did
not mean that they were forever renouncing hostilities. Most tribes on the
turbulent plains had enemies enough among rival Indians without adding
Americans to the list. But travelers who entered contested country, or territory that a tribe claimed as its own, without reaching some accommodation
with that tribe exposed themselves to the same treatment that the Pawnees,
Comanches, and other assertive groups meted out to their native rivals. And
animosities increased when blood was spilled and the principle of revenge
came into play. As Storrs observed, warriors out for revenge were prepared
to take greater risks and were harder to conciliate as a result. Similarly, whites
whose parties suffered mortal injuries at the hands of Indians were no less
intent on making up for their losses.

One such vendetta in 1828 had far-reaching consequences, leading to the
first confrontations along the Santa Fe Trail between tribal warriors and American troops. A company of traders heading home from New Mexico that fall,
Gregg related, lost two young men who ventured off on their own and fell

asleep, whereupon they were attacked by warriors of an unidentified tribe. (The two victims were named Daniel Monroe and Robert McNees, and the incident occurred in what is now northeastern New Mexico alongside a stream that became known as McNees Creek.) Both men died, and their traveling companions took vengeance on the next Indians they met, a party of six or seven men encountered along the Cimarron River. Some of the traders "proposed inviting them to a parley," Gregg noted, but others opened fire on the Indians, killing all but one, who "escaped to bear to his tribe the news of their dreadful catastrophe!"⁹ Predictably, the aggrieved tribesmen struck back at the offending company a few days later, making off with nearly a thousand mules and horses. Not long afterward, in what was probably a related incident, Indians described as Comanches clashed with a second party of traders returning to Missouri and killed their captain, John Means. The survivors of this attack abandoned their wagons in the night and fled on foot in the direction of the Arkansas, where they lightened their burden by burying on Chouteau's Island much of the silver they had acquired through trade in New Mexico.

Such violent give-and-take mimicked commercial dealings in that each side was concerned with settling scores and balancing accounts, but unlike peaceful trades, these hostile exchanges seldom if ever satisfied both sides. One party or the other invariably felt wronged and called for reprisals. In this case, outraged traders sought to strengthen their hand against the hostile Indians—whose tribal identity throughout this crisis remained uncertain—by appealing for federal troops to protect them.

It was this mission that brought Lieutenant Cooke west in the summer of 1829 with a detachment of soldiers from Fort Leavenworth commanded by Major Bennet Riley. Cooke was not much impressed with the traders that he and his men were assigned to escort. To be sure, they had a capable captain in the person of twenty-nine-year-old Charles Bent, who would later establish the firm of Bent, St. Vrain & Co. and become the first civil governor of American-occupied New Mexico. Bent was making his maiden journey along the Santa Fe Trail, but he had already proven his mettle in harsh circumstances as a fur trader in the West. In Cooke's view, however, strong leadership was wasted on civilians who lacked the sense to subordinate their selfish whims to the good of the outfit:

> The traders were about seventy in number, and had about half that number of wagons, with mule and a few horse teams. They organized themselves into a company and elected Mr. B. of St. Louis, their "captain," an office that experience had pronounced indispensable, but was nevertheless little honored; for danger itself, uncredited, because unseen, could not overcome the

self-willed notions and vagrant propensities of the most of these border inhabitants—self-willed and presumptuous, because ignorant.[10]

Cooke was severe in his judgments and overstated the traders' shortcomings.
Joining Bent on this venture were men of some experience and savvy, including Dr. David Waldo, soon to emerge as a leader on the trail in his own right,
and Milton E. Bryan, who had come under attack in 1828 on his way back
from New Mexico and was returning now to retrieve the silver he and others
had buried along the Arkansas and to try his luck again as a merchant in Santa
Fe. Collectively, however, the traders indeed lacked the cohesion and resolve
that a professional officer might expect of a group calling itself a company,
and they proved to be no small burden for their escorts, who were laboring
under various handicaps and restrictions as it was. For one thing, the two hundred or so enlisted men in Riley's command made the journey on foot rather
than on horseback. The army as yet had no cavalry, and only the officers had
mounts—a serious handicap on a mission that would bring the troops up
against Indians adept at fighting from horseback. Furthermore, the command
carried with it only part of what it required in the way of provisions, loaded
in wagons hauled by oxen (whose durability on this their pioneering journey
led others to adopt them as draft animals on the trail). Thus the soldiers, like
the traders, relied largely on hunting for subsistence, and as Cooke observed,
buffalo hunting, for all its thrills, also exposed men and horses to injury and
diverted the command from its main task of guarding against Indians. Furthermore, the troops could not accompany the traders south of the Arkansas
without trespassing on territory that officially belonged to Mexico.

In truth, the real powers to be reckoned with below the Arkansas were
not Mexicans but Comanches and Kiowas, both of whom may have been
involved in the 1828 disturbances. The traders knew that the most dangerous stretch of their journey lay ahead and would have liked the troops to
accompany them across the Arkansas, but Riley lacked authority to oblige
them. As Cooke put it: "Our orders were to march no farther; and as a protection to the trade, it was like the establishment of a ferry to the mid-chan-
nel of a river."[11]

On July 10, 1829, Bent's company reluctantly left Riley's troops behind
on American soil and forded the Arkansas at Chouteau's Island, where trader
Bryan had recovered the buried silver and, by his own account, entrusted it
to Major Riley for safekeeping. Riley visited the traders at their camp on the
south bank the next morning before they continued on and cautioned them
in parting never to let down their guard. As he noted in his official report,
however, his warnings were of little avail:

I had given them my views and advice of the manner they should proceed, and they promised to adhere to it, but it was soon forgotten. I told them they must stick together, and not leave their wagons more than one hundred yards, without they sent out a party to hunt, but it had no effect: for at about half past six of the same evening, an express arrived from them, stating that Mr. Lamme, a merchant from Liberty, was killed, and they were only six miles off, and the Indians were all around them, and if I did not go to their assistance, that they expected to be all killed and scalped. I could not hesitate, but struck my tents immediately and commenced crossing.[12]

Cooke, in his own account, added that the victim, Samuel C. Lamme, and some other traders, "in spite of all remonstrance or command," had ridden out recklessly ahead of the rest and come under attack by "about fifty mounted Indians," who chased the survivors back to the main party of traders but "dared not attack them when they made a stand among the wagons."[13] Here again, Cooke may have been too quick to fault the traders. William Waldo, who formed part of the company along with his older brother David, recalled many years later that the men of Bent's company tried their best to maintain cohesion and guard against attack but were frustrated by the terrain, consisting of sand hills that gripped at the wagon wheels and provided attackers with ample cover:

> It was nearly impossible to keep the wagons closed up together, in consequence of the depth of the sand and the stalling of many teams, and our train was extended over a space of more than a mile. Capt Bent had thrown out sixteen men in van and rear, to guard against surprise; but notwithstanding his prudent precautions, our surprise was complete. The Indians had concealed themselves and their horses in deep ravines, and seemed to spring out of the ground like swarms of locusts.[14]

Waldo added that Charles Bent averted further casualties by riding out alone to defend a man being hotly pursued by the same band of Indians that killed Lamme. "I can see him now as plainly as I saw him then," Waldo recalled of Bent, "mounted on a large black horse, I think bare-headed, with his long black hair floating in the wind." Such bravery, combined with ceaseless vigilance, enhanced Bent's stature as a leader on the trail, one whose commercial acumen was matched by his combative instincts.

In all likelihood, Bent's company and its military escort had been under surveillance by Indian scouts for some time. Cooke was later informed by Mexican traders familiar with these Indians and their tactics "that our motions had been watched the whole route from Council Grove; whilst we, concluding from appearances, scarcely conceived that a human being could be within hundreds of miles of us."[15] This seemingly confirmed what some had feared from the start—that the presence of troops on the trail would only alarm watchful war parties and incite them to attack as soon as a favorable opportunity presented itself. (In May, the editor of the *Missouri Intelligencer* had warned that "the exhibition of an armed force may excite the Indians . . . and probably provoke them to an attack after the protection shall be withdrawn.")[16]

Once Riley's troops crossed the Arkansas to aid Bent's beleaguered company, they found themselves on that notorious stretch of the trail known as the Jornada, which on this occasion was truly a "Journey of the Dead." Amid the bleak sand hills, Cooke related, the soldiers linked up with the frightened traders and disposed of the unfortunate Lamme:

> Having buried the poor fellow's body, and killed an ox for breakfast, we left this sand-hollow, which would soon have been roasting hot, and advanced through the defile—of which we took care to occupy the commanding ground—and proceeded to escort the traders at least one day's march further.
>
> These "sand-hills" compose a strip of country found occasionally a few miles off, on the Mexican side of the river, and where its valley has no abrupt boundary; they are irregular hillocks of the loosest sand, seemingly formed by the sport of the wind. There is scarce a sign of vegetation, and they present an aspect as wild and desolate, and as little *American*, as possible.
>
> Emerging from the hills, we found ourselves on the verge of a vast plain, nearly level, where it seemed nature had ineffectually struggled to convert a sandy desert into a prairie. There was a scanty and dwarfish growth of wiry grass, brown and withered, amid the white sand. On we marched, under a fiery sun, facing a burning wind. Not a tree, not a shrub, nor the slightest indication of water, could be seen in a view apparently illimitable in every direction. Thus we struggled on until noon, when the panting oxen, with lolling tongues, seemed incapable of proceeding. A halt was made, and they were taken from the wagons, but stood motionless. The wind blew a gale, a true sirocco. We sought every cover to avoid it. A messmate—one of those unfortunates who prefer the dark side of a picture, and croak when a cheerful word of encouragement is needed—gave vent to his despondency, and sought to engender discontent and fearful apprehensions; he predicted we would lose our baggage train, if not our lives, in the desert. Indignant, and without a better answer, perhaps, I undertook to prophesy, and actually foretold the exact event, viz.: that, pushing on, within ten miles we would find water and grass in some hollow, and buffalo too. After marching about that distance, we came to the sandy bed of a dry creek, and found in it, not distant

from our course, a pool of water, and an acre or two of fine grass. On the surface of the water floated thick the dead bodies of small fish, which the heat of the sun had that day destroyed. After encamping we saw a few buffalo, attracted doubtless by the water; and several were killed. Beyond our hopes, all our necessaries were thus ministered to; it seemed a special providence.[17]

There was something about this harrowing country that made even men who seldom raised their voices in prayer think in biblical terms and give thanks for their deliverance. Major Riley was not about to tempt Providence, however, by proceeding further against instructions, and he prepared to march back to Chouteau's Island, where he and his men would await the return of Bent's company from New Mexico that fall.

When the traders learned that they would once more have to fend for themselves, a number of them wanted to stay behind with Riley's command. As David Waldo wrote to Riley in a letter cosigned by Bent: "Many of our Caravan are now determined on remaining with you, to venture no farther; the balance are urged ahead, more by a sense of honor than propriety and cannot risk having the finger of scorn pointed at them for retreating after having so nearly accomplished their expedition, and sooner would they crimson the sands of the Semirone with their blood than have their Courage suspected."[18] Waldo and Bent asked Riley to accompany the caravan at least as far as the Cimarron, if only to encourage the civilians who had lost heart to continue on. But Riley held firm, and in the end, as Cooke put it, the traders inclined to hold back were "talked and shamed out of it" and the caravan proceeded alone and intact.[19]

Returning to American territory in no way exempted Riley's men from attack. The Indians found their presence as provocative on one side of the Arkansas as the other. The recent attack should have demonstrated to all concerned that this was no time for men to go off in small groups, but on July 31 four of Riley's infantrymen, their terms of enlistment having expired, ignored their commander's warnings and headed back to Missouri on foot. Three of the four returned that same night, Riley reported, and told of the death of their comrade, George Gordon:

> They stated that they had not gone more than 8 or 10 miles, when they discovered about 30 Indians, riding across the river. They landed and soon galloped up to them, when one of the men made a sign of peace, which they returned, and the parties shook hands. Then the Indians made sign for them to go across the river, which they declined, and started on their journey. . . . George Gordon looked back and said they were all friends, and that he would go and shake hands with them again; the others told him not; but in the act

of shaking hands with them a second time, he was killed by another Indian with a gun. The other three immediately took off their packs and prepared to defend themselves. The Indians began to ride round and cut capers on their horses, the three men fired one a time at them, and retreated towards my camp.[20]

This was similar to the incident of 1828, in which Indians were attacked by vengeful whites, some of whom appeared peacefully inclined. This too may well have been an act of revenge, for these foot soldiers had little worth plundering and Indians did not routinely attack people they made friendly gestures to, any more than whites did. Whatever the motive for the attack, it did not bring an end to hostilities. Riley's men remained encamped in force along the Arkansas. Even Indians who bore no grudge toward Americans could savor the challenge of depriving such intruders of their animals—among them light-skinned oxen that, according to Cooke's Mexican informants, were mistaken by Indian spies for white buffalo, prodigies revered for their wondrous medicine, or spirit power. "It would seem that these Indians had never seen the ox before," Cooke noted. He and his men later found the carcasses of oxen that the Indians had seized, "with all the white spots carefully cut out from the rest of the hide" and presumably carried off as trophies.[21]

The death of Gordon provided the watchful Indians with a golden opportunity to raid Riley's encampment, for on August 1 and again two days later the major sent sizable detachments to search for Gordon's body, leaving Riley's main force and its livestock vulnerable to a concerted attack. On the afternoon of August 3, Cooke was serving as officer of the guard outside camp when all hell broke loose:

> About 2 o'clock, when all the cattle and our few horses were grazing about a mile off above, under a charge of five men, an alarm of great uproar and yelling was suddenly heard. I and my guard sprang into ranks, and looking to the left, saw the cattle rushing towards the camp, followed by between 400 and 500 mounted Indians, who, decked in paint and feathers, uttering horrid yells, brandishing spears, and firing guns, and riding at full speed, seemed about to make an intrepid charge. . . . As we were about to meet the foremost, they branched off, firing on us as they ran, which, in view of the main body, I scarcely noticed, but kept steadily on, until I found they were all playing the same game; and the whole opened out at a respectful distance, like buffalo, and fled, or charged far clear of my flanks, except a body of them which seemed stationary, more than a half mile in advance. . . . I looked back, and saw the camp surrounded, at a respectful distance, by the Indians, all in rapid motion, a part still in pursuit of a body of cattle, rushing along the sandbars and island.[22]

What Cooke described here was a classic charge by mounted warriors in which they branched out as they approached an opposing force and swept around either flank, harassing their foes without risking a frontal assault. Whites sometimes belittled such tactics, as Cooke seemed to when he compared the warriors to skittish buffalo and noted that they "seemed about to make an intrepid charge," implying that they never quite delivered on that threat. Cooke knew enough about his opponents, however, to recognize the attack for what it was—a calculated maneuver by well-trained warriors aimed at intimidating the soldiers and separating them from their animals at minimal cost. As he conceded: "These Indians, who thus, from education and on principle, avoided our bold opposition, had we wavered or fled, would have proved the fiercest and most formidable pursuing enemy perhaps in the world."[23] His estimate of up to five hundred Indians may have been high (forces of that magnitude were rare on the plains, and mounted warriors had a way of seeming more numerous than they were). In any case, a headlong charge would have exposed the attackers to dreadful casualties at the hands of soldiers whose assets included a small cannon. As it was, that 6-pounder found the range of the circling Indians, and they paid dearly for their initiative. "They carried off their dead, afterwards ascertained to be nine in number," Cooke wrote, "Our loss was one man mortally wounded, and fifty oxen and twelve horses killed or driven off."[24] He paid due tribute to their remarkable horsemanship:

> On my first advance I saw an Indian handsomely mounted on a gray horse, gaudily ornamented with feathers, conspicuous for his rapid action and loud commands. A corporal on the right of my detachment was so much struck with him, that, unobserved, he came to a halt, and took a deliberate shot, but, I believe, came much nearer hitting myself. The Indians who dashed by the rear—their left flank exposed to a sharp fire—extended themselves along the right sides of their horses, hanging by the left foot and arm; this last, with a bull's-hide shield attached, passed around the horse's neck, from beneath which they rapidly discharged their arrows—the shield covering arm, horse's neck, the head, and right arm below! Excited as they were, they seemed the best of horsemen; and rushed up and down places which few persons in cool blood would think of attempting.[25]

The feat of firing from beneath the horse's neck was one at which Comanches and their allies excelled (artist George Catlin, visiting among Comanches in 1834, saw warriors practicing that move along with other deft maneuvers). In all likelihood, this was another in a series of hot scrapes extending back to the autumn of 1828 involving Comanches and Kiowas, who may have combined forces here to swell their numbers and teach the American soldiers a lesson.

What did the opposing parties glean from these violent exchanges? For Major Riley, the moral was that soldiers patrolling the plains against hostile Indians had to be mounted like their foes to be truly effective. "Think what our feelings must have been to see them going off with our cattle and horses," he wrote after the battle, "when, if we had been mounted, we could have beaten them to pieces."[26] Cooke was of the same opinion. "It was a humiliating condition to be surrounded by these rascally Indians, who, by means of their horses, could tantalize us with the hopes of battle, and elude our efforts," he concluded after a subsequent skirmish near the camp. "Much did we regret that we were not mounted too."[27]

Riley's travails of 1829 did much to prompt the army to develop units of mounted infantry, or dragoons, to patrol the plains. Yet that logical response failed to address the underlying problem exposed by Riley's escort. The presence of troops on the trail, meant to allay trouble, could in fact incite opposition. As Cooke put it, the soldiers found themselves "in the midst of many thousands of Indians, whose concentration our long stay seemed to invite."[28] The army hoped that by fielding more troops and placing them on horseback, they would reach a point where Indians no longer found resistance rewarding. After all, the traders had not been attacked so long as they remained under Riley's protection, and future escorts by mounted infantry might be even more effective in suppressing hostilities. But if troops continued to escort traders only part of the way to their destination, they would simply be drawing attention to the caravan and exposing traders to heightened risks once the soldiers turned back. In any case, conducting every caravan to and from the Arkansas River was more of a commitment for the small U.S. Army than authorities in Washington were willing to make, and Mexican officials seemed even less inclined to place additional burdens on their overtaxed troops by providing regular escorts between the Arkansas River crossings and Santa Fe. Rules of economy governed military as well as commercial dealings on the trail, and it simply did not pay at this point for either nation to protect a trade of modest proportions by mounting long and costly expeditions year after year against determined tribal foes who were always seeking new ways to settle old scores. Lacking strong economic ties with the disaffected tribes that might channel those competitive energies in more fruitful directions, traders and any troops escorting them who hoped to overawe such defiant warriors risked becoming embroiled in a relentless give-and-take that drew payment in blood from both sides and profited neither.

The expense of mounting escorts on a regular basis might have been deemed worthwhile if anything like a state of war had existed between Americans and the Comanches and Kiowas at this juncture. William Waldo, looking back on these events a half century later, asserted without foundation that ever since the disturbances along the trail in 1828, "the Comanches have waged war against the whites."[29] In truth, Comanches and Kiowas in the late 1820s were far from conducting a wholesale campaign against Americans aimed at eradicating the Santa Fe trade, which at this early stage in its development may well have offered Indians along the route more in the way of opportunity than aggravation. Up until the Mexican War, when American troops and supply wagons filed down the trail in unprecedented numbers and provoked substantial opposition, Comanches and Kiowas clashed sporadically with travelers on the trail but remained receptive to trade and talks with Americans. The U.S. Army, for its part, was far more concerned at this point with appeasing restive Indians than with challenging them. The army did not abandon efforts to protect traders on the Santa Fe Trail after 1829, but escorts were provided only intermittently and were largely confined to American territory.[30]

Among those who came to doubt the value of such halfway escorts was an officer entrusted with that task in 1834, Captain Clifton Wharton. The caravan he and his dragoons were assigned to protect was captained by Josiah Gregg and included traders who showed little respect for Wharton's authority when it came to dealing with Indians. On one occasion, Wharton reported, "several irresponsible persons" in Gregg's company nearly opened fire on a band of Kansas whom Wharton regarded as friendly and was trying to engage in talks. Later, after encountering Comanches along the Arkansas who called out "*buenos amigos, buenos amigos,* good friends, good friends," Wharton made plans to meet with several of their representatives for "a friendly talk and a Smoke," only to have his plans thwarted by traders who regarded those Comanches as hostile. As Wharton reported:

> I was informed that many of the traders were in the act of conducting a piece of artillery to a point opposite that at which the Indians were Quietly standing in a large group with the avowed intention of firing on them. I hastened immediately to the Captain of the Caravan to remonstrate against the measure, not only as a violation of my pledge of a friendly disposition towards the Indians and one which would effectually prevent the meeting which I had proposed should take place between us, as an act of positive cruelty.[31]

Gregg restrained the traders from firing the weapon after they threatened one of Wharton's subordinates with "personal violence" for denouncing their provocative gesture. A short time later, however, Gregg undercut Wharton by meeting with Comanches while Wharton was otherwise occupied and issuing them a warning as the self-proclaimed commander of the American force. "We are disposed to be friends," he told the Comanches by Wharton's account, "but you must keep off, and if you do not, the Soldiers, meaning my command, will fire upon you."[32] Gregg was claiming powers here as captain of the caravan that rightfully belonged to Captain Wharton. Perhaps he recognized that he was out of bounds, for he soon resigned his position, informing Wharton by letter that he considered himself "unworthy" of leading the caravan.[33]

Wharton was plainly exasperated by the interference of civilians in his peace-keeping efforts, but he nonetheless escorted the traders across the Arkansas into Mexican territory and offered to accompany them as far as the Cimarron River, an offer politely rejected by Gregg's successor. Privately, Wharton may have wondered why the army should go to any further trouble to protect traders who called their own shots and paid little heed to military authority. But he confined himself in his report to the pointed observation that escorts proceeding no farther than the Arkansas River were worse than none at all, for they encouraged "a habit of negligence and lack of vigilance on the part of the traders" while inspiring "confidence in the Indians" once the troops withdrew.[34]

On the Mexican side, the forbidding costs of escorting traders hundreds of miles through hostile territory between Santa Fe and the Arkansas River had been painfully demonstrated five years earlier in 1829, when Mexican forces offered such protection to the caravan returning to Missouri that fall and paid a steep price in blood and toil. That escort came in response to a request from Major Riley, who gave the Americans he accompanied that summer a letter to New Mexico's governor asking that Mexican troops conduct the traders back to the Arkansas, where Riley would await their arrival and see them safely to their destination. Mexicans were becoming increasingly involved in the Santa Fe trade and shared the American interest in safeguarding travelers on the trail. Colonel José Antonio Vizcarra duly assembled an international force of some two hundred men—including American volunteers, a company of regular Mexican troops, and Pueblo recruits—and set out in September with the eastbound caravan, which contained a number of Mexican civilians as well as American traders. Despite this impressive show of force, trouble arose along the Cimarron when Vizcarra came up against a large force of Indians, most likely Kiowas and Comanches, whose relations with Mexicans and Pueblos had deteriorated in recent years.[35] (The mutual hostility of Pueblos and Mexicans toward Comanches, Kiowas, and other troublesome tribes was such that Pueblo warriors were prepared to risk their lives for respected Mexican officers like Vizcarra, just as they were for their own chiefs.) Cooke described the confrontation that ensued, as detailed to him by the traders after they rejoined their American escorts at the Arkansas in October. The Indians who came up against Vizcarra were on foot, Cooke wrote, and appeared to the traders to be on a horse-stealing foray:

They pretended friendship, as the best way, doubtless, of effecting their purposes. A guarded intercourse took place, and Col. V. was warned by some of his Indians, and the traders, not to trust them: at last, as Col. V. was talking to their chief, the latter, being a few feet off, presented his gun and fired. One of the Colonel's Indians, who had been most suspicious, and stood by watching, with heroic devotion, sprang between, just in time to receive the ball through his own heart. He had a brother near by, who, as the Indian chief turned to fly, sprang upon him like a tiger, and buried his knife to the hilt in his back. Almost at the same instant another chief fell, by a shot from a trader, who had marked him in anticipation of the result. The Indians fled, and many of the Mexican militia and the traders pursued them on horseback. The ammunition of the Indians soon gave out, and their pursuers would overtake them in succession, dismount, fire, take the scalp—without being particular whether the man was dead or not—reload, and pursue again; several of the traders were mentioned as having killed three or four in this manner—like turkey shooting—and perhaps nothing but nightfall saved the whole party from destruction. It was not ascertained that the Mexican regulars shed any blood on the occasion; but on the other hand, we were assured that the cruelty and barbarity of some of the Americans disgusted even the Mexicans and Spaniards; that they scalped one Indian at least, who had life enough left to contend against it, though without arms; and they undoubtedly took the skin from the bodies, and stretched it on their wagons. I, myself, saw several scalps dangling as ornaments to the bridle of a trader.[36]

Perhaps the Americans who committed these deeds thought they were treating the opposing Indians, who killed three men in this battle, to some of their own medicine. But the lesson learned may not have been the one intended. Scalp taking and other forms of mutilation were spiritual affronts to the victims that heightened the longing for revenge among their comrades and kin, making the trail all the more hazardous for future travelers, who might be innocent of any offense to tribesmen but who paid nonetheless.

Conceivably, resentments stirred up among Comanches by the events of 1829 contributed to the killing two years later of Jedediah Smith, among the greatest of the mountain men. Making his first venture in the Santa Fe trade, Smith and his companions lost their way below the Arkansas, not far from the site of the bloody exchanges of 1828 and 1829. Smith came to grief after riding off on his own in an attempt to find water for the party. His brother, Austin Smith, later wrote to their father telling of his fate, as related by some Mexican traders who dealt with the Comanches involved:

Your Son Jedediah was killed on the Semerone the 27th of May on his way to Santa Fé by the Curmanch Indians, his party was in distress for water, and he had gone alone in search of the above river which he found, when he was attacked by fifteen or twenty of them—they succeeded in alarming his animal not daring to fire on him so long as they kept face to face, so soon as his horse turned they fired, and wounded him in the shoulder he then fired his gun, and killed their head chief it is supposed they then *rushed* upon him, and despatched him.[37]

Josiah Gregg later recast this episode for his readers in a manner that heightened the pathos of Smith's last moments and reflected even less favorably on the Comanches responsible:

> He had already wandered many miles away from his comrades, when, on turning over an eminence, his eyes were joyfully greeted with the appearance of a small stream meandering through the valley that spread before him. It was the Cimarron. He hurried forward to slake the fire of his parched lips—but, imagine his disappointment, at finding in the channel only a bed of dry sand! With his hands, however, he soon scratched out a basin a foot or two deep, into which the water slowly oozed from the saturated sand. While with his head bent down, in the effort to quench his burning thirst in the fountain, he was pierced by the arrows of a gang of Comanches, who were lying in wait for him! Yet he struggled bravely to the last; and, as the Indians themselves have since related, killed two or three of their party before he was overpowered.[38]

Whites saw such murderous incidents as proof of the innate savagery of the Comanches and other "warlike" tribes and concluded that they would kill without compunction any defenseless strangers they happened upon. Alphonso Wetmore implied as much with biting sarcasm in his diary when he wrote of a grim landmark at the Upper Spring of the Cimarron, evidently commemorating the attack on Monroe and McNees that triggered all the trouble below the Arkansas: "a very abrupt rocky hill, on the summit of which is a cross standing over the bones of two white men, who were slain while asleep by the gallant, high-minded, persecuted, gentlemen Indians."[39] Yet such incidents did not prove that those who condemned Indians for their barbarity were any closer to the truth than those who idealized their character. Comanches had long welcomed those New Mexican traders known as Comancheros, who traveled with their wares from band to band and would have made easy targets for any war party. (Even after relations between the two sides deteriorated, vulnerable parties of Comancheros continued to ply their trade in tribal territory without meeting with undue hostility.)[40] Prohibitive assaults were reserved for members of rival factions who declined to treat or trade with Comanches or actively antagonized them. Gregg's account of Comanches treacherously "lying in wait" for Smith at the water hole was well calculated to arouse the sympathy and indignation of readers. But however innocent Smith's intentions, Comanches in this area had some reason to regard him and his kind as enemies. Attacks like the one on Smith might appear unprovoked, but they often had their origins in past intrusions and bloodlettings that remained fresh in tribal memory.

For now, at least, Americans and Mexicans found common cause in their opposition to Comanches and other vexing plains-dwellers. When Colonel Vizcarra and the caravan at last linked up with Riley's troops in October of 1829, the Americans played host to a diverse contingent from New Mexico, which included Mexican troops and civilians (whom Cooke referred to as "Creoles") along with the Pueblo auxiliaries, some French-speaking trappers, and a well-stocked group of civilians of Spanish birth who had been banished as aliens under Mexican law (a reflection of the hostility toward Spain that persisted in Mexico for some time after it won independence). Several of those exiles were women, perhaps the first women ever to travel the Santa Fe Trail.[41] Cooke described this remarkable assemblage along the Arkansas:

> The next day we had time to look about us, and admire the strangest collection of men and animals that had perhaps ever met on a frontier of the United States. There were a few Creoles—polished gentlemen, magnificently clothed in Spanish costume; a large number of grave Spaniards, exiled from Mexico, and on their way to the United States, with much property in stock and gold—their whole equipage Spanish; there was a company of Mexican Regulars, as they were called, in uniform,—mere apologies for soldiers, or even men; several tribes of Indians, or Mexicans, much more formidable as warriors, were grouped about with their horses, and spears planted in the ground; Frenchmen were there *of course*; and our 180 hardy veterans in rags, but well armed and equipped for any service: four or five languages were spoken; but to complete the picture, must be mentioned the 2000 horses, mules, jacks, which kept up an incessant braying. The Spaniards and their attendants were in motion, throwing the lazo, catching the wild mules; and others dashed off after buffalo, which seemed disposed to send representatives to this Congress of the men and animals of two nations. I remember, too, that some Camanche dogs came over the hills into camp, from a direction opposite to that of the march of the Mexicans; but this strange circumstance was hardly noticed, though I did hear some one ask, "Where the d——l did those wild geese come from?" as a pair of them were seen dodging about.[42]

It was a rare moment of international accord in a place notorious for conflict. Yet Cooke, in this otherwise benign passage, offered a hint of hostilities to come between Americans and Mexicans in his reference to Vizcarra's regulars as "mere apologies for soldiers, or even men," a low blow at troops who had undertaken this thankless errand for the protection of a party that included many Americans as well as Mexicans. On the Santa Fe Trail, it seems, the line between partnership and partisanship, between trading favors and exchanging insults, was narrow and all too easily crossed.

11

Out along the Cimarron

fter the upheaval of 1829, traders concerned for their safety recognized that military escorts were no cure-all. Not until the Mexican War would the army begin to patrol and establish forts along the trail. Until then, travelers would be largely responsible for their own defense. They became better at that task with experience, learning to avoid casualties by remaining vigilant and avoiding rash acts that might provoke a hostile response. For all the talk of Indian savagery and scalp-taking, Alphonso Wetmore reported to Secretary of War Lewis Cass in 1831 that no more than ten lives had been lost in the "Mexican trade" since its inception a decade earlier.[1] To be sure, travelers who ventured alone or in small groups through hostile country risked meeting the same fate that befell Jedediah Smith in 1831, but two other companies traveled the Cimarron Route to New Mexico that same year without coming to grief. One was the group headed by Elisha Stanley and accompanied by Josiah Gregg, on his first trip to New Mexico. The other party, organized in the fall of 1831, was captained by Charles Bent, who had played the same role in 1829, and included among its members Albert Pike, who documented the journey briefly in writing.

Stanley's company came armed for trouble with two small cannons like the one Riley's command had carried. They had no use for artillery before they crossed the Arkansas in mid-June, and even then the opposition they faced came more from the country itself than from its native inhabitants. As Gregg recalled, they forded the Arkansas after passing the celebrated Caches, where a pioneering party of traders had buried their goods for future retrieval after becoming stranded there over the winter. ("Few travellers pass this way without visiting these mossy pits," Gregg wrote, "some of which remain partly unfilled to the present day.")[2] Crossing the Arkansas could be treacherous, for the riverbed consisted of quicksand in places, and snowmelt from the Rockies in late spring created a "June freshet" that could swamp wagons and drown skittish animals. Gregg and company escaped those hazards, but as Cooke could attest, the real trial for travelers lay ahead on the south side. Mindful of the desert that the company would have to cross before reaching the Cimarron and its springs, Captain Stanley reminded the men to "fill up the water kegs,"[3] casks holding at least five gallons, before they embarked on the hard pull through the sand hills and on across the sunbaked plain. The following day they came under a heavy downpour that proved to be a mixed blessing, allowing them to refill their kegs but causing a flash flood that upset one of the wagons. By the time Bent's company undertook this same Jornada in October, Pike related, drought had reduced the terrain to its bare essence:

> After following the Arkansas, about eighty miles, we forded it with our wagons, and took a more southerly course toward the Semaron [Cimarron River]. . . . When we crossed, the water was nowhere more than two feet in depth, rather muddy, but sweet. After crossing, we travelled about twelve miles through the sand-hills, and then came into the broad and barren prairie again. The prairie, however, between the Arkansas and Semaron, (a distance, according to our route, of about a hundred miles), was not level, but rather composed of immense undulations, as though it had once been the bed of a tumultuous ocean—a hard, dry surface of fine gravel, incapable, almost, of supporting vegetation. The general features of this whole great desert—its sterility, dryness and unconquerable barrenness—are the same wherever I have been in it. Our oxen were daily decreasing in number, and our train of wolves enlarging. I can give the reader some idea of their number and voracity, by informing him, that one night, just at sunset, we killed six buffaloes, and having time to butcher and take to camp only three, we left the other three on the ground, skinned and in part cut up. The next morning there was not a hide, a bone, or a bit of meat, within fifty yards of the place.[4]

Gregg and company, while undertaking this Jornada earlier in the year, had been largely concerned with the possibility that warriors might be on their trail. They had their first encounter with Indians shortly before reaching the Cimarron, when they met with about eighty Sioux who displayed a U.S. flag—often used by tribal bands to signal their good intentions to Americans. "Our communications were carried on entirely by signals," Gregg wrote, "yet we understood them perfectly to say, that there were immense numbers of

Indians ahead, upon the Cimarron river, whom they described by symbolic language to be Blackfeet and Comanches; a most agreeable prospect for the imagination to dwell upon!"[5] The formidable Blackfeet occupied a position on the far northern plains roughly comparable to that of the Comanches on the southern plains. Would the Comanches have welcomed them here with open arms, or did the Sioux mean that there were separate parties of Comanches and Blackfeet along the Cimarron? The latter appears more likely, for Gregg later learned that the Indians his company subsequently encountered in large numbers down by the Cimarron were Blackfeet and Gros Ventres, a French term sometimes applied to the village-dwelling Hidatsas of the upper Missouri but more likely referring in this case to the Atsinas, who lived close to the Blackfeet and sometimes traveled with them. If Gregg was well informed (such tribal identifications were often uncertain), then the Blackfeet and Gros Ventres were most likely on a lengthy hunting expedition, as evidenced by the fact that the men were accompanied by women and children. At first encounter, however, the traders thought they were dealing with a war party, and fighting nearly erupted:

> The Indians who were in advance made a bold attempt to press upon us, which came near costing them dearly; for some of our fiery backwoodsmen more than once had their rusty but unerring rifles directed upon the intruders, some of whom would inevitably have fallen before their deadly aim, had not a few of the more prudent traders interposed. The savages made demonstrations no less hostile, rushing, with ready sprung bows, upon a portion of our men who had gone in search of water; and mischief would, perhaps, have ensued, had not the impetuosity of the warriors been checked by the wise men of the nation.[6]

As Gregg noted here with an evenhandedness that transcended his habitual use of the term "savages," those "prudent traders" who restrained the "fiery backwoodsmen" had their worthy counterparts in tribal "wise men" who cooled tempers on the other side.

Soon, Captain Stanley was smoking a peace pipe with the opposing chief, and the traders found themselves camped beside "an immense Indian village" of from two to three thousand men, women, and children who had pitched their tepees along a dry riverbed.[7] Still fearing for their safety and blaming the loss of one of their horses on Indian thievery, the traders slipped away unceremoniously from their newfound tribal companions in hopes of finding the Cimarron, ignorant of the fact that they had already reached that goal in the form of the riverbed they camped along. They traveled far before realizing their blunder and reversing course, and they might have been overcome by

"Indian Alarm on the Cimarron River," from Gregg's *Commerce of the Praries*. Courtesy Library of Congress, Prints and Photographs Division.

thirst had they not been met and guided to water—at one of the Cimarron springs that served as oases in this desert even when the river ran dry—by some of the same Indians they had taken for villains:

> We had just set out, when a couple of Indians approached us, bringing the horse we had lost the night before; an apparent demonstration of good faith which could hardly have been anticipated. It was evidently an effort to ingratiate themselves in our favor, and establish an intercourse—perhaps a traffic. But the outrages upon Major Riley, as well as upon a caravan, not two years before, perpetrated probably by the same Indians, were fresh in the memory of all; so that none of us were willing to confide in their friendly professions. On inquiring by means of signs for the nearest water, they pointed to the direction we were travelling: and finally taking the lead, they led us, by the shortest way, to the valley of the long-sought Cimarron, which, with its delightful green-grass glades and flowing torrent (very different in appearance from where we had crossed it below), had all the aspect of an 'elysian vale,' compared with what we had seen for some time past. We pitched our camp in the valley, much rejoiced at having again 'made a port.'[8]

This was reminiscent of that moment when Cooke and his thirsty troops came upon water in the desert and felt blessed by a "special providence." In Gregg's case, however, the deliverance was all the more surprising for having come at the hands of Indians deemed hostile. (If, in fact, they were Blackfeet and Atsinas, then they were probably not responsible for the earlier incidents Gregg referred to.) No doubt these Indians hoped for something in return, but it was not too much to ask—some sort of exchange or consideration that would relate the two sides peacefully. What Gregg and his companions had stumbled upon here was a principle that worked to the advantage of travelers more often than it caused them harm—the insistence of Indians that strangers in their midst honor or engage them in some way. That engagement might be bloody, but more frequently the requirement was satisfied by an exchange of gifts, goods, or other courtesies. Belatedly, Gregg and company recognized that they had failed to ratify their "treaty of peace" with these Indians, signaled earlier by the smoking of the pipe, an oversight remedied in a meeting with several chiefs: "The truth is, the former treaty had never been 'sealed'—they had received no presents, which form an indispensable ratification of all their 'treaties' with the whites. Some fifty or sixty dollars' worth of goods having been made up for them, they now left us apparently satisfied; and although they continued to return and annoy us for a couple of days longer; they at last entirely disappeared."[9] Not all Indians encountered along the route could be appeased in this fashion, of course, particularly if they bore active grudges against whites. After continuing westward up the Cimarron for a while, the traders were challenged by about one hundred warriors, presumed to be Comanches, and repulsed them with cannon fire in a brief skirmish that left both sides unscathed.

Despite such run-ins, companies that kept careful watch, held their fire until they knew for sure they were under attack, and paid due tribute to Indians who remained friendly stood an excellent chance of reaching Santa Fe without losing any of their men. Indeed, some journeys were so tranquil that men new to the trail questioned the need for continued guard duty. Such was Albert Pike's reaction that fall when Captain Bent and his lieutenants insisted on maintaining vigil through the chill nights in the absence of any apparent threat. Men of Bent's company had come equipped for the cold with tents, but that was no consolation for those on guard:

> After striking the Semaron, that saltest, most singular, and most abominable of all the villanous streams of the prairie, we went crawling up it for forty miles, with our jaded oxen, at the rate of about eight miles a day, and about the first of November we reached the middle spring of the Semaron. Before reaching this point, my horse ran off in a storm, one night, and left me to walk the rest of my way to Santa Fe. I had no particular objection, for the Indian Summer was over, and it was altogether too cold to ride. . . . We reached the spring in the middle of a light snow, accompanied as it had been heralded, by a keen, biting north wind, fresh from the everlasting ice-peaks that guard the springs of the Arkansas. We camped, and commenced gathering the dry ordure of the buffalo for fuel—the only salvation of the journeyer in the prairie. We piled a quantity under the wagons, and with difficulty having satiated our hunger, I for one rolled myself in my blankets and coiled myself in the tent. As the hours of night wore away, the snow fell thicker, and the cold grew more intense. At half past one, I was called out to stand guard. I strapped my blanket round me, shouldered my gun, and was ready to stand as sentry till nine in the morning—for what purpose, the wise commanders of the party knew best. Indians never attack on such nights. I stood at the west end of the camp—in front of the tent belonging to our mess. On the east end was another tent, and by it a small fire, where the captain of our guard, quaking, half with cold and half with fear of Indians, *stood* guard *sitting*. For about half an hour, I paced back and forth on the rod and half of line allotted me—in snow about a foot deep. The storm was over, and the wind every moment grew more intensely cold. At length my feet forced me to the fire. I warmed them, and they were cold before I was at my stand again. I tried the fire again, but with no better fortune and then I resolved

to build a fire for myself. I piled some of our fuel together, and sat down to watch it ignite. It was then about three in the morning—and in about an hour it gave me sufficient heat to keep tolerably warm by bending over it— which I did, with a sovereign contempt for every tribe of heathen Indian between the Mississippi and the mountains. In the morning my feet were so swollen that I could with difficulty move—and the reader, and you also, may judge of the degree of cold, when I tell you that a horse froze to death within ten feet of me. Great God! how those animals suffered. I have seen oxen come and stand by the fire, till it scorched the skin from them. You could not drive them away—and no wonder.[10]

Given the recent disturbances along the Cimarron, Bent had ample reason to subject the company to such punishing duty. Still, Pike's bleak and uneventful vigil illustrated the fundamental challenge that faced travelers on this arduous pilgrimage. By and large, they met with far less grief from unfriendly Indians than from hostile elements—forces that could not be appeased or conquered but simply had to be endured.

From the Middle Spring of the Cimarron, flanked to the north by steep bluffs "with just breaks enough between them for the wind to whistle merrily between their rough teeth,"[11] as Pike put it, his party and other westbound travelers on the trail continued along the often-dry riverbed for some forty miles to the Upper Spring and thence to the nearby Cold Spring, where they left the Cimarron and cut southwestward through what is now the western tip of the Oklahoma panhandle to the upper Canadian River in New Mexico. That lonely stretch of the journey took them beyond prime buffalo country into the range of antelope, whose far-off forms were often "mistaken for droves of elk or wild horses," Gregg noted, "and when at a great distance, even for horsemen; whereby frequently alarms are occasioned."[12] In fact, this area was not much frequented by Plains Indians, who preferred country where buffalo abounded. Now and then, however, travelers might come upon Indian raiding parties returning from encounters with rival tribes. In July 1828, for example, Alphonso Wetmore and his westbound party met with some war-weary Kiowas while traversing this bleak portion of the Cimarron Route:

Yesterday morning after we encamped, a small party of red gentlemen called on us; smoked, ate, drank, and slept with us; one of them, at the first setting, drank nine pints of water; he was probably a secretary of some cold water conventicle. The chief of this little band claimed the honor for them of being Kiawas. Through the medium of the Pani language, we learned that they had been on a gentleman-like horse stealing expedition against the Chians

[Cheyennes], in which they were at first successful, but when they believed they had escaped with their booty, the Chians were down upon them, and retook the cavalry and a few scalps. They had walked at double quick for the last two or three days; finding themselves at ease and secure in our camp, they "slept fast."[13]

Hosting these "red gentlemen" was evidently something of a strain on Wetmore and company. "This morning, we parted with our guests, with mutual expressions of esteem and good will," he wrote sarcastically the next day; "our old trapper told them that when he returned their visit, he would leave his card, meaning a ball cartridge."[14] But even those who considered Indians bad company were well advised to put up with such visits rather than provoke warriors who wanted nothing more from the passing traders than refreshment.

As companies bound for the New Mexican settlements neared their objective, they often detached "runners," or small advance parties, to ride ahead and make arrangements with officials there or obtain provisions for their lagging comrades, who sometimes ran short of food unless they had laid by a large store of buffalo meat earlier on. Fatigue, hunger, and thirst could make this last stretch of the journey across the high desert country disorienting, an effect heightened by mirages that sent travelers racing toward beckoning ponds of water, only to see those tantalizing illusions vanish. The only relief for the eye, or solace for the mind, came from such prominent landmarks as the jagged Rabbit Ears and the nearby Round Mound that rose from the tedious expanse and reminded wayfarers that they were nearing the Rockies and the end of their ordeal. Gregg and others in his company climbed to the top of the Round Mound and beheld off to the west "the perennially snow-capped summit of the eastern spur of the Rocky Mountains."[15] For many travelers, that sight was like the first glimpse of land at the end of a long, hard voyage. As Pike put it eloquently, parties traversing the plains were like souls lost at sea, and not until they came within sight of the mountains did they glimpse redemption:

In the prairie we are alone; we have that same desolate, companionless feeling of isolation, so well expressed by Coleridge. We separate ourselves from our companions, and turning our mind inward to a consideration of its own hidden joys or miseries—its memories or anticipations, we pass over the desert as men pass through a glimmering and lonely dream. But the mountains are our companions. We lose that feeling of solitude and oppression at the heart, and in its stead is an expansion and an elevation of the mind, as though the great spirit which, as Fancy might imagine, inspires the mighty mountains, was entering into the heart and abiding there.[16]

"March of the Caravan," as viewed from atop Round Mound, from Gregg's *Commerce of the Prairies*. Used by permission, State Historical Society of Missouri, Columbia, all rights reserved.

Such uplifting moments repaid travelers for weeks of toil and privation. The sense of deliverance evoked by the prospect of the distant mountains came only to those who first set out across the desert and braved that errand into the wilderness, as the Puritans conceived of their exodus to the New World. Most pilgrims on the Santa Fe Trail undertook their errands for worldly profit, but did that not prevent them from feeling at times that they were being guided through the wilderness by a transcendent power that Pike referred to graciously in tribal fashion as "the great spirit."

For Mexicans heading west on the trail, the first glimpse of the mountains was all the more inspiring, for it meant that they were nearly home. Wetmore described one such poignant moment that occurred when his party reached the Point of Rocks, not far from where the Cimarron Route rejoined the Mountain Route: "We were to-day gratified with a full view of the Rocky mountains ranging along to the right. When our Mexican, from a hill top, caught a distant view of the mountain, he lept for joy, discharged his carabine, and exclaimed, 'Las luz de mis ojos, mi casa, mi alma'; light of my eyes, my house, my love. Such emotions as these, we call in Spanish, amor de la patria."[17] Among the worthiest of exchanges on the Santa Fe Trail was this linguistic give-and-take that allowed diligent travelers like Wetmore to master the terms of their foreign traveling companions and gain precious insights into their world.

No less gratifying than the first view of the distant mountains was the sight of a friendly party approaching from the Mexican settlements—perhaps the "runners" returning with much-needed provisions, or a companionable band of Mexican *ciboleros* (buffalo hunters), heading east to pursue their prey. Gregg met such a party shortly after his company passed the Rabbit Ears, and he remarked on their distinctive regalia:

> These hardy devotees of the chase usually wear leathern trousers and jackets, and flat straw hats; while, swung upon the shoulder of each hangs his *carcage* or quiver of bow and arrows. The long handle of their lance being set in a case, and suspended by the side with a strap from the pommel of the saddle, leaves the point waving high over the head, with a tassel of gay parti-colored stuffs dangling at the tip of the scabbard. Their fusil, if they happen to have one, is suspended in like manner at the other side, with a stopper in the muzzle fantastically tasselled.[18]

These obliging ciboleros furnished Gregg's hungry party with dried buffalo meat and some hard bread that yielded to the tooth when steeped in water or coffee. Among their trademarks were their creaking *carretas*: carts made entirely of wood that in the words of a later American visitor emitted a "siren song which wakened the dead for five miles or more."[19] Aside from these vehicles, used to carry buffalo meat, the ciboleros employed much the same tools and techniques as their Indian counterparts, whose success they emulated. For companies nearing the settlements, they were heralds of what Cooke called a "Creole" society, one in which Spanish culture had been substantially modified by close and prolonged contact with Pueblos and other Indians. Americans, accustomed to refashioning the lands they occupied in their own image and remaining apart from native populations, found this hybrid culture strange and backward. But they would have to reckon with these ever-adaptable New Mexicans—and learn from them—before they could call this land their own.

12

Bent's Fort and Beyond

Not every party bound for Santa Fe braved the hazards of the Cimarron Route. The founding in the early 1830s of Bent's Fort lured more than a few travelers down the Mountain Route, which followed the Arkansas River upstream to the fort before veering southwestward through Raton Pass to the settlements beyond. The fort itself became a destination and turnaround point for wagon trains carrying trade goods to the busy outpost and returning to Missouri with buffalo hides and other pelts purchased there from Indians or white trappers. In addition, parties heading for New Mexico with pack animals or with wagons that were not too heavy to negotiate Raton Pass often preferred the Mountain Route because the fort offered them welcome sanctuary en route and rendered tribes that traded there more receptive to whites. Indeed, Bent's Fort was the one spot on the Santa Fe Trail where exchanges with Indians were systematically welcomed and encouraged, and the effects of that intercourse on both sides were profound and far-reaching. Cheyennes and allied Arapahos, whose territory embraced the western reaches of the plains from the Arkansas River north to the Platte River and beyond, entered into a close trading relationship with the fort's manager, William Bent (linked to the Cheyennes by marriage), and they were more hospitable to Americans as a result. Travelers continuing on from Bent's Fort to New Mexico still had to negotiate the barren and potentially dangerous stretch of the trail from that outpost to Raton Pass, but overall the Mountain Route was a prudent alternative to the Cimarron Route, particularly for smaller groups that lacked the firepower of larger companies or big wagons to use as shields against attackers.

Parties might be safer on the Mountain Route, but that did not protect them from internal strife. Thomas Farnham, while leading his Peoria party to Oregon via Bent's Fort in 1839, encountered far more trouble from within his own ranks than from any external threat. Along the way, he also had occasion to observe how companies of greater experience and discipline than his own held together in the face of adversity. In mid-June, as Farnham and his men approached the Arkansas amid a series of downpours that swelled the river's tributaries and impeded their progress, they met with an eastbound wagon train operated by the firm of Bent, St. Vrain & Co. traveling to Missouri with furs from the fort and livestock from New Mexico. As Farnham related:

> One of the partners and thirty-odd men were on their way to St. Louis, with ten wagons laden with peltries. They were also driving down 200 Santa Fe sheep, and 40 horses and mules for the Missouri market. These animals are usually purchased from the Spaniards for the merest trifle; and if the Indians prove far enough from the track to permit the purchaser to drive them into the States, his investment is unusually profitable.[1]

The "partner" Farnham encountered here was none other than Charles Bent, the driving force behind the company. Bent's Fort was the hub of his firm, but as this shipment illustrated, its operations extended from St. Louis to Santa Fe. While younger brother William supervised the fort, Charles resided in Taos and oversaw the company's Mexican interests along with partner Ceran St. Vrain, an enterprising Missourian of French ancestry. Periodically, Charles Bent led company caravans like the one Farnham encountered to and from Missouri. The risk of losing goods or livestock en route, either because of Indian raids or because the animals simply strayed from camp, was a constant worry for him and his partners. Bent informed Farnham, for example, that he had lost "thirty Mexican mules and seven horses" on the way east. A less experienced trader might have engaged in a lengthy pursuit of the runaways—or their Indian captors—at the risk of even greater losses. The seasoned Bent, however, understood that such were the tolls of the trail and forged ahead, after asking Farnham as a favor to return to Bent's Fort any of those animals that he chanced to recover on the way west. Farnham promised to do so, for as he put it, "A request of any kind from a white face in the wilderness is never denied."[2] A few days later, Farnham's skittish company, new to the plains and fearful of attack, received an alarming visit around dusk:

We were suddenly roused by the rapid trampling of animals in such numbers that made the ground tremble as if an earthquake were rustling beneath it. "Indians!" was the cry from the guard "Indians!" We had expected an encounter with them as we approached the Buffalo, and we were consequently not unprepared for it. Each man seized his rifle and was instantly in position to give the intruders a proper reception. On they came, rushing furiously in a dense column till within 30 yards of our tent; and then wheeling short to the left, abruptly halted. Not a rifle ball or an arrow had yet cleft the air. Nor was it so necessary that there should, as it might have been, had we not discovered that instead of bipeds of bloody memory, they were the quadrupeds that had eloped from the fatherly care of Mr. Bent, making a call of ceremony upon their compatriot mules &c. tied to stakes within our camp.[3]

This incident was characteristic of the journey across the plains in that travelers often found that hostile Indians were the least of their worries. (Farnham referred to the Arkansas River as the "American Nile," haunted by swarms of mosquitoes and other "Egyptian plagues" that compounded the problems he and his followers experienced with their animals and with each other.)[4] After corralling Bent's strays, Farnham remained deeply concerned about the possibility of an Indian attack, despite the fact that his party met with reinforcements at Pawnee Fork in the form of a large company of traders bound for Santa Fe and spotted no Indians in the vicinity other than an encampment of Kansas on a buffalo-hunting expedition:

The owners of the Santa Fe wagons were men who had seen much of life. Urbane and hospitable, they received us in the kindest manner, and gave us much information in regard to the mountains, the best mode of defence, &c., that proved in our experience remarkably correct. During the afternoon, the chiefs of the Kauzaus sent me a number of buffalo tongues and other choice bits of meat. But the filth discoverable upon their persons generally deterred us from using them. For this they cared little. If their presents were accepted, an obligation was by their laws incurred on our part, from which we could only be relieved by presents in return. To this rule of Indian etiquette, we submitted; and a council was accordingly held between myself and the principal chief through an interpreter, to determine upon the amount and quality of my indebtedness in this regard. The final arrangement was, that in consideration of the small amount of property I had then in possession, I should give him two pounds of tobacco, a side-knife, and a few papers of vermillion; but that, on my return, which would be in fourteen moons, I must be very rich, and give him more.

To all which obligations and pleasant prophecies, I of course gave my most hearty concurrence.[5]

Obadiah Oakley, in his journal of this same expedition by the Peoria party, reported that their dealings with the Kansas were not as one-sided as Farnham implied. Some of the Kansas bought articles from them "for money, of which they seemed to have plenty," Oakley noted. "The price of a common butcher knife, for which the company paid 25 cents at Independence, was out here $1.50."[6] Farnham, however, worried that his costly bargain with the principal chief, reminiscent of his earlier encounter with a member of the same tribe who exacted presents from him near Council Grove, might not exempt the party from further impositions by the Kansas. "The Caws are notorious thieves," he contended. "We therefore put out a double guard to-night to watch their predatory operations, with instructions to fire upon them if they attempted to take our animals."[7]

A violent storm that night precluded any such raid, and the threat may have been less than Farnham imagined, for the Kansas were preoccupied with hunting and processing buffalo. The following morning, the Santa Fe traders harnessed their teams and headed out, leaving Farnham's party to reckon with the less-than-formidable Kansas and follow at their own pace:

A noble sight those teams were, forty-odd in number, their immense wagons still unmoved, forming an oval breastwork of wealth, girded by an impatient mass of near 400 mules, harnessed and ready to move again along their solitary way. But the interest of the scene was much increased when, at the call of the commander, the two lines, team after team, straightened themselves into the trail, and rolled majestically away over the undulating plain. We crossed the Pawnee Fork, and visited the Caw camp. Their wigwams were constructed of bushes inserted into the ground, twisted together at the top, and covered with the buffalo hides that they had been gathering for their winter lodges. Meat was drying in every direction. It had been cut into long narrow strips, wound around sticks standing uprightly in the ground, or laid over a rick of wicker-work, under which slow fires were kept burning. The stench, and the squalid appearance of the women and children, were not sufficiently interesting to detain us long; and we travelled on for the buffalo which were bellowing over the hills in advance of us. There appeared to be about 1,500 souls: they were almost naked; and filthy as swine. They make a yearly hunt to this region in the spring—lay in a large quantity of dried meat—return to their own Territory in harvest time—gather their beans and corn, and make the buffalo hides taken before the hair is long enough for robes, into conical tents; and thus prepare for a long and jolly winter.[8]

As evidenced in this and other passages, Farnham was deeply ambivalent toward these Indians and their way of life. He admired their solidarity and resourcefulness and compared their pleasures and pursuits favorably to the preoccupations of a "fantastic, mawkish civilization—that flattering, pluming, gormandizing, unthinking, gilded, clamlike life, that is beginning to measure mental and moral worth by the amount of wealth possessed, and the adornments of a slip or pew in church."[9] At the same time, he feared and distrusted these "filthy" Kansas, blaming them for stealing three of Bent's mules that may simply have strayed from camp (as they had before) and insisting that once the Santa Fe traders departed, the Kansas "would without scruple use their superior force in appropriating to themselves our animals."[10]

Only gradually did Farnham come to realize that the real threat to the welfare of his party came not from without but from within. While he was off trying in vain to retrieve the missing mules from the Kansas, who professed ignorance of the animals' whereabouts, a dispute broke out back in camp that left one man seriously wounded and demoralized the entire party. This argument arose "between two of the most querulous of the company," Farnham noted— one of whom, Sidney Smith, tried to enforce his point by grabbing his loaded rifle by the muzzle and pulling it from among some baggage, at which the "hammer of the lock caught, and sent the contents of the barrel into his side." Fortunately for Smith, Dr. David Waldo (referred to here by Farnham as Walworth) was with the trading company that had recently moved out ahead of the Peoria party and returned promptly to treat Smith's self-inflicted wound. Waldo was not the only healer to offer his services. As Farnham related:

> Every thing was done for the wounded man that his condition required, and our circumstances permitted. Doctor Walworth, of the Santa Fe caravan, then eight miles in advance, returned, examined, and dressed the wound, and furnished a carriage for the invalid. During the afternoon the high chief of the Caws also visited us; and by introducing discolored water into the upper orifice, and watching its progress through, ascertained that the ball had not entered the cavity.[11]

This procedure, which seemingly indicated that Smith had not been wounded in the intestines, was certainly a kind gesture on the part of "our friend the chief," as the author referred to him. Yet Farnham remained convinced that his small party was in grave danger from the Kansas—not to mention the Pawnees and Comanches who were said to be in the area—and decided to forge ahead to Bent's Fort at as rapid a pace as Smith's condition would permit. For some in the party, that was not fast enough. They resented being burdened with an invalid who had shown himself to be a troublemaker, and made their feelings clear to Farnham in late June, just as the Santa Fe traders, who had done all they could to help Smith, were about to cross the Arkansas and follow the Cimarron Route to New Mexico:

> To-day a mutiny, which had been ripening ever since Smith was wounded, assumed a clear aspect. It now appeared that certain individuals of my company had determined to leave Smith to perish in the encampment where he was shot; but failing in supporters of so barbarous a proposition, they now endeavored to accomplish their design by less objectionable means. They said it was evident if Smith remained in the company, it must be divided; for that they, pure creatures, could not longer associate with so impure a man. And that in order to preserve the unity of the company, they would propose that arrangements should be made with the Santa Feans to take him along with them. In this wish a majority of the company, induced by a laudable desire for peace, and the preservation of our small force entire in a country filled with Indian foes, readily united. I was desired to make the arrangement; but my efforts proved fruitless. Gentlemen traders were of opinion that it would be hazardous for Smith, destitute of the means of support, to trust himself among a people of whose language he was ignorant, and among whom he could consequently get no employment; farther, that Smith had a right to expect protection from his comrades; and they would not, by any act of theirs, relieve them from so sacred a duty. I reported to my company this reply, and dwelt at length upon the reasons assigned by the traders.[12]

Some others in Farnham's company saw the matter as he did. Oakley, for one, was appalled that the majority of his fellow travelers endorsed the "horrid proposition" to leave Smith "on the plain to perish, or to take care of himself as he could."[13] Farnham and Oakley, by their own accounts, were among the minority in the company who pledged to honor the oath they had taken "to protect each other to the last extremity," as Farnham put it, and they resolved that "however unworthy Smith might be, we could neither leave him to be eaten by wolves, nor upon the mercy of strangers; and that neither should be done while they had life to prevent it."[14] They mounted Smith on a gentle mule and did their best to keep him upright as the party continued on to Bent's Fort. Farnham, seeing that he no longer had the support of the majority, resigned command, and his place was taken by a man he declined to name but described as a "hard-faced villain," who set a punishing pace, as if intent on leaving Smith and his caretakers behind. (If such was his intention, he failed, for Smith rallied and kept up with the rest.)

The man who replaced Farnham as captain was Robert Shortess, whom Oakley identified as one of the first to propose abandoning Smith. A letter to the press written in 1840 in response to published charges by Oakley and signed by Shortess and four other members of the company denied that they had any intention of leaving Smith behind and attributed the so-called mutiny to "the low intriguing disposition" of Farnham, Oakley, and Smith, which "resulted in their expulsion from the company."[15] Shortess later portrayed Farnham as a little Napoleon who imagined that his "Oregon dragoons," as he styled the company, could single-handedly take possession of the contested Oregon country for the United States and drive out the competing British. Shortess claimed that he tried unsuccessfully to make clear to Farnham the folly of this improbable takeover scheme: "'But, captain, part of your force are Englishmen; do you think they will fight against their countrymen?' 'Oh, yes, they will not turn traitors; if they do, by God, we'll shoot them.' This conversation gave the writer a pretty good idea of Captain Farnham's character, morally and intellectually."[16]

Farnham was indeed an avid American expansionist, and that attitude may have grated on some men in his company, several of whom were born in England. But the trigger-happy captain described by Shortess bears no relation to Farnham as he portrayed himself or as others in the party perceived him. Even Joseph Holman, who signed the 1840 letter siding with Shortess, conceded later that Farnham's "duties as captain were well discharged and satisfactory to the company."[17] Plainly, Shortess and Farnham despised each other, and neither can be considered an objective witness in matters relating to their dispute. Oakley, however, offers compelling testimony supporting the case against Shortess, who was described by another acquaintance in later years as a man of "inflexible purpose," capable of "strong hate" as well as acts of kindness. "His whole life is a mystery," that acquaintance concluded, "his combinations a riddle."[18]

Farnham characterized the unnamed "villain" who replaced him as captain as one who felt bound by no other rule than the principle of might makes right. "These democratic parties for the plains!! what are they?" he declared by Farnham's account, "what is equality anywhere? A fudge. . . . One must rule; the rest obey, and no grumbling, by G**!"[19] Yet this aspiring despot exercised little real authority over his demoralized followers. While they were drying buffalo meat on a rack over the fire one evening, Farnham related, the captain made the mistake of stirring up the flames too high, then ordered others to remove the sizzling flesh before it burned to a crisp:

> "Take that meat off," roared the man of power. No one obeyed, and His Greatness stood still. "Take that meat off," he cried again, with the emphasis and mien of an Emperor; not deigning himself to soil his rags, by obeying his

own command. No one obeyed. The meat burned rapidly. His ire waxed high; his teeth ground upon each other; yet, strange to record, no mortal was so much frightened as to heed his command. At length his sublime forbearance had an end. The great man seized the meat, fat, and blazing gloriously, in the spirit in which Napoleon seized the bridge of Lodi, dashed it upon the ground, raised the temperature of his fingers to the blistering point, and rested from his labors.[20]

This may or may not be a fair portrait of Shortess, but the anecdote serves nonetheless as an instructive tale on the plight of companies that lost cohesion. The men around the fire appeared content to let their irksome new captain pay for his own blunder. Any idea of collective sacrifice, of pitching in to rescue a fellow traveler from the consequences of his mistakes, had seemingly been discarded when much of the company tried to deny responsibility for Smith. In essence, they chose not to pay the price expected of all groups that hoped to cross the plains intact, be they bands of warriors or parties of traders—the commitment to protect and defend their companions wholesale, regardless of their individual merits. Plains warriors, however guarded they might be in other circumstances, took great risks to rescue their wounded comrades, and whites traveling together who cared for their reputation and their mutual welfare did the same. The malcontents in this Peoria party were fortunate not to encounter any concerted challenge on their way to Bent's Fort that exposed their incoherence as a company.

Farnham noted that two of the Bents were present at the fort when he and others in his fractious party arrived there in early July—most likely William and his younger brother Robert—and he likened the pair in appearance and attitude to tribal chiefs:

> They seemed to be thoroughly initiated into Indian life; dressed like chiefs; in moccasins thoroughly garnished with beads and porcupine quills; in trowsers of deer skin, with long fringes of the same extending along the outer seam from the ancle to the hip; in the splendid hunting-shirt of the same material, with sleeves fringed on the elbow seam from the wrist to the shoulder, and ornamented with figures of porcupine quills of various colors, and leathern fringe around the lower edge of the body. And chiefs they were in the authority exercised in their wild and lonely fortress.[21]

The paradox of Bent's Fort and its overseers, as Farnham recognized, was that they were much influenced by tribal culture while serving at the same time as a bastion against hostile Indians and their designs. The fort, situated on the north bank of the Arkansas, was built by Mexicans and framed in Mexican fashion, with adobe walls up to seven feet thick by Farnham's reckoning, and a stout gate that offered access to the *placita*, or central courtyard, around which were arrayed two stories of workshops, storerooms, and living quarters. Friendly Indians were allowed in during the day to trade, but guards kept watch from two bastions at opposite corners that were "properly perforated for the use of cannon and small arms," Farnham observed, "and command the fort and the plains around it."[22]

In sum, the fort, much like the wagons traders traveled in, embodied the dual nature of exchanges on the Santa Fe Trail, functioning both as a medium for peaceful intercourse and as a bulwark against potential opposition. By and large, peace prevailed and diverse elements of Anglo, Mexican, and Indian society found common ground here, as elaborated by Farnham in one of the most evocative passages in his book:

> A trading establishment to be known must be seen. A solitary abode of men, seeking wealth in the teeth of danger and hardship, rearing its towers over the uncultivated wastes of nature, like an old baronial castle that has withstood the wars and desolations of centuries; Indian women tripping around its battlements in their glittering moccasins and long deer skin wrappers; their children, with most perfect forms, and the carnation of the Saxon cheek struggling through the shading of the Indian, and chattering now Indian, and now Spanish or English; the grave owners and their clerks and traders, seated in the shade of the piazza smoking the long native pipe, passing it from one to another, drawing the precious smoke into the lungs by short hysterical sucks till filled, and then ejecting it through the nostrils; or it may be, seated around their rude table, spread with coffee or tea, jerked buffalo meat, and bread made of unbolted wheaten meal from Taos; or after eating laid themselves comfortably upon their pallets of straw and Spanish blankets, and dreaming to the sweet notes of a flute; the old trappers withered with exposure to the rending elements, the half-tamed Indian, and half civilized Mexican servants, seated on the ground around a large tin pan of dry meat, and a tankard of water, their only rations, relating adventures about the shores of Hudson's Bay, on the rivers Columbia and Makenzie, in the Great Prairie Wilderness, and among the snowy heights of the mountains; and delivering sage opinions about the destination of certain bands of buffalo; of the distance to the Blackfoot country, and whether my wounded man was hurt as badly as Bill the mule was, when the "meal party" was fired upon by the Cumanches; present a tolerable idea of every thing within its walls. And if we add, the opening of the gates of a winter's morning—the cautious sliding in and out of the Indians whose tents stand around the fort, till the whole area

Bent's Fort, from Lieutenant J. W. Abert's report on his 1845 reconnaissance, in Sen. doc. 438, 29th Cong., 1st sess., Serial 477. Courtesy Museum of New Mexico, negative no. 1673.

is filled six feet deep with their long hanging black locks, and dark wakeful flashing eyes; and traders and clerks busy at their work; and the patrols upon the battlements with loaded muskets; and the guards in the bastions standing with burning matches by the carronades; and when the sun sets, the Indians retiring again to their camp outside, to talk over their newly purchased blankets and beads, and to sing and drink and dance; and the night sentinel on the fort that treads his weary watch away; we shall present a tolerable view of this post in the season of business.[23]

At every corner here, Farnham found evidence of the give-and-take that linked hosts to guests, traders to clients, and Americans to Mexicans and Indians (connections he emphasized artfully in writing by stringing his clauses together to form sentences of epic proportions). The hint of "Saxon" blood in the Indian cheek, the passing of the "native pipe" from owner to trader, the "Spanish blankets" around the shoulders of merchants, and their blankets and beads in the appreciative hands of Indians—all testified to the transforming power of the exchanges that occurred here and elsewhere along the Santa Fe Trail, intercourse that infused each side with something of the spirit of their trading partners along with their property. And yet none of this erased the fundamental distinctions between the various parties. The withered old trapper might look and talk like an Indian—and even think like one at times—but that did not make him any less hostile to Indians when the lines were drawn. Fittingly, Farnham ended his otherwise idyllic passage with a reminder of the tensions that persisted amid the trading, tensions that kept the guards at their posts through the day and separated Indians from whites at nightfall, when men reverted to their fears and disdained all those beyond the pale.

Farnham himself seemed to be of two minds about the proximity of Indians to Bent's Fort, asserting at one point that "in the months of June, July, August and September, there are in the neighbourhood of these traders from fifteen to twenty thousand savages ready and panting for plunder and blood."[24] The occupants of the post escaped annihilation, he added, only because the Indians were ignorant "of the weakness of the Post," an assertion that slighted both the intelligence of the Indians and the precautions taken by the owners, who maintained as strong a defense as they could without driving away the very tribespeople on whom their trade depended. Here as elsewhere in his narrative, Farnham displayed a deeply ambivalent view of Indians, one in which his nightmarish fears of native savagery vied with brighter visions of their noble and generous impulses.

Farnham had some reason to regard Bent's Fort—or at it least its outskirts—as vulnerable to attack. A raid conducted by Comanches, who had a long-standing dispute with the Cheyennes and saw no reason to be kind to their white trading partners, had occurred in mid-June of 1839, a few weeks before he arrived at the outpost, and he described the deadly incident as others related it to him. A band of sixty or so Comanches had crossed the Arkansas from the south bank under cover of darkness and hidden among some bushes, he reported, until a Mexican employed at the fort to watch over the mules and horses came out through the gate in the morning to graze the animals (the owners kept animals corralled within the walls but could not afford to feed them regularly on stored grain and had to risk such outings). Like most attacks along the Santa Fe Trail, this one was aimed at stealing animals rather than killing their keepers, but as Farnham related, the Comanches did not hesitate to target the Mexican when he got in their way:

> The faithful guard at Bent's, on the morning of the disaster I am relating, had dismounted after driving out his animals, and sat upon the ground watching with the greatest fidelity for every call of duty; when these 50 or 60 Indians sprang from their hiding places, ran upon the animals, yelling horribly, and attempted to drive them across the river. The guard, however, nothing daunted, mounted quickly, and drove his horse at full speed among them. The mules and horses hearing his voice amidst the frightning yells of the savages, immediately started at a lively pace for the fort; but the Indians were on all sides, and bewildered them. The guard still pressed them onward, and called for help; and on they rushed, despite the efforts of the Indians to the contrary. The battlements were covered with men. They shouted encouragement to the brave guard—"Onward, onward," and the injunction was obeyed. He spurred his horse to his greatest speed from side to side, and whipped the hindermost of the band with his leading rope. He had saved every animal: he was within 20 yards of the open gate: he fell: three arrows from the bows of the Cumanches had cloven his heart. And relieved of him, the lords of the quiver gathered their prey, and drove them to the borders of Texas, without injury to life or limb. I saw this faithful guard's grave. He had been buried a few days. The wolves had been digging into it. Thus 40 or 50 mules and horses, and their best servant's life, were lost to the Messrs. Bents in a single day.[25]

Plainly, the occupants felt for the guard and regretted his death, but they did not venture out in response to his call for help or seek retaliation by pursuing his assailants. Admittedly, they were short of mounts as a result of the raid, but presumably they had taken the precaution of keeping at least some of their animals safely within the walls when the rest were let out to graze. That, at least, was the implication of another account of this same raid, related by

Obadiah Oakley. He stated that thirty-seven animals were lost in the attack and added that the Indians had driven the captured horses "across the river before the men in the fort took the alarm, being at dinner when it happened. As the garrison numbered only 18 men, they did not deem it prudent to go in pursuit."[26] Perhaps Farnham invented the scene in which the men stood at the battlements shouting encouragement to the guard, or perhaps he was simply passing along a different version of the episode than the one related to Oakley. Nothing in Farnham's account, however, contradicts Oakley's assertion that the occupants of the fort deemed it imprudent to mount a pursuit, which implied that they had the means to do so but feared they would be outnumbered or outmaneuvered by the Comanches if they ever managed to catch up with them. (Oakley's informant went on to explain to him in considerable detail that most of the fort's garrison was away at the time on various errands.) The harsh calculus of risks and rewards at this vulnerable outpost impelled men in such situations to cut their losses, and perhaps the life of a Mexican employee was more easily written off than that of a prominent Anglo trader.

Another version of this incident was related by Matt Field, who arrived at Bent's Fort several weeks after Farnham left for Oregon with a few companions, his disgruntled party having disbanded. Aside from occasional battles with bison, Field's journey to the outpost was relatively peaceful and harmonious. His party did lose one member along the way to illness, however, their young Mexican cook Bernardo, who had scarcely spoken a word since their departure. "We could never learn whether he was ignorant entirely of English, or what other reasons caused his reserve," wrote Field, "but it was evident that sickness or melancholy, or perhaps both, were preying sadly upon his spirits."[27] He came down with a fever, accompanied by raging thirst, and was buried along the Arkansas near Chouteau's Island. Like many other Mexicans who toiled in the trade, he might have gone unnoticed in its annals, if not for Field's poignant elegy to him: "Poor Bernardo! Among strange men, speaking a strange tongue in the lone wilderness, he breathed his last. Where had been his thoughts in that long silence he had kept during our thirty days travel? He had doubtless felt the approaches of death, and in lonely hopelessness had brooded over remembrances of a mother's tones of love, a sister's kind caresses."[28]

As demonstrated by such passages, Field was one of the more sympathetic observers of the Mexicans involved in the Santa Fe trade. He was also a professional storyteller, however, and recognized the plight of a sufferer like Bernardo as an opportunity to be seized and embellished with romantic flourishes of the sort his readers savored. "Perhaps some young affection blighted lay in his heart like a withered leaf preserved in the pages of a favorite book," he wrote of Bernardo. "Many sweet thoughts are daily buried in the grave that have never yet been enshrined in song."[29] There was nothing unseemly in this, for audiences of the day took it for granted that the role of the story-teller was to improve on the raw material of experience. Field admitted as much in his account of his stay at Bent's Fort, where he and his companions received a hearty welcome:

> To the hospitable courtesy of Robert Bent we were indebted for several days courteous and really delightful entertainment. The fatted calf was killed for us and the hoarded luxuries of Fort William were produced. The tenants of the fort were merry fellows, we were a set of youths well worthy to shake hands with them, and as such meetings, to the lonely sojourners in the desert, were indeed much like "angels' visits," the time was mutually appreciated, and by no means suffered to pass unimproved.—Among many stirring incidents pertaining to this adventurous life, related to us while at the fort, Mr. Bent told us of the death of one of his men and the severe loss he had sustained by the Camanches a few months before.[30]

One way to "improve" the time, in other words, was with rousing stories, which themselves were often improvements on earlier versions of the same tale, as indicated by the rendition of the recent Comanche attack that Field attributed to Robert Bent and no doubt embellished some himself in the retelling. Field put the Comanche force at some three hundred men—more than four times the number estimated by Farnham—and described the attack as occurring not in the morning but at midday, a circumstance the author put to good use in his rendition:

> The brothers were at the time absent on one of the upper forks of the Platte, trading with the Pawnees, and the fort numbered only twenty tenants. It was just at sultry noon day, when the full flood of heat and light poured over the scene, the voice of the wind was mute, the insect ceased to hum, the wave of the Arkansas to murmur, and mid-day rivaled the night in hushed and breathless repose. The huge gate of the fort swung wide upon its hinges, and the whole stock of valuable animals—swift horses for hunting buffalo, strong mules for labor, etc., under care of a single Spanish guard—grazed in confident security, at some distance, but within sight of the watchman on the battlement. Demonstrations of danger had been of late unusual at the fort, and a degree of carelessness had grown upon the inmates, which, combined with the rapid movement of the marauders, was the cause of the fatal result which followed.

> Suddenly the dozing inmates of the fort were startled by the war shriek of three hundred Camanches, who appeared upon the opposite bank of the Arkansas. This was exactly in the wrong place either to attack the fort or capture the stock; but the cunning Indians had skilfully laid their scheme. Almost in the same instant a faint cry reached the fort from the cattle guard, and before the alarmed tenants of the fortress had issued from the gate, all the animals were seen in full flight down to the green bank, over the Arkansas, and away, driven before some twenty red devils on wild horses, while the hapless Spaniard who had been on duty was seen to stagger towards the fort, and fall with three barbed arrows quivering in his body.[31]

The main force of Comanches across the Arkansas had raised their war cries as a diversion, Field explained, enabling the twenty warriors hiding near the fort to take the guard by surprise and drive the animals across the water. This was a plausible stratagem, and something of the sort may well have occurred. Yet other elements of the tale, when compared to Farnham's and Oakley's versions, suggest that Robert Bent—or whoever Field's informant was—may have been trying to counter the impression that the Mexican guard had been abandoned to his fate by the occupants of the fort. Farnham wrote that the guard "called for help" to the men in the fort, who remained within the walls, while Field reported only a "faint cry" from the victim and added that the damage was done "before the alarmed tenants of the fortress had issued from the gate." This might seem consistent with Oakley's version, but Oakley stated that the occupants decided that any pursuit would be imprudent, not impossible. Field, by contrast, closed his anecdote with a passage that denied that possibility and seemed designed to absolve the fort's occupants of any charge of callousness or neglect:

> Seventy-five valuable animals were thus swept away from the fort, and five minutes scarcely elapsed from the first cry of alarm until the receding Camanches disappeared with their booty on the far horizon. The men at the fort were left without an animal to mount in pursuit, and so like a swift stroke of lightning came the misfortune, that, save bringing in the dying Spaniard and closing the gates, not another action of the inmates followed the alarm.[32]

Field's figure of seventy-five lost animals was significantly higher than the tallies offered by Farnham and Oakley, and Field was the only one of the three to state that the fort's occupants were left entirely without animals for a pursuit.[33] If his version faithfully reflects what he was told at the fort, then it appears that the story evolved there over time in a way that served to obscure a realistic but less than heroic response by the fort's "inmates" to the attack that cost the Mexican his life.

That Field himself played some part in embellishing the story is suggested by the artful contrast between the "hushed and breathless repose" of the scene at high noon, with the inmates "dozing" heedlessly within the walls and the animals grazing in "confident security" without, and the nightmarish bedlam that followed. Among Field's recurring themes was the deceptive nature of appearances on the trail. The tranquil semblance of this "sultry noon day" offered no hint of what lay in wait. It seemed that nature herself had been tamed, or domesticated, like the Frenchman Field met on the steamboat, but those who were fooled by the fine show and lulled into letting down their guard were in for a rude awakening.

In other stories, Field told of white men who disguised themselves as Indians so adroitly that close acquaintances were unable to recognize them for who they were. In one case, an army officer "famous for his power of imitating Indian character" played the part of a chief named Imallahokes so successfully at a dinner party that his own wife failed to see through him and fainted when he kissed her. Casting off his disguise, he revived her with words that perhaps said more about him than he realized: "*I'm all a hoax!*—do you not understand—*I'm all a hoax!*"[34] This was more than a play on the name of the chief he impersonated. A man who crossed the line in this way risked blurring his identity to the point that his true nature became as much of a hoax as his assumed one. The author made a similar point in humorous terms when he described a prank several drivers in his party played on another, a young man named Joseph, or Jo, who cloaked his naturally "soft and kind" disposition by pretending to bravado and boasting of what he would do to the "red devils" if challenged. After leaving Bent's Fort and camping on the south bank of the Arkansas, three men fed up with his pretenses disguised themselves as Comanches and ambushed Jo as he was gathering plums in the woods. The mock warriors raised shrill war cries that caused the butt of their joke to flee in terror and fall on his face, bloodying his nose. Unfortunately, the pranksters had neglected to inform the rest of the party of their intentions, and the stunt nearly ended in calamity when Field and others returned from a parting visit to Bent's Fort and found their camp in an uproar:

> We had been dining at the fort, five of us, and had just rode across the river when the firing took place, and Jo came rushing into camp covered with blood. We made instantly for the wood with our rifles in rest, and the three drivers seeing us coming, were filled at once with the utmost consternation, fearing to be shot down for Camanches before they could make themselves known.

Explanations were soon arrived at and the joke understood, but to Jo the trick was never revealed, and during the remainder of our travel we were continually amused with poor Jo's recital of the perilous adventure; he assuring us upon his honor that he distinctly saw seventeen naked Indians, and showing us a wound upon his ear where a ball had whizzed past and scratched him.[35]

Jo had the misfortune of peddling this inflated tale to men who knew the truth of the matter and recognized his improvements for what they were, but few storytellers on the trail had to reckon with such wary and well-informed customers. One element of the Santa Fe trade was this traffic in tales, many of them so altered in the exchange from one purveyor to another that the truth of the matter soon became muddled. But if these stories were not always accurate reflections of the events that inspired them, they were nonetheless revealing of the fears and longings of those who sustained this busy trade in anecdotes. Jo's story, for example, as retailed by Field (who surely burnished it some before offering it to his readers), told eloquently of how the specter of the "red devil" haunted travelers to the point that it sometimes possessed them. In confronting that specter, Jo became something of a demon himself, and his companions could think of no better way of exorcising that swaggering, boastful spirit in him than by playing the part of red devils themselves, which they did so effectively that they were nearly targeted as such. The truth such tales hinted at but never quite broached was that the savage part played by Indians in western lore was easily assumed by whites and seemed to suit them as well as it did their tribal foes. Dick Wootton related a similar story, in which he and another man in Bent's employ, while working at Fort St. Vrain along the Platte River, taught a "party of fellows there, who had come out from St. Louis to see the wild west," to quit boasting idly of killing Indians when they had yet to see a fight. Wootton and friends crept up on the "eastern Indian slayers" while they were picking cherries, he related:

About the time they had gotten interested in their work, we commenced shooting off our pistols and yelling like Comanche Indians; and then you ought to have seen those Indian fighters run. They never fired a shot, and didn't even stop to pick up their guns, but made the best possible time in getting to the fort. When they got in they reported that they had been attacked by a large force of Indians; they had killed a good many of them and had only sought safety in flight, when they found that they could not contend against the overwhelming numbers of the savages. To account for the loss of their guns, they said they had to swim the Platte River, and had been compelled to leave their weapons behind them.

My companion and I rode in shortly after they had finished the story of their thrilling adventure, and in a day or two the facts leaked out. Then those St. Louis braves wanted to go home, and they embraced the earliest opportunity afforded them of making a safe trip to the east.[36]

Among many intriguing parallels between white "braves" like mountain man Wootton and real Indian warriors was the concern both groups had for verifying legitimate coups and exposing false claims. A certain amount of embellishment or improvement was accepted in tribal circles, as it was around the campfires of traders or trappers, particularly when storytellers were dealing with incidents long past. But neither Indians nor whites tolerated an informant who lied extravagantly about recent encounters with enemies, for they needed to assess such challenges accurately and prepare to meet them. Among many tribes, warriors who were shown to have invented coups were publicly disgraced, and steps were taken to ensure that raids and battles were related truly. Missourian James Hobbs—who told of being seized by Comanches in the mid-1830s when he was sixteen and he and a companion strayed from a wagon train bound for Bent's Fort—explained how the Comanche warriors he later joined on a raid into Mexico kept a faithful account of that expedition. As Hobbs recalled, they made sure that their leader (referred to here as the war-chief) accurately recounted the results of the foray to his father, Old Wolf, the chief of the band, who had remained behind:

> Our report to "Old Wolf" was made somewhat as follows; All of the war-party sat in a circle in front of the chief's tent, so that the door of the tent was within the line of the circle. "Wolf" sat in the doorway on a buffalo robe, and by his side his son, the war-chief. The medicine pipe passed around for good luck, and then, in a loud voice, so that all the four hundred warriors could hear it, every event was narrated by the war-chief, from the setting out of the party till its return. During this narration there was the most profound silence. When he concluded he asked the warriors if he had stated the events correctly. These reports are meant to be very accurate, but, if any mistake is made, the warriors correct it.[37]

Unfortunately, Hobbs himself was not the most accurate of witnesses. His account of his western adventures, set down a quarter century or more after the events in question, was riddled with inaccuracies and inventions.[38] Yet his recollections of life among the Comanches were largely consistent with other reports by more reliable sources who were captured, harbored, or hosted by members of that tribe. If in fact he was not adopted by Comanches, he was nonetheless well informed on their customs and capabilities—and on their interactions with traders at Bent's Fort. Unlike those who knew Comanches only by their grim reputation, for example, Hobbs did not claim that they were uniformly cruel to their captives. He described himself more as a ward of the Comanches than as their prisoner, having been taken in by them with his young companion, John, or Jean Batiste, when the two pursued a wounded buffalo across the Arkansas against the warnings of their elders and became lost. ("Better go with us awhile," said the English-speaking chief who found them.)[39] Nor did Hobbs romanticize the Comanches and their treatment of captives. They made it clear to him early on that they would kill him if he tried to escape, and he knew that he might have fared worse at their hands had he been a Texan, with whom Comanches were embroiled in a long and brutal vendetta.

In essence, Hobbs had a choice between remaining aloof from the tribe and suspect, as John did by refusing to join Comanche war parties, or embracing the ways of his tribal overseers and earning their respect. He chose the latter path and, by his own account, so distinguished himself in battle against the Pawnees that he won Chief Old Wolf's daughter as his wife:

> Upon our arrival back in camp, "Old Wolf" helped me off the horse himself, hugged me, and said I had a big heart, but John had a little heart, because he would not go and fight. A procession was formed, and the Indian who had the Pawnee scalp led off, while I was second, the chiefs following, with the warriors in the rear; after which there was a big dance and pow-wow. "Old Wolf" brought out his daughter, a really beautiful Indian girl about my own age, with whom I had become slightly acquainted, and offered her to me for a wife! Of course I consented; what else could I do?[40]

Here again, one must ask if Hobbs was improving on his experiences, or perhaps fabricating the entire episode. After all, many whites who "went native," whether by force or by choice, thought themselves so far superior to the average tribesman that they expected to become chiefs or the favorites of chiefs— and might be tempted to claim as much, whatever the facts of the matter. Dick Wootton, for example, although no friend of Indians in general, dealt cordially with Arapahos as an employee of Bent, St. Vrain & Co. and lived among them long enough to feel like a member of the tribe, albeit one of great distinction. "I was in high favor among the Arapahoes at that time," he claimed, "and if I had had a fancy for it, they would have made me a 'big chief' without hesitation."[41]

This may have been wishful thinking on Wootton's part, but the idea that an outsider could rise to a lofty position within a tribe was not pure fantasy. Whites captured by Indians, or the offspring of such captives, sometimes achieved prominence in tribal settings. In 1834, while visiting among Comanches, artist George Catlin encountered an honored warrior named Hi-soo-san-ches, or Jesús Sánchez, whom Catlin described as "half Spanish."[42] Incorporating people of foreign ancestry in this way gratified the Comanches and other tribal groups because they felt that they gained fresh medicine, or spirit power, from the outsider and infused that newcomer with some of their own power in return. Indeed, the adoption of captives and the resulting intermarriages were among the deepest of exchanges between Indians and outsiders. If, as Hobbs claimed, Old Wolf chose him as his son-in-law, then he was bound to the chief by the firmest of deals, one that obliged and obligated him at the same time. Hobbs testified that he was ultimately released from those obligations by the chief and allowed to rejoin white society, but Old Wolf did not make that concession lightly. He parted with his coveted son-in-law only as part of a larger bargain between Comanches and the outside world—a pact that was sealed, fittingly, at Bent's Fort.

Hobbs recalled that he was ransomed at Bent's Fort in 1839, the same year Field and Farnham visited the post, but his memory for dates was faulty and the exchange may have occurred in 1840, when the fort's proprietors invited Comanches to trade there and talk peace with Cheyennes and Arapahos. The larger objective of this conclave was to draw Comanches peacefully into the company's orbit, clearing the way for trading posts in Comanche territory and reducing, if not eliminating, costly raids like the one in 1839 that depleted the fort's stock of horses and mules. By Hobbs's account, he and John were ransomed there from Old Wolf by a man he identified simply as Bent—presumably either Charles or William—for a small sum in trade goods, suggesting that Old Wolf recognized these transactions as goodwill gestures that would bring the two sides closer together and promote trade, if not peace:

> Next morning Bent gave our chief eight yards of curtain calico for John Batiste, and took possession of his property at once. Old Wolf made many objections to disposing of me, but I was finally ransomed from the Indians for the trifling consideration of six yards of red flannel, a pound of tobacco, and an ounce of beads.
>
> My wife, who sat looking on was greatly distressed, cried bitterly, and would have gone with me if the chief had given permission, but he refused, saying he preferred to keep her, and that I could visit her often, if I chose, as I promised faithfully to do. I tried to comfort her by rigging her out gaily, giving her a variety of beads and a red dress, but this, although very pleasing to her Indian taste, hardly reconciled her to the separation.[43]

In both cases here—Old Wolf's reluctant decision to accept the "trifling" ransom payment for Hobbs and his wife's refusal to be assuaged by the

His-oo-san-ches (Jesús Sánchez), Comanche warrior, from Catlin's *Letters and Notes*. Courtesy Library of Congress, Prints and Photographs Division, LC-USZ62-1301.

handsome presents he offered her—the value of the goods themselves mattered less to the recipient than the spirit in which they were given. Old Wolf
sensed that he was being courted by Bent, and his daughter knew she was being
forsaken by her husband, and the goods that changed hands simply confirmed
those assessments. For Comanches as for other tribal groups, trade was conducted more for honor and satisfaction than for profit. Parting with Hobbs on
generous terms was thus a good exchange for Old Wolf because it left him feeling not enriched but esteemed. Through this transaction, he and his people
secured a measure of trust and respect from the traders at Bent's Fort, as the
events of the next several days demonstrated. According to Hobbs, Old Wolf
was given a tour of the fort and allowed to spend the night there along with a
Cheyenne chief (a rare honor for Indians) while Old Wolf's followers camped
outside the walls. Soon after Hobbs was ransomed, he related, they were
invited to trade at Bent's Fort and responded almost too enthusiastically:

> The Indians wished to come into the fort, but Bent prohibited the entrance
> of any but chiefs. At the back door he displayed his wares, and the Indians
> brought forward their ponies, buffalo robes, and deer and other skins, which
> they traded for tobacco, beads, calicoes, flannels, knives, spoons, whistles,
> jewsharps, &c., &c.
>
> He sold them whisky the first day, but it caused several fights among
> themselves before night, and he stopped its sale by my suggestion and with
> "Old Wolf's" consent. Indians do not waste time in fighting with their fists,
> but use knives and tomahawks, and a scrimmage among themselves is seri-
> ous. There was considerable difficulty the first day, with drunken Indians out-
> side the fort, and two or three deaths resulted.
>
> The trading continued eight days and Bent reaped a wonderful harvest
> of what would turn to gold when shipped to St. Louis. "Old Wolf" slept in
> the fort every night except one, and every time he did, his warriors aroused
> him during the night and compelled him to show himself on the walls to sat-
> isfy them of his safety.
>
> On the morning of the ninth day the chiefs met and told Bent they were
> going home and would send out hunting parties, collect more skins and furs
> and come to trade with him every two or three months. "Old Wolf" told Bent
> that his goods were splendid, his whisky excellent and he should furnish him
> with all the horses and mules he wanted by sending out parties and making
> raids into Mexico. Bent offered to give him the market price for all such stock,
> and had no conscientious scruples about the way the Indians obtained them.[44]

Hobbs touched here on two controversial aspects of the trade at Bent's Fort
and other outposts owned by the company—the sale of liquor to Indians and

the acceptance of stolen animals from them in payment. In general, whites who traded with Indians neither knew nor cared whether the horses and mules they received were bred by the tribe, snared in the wild, or seized in raids. As Dick Wootton said of a foray he made into New Mexico in the 1840s to barter for animals with the Utes:

> The Indians were at war with the Mexicans about that time, and that was a good time for an American to trade with them. That was the time when they always had plenty of mules and ponies. That they ran a great many of them away from the ranches of the Mexicans I had no doubt, but they were shrewd horse thieves and had a way of effacing the brands, so that I had no means of knowing what animals rightfully belonged to them, and what ones were stolen. Even if I had known, I could not have refused to trade for anything that they wished to dispose of, without giving them great offense, and perhaps getting into serious trouble. They didn't set a very high price on either their mules or the ponies. The mules usually cost me ten or twelve dollars a piece in trade, and the ponies a little less.[45]

The principals of Bent, St. Vrain, for whom Wootton worked when he was not off on his own trading expeditions, took a similarly loose, or pragmatic, approach when trading for animals, and Charles Bent became the target of resentment among Mexicans in his hometown of Taos as a result. Were he and his partners also lax about plying Indians with liquor? Here Hobbs seemed to contradict himself, asserting at one point that Charles Bent was honorable in his dealings with Indians and would never furnish them liquor "for the purpose of making more advantageous bargains with them."[46] But that was not to say that Bent and company refused to sell liquor to Indians who sought it. The fort's proprietors were not the worst offenders in this regard and curbed the practice when it threatened to get out of hand, as when fights broke out in the episode related by Hobbs, but they trafficked in liquor when they felt it necessary to attract and hold Indian trading partners.[47]

Thus the seemingly peaceful exchanges cultivated at Bent's Fort and other outposts had potentially destructive consequences for Indians, manifested not only in deadly drinking bouts but also in heightened competition for the horses, mules, and buffalo hides that tribesmen offered in trade and in a demoralizing dependence on the white traders who purchased those articles. So strong was the lure of Bent's Fort that it contributed to the division of both the Cheyennes and the Arapahos into northern and southern branches, with the latter gravitating toward the fort. Bands that dealt regularly with Bent, St. Vrain no longer hunted merely for subsistence. They killed as many buffalo as they could track down and bartered their hides for commodities

like cloth or liquor that they had once lived happily without—or for traditional trade goods like knives, beads, or tobacco that they had long produced
themselves or obtained from other tribes.

Buffalo hides became more important to the company in the early 1840s
as the beaver trade dried up, impelling gifted mountain men like Dick Wootton and Kit Carson to give up trapping and offer their services to Bent, St. Vrain
as hunters or scouts. In 1842, Bent's Fort took in 1,670 beaver skins valued
at $7,836.12, compared to nearly 3,000 buffalo robes valued at $7,535.80.[48]
Before long, the fort's fur inventory consisted almost entirely of buffalo hides,
flattened in a press and bundled in packs of ten for transportation to market
by wagon. This shift in the trade entailed a significant change in tribal life-
ways, one that was often materially rewarding at first but proved disruptive
and dispiriting in the long run. The Comanches may have been fortunate in
that they never came close to rivaling the southern Cheyennes and Arapahos
as trading partners of the company and remained among the toughest customers Americans had to deal with on the plains.

Several witnesses documented in writing this time of transition in and
around the fort. In 1840, Alexander Barclay, the fort's bookkeeper and superintendent of stores, wrote a revealing letter to his brother back in England in
which he told of bidding unsuccessfully for a Cheyenne wife. The episode
illustrated that the Cheyennes retained considerable bargaining power in their
dealings with the fort's occupants and were not afraid to spurn their offers if
a rival party offered better terms. As Barclay related:

> I had conceived a liaison for the prettiest girl among the Cheyenne tribe, and
> would have bought her at any price, but her father's cupidity overreached itself,
> having a competition for the girl in the tribe who he represented as willing to
> give eight horses for her, and stated the preference he gave the young Indian,
> I offered more than on calm reflection I can own without a blush. He gave
> the finishing touch by requesting me to add another American horse to the
> offering. As this exceeded fair trade, the additional horse he wished being
> worth (200) two hundred dollars, I declined any further conference on the
> subject telling him in his own tongue "that all the world did not live for me.
> I loved his daughter, but he could keep her and I could keep my presents."[49]

This custom of soliciting a handsome gift of horses from a suitor, practiced
by various plains tribes, served the interests of the bride as well as her father
by ensuring that her husband was a man of some accomplishment and generosity. Perhaps Barclay's offer would have been regarded more favorably had
he been a trader of the stature of William Bent, whose marriage to the Cheyenne
Owl Woman brought credit both to her family and to the tribe as a whole.

William Bent. Courtesy Museum of New Mexico, negative no. 7029.

The importance of that alliance was attested to by William Boggs, who went west on the Santa Fe Trail in the summer of 1844, at the age of seventeen. Boggs, who had family ties to the Bents, spent much of the ensuing winter with William Bent and Owl Woman at the Cheyenne encampment in the Big Timbers, an extensive cottonwood grove along the Arkansas east of Bent's Fort that also served travelers on the trail as a campground. Many years later, Boggs described the central position William Bent occupied in that village and the extent to which his marriage reinforced his commercial ties with the Cheyennes:

> We had a successful trade that winter, as buffalo was very plenty, and fat. William Bent lived in a tepee, or lodge, with his wife, a full-blood Cheyenne and a most excellent good woman. She was the daughter of a Cheyenne chief or brave that had been killed in some of the fights with some tribes that they

were at war with. Her mother was living in this village also, but in a separate lodge. . . .

The old chief, "Cinemo," had the largest lodge or tepee in the village and tendered the use of one-half of it to William Bent, to keep the goods in that we had brought down from the Fort, and we received the buffalo robes as fast as they were dressed, and gave them goods. The Cheyenne village was located, for the fall and winter of 1844, to surround and kill buffalo and make dress robes for the trade of the Fort at the request of William Bent.[50]

In exchange for the buffalo hides that women of the encampment stretched and dried, Boggs added, the villagers received a rich assortment of trade goods, including "red cloth, beads, tobacco, brass wire for bracelets, hoop iron for arrow points, butcher knives, small axes or tomahawks, vermilion, powder and bullets."[51] The manufactured items came by caravan from Missouri, but the company also offered the Cheyennes such traditional Indian trade goods as Navajo blankets and seashells. One abalone shell might be worth as many as four buffalo robes, Boggs observed, and served to adorn the ears and garments of the villagers:

> Their dresses were made of antelope or deer skins, dressed, and were neatly fringed and trimmed around with beads and fragments of these shells or ante-lope hoofs, all polished. Their moccasins were of the most beautiful make and were highly ornamented with various colored beads and colored porcupine quills, that were worked in various shapes, of ornamental patterns, according to their taste, and with a Navajo blanket and their faces tinged with vermilion, the young squaw or girl presented a very neat appearance.[52]

Cheyennes felt much enhanced by the many useful and alluring items they received through this trade, and they repaid the men who offered those goods in more ways than one. On one occasion that winter, Boggs recalled, William Bent was suffering from a severe cold that so clogged his throat that he could consume no other food than broth, fed to him by his wife through a quill. An Indian doctor named Lawyer cleared his congestion by forcing burrs that were coated with marrow fat and threaded on braided sinew down his throat. Bent later told Boggs that he "certainly would have died if that Indian had not come to his relief and saved his life."[53]

Another visitor who stopped at Bent's Fort a short time later offered fur-ther testimony to the attractions of the outpost and its goods for the Chey-ennes, although he also saw signs that the trade might be taking a toll on tribal morale. In the summer of 1845, Lieutenant James W. Abert of the Topo-graphical Engineers stopped at Bent's Fort before embarking on a military reconnaissance of the Southwest that infringed on Mexican territory. Abert took the opportunity at the fort to observe and sketch what he called "wild Indians," as opposed to those who lived around "settlements."[54] In fact, Bent's Fort resembled a small settlement in its effect on the Indians who traded there. As Abert noted, however, the Cheyennes who frequented the outpost persisted in many of their traditional activities, including raids on tribal enemies. On August 7, he wrote in his journal, a large party of Cheyennes approached the fort and proceeded to celebrate a recent victory in rousing fashion:

> They were all, both men and women, mounted astride of their horses, and came galloping up abreast, singing a song of triumph in honor of the success of a war party which had just returned with a Pawnee scalp. Their song was accompanied by the music of four tambourines, and all the sounds seemed jerked out by the motion of the horses, which galloped in perfect time. They then collected around the fort, and we had a fine opportunity of observing them. The successful warrior and his relatives were covered with black paint; he was called "Little Crow," or "O-co-chee-ta-nah-hun." In the afternoon I was kindly invited by the gentlemen of the fort to see a scalp dance. On going up I found about forty women, with faces painted red and black, nearly all cloaked with "Navahoe" blankets and ornamented with necklaces and ear rings, dancing to the sound of their own voices and the four tambourines, which were beat upon by the men. I was informed that the songs were in honor of those who had distinguished themselves, holding them up for imitation, and deriding one whose behaviour had called his courage in question. In dancing they made a succession of jumps, in which the feet were raised but little from the ground. When they first commenced, they were placed shoulder to shoulder on different sides of a square; they then moved forwards towards the centre, raising a yell resembling the war whoop; they then dispersed and retook their stations, in order to repeat the same movements; some had lances, some war clubs, whilst the mother of "Little Crow" had the honor of bearing the scalp. I never in my life saw a happier set. The women laughed and jumped in rapturous delight, whilst their husbands and lovers were grouped around on the roofs of the fort, looking on most complacently. Again the figure of the dance was changed; the dancers placed in one continuous ring move slowly round. I happened to be near the press for packing furs, in the centre of the square, and had a fine opportunity for taking sketches.[55]

This fervent scalp dance demonstrated dramatically the extent to which the Cheyennes and their customs found accommodation at Bent's Fort. Evidently, the dancers felt that to have the fort's occupants witness the ceremony along with their fellow tribespeople was to validate the coup; otherwise, they might have kept the ritual to themselves.

In a similar fashion, Cheyennes in and around the fort welcomed being portrayed by Abert, so long as he honored them with a faithful likeness. One chief expressed dissatisfaction with the preliminary sketch Abert did of him, only to be reassured by the artist that the final portrait would bring him to completion. Abert's Indian models were proud of their finery—some of which, like the beads that adorned their garments, came to them through trade with whites—and they recognized that his work was a further tribute to them from the white world. One of the subjects who impressed him most was a Cheyenne woman married to a white man (this was probably William Bent's wife, Owl Woman). She seemed in his eyes to represent an elusive ideal—the Indian modified and softened by civilization but still possessed of native charms:

> Having a white man for her husband, she has not been obliged to work, therefore her hands are in all their native beauty, small, delicately formed, and with tapering fingers; her wavy hair, unlike the Indians' generally, was fine and of silken softness. She put on her handsomest dress in order to sit for me. Her cape and under garment were bordered with bands of beads, and her beautiful leggins, which extended only to the knee, were so nicely joined with the moccasin that the connexion could not be perceived, and looked as neat as the stockings of our eastern belles.[56]

This Cheyenne "belle," who admittedly led an easier life than most Indian women who became wives of white men on the frontier, seemed to advertise the material benefits that came to her people through dealings with whites. Even those women who married within the tribe and continued to toil at their traditional occupations had access through trade to new tools and ornaments that lightened some of their tasks and embellished their costume. Men, too, felt the powerful allure of trade goods and used them in sundry ways to enhance their personal charms and sharpen their skills as hunters and warriors. But such acquisitions came at a cost that mounted over the years. One Cheyenne chief whose words Abert recorded suggested that his people might be losing more than they gained from their seemingly harmonious intercourse with whites. The speaker, named Old Bark, expressed those sentiments in peace talks at the fort between the Cheyennes and rival Delawares, a displaced tribal group from the eastern woodlands that furnished scouts and hunters for various army expeditions and trading companies crossing the plains. In 1844, Cheyennes had joined in an attack that left fifteen Delawares dead, and Old Bark now sought to assure their aggrieved representatives at Bent's Fort that his tribe was in no condition to prosecute a war and longed for peace:

We have been in great dread lest you should make war upon us, and, although our women and children have been suffering for food, were afraid to venture forth, for we are now weak and poor, and our ground diminished to a small circle. The whites have been amongst us, and destroyed our buffalo, antelope, and deer, and have cut down our timber; but we are so desirous to keep peaceful that we take no notice of it, for we regard the Delawares and whites as one people.[57]

Perhaps Old Bark exaggerated the plight of his people somewhat to arouse the sympathy of the Delawares and mute their anger, but in councils as in victory celebrations, there were limits to how far a speaker could stretch the truth without being ridiculed and rejected. Old Bark was evidently speaking from the heart about unsettling changes that befell the Cheyennes at least in part because of their proximity to whites. The cottonwood groves along the Arkansas offered an abundant but not unlimited supply of timber, and the caravans that stopped and kindled fires there were evidently diminishing that resource. And despite William Boggs's observation that buffalo were "very plenty" near the Big Timbers in late 1844, Old Bark was not the only one to complain that game was growing scarce in the area. In the spring of 1844, mountain man Solomon Sublette wrote from the fort that if "Bufalo do not come in more plentifully than they have been for the last year it will be starving times."[58] Conceivably, increased hunting in recent years by travelers, hunters from the fort, and Indians seeking hides to offer there had reduced the herds locally or scared them away. If Cheyennes ranged farther afield in pursuit of game, they risked running afoul of rival tribes. Old Bark's reference to their ground being "diminished to a small circle" aptly described the situation of tribal groups that gravitated toward trading centers like Bent's Fort and found their universe shrinking.

In late 1846, another discerning visitor reached Bent's Fort and spent time among the Cheyennes camped in the vicinity—young Lewis Garrard, who arrived from Missouri around the first of November with a company caravan led by Ceran St. Vrain. The war with Mexico was well under way, and Garrard and others at the fort would soon be caught up peripherally in that conflict. But his journey as far as Bent's Fort differed little from the trips made by his predecessors before the war began. The men in his party feared hostility from Indians, not Mexicans. In fact, Garrard's party included Mexicans, among them the expert muleteer Blas, who on one occasion retrieved Garrard's runaway horse Paint, "for which service I gave him *dos pesos* (two dollars) and *muy gracias* (many thanks)."[59] Attached to the company unofficially, Garrard visited Cheyenne encampments near the fort for extended periods and took part in the trading there. In the process, he caught glimpses of the problems attested to by Old Bark. On one occasion, a small party of company men that included Garrard and John Simpson Smith—an accomplished mountain man with a Cheyenne wife—encountered a band of thirty or so Arapahos returning from a raid into New Mexico. The leader of the band seemed ill-inclined to shake hands with them, and they asked the Arapaho what the problem was in the language of his Cheyenne allies:

> *Ten-o-wast?* "What is it you wish?"
> He looked silently at us, and again we chidingly asked, in the Cheyenne tongue, "Ten-o-wast?"
> *Ni-hi-ni, veheo, matsebo, esevone Arapaho,* answered he. The amount of his answer was, that the "whiteman was bad, that he ran the buffalo out of the country, and starved the Arapaho."
> Smith explained, that he had been trading a long time with the Cheyenne, whom he loved, and who was brother to the Arapaho; that he only took what meat he wanted, and, pointing to his squaw, that his wife was a Cheyenne. The Arapaho must not blame him. It was the whiteman from the States (Government men) with wagons, who scared the buffalo from him and his children. It was always his intention to live and die with the Cheyenne, for he had thrown away his brothers in the States. The Cheyenne lodge was his home— they smoked the same pipe—the broad prairie supported them both.
> "The whiteman has a forked tongue," replied the chief, impatiently, raising his hand to his mouth, and sending it in a direct line with two of the fingers open, and stretched far apart, to signify a fork or divergence.[60]

As Smith indicated, the government troops and wagons bound for Mexico in recent months to support the war effort there may indeed have scattered herds and exacerbated the problem that Old Bark had complained of more than a year earlier. But the fur trade that Smith was involved in may also have contributed to the apparent scarcity of game. Try as they might, neither Smith nor others who trafficked with Indians around Bent's Fort could disclaim responsibility for the troubles that beset their trading partners. Smith was seemingly sincere, however, in his claim that he felt closer to the Cheyennes than to his discarded "brothers in the States." Like William Bent, he was bound to the Cheyennes by marriage and could not easily separate the tribe's prospects from his own. The trade around Bent's Fort was not a simple matter of whites profiting at the expense of Indians—if only because the lines between the two sides had been blurred by an intimate pattern of exchange that went far beyond the transfer of goods. Perhaps there was something two-sided about Smith, as the Arapaho implied with the forked-tongue signal.

After all, he had one foot in the white man's camp and another in the Indian's. But then so did many Cheyennes around the fort who welcomed the traders and shared quarters with them.

Garrard himself harbored kindred feelings for his Cheyenne hosts, sentiments that clashed with his lingering revulsion for a tribal way of life that seemed utterly alien to his own upbringing. A chief named Mah-ke-o-nih, or "Big Wolf," who was in mourning for a lost relative, took a liking to Garrard and bestowed his name on him, an informal kind of adoption that gave him a certain standing within the tribe (although Cheyennes also called him Veheo-kiss, or "Young Whiteman"). At times he fancied himself a young brave and felt that he had joined a select company. "I thought, with envy, of the free and happy life they were leading on the untamed plains, with fat buffalo for food, fine horses to ride, living and dying in a state of blissful ignorance," he wrote of the Cheyennes early on.[61] Yet he later portrayed their unfettered existence in a much harsher light: "It seems strange that these people remain the same untutored, blood-thirsty savages as ever; and so untamable are their natures, that contact with missionaries and white men, make them only the greater demons."[62] So deeply ingrained were such biases that they persisted even in a conscientious observer like Garrard, who witnessed and reported various ways in which these supposedly "untutored" and "untamable" Indians subjected themselves and their children to rigorous discipline. To be sure, Garrard also saw them give vent to their demons on occasion, as when under the influence of alcohol, but in that case their contact with whites was not a lost opportunity, as he implied, but a singular misfortune. Garrard confessed that he and others from the company took to offering the Cheyennes liquor after some competing traders did the same, but he expressed no remorse. To the contrary, he reacted with lofty contempt when two drunken Cheyenne women, after a noisy all-night revel, tumbled laughing and weeping into the lodge he was sharing with his fellow traders:

> We finally succeeded in making them vacate the premises, by dint of threats and persuasion, though sleep was chased effectually, for the time, from our eyelids. There are two objects most repugnant to my feelings—a drunken or an angry woman. She seems to descend from the position of a ministering angel, down, down below any scale of degradation conceivable; and imprints such a hideous image of contorted passion, which, notwithstanding the subsequent blandishments of grace and smiles, can never be effaced from the memory.[63]

Garrard's sojourn in and around Bent's Fort brought him in contact with many such fallen angels, and they were not all women or Indians. The mountain men he consorted with seemed to him, in many ways, lost souls:

My companions were rough men—used to the hardships of a mountaineer's life—whose manners are blunt, and whose speech is rude—men driven to the western wilds, with embittered feelings—with better natures shattered—with hopes blasted—to seek, in the dangers of the warpath, fierce excitement and banishment of care. The winter snow wreaths drift over them unheeded, and the nightwind, howling around their lonely camp, is heard with calm indifference. Yet these aliens from society, these strangers to the refinements of civilized life, who will tear off a bloody scalp with even grim smiles of satisfaction, are fine fellows, full of fun, and often kind and obliging.[64]

Garrard's capacity to fathom his companions' cruel desperation as well as their dignity—to encompass in one passage the baffling contradictions in their character—was truly remarkable in one so young. His appreciation for his Indian hosts was not as comprehensive and tended to veer back and forth between admiration and contempt, yet for all his misgivings and misperceptions he had a rare ability to suspend judgment and enter into the spirit of tribal life. The women and girls he met with among the Cheyennes may not have lived up to his high ideal of ministering angels, but they lavished him with kind attentions and he often obliged them by dropping any pretense of superiority and joining freely in their ceremonies: "The trader is treated with much respect by the Indians, and is considered a chief—a great man. To retain this respect, he acts with as much dignity as the circumstances permit. Caring for none of the trader's assumed reservedness, I danced with the squaws, mixed in the gayeties, and, in everyway, improved my time."[65]

It might be said that this in itself was an improvement over the way in which Matt Field and his hosts improved their time at Bent's Fort—by telling of their harrowing run-ins with Indians. Garrard entered into the dance and offered the Cheyennes not just blankets or beads but personal tribute by conforming to their customs. Such recognition knit together the diverse elements that congregated in and around the fort and lent to their exchanges an element of grace and spontaneity. The fort's employees made a similar concession when they danced at their evening revels with the black cook Charlotte, acknowledging thereby that she was not merely a slave but the hostess of the establishment and a valued figure in her own right: "The grand center of attraction, the belle of the evening, she treated the suitors for the 'pleasure of the next set,' with becoming ease and suavity of manner. She knew her worth, and managed accordingly; and, when the favored gallant stood by her side, waiting for the rudely-scraped tune, from a screaking violin, satisfaction, joy, and triumph, over his rivals, were pictured on his radiant face."[66]

Such cordial moments could not abolish the distinctions that persisted here. Eventually, the music stopped and the parties returned to their corners. For all its congeniality, Bent's Fort remained a company outpost, with a well-defined hierarchy that placed the owners and their honored guests far above the slaves and hired hands. Trusted employees like Alexander Barclay occupied an intermediate position between the bosses and those who performed menial tasks for low wages or no wages, but even Barclay felt ill at ease with the fort's proprietors. "Here I forego all kind of reciprocal society," he wrote his brother, adding that the hired hands were "of the most uneducated and reckless class and there is something which I cannot explain, a sort of restraint which prevents the full social enjoyment with those who, from their position in life, have the power of controul over us, even though by education and general information we may be satisfied with our own superiority."[67] The distance that separated Barclay from the owners was slight, however, compared to the gulf between the better-paid employees and the Mexicans who toiled there. Their lowly position in the hierarchy was spelled out in disparaging terms by an anonymous correspondent who filed a dispatch from the fort in the spring of 1846:

> The company keep a large stock of cattle, employing Mexicans to herd them. These men can be had for from six to eight dollars per month, payable in goods, at an advance, on an average, of five hundred per cent. They are good workers, and attentive to their business, which is all that can be said in their favor. To show you how very choice they are in names, I will introduce you to Maria Jesus Arriano, our cow-herd; a more sinister-looking, dirty scamp you could never wish to meet with. They are all a poor, cowardly, despicable, thievish, gambling set—but little removed from the Indian, and only fit to drudge, break wild horses and mules, and herd cattle and sheep in this world, and be ———— in the next; which latter fate inevitably awaits them, unless they speedily reform, of which, at present, there are no hopes.[68]

Garrard was not immune to such arrogance, but he was less inclined than most observers to deprecate Mexicans or Indians, if only because he himself was "but little removed from the Indian" at this point in his odyssey. He saw signs of trouble on the horizon for the fort's owners and their trading partners, but the exchanges he witnessed and took part in here were idyllic compared to what he would experience in the months to come. Soon, he would travel to embattled New Mexico, where Anglos and Hispanics who had once swapped goods and courtesies were now trading blows. And while returning to the States, he would serve briefly at the first military post established along the Santa Fe Trail—a grim portent of a deepening conflict between whites and Indians for control of the vital pathways across the plains and the precious resources those routes commanded.

Bent's Fort was not the only outpost along the upper Arkansas where the disparate threads of American, Mexican, and Indian cultures intertwined.[69] Travelers continuing on the Mountain Route to Santa Fe, as Matt Field did in 1839, sometimes stopped at Pueblo de Leche, or Milk Fort, located about five miles upriver from Bent's Fort on the south bank. Established and occupied largely by Mexicans, it was more of a colony than a trading post, containing "about thirty houses, of small dimensions," Field wrote, "all built compactly together in an oblong square, leaving a large space in the centre, and the houses themselves forming the wall of the fort, into which there is but one entrance, through a large and very strong gate."[70] The resident families raised some crops to supplement what they gleaned through hunting, herding, and trading with Indians. It was Field's first immersion in Mexican society, and he confessed to "some awkward sensations relative to the black-looking fellows who were around us."[71] But he had heard they were friendly and made the most of their hospitality, spending a snug night inside the fort's sealed gate along with the colony's horses and mules, which were brought in at sunset and "completely filled the corral."[72] Field's visit to Pueblo de Leche was much like Josiah Gregg's initial encounter with those *ciboleros* on the Cimarron Route—an object lesson in how Mexicans adapted to alien circumstances and accommodated rival cultures and customs.

Officially, Pueblo de Leche was in Mexican territory, but Mexico exercised no more authority on the south side of the Arkansas here than the United States did on the north side. Travelers bound for Taos, Santa Fe, or other settlements still had to traverse what was in effect a no-man's-land before they reached Raton Pass, the true threshold to New Mexico. Most followed a path that took them southwestward along Timpas Creek, which was often dry with the welcome exception of Hole-in-the-Rock, a popular watering spot at the head of the Timpas. From there, they proceeded across the desert before fording the Purgatoire River, fed by snowmelt from the Rockies, and following that waterway to the base of Raton Pass. The Santa Fe Trail featured many a dramatic transition—from woodlands to prairie, from prairie to plains, and from plains to desert below the Arkansas. But this climactic passage up through the mountains and down into the Mexican mesaland was the most poignant transformation for westbound travelers because it came after a long, hard journey and took them across a frontier that was both geographical and cultural. James Abert waxed poetic when he and the men of his reconnaissance headed up Raton Pass in late August of 1845 alongside the clear, rushing waters of Raton Fork, a tributary of the Purgatoire:

Our road now became exceedingly rough, leading along a tortuous valley, sometimes passing on one side of the Raton fork, sometimes on the other, whilst occasionally the narrowness of the banks forced us to seek a passage in the rocky bed of the creek itself. Travelling in the deep ravine of a mountain stream, our horses' feet splashed in its cool waters, so tempting, that the ferns bent forward to lave their dark fronds in the limpid stream. Luxuriant vines, and trees of healthiest green, formed arbors for our heads. It appeared like passing through tunnels formed by the goddess Flora, and we looked around as if expecting to see the Naiads of the Purgatory spring from some nook in the moss-covered banks. We were almost wild with excitement. Having suffered so much from drinking the nauseous salt-water of the plains, we could have wished for the days of the metamorphosis, and prayed to be changed into one of these cool mountain streams.[73]

Raton Pass was indeed a place of metamorphosis, or transformation, one that harbored perils for travelers as well as the prospect of renewal. Up near the crest of the pass, Abert saw the debris of wagons that had come to grief on the steep, rocky trail. And hunters who went off from their encampments at day's end in pursuit of elk or deer risked running afoul of the formidable grizzly bear, a former denizen of the high plains that had retreated in recent times up into mountainous country. Dick Wootton, an habitué of Raton Pass who later improved the trail here into a serviceable toll road for wagons, once fired an errant shot at a mother bear and escaped being mauled only scrambling up a pine tree. But he took issue with the notion that the grizzly was a man-killer by nature: "That he has been guilty now and then of staining his 'chops' with human gore is true, but it was usually under circumstances which would have made 'justifiable homicide' a proper verdict, if the affair had been between man and man."[74]

The rigors of Raton Pass failed to deflate the buoyant spirits of travelers as they left the dusty plains behind and ascended the forested slopes amid the majestic prospect of the Spanish Peaks, known to Utes as Wah-to-ya, or the "Breasts of the World." For Matt Field, the metamorphosis began a bit earlier in the journey when he crossed the Purgatoire. (More prosaic travelers called this river the "picketwire," but the imaginative Field referred to it as the Styx.) He and his companions immersed themselves gratefully in its cool waters, like lost souls who had served their time in limbo and seemed destined for a better place:

We footed up our accounts with fortune and chuckled with the thought that the balance of enjoyment was in our favor. There we were, a set of reckless, aimless wanderers, floundering in the river Styx, as happy a set of care-for-naughts as ever drank rapture from the eye of beauty or the bowl of Bacchus.

A long, striped snake glided past us in the water, and slipped in among the flowers upon the green bank. So poison is ever creeping through the regions of delight, watching a chance to sting.[75]

Field amplified on this evocative theme of promise mingled with peril in his account of Raton Pass and a noontime idyll he spent there with his party by the rushing stream:

The whole scene was a most admirable mingling of the lovely with the wild and terrible. Splintered and rifted trees and tottering rocks above, hung beetling over the ravine, while, like a very laughing child sporting unconsciously near some object of fear, the bright little stream danced gaily over the pebbles. Huge stones were lying around, from whose forms we could trace the gaps above from whence they had fallen. Dark and tangled thickets were near, where hung the berries sought for food by the grizzly bear. Like the lion and the lamb lying down together seemed this singularly fascinating yet unsafe retreat. We thought of paradise, where woman and the snake, man's best good and greatest ill, breathed the same air together.[76]

In such probing passages, Field came as close as any early traveler on the trail to encompassing the journey in all its conflicting possibilities. Here, as in his account of crossing the Purgatoire, he conveyed both the bright hope of gain and the brooding sense of loss that attended this fateful transition from one world to the next. Like all those on long and perilous pilgrimages, travelers bound for Santa Fe hoped to achieve redemption at the end of the trail, if only in financial terms. But as Matt Field emphasized here, those who crossed frontiers in search of fulfillment were as likely to find perdition as paradise. Indeed, to enter paradise and taste its charms was to know evil as well as good and lose forever the innocent hope of being made anew.

These were not idle theological musings on Field's part. They were, rather, the logical extension of a theme he explored time and again in his articles—the thin line separating soft appearances from harsh realities, the civilized man from the savage, the lover of nature from the avid hunter and killer, the pilgrim bound for a better place from the lost soul drifting in the wilderness. Field was pondering questions that, in one form or another, concerned all travelers on the trail as they neared their goal. Would the evil spirits that haunted them on their taxing journey across the plains, whether in the guise of "red devils" in the distance or demons within, be banished by the cleansing waters of the Purgatoire and the rarefied air of Raton Pass, leaving these weary pilgrims fit to reap their due rewards in Santa Fe, the city of Holy Faith and resurrected fortunes? Or would they instead be lost irretrievably on the far side of the divide and end up like Field's tortured traveling companion on the steamboat, "wandering forever like a thing accursed," outcasts from their people, their kin, and their God? Field seemed to sense prophetically that the road to Santa Fe harbored both prospects for his countrymen, beckoning them to a place of beauty and peril where their "best good and greatest ill" lay intertwined, an apt description of the tangled American affair with New Mexico.

If Field suspected that this journey promised travelers as much disillusionment as delight, he was no less impatient to reach the land beyond and see for himself. Like other adventurers who paused at this lovely and fearful pass to ponder what lay in store for them, he relished the sense of standing at the threshold of something grand and indeterminate—and forged eagerly ahead.

13

Coming into New Mexico

B y whichever path they approached it, Americans coming fresh to New Mexico discovered that the challenges of their journey were far from over when they reached the settlements. For all the hardships they endured while crossing the plains, untutored travelers found few obstacles on the journey more perplexing than the cultural divide between the Anglo and Hispanic worlds. It was not that the two sides were constantly at odds. But even as Americans traded with Mexicans and enjoyed their hospitality, they often expressed puzzlement and exasperation at their customs and habits. That mixture of cordiality with cultural bias, or sheer bewilderment, was evident from the start in the reports of the Americans who inaugurated trade on the Santa Fe Trail. William Becknell, in his edited account of his pioneering trading expedition to New Mexico in 1821, wrote of the friendly troops he and his party encountered that November near the town of San Miguel del Vado—located on the Pecos River southeast of Santa Fe and destined to become a port of entry for visiting Americans—with affectionate gratitude, tinged with a measure of disapproval:

> On Tuesday morning the 13th, we had the satisfaction of meeting with a party of Spanish troops. Although the difference of our language would not admit of conversation, yet the circumstances attending their reception of us, fully convinced us of their hospitable disposition and friendly feelings. Being likewise in a strange country, and subject to their disposition, our wishes lent their aid to increase our confidence in their manifestations of kindness. The

discipline of the officers was strict, and the subjection of the men appeared almost servile.[1]

In another context, such deference to one's superiors might have been seen as a sign of good military discipline. But Becknell, like many later American visitors, looked askance at the powers high-ranking Mexicans exercised over their inferiors. The troops he encountered were mostly recent recruits from various towns and pueblos in northern New Mexico under the command of Captain Pedro Ignacio Gallego, who wrote in his diary of encountering "six Americans" and attempting to parley with them, although he could understand neither "their words nor any of the signs they made."[2] Gallego and company were on their way to patrol for hostile Comanches, whose raids had increased recently as the struggle for Mexican independence interrupted gift-giving and other diplomatic gestures and undermined the long-standing truce between Comanches and the settlers. Officers leading such nerve-racking forays had good reason to keep their men under strict control.

Becknell was fortunate in arriving with his party as Mexican officials were severing ties with Spain and seeking better relations with the United States, and he was well received in Santa Fe by Governor Facundo Melgares. Overall, Becknell was inclined to blame the problems he perceived there less on the obliging New Mexicans themselves than on the inherent backwardness of their country and culture:

> The next day, after crossing a mountain country, we arrived at SANTA FE and were received with apparent pleasure and joy. It is situated in a valley of the mountains, on a branch of the Rio del Norte or North river, and some twenty miles from it. It is the seat of government of the province; is about two miles long and one mile wide, and compactly settled. The day after my arrival I accepted an invitation to visit the Governor [Facundo Melgares], whom I found to be well informed and gentlemanly in manners; his demeanor was courteous and friendly. He asked many questions concerning my country, its people, their manner of living, etc.; expressed a desire that the Americans would keep up an intercourse with that country, and said that if any of them wished to emigrate, it would give him pleasure to afford them every facility. The people are generally swarthy, and live in a state of extreme indolence and ignorance. Their mechanical improvements are very limited, and they appear to know little of the benefit of industry, or the advantage of the arts.[3]

In fact, New Mexicans applied themselves energetically to their chosen occupations, notably the cultivation of irrigated fields along rivers and streams and the herding of cattle and sheep, whose wool they wove into coarse cloth.

Becknell was not alone, however, in noting the lack of "industry," or mechanical arts, in New Mexico. Antonio Barreiro, a Mexican lawyer who arrived in Santa Fe from the south a decade after Becknell, reported that such arts were "in the worst state imaginable." Those who worked as carpenters, blacksmiths, and gunsmiths and at other skilled trades in the settlements were largely Anglo-Americans, he added, "and doubtless we must look to them to improve the arts in New Mexico."[4] Notwithstanding such openings for skilled workers, the greatest opportunity here for venturesome Americans came from the steep prices that prevailed in New Mexican markets for fine fabrics and other imports. The locals resented having to pay high prices for the sometimes inferior merchandise that reached them from Chihuahua and more distant parts of Mexico. And they were glad to traffic with Americans, so long as the newcomers obliged them with worthy offerings. After his first visit, Becknell returned to New Mexico in 1822 with three wagons full of cloth and other goods—the first such wagon train to ply the Santa Fe Trail—and he later offered sound advice to all those who hoped to follow in his path and profit as he did:

> Those who visit the country for the purpose of vending merchandise will do well to take goods of excellent quality and unfaded colors. An idea prevails among the people there, which is certainly a very just one, that the goods hitherto imported into their country, were the remains of old stock, and sometimes damaged. A very great advance is obtained on goods, and the trade is very profitable; money and mules are plentiful, and they do not hesitate to pay the price demanded for an article if it suits their purpose, or their fancy.[5]

After complimenting New Mexicans on their commercial sense, Becknell felt compelled to add that their system of government remained "very arbitrary" and that the lingering effects of despotism were painfully evident in "the servility of the lower orders to the wealthy." There were indeed many people in New Mexico who had to defer to their masters as servants or peons, but visitors from Missouri and other slaveholding states had little reason to feel morally superior to Mexicans in that regard.

Becknell's view of New Mexico was positively idyllic compared to the portrait offered by Thomas James, who took a more southerly route west than Becknell did in 1821 and reached Santa Fe perhaps two weeks later. Although he was not a pioneer of the Santa Fe Trail, James helped to inaugurate the Santa Fe trade and later offered a detailed if highly subjective account of conditions in New Mexico at the time it opened its doors to Americans. He found Santa Fe itself, with its whitewashed adobe houses, "a very neat and pleasing sight to the eye,"[6] but he had few kind words for its inhabitants, who, among their other faults, were short of cash to offer for the goods he hauled to New Mexico across the southern plains at great trouble and expense (including exorbitant "presents" to imposing Comanches). James summed up his bleak impressions of the populace in a memoir he dictated roughly a quarter century later, around the time of the Mexican War, to Nathaniel Niles, who may have cleaned up the narrator's prose but evidently made no attempt to sanitize his opinions: "I continued my trading, though without much success on account of the scarcity of money. I had seen enough of Mexican society to be thoroughly disgusted with it. I had not supposed it possible for any society to be as profligate and vicious as I found all ranks of that in Santa Fé. The Indians are much superior to their Spanish masters in all qualities of a useful and meritorious population."[7]

Throughout his account of his visit to Santa Fe, James would elaborate on this theme of the inferiority of the Spanish settlers to the native peoples of the region. A month or so after he arrived, the inhabitants of the capital staged a festival to mark their newly won independence. James claimed credit for showing them how to observe the occasion in proper American fashion by raising a liberty pole, hoisting a flag, and firing a salute for each state or province. He had nothing to teach them, however, when it came to celebrating their freedom:

As the flag went up, the cannon fired and men and women from all quarters of the city came running, some half dressed, to the public square, which was soon filled with the population of this city. The people of the surrounding country also came in, and for five days the square was covered with Spaniards and Indians from every part of the province. During this whole time the city exhibited a scene of universal carousing and revelry. All classes abandoned themselves to the most reckless dissipation and profligacy. No Italian carnival ever exceeded this celebration in thoughtlessness, vice and licentiousness of every description. Men, women and children crowded every part of the city, and the carousal was kept up equally by night and day. There seemed to be no time for sleep. Tables for gambling surrounded the square and continually occupied the attention of crowds. Dice and faro banks were all the time in constant play. I never saw any people so infatuated with the passion for gaming. Women of rank were seen betting at the faro banks and dice tables. They frequently lost all their money; then followed the jewelry from their fingers, arms and ears: then the ribose or sash edged with gold, which they wear over the shoulders, was staked and lost, when the fair gamesters would go to their homes for money to redeem the last pledge and if possible, continue the play. Men and women on all sides of me were thus engaged, and were all equally absorbed in the fluctuating fortunes of these games. The demon of chance and of avarice seemed to possess them all, to the loss of what little reason nature had originally made theirs. One universal jubilee, like bedlam broke loose, reigned in Santa Fé for five days and nights. Freedom without restraint or license was the order of the day; and thus did these rejoicing republicans continue the celebration of their Independence till nature was too much exhausted to support the dissipation any longer. The crowds then dispersed to their homes with all the punishments of excess with which pleasure visits her votaries. I saw enough during this five days' revelry to convince me that the republicans of New Mexico were unfit to govern themselves or anybody else. The Indians acted with more moderation and reason in their rejoicing than the Spaniards.[8]

The truth of the matter probably lay somewhere between this scathing account by James and the glowing report on the festivities written for the official government newspaper in Mexico City by Governor Melgares, who portrayed the celebration as profligate only in its outbursts of patriotism. Melgares, like others in remote Santa Fe, had learned of the revolution in Mexico City belatedly and reacted to the news cautiously, and he may have been attempting in this article to allay any concerns among his superiors about his own loyalty and that of the territory he governed. The crowd surged through the streets "singing sweet hymns of thanksgiving," he reported, and the ball held that night for "all persons of distinction" was well choreographed to suit the patriotic occasion:

> The fair sex attended wearing skirts of sky blue, and green laurels worn across the breast like a sash, with white letters reading "Long live the Independence of the Mexican Empire." The floor of the hall was pleasingly adorned. The refreshment was served with the lavishness required by so large an attendance. And the entertainment ended at four-thirty in the morning as merrily as it had begun at eight in the evening.[9]

A dance like this one that went on late into the night was neither unusual nor unseemly in Santa Fe, but Melgares made a point of vouching for its propriety. "Moderation prevailed so powerfully throughout these events," he insisted, "that both men and women decidedly proclaimed the sanctity of our cause." One point on which Melgares and James agreed in their accounts was that Pueblos from the surrounding area honored the occasion by performing dances. While Melgares described the dancing simply as "splendid," however, James elaborated on the performance by groups from the Pueblos of San Felipe and Pecos (or "Peccas," as he put it) and drew a sharp contrast between

their grace and nobility and the deficiencies of their Spanish "masters," a deceptive term for the less-than-absolute authority that New Mexican officials exercised over the Pueblos:

> On the second day of the celebration a large company of men and women
> from San Felipe, an Indian town forty miles south of Santa Fé, marched into
> the city, displaying the best-formed persons I had yet seen in the country.
> The men were a head taller than the Spaniards around them, and their
> women were extremely beautiful, with fine figure and a graceful, elegant car-
> riage. They were all tastefully dressed in cotton cloth of their own weaving
> and decorated with coral beads of a brilliant red color. Many wore rich pearl
> necklaces and jewelry of great value. . . .
>
> This Indian company danced very gracefully upon the public square to
> the sound of a drum and the singing of the older members of their band. In
> this exercise they displayed great skill and dexterity. When intermingled in
> apparently hopeless confusion in a very complicated figure, so that the dance
> seemed on the point of breaking up, suddenly at the tap of the drum, each
> found his partner and each couple their place, without the least disorder and
> in admirable harmony. About the same time the Peccas Indians came into
> the city, dressed in skins of bulls and bears. At a distance their disguise was
> quite successful and they looked like the animals which they counterfeited so
> well that the people fled frightened at their appearance, in great confusion
> from the square.
>
> I have spoken before, in favorable terms of the Mexican Indians. They are
> a nobler race of people than their masters, the descendants of the conquerors;
> more courageous and more generous; more faithful to their word and more
> ingenious and intellectual than the Spaniards. The men are generally six feet
> in stature, well formed and of an open, frank and manly deportment. Their
> women are very fascinating, and far superior in virtue, as in beauty, to the
> greater number of the Spanish females.[10]

Even the Comanches and Utes, or Utahs—tribes with warlike reputations—fared
significantly better in James's account than did the maligned "Spaniards," or
Mexicans. He described a visit to Santa Fe early in 1822 by the Comanche chief
he called Cordaro—referred to properly in other accounts as Cordero—who had
befriended and protected James during his journey to New Mexico and who
now invited the Americans to visit his people and trade with them. "Come with
your goods among us; you shall be well treated," he declared according to James,
"I pledge you my word, the word of Cordaro, that you shall not be hurt nor
your goods taken from you without full payment." James went on to contrast
the chief's sense of honor to the deviousness of the Mexicans:

The old warrior spoke like an orator and looked like a statesman. He appeared conscious of the vast superiority of the whites, or rather of the Americans, to his own race and desired the elevation of his countrymen by adopting some of our improvements and customs. For the Spaniards he entertained a strong aversion and dislike; not at all mingled with fear, however, for he spoke to them always as an equal or superior. They refused to trade with his nation in arms and had nothing besides which his people wanted. Their remarkable disposition to treachery appeared to be perfectly known to the old chieftain.[11]

James was evidently unaware that this chief had once been on excellent terms with Spaniards. Indeed, Cordero took his name from a former Spanish governor of Coahuila. Whatever caused him to turn against his erstwhile Spanish allies, he was far from typical of Comanches in acknowledging the "vast superiority" of Americans, who would never achieve an understanding with the tribe of the sort reached by Spanish colonial authorities at great effort in the late eighteenth century.

The Utes James met with in Santa Fe resembled Cordero in professing admiration and friendship for Americans and contempt for Mexicans. James paraphrased the appeal of a Ute chief named Lechat, who addressed him in fluent Spanish:

"You are Americans, we are told, and you have come from your country afar off to trade with the Spaniards. We want your trade. Come to our country with your goods. Come and trade with the Utahs. We have horses, mules and sheep, more than we want. We heard that you wanted beaver skins. The beavers in our country are eating up our corn. All our rivers are full of them. Their dams back up the water in the rivers all along their course from the mountains to the Big Water. Come over among us and you shall have as many beaver skins as you want." Turning round and pointing to the Spaniards, in most contemptuous manner and with a scornful look, he said, "What can you get from these? They have nothing to trade with you. They have nothing but a few poor horses and mules, a little puncha, and a little tola (tobacco and corn meal porridge) not fit for anybody to use. They are poor—too poor for you to trade with. Come among the Utahs if you wish to trade with profit. Look at our horses here. Have the Spaniards any such horses? No, they are too poor. Such as these we have in our country by the thousand, and also cattle, sheep and mules. These Spaniards," said he, turning and pointing his finger at them in a style of contempt which John Randolph would have envied, "what are they? What have they? They won't even give us two loads of powder and lead for a beaver skin, and for a good reason, they have not as much as they want themselves. They have nothing that you want. We have

everything that they have, and many things that they have not." Here a
Spaniard cried out, "You have no money." Like a true stump orator the Utah
replied. "And you have very little. You are *depicca*." In other words, you are
poor, miserable devils and we are the true capitalists of the country. With this
and much more of the same purport, he concluded his harangue, which was
delivered in the most independent and lordly manner possible.[12]

No doubt, the Utes and Comanches James encountered sensed the budding
rivalry between Americans and Mexicans and were trying to exploit it, much
as white traders sometimes tried to play one tribe off against another. Among
the goods the Utes and the Comanches hoped to obtain from the Americans
were guns and ammunition—rare commodities among New Mexicans, who
still relied largely on lances and bows for hunting and fighting and had laws
against trading what few firearms they possessed to Indians given to raiding
their settlements. For the most part, James seemed to accept at face value the
calculated appeals to American vanity made by cunning chiefs like Lechat and
Cordero while regarding the claims of the Mexicans with deep skepticism. He
even portrayed the remorseless conflict between New Mexicans and Navajos—
marked by bloody provocations and reprisals on both sides—as one that Mexican authorities might perhaps have resolved with a little Christian forbearance:

> What was the immediate cause of this war, I did not learn, but I saw and
> heard enough of it to enlist my sympathies with the Navahoes. A few days
> after the visit of the Utahs, I saw a solitary Indian of that tribe crossing the
> public square in the direction of the Governor's house, and driving before
> him a fat heifer. He went up to the Governor's door, to whom he sent word
> that he had a present for him, and was admitted. What followed, I learned
> from Ortise, an old Alcalde, with whom I boarded during the time of my
> stay in Santa Fé. As he entered the room of the Governor the Navaho pros-
> trated himself on his face. The Governor stepped towards him and with a
> spurning motion of the foot which touched the Indian's head, asked him
> who he was and what he wanted. The poor Indian arose on his knees and
> said he was a Navaho, and had come to implore peace for his nation. "We
> are tired of war and we want peace," said he; "our crops are destroyed, our
> women and children are starving. Oh! give us peace!" The Governor asked
> the interpreter what he said, and being told, the *christian* replied, "Tell him
> I do not want peace, I want war." With this answer the Indian was dismissed,
> the Governor keeping his heifer. The poor fellow came to my store, announced
> his name and nation, and requested me to go among his tribe and trade. He
> said the rivers were full of beaver and beaver dams—that they had horses and
> mules which they would exchange for powder, lead and tobacco. The Indians

are destitute of ammunition and guns, and Spanish laws prohibit all trade with them in these articles. I gave him several plugs of tobacco, a knife and other small articles, and told him when he went back to his country to smoke my tobacco with his chiefs and tell them if any Americans came to their country to treat them like brothers. He went off with a guard as far as the outposts on the route to his country. But I have no doubt he was murdered by the Spaniards long before reaching his home.[13]

Implicit in James's account was the notion that Spanish pride and arrogance were perpetuating this conflict and that Americans with their sense of decency and fair play could do better. But experience would teach otherwise. The "poor fellow" who abased himself before the governor and begged for peace was hardly representative of the proud Navajo nation, whose warriors regarded the settlers and their sheep as fair game and raided them persistently and unapologetically. Far from being accepted as brothers, the Americans would ultimately inherit the hostility once reserved for Spanish settlers and would end up waging their own punishing war against the Navajos.

By the spring of 1822, James was eager to return to Missouri and managed to unload most of his remaining goods wholesale. Before leaving, however, he had a bitter confrontation with Governor Melgares in Santa Fe that deepened his distrust of Mexican authorities and foreshadowed the difficulties some other American traders would experience there with officials in years to come:

I was now ready to depart for home, having disposed or got rid, rather, of my goods and collected all my debts except one from the Governor. During the winter his Excellency had sent his Excellency's secretary to my store for some samples of cloth. The secretary after taking these with some shawls for the examination of his master, returned and purchased goods for his Excellency to the sum of eighty-three dollars and told me to charge them to his Excellency. I did so, and on the day before my departure I called at his Excellency's house and found his Excellency looking every inch a Governor, and very pompously pacing the piazza as was the custom of his Excellency. I remarked that I was going home. "Very well," said his Excellency, "you can go"; and walked on. I awaited his Excellency's return, and again remarked that I was going home; that I did not expect to return, and would be thankful for the amount of his Excellency's account with me. "I have not a dollar. The government has not paid me in ten years, and how can I pay my creditors." I offered to take two mules. "I have no more mules than I want myself," said his Excellency. With this I parted forever with Gov. Malgaris of New Mexico. Ortise told me I could not sue him, as he was "the head of the law."[14]

At that, James turned his back on Santa Fe, "perfectly content never to repeat my visit to it or any other part of the country."[15] No doubt, Mexicans were just as glad to see the last of this irascible American, who got along little better with his countrymen than he did with foreigners (his memoir was suppressed shortly after it appeared because of his scurrilous remarks about rival American traders).

Perhaps James's derogatory treatment of Hispanic New Mexico was calculated in part to appeal to American sentiment around the time of the Mexican War, when his account was published. While he may not have been the most objective of observers, however, he nonetheless bore witness to some of the genuine problems plaguing Mexico, including neglect of the remote northern territories by the central government, which did little to provide for the defense of vulnerable outposts like Santa Fe or regulate the arbitrary dealings of provincial "Excellencies." The political turmoil in Mexico City that would allow such problems to fester was evident early on when the leader of the revolution, Agustín de Iturbide, went abruptly from being a liberator to an emperor and perceived tyrant who was forced to abdicate in 1823 and executed the following year. The Mexican republic that emerged in the wake of that debacle lacked cohesion and left authorities at frontier outposts like Santa Fe largely to their own devices.[16] Such factors made coping with New Mexico as trying for some Americans as the journey that brought them there. At the same time, however, the political and economic isolation of Santa Fe from the Mexican heartland created openings for Americans that they would shrewdly exploit, first for private gain and ultimately for the enhancement and enlargement of their native country.

By the mid-1820s, Americans were venturing regularly to Santa Fe on the trail William Becknell pioneered. The trade was becoming formalized—as were the attitudes of the visitors toward their hosts. Typical was the response of M. M. Marmaduke, whose party reached Santa Fe from Missouri in the summer of 1824 after a hot and harrowing journey along the Cimarron Route. Marmaduke, later governor of Missouri, encapsulated the attractions and repulsions of Santa Fe in his journal entry for July 28:

> Santa Fe is quite a Populous place, but is built entirely of Mud houses, there being not a brick or wood house in the whole City . . . some parts of the City are tolerably regularly built, other parts very irregular—The inhabitants appear to be friendly—and some of them are very wealthy, whilst by far the greater part of them are the most wretched, poor miserable Creatures that I have ever seen—Yet they appear to me to be quite happy & contented in their

miserable Priest-ridden situation—This city is well supplied with fine water. Provisions very scarce and many—very many beggars walking the streets.[17]

American traders like Marmaduke profited by the purchases of the wealthy Mexican minority (the so-called *ricos*), yet that did not stop them from expressing dismay at the glaring disparities between rich and poor. Similarly, they often faulted Mexican officials for being arbitrary, even though such official inconsistency could work to their advantage. Shortly before reaching Santa Fe, for example, Marmaduke and others in the company heard that officials there were charging a tariff of 39 percent on imports and resolved to "make some arrangements on the Subject." A week later, he reported the results:

> Remained in Town, entered our goods, and arranged the Taxes with the Collector, who appears to me to be an astonishingly obliging man as a public officer, and proceeded to offer our goods for sale—The duty imposed by law on all traders appears to be 25 pct. which is considered exceedingly high and unreasonable and was the Cause of Considerable discontent among the Americans—who however succeeded in arranging their taxes very satisfactorily with the Collector.[18]

Perhaps what made that collector so obliging was his willingness to accept less than the official tariff on the imported goods in exchange for some sort of "gift" or consideration from the traders. Antonio Barreiro, writing in 1832, complained of scandals surrounding the collection of duties from American traders and recommended that those overseeing the process be better paid so as to "protect them from the corrupting gold of the fraudulent merchant."[19] Such illicit arrangements with local officials often served the traders' interests but left them feeling uneasy. In this and other respects, the customs of New Mexico challenged their values and assumptions. Things that many of them considered suspect or unworthy—including the Roman Catholic faith—seemed necessary and even appropriate here. As Marmaduke remarked in his journal on May 31, 1825, at the end of a ten-month stay in Santa Fe and environs:

> On my arrival in the Territory of N. Mexico I was a little astonished at the blind zeal and enthusiasm of the people, all professing the Catholic religion which I found to be the only religion tolerated in this Country, and which I do verily believe is the best religion that could possibly be established among them as they appear to live more happily under their religious yoke than any other profession I have ever known and I verily believe they die as happily as any people in this world do. The homage and adoration which they pay to their priests far surpass that, which any other religious Sect that I have any knowledge of pay their God, and is much greater than they themselves pay

to their God as all their worship of their God consists in the most unmeaning Ceremony that can possibly be conceived.[20]

Life in Santa Fe plainly did little to lessen Marmaduke's aversion to Catholicism—a common prejudice among Protestants in those days—but it nonetheless forced him to confront certain moral quandaries, including the ability of a religion he regarded as false to provide people with great solace and the capacity of the supposedly unscrupulous New Mexicans to perform acts of conspicuous kindness and charity:

> Thieving, lieing, whoring—gambling &c. in a word every vice reigns among this people to the greatest extent that this poor miserable situation will possibly permit—In justice however I cannot forbear to remark that there does exist among them one solitary virtue—and that is hospitality to Strangers— for when I consider the very unequalled scarcity that does exist at all times in their Country of human diet, I am compelled to declare that I do not believe there are any people who would more willingly divide their morsel with the stranger, than these people would do—and that too, without any demand or expectation of Compensation for it, but if you offer to return them the value or ten times as much it will at all times and by nearly or quite all persons be received.[21]

Marmaduke and his fellow traders were used to drawing up ledgers and making precise evaluations, but they found these New Mexicans hard to account for in moral terms.

Among the first American visitors to view the country and its people more generously was George Champlin Sibley, who spent the winter of 1825–26 in Taos and Santa Fe awaiting permission from Mexico City to complete his official survey of the Santa Fe Trail through Mexican territory. The town of Taos that Sibley entered on October 30, 1825, was a considerably smaller place and less of a commercial center than Santa Fe, situated some seventy miles to the south. But its proximity to the mountains made Taos attractive to American trappers and fur traders, and Sibley deemed it worth a visit, if only to prove that his wagons, once their contents had been transferred to pack mules, could negotiate the steep path through the mountains that linked Taos to the plains and the Santa Fe Trail. He succeeded in that experiment, and his party entered the town with a sense of accomplishment that was shared by man and beast alike. "Our Poor Horses seemed to pluck up fresh Spirits, on sight of fields and Houses," he wrote in his journal; "they entered the Village merrily at a good Trot as if they meant to enjoy their *full* Share of the honour of bringing the First Waggons over the Mountains into the Valley of Taos."[22] Later that day, after renting quarters for himself and his party not far from town, he met with the alcalde of Taos, Severino Martínez, one of the leading landholders in the area and the father of Antonio José Martínez, a strong-willed young priest and Mexican patriot who would clash in years to come with trader Charles Bent and other American residents of Taos. Severino Martínez was under orders to intercept and impound the goods of any American traders who tried to avoid paying duties on their merchandise by skirting Santa Fe and bring in their wares through Taos, which had no customs officer.[23] Sibley handled this confrontation with the alcalde and his son the padre with a diplomatic poise that reflected his experience in dealing with tribal leaders and other demanding dignitaries:

> It was near night when I returned to the Village, where I found the Alcalde & the Curate waiting for me—who it seems had called on me officially to enquire my business &c. Altho' I suspected that these Men were acting a little arrogantly, yet I deemed it proper to treat them with proper civility. I therefore gave them to understand, as briefly as I could, why I had come here and told them that I should explain myself more fully to the Governour of the Territory, as soon as I conveniently could. After some consultation between themselves, they took leave of me very civilly, without asking any more questions. A very fine day.[24]

In late November, Sibley moved on to Santa Fe and met with the new governor there, Antonio Narbona, who was all graciousness but could offer no official assurances on the matter of the survey. Sibley would have to wait until the following summer for an answer to his request for permission from Mexico City.[25] In the meantime, he enjoyed the hospitality of Santa Fe, attending many a fandango—balls at which men and women smoked and danced together with an abandon that some visiting Americans found shocking. Sibley's busy social schedule was reflected in his diary—a more informal and abbreviated record of events than his official journal—for the latter part of December 1825, a time of sacred as well as patriotic observances:

> *Sunday 18th Decr.*
> Dined today with Gov[erno]r Narbona's. Fine day.
> *Monday 19th.*
> Kept as a Religious and Political festival—the people all very merry and Noisy. Bonfires &c. &c.
> *Wednesday 21t.*
> The Priest gave a Fandango, to which I went and Staid till 12.
> *Saturday 24.*
> Fandango all night—the People danced and Prayed all night.[26]

The festivities reached a peak at month's end, after Santa Feans received word that the last stronghold of the Spanish royalists had fallen, ending resistance to the Mexican Revolution. "There seems to be Something like Rejoicing every day," Sibley wrote on New Year's Eve, "& at Nightfall Bonfires are lighted up around the Public Square."[27] He may have lost some sleep, but unlike Thomas James, he did not begrudge the locals their spirited celebration. Indeed, for one who spent less than a year in New Mexico, he demonstrated considerable appreciation for his hosts and their customs. Some visitors were put off by the elaborate funerals Santa Feans staged for children who had been baptized before death and were thus thought to be destined for heaven, concluding that the music and pageantry accompanying these ceremonies signaled that the passing of the *angelito*, or "little angel," was more to be celebrated than mourned.[28] But Sibley observed otherwise in his diary on January 27, 1826:

> Funeral of Juan Baca's oldest child, a Daughter, at 10 o'Clock. The child died Night before last of Dysentery after the Measles—the family very much afflicted. The Corpse was very richly dressed and carried above the heads of the People Standing upright. The procession was a very long one chiefly composed of the most Respectable Inhabitants, many of whom marched in front of the Body, carrying lighted Tapers and wreaths of Flowers. The Priest was dressed in his Richest Robes and the whole moved with a Solemn pace. Several Voices Singing and Several Violins playing.[29]

Later, while returning to Taos, Sibley had occasion to remark upon the kindness of his hosts in language far more generous than the terms used earlier by Marmaduke. He left Santa Fe on March 6, still suffering from a severe cold and fever, and was taken in that night by the priest of the village of Santa Cruz, twenty-five miles distant. As Sibley noted in his diary: "Stopped at the Priest's who Received me with much politeness & kindness, & treated me with the utmost hospitality." He went on to detail that gracious reception the following day:

> I indulged myself in bed 'till it was pretty late this M[ornin]g. When I arose, found a Servant with Water, Napkin & c. & after I had finished Washing, was Served with a Cup of very fine, Rich chocolate—& in half an hour Breakfast was Ready.
>   I left the hospitable Priest's at ½ past 9, and felt every way the better.[30]

Such gratitude stood in marked contrast to the aspersions other American visitors to New Mexico cast on the local priests. (As Marmaduke put it, "I do verily believe 9/10 of them to be the most abandoned scoundrels that disgrace human nature.")[31] Were these holy men angels of mercy or agents of corruption? The answer depended in part on whether the visitors saw their New Mexican hosts as equal trading partners, whose terms had to be honored, or as prospective clients, who would fulfill their destiny only if they renounced their outdated allegiances and embraced Anglo-American principles and patronage.

Some early American visitors to New Mexico were more interested in spinning yarns than in selling goods. The place offered rich material for storytellers, and most readers back home knew so little about the Spanish Southwest that they found the humblest details entrancing and the wildest assertions faintly plausible (although plausibility was not always required in an age when many readers preferred romantic fancies). Albert Pike, who arrived here in 1831, was the first accomplished literary adventurer to mine the possibilities of New Mexico, but there were others before him who strayed across the line from reporting into storytelling—and made imaginative claims on the land and its people in the process. American visitors who romanced New Mexico in writing tended to regard the hospitality they enjoyed there as an appeal for help from a benighted people who saw Anglos as their potential champions. Such at least was the perspective of James Ohio Pattie, a lively chronicler who peppered his wide-ranging account of his western travels with improbable flourishes and borrowed anecdotes. He reached Taos with a party of trappers and traders in 1825 shortly before Sibley arrived there, having journeyed from the vicinity of Fort Atkinson across present-day Nebraska and down to the Arkansas River, where they evidently picked up some portion of the Santa Fe Trail. (Along the way, Pattie claimed, he and his companions encountered 220 grizzly bears in a single day.) He was barely twenty-one when he embarked on the journey with his father, Sylvester Pattie, and so ignorant of what lay ahead that he knew almost nothing of the differences between Mexicans and Americans. When he and his companions rode down through the pass into Taos on October 26, after caching some of their goods to avoid paying full duties, they encountered the same stern alcalde, Severino Martínez, who would confront Sibley a few days later:

> The alcaide asked us for the invoice of our goods, which we showed him, and paid the customary duties on them. This was a man of a swarthy complexion having the appearance of pride and haughtiness. The door-way of the room, we were in, was crowded with men, women and children, who stared at us, as though they had never seen white men before, there being in fact, much to my surprize and disappointment, not one white person among them. I had expected to find no difference between these people and our own, but their

language. I was never so mistaken. The men and women were not clothed in our fashion, the former having short pantaloons fastened below the waist with a red belt and buck skin leggins put on three or four times double. A Spanish knife is stuck in by the side of the leg, and a small sword worn by the side. A long jacket or blanket is thrown over, and worn upon the shoulders. They have few fire arms, generally using upon occasions which require them, a bow and spear, and never wear a hat, except when they ride.[32]

The women, Pattie added, wore "a short petticoat fastened around the waist with a red or blue belt,"[33] and a blouse covered with a kind of scarf, or rebozo, draped about the shoulders in much the same fashion as a serape, or shawl. He was struck less by their beauty than by their fetching congeniality:

> Although appearing as poorly, as I have described, they are not destitute of hospitality; for they brought us food, and invited us into their houses to eat, as we walked through the streets.
>
> The first time my father and myself walked through the town together, we were accosted by a woman standing in her own door-way. She made signs for us to come in. When we had entered, she conducted us up a flight of steps into a room neatly white-washed, and adorned with images of saints, and a crucifix of brass nailed to a wooden cross. She gave us wine, and set before us a dish composed of red pepper, ground and mixed with corn meal, stewed in fat and water. We could not eat it. She then brought forward some tortillas and milk. . . . We remained with her until late in the evening, when the bells began to ring. She and her children knelt down to pray. We left her, and returned. On our way we met a bier with a man upon it, who had been stabbed to death, as he was drinking whiskey.[34]

Pattie left much unexplained here. Was this woman who "accosted" the two men in the street and invited them in for dinner expecting something from them in return? Jacob Fowler, who visited Taos in 1822 with Hugh Glenn's party of trappers, told of one woman in town who was so taken by a companion of his that she barely let him out of her grasp. But this mother, kneeling down to pray with her children amid crucifix and icons, seemed innocent enough. Perhaps she expected nothing more than a gift of some kind from them—or the simple satisfaction of hosting well-mannered visitors in a town with more than a few rough customers, who binged on "Taos lightning" and brawled with sometimes deadly consequences.

After several days in Taos, Pattie and his party moved on to Santa Fe in the hope of obtaining from the governor permission to trap on the Gila River in southwestern New Mexico. Their timing was poor, for officials in Mexico

City had recently soured on the idea of allowing American trappers to reap gain in Mexican territory.[35] According to Pattie, the governor in Santa Fe informed them that nothing in the law permitted him to grant their request, but he seemed open to inducement: "We then proposed to him to give us liberty to trap upon the condition, that we paid him five per cent on the beaver we might catch. He said, he would consider this proposition, and give us an answer the next day at the same hour. The thoughts of our hearts were not at all favorable to this person, as we left him."[36]

Before they could receive the governor's answer, Pattie claimed, they were drawn into a retaliatory expedition against a band of Comanches who had attacked Mexican ranches along the Pecos, killing a number of people and taking several women captive, including Jacova, the daughter of the former governor. When the avengers finally tracked down the Comanches and met them in battle, the Mexicans supposedly broke and ran, leaving it to Pattie and his fellow Americans to repulse the Indians on their own and reclaim the captives. The former governor then invited young Pattie to his home and led him to a room where the grateful Jacova seemed intent on hosting him for the night. Pattie tried to excuse himself:

> But Jacova, showing me a bed, prepared for me, placed herself between me and the door. I showed her that my clothes were not clean. She immediately brought me others belonging to her brother-in-law. I wished to be excused from making use of them, but she seemed so much hurt, that I finally took them, and reseated myself. She then brought me my leather hunting shirt, which I had taken off to aid in protecting her from the cold, and begged the interpreter who was now present, to tell me, that she intended to keep it, as long as she lived. She then put it on, to prove to me she was not ashamed of it.
>
> I went to bed early, and arose, and returned to my companions, before any of the family were visible.[37]

The heroic battle that earned Pattie such gratitude from the daughter of that unnamed—and possibly fictitious—-governor may have been one of several tall tales that the author or his editor, Timothy Flint, added for dramatic effect to his narrative before it was published in 1831.[38] Conceivably, Pattie was inspired by the same yarn that fired the imagination of a more gifted storyteller, Albert Pike, who reached Taos in the same year that Pattie's book appeared, after traversing the Cimarron Route with a party captained by Charles Bent. Pike, who made the journey largely in search of literary inspiration and found plenty of it in New Mexico, told of a battle similar to the one described by Pattie that reportedly occurred outside Taos not long before Pattie arrived there in 1825.

Pike's version of the event was admittedly secondhand, and the author passed it along to his readers not as the plain truth but as part of what he termed a prose sketch, entitled "The Inroad of the Nabajo." He began that semifictional tale in realistic fashion, with a vivid description of Taos and its inhabitants as they appeared to him at first encounter in the fall of 1831:

> Directly in front of me, with the dull color of its mud buildings, contrasting with the dazzling whiteness of the snow, lay the little village, resembling an oriental town, with its low, square, mud-roofed houses and its two square church towers, also of mud. On the path to the village were a few Mexicans, wrapped in their striped blankets, and driving their jackasses heavily laden with wood towards the village. Such was the aspect of the place at a distance. On entering it, you found only a few dirty, irregular lanes, and a quantity of mud houses.
>
> To an American, the first sight of these New Mexican villages is novel and singular. He seems taken into a different world. Everything is new, strange, and quaint: the men with their pantalones of cloth, gaily ornamented with lace, split up on the outside of the leg to the knee, and covered at the bottom with a broad strip of morocco; the jacket of calico; the botas of stamped and embroidered leather; the zarape or blanket of striped red and white; the broad-brimmed hat, with a black silk handkerchief tied around it in a roll; or in the lower class, the simple attire of breeches of leather reaching only to the knees, a shirt and a zarape; the bonnetless women, with a silken scarf or a red shawl over their heads; and, added to all, the continual chatter of Spanish about him—all remind him that he is in a strange land.
>
> On the evening after my arrival in the village, I went to a fandango. I saw the men and women dancing waltzes, and drinking whiskey together; and in another room, I saw the monti-bank open. It is a strange sight—a Spanish fandango. Well dressed women—(they call them ladies)—harlots, priests, thieves, half-breed Indians—all spinning round together in the waltz. Here, a filthy, ragged fellow with a half shirt, a pair of leather breeches, and long, dirty woollen stockings, and Apache moccasins, was hanging and whirling round with the pretty wife of Pedro Vigil; and there, the priest was dancing with La Altegracia, who paid her husband a regular sum to keep out of the way, and so lived with an American. I was soon disgusted; but among the graceless shapes and more graceless dresses at the fandango, I saw one young woman who appeared to me exceedingly pretty. She was under the middle size, slightly formed; and besides the delicate foot and ancle and the keen black eye, common to all the women in that country, she possessed a clear and beautiful complexion, and a modest, downcast look, not often to be met with among the New Mexican females.

Street scene in Taos, from Albert D. Richardson, *Beyond the Mississippi* (1867). Used by permission, State Historical Society of Missouri, Columbia,

I was informed to my surprise, that she had been married several years before, and was now a widow. There was an air of gentle and deep melancholy in her face which drew my attention to her; but when one week afterward I left Taos, and went down to Santa Fe, the pretty widow was forgotten.[39]

As Pike learned later from an American friend of long tenure in New Mexico, this melancholy young beauty, before being widowed, had lost her father in battle against Navajo raiders, a fight that occurred some "six or eight years" before Pike reached New Mexico (or between 1823 and 1825) and resembled in some respects the contest with the Comanches described by Pattie. In both accounts, a small group of Americans volunteered to aid Mexicans against their Indian foes and ended up doing the bulk of the fighting when the Mexicans lost heart. In Pike's version of the battle against the Navajos at Taos—told from the perspective of his friend, who claimed to have participated in the fight—the Americans rushed unbidden to the defense of their Mexican hosts as soon as they learned of the Navajo threat:

Through the tumult, we proceeded towards the outer edge of the town, whither all the armed men seemed to be hastening. On arriving in the street which goes out towards the cañon of the river, we found ourselves in the place of action. Nothing was yet to be seen out in the plain, which extends to the foot of the hills and to the cañon, and of which you there have a plain view. Some fifty Mexicans had gathered there, mostly armed, and were pressing forward towards the extremity of the street. Behind them were a dozen Americans with their rifles, all as cool as might be; for the men that came through the prairie then were all braves. Sundry women were scudding about, exhorting their husbands to fight well, and praising 'Los Señores Americanos.' We had waited perhaps half an hour, when the foe came in sight, sweeping in from the west, and bearing towards the cañon, driving before them numerous herds and flocks, and consisting apparently of about one hundred men. When they were within about half a mile of us, they separated; one portion of them remained with the booty, and the other, all mounted, came sweeping down upon us. The effect was instantaneous, and almost magical. In a moment not a woman was to be seen far or near; and the heroes who had been chattering and boasting in front of the Americans, shrunk in behind them, and left them to bear the brunt of the battle. We immediately extended ourselves across the street, and waited the charge. The Indians made a beautiful appearance as they came down upon us with their fine looking horses, and their shields ornamented with feathers and fur, and their dresses of unstained deer-skin. At that time, they knew nothing about the Americans; they supposed that their good allies, the Spaniards, would run as they commonly do, that they would have the pleasure of frightening the village and shouting in it, and going off safely. As they neared us, each of us raised his gun when he judged it proper, and fired. A dozen cracks of the rifle told them the difference; five or six tumbled out of their saddles, and were immediately picked up by their comrades, who then turned their backs and retreated as swiftly as they had come.[40]

The Americans could not claim all the credit for punishing the raiders, however. The retreating Navajos were pursued by a party of some sixty warriors from Taos Pueblo, "all fine looking men, well mounted, large, and exceedingly brave."[41] Even a few of the maligned Mexicans joined in the chase, and one of them—the father of the young woman who would later catch Pike's eye—died at the hands of a Navajo chief. The dead man's grieving daughter, Ana Maria, then purportedly offered her hand to whichever of her two lovers, a Mexican named Victorino and a young American trapper named Hentz, succeeded in avenging her father. To that end, the two suitors joined a punitive expedition against the Navajos led by a Mexican officer referred to in Pike's tale as Viscara. (José Antonio Vizcarra in fact carried out such a campaign in 1823, one of many expeditions that the supposedly fainthearted Mexicans mounted over the years to discourage raids on their settlements.) Hentz claimed the honor of avenging Ana Maria's father after his rival Victorino tried and failed. Then, in an improbably sporting gesture, the American took pity on the forlorn Mexican and offered him the scalp of the Navajo chief to present to Ana Maria:

> 'Victorino looked fiercely up, and seemed inclined to resent it, but Hentz, without regarding the glance, proceeded with a mass of immensely bad Spanish, which I know not how the poor fellow ever understood. "Here," said he, "you love Ana better than I do, I know—you have known her longer, and will feel her loss more; and after all, you would have killed the chief if you could have done it—and you did help me save the body. Take this bunch of stuff," holding out the hair, "and give me your hand." Victorino did so, and shook the offered hand heartily; then taking the scalp, he deposited it in his shot-pouch, and dashing the tears from his eyes, rode off towards his comrades like a madman. So much for the inroad of the Nabajos.'
>
> 'But what became of Victorino?' inquired I.
>
> 'He married Ana Maria after she had laid aside the luto, (mourning,) and two years ago, he died of the small pox, in the Snake country. Poor fellow—he was almost an American.'[42]

Pike's literary assessment of the New Mexicans and their dealings with Americans was not always so blunt or belittling. He offered shrewd insights into how traffic with Americans was gradually transforming the locals and their ancestral culture. He noted that the wealthy Ana Maria's adornments, for example, consisted largely of traditional Mexican items, enhanced by such American-imported luxuries as calico dresses:

> Ana was in truth, not a girl to be slighted. She was pretty, and rich, and sensible; her room was the best furnished mud apartment in Taos; her zarapes were of the best texture, some of them even from Chihuahua, and they were piled showily round the room. The roses skewered upon the wall, were of red silk; and the santos and other images had been brought from Mexico. There were some half dozen of looking-glasses, too, all out of reach, and various other adornments common to great apartments. The medal which she wore round her neck, with a cross-looking San Pablo upon it, was of beaten gold, or some other kind of gold. She had various dresses of calico and silk, all bought at high prices of the new comers; and her little fairy feet were always adorned with shoes. That was a great extravagance in those days.[43]

In another of his prose sketches, "A Mexican Tale," Pike evoked the mixed reactions of the inhabitants of the small town of Embudo to the arrival of an American merchant with his exotic wares:

> The trader, as he approached the town, seemed an object of curiosity to various individuals who were to be seen seated at the doors of the houses, all of them, of both sexes, with their never-failing companion, a segar of *punche* (their country tobacco) rolled in a slip of corn-husk. At this time, which was just at the commencement of the American trade to the country, the common people were not so well accustomed to the sight of Americans as at present. Then, the high hat, the long coat, the boots, the full pantaloons, seemed to them odd and *outre*; and they gazed upon the wearer as a singular curiosity. Amid various ejaculations—for the New Mexicans are not a people to restrain or hide their surprise or admiration—the foreigner moved steadily through the town towards the outer edge of it, obedient to a mute sign of direction given by his servant. One group, particularly, by which he passed, seemed interested by his arrival. There were two old men with their dress of leather and coarse woollen, a woman with her hair turned gray, and one of middle age, a young man, and a girl of some fifteen years. In the door-way, too, stood an Indian girl with her Nabajo blanket, black, with a red border, just around her middle, and answering for a gown.
>
> 'Mira! Don Santiago!' said one of the old men to the other—'there comes one of these strangers that have arrived now for years to our land.' 'Yes, brother,' was the answer, 'and no doubt he comes well laden with goods

to fish away the *pesitos* (little dollars) of us poor.' 'And a good exchange,' resumed the other, 'to barter our musty gold and silver for the useful and beautiful things he brings. Every pelayo has his hands full of dollars, and his legs cased in leather—ay, and his back, for not till now has he been offered a shirt.' 'As to your gold, Amigo Ramon,' answered Don Santiago, 'I know and see but little of it; but what little silver I have, Valgame Dios y La Virgen! is better bestowed in my big chests than in the pockets of that picaro.'

'Nay,' interrupted the oldest woman, 'they are no picaros, these Americans. I have been told by the Doña Imanuela, in Santa Fe, that she would place her dollars in their hands without counting them, and have no fear of losing one. Nay, compadre, an American cannot steal.'

'Quien sabe?' (who knows?) ejaculated the old man, 'every rascal has a good face till he is found out.'

'And then they are such ingenious men!' went on the dame, 'Tata dios! such strange things as they know how to make,—they know everything,—calico and balls of thread, and a thousand things more strange.'

'And, Señora,' said the young man, 'what beautiful guns—not like our old fusees—some with two barrels, and some that have no flints. Nay, it is true, Inacia! Have you not seen them, Tata Ramon?'

'Yes, indeed I have—and so strange they are, too! Ah! they are great men, these Americans! they can all read and write like a priest. Lastima! (pity) that they are heretics.'[44]

In such passages, Pike came as close as any contemporary observer to defining the true nature of American infiltration in the early years of the trade—a campaign that succeeded not through acts of force or deeds of heroism but through peaceful commercial overtures that slowly loosened the attachment of New Mexicans to their native ways and wares and left them increasingly susceptible to Americans and their goods.

This story of gradual economic seduction was perhaps too prosaic to hold Pike's attention for long. After dwelling briefly on the successful courtship of these townspeople by the visiting merchant, the author shifts focus in "A Mexican Tale" to a more conventional romance—that between the young man, Rafael Mestes, and his sweetheart, Inacia Martin, who hopes to marry Rafael but instead becomes engaged to a rich old wastrel with the connivance of a corrupt priest willing to exert his influence on behalf of the elderly suitor in exchange for an offering of "three ounces of gold and a jar of Velarde's best vintage."[45] Like the lovestruck Victorino in "The Inroad of the Nabajo," young Rafael manages to win the object of his desire only with the help of a stouthearted American, in this case a Kentuckian named Lem, who learns of

Rafael's plight and boldly intervenes to free Inacia from the clutches of her menacing fiancé and the sinister priest:

> On reaching the door of the church, Lem dismounted, and signing to Rafael to remain in his saddle, he entered into the church with his never failing companion, his rifle, in his hand. His entrance disturbed the ceremony which the Frai Luis had just commenced, and the priest's voice hushed as the careless American walked heavily towards the altar with his hat upon his head. Unmindful of everything about him, he drew the pale and weeping Inacia aside, and whispered with her a moment; then, suddenly grasping her by one arm, he bore her towards the door. Some of the bystanders attempted to interfere; but Lem threw them rudely aside, and continued his course. Handing his burden to the expectant Rafael, he pointed to the mountains, and Rafael, with a brief expression of thanks, darted forward again, and was soon out of sight. Some motion was made to follow him; but it was quickly prevented by Lem, who, placing himself in his saddle, menaced any one with death who should dare to stir. He maintained his place steadily for two hours or more, as if he were on guard, in spite of the maledictions of the Frai Luis, few of which, though delivered in very excellent Castillian, did he understand, and none of which did he care for.[46]

In the end, Lem's heroic intervention only postpones the cruel fate awaiting the young lovers (tracked down by Inacia's fiancé, Rafael takes her life before surrendering his own). But the arresting image of the Kentuckian holding off the alien forces of greed and corruption at the door of the church stands as a dramatic instance of the way in which Americans staked a claim to New Mexico in writing long before they occupied the country in force.

It remained to Matt Field to offer a more complex and balanced portrait of the American courtship of New Mexico. Field's prose sketches for the *New Orleans Picayune* resembled Pike's in that he sometimes blended fact with fancy. But while Field was not necessarily a more gifted writer than Pike, he was more faithful to the terms of the culture he encountered in New Mexico and more sympathetic to the concerns of the people. To come into this country, he recognized, was not a right but a privilege for Americans, who if they were in fact going to inherit this land—an outcome that was by no means inevitable—would have to assume the many responsibilities and obligations that came with that bequest. Although Field was sometimes dismissive of local customs, referring to a mass he attended in San Miguel, for instance, as "an offensive libel on sacred things,"[47] he understood that these New Mexicans knew what they were about and hoped for no savior other than God. Indeed, Field recognized that the Anglo intrusion could be a singular misfortune for locals who surrendered to the material or personal charms of venturesome Americans and lost their bearings. In one article, he told of a crazed young mother in Taos named Maria Roméro, who had been abandoned by the American she loved. At first, she was told that her darling John had been killed by Comanches:

> This affliction the poor girl bore only in melancholy, bending over her infant in silent anguish; but when subsequently she heard that he had designedly abandoned her, and had gone forever back to the United States, her reason failed, and poor Maria, the beauty of Taos, became a lunatic. When traders were leaving the valley for the States, she invariably came and entreated to be taken with them; and when she found her pleadings useless, she would pray that John should be brought back with them when they would return. Poor Maria! Death she had heard of before; she knew that it was an affliction sooner or later to be expected, but the idea of desertion never entered her mind until it came to dethrone her reason.[48]

Maria's plight was a poignant reminder of the potential risks for New Mexicans of yielding wholeheartedly to American overtures. Even the tenderest exchanges could take on aspects of a conquest and leave devastation in their wake.

Field did not conclude that all such relationships were doomed, however. In a later article, entitled "A Wedding," he described the festive union of a Mexican woman with her American beau of long standing. The author framed the tale as a comic piece with wry observations on Mexican customs, including the fondness of the women for smoking their hand-rolled *cigarillos*. (As he wrote of the bride: "She was a creature to love—just such a creature as was calculated to win the impulsive and adventurous young American—and there she sat with a cigar in her mouth!")[49] Yet Field transformed the story at the end into a parable of acceptance and redemption:

> Just as this ceremony concluded, three merry little children came bouncing into the room, the oldest a girl, and the other two dark haired and dark eyed boys, bearing a strong resemblance to the bride. They flew to our American friend, the bridegroom, and he seemed to receive their caresses with every mark of paternal solicitude and delight, which exciting our surprise, we made enquiry, and were told, to our no little wonder, that the children were his own, and that for five years he and the bride had been man and wife in all but the ceremony.[50]

Like Maria Roméro's faithless suitor, this young American had parted with his sweetheart and headed home to the States, "intending to abandon his dark eyed enchantress and join his relatives," but he found his attachment to her unbreakable and returned to Santa Fe:

> Nearly three years more he dwelt away from home, and at the time that we attended his wedding, he had just returned from another visit to the States, having bidden farewell forever to friend and relative, resolved to give his wife a husband and his children a father.
>
> When made acquainted with these circumstances, we very naturally experienced a lively interest in our new friends, and upon calling on them we found our young countryman in a situation which we were far more inclined to envy than to commiserate. The Mexican girl, it was evident, stored up the whole treasure of her young affections in her American husband, and he seemed to love his children the more for possessing the dark eyes of their mother.[51]

As Field illustrated here, the exchange between these two cultures was not always dominated by Anglos. The greater assets of this union came from the bride, from the precious and persistent affection she invested in her prodigal husband and from the dark features that she bequeathed to her children and that were more becoming to them here than their father's endowments. As Field remarked of the bride, "She would pass for handsome among all who do not consider a fair skin absolutely indispensable to beauty,"[52] a bias the author seemed blessedly free of. If more Americans had conducted their affairs with New Mexico in the appreciative manner of Matt Field and his friend the bridegroom, the two sides might have avoided a bitter reckoning.

14

Accommodation in the Marketplace

In economic as in cultural exchanges, visitors to New Mexico derived more satisfaction, if not more profit, from their dealings with the locals if they honored their terms. Few Americans involved in the Santa Fe trade made a better bargain with New Mexico in writing in the early years than Josiah Gregg. Like other visitors from the States, he brought with him cultural biases, and his prejudices carried extra weight because the book he wrote was so influential.[1] Far from clinging blindly to his preconceptions, however, Gregg mastered the language of his hosts, studied their history and traditions, and showed some appreciation for the burdens they labored under at the far northern fringe of their young and unstable republic. His account, published in 1844, was unparalleled in its time. But another trader, James J. Webb, who first reached New Mexico that same year, produced a memoir several decades later that was more tolerant of the locals and their customs in some respects. In both cases, the authors were informed by the spirit of accommodation intrinsic to their trade.

Like many early visitors, Gregg was rather disillusioned by his first encounter with Santa Fe. In the summer of 1831, after journeying down the Cimarron Route with Captain Stanley's caravan and encountering scattered bands of *ciboleros* and *rancheros* (buffalo hunters and ranchers) east of the mountains, Gregg and company arrived at San Miguel, "the first settlement of any note upon our route."[2] This small town was now a port of entry, meaning that Mexican officials sometimes met incoming Americans there and made a preliminary inspection of their goods. Duties were collected in Santa Fe, however,

and newcomers like Gregg assumed that San Miguel, with its "irregular clus-
ters of mud-wall huts," was as nothing compared to the provincial capital.
Not until they made their way past dwindling Pecos Pueblo, which would be
abandoned by its last remaining residents in 1838, and threaded narrow
Apache Canyon through the mountains to the west—"where the road winds
and turns," noted Webb, "crossing steep pitches and ravines, over rocks, and
around boulders, making short and difficult turns, with double teams to make
an ascent"[3]—did they catch sight of their long-sought goal and surrender
their lofty expectations. As Gregg recollected in a passage echoed by many
newcomers to Santa Fe in those days: "'Oh, we are approaching the suburbs!'
thought I, on perceiving the cornfields, and what I supposed to be brick-kilns
scattered in every direction. These and other observations of the same nature
becoming audible, a friend at my elbow said, 'It is true those are heaps of
unburnt bricks, nevertheless they are *houses*—this is the city of Santa Fé.'"[4]
The humble appearance of the capital with its adobe buildings and narrow
streets did not discourage Gregg and his companions from staging a grand
entry of the sort Santa Feans had come to expect of visiting caravans:

> The arrival produced a great deal of bustle and excitement among the natives.
> *"Los Americanos!"*—*"Los carros!"*—*"La entrada de la caravana!"* were to be
> heard in every direction; and crowds of women and boys flocked around to
> see the new-comers; while crowds of *léperos* hung about as usual to see what
> they could pilfer. The wagoners were by no means free from excitement on
> this occasion. Informed of the 'ordeal' they had to pass, they had spent the
> previous morning in 'rubbing up;' and now they were prepared, with clean
> faces, sleek combed hair, and their choicest Sunday suit, to meet the 'fair eyes'
> of glistening black that were sure to stare at them as they passed. There was
> yet another preparation to be made in order to 'show off' to advantage. Each
> wagoner must tie a bran new 'cracker' to the lash of his whip; for, on driv-
> ing though the streets and the *plaza pública*, every one strives to outvie his
> comrades in the dexterity with which he flourishes this favorite badge of
> authority.[5]

This ceremony, with its whip-cracking and other aggressive posturing, was
similar in nature to the mock attacks staged on horseback by Indians of various tribes to impress members of rival parties before the two sides settled
down to talk or trade. Such harmless demonstrations of force at the volatile
time of entry, or *entrada* (a word with militant associations in Spanish usage),
helped release tensions and set the stage for commerce and more intimate
exchanges. Preparations for this disarming ritual at Santa Fe were much the
same when Webb and his companions arrived there in 1844:

"Arrival of the Caravan at Santa Fé," from Gregg's *Commerce of the Prairies*. Courtesy Library of Congress, Prints and Photographs Division, LC-USZ62-25701.

The men here wash their faces and hands, and those possessed of that luxury would don a clean shirt. But those having no spare clothes would content themselves with fixing up shirts and trousers by substituting splinters for buttons and tying a handkerchief around their necks in such a way that it would cover the holes in their shirts as much as possible. But the most important preparation for the drivers was to put on new and broad crackers, so as to be able to announce their arrival by the cracking of their whips, which would nearly equal the reports made by the firing of so many pistols.[6]

After winning entry to Santa Fe in this rousing fashion, the drivers and other employees of the caravan often joined in fandangos around town, but the traders engaged in a dance of a different sort with customs officials—one marked by the greasing of palms. Gregg confirmed Marmaduke's earlier observation that such officials could be quite obliging to those who paid them due consideration. The official tariffs demanded by the government by the 1840s were quite steep, Gregg noted, averaging nearly 100 percent of the cost of the goods to the traders:

> But it is scarcely necessary to add that there are believed to be very few ports in the Republic at which these rigid exactions are strictly executed. An 'arrangement'—a compromise is expected, in which the officers are sure at least to provide for themselves. At some ports, a custom has been said to prevail, of dividing the legal duties into three equal parts: one for the officers—a second for the merchants—the other for the government.[7]

Manuel Armijo, who served three inconsecutive terms as governor of New Mexico between 1827 and 1846, made his own "arrangement" for customs at one point, Gregg added, by charging $500 per wagonload: "As might have been anticipated, the traders soon took to conveying their merchandise only in the largest wagons, drawn by ten or twelve mules, and omitting the coarser and more weighty articles of trade." This led Armijo "to return to an *ad valorem* system," the author noted. "How much of these duties found their way into the public treasury, I will not venture to assert."[8]

Armijo and his collectors were not the only ones suspected of skirting the law in such matters. There were numerous reports of traders caching part of their goods outside Santa Fe and arranging for their sale or shipment without paying duties. If Gregg was among those who resorted to such expedients, he was not in the best position to criticize Armijo at length for financial irregularities. But he felt free to indict the governor for offenses in other areas, including his ruthless suppression of a revolt in 1837 by New Mexicans who vented their resentments against the central government by ousting Governor Albino

Pérez from office and taking his life. Gregg claimed that Armijo had helped incite the uprising, before turning against the rebels when they declined to name him governor to succeed Pérez. Armijo in fact put down that revolt by executing several of the ringleaders, but accusations by Gregg and other American critics that he encouraged the uprising were unfounded.[9]

Gregg was not the only trader to suggest that Armijo may have profited personally from the duties he and his customs agents collected. Merchant William Henry Glasgow, who passed through Santa Fe in early 1843 on his way back to Missouri from Chihuahua and points beyond, arranged with Armijo to pay export fees on the Mexican currency he was transporting to St. Louis on behalf of his father's firm. His exchange with the governor left little doubt in his mind that Armijo had a vested interest in the fees he assessed:

> The Gov[r] is a large fine looking man of about 50 years of age, very portly, has a high & wide forehead & a penetrating eye.
>
> He arose upon our entrance and shook each of us by the hand & requested us to be seated. After a few moments Conversation we broached our business, which was to make arrangements for the payment of as little duty as possible upon the money we were to take out of the country. He told us he had nothing to do, with the administrations of the Custom House, and referred us to the Collector whom he supposed would charge us about 1½%.
>
> As we knew this was all gammon we left him and did not return again until 3 oclk when we called in company with the collector. and the affair was arranged by our paying 1 ½ Pr ct export duty. The legal charge for exporting coined money from the Mexican Republic is 6 pr ct. It is Contrary to law to export bullion and can only be done by smuggling or the connivance with the Custom House officers. I pulled out my purse to pay my duties, & tendered the money to the Gov[r] but he declined receiving it & told me that it must be paid to the Collector at the Custom House. That Gent being present said it was useless trouble to go to the Custom House and would receive it then. The money was counted down upon the Gov[r]'s table and considering *he had nothing to do with it*, I thought he appeared to take considerable interest in the matter as he picked up and examined seperately each doubloon as I laid it down—remarking that there was a great many Counterfeits in circulation.[10]

Glasgow's dim view of Armijo was shared by a number of American traders, who complained that the governor exacted higher duties from them than he did from Mexican merchants importing goods from the States. Some others in the trade, however, regarded Armijo as more of an ally than an adversary. After all, he consistently charged them less than the law required, and he understood the nature of their business. He himself was one of those Mexicans who joined in the commerce of the prairies by transporting goods between Missouri and New Mexico or by commissioning agents to do so for them. James Webb, for one, found Armijo to be someone he could deal with. Webb recalled an amicable exchange in which Armijo obtained a pair of horses he coveted from Webb by forgiving the tariff on one of his wagons, an arrangement that Webb regarded as reasonable and defended with some fervor:

> Well, were we smugglers? Were we guilty of any fraud? We entered the country with our goods and paid the duties demanded by the legal authorities according to a custom prevailing for years, which had become recognized as law by the authorities throughout the country, without any misrepresentation, prevarication, or deceit. And if there was fraud or evasion, the governor never shirked the responsibility or attempted to throw it on the shoulders of others.[11]

In Webb's view, the irregular tariff system, which sometimes included small loans to the officers in charge, who invariably forgot to repay them, or "presents" amounting in value to less than $100, was like other customs of the country—something beyond his control that he simply had to live with.[12]

Neither Gregg nor Webb had much to say about how traders sold their wares in and around Santa Fe, but Matt Field, with his fine eye for detail, kindly filled out the picture. All goods, he noted, were unloaded from the wagons in the plaza and underwent at least a cursory inspection in the customhouse, despite the fact that when Field visited Santa Fe the flat rate of $500 per wagon was in effect:

> The next day the goods are released from the customhouse, and the owners having duly engaged themselves to pay five hundred dollars for each wagon; having undergone a scrutinizing cross-examination before the Governor to ascertain that no goods have been *cached* or otherwise secretly disposed of; and having laid a *douceur* of some kind before his eminence—proceed to open their shops and arrange their merchandise for sale.[13]

Not all traders opened shops in town. Some sold out their stock to retailers in Santa Fe or to merchants bound for other markets where they hoped to fetch higher prices for the goods. Those traders who chose to offer their goods to the public in Santa Fe, however, generally did so from one of the many shops lining the plaza, as described by Field:

> A large square, comprising about three hundred square yards, is situated in the centre of the town of Santa Fé. The row of houses on one side is occupied entirely by the public offices, the custom house, and armory, and quarters for the military. The other three sides are used for shops for the sale of

merchandise brought from the United States, and are kept by Americans. The houses are built of clay, and with very few exceptions are but one story high. Shops are rented to traders in this square, the best situation in the place at from ten to twenty dollars a month. The store keepers, in dull times, sit at their doors all day smoking cigars, cracking jokes with the Spaniards, and peeping under the veils of the Señoras and Señoritas as they pass.[14]

Americans trading in Santa Fe were quick to learn Spanish since few of their customers spoke English, Field added, and some visiting merchants who settled down in the capital became quite prominent there. One such immigrant from St. Louis, Louis Robidoux, a trader of French ancestry married to a Mexican woman, was serving as the principal alcalde of Santa Fe when Field visited. "He shares the rule over the people almost equally with the Governor and priests," Field claimed.[15] Other traders preferred to make their profits in Santa Fe over the summer and return to the States for the winter. To cover the costs of rent and transportation, they had to be sharp in their dealings with the locals without antagonizing them. Field portrayed the scene at one American shop in the plaza:

> Around the door, outside, sat upon the ground some half dozen ragged Mexicans, men and women, with baskets before them, containing grapes, melons, peaches, and other fruits for sale. Stepping over the bare legs of these fruiterers, we entered the store, and found ourselves in an apartment of about fifteen by eighteen feet dimensions. Two sides of the room were covered with shelves, upon which calicoes and domestics, and a variety of dry goods and nic-nacs were disposed in much the same manner as is customary in the States. A plain counter stood in front of these shelves, serving to show the goods upon and keep off meddlers, and upon the counter we found our friend, the trader, seated smoking a cigar.
>
> We had scarcely exchanged civilities before a young *cavallero*, on a remarkably large and well fed mule, with saddle and other gear gorgeously decorated with silver, and little bells and ornaments jingling as he approached, rode up, dismounted, and came into the house.[16]

Such *ricos* were the traders' best customers and sought out their finest fabrics and adornments. This *cavallero* (cavalier, or gentleman), "educated in the more civilized part of Mexico," was already wearing "a shirt of American make," Field observed, and "a very elegant black silk handkerchief," and he needed little encouragement to make further purchases of similar quality:

> His business showed him to be a lady's messenger, for he wanted silk for a dress, and other things for female use. Besides which he suffered himself to

"East Side of the Plaza—Santa Fe," from J. H. Beadle, *The Undeveloped West; or, five Years in the Western Territories* (1873). Used by permission, State Historical Society of Missouri, Columbia, all rights reserved.

be seduced by the store keeper into the purchase of sundry new handker-chiefs and other matters just received from the States.

Having spared as many golden pieces from his net purse as he thought prudent, he took leave of us with much politeness, and mounted his noble mule.[17]

Traders could not rely exclusively on such well-heeled customers. For one thing, even those with expensive tastes did not always have enough cash on hand to cover their purchases. Artist Alfred Waugh, who reached Santa Fe in the summer of 1846 shortly before American troops occupied the town, told of a "swarthy-looking member of the dragoon corps," presumably an officer, who found himself unable to a pay for a draft of liquor he obtained in the store of an American merchant and promptly removed both his coat and shirt and offered them in pledge. "Don Henrico," he said to the storekeeper, "I am a *caballero*, my honor is at stake!" The storekeeper professed to be "touched with deep humiliation for the wrong which he had done a *Mexican gentleman*, in doubting *his honor*," Waugh related, and assured him "*his* word was sufficient."[18] Customers who failed to honor their word and settle their accounts with traders in due time, however, sometimes faced legal action. In one such case, American merchant Alexander Le Grand went to court to collect on a bill amounting to more than a thousand pesos from Manuela Baca, a substantial local property owner who nonetheless made purchases on credit, either by necessity or by choice. She and her husband were trading on the side with Navajos and Pueblos, it turned out, and they may have been short on cash between the time they purchased their trade goods and the time they sold them. In any case, they eventually reached a settlement with Le Grand.[19]

Aside from extending credit occasionally to such cash-poor ricos, American merchants in Santa Fe adapted to the requirements of their market by buying and selling an assortment of inexpensive household items that were within the means of many if not most residents. Field observed that the same American trader who sold silks and handkerchiefs at his shop in the plaza to that well-appointed cavalier proceeded to drive hard bargains with locals who had far less to offer:

> He had scarcely departed when a little bare footed girl came in, with a dozen most bilious looking candles hanging together by a string. These she sold to the shop keeper for an old rusty steel thimble for her *madre*. The thimble cost the trader about the forty-ninth part of a cent, and he sold the candles before we left the shop for a good Spanish shilling, which was making, certainly, a small trifle above first cost. The old women all understood making candles, and one of them will often spend half a day boiling grease and dipping a dozen, only to realize sixpence worth of tobacco from a shop keeper.[20]

The terms of exchange in Santa Fe did not always favor visiting merchants at the expense of the locals. By late summer, itinerant American merchants in Santa Fe often slashed prices as they prepared to close up shop and return to Missouri before the grass that nourished their animals withered and the weather turned nasty. Other traders passing through town at this time on their way back from Chihuahua added their remaining goods to the glut, creating a buyer's market described appreciatively by Mexican Antonio Barreiro:

> That is the time when all the Anglo-American merchants are returning who, during the year, have gone to the neighboring states to transact business, and

then in short is when one beholds a traffic which is truly pleasing. Goods become extremely cheap, for many merchants "burn their profits" so as to return to the United States in August, and purchases are made with the greatest ease. Upon the invoices from Philadelphia or Saint Louis goods are sold wholesale at an advance of scarcely 80, or 90, or 100%, and indeed they are often sold at an advance of only 50%.[21]

An advance of 50 percent was a paltry return for merchants who paid premiums of up to 25 percent over eastern prices on goods they purchased in Missouri and who then had to spend up to two months conveying wares to New Mexico with hired help.[22] As Barreiro observed, the "crazy bargains" some traders offered at summer's end could ruin them. Among those who profited by their misfortune were Mexicans who bought merchandise from departing Americans wholesale and sold the goods in Santa Fe, Chihuahua, and other markets at better terms over the winter, when there were fewer foreign merchants abroad. The Americans who survived and flourished in this highly competitive environment tended to be those who had the resources and the initiative not only to purchase goods at bulk rates in Philadelphia and other eastern cities but also to extend their operations at the Mexican end, either by remaining there for long periods and exploiting opportunities at one or more markets through the year or by establishing partnerships with Mexicans who could do the same.

Aside from the Mexicans actively involved in the trade, there were other local entrepreneurs who specialized in parting visitors from their cash. No one fared better at that business in Santa Fe than the celebrated Gertrudis Barceló, also known as La Tules (the diminutive form of Gertrudis), who made her fortune as a saloon owner and dealer at monte, a card game played with a special deck for stakes that were often steep. Frank Edwards, after entering Santa Fe in 1846 with the occupying American army, offered a pithy if somewhat cryptic description of that game, which few seemed to profit from with the notable exception of the dealers, who claimed what the players ventured and lost:

> The universality of the cigarito is only equaled by that of the eternal game of monte, played with cards. The suits whereof are clubs, swords, suns, and cups, all delineated in their own proper colors and figures. Each suit numbers ten cards, namely, (like the American,) from ace to seven, and then knave, horse standing in the place of queen, and king. The mysteries of the game can only be learnt by losing at it.[23]

Few chroniclers of Santa Fe in the years leading up to the Mexican War failed to pay sardonic tribute to Gertrudis Barceló and her remarkable gift for initiating spendthrift newcomers into the mysteries of monte. Josiah Gregg, whose own occupation involved taking a gamble now and then, had reason to admire the pluck of La Tules, who had purportedly worked her way up from the rough alleys of Taos to the fashionable parlors of Santa Fe:

> Some twelve or fifteen years ago there lived (or rather roamed) in Taos a certain female of very loose habits, known as *La Tules*. Finding it difficult to obtain the means of living in that district, she finally extended her wanderings to the capital. She there became a constant attendant on one of those pandemoniums where the favorite game of *monte* was dealt *pro bono publico*. Fortune, at first, did not seem inclined to smile upon her efforts, and for some years she spent her days in lowliness and misery. At last her luck turned, as gamblers would say, and on one occasion she left the bank with a spoil of several hundred dollars! This enabled her to open a bank of her own, and being favored by a continuous run of good fortune, she gradually rose higher and higher in the scale of affluence, until she found herself in possession of a very handsome fortune. In 1843, she sent to the United States some ten thousand dollars to be invested in goods. She still continues her favorite 'amusement,' being now considered the most expert 'monte dealer' in all Santa Fé. She is openly received in the first circles of society: I doubt, in truth, whether there is to be found in the city a lady of more fashionable reputation than this same Tules, now known as Señora Doña Gertrudes Barceló.[24]

Gregg implied that the honorific title *Doña*—the feminine of *Don*, or "Sir," reserved for Mexican gentry—was something the formerly footloose Barceló acquired along with her profits at the monte table. In fact, she was well bred and well educated. Born in Sonora in 1800, she learned to read and write—something few girls accomplished on Mexico's northern frontier—and went on to marry a prominent New Mexican, retaining her maiden name and her property as wives were entitled to under Mexican law.[25] She may have lived for a while in Taos, but she had no need to roam the streets there or work as a prostitute, as Gregg implied by referring to her "very loose habits." Señora Doña Barceló was a woman of legitimate resources—and a more advanced capitalist than most American traders frequenting Santa Fe, some of whom tried their luck at monte and other games of chance now and then. They were inveterate risk takers, while she preferred to leave risks to others and benefit by their inevitable failures. "Traders often lose the profits of a whole season in an hour's play," claimed Matt Field, and such losses helped Barceló to become a conspicuous consumer of the best the Americans had to offer. As Field noted after touring her home:

> A very rich clock of American manufacture hung on the wall, completely out of order, and the hands were pointing with great constancy one at twelve and the other at six, they having been placed so probably to look uniform. The Señora told us facetiously that she was economical with her clock, it being too handsome to work, and not wishing it to grow old too fast, she only let it go on holidays.[26]

This was her prerogative as one who belonged to the enviable ranks of the ricos, to have objects about that were "too handsome to work" and were simply there for display. Few of the Americans who ventured to Santa Fe would attain that level of luxury, and Field detected a subtle element of contempt in the way she manipulated visitors and deprived them effortlessly of their hard-earned gains. One player, whom Field described as a "sturdy Kentuckian," was so emboldened by a brief winning streak that he objected when she requested a fresh pack of cards:

> Toulous smiled as courteously as though she had received a compliment, although the abrupt objection and the tone of its delivery, evidently betrayed a suspicion of foul play. Yet, although even the victim might have fallen in love with that polite expression of feature, to a reader of hearts there was in it the dark designing of one who despised both her fools and the tools by which she ruled them.[27]

The local tolerance for gambling and the involvement of women in that pastime were among various irregularities that led Americans to view New Mexico in general, and Santa Fe in particular, as morally deficient. Not only did women there smoke and gamble, but some engaged in affairs that seldom escaped notice for long in a town with few secrets. In one case, American trader John Scolly took his Mexican wife, Juana Lopes, to court in Santa Fe, charging her with repeated acts of adultery. "In my very house," he testified, "I have heard said adulterers knock on the window when they want my wife to go out." His wife made no attempt to deny the accusations or apologize for her lapses, insisting bluntly that "it was her ass, she controlled it, and she would give it to whomever she wanted."[28] She was ordered to quit "roving" and stay by her husband and children. Wives in Santa Fe leveled similar charges of infidelity in court against their husbands, who were instructed to mend their ways and honor their obligations to their families. Josiah Gregg was one of several American observers who claimed that New Mexicans of both sexes were lax when it came to their marriage vows, but he was more interested in explaining their behavior than in denouncing it:

"Lady Tules," or Gertrudis Barceló, from *Harper's Monthly*, April 1854. Courtesy Museum of New Mexico, negative no. 1854.

In New Mexico, the institution of marriage changes the legal rights of the parties, but it scarcely affects their moral obligations. It is usually looked upon as a convenient cloak for irregularities, which society less willingly tolerates in the lives of unmarried women. Yet when it is considered that the majority of matches are forced and ill-assorted, some idea may be formed of the little incitement that is given to virtue. There are very few parents who would stoop to consult a young lady's wishes before concluding a marriage contract, nor would maidens, generally, ever dream of a matrimonial connexion unless proposed first by the father. . . .

Among the humbler classes, there are still more powerful causes calculated to produce irregularity of life; not the least of which is the enormous fee that must be paid to the curate for tying the matrimonial knot. This system of extortion is carried so far as to amount very frequently to absolute prohibition: for the means of the bridegroom are often insufficient for the exigency of the occasion; and the priests seldom consent to join people in wedlock until the money has been secured to them.[29]

No less burdensome, Gregg added, were the fees priests charged for performing baptisms and burials. Some bereft parents, he noted, furtively left their dead children in the church at night so that the priest would have no choice but to perform the burial without charge. Parents of means, on the other hand, staged elaborate funeral processions for their heaven-bound *angelito*, "accompanied by musicians using the instruments and playing the tunes of the fandangos; and the little procession is nothing but glee and merriment."[30]

Although Gregg was severe in his assessment of the priests and the ceremonies they presided over—Sibley, for one, saw nothing gleeful in such funeral processions—the church in New Mexico was undeniably in need of some repair. James Webb was not one to disparage the moral character of New Mexicans. He noted, for example, that he had never witnessed any "want of decorum and self-respect in any woman in a *fandango*, whatever might be her reputation for virtue outside," and he blamed disorders at the dances largely on "Americans and whiskey."[31] Yet the local priests and their parishioners did not strike Webb as especially pious. He passed along a sarcastic tale told of the esteemed New Mexican official Pedro Baptista Pino, author of the *Exposition on the Province of New Mexico*, who reportedly reached the gates of paradise after his death by virtue of his good conduct but was nearly denied admission by a skeptical St. Peter, who had never heard of New Mexico or welcomed a single soul from that benighted province. Fueling such stories were reports of priests who had one or more common-law wives or indulged in drinking bouts like the padre at San Miguel, who dined there with acquaintances of Webb's and made a spectacle of himself:

> They had a good supper, with a good supply of liquors for the entertainment of their reverend guest, of which he partook quite freely and became rather hilarious. On leaving camp, he mounted his pony and rode around the camp at the fastest run of his horse (two or three times), and coming to the road leading to town, struck off on it, raising his hat with a grand flourish, [and] gave us the parting "*Adíos!* Good-bye! Go to hell!" and went off satisfied and happy.[32]

Local Catholics were themselves distressed by such pastoral excesses and by the fees charged for marriages, baptisms, and burials (fees that some priests, at least, lowered or eliminated for the poor). Antonio Barreiro lamented the "abuses which are committed in New Mexico in the nurture and cure of souls,"

and added that "charity requires a veil to be thrown over many things the relation of which would occasion scandal."[33] Yet Barreiro understood better than
most Americans how difficult it was for priests educated in more comfortable
surroundings to the south to adjust to life on the lonely New Mexican frontier:

> The curates and missionaries of this Territory have to subsist on a scanty com-
> petence; they find themselves separated from cultured intercourse with other
> people, isolated in these corners of the Republic where only disagreeable
> objects and oftentimes dangers are near them; they are deprived of the pleas-
> ures with which civilized places allure them; they come to live on some mis-
> erable ranch and to endure privations which weigh not a little on the spirits
> of men who are used to a different order of things.[34]

The shortage of priests in New Mexico that Pedro Baptista Pino had complained of in 1812 had only been exacerbated by the government's recent
efforts to secularize the missions, which meant replacing friars of the Franciscan order with parish priests. Some Franciscans stayed on as parish priests in
New Mexico, but others departed or died, and few young priests arrived from
the south to fill the void. Those who did answer the call had little choice but
to charge fees for their services. In 1833 the government abolished the unpop-
ular practice of compulsory tithing, and New Mexicans were not much inclined
to pay tithes voluntarily, complaining that the church hierarchy funneled much
of their offerings southward to Mexico's large population centers. Some in
New Mexico responded to the crisis by forming a lay brotherhood known as
the Penitentes, whose members ministered to the poor and also engaged in
the controversial practice of flagellation to atone for their sins. In 1851, Rome
would belatedly acknowledge the need for closer attention to the spiritual problems of New Mexico by granting the territory its first bishop, Jean Baptiste
Lamy. In the interim, however, the neglected state of the church there reinforced the impression of visitors from the United States that their hosts were
in poor hands and might be better off under American auspices.[35]

A more accurate assessment might be that the New Mexicans were compromised by circumstances. Life on the frontier did not lend itself to moral
absolutes. Hardship, loneliness, and want impelled all but the most saintly of
settlers to seek consolation where they could find it and to reach accommodations with those who were not always the best of neighbors. New Mexicans could ill afford to cast out sinners from their midst, any more than they
could afford to cease trafficking with nearby Indian tribes whose members
were sometimes hostile. Josiah Gregg understood the necessity of such compromises and wrote insightfully of the complex manner in which the locals
dealt with the various tribal groups in their vicinity, trading and sometimes

intermarrying with them when they were not actively engaged in fighting them. The most durable and successful of those accommodations was the one that the New Mexicans had reached with the Pueblo peoples. Once violently opposed to the intrusive Spaniards, Pueblos were now largely reconciled to outside authorities, although they remained deeply suspicious of any attempt by the Mexican government to infringe on their prerogatives—a fear that led a number of them to back the revolt of 1837. Among the rights they cherished and were prepared to defend with their lives was the control they exercised over their own communities. As Gregg observed:

> Although nominally under the jurisdiction of the federal government, as Mexican citizens, many features of their ancient customs are still retained, as well in their civil rule as in their religion. Each Pueblo is under the control of a *cacique* or *gobernadorcillo*, chosen from among their own sages, and commissioned by the governor of New Mexico. The cacique, when any public business is to be transacted, collects together the principal chiefs of the Pueblo in an *estufa*, or cell, usually under ground, and there lays before them the subjects of debate, which are generally settled by the opinion of the majority. No Mexican is admitted to these councils, nor do the subjects of discussion ever transpire beyond the precincts of the cavern. The council has also charge of the interior police and tranquility of the village.[36]

The *estufa*, or underground cell, referred to here was the Pueblo kiva, where those privileged to enter gathered around a fire. That secret and sanctified place aroused much interest and speculation among outsiders. Both Gregg and Field told of a legend associated with Pecos Pueblo that portrayed the inhabitants as guardians of a sacred fire dedicated to the last Aztec king, Montezuma, who, as Gregg wrote, had "enjoined their ancestors not to suffer it to be extinguished until he should return to deliver his people from the yoke of the Spaniards."[37] Legends portraying Montezuma as a savior were in fact widespread among the Pueblos. Some believed that Montezuma had been born on a pueblo in New Mexico and that he would return one day with the rising sun to redeem his people.[38] But the story that occupants of Pecos Pueblo tended an eternal fire in honor of the Aztec king may simply have been another facet of the Montezuma myth that beguiled Mexicans and Americans as well as Pueblos. James Webb's account of the abandonment of Pecos Pueblo, whose last remaining residents moved to Jémez Pueblo in 1838, makes much of the sacred fire but includes no mention of Montezuma:

> The migration was made with great formality, the sacred fire not being allowed to become extinguished, but was kept burning and borne upon the shoulders

of the old men who had formerly had charge of it and [who had] directed the ceremonious worship of the Indians in the *estufa*. The Pueblo Indians are good Catholics, each having a church and paying the parish priest his tithes and firstlings and the legal fees for marrying, baptizing, and burying. Yet in each pueblo the ancient mode of worship was maintained in the *estufa* in all its forms as handed down by tradition, and seldom or ever was a Mexican permitted to enter the *estufa* even to gratify curiosity, much less to be present during the performance of any religious ceremonies.[39]

This cogent interpretation of the "sacred fire" as a symbol of ancient religious and communal rituals that the inhabitants faithfully preserved even as they reached an accommodation with outsiders was more in keeping with Pueblo tradition than the idea that worshipers in the kiva kept the flames alive eternally in Montezuma's honor. Field remarked that a version of the Montezuma story "was current among all the Americans residing in Santa Fé,"[40] suggesting that the legend, whatever its origins, may have held some special meaning for Americans and perhaps been refashioned by them in the telling. When American forces occupied New Mexico in 1846, it was said that Pueblos linked their arrival from the east with the promised return of Montezuma and saw the American conquest as a godsend—a strange twist, indeed, on the story of a sacred fire that symbolized the determination of Pueblos to preserve their ancestral identity in the face of any and all intrusions.

If Hispanic New Mexicans had succeeded over the years in coming to terms with the Pueblos, they were far from reaching a similar accommodation with the Navajos. Gregg noted, however, that the frequent clashes between the two sides did not preclude peaceful exchanges. Among the items the local settlers sought from the resourceful Navajos—who raised cotton and other crops and tended sheep—were their splendid weavings, including woollen serapes so densely woven that they were virtually waterproof and were "sold among the Mexicans as high as fifty or sixty dollars each."[41] Campaigns led by José Antonio Vizcarra in the 1820s had kept the Navajos "in submission for some time," Gregg added, but they had since renewed their raids against the New Mexicans on a seasonal basis:

When the spring of the year approaches, terms of peace are generally proposed to the government at Santa Fé, which the latter never fails to accept. This amicable arrangement enables the wily Indians to sow their crops at leisure, and to dispose of the property stolen from the Mexicans during their marauding incursions, to advantage; but the close of their agricultural labors is generally followed by a renewal of hostilities, and the game of rapine and destruction is played over again.[42]

Mexicans even traded sporadically with Apaches, Gregg remarked, despite the fact that repeated Apache raids had forced settlers to abandon many remote villages and ranches, particularly in the department of Chihuahua to the south:

> In 1840, I witnessed the departure from Santa Fé of a large trading party freighted with engines of war and a great quantity of whiskey, intended for the Apaches in exchange for mules and other articles of plunder which they had stolen from the people of the south. This traffic was not only tolerated but openly encouraged by the civil authorities, as the highest public functionaries were interested in its success—the governor himself not excepted.[43]

As an outsider, Gregg felt free to criticize such dealings, which he felt rewarded the Apaches for their predations. But Americans would soon inherit such problems when they claimed New Mexico, and they too would vacillate between bargaining with the defiant tribes and fighting them. Indeed, that pattern of hostilities intermingled with diplomatic and economic exchanges was a long-standing tribal tradition here and in much of the West and had certain advantages over a policy of relentless warfare that might result ultimately in the annihilation of one side or the other and the loss of a useful trading partner.

Like it or not, Americans were being drawn ever deeper into this world of vacillation and compromise through the ventures of traders like Gregg, whose interests carried him not only to Santa Fe but southward to the city of Chihuahua, a journey of some 550 miles through largely arid country haunted by Apaches. The incentive for following that rough road to Chihuahua was much the same as for plying the Santa Fe Trail—the lure of Mexican customers who had no ready supply of manufactured goods, living as they did far from the major seaports of their own country, and who would pay handsomely for well-made American imports. To be sure, the trip south involved extra expense and risk for American traders, but Chihuahua was roughly twice the size of Santa Fe and boasted a sizable concentration of ricos who were drawn to the safety and comfort of that impressive urban oasis. Gregg described the journey as he made it in 1839, when a French blockade of Mexican ports made the trip all the more worthwhile, but other American traders had been following that trail south assiduously since the 1820s.

The first stretch of the trip, down along the Rio Grande, was through country long occupied by Spanish settlers, Gregg noted, but one that remained largely a backwater by American standards:

> The road we travelled passes down through the settlements of New Mexico for the first hundred and thirty miles, on the east side of the Rio del Norte. Nevertheless, as there was not an inn of any kind to be found upon the whole

route, we were constrained to put up with very primitive accommodations. Being furnished from the outset, therefore, with blankets and buffalo rugs for bedding, we were prepared to bivouac, even in the suburbs of the villages, in the open air; for in this dry and salubrious atmosphere it is seldom that travellers go to the trouble of pitching tents. When travelling alone, however, or with but a comrade or two, I have always experienced a great deal of hospitality from the rancheros and villageois of the country. Whatever sins these ignorant people may have to answer for, we must accord to them at least two glowing virtues—gratitude and hospitality.[44]

In the vicinity of Fray Cristóbal, Gregg and company left the Rio Grande—which bends to the west at that point—and traveled due south across the desert for eighty miles or so before rejoining the river's path. This was the genuine *Jornado del Muerto*, traversing desert even more severe than the Jornada on the Cimarron Route. Gregg and company avoided the worst of the heat by traveling that desolate stretch mostly in the evening. After rejoining the Rio Grande, they continued south along the east bank before fording the river, whose waters were unusually high, requiring the traders to empty their wagons of goods and ferry the merchandise across in dugouts.

On reaching El Paso, the traders entered the department of Chihuahua and underwent a brief inspection of their wares by a customs officer. Gregg described the place as "so thickly interspersed with vineyards, orchards, and cornfields, as to present more the appearance of a series of plantations than of a town."[45] This was the last fertile ground the travelers would see for many days. Departing El Paso, they left the Rio Grande for good and headed due south through the bleak sand hills known as Los Médanos, where the footing was so poor that pack mules had to be enlisted to lighten the wagons. Beyond lay high desert country watered only by murky springs that were thoroughly uninviting, with the notable exception of Ojo Caliente, a favorite bathing spot roughly midway between El Paso and Chihuahua. At length, the traders descended into the lush valley of Encinillas, whose once-prosperous ranches had been ravaged by Apache raids in recent times. Finally, forty days after setting out, Gregg and company reached Chihuahua, which, while less hospitable to Americans than Santa Fe, the author observed, surpassed that town both in the elegance of its architecture and in its opportunities for amusement and expenditure:

> Besides the cock-pit, the gaming-table, and the *Alameda*, which is the popular promenade for the wealthy and the indolent, one of the most favorite pastimes of the females generally is shopping; and the most fashionable time for this is by candle-light, after they have partaken of their chocolate and their

cigarritos. The streets and shops are literally filled from dusk till nine or ten o'clock; and many a time have I seen the counter of a store actually lined till a late hour, with the fairest and most fashionable señoritas of the city.[46]

Merchants had to keep a sharp eye out, Gregg added, for some of those ladies were "painfully afflicted with the self-appropriating mania." But that was just another of the nagging irregularities that foreigners who sought the fruits of the trade learned to put up with. For Gregg, it was all part of a rich and rewarding exchange, and he remained hopeful as late as 1843, when he set down his account, that the common interests of commerce would transcend any differences that arose between the United States and Mexico. But even as he wrote, representatives of a third party—the independent Republic of Texas, soon to enter the Union as a state—were probing their disputed border with Mexico and sowing seeds of discord.

15

Paths to Conflict

Josiah Gregg's *Commerce of the Prairies* reached a wide audience and did much to influence the way Americans viewed New Mexico. But his book was rivaled in impact by an account published the same year that was more provocative in its portrait of Mexicans—George Kendall's *Narrative of the Texan Santa Fé Expedition* (1844), which became a best-seller. Kendall was an accomplished journalist and editor, and his gripping narrative helped transform the ill-fated expedition in which he participated into a cause célèbre not just for Texans but for sympathetic Americans, whose nation would inherit the claims and grievances of Texas when that republic was willingly annexed by the United States in 1845.

The venture Kendall chronicled did not follow the Santa Fe Trail, but it was prompted in part by the lucrative traffic on that route and included a forced march by Kendall and company down the Chihuahua Trail, a vital extension of the road to New Mexico and an increasingly important link between the fortunes of Mexico and the United States. By 1841, the Republic of Texas, which had won independence from Mexico just five years earlier, was in dire financial straits, having accumulated a debt of over $7 million.[1] President Mirabeau Buonaparte Lamar proposed that Texans establish their own road to New Mexico, a trade route suitable for wagons that would divert to the coffers of the republic some of the coveted currency that was being funneled to Missouri on the Santa Fe Trail. But Lamar's ambitions were not limited to trade. Encouraged by New Mexico's unsuccessful revolt against the central government in 1837 and by reports that New Mexicans remained resentful of higher authorities and hungry for independence, Lamar hoped that if Texans reached Santa Fe in force, the populace would join forces with them and cast off their Mexican overlords. The boundary between Mexico and Texas remained in dispute, and Texans claimed everything east of the Rio Grande, including Santa Fe. Lamar went so far as to invite New Mexicans to help Texans assert that claim in a letter he entrusted to William G. Dryden, an American trader who had settled in Santa Fe: "We tender to you a full participation in all our blessings. The great River of the North, which you inhabit, is the natural and convenient boundary of our territory, and we shall take great pleasure in hailing you as fellow-citizens, members of our young Republic, and co-aspirants with us for all the glory of establishing a new and happy and free Nation."[2]

Zebulon Pike had expressed similar sentiments as early as 1810, when he imagined circumstances in which American forces might be welcomed by Mexicans as liberators. It was not just visions of wealth or empire that lured Anglo adventurers to Santa Fe over the years but the flattering prospect of freeing Mexicans from their political and economic restraints and being hailed as champions. Yet that elusive dream—and Lamar's specific hopes for a take-over of the disputed territory with the consent of the populace—ignored the cultural boundaries that divided Hispanics from Anglos and linked Spanish-speaking people on either side of the Rio Grande to their compatriots to the south. Like others on their nation's troubled northern frontier, New Mexicans indeed yearned for greater autonomy. The chief consequence of the Texan Santa Fe expedition, however, was not to satisfy that yearning but to render New Mexicans more vulnerable to hostile incursions by outsiders, including troops from Texas and the United States intent on avenging the mistreatment of those captured during Lamar's ill-conceived venture and herded down the Chihuahua Trail. In the process, that trail ceased to be strictly an avenue of commerce and fostered exchanges of a more disruptive nature that recalled earlier episodes of confrontation and conquest on Mexico's Royal Road.

Lamar recognized the possibility that Texans might not be welcomed as liberators in Santa Fe and issued instructions to the leaders of the expedition to avoid hostilities in the face of popular resistance: "The President anxious as he is to have our National flag acknowledged in Santa fé, does not consider it expedient at this time to force it upon that portion of the Republic. If the Mexican authorities are prepared to defend the place with arms, and if you can satisfy yourselves that they will be supported by the mass of the people . . . you will not be authorized to risk a battle."[3] Like Zebulon Pike's reconnais-sance of 1806–7, the Texan Santa Fe expedition was an ambiguous venture whose possibilities ranged from promoting trade and other forms of harmonious intercourse to clearing the way for a takeover. The expedition included more than three hundred Pioneers, as the volunteers were called, some of them merchants but most of them soldiers, or men prepared to fight, officially recruited to defend the caravan against attack by Comanches, Kiowas, and other tribes whose territory the Pioneers would traverse on their way to Santa Fe. That these soldiers might also play a part in the taking of New Mexico was supposed to remain a secret, but it did not long remain so. Critics of the expedition would contend that the commercial objectives were a smoke screen and that the venture was essentially an act of aggression. George Kendall, who maintained his American citizenship and joined the expedition as a journalistic observer, staunchly denied those charges:

> The idea, which has obtained credence to some extent in the United States, that the first Texan Santa Fé pioneers were but a company of marauders, sent to burn, slay and destroy in a foreign and hostile country, is so absurd as not to require contradiction; the attempt to conquer a province, numbering some one hundred and fifty thousand inhabitants within its borders, was a shade too Quixotical to find favour in the eyes of the three hundred and twenty odd pioneers who left Texas, encumbered with wagons, merchandise, and the implements of their different trades and callings.[4]

In fact, New Mexico had less than half as many inhabitants as Kendall claimed, and it was so poorly defended that in 1846 an invasion force of fewer than two thousand hastily assembled American volunteers would occupy Santa Fe without firing a shot. Yet Kendall had a point. The expedition was not strong enough for purposes of conquest; nor was it innocent enough to be accepted by New Mexican authorities as a simple trading venture. It was a study in contradictions, embodying the mix of peaceable and predatory motives that drew not just Texans but Americans to Santa Fe in large numbers and culminated in a military takeover in 1846 that was fraught with commercial overtones.

The men of the Texan Santa Fe expedition encountered many of the same problems faced by travelers on the Santa Fe Trail, difficulties compounded by the fact that these Pioneers had only the vaguest idea of how to reach their goal. Preparations delayed their departure from the vicinity of Austin until the latter part of June, and their leaders then elected to travel due north before turning west, a course that took them into the tangled Cross Timbers region above the Brazos River, where men had to clear a path through the brush on foot to make way for the wagons. Not until late July did they extricate themselves from that maze, which meant that they would be crossing the arid plains of north Texas at the hottest time of the year. Only fitfully successful at buffalo hunting and short of food, they sent guide Samuel Howland and two other men ahead to purchase provisions in New Mexico and see what sort of welcome they might receive there. Then in late August, having heard nothing from those three scouts and having recently lost five members of the expedition in a clash with Kiowas below the Red River, the Pioneers divided their command. Kendall went ahead with a group of one hundred or so men on horseback to find the way to the New Mexico settlements as quickly as possible and secure food, while the rest of the expedition remained behind with the wagons, which were greatly impeding progress. Carrying only five days' provisions in their packs, Kendall and company traveled northwestward for nearly two weeks through the bleak, broken terrain of the Staked Plains (Llano Estacado) and the desert beyond before finally encountering a New Mexican trading party returning home from Comanche and Kiowa territory. Those venturesome Comancheros had little food to offer the famished Texans, Kendall related, but directed them to nearby shepherds, who gladly sold the pioneers some of their stock:

> Here a scene of feasting ensued which beggars description. We had been thirteen days upon the road, with really not provisions enough for three, and now that there was an abundance our starving men at once abandoned themselves to eating—perhaps I should rather call it gormandizing or stuffing. No less than twenty large, fat sheep had been purchased and dressed, and every ramrod, as well as every stick that could be found, was soon graced with smoking ribs and shoulders, livers and hearts. Many made themselves sick by overeating; but an attempt to restrain the appetites of half-starved men, except by main force, would be the very extreme of folly.[5]

Once they recovered from these excesses, the men felt optimistic that their hardships were behind them. The locals were trafficking with them enthusiastically, Kendall noted, and it seemed possible that the faltering expedition might yet succeed as a trading venture:

> The morning after our feast we made another hearty meal of broiled mutton, with *atole con leche*, a mush compounded of flour and goats' milk. The Mexican shepherds, finding the Texans excellent customers, and disposed to pay the highest prices for anything in the shape of bread, had sent to their *rancho*, or farm, during the night, a distance of some twelve miles, and supplied themselves abundantly with flour.[6]

But the hopes of the Pioneers were soon dashed. The shepherds informed them that Howland and the two other Texans sent ahead as scouts were being held captive in Santa Fe. Although Kendall and his companions initially dismissed this and other ominous reports as mere rumors, they soon received confirmation that Governor Manuel Armijo had learned of the expedition and regarded it as hostile, having informed the populace that the Texans, as Kendall put it, were out to "burn, slay, and destroy."[7]

Nonetheless, Kendall went ahead with several other Pioneers to San Miguel to purchase provisions for the men who had remained behind on the plains and to assure authorities that their intentions were "in every way pacific."[8] Unfortunately, one of the Texans accompanying Kendall carried copies of a proclamation from President Lamar in Spanish and English that revealed the ulterior motive of the expedition, stating by Kendall's account that "if the inhabitants of New Mexico were not disposed to join, peacefully, the Texan standard, the expedition was to retire immediately."[9] Weakened and divided as they were, the Pioneers had no hope now of leading the populace in a revolt against Mexico, yet this proclamation betrayed that quixotic ambition and defined them as enemy agents, albeit not very dangerous ones. Kendall and the others in his advance party were apprehended by New Mexican troops before they reached San Miguel. A similar fate awaited all the other Pioneers who survived the harsh journey across the plains and reached New Mexico—some of whom might have resisted arrest had they not been assured by a Texan-turned-traitor that they would be well treated if they surrendered. In fact, they were sorely mistreated, and the punishments and privations they suffered, as detailed by Kendall and other witnesses, did more to incite Texans and Americans and contribute to the eventual overthrow of Governor Armijo than anything the bedraggled Pioneers could have hoped to accomplish had they somehow evaded arrest.

Kendall's captivity narrative was much more than a litany of abuses, however. He interspersed his denunciations of his captors with tributes to those New Mexicans who took pity on the prisoners. In particular, he paid tribute to the merciful women of New Mexico—in strong terms that heightened the contrast between their charity and the callousness of the men and implied that the better half of the population (as he regarded the women) might be better off under American guardianship. When Kendall and his fellow captives were stripped of their weapons and marched off to San Miguel, for example, women along the route showered them with sympathy and gifts, prompting Kendall to offer the first of several sweeping generalizations about the relative virtues of the two sexes in New Mexico:

> That the women all pitied us was evident; for the commiserating exclamation of *pobrecitos*! as they gave us bread, cheese, and such food as they had at hand, fell from their tongues in softest and most feeling tones. They knew their husbands and brothers, and knowing them, felt that little of mercy or kindness could we expect at their hands.[10]

Later in their grueling journey, Kendall and his fellow captives received further considerations from a female sympathizer, and the author expanded on his theme:

> We had not traveled more than a couple of miles before a tolerably well-dressed woman came running towards us from a small house, bringing a bottle of the country whiskey, and saying that it was for our use. This we drank upon the spot, and as we thanked the good-hearted creature for her kindness she appeared to feel deeply for us in our misfortunes. Even after we had been hurried off by our inhuman guard, the woman still remained to gaze upon us, looking her last at the *pobrecitos*, whom she really thought the sun would not set upon alive. The almost universal brutality and cold-heartedness of the men of New Mexico are in strange contrast with the kind dispositions and tender sympathies exhibited by all classes of the women.[11]

Elsewhere, however, Kendall offered testimony to the contrary, indicating that the men of the province were not all so coldhearted. The priest in San Miguel, for example, sent each of the prisoners "a generous bowl of hot coffee," noted Kendall, who later attested that the Mexican priests he encountered while in captivity were on the whole "liberal and enlightened men, and disposed to assist us as far as was in their power."[12] And several of the author's fellow prisoners were comfortably confined at a "rancho some three miles from San Miguel, and there quartered in the family of a kind-hearted old Mexican, named Don Antonio Baca, a man who had frequently visited us during our imprisonment, and who had never called without bringing us eggs or some little delicacy."[13] Yet Kendall was even more impressed by the affection bestowed on one handsome young Texan by a daughter of this same obliging Mexican:

> Don Antonio had two or three daughters, pretty, and accomplished too, for that country; we afterward learned that one of them formed an ardent attachment—fell in love, in more common parlance—with one of our young friends, and was affected even to tears and hysterics when he was ordered to the city of Mexico. It is said that no attachment can be stronger, no love more enduring, than that of the better-informed Mexican doncella, when once her heart is touched by the blue eyes, light hair, and fair complexion of some roving Anglo-Saxon.[14]

Much like Albert Pike in his prose sketches, Kendall portrayed the "roving Anglo-Saxon" as exercising an irresistible allure for the discriminating Mexican woman, who if given a choice would naturally prefer a suitor who was light and fair (in conduct as well as complexion) to one who was dark and devious. To his credit, Kendall did not dismiss Mexicans as entirely unappealing, as some Anglos did. To the contrary, he found the women of the country more fetching in their dress and demeanor than their counterparts back in the States:

> Among the Mexican women, young and old, corsets are unknown, and, by a majority of them, probably unheard of. I traveled nearly seven hundred miles through the country, without seeing a single gown—all the females were dressed in the same style, with the same *abandon*. The consequence any one may readily imagine: the forms of the gentler sex obtain a roundness, a fulness, which the divinity of tight lacing never allows her votaries. The Mexican belles certainly have studied, too, their personal comfort in the costume they have adopted, and it is impossible to see the prettier of the dark-eyed *señoras* of the northern departments without acknowledging that their personal appearance and attractions are materially enhanced by the *negligé* style.[15]

Kendall saw something uncommonly generous in these women—an easiness and liberality that gratified the beholder even at a distance. Such hospitality, while often enthusiastic and heartfelt, also served the interests of the host country, however, by disarming potentially hostile visitors and drawing them safely into the realm of peaceful exchanges. Overtures of this sort were easily misinterpreted. When Mexican women were sympathetic and obliging to their Anglo visitors, some on the receiving end took that as an invitation to make themselves at home, as it were, and to claim superiority over their hosts. That, at least, was how Kendall seemed to interpret the situation. He not only suggested that Mexican women were romantically susceptible to American mastery but insisted that Mexican men, for all their bluster, had little chance against stout-hearted Anglo-Saxons in a fair fight. He derided the guards who watched over him and his fellow prisoners, claiming at one point that a "determined rush, accompanied by a true Anglo-Saxon shout of defiance, would have brought every one of the cowardly wretches to his knees begging for mercy."[16] (Only the impossibility of returning safely to Texas on foot through passes patrolled by mounted men deterred the prisoners from making such an attempt, he added.) In a similar vein, Kendall denounced Armijo as a craven despot who resorted to treachery against Texans and Americans because he dreaded their superiority: "He is afraid of Anglo-Saxon blood, and he seeks to spill it by protecting the knife of the secret assassin, or by influencing, to most outrageous decisions, his farcical courts of law."[17]

That Kendall's verbal assaults on Armijo and his countrymen were sometimes tainted by bigotry should not obscure the fact that the author had deep and legitimate grievances. Not long after he was taken prisoner, he and other captives witnessed the execution of Samuel Howland and Alexander Baker, who had escaped from prison in Santa Fe only to be recaptured by Armijo's troops. (The third member of their advance party, William Rosenberry, died resisting those troops.) Baker's execution went dreadfully awry, Kendall related:

> His cowardly executioners led him to a house near the same corner of the square we were in, not twenty yards from us, and after heartlessly pushing him upon his knees, with his head against the wall, six of the guard stepped back about three paces, and at the order of the corporal *shot the poor fellow in the back*! Even at that distance the executioners but half did their barbarous work; for the man was only wounded, and lay writhing upon the ground in great agony. The corporal stepped up, and with a pistol ended his sufferings by shooting him through the heart. So close was the pistol that the man's shirt was set on fire, and continued to burn until it was extinguished by his blood![18]

Howland was shot to death a short time later, having earlier been maimed by his captors, according to Kendall. He and others feared that they too might be executed, but Armijo informed them that they would be spared so long as they did not attempt to escape. Not all of them survived the ordeal that lay ahead, however. They were dispatched to Mexico City, and the officer Armijo assigned to escort them, Captain Dámaso Salazar, saw to it that their trek south to El Paso, where they were to be transferred to Chihuahuan authorities, would be as punishing as possible.

The arrival and capture of the Texans brought a sudden chill to relations between resident Americans and their New Mexican hosts. Armijo feared that Americans were behind the intervention and used charges to that effect to alarm and arouse the populace, whom he considered all too vulnerable to the seditious appeals of foreigners.[19] That, at least, was how Manuel Alvarez, the Spanish-born American consul in Santa Fe, viewed the situation. Two deserters from the Texan force had accused prominent Americans in New Mexico of conspiring with the invaders, Alvarez noted, and "some respectable citizens of Santa Fe had denounced several Americans as being engaged in a plot to assassinate the Governor." Alvarez implied that Armijo was using these "false reports" to whip up hostility toward "peaceable and unoffending American merchants who were in no way connected with the Texan invasion."[20] Before departing Santa Fe in September to inspect the captured Texans, Armijo issued an order forbidding Alvarez and other foreigners in Santa Fe to leave the capital. A short time later, Armijo's nephew, Ensign Thomás Martín—described by Alvarez as the governor's "most intimate friend and confidant"—confronted the American consul and abused him "in the grossest and most insulting manner."[21] Backed by an angry crowd, Martín brandished a knife and wounded Alvarez in the face before Armijo's secretary, Guadalupe Miranda, intervened and restored peace. Alvarez considered himself lucky to escape with his life.

In this Texan Santa Fe crisis, as in other instances where commerce gave way to conflict along the trail, differences that rival parties customarily settled through exchanges of cash, goods, or favors were no longer so easily resolved. When Alvarez learned that Kendall, an American citizen, was among the captured Pioneers, for example, he pooled resources with traders Charles Bent and James Wiley Magoffin, a native Kentuckian with strong commercial ties to Mexico, and offered Armijo a hefty price to free Kendall and José Antonio Navarro, one of the few Texans of Mexican heritage to participate in the expedition. Alvarez and company fully expected Armijo to come to terms, as he usually did when the price was right, but the governor was in no mood to bargain. As Alvarez reported:

> Mr. Kendall being known to the American residents in Santa Fe, as a popular editor, and a highly honorable man, Mr. C. Bent, Mr. J. Magoffin and myself feeling very anxious for his liberation, thought that the only efficient means in our present circumstances was money. We therefore, authorized Mr. J. Magoffin (he being on good terms with the Governor) to offer three thousand dollars for the release of Mr. Kendall and a Mr. Navarro (a Mexican, to show that we were not altogether partial to the Americans alone). Contrary to our expectations the offer was declined.[22]

Armijo no doubt felt that in rejecting this compromising offer he was doing himself credit, but he would have done better in the long run by releasing Kendall, with or without financial incentive. Generally shrewd in dealing with Americans, Armijo made a serious miscalculation in this case, perhaps because he was truly incensed by what he saw as American collusion in an abortive uprising. By refusing to bargain for Kendall's release and subjecting him to the same treatment as the other prisoners, Armijo exposed himself to the barbs of an influential journalist who proceeded to skewer the governor in writing. Kendall's description of Armijo as he departed San Miguel after inspecting the prisoners was a small masterpiece of caustic portraiture:

> His appearance was certainly imposing, even unto magnificence. On this occasion he was mounted on a richly-caparisoned mule, of immense size and of a beautiful dun colour. In stature Armijo is over six feet, stout and well built, and with an air decidedly military. Over his uniform he now wore a *poncho* of the finest blue broadcloth, inwrought with various devices in gold and silver, and through the hole in the centre peered the head to which the

Governor Manuel Armijo. Courtesy Museum of New Mexico, negative no. 50809.

inhabitants of New Mexico are compelled to bow in fear and much trembling. Armijo is certainly one of the best-appearing men I met in the country, and were he not such a cowardly braggart, and so utterly destitute of all moral principle, is not wanting in the other qualities of a good governor.[23]

Travelers on the Santa Fe Trail may have come to respect mules as mounts, but Kendall could rest assured that many of his readers would regard a governor riding even a "richly-caparisoned" mule as a ludicrous figure. This was just one of several instances in which Kendall settled the score with Armijo by subjecting him to a journalistic treatment, a makeover that transformed a complex historical figure into a caricature. Kendall claimed without foundation, for example, that Armijo was born "of low and disreputable parents" and got his start in life by stealing sheep from a wealthy New Mexican rancher, Francisco Chávez:

> When among his intimate friends, General Manuel Armijo boastingly relates the exploit of having sold to "Old Chavez" the same ewe *fourteen different times*, and of having stolen her from him even in the first instance. By this means, and by having what is termed a good run of luck at dealing *monte*, he amassed no inconsiderable fortune, and as his ambition now led him to learn to read and write, the foundation of his future influence and greatness among his timid and ignorant countrymen was substantially laid.[24]

In fact, Armijo belonged to one of New Mexico's wealthiest families and had little need to enrich himself at the expense of "Old Chavez," a man to whom he was related by marriage. As George Ruxton observed in 1848, the Armijo and Chávez families were prominent among the "*ricos* of New Mexico."[25] Perhaps Kendall was honestly misinformed as to Armijo's origins, but he did his best here to portray the governor as an unscrupulous upstart, lording it over countrymen who were only slightly more ignorant than he was. This was much the same treatment accorded Gertrudis Barceló in American accounts. She and Armijo wielded considerable power over visitors to New Mexico and sometimes profited at their expense, and the unfounded assertions that both were social climbers of base origins seemed designed to cut them down to size. Kendall filled out his scathing portrait of Armijo by attributing to the governor and his wife vices and vanities of the sort often associated with the New Mexican elite by disapproving Americans but seldom expressed in such strong language:

> When his majesty is in the street, each dutiful subject takes off whatever apology for a hat he may have on his head. Should the governor's wife, a gross, brazen-faced woman, issue from the building, the form is even more ridiculous, for then the cry of "*La gobernadora!*" or "*La commandante generala!*" resounds on every side. This woman is contaminated with every depraved habit known to human nature; and as her husband is a debauchee by "special prerogative," she does not scruple to act as his *alcahueta* in all his amours. In the mean time she is not without her own lovers—a worthy couple, truly![26]

Kendall added that he might, at the risk of sickening his readers, relate many a story of Armijo's "abuse of the rights of women, that would make Saxon hearts burn with indignant fire; for Saxon hearts enshrine the mothers of men as objects sacred and apart."[27]

Kendall's most damning charge against Armijo was more cogent—that he sanctioned the mistreatment of prisoners. On one occasion, the author asserted, Armijo told an officer under his command that if any of the prisoners "*pretends* to be sick or tired on the road, *shoot him down and bring me his ears!*"[28] For Texans as for Americans down through their history, reports of the capture and abuse of their compatriots by hostile powers touched deep chords of shame and outrage that continued to resonate until the offenses were somehow avenged. It was this aspect of Armijo's grim legend, as detailed by Kendall, that most aroused those readers who later volunteered to march on Santa Fe in 1846 and who went on to retrace in triumph the route south that the ill-fated Pioneers had followed as captives in 1841.

Armijo himself did not conduct the prisoners to El Paso, but Kendall held the governor responsible for the misdeeds of the officer he entrusted with that task, Captain Salazar, characterized by the author as "the greatest brute among Armijo's officers."[29] Salazar kept the prisoners on the brink of starvation, the author attested, doling out meager rations on one occasion in a fashion well calculated to degrade his captives:

> Early in the morning we were ordered to continue the march, and without food. Salezar did, previous to starting, distribute some fifty small cakes among one hundred and eighty-seven half-starved men; and the manner of this distribution showed the brutal nature of the wretch. Calling the prisoners around him, each with the hope that he was to receive something to allay the sharp cravings of hunger, he would toss one of these cakes high in the air, and then, with a glee absolutely demoniacal, watch the scramble that ensued as it fell among the suffering throng. It was a game of the strong against the weak, this struggle for the few mouthfuls of food which Salezar threw among them.[30]

The prisoners suffered not just from hunger but from exposure, for they began their march south in mid-October and the nights were bitterly cold. On one bone-chilling evening, after a long day's march to the little town of Valencia, Kendall and a companion, Archibald Fitzgerald, profited by an act of charity; but another man in their party, Felix Ernest, fared far worse:

> Fitzgerald and myself had better quarters, or rather a better bed, that night, than our fellows. We were about lying down, immediately in front of a small house, when an old woman threw us out a couple of sheepskins with the wool

still on. With these between us and the cold ground we really passed a comfortable night.

Not so one of our unfortunate companions. On rising in the morning, it was found that a man named Ernest had died during the night—died from hunger, cold, and fatigue, and without even the knowledge of the man sleeping by his side! . . . Salezar immediately ordered one of his men to cut off and preserve the dead man's ears, as a token that he had not escaped, and by the orders of the same brute the body was thrown into a neighboring ditch.[31]

In another act of kindness that contrasted sharply with Salazar's cruelty, the alcalde of Valencia provided a cart for the transportation of sick and lame prisoners. But the vehicle was rickety, and it proved unequal to the task. Captive John McAllister, who had a sprained ankle, was forced to dismount from the cart and walk, and Salazar threatened to kill him if he failed to keep up with the others:

> "Forward!" said Salezar, now wrought up to a pitch of phrensy. "Forward, or I'll shoot you on the spot!" "Then shoot!" replied McAllister, throwing off his blanket and exposing his manly breast, "and the quicker the better!" Salezar took him at his word, and a single ball sent as brave a man as ever trod the earth to eternity! His ears were then cut off, his shirt and pantaloons stripped from him, and his body thrown by the roadside as food for wolves![32]

Another prisoner who chronicled the ordeal, Englishman Thomas Falconer, described this incident somewhat differently than Kendall, attributing the shooting to one of Salazar's subordinates. But Falconer confirmed that McAllister was one of several Pioneers who died during the march either at the hands of their captors or of natural causes—and that each victim had his ears cut off, "to be presented, by our captain [Salazar], to his superior officer, as evidence that the man had not escaped."[33] Salazar seemed perversely intent on making the prisoners pay dearly for any charitable offerings they received from his merciful compatriots. As Falconer reported:

> Some days no food was distributed, and sometimes only two heads of corn to each man. At Algodonez and San Dia, and their neighborhood, the inhabitants came out and gave the men water-melons, eggs, tortillas and bread, but it was not all who obtained even a part of this charity. When, in the evening, the Captain was asked, if rations would be given, he replied, "No, the men have had excellent grazing to-day." The joke was a cruel one to those who had to wait until the next evening for a meal.[34]

Salazar's anger may have stemmed in part from the knowledge that he could never settle matters with the Texans to his satisfaction so long as New Mexicans along the route continued to treat the prisoners generously. He tried to penal-ize the captives for any such blessings they received—and some of his cruelest outbursts came in response to favors bestowed on the Texans—but he failed to negate the effect of that deep fund of hospitality New Mexicans reserved for wayfarers in need, even in times of unrest. Perhaps, like Governor Armijo, Salazar misinterpreted fellow feeling for the beleaguered Texans as sympathy for their cause. If there was any ulterior motive in the kindness shown to the prisoners, however, it was the simple desire of New Mexicans not to add more enemies to their list by degrading and provoking intruders who no longer posed a threat. That instinct for conciliation ran deep, and it had done as much to preserve the settlers and their communities over the centuries as their willingness to fight when pressed.

Overall, Falconer and Kendall provided ample evidence that Salazar's cru-elty was far from typical of the populace as a whole. Even within Salazar's command there were men who were often willing to accommodate the cap-tives. Throughout the march, Kendall noted, guards traded favors with the prisoners in exchange for coins, buttons, and articles of clothing. (Merchant Amos Golpin was in the act of offering his shirt to a guard for a ride on the Mexican's mule, Kendall reported, when Salazar noticed the transaction and ordered Golpin shot to death.) Furthermore, Kendall acknowledged that at least some of the hardships that he and his companions endured on the march were experienced routinely by Mexicans. On their way to El Paso, for exam-ple, the captives traveled the dreaded Jornada mostly at night—even in autumn that virtually waterless stretch of the trail could be deadly in the day-time—and consequently suffered terribly from the cold. Along the way, how-ever, they met with a party of soldiers and camp followers from Durango who seemed even more susceptible to the elements:

> Being from a more southern and temperate climate, they suffered excessively from the cold, so much so that many of them were leading their horses and setting fire to every little tuft of palm or dry grass on either side of the road. Around these blazing tufts, and scattered along the road for miles, were to be seen knots of half-frozen dragoons, mingled with a large number of women, who always follow the Mexican soldiery on a march. How the latter, who were but half clad even in the warmest climate, could withstand the bitter cold of that night, is to me incomprehensible.[35]

It was not until the prisoners reached El Paso, however, that Kendall truly gained perspective on their ordeal. Captain Francisco Ochoa, the Chihuahuan officer who took charge of them there, "expressed the greatest abhorrence of Salezar and his herd of *ladrones* and *picaros*,"[36] Kendall noted, and treated the captives with consideration. More gratifying still were the kind attentions the author received from a local priest, Ramón Ortiz, who invited Kendall into his home, receiving in return a gold pen that the author had managed to conceal from his captors:

> During a visit of some two hours, young Ortiz seemed to be studying my every want. In addition to an excellent dinner, with wine of his own making, which he gave me, he invited me into his private study, where a bath was provided. Hardly had I partaken of this luxury, before a girl brought me clean flannel and linen throughout—and when I say that for the previous seven weeks I had had no change of clothing, and that the vermin which infest the lower orders of Mexico had taken forcible possession of all my ragged and dirty vestments, the luxury of once more arraying myself in clean linen will be appreciated. But the liberality of Ortiz did not stop here, for, notwithstanding I told him I had a sufficiency, and obstinately refused taking it until farther resistance would have been rude and almost insulting, he still pressed a sum of money into my hands. It was carefully wrapped in paper, and the amount I did not at the time know. From its weight I knew, however, that it was specie, and hence my extreme reluctance to receive it at his hands. He may have thought it an imperative duty thus to press it upon my acceptance, in order to cancel the obligation he evidently considered himself under for the pen I had presented him.[37]

Ortiz was probably trying to make things up to Kendall in more ways than one, for the priest was a devout Mexican patriot who had no desire to see his homeland overrun by angry Americans. He likely recognized that Kendall was a special prisoner—one in a strong position to influence American opinion—and did his best to reassure the author that Salazar and other *picaros* ("scoundrels") were in no way representative of the nation as a whole. For this priest, as for others who dealt kindly with the prisoners, charity was a matter of policy as well as principle, a way of canceling debts and of restoring a sense of courteous give-and-take to an exchange that threatened to become irretrievably hostile.

As it happened, Kendall soon had an opportunity to repay Captain Salazar in bloodless fashion. In addition to the money he received from Ortiz, Kendall had concealed a stash of gold coins from the grasping Salazar during the march by baking them into cakes. While still under the protective custody of Ortiz in El Paso, Kendall encountered his nemesis in the plaza and flaunted the wealth that Salazar had failed to confiscate:

> Telling Ortiz that I wished to purchase a handkerchief, or some trifling article, he kindly held my horse while I dismounted. As I walked directly towards

the little knot of our former oppressors I placed a hand in each pocket of my pantaloons, which were now tolerably well filled with the doubloons and other gold pieces I had taken from the cakes after reaching El Paso. Grasping as many of them as I could in either hand, I let them drop jingling to the bottom of my pockets when within five yards of Salezar, and so that he could plainly hear them. The sound, I am confident, entered his soul. . . . His face was a perfect index to the workings of his selfish mind, and with a pleasure, malicious perhaps, I watched it. That he would not close his eyes in sleep that night I felt confident, so well I knew his nature.[38]

Ortiz made no complaint to Kendall about his vengeful gesture. After all, this was a reckoning of the sort the priest might approve of, a settlement in coin. But the larger resentments aroused by the disastrous expedition would not be so easily satisfied. Both sides felt deeply aggrieved by the incident. Even Mexicans who regretted the mistreatment of the captives believed that their intentions were subversive and feared further intervention by Texans. Rafael Chacón, whose father served as an officer under Salazar on the march to Chihuahua, knew from comments his father made that reports of the mistreatment of prisoners were well founded: "He said that some of those poor men could hardly walk on account of their blistered and sore feet and that when pain and fatigue overpowered them and they could travel no longer, Salazar would have them shot." But Chacón also recalled verses composed by a local poet, Jorge Ramírez, that summed up the widespread resentments of New Mexicans toward the intrusive Texans:

A constitution and laws
They pretended to bring with them,
But to plant slavery with us
Was all they had in mind.[39]

The ill will fostered by the expedition, both in New Mexico and in Texas, raised the stakes for both sides in this dangerous contest. Ultimately, there would be hell to pay. Although the immediate prospects of the prisoners improved with their arrival in El Paso, bitter days lay ahead for them. Many fell ill of smallpox and other diseases on their way south to Mexico City, where Kendall and other ailing captives were confined in a lepers' prison. He and a number of others were released at the urging of diplomats from various countries in April 1842, and the rest of the captives were freed in June.

By then, Texans and Mexicans were up in arms. In early 1842, legislators in Austin had reacted to news of the capture of the Pioneers by passing an incendiary resolution annexing to Texas not just New Mexico but also Chihuahua,

Sonora, Alta and Baja California, and sundry other parts of Mexico. In March, Mexican forces launched attacks on Texas, and fighting continued into 1843, when Texans recruited a number of Americans to their cause. In April of that year, a raiding party prowling the Santa Fe Trail under the direction of John McDaniel, a Missourian with a captain's commission from Texas, robbed and murdered Mexican merchant Antonio José Chávez, the son of a former governor of New Mexico, after he had entered American territory with a small trading party on his way east to Missouri. McDaniel's crime was not sanctioned by anyone in Texas and could not be construed as just retribution for the mistreatment of the captive Pioneers. Although the Chávez and Armijo families were linked by marriage ties, they differed on matters of policy. As recounted by Josiah Gregg, a brother and sister-in-law of the murdered Chávez had aided the captive Texans in New Mexico by providing them with provisions and blankets, among other comforts.[40]

The widespread revulsion that McDaniel's deed inspired among the people of Missouri demonstrated that the spirit of accommodation fostered by the Santa Fe trade still prevailed there despite the recent tensions. To be sure, traders from Missouri feared competition from venturesome Mexicans like Chávez, but no one in the trade at this juncture wanted to see disputes with competitors resolved by brute force, and artisans and shopkeepers in Missouri who profited by the influx of silver from Santa Fe welcomed prosperous Mexican visitors and tried to safeguard them. A month before Chávez was murdered, residents of Independence had learned that McDaniel was out after Mexican merchants and had warned the superintendent of Indian Affairs in St. Louis of trouble along the trail west of the Missouri border (that unorganized territory was still Indian country in 1843 and under the jurisdiction of the department of Indian Affairs). After the murder, posses organized in and around Independence went after McDaniel and nabbed him when he returned to his hometown of Liberty, Missouri. An editorialist in St. Louis—where McDaniel and Joseph Brown, his chief accomplice, were executed for the crime in 1844—spoke for many Missourians when he denounced the idea that McDaniel's commission from Texas had given him any right to murder an unsuspecting foreigner on American territory, where the victim "was as much entitled to the protection of our laws as the president of the United States himself."[41]

The officer who had recruited McDaniel on behalf of Texas was himself an American citizen, Charles A. Warfield of New Orleans. Warfield had accepted a commission as colonel for the Lone Star Republic and had delegated McDaniel to raise a company in Missouri, not for the purposes of robbery and murder on American soil but for an invasion of New Mexico that

Warfield was organizing. Warfield may have dreamed of succeeding where the Pioneers had failed by occupying Santa Fe, but he met with little success in his own recruiting efforts and was reduced to carrying out a hit-and-run raid in May 1843 on an isolated encampment of New Mexicans outside the frontier settlement of Mora, during which the attackers killed several men from the town and captured eighteen. Rufus B. Sage, who enlisted with Warfield's company and later described the attack in writing, reported that the raiders decided in council after the battle not to attack the town itself because the occupants were now fully alerted to the threat. Before retreating, Sage added, the raiders released their captives with words that underscored the bitter legacy of the Texan Santa Fe expedition: "You are now free. Bury your dead, and remember in future how vain it is to resist the arms of Texas. Tell Amijo, your General, the Texans are men, and not wild beasts. They never kill an unresisting enemy,—they never kill a prisoner of war. He has done both,—but let him beware how he does it again, for the lives of ten Mexicans shall be the forfeit for each offense."[42]

Unlike McDaniel, Warfield could claim license for his attack, having been instructed by Secretary of War George W. Hockley of Texas to take "just retribution" for "injuries and cruelties" inflicted on Texans by their Mexican foes.[43] But were the Mexicans killed at Mora in any way liable for the misdeeds charged to Armijo and his subordinates? Americans had been among Mora's earliest residents, Gregg wrote, and the town had a reputation for being receptive to foreigners: "The inhabitants of that place are generally very simple and innocent rancheros and hunters," he added, "and, being separated by the snowy mountains from the principal settlements of New Mexico, their hearts seem ever to have been inclined to the Texans."[44] Whatever their attitude toward Texans before the attack, they had good reason to resent and distrust Anglo intruders afterward.

Following the attack at Mora, Warfield joined up with Colonel Jacob Snively of Texas and routed a poorly armed detachment of Mexican troops below the Arkansas River in June 1843, killing at least eighteen men, many of them Pueblos who had been recruited at Taos to help repulse the invaders. The loss embittered Taos Pueblos toward Anglos in the area who were thought to be in league with the Texans. (In fact, a number of Americans campaigned for Texas that year under Warfield and Snively.) When news of the defeat reached Taos, Gregg related, "the friends and relatives of the slain— the whole population indeed, were incensed beyond measure; and two or three naturalized foreigners who were supposed to favor the cause of Texas, and who were in good standing before, were now compelled to flee for their lives; leaving their houses and property a prey to the incensed rabble."[45]

People on the vulnerable Mexican frontier did not soon forgive hostile intrusions or bury their grievances. Resentments stirred up in 1843 may well have contributed to violent resistance encountered four years later by American occupation forces in settlements antagonized by the Texans and their confederates from the States. In the short term, however, tensions were eased by the actions of U.S. troops under Captain Philip St. George Cooke, who had orders to prevent troops under the Texas banner from assailing traders along the Santa Fe Trail in American territory and harming any more Mexicans. Cooke knew this country well, having escorted traders to the Arkansas River and back as a lieutenant in 1829 during Major Bennet Riley's pioneering expedition to safeguard travelers on the trail. When Cooke confronted Snively's forces on June 30, they were in an ill-defined zone on the south side of the Arkansas near the one hundredth meridian, the unmarked dividing line between American territory to the east and Mexican territory to the west. Cooke felt certain they were on the American side of that frontier, however, and laid down the law. "Gentlemen, You are in the United States," he declared by his own account, adding that he had the right to disarm them in any case because a number of them had ventured north of the Arkansas River into what was indisputably American territory with the intent to harm "a caravan of *peaceful* traders between the United States and a friendly power; a trade which it is our wish to protect; and which you profess your determination to attack." He demanded that they cross the river and lay down their arms. If any of them failed to do so and sought shelter amid the trees on the south bank, he added, he would fire his howitzers, "and thus drive you from the woods, and attack you in the plains!"[46]

Cooke's forceful measure helped to resolve the crisis not only by depriving the raiders of their arms but also by making it clear to Mexicans that American authorities as yet had no intention of embracing the combative Texans and their claims. But all that changed two years later with the annexation of Texas. Suddenly, Cooke and Snively were compatriots. Americans inherited a vast area bordering Mexico and assumed an explosive territorial dispute with that nation. Mexican officials, who had never acknowledged the independence of Texas, warned that its annexation by the United States would mean war, and such was the case. Soon American forces would set out for Santa Fe to seize the objective that had eluded the Texans. Once in possession of the capital, however, Americans would face sharp opposition at two spots where memories of the recent disturbances were painfully fresh—Taos and Mora.

It was not just Texans who feuded with New Mexicans and dreamed of claiming their country in the years leading up to the war. As underscored by the furor surrounding the Texan Santa Fe expedition, more than a few Americans who did business in New Mexico and settled there felt estranged from their adopted country and at odds with local authorities. Some of these resident merchants came to welcome the prospect of an American takeover. For Charles Bent, who made his home at Taos when he was not conducting caravans to and from Bent's Fort for the firm of Bent, St. Vrain & Co., life under Mexican rule was rife with obstacles and frustrations, and he eventually reached the conclusion that New Mexicans were "not fit to be free" and should be "ruled by others than themselves."[47] That implicit endorsement of an American conquest, expressed by Bent in early 1846, was not a position he adopted quickly or lightly. Bent had close ties to his host country, including a Mexican wife and friends and business associates among her relatives and other local families. But he also had powerful Mexican enemies, and his clashes with them, chronicled in his correspondence with Manuel Alvarez, the American consul in Santa Fe, offered a preview of the larger conflict to come—a war that would claim Charles Bent among its most prominent victims.

Chief among Bent's foes at Taos was Padre Martínez, who blamed many of his country's problems on the intruding Americans. The sources of conflict between Martínez and Bent were numerous, including massive land grants that Bent's Mexican associates sought from Governor Armijo and which Martínez (whose relatives were also maneuvering to expand their landholdings) vehemently opposed. But what most aroused Bent were accusations by Martínez and his allies at Taos that Bent was profiting at their expense by purchasing horses, mules, and cattle stolen by hostile Indians from Mexicans in raids. If it were not for traders like Bent, Martínez reasoned, those Indians would have no market for their ill-gotten gains and would cease their attacks. Martínez summed up his case against Bent and others who trafficked with Indians at American trading posts like Bent's Fort in a report to Mexican president Antonio Lopez de Santa Anna in 1843:

> Besides the useful and necessary articles, the traders sold the Indians also liquors and ardent spirits, which were prohibited. The result was that these Indian nations became extremely demoralized, and were prompted to greater destruction of buffaloes, in order to satisfy their appetite for strong drinks, which they obtained in exchange. They also made raids in our Department of New Mexico, in order to steal cattle which were bought of them by the proprietors of these forts, thus encouraging and inducing the idle and ill intentioned ones among us to follow their example, and become cattle robbers; selling their booty to the inhabitants or proprietors of the forts.[48]

Padre Antonio José Martínez. Courtesy Museum of New Mexico, negative no. 174508.

Bent, for his part, blamed the Indian raids on the failure of local authorities to deal forcefully with bands whose motives were purely mercenary and to address the legitimate grievances of other tribes against Mexicans. He bristled at charges that he was dealing in stolen goods, accused Mexicans of doing the same with animals taken from him—in fact, those who purchased stolen animals did not always know they were doing so—and denounced Martínez and company as rabble-rousing slanderers. In a letter to Alvarez penned on January 30, 1841, Bent (a man of some literary eloquence despite his irregular syntax and spelling) wrote sarcastically of the priest's hold over his followers:

> He is a prodigy, and his greate name deserves to be written in letters of gold in all high places that this gaping and ignorant multitude might fall down and worship it. . . . It is certainly a great blessing to have such a man amongst uss, theas people canot help but find favor in this and the other world in consiquence of having such a man to leade and direct them; If the days of miricals had not gon by I should expect that God would bestow some great blessing on theas people, through this greate man.[49]

Bent went on to address charges made against him in Taos that he had purchased animals stolen from a local Mexican who was asking to be reimbursed by Bent for his losses. Bent had heard that Martínez intended to put the matter before the governor in Santa Fe and, if so, wanted to offer his own testimony there in defense, supported by witnesses.

Another man in Taos whom Bent blamed for making false charges against him was one Juan B. Vigil. What Bent called "false representations" on Vigil's part may have had to do with a matter even more serious than stolen livestock—charges that Bent and associates were involved in the plotting that led up to the Texan Santa Fe expedition in the summer of 1841. A year before that expedition materialized, Texas president Mirabeau Lamar had appointed William Dryden of Santa Fe as a commissioner of sorts to New Mexico to function as a kind of advance agent for the takeover scheme later entrusted to the Pioneers. Named to serve in a similar capacity were John Rowland and William Workman, who had earlier arranged with his brother David to open an unauthorized distillery in Taos. William Workman, now a Mexican citizen, may not have sought this cryptic assignment as an agent for Texas or done anything seditious to justify the appointment, but it placed him and those associated with him in a precarious position. He was close to Charles Bent, and suspicions that attached to one man had a way of rubbing off on the other. By early 1841, New Mexicans had inklings of Lamar's not-so-secret ambition to attach their homeland to Texas, peacefully or otherwise. Perhaps the "false representations" that so enraged Bent were accusations by Juan Vigil that Bent was somehow involved in that takeover scheme.[50] In any case, Bent and William Workman proceeded to confront Vigil, with dire results that Bent detailed to Alvarez on February 19:

> To day about mid day Workman and myself called on Juan B Vigil. I presented the coppy of the representation he made against uss. I asked him after he red it if that was a coppy of the one he had made to the Govenor he said it was. I then asked him how he dare make such false representations against uss he denied them being false. The word was hardly out of his mouth, when Workman struck him with his whip, after whiping him a while with this he droped it and beate him with his fist untill I thought he had given him enough, where-

upon I pulled him off. he [Vigil] run for life. he has bean expecting this ever since last eavening, for he said this morning, he had provided himself with a Baui Knife for any person that dare attack him, and suting the word to the action drue his knife to exhibit, I supose he forgot his knife in time of neade. . . . I doubt wether you will be able to reade this I am much agitated, and am at this time called to the Alcalde's I presume at the instance of Juan Vigil.[51]

The alcalde in Taos placed Bent under house arrest for forty-eight hours before referring the case to higher authorities. Bent found himself in an awkward position. He defended the attack on Vigil in a letter to Alvarez as a matter of honor that called for a direct and forceful response, without appeal to a court of law. But at the same time, he wanted the governor and local authorities to respect the law when it came to his own rights as a defendant:

> I had rather have the satisfaction of whiping a man that has wronged me than to have him punished ten times by the law, the law to me for a personal offence is no satisfaction whatever, but Cowardes and wimen must take this satisfaction. I could posibly have had Vigil araned for trial for Slander but what satisfaction would this have bean to me to have had him fined, and morcover I think he has nothing to pay a fine with he is a vagabond that lives by flitching his neighbor
>
> If you think that you can doe anything with the Govenor for uss you will pleas doe so. You will recollect the promises I told you that had bean made to me in Santafe. now they will be tested. The law requires that I should be araigned for t[r]ial within 48 howers, this has not bean done, I have not sean a scrach of a pen on that subject. the law requires that all should have bean concluded and sentenced within 72 howers nothing definitive has bean done.[52]

How the attack on Vigil—carried out by another man while Bent looked on—rendered him superior to those "Cowardes and wimen" who took their grievances to court was a point that Bent failed to address. Perhaps he regretted not dealing with Vigil himself, for on March 15, while the Mexican was out of town, Bent wrote Alvarez that he was ready to take up the quarrel where Workman left off:

> If you know what that mighty man Juan Vigil is about pleas let uss know, we are geting somewhat anctious to have the light of his countanance amongst uss again, he sayed before he left heare that he would not be satisfyed untill he had me publicly whiped. . . . At all events If Juan Vigil is not satisfyed I am redy to give him any satisfaction one Gentleman can ask of an other. I doe not mean by this to insult him by calling him a gentleman, he is not entitled to the apalation, and posibly he may have to answer again for his missdeades.[53]

As it turned out, Bent did not deal with Vigil man to man. Instead, a masked party of four—perhaps including Bent and most likely acting with his approval—did their best to silence the Mexican, as Bent informed Alvarez on March 22:

> On the night of the 20 thare ware four men armed (so says report) went to Manuel Andress, that lives betwean this place an cordova Town, in serch of Juan Vigil, but he made his escape before they got to the house as the dogs gave notice of thare coming, theas men it is said ware disguised. I have heard that Vigil left nearly naked and crosed the prairie to the Del Norte, and laid thare all day a Sunday. . . .
>
> I think that Juan Vigil will be heartely tired of the vally of Taos if he is scarte onse or twice more, I think if he gets fairly away this time, he will be verry apt to ceape away.[54]

Bent's role in this tawdry affair represented just one facet of his complex relationship with his host country. He kept faith with his Mexican friends and kin and often advised the governor through Alvarez as to how to allay Indian resentments that might spell trouble for New Mexicans and their settlements. And he was not alone in complaining about the local brand of justice, which deputized the alcalde to serve, in effect, as judge and jury and sometimes left those who appealed his sentences to languish in jail while awaiting a ruling from the governor. (Severino Martínez, father of Bent's nemesis and one of the leading citizens of Taos, once spent nearly two weeks in jail for insulting the alcalde in a dispute over ownership of a mule.)[55] Bent's differences with his adopted country were of greater severity and consequence than most such altercations, however. The mounting tensions at Taos seemed to bring out the worst in this influential American and in his Mexican antagonists, who made him a scapegoat for problems that went well beyond his realm of responsibility. Later in 1841, when the Texas Pioneers reached New Mexico and fell into Armijo's grasp, Bent was arrested in Taos on suspicion of abetting the incursion and was hauled off to the capital, only to be released a short time later without facing any charges. (William Workman and John Rowland, for their part, fled to California rather than face reprisals for their nebulous role as Texas "commissioners.")

In the years that followed, the rift between Bent and his critics in Taos widened. In their view, he was a parasite who flourished at the expense of his Mexican hosts. A more objective assessment might be that his relationship with the locals was symbiotic, in that he profited significantly from dealings with his host country but also brought New Mexicans benefits in the form of the duties he paid and the knowledge he imparted to those who trusted him

Charles Bent. Courtesy Museum of New Mexico, negaitve no. 7004.

and heeded his advice. Whether for good or for ill, however, Bent and others from the States had clearly succeeded in colonizing Taos, which is not to say that they controlled the town but that they were established there in sufficient strength to alter the terms of the exchange between Americans and New Mexicans. Compared to merchants who visited New Mexico for a season and then departed, Americans who settled down there engaged in give-and-take with their hosts that was deeper, broader, and more volatile, involving a greater potential for fruitful alliances and partnerships, on the one hand, and for disruptive tensions and conflicts, on the other hand. The fact that a powerful

American like Bent had a local wife and local associates did nothing to reassure his Mexican opponents, who saw such intimacy as a calculated way for intruders to gain a tighter grip on their country.

Bent, for his part, drew an increasingly sharp distinction between those Mexicans within his trusted circle and those who declined to bargain with him on favorable terms and seemed, in his view, to be inviting hostilities. By early 1846 he had come to regard war between Mexico and the United States as inevitable—and perhaps even desirable. The preliminary skirmishing was already under way that spring in Taos, where in April Bent reported on hearsay that Padre Martínez suspected him of digging a mine from his house to the church and filling it with "three Kegs Powder, for the purpus of blowing them up on Good friday."[56] In early May, Bent's younger brother George and a tipsy companion—the well-connected Missourian Francis P. Blair, Jr., who had ventured west to improve his health—ran afoul of a large group of Mexicans in the plaza at Taos and were badly beaten. Having seen other crimes against Americans go unpunished, Bent doubted that those responsible for enforcing the law in Taos would bring to justice assailants who included "serventes of the big famely"[57] or that of Padre Martínez, and he asked Governor Armijo to intervene. But Bent no longer had much faith in Mexican authorities, whether in Taos, Santa Fe, or Mexico City. Recently, General Mariano Paredes, no friend of the United States, had seized control of the Mexican government. Adapting to circumstances, Armijo and others who had earlier pledged to support the president ousted by Paredes quietly submitted to the new regime, eliciting from Bent a tirade against the Mexican national character that summed up all the fulminations of disgruntled American observers over the past quarter century:

> They are intirely governed by the powers that be, they are without exception the most servile people that can be imagined. They are compleately at the will of those in power let theas be as Ignorant as may be they dair not express an oppinion contrary to that of thare rulers, they are not fit to be free, they should be ruled by others than themselves, Mexico has tryed long enough to prove to the world that she is not able to govern herself, whare thar is no morality, honesty, or Patriotesim of caracter that people ar not fit for self-government. On the contrary every speses of vise in this country is a recomendation to public office; and such officers as they are corrupt, destitute of all principal, lasy indolent Ignorant and base to the last degreee, thare is no confidenced to be placed in them, with gold, anything let it be unjust and unreasonable—can be accomplished, through theas vile reches. . . . thare religion consists intirely in [?] show, they have no idea a sinsear devotion they are taught to believe

that thare priests are the only meadiator betwean the supriem being and themselves, and eaven in this, you can acheave greate benifits (nominly) by a lavesh presant of gold, thare vallor consists of Boasting, and show whare thare is no dainger, thare tallence is superfitial, and consistes, of what is called in this country *dilihentia*, that is to cheate steal lye and defraud all that are suseptible of being envagled by them in any way.

Officers, and justices perticularly eaqually ignorant, insolent & aviritious are easily bribed justice is badly administered, and is rendered with extream delay. . . . The Mexican caracter is made up of stupidity, Obstanacy, Ignorance duplicity and vanity.[58]

This outburst was all the more remarkable in that came from a man who before the year was out would be granted authority over the very people he dismissed here as unfit to be free. Bent's words marked a sad departure from the spirit of accommodation that in quieter times had brought American traders in New Mexico a measure of respect from the populace as well as material rewards and helped keep the volatile exchange between the two cultures within peaceful and productive bounds. Unwilling to extend any further credit to those with whom he had long bargained and bickered, Bent was in effect calling in his debts, knowing as he did so that the sweeping claims he made against the New Mexicans could only be satisfied if they forfeited control of their homeland.

The bitter irony here was that Bent was imposing this harsh judgment on a people to whom he was now so closely linked by family ties and other bonds that he was slighting his own kind. From the beginning, the American odyssey to New Mexico had been a journey of self-discovery. As Zebulon Pike had asserted to Governor Alencaster in Santa Fe four decades earlier, he had come to reconnoiter his own country. The troubled social landscape that Bent was surveying here with such disdain was now his own domain, and he shared substantially in its assets and liabilities. In all of New Mexico, there were few more accomplished embodiments of that quality known as *diligencia*, or diligent cunning, than Bent himself. He used that word disparagingly in denouncing the Mexican character, but it was highly ambiguous and could be as much of a compliment as an insult. Adventurers needed a large measure of diligencia to survive and prosper in this land of calculation and compromise. As Matt Field had sensed when coming into New Mexico, this was a realm where "man's best good and greatest ill, breathed the same air together." Good and ill lay intertwined in the restless heart and resourceful mind of Charles Bent. But as war loomed, he reckoned as others did in such divisive times and charged all moral delinquencies to his enemies.

Given his dismal evaluation of his hosts, it was little wonder that he lent aid and counsel to Stephen Watts Kearny, commander of the American army that invaded New Mexico in the summer of 1846. Much obliged, Kearny would return the favor later that year by naming Charles Bent governor of the occupied territory—a fateful appointment that further alienated the opponents of Anglo rule in Taos, among other bastions of resistance, and set the stage for an American tragedy.

Part 3

The American Conquest
(1846–1848)

16

Gathering at Bent's Fort

On July 26, 1846, more than two months after the United States declared war on Mexico, a merchant caravan including veteran Missouri trader Samuel Magoffin, accompanied by his young bride of less than a year, Susan Shelby Magoffin, approached Bent's Fort en route to Santa Fe. That sturdy adobe trading post on the north bank of the Arkansas River, managed by Charles Bent's brother William, was always a lively place in summer, when parties of traders and other adventurers heading to and from New Mexico on the Mountain Route of the Santa Fe Trail paused there to rest and refit, mingling with a motley assemblage of clerks, hired hands, mountain men, and visiting Indians. But in this year of gathering conflict, Bent's Fort was busier than ever. Military and economic interests converged here in the summer of 1846, and troops by the hundreds shared the fort and its environs with scores of merchants, intent on pursuing their own potentially profitable sorties into Mexico, war or no war. A sentinel challenged the Magoffins as they neared the fort, but they soon received clearance to proceed. Far from placing an embargo on trade with Mexico, the army was charged with protecting the merchants and their interests and affording them safe passage to Santa Fe in the wake of the advancing troops. In this campaign, commerce and conquest went hand in glove.

For Susan Magoffin, the sheltering walls of Bent's Fort were a welcome sight after a grueling journey across the plains. She had prepared for the ordeal by reading Josiah Gregg's meticulous account of life on the trail, and her trip had been eased somewhat by advantages that most other travelers did without, including a tent to sleep in, a servant named Jane to look after her, and a pet greyhound called Ring to keep her company. But her usually buoyant spirits had been deflated in recent days by an obscure malady that persisted despite the attentions of a traveling doctor, whom she described in her diary as "an excellent physician '*especially in female cases.*'"[1] Under the circumstances, she was a glad to have a roof over head and a modest room at the fort that she and her husband could call their own, amid conditions that bordered on the civilized. As she wrote in her diary:

> They have a well inside, and fine water it is—especially with ice. At present they have quite a number of boarders. The traders and soldiers chiefly, with a few *lofers* from the States, come out because they can't live at home.
>
> There is no place on Earth I believe where man lives and gambling in some form or other is not carried on. Here in the Fort, and who could have supposed such a thing, they have a *regularly established billiard room*! They have a regular race track. And I hear the cackling of chickens at such a rate some times I shall not be surprised to hear of a cock-pit.[2]

Men at the post relaxed in the billiard room and sipped frosty juleps concocted in the fort's well-stocked icehouse, but there was little in the way of diversion here for a well-bred young lady from Kentucky. She and Samuel had their own room with a few furnishings, and she dutifully sprinkled water on the dirt floor through the day to keep the dust down. She noted wryly that she was "keeping house regularly, but I beg leave not to be allowed *that* privilege much longer."[3] Other than Susan and Jane, the only women on the premises were Indians or Mexicans like the wife of George Bent, brother to Charles and William. She was among several "*senoritas*" Magoffin met on her first night at the fort, one of whom sat in the parlor oiling her hair in a manner the diarist found astonishing: "After the combing she paid her devoirs to a crock of oil or greese of some kind, and it is not exaggeration to say it almost *driped* from her hair to the floor."[4]

Yet Susan Magoffin was not one to waste much time lamenting her lot in life or complaining of the circumstances that exposed her to strange company. She was only eighteen, and her comfortable upbringing had hardly prepared her for the shocks of this long journey into alien country. But she met adversity with the forbearance of a devout Christian and a determined frontierswoman. When her doctor administered medicine to her at the fort on July 28 and advised her that it might be better for her health if she traveled to Europe—life on the trail had not been the cure-all she had hoped for—she allowed herself only a brief moment of self-pity:

The advice is rather better to take than the medicine, anything though to restore my health. I never should have consented to take the trip on the plains had it not been with that view and a hope that it would prove beneficial; but so far my hopes have been blasted, for I am rather going down hill than up, and it is so bad to be sick and under a physician all the time. But cease my rebellious heart! How prone human nature is to grumble and to think his lot harder than any one of his fellow creatures, many of whom are an hundred times more diseased and poor in earthly assistance and still they endure all, and would endure more.[5]

She maintained that sense of proportion and perseverance even after the cause of her discomforts became clear to her. On the night of July 30, her nineteenth birthday, she suffered a miscarriage. A week later, she wrote of that loss with resignation:

The mysteries of a new world have been shown to me since last Thursday! In a few short months I should have been a happy mother and made the heart of a father glad, but the ruling hand of a mighty Providence has interposed and by an abortion deprived us of the hope, the fond hope of mortals! But with the affliction he does not leave us comfortless![6]

Her pilgrimage had thus far brought her little but hardship and heartbreak, but she accepted this mysterious "new world" as she found it and heeded its stern lessons. She had good reason to feel that her sufferings were neither unusual nor disproportionate, for many were making their first perilous journey west on the same trail that summer as volunteers with the U.S. Army, and a number of them would fall prey to disease without ever exchanging shots with the enemy. Others would survive but find themselves bedeviled by the same sort of problems that had long plagued inhabitants of New Mexico: loneliness, deprivation, and a sense of neglect at the hands of distant authorities.

The struggle that these volunteers recorded eloquently in their journals, memoirs, and dispatches—and which Susan Magoffin and other noncombatants chronicled in their own compelling accounts—was not an impromptu invasion but the culmination of the economic and cultural infiltration begun by the pioneers of the Santa Fe trade a quarter century earlier. In this *entrada*, as the Spanish referred to their first armed entry into New Mexico in the sixteenth century, the conquistadores of the U.S. Army would simply finish what those American merchants had started, albeit peacefully and with little thought for what the long-term consequences might be for the local populace. Armed conflict had always been one of the ways for rival groups to resolve or exploit their differences along the trail, and while it briefly became the dominant form of exchange during this confrontation, it by no means precluded the trading of goods or favors between the opposing sides. The laws of exchange that set a price for every purchase on the trail applied even to the gains of armies. Like all successful takeover bids, the conquest of New Mexico would come at a cost, one measured not only in lives lost and treasure expended but in the heavy liabilities assumed by the conquerors, who would inherit the hostility of Navajos, Apaches, and other determined tribal groups and the resentments of a largely impoverished Hispanic population that felt let down by their former rulers and duly suspicious of their new overlords.

If this conquest was in some ways an "affliction" for Americans, in Susan Magoffin's words, it did not leave them comfortless. For in the end, the victors acquired more than territory or economic opportunities. Their complex dealings with New Mexico and its people offered those intruders inclined to be oversure of themselves and their virtues useful lessons in reckoning with a world of competing values, where even the proudest of conquerors had to make humbling concessions. Not all who confronted the mysteries of this new world came to terms with it, but those who did profited in ways that transcended any material gain.

That the taking of New Mexico would have strong commercial overtones was clear to American authorities from the start. On May 14, Missouri senator Thomas Hart Benton, long an ardent supporter of the Santa Fe trade, dispatched a letter to an aide to Missouri governor John C. Edwards in which he stressed the importance of protecting that trade during the forthcoming New Mexico campaign:

> The morning papers will let you see that the state of war was declared to exist yesterday, between the United States and Mexico. Our first care in this sudden change in our relations with that country was to try and take care of our Santa Fe trade. For this purpose, it will be proposed to the people of New Mexico, Chihuahua and the other internal provinces, that they remain quiet and continue trading with us as usual, upon which condition they shall be protected in all their rights and be treated as friends. . . . This military movement will be to make sure of the main object, to wit: peace and trade, to be secured peaceably if possible, forcibly if necessary. For unless they accept these conditions, the country will have to be taken possession of as a conquest. This, however, we hope will not be necessary, as it will be so obviously to the interest of the inhabitants of that part of Mexico (too far off from the Central Government to have any effect on general hostilities), to enjoy the benefits of peace and trade, with the full protection of all their rights of person, property, and religion.[7]

Benton, who backed the war reluctantly and feared that hostilities would disrupt trade, was shading the truth here in an effort to portray the military objectives of the United States in a soft commercial light. To be sure, the task of the army would be greatly eased if the people of New Mexico remained quiet and continued trafficking with the Americans as usual. But whether they chose to adopt that obliging stance or not, their country would still be "taken possession of as a conquest." As Benton conceded rather awkwardly, American forces were prepared to impose "peace and trade" on their own terms, "forcibly if necessary." Promises of protection could not disguise the fact that this was, in effect, a hostile takeover. If all went as planned, the Mexicans would have little choice but to accept the deal.

Benton and others in high positions were sincere in hoping for a bloodless campaign, however. Most of America's military might would be devoted to the task of subduing opposition in the Mexican heartland, and the army would have few resources to spare for the occupation of New Mexico and Alta California, both of which President James K. Polk hoped to seize during the war and to incorporate as American territories or states once the Mexicans conceded defeat. The daunting task of first crossing the plains to invade New Mexico and then traversing the desert to support the navy's Pacific Squadron in claiming California was assigned to Colonel Stephen Kearny and his so-called Army of the West, which consisted of around 1,650 soldiers, most of them volunteers raised in Missouri but including a few hundred men from the Regular Army. (How many of those troops would remain in occupied New Mexico and how many would continue on to California with Kearny was yet to be determined.) Secretary of War William Marcy drew up orders for Kearny based on these instructions from President Polk:

> After you shall have conquered & taken possession of either New Mexico & Upper California, it will be necessary that you should establish a temporary civil Government in each of these Provinces abolishing all arbitrary restrictions which may exist at present so far as this can be done with safety. In performing this duty, it would be wise & prudent to continue in their employment all such of the existing officers as are known to be friendly to the United States & will take the oath of allegiance to them. The duties at the Custom Houses ought at once to be reduced to such a rate as may be barely sufficient to maintain the necessary officers, without yielding any revenue to the Government.[8]

The prospect of virtually duty-free trade with New Mexico was sure to appeal to volunteers in Missouri, where that trade benefited not only the merchants involved and those who supplied them but the economy as a whole by providing a cash-poor state with regular infusions of Mexican silver. Indeed, some of those who enlisted in Kearny's army saw their campaign as more than just an outgrowth of the bitter border dispute with Mexico that the United States inherited in 1845 when it brought Texas into the Union. They linked their efforts to specific grievances accumulated over the years by American merchants bound for Santa Fe and Chihuahua. As one volunteer, Frank Edwards, put it: "The governor of New Mexico, Manuel Armijo, had subjected the American traders to numerous extortions; for instance, collecting a duty of five hundred dollars on each wagon load of goods. Now this, as the goods mostly sold by them were the coarser kinds, was a serious imposition."[9]

Edwards was not involved in the trade himself and knew of Armijo's "extortions" only secondhand. In fact, the duties Armijo exacted were less than he might legally have imposed, and some Americans made his system work to their advantage. But thanks in part to a scathing portrait of him by George Kendall and unflattering words by Josiah Gregg, Armijo had earned notoriety as the portly embodiment of Mexican misrule—an official of inflated pretensions and few if any scruples—and he made a convenient foil for those who enlisted under Kearny. Not all of the volunteers were Missourians by birth or upbringing (the English-born Edwards, for example, had recently moved to St. Louis from New York). But as he observed, they felt that their adopted state had a certain claim to New Mexico, and by enlisting they hoped to share in the adventures and opportunities long associated with the Santa Fe Trail:

> Perhaps no place could be found which would so readily respond to such a call as St. Louis: for, it being the point where the Santa Fé traders procure their goods, it is a common thing to observe their arrival with numerous packages of specie, which they freely use in making their purchases. This naturally gives the idea of vast mines of gold and silver at Santa Fé; and the young men of all classes were eager to go—indeed, it became a question of who must be left; as, besides gold and silver and visions of flowery prairies, buffalo hunting and Indian skirmishing, General Kearney was well known to be a kind officer to his men, although a strict disciplinarian.[10]

By early June, the volunteers were streaming into Fort Leavenworth, some twenty miles upriver from Independence. There Kearny and his subordinates did what they could to mold these enthusiastic but unpolished recruits into something resembling soldiers in short order. The volunteers admired the suave and seasoned Kearny, a fifty-one-year-old veteran of the War of 1812 and various western expeditions who knew the road to Santa Fe, having traveled the trail in command of a regiment of dragoons (mounted infantry). But as much as the recruits revered Kearny, they resented his junior officers, stern young West Pointers intent on imposing discipline on volunteers who felt that their present duties as soldiers should not obscure their enduring rights as citizens. Among the privileges they retained was that of electing their own commanders. The men of the First Regiment Missouri Mounted Volunteers—the core of Kearny's army—chose as colonel thirty-seven-year-old Alexander Doniphan, an accomplished trial lawyer and politician whose only military experience consisted of commanding Missouri state militiamen in the so-called Mormon War of 1838. Doniphan's chief role then had been to quell hostilities between the Mormons and their civilian antagonists, and he helped to keep the peace now at Fort Leavenworth by sympathizing with the sometimes restive volunteers while deferring cordially to his superior Kearny, who would soon be promoted to brigadier general. As Doniphan wrote in later years to an acquaintance: "I did not fear the Genls criticism—for they would be kind if not complimentary—and he would have courteously corrected my blunders—but I did fear the host of Lieuts and Subs fresh from West Point— always envious, jealous & disrespectfully contemptuous of Volunteers."[11] Those junior officers may have rubbed Doniphan and his men the wrong way, but they were faithfully executing their orders from Kearny, who had little time to prepare the volunteers for battle and compensated by drilling them long and hard.

Although the fighting caliber of these volunteers was not readily apparent on the parade ground, they brought several assets to the campaign, including youthful adventurism—most were in their late teens or twenties—and a determination to earn the respect of their comrades in the field and their loved ones back home. One older volunteer, George Gibson, editor of the short-lived *Independence Journal*, told of the persuasive power of the "tears trickling down some father's cheek as he takes his son by the hand and tells him to do his duty and above all things to have a Spartan's courage and never to come back dishonored or disgraced."[12] And another volunteer, John T. Hughes, a college graduate who composed a lively history of the Army of the West, related the equally Spartan words of the spokeswoman for a delegation of ladies from Clay County, Missouri, who visited Fort Leavenworth in June to present a flag to a company of volunteers from that county:

> In presenting to you this token of our regard and esteem, we wish you to remember that some of us have sons, some brothers, and all of us either friends or relatives among you, and that we would rather hear of your falling in honorable warfare, than to see you return sullied with crime, or disgraced by cowardice. We trust, then, that your conduct, in all circumstances, will be worthy the noble, intelligent and patriotic nation whose cause you have so

Brigadier General Stephen Watts Kearny. Courtesy Library of Congress, Prints and Photographs Division, LC-USZ62-17905.

generously volunteered to defend; your deportment will be such as will secure to you the highest praise and the warmest gratitude of the American people—in a word—let your motto be: "DEATH BEFORE DISHONOR." And to the gracious protection and guidance of HIM who rules the destinies of nations, we fervently commend you.[13]

Such urgings brought the weight of entire communities to bear on the volunteers and strengthened their resolve to fulfill their duties and avoid disgrace. Determination and dedication were not their only strong points. Many of the recruits were already adept at handling firearms when they enlisted, and the

Colonel Alexander William Doniphan. Used by permission, State Historical Society of Missouri, Columbia,

army capitalized on their marksmanship by equipping them with rifles that were far superior in range and accuracy to the smoothbore muskets carried by most Mexican troops.[14] The Missourians also boasted an artillery battalion that reached a high level of proficiency under the direction of Major Meriwether Lewis Clark of St. Louis, son of explorer William Clark and a graduate of West Point.

In other respects, however, the volunteers were ill equipped for the ordeal that awaited them. They lacked resources that often helped to knit units together and uphold their spirits, including a common uniform, dependable rations, and regular pay. They received a clothing allowance when they reached camp but dressed largely as they pleased and supplemented their meager provisions by purchasing food from camp sutlers, Indians, and others they encountered along the trail. When they ran out of cash—and few received any compensation from the government before their discharge—they tore the buttons off their jackets and offered them in trade.

Although idealistic volunteers like John Hughes portrayed the campaign as a moral crusade that would bring the "principles of republicanism and civil liberty" to a Mexican nation "fast sinking in slavery's arms,"[15] the Missourians brought along a dozen or so of their own slaves, one of whom served as an attendant to Colonel Doniphan. (Slaves attached to the regiment would later receive permission from Doniphan to form their own company in support of the volunteers.)[16] Most Missourians in the ranks, of course, had no slaves to look after them and had to cope as best they could with the demands of life at Fort Leavenworth—an unappetizing regimen that they were eager to put behind them. As Marcellus Ball Edwards, an eighteen-year-old Virginia-born volunteer who wrote with the poise and perception of a veteran reporter, remarked sardonically in his journal:

> One of our greatest enjoyments here was to get up by day's dawn and drill for two hours on horseback, amidst clouds of dust; then the next, after feeding and currying horses, was to sit down to breakfast, provided we could get a seat. We had a dining room next the kitchen, the doors of which were well fastened until the call of "come to breakfast" was sounded by the cook; and then such rushing and crowding as was never before seen was made by those who had been waiting at the doors the last half hour. Indeed this was policy, as the table was not sufficiently large to contain the company. Part must necessarily be excluded, and the maxim here is, "The first come, best served." But a homely fare this, soldiers' rations, consisting of sour loaf bread made up by a Dutchman's foot, who was not particular about washing it. Then came our pickled pork without a shadow of lean, or some badly cooked beef, which to

eat was well earned by the labor of so doing; the whole to be washed down by coffee made by cooks who had so far learned economy as to know exactly how many grains it took to color a pint of water.[17]

Such fare was lavish compared to what the volunteers would have to make do with on the trail in the months to come. Marcellus Edwards's unit, Company D, from Saline County, was in camp at Fort Leavenworth for only about two weeks before it moved out with Company A, from Jackson County—hardly enough time for the volunteers to acquire much in the way of polish. Their rousing but unruly departure on June 22 was described with characteristic objectivity by one of the campaign's more discerning witnesses, Richard Smith Elliott, journalist and former Indian agent, who joined a mounted company in St. Louis called the Laclede Rangers that succeeded in attaching itself to Kearny's army by sheer persistence:

> The moving out of the Saline and Jackson companies, this morning, was characteristic of Missouri volunteers—all enthusiasm and cheers. They marched round the parade, waving their flags, and giving vent most lustily to their patriotism. To be sure, it was not a very *soldier-like* way of going off, and a certain gentleman of some authority here looked very grave while the proceeding was in train; but then it is their way, and I suppose that when they become disciplined—if they ever do become disciplined—they will make tolerably good soldiers. The raw material is good enough, but then it is, in truth, *very raw*.[18]

Kearny had less than a month to mold such raw stuff into something impressive enough to daunt the Mexicans. But then much of the material his adversaries had to work with if they chose to contest his bid was even less polished. In this respect, as in others, the New Mexico campaign was not unlike a contest in the marketplace, with the Americans rushing out a product that was unfinished and untested in the hope of winning the battle of appearances and precluding opposition.

At the same time, Kearny had to deal with traders on the Santa Fe Trail who were maneuvering for advantage in their own way by trying to beat their rivals to New Mexico. The last few months had been unusually hectic in the streets of Independence, as veteran trader Edward James Glasgow noted in the letter he wrote from that town to his sister in late May before heading west with his own caravan of goods: "All the traders are busy, hurrying to get off," he reported. "The Emigrants to Oregon and California are passing through daily in numbers, and it appears that very soon there will hardly be enough people left to take care of the town."[19] Fortunately for Kearny, those emigrants would be following the Oregon Trail across Nebraska and would

"A Camp Washing Day," near Fort Leavenworth, 1846, from William H. Richardson, *Journal* (1848). Courtesy Library of Congress, Prints and Photographs Division, LC-USZ62-127.

not be clogging his own route. As for the merchants, those like Edward Glasgow and Samuel Magoffin who started out shortly before the army embarked from Fort Leavenworth and were overtaken by Kearny's vanguard would have to wait at Bent's Fort for the troops to gather there and proceed in force, with the traders following safely behind.

Other westbound caravans, however, had a big lead on the army, having left Independence earlier in the season, and would be difficult, if not impossible, to catch up with. James Webb and his partner George Doan, for example, left Independence with five wagons on May 9 and reached Santa Fe in late June, unrestrained by Kearny's troops. Two westbound caravans that left for Mexican territory well ahead of the army were of special concern to Kearny because they contained arms and ammunition. One was led by the foreign trader Albert Speyer, who had a contract to deliver armaments to the governor of Chihuahua; the other was consigned to Governor Armijo of New Mexico. Kearny dispatched Regular Army units in early June to chase after those caravans and reinforced that task force a few weeks later by sending out the two volunteer companies, A and D, that left Fort Leavenworth on June 22 as described by Richard Elliott. Jacob S. Robinson, a company mate of Marcellus Ball Edwards, recalled that intoxicating moment of departure in his journal:

> Our men, glad to escape from the strict discipline and monotonous confinement of the fort, sent up a shout of joy that ran through all their ranks, as they inhaled the clear air of the green and sunny prairie. That joyous shout rings in my memory yet; and though connected with much of our subsequent travel amid hunger and thirst and suffering in a thousand forms, still its remembrance shall be cherished as that of a golden moment, when life and youth and health break over forms, and rejoice in hope, even though that hope may never be realized.[20]

Neither these eager volunteers nor the regulars who preceded them had any chance of intercepting the elusive caravans that so worried Kearny. (By June 22, Speyer's party had hurried down the Cimarron Route and was approaching the Wagon Mound in New Mexico, little more than a week's journey from Santa Fe.)[21] Whatever lay ahead of them, however, the Missourians were delighted to be free of the fort and its constraints.

The path leading southwest from Fort Leavenworth to the Santa Fe Trail was new and poorly marked, and Robinson's company, like other units that followed, had difficulty finding their way. To make matters worse, they were plagued by heavy downpours for the first few days. But they still had occasion to admire the countryside, described by Robinson as "flower-covered prairie, spotted here and there with fine groves of walnut and plum, as though planted by the hand of man to make it a magnificent garden."[22] Among the settlers tending this well-traveled garden country along the Kansas River that offered access to both the Oregon and Santa Fe Trails were Shawnee and Delaware Indians, exiles from the East who had learned almost too well for Robinson's taste how to profit by their opportunities:

> The Shawnees have fine farms, and are quite a civilized people: the Delawares are a little behind them: both tribes speak the English language more or less. They keep a ferry-boat here, in which we crossed the river. The keeper of the boat said he had made four hundred dollars this season, by the crossing of emigrants bound to Oregon. We purchased a beef steer of them for four dollars, paying for it ourselves; for Uncle Sam finds us no beef. These half-civilized Indians differ very widely in character from those in their native wildness. Having learned from us the virtue of avarice most perfectly, you can get nothing of them, not even a cup of milk or an onion, without paying them the most extravagant prices.—We were surprised at the neatness of their houses, and their fine gardens and fields, in which they equal if they do not excel us.[23]

In fact, four dollars was not so much to ask for a hefty steer (Marcellus Edwards noted in his journal that the price amounted to a penny a pound). But where better for Indians to learn the "virtue of avarice," as Robinson put it, than along paths pursued by whites seeking profit and advantage?

By the Fourth of July, Robinson and company had picked up the Santa Fe Trail, passed through Council Grove with barely a pause, and were approaching the Arkansas River. All of Kearny's units would be on their way within a few days. (A second regiment of Missouri volunteers would follow later in the summer to reinforce Doniphan's regiment in New Mexico, as would a battalion of Mormon recruits assigned to follow Kearny to California.) The journey the Army of the West had embarked upon could be trying in any season, but it was hellish in high summer, with shriveling heat waves punctuated by torrential downpours that transformed sluggish streams into raging torrents. Many of Kearny's men would remember the Fourth of July as Robinson did— as a day of hunger, thirst, and hard traveling, relieved by only the briefest of revelries:

> This morning we all took a drink of whiskey in honor of the day; but are obliged to march on, as the rations we have are nearly gone, and if we cannot overtake the commissary wagons we shall have nothing to eat but our horses. We reduced our ration one-third, travelled twenty-five miles, and encamped at Good Water. The prairie has become drier, and the eye tires with its monotony.[24]

Kearny had earlier dispatched wagons to haul provisions to designated points along the route. Feeding even a small army as it crossed the barren plains was a formidable logistical challenge, however. The supply wagons, many of them driven by inexperienced teamsters, frequently broke down or overturned. Reductions in rations of one-third or more were commonplace for the troops, and some men might well have starved had it not been for buffalo, encountered in abundance near the Arkansas and targeted by designated teams of hunters. For one new to the plains like Robinson, a native of New Hampshire who spied his first great herd atop Pawnee Rock on July 8, the sight of the bison approaching in force was both splendid and fearsome and evoked thoughts of battle:

> Far over the plain to the west and north was one vast herd of buffaloes: some in column, marching in their trails, others carelessly grazing. Every acre was covered, until in the dim distance the prairie became one black mass, from which there was no opening, and extending to the horizon.—Every man was astonished. We had heard of the large numbers frequently seen, but had no idea such an innumerable herd could be gathered together. Most of them were travelling south, (probably for water) so as to come across our path. Their front ranks very obligingly made way for us for about two miles; but as the main body moved on they could be kept off no longer. They rushed through our ranks, throwing us into complete confusion; stopped the further progress of our wagons; and though an hundred shots were fired at them, we could not drive them away until the crowd passed. We killed 40 of them—cooking our meat by fires made of buffalo-dung, which burns as well as charcoal.[25]

Marcellus Edwards offered a somewhat different account of this incident in his journal, noting that the bison were driven into the ranks of Company D by careless hunters and describing the ensuing fracas in terms that reflected little glory on the men involved. Soldiers fired randomly among the "bellowing throng," he wrote, "endangering the lives of their companions as much as those of the buffaloes." So many hotheads joined in the chase, Edwards added, that the ranks were left "as thin as if there had been a real battle."[26]

The volunteers may not have distinguished themselves in this encounter, but they had good reason to liken such experiences to battle. Although many would see some action in Mexico, the struggle with the forces of nature was for most the essence of the campaign and the real test of their fiber. John Hughes wrote in a similar vein of the bugs that assailed the troops in buffalo country that July:

On the 9th, after a hurried march of twenty-five miles, we arrived upon the banks of the Little Arkansas, about ten miles above its confluence with the main Arkansas river. Here the mosquitoes, and their allies, the black gnat, in swarms, attacked us in the most heroic manner, and annoyed us as much, if not more than the Mexican lancers did at a subsequent period.[27]

Although Hughes and his comrades responded to such travails in retrospect with healthy doses of frontier humor, assaults by insects along the well-watered sections of the trail could be truly maddening—as could the prospect of waking in the morning on the hard sod to find a rattlesnake curled up under one's blanket. Frank Edwards, whose light artillery company formed part of Doniphan's regiment, noted that close encounters with those venomous reptiles became almost habitual on the plains:

It was, by no means, an unusual occurrence for us, after a heavy dew, to kill, in the morning, within a quarter mile of camp, more than twenty rattlesnakes, which, having come out to imbibe the dew, had become benumbed by the cool night air and, so, were an easy prey. One Major awoke one morning with one of these reptiles coiled up against his leg, it having nestled there for warmth. He dared not stir until a servant came and removed the intruder.[28]

For Edwards, who had enlisted in St. Louis partly to restore his health (influenced as Susan Magoffin was by Gregg's account, perhaps) and who in fact found the "soft delicious air" of the prairie invigorating, that cure had its costs in the form of myriad annoyances, including swarms of gnats that "got into the nostrils, eyes, and ears, creating a singularly pricking sensation, and making our horses almost frantic with pain," the "strong ammoniacal odor" of the buffalo chips that flavored the meat the men ate, and the insistent wolves that lurked about the camp after animals had been slaughtered there, howling "in the most mournful manner all night long."[29] Such aggravations made men callous and trigger-happy. Edwards recalled an incident that occurred one night in July as he was standing guard at the company's campsite along the Arkansas:

I was leaning upon my carbine, with my back to a small ravine along the edge of which my post extended and my mind in a quiet reverie, when, suddenly, from behind a bush, not three feet from me, a big gray wolf set up his dismal cry unconscious of my presence. It, annoyingly, took me by surprise;—snatching up a stone, I hurled it after his howling wolfship as he dashed precipitately down the ravine. I would have given something to have been allowed to shoot him, but as orders were to shoot nothing of less size than an Indian, I dared not alarm the camp by a shot.[30]

Indians, it seems, ranked first among the annoyances the troops had to guard against and were treated largely with contempt. Not only were they shot at if they approached the camp at night, but their gravesites were tampered with and their remains were used in at least one instance as a prop in a cruel joke. On Chouteau's Island in the Arkansas, Edwards recollected, "two of our men found a dead Indian lying on the ground, which, by means of sticks, they made to stalk about the Island to the surprise and terror of some who were not aware of the motive power."[31] The conscientious Marcellus Edwards of Company D complained of a similar sacrilege that occurred near Bent's Fort, involving the remains of an Indian wrapped in buffalo hide and exposed to the sky (a form of burial practiced by various tribes):

> We nooned under some scattering cottonwoods, in the branches of one of which was a scaffold, on which was placed the dead body of an Indian wrapped in a buffalo rug. The flesh was entirely decayed except a portion of the scalp, as was also the rug. Some persons climbed up and dislodged it. This was very wrong, for it being their mode of disposing of their dead, should be held as sacred as ours. Let some Indians be passing through our country and go to our place of interment and break them open, we would at once say they were the worst of savages and not one whit above the brute creation, and be for murdering them at once.[32]

By and large, Comanches, Cheyennes, and other plains-dwellers commonly encountered along the trail kept clear of the troops that summer. But scouts from those various tribes could hardly have overlooked the ominous procession of soldiers and the litter of carcasses they left in their wake. Soldiers who gunned down buffalo along the trail often butchered their prey hastily and incompletely, leaving many potentially useful parts to waste. Adding to the debris were the remains of dead horses and oxen cast aside by Kearny's men. The observant George Gibson reported that the "whole country from the Little Arkansas is like a slaughter pen, covered with bones, skulls, and carcasses of animals in every state of decay."[33] Such refuse, which had the effect of scaring away buffalo herds, and the presence of so many soldiers vying for the assets of this vital hunting ground were plainly provocative to tribes of the region, for travelers heading to and from New Mexico in the months and years to come would face Indian attacks on an unprecedented scale, forcing the army to patrol the Santa Fe Trail with troops that might otherwise have been used against the Mexicans. Such were the hidden costs of an expedition that pitted raw soldiers against an environment whose vistas might seem limitless but whose resources were finite.

Few faced a tougher battle with the elements on the way west than the two companies of volunteer infantry that Kearny recruited to supplement

Doniphan's mounted regiment. Kearny requested those infantrymen because he knew how hard it would be to keep horses fed and fit in barren country and wanted soldiers at hand who were used to campaigning without mounts. As it turned out, the infantrymen matched or exceeded the pace of the mounted men—but only by enduring marches of up to thirty miles or more a day in blistering heat that left some of the men lame and many of them cursing their superiors. Among those volunteer infantrymen was journalist Gibson, serving as second lieutenant. True to his calling, he kept a meticulous record of the march, replete with editorial blasts at the battalion's commander, Captain William Z. Angney, who lacked the support that the men might have placed in their leader had they been allowed to elect him, as other units did. As Gibson noted on July 1 in the vicinity of the Kansas River, a day after the battalion left Fort Leavenworth:

> The men were very much fatigued by the long march, and many had sore feet; and all of our teams were completely used up without anything to eat, as there was no grass in the bottom. . . . The men were not sparing of imprecations upon Captain Angney, who required us to make such a forced march to the great injury of men and teams, merely to have the reputation of keeping up with mounted troops. Several of our men were on the sick report but none dangerously ill, as they had all been sent to the wagons when taken [sick]. Both companies were regretting that we were prevented from electing a major and were thus deprived of the services of a man who could use more judgment.[34]

An elected officer might have asked no less of the men, given Kearny's demands and expectations, but Gibson and company felt that the army had not honored its side of the bargain with them as citizen soldiers and Angney bore the brunt of their resentments. Mercifully, the rigors of marching were offset by moments of frivolity and good cheer. Only a day after lamenting the cruelty of the march, Gibson struck a different note when Kearny allowed the men to recuperate after crossing the Kansas River and replace the worn animals hauling their supply wagons: "In the evening the camp presented a pretty appearance, the weather was fine, the men all merry and exchanging visits to know how the military life pleased them; and the sound of the bugles at retreat gave a military air to the surrounding country."[35]

And so it went for Gibson and his mates all the way to Bent's Fort, with long days of toil and resentment salvaged by precious interludes of harmony and tranquillity, one of which occurred when they reached the Arkansas River on July 14 and camped "at an early hour," after a march of a mere eighteen miles. "Sunset was magnificent," Gibson exulted, "the air balmy, and all the company enjoyed it, bathing, smoking, writing, cooking, laughing, and talking."[36] The men owed such charmed moments in part to the willingness of their commanders to give them a break now and then. When the grind resumed, they voiced their grievances anew, complaining as they did a week or so later that "Captain Angney did not treat them well, and that he marched faster than necessary, as in a day we could only go as far as our teams."[37] The troops had to reckon not just with the demands of their officers, however, but with the exactions of the country itself, which taxed travelers to the breaking point— and then afforded them moments of beauty and contentment that seemed to redeem all their pains. Gibson was not the sort to find spiritual solace in such trials and rewards. But like Susan Magoffin, he and other pilgrims on the trail that summer were confronting the mysteries of a new world and finding that there was more to this journey than they had calculated. As an editor, Gibson was probably familiar with journalist John O'Sullivan's memorable proclamation in 1845 that it was America's "manifest destiny to overspread the continent allotted by Providence for the free development of our yearly multiplying millions."[38] As Gibson and his mates discovered, however, Providence drove a hard bargain with those hoping to fulfill that destiny on the road to New Mexico in 1846. It remained to be seen whether the gains they achieved would outweigh the sacrifices demanded of them. And yet they persisted on the trail, and some acquired along the way a deeper sense of purpose.

On July 28, after suffering for two days from a fever that forced him to ride in the wagons with others who were too lame or ill to walk, Gibson fortified himself with "a pocket full of quinine pills"[39] and traveled fifteen miles with the company to their designated camp near Bent's Fort, arriving there two days after Susan Magoffin. Along the way, the men caught their first view of the Rockies, far to the west, and raised a cheer. By the time they reached camp that day, most of Kearny's army had gathered in the vicinity of Bent's Fort. Gibson's unit would be among the first to move out for Santa Fe, but they would still have a few days to relax—time enough to shave, bathe, clean their clothes, and pay a visit to the fort, where Gibson marveled at the diverse crowd of "citizens, soldiers, traders to Santa Fé, Indians, Negroes, etc." Still recuperating, Gibson could not bear the fort's "confined air" and "saw but little of its interior arrangements."[40] Far from complaining when it was time to resume the march, he and his mates gladly took to the road on August 1, short of provisions as usual but eager to cross those distant mountains and come into a country that was seemingly theirs for the taking. "After nearly four days' rest we all became anxious to reach the place of our destination," he wrote; "so we drew rations, the sugar and coffee being short (only half), broke up camp, and today turned our faces once more towards Santa Fé."[41]

A similar sense of duty and anticipation moved Susan Magoffin several days later to rise from her sickbed and prepare to resume the journey to Santa Fe with her husband in the wake of the army. If she needed a lesson in fortitude after her miscarriage, she found one close at hand:

> My situation was very different from that of an Indian woman in the room below me. She gave birth to a fine healthy baby, about the same time, *and in half an hour after she went to the River and bathed herself and it*, and this she has continued each day since. Never could I have believed such a thing, if I had not been here, and *mi alma's* own eyes had not seen her coming from the River. And some gentleman here tells him, he has often seen them immediately after the birth of a child go to the water and *break the ice* to bathe themselves![42]

Bent's Fort was nearly deserted by now, except for the soldiers who were rendered too ill to travel by fevers, intestinal disorders, or contagious diseases like measles.[43] Two of them had died recently, Susan noted, and been buried in the sand hills along the river. She hoped that when her own time came to face death, she would be "as well prepared to leave this mortal, this earthen body as I am to leave this earthen house."[44] Departing the fort on August 7, she marked the "second start" of her journey, as she put it in her diary, by fording the shallow Arkansas River with her party and leaving her homeland for Mexican territory:

> The crossing of the Arkansas was an event in my life, I have never met with before; the separating me from my own dear native land. . . . Perhaps I have left it for not only the first, but the last time. Maybe I am never to behold its bright and sunny landscape, its happy people, my countrymen, again. It is better always to look on the *bright* side, and it is certainly *wiser* to rely more fully on the Wisdom and Goodness of Providence.[45]

Crossing the Arkansas, where birth and death had alike been commemorated in recent days, Susan Magoffin could only pray that she would find new life on the far side. Hers was no manifest destiny. She hoped for the best and trusted in Providence, but perhaps Providence in its wisdom frowned on this undertaking. She and her countrymen were leaving the land they cherished in pursuit of another, little knowing if the world they gained would truly profit them in the end.

17

A Bloodless Bid for Santa Fe

Before leaving Bent's Fort with most of his forces on August 2, Stephen Kearny had taken several steps designed to lessen the likelihood that his army would be opposed by Governor Armijo and the troops under him. Some of Kearny's subordinates may have been hungry for a fight, but the commander and his superiors in Washington dearly hoped to acquire New Mexico without bloodshed and thus conserve the army's strength for the march to California. In a proclamation to the citizens of New Mexico, issued July 30, Kearny declared that he was entering their country "with a large military force for the purpose of seeking union with, and ameliorating the condition of the inhabitants."[1] To facilitate that merger, he enlisted the services of several American traders with long experience in dealing with Mexicans. At Fort Leavenworth in late June, he had conferred with Charles Bent, who had agreed to place Bent's Fort at the army's disposal and had informed Kearny of the situation in Santa Fe, where Armijo was expecting reinforcements from the south.[2] Then on August 1, after haggling over terms, Kearny dispatched William Bent and six others at Bent's Fort to serve as scouts for the march to Santa Fe. They would collect intelligence for the army, riding out ahead to talk with Mexican civilians, watch for Mexican troops, and detain spies. Three Mexicans suspected of spying for Armijo had already been apprehended at Bent's Fort. Rather than have them imprisoned or executed, Kearny ordered that they be given a tour of the assembled forces to impress them with American might before being sent on their way. "My God!" their leader exclaimed as they departed for Santa Fe, "What is to become of our republic?"[3] Kearny also sent trader Eugene Leitensdorfer—husband of one of the Mexican women Susan Magoffin met at the fort—with a military escort to Taos to try to conciliate the Pueblos there.

Kearny entrusted an even more sensitive mission to another American merchant who had long lived and trafficked in Mexico, James Magoffin, Susan's brother-in-law. Shrewd, convivial, and well connected, James had recently held council in Washington, D.C., with Senator Benton and President Polk and had arrived at Bent's Fort in late July with a letter from the president recommending him as an envoy to Armijo. Kearny was duly impressed and sent James Magoffin ahead on August 2 to parley with the governor in Santa Fe and implore Armijo to submit peacefully to an American takeover. Accompanying Magoffin were Captain Philip St. George Cooke and a detachment of twelve dragoons, who would enter the capital under a flag of truce.

Cooke was a natural choice for the assignment. A few years back, while patrolling the Santa Fe Trail, he had detained and disarmed Texans of the Snively expedition who were out prowling for Mexican caravans, an action that virtually ensured Cooke a polite reception in Santa Fe.[4] But he was not entirely happy campaigning for Kearny under a white flag. He had hoped to figure in "stirring war scenes," he wrote later in a memoir based on his wartime journal. Instead, he was being asked to bear an olive branch. By way of compensation, the normally secretive Kearny informed him that there was more to the upcoming campaign than the occupation of New Mexico. As Cooke characterized his briefing by Kearny:

> At a plaintive compliment, that I went to plant the olive, which he would reap a laurel, the general endeavored to gloss the barren field of toil, to which his subordinates at least, were devoted; and rather unsuccessful, he then revealed his ulterior instructions for the conquest of California. He had been promised the grade of brigadier general, to date with the march for that territory. A regiment or two would follow us to New Mexico.
>
> New deserts to conquer! That was giving to our monotonous toils a grandeur of scale that tinctured them with adventure and excitement.[5]

Another consolation for Cooke was the company of James Magoffin, with whom the captain first fraternized over chilled punch concocted in the icehouse at Bent's Fort. Magoffin's fondness for fine spirits was boundless, Cooke noted, and his "provision of wine defied all human exigencies."[6] He would share some of his stock with Cooke and a Mexican traveling companion, trader José Gonzales, on the way to Santa Fe. The rest he would reserve for the entertainment of Armijo and other Mexican officials. A few days out from the fort, after winding their way up Raton Pass, Cooke's party paused for refreshment in view of the Spanish Peaks. As Cooke related, Magoffin made the most of the occasion:

> He was in the vein to-day; reclining on the grass, after lunch, he made a long speech to Gonzales, in the most sonorous Spanish, about liberty and equality, and the thousand advantages of being conquered by our arms. Then, chuck-ling, he swore the old rascal would get himself in the calaboose as soon as he got to Chihuahua. He then held up, and addressed a pocket cork-screw, which, he said he had carried eight years. "You have cost me a thousand—five thou-sand dollars; but what do I care except for a bottle of wine every day; I work this way on purpose to keep you; what is money good for? I would not say to a bottle of champagne, 'I won't, I cannot use you,' for a million of dollars. I travel this way every year over deserts just to be able to have my wine and edu-cate my children."[7]

Those cherished pursuits might be disrupted if New Mexicans resisted the American incursion, and Magoffin would do all in his power to ease Kearny's advance.

Hurrying on, Cooke's party reached the budding New Mexican town of Las Vegas on August 9. A lonely outpost at the eastern fringe of the Spanish settlements, Las Vegas was vulnerable to Indian raids, as Cooke discovered when he and his men approached:

> Then we saw the people running and riding about in excitement and appar-ent confusion; mounting in hot haste, driving in herds of ponies, cattle, goats. I hardly believed the appearance, on the bluff, of my party of horse to be the occasion of it all; and as I drew nearer I doubted more and more, for a large party came galloping in my direction. . . . All doubt was soon solved by these eccentric cavaliers, formidable at least in appearance, passing at the gallop to our left. I marched on with increasing astonishment, tinged with a shade of mortification. I soon learned that this very characteristic introduction to New Mexican life, was caused by the wild Indians having killed a shepherd or two, at a distance of two leagues, and driven off their flock. And such was the meas-ure of New Mexican efficiency—to gallop off in confusion, and without pro-vision, to a pursuit, in which, if the robbers were overtaken, it would be at the moment when their own horses were quite blown, or exhausted.[8]

Had the New Mexicans failed to respond promptly to the assault, on the other hand, the fastidious Cooke might have questioned their courage, as other Americans did in such circumstances. In any case, the incident illustrated how preoccupied the settlers were with the Indian threat. Isolated on the frontier, they could ill afford to antagonize these well-armed Americans. Cooke and

Magoffin were politely entertained at the home of the local alcalde, where "some whiskey was handed around in an earthen cup" and they dined on cheese, tortillas, and poached eggs amid surroundings that Cooke sketched with the skill of a practiced observer:

> The room had a smooth earthen floor; it was partly covered by a kind of car-peting of primitive manufacture, in white and black—or natural coloring of the wool;—it is called Jerga; around the room, mattresses, doubled pillows, and coverlids, composed a kind of divan; the walls were whitewashed, with gypsum,—which rubbing off easily, a breadth of calico was attached to the walls above the divan; there was a doll-like image of the virgin, and two very rude paintings on boards and some small mirrors; the low room was ceiled with puncheons, supporting earth;—there were several rough board chairs. The alcalde's dress was a calico shirt,—very loose white cotton drawers or trowsers, and over them another pair—also very loose,—of leather, open far up at the outer seams. There appeared to be servants,—wild Indians of full blood. This may serve for a general picture.
>
> The alcalde—profanely surnamed Dios—gave me a very singular missive to his inferior magistrate of the next village; it required him to furnish ten men to watch my camp, that the Utahs should not steal my horses, and my men might sleep. He sent as I afterward learned, a swift express by the moun-tain paths, to the Governor at Santa Fe.[9]

This alcalde was evidently wary of Cooke, but he was in no position to chal-lenge the Americans directly. Instead, he used the conventions of hospitality to keep the visitors in line, providing a watch for their camp that would also place them under guard.

After passing through the town of San Miguel on August 10, Cooke's party reached the abandoned Pecos Pueblo the following day. The crumbling adobe walls of that Indian village and the adjacent Spanish mission church were a source of fascination to many who passed them on their way to Santa Fe that summer. Cooke, in his account, did not elaborate on the legend recounted by Gregg and others linking the former inhabitants of Pecos to a sacred fire dedicated to the Aztec king Montezuma. But he did draw a sharp distinction between the Pueblos and their vigorous "Aztec" heritage, as sym-bolized by their "unceasing altar fire," and the "degenerated" faith imposed on them by their Spanish conquerors:

> Here we see, only partially ruined, the temples of two religions which met in rivalry—the Aztec, with unceasing altar fire, and that of Rome, with its graven images; the former an ignorant, honest superstition with a basis of morality;

the latter, degenerated in this far isolation, steeped in immorality, embodied in spectacles and ceremonies, and degrading all that is high and holy to the level of sense—the depths of superstition.[10]

Cooke, as he often did after one of his rhetorical outbursts, qualified his argument by conceding that the Roman Catholic and "Aztec" traditions were now "harmoniously blended" among the Pueblos. (In fact, Pueblos were linguistically and culturally distinct from the Aztecs.)

Other chroniclers of the campaign surmised that Pueblos were seeking deliverance from Spanish oppression—redemption expected to come from the east with the rising sun, according to the Montezuma legend, suggesting that the advancing American army might be the fulfillment of that promise. As John Hughes wrote:

> Most of the Pueblos of New Mexico have similar traditions among them, respecting their great sovereign, Montezuma, and to this day look for him to come from the east to deliver his people from Mexican bondage. After our arrival in Santa Fé, an intelligent New Mexican declared to me, "that the Pueblo Indians could not be induced to unite their forces with the Mexicans in opposing the Americans, in consequence of an ancient and long cherished tradition among them, that at a certain period of time, succor would come from the east to deliver them from their Spanish oppressors, and to restore to them the kingdom of Montezuma; and that they hailed the American army as the long promised succor."[11]

If, in fact, a well-informed New Mexican made such a remark to Hughes, it must have been before the Pueblos at Taos joined in the uprising there against the American occupiers in January 1847—an event that dispelled any thoughts that the conquest marked some sort of liberation for Pueblos. In the heady summer of 1846, however, before disillusionment set in, Americans could gaze on the ruins of Pecos Pueblo and feel that they were part of a legendary enterprise. This was as close as they would get to reveling in the halls of Montezuma.

On August 12, after threading Apache Canyon—a treacherous pass west of Pecos that offered the New Mexicans a fine opportunity for contesting Kearny's advance if they so desired—Cooke entered Santa Fe, where he and his men were confronted by Armijo's guards near the Palace of the Governors:

> For the first time, I thought it would not be amiss to air my flag of truce; so I placed a white handkerchief on the point of my sabre, and the officer of the guard advancing to meet me, I announced my mission in a sentence of very formal book-Spanish; he gave me a direction, to the right I thought, and

looking up a narrow street, I saw a friendly signal, pushed on, and emerging, found myself and party on the plaza, crowded by some thousands of soldiers and countrymen, called out en masse, to meet our army. We made our way with some difficulty, toward the "palace," and coming to a halt, my trumpeter sounded a parley. It was some time before I was attended to; and it was a feeling between awkwardness and irritation that was at last relieved by the approach of an officer, the "Mayor de Plaza"; and he again went into the palace and returned, before he was ready to conduct me thither.

I entered from the hall, a large and lofty apartment, with a carpeted earth floor, and discovered the governor seated at a table, with six or eight military and civil officials standing. There was no mistaking the governor, a large fine looking man, although his complexion was a shade or two darker than the dubious and varying Spanish; he wore a blue frock coat, with a rolling collar and a general's shoulder straps, blue striped trowsers with gold lace, and a red sash. He rose when I was presented to him; I said I was sent to him by the general commanding the American army, and that I had a letter, which I would present at his convenience. He said he had ordered quarters for me, and that my horses should be grazed near the town, by his soldiers, there being no corn; he hoped I would remain as long as it pleased me. I then took my leave.[12]

These elaborate courtesies were merely a preamble to more serious discussions conducted later in the day. Cooke's interview with Armijo, now serving in a dual capacity as governor and general, did not yield any great diplomatic breakthrough. Armijo inquired as to whether Kearny was a colonel or a general (Kearny's promotion to general took effect when word reached him on August 15). Armijo seemed to be assessing the strength of the opposition, but he offered Cooke no hint as to his possible response.

More significant, perhaps, were talks James Magoffin held later with Armijo and his aide, Colonel Diego Archuleta, thought to be more militant than the governor when it came to meeting the American challenge. What exactly transpired at those talks was never revealed, but Magoffin later claimed credit in vague terms for appeasing the authorities in Santa Fe:

I engaged, at the request of President Polk, to go to Mexico, where I had been for many years, to be of service to our troops, and I took what they gave me, *to wit*: letters to accredit me to the Generals. They did accredit me and imploy me. I went into Santafe ahead of Genl. Kearney and smoothed the way to his bloodless conquest of New Mexico. Col. Archulette would have fought: I quieted him.[13]

Senator Benton later claimed that Magoffin won Archuleta over by assuring him that Kearny intended to appropriate for the United States only that part of New Mexico claimed by Texas before it joined the Union—east of the Rio Grande (the letter Cooke delivered from Kearny to Armijo stated as much, but the American claim would soon be extended to cover all of New Mexico). Magoffin advised Archuleta to "make a *pronunciamiento*," Benton wrote, and claim for himself the country west of the Rio Grande. That idea reportedly appealed to the ambitious Archuleta, Benton added, and the colonel "agreed not to fight."[14]

Benton further attested—and Magoffin tacitly implied—that Armijo was disinclined to oppose Kearny's advance, leaving open the question of whether Magoffin offered the governor some inducement to maintain that obliging stance. Magoffin later submitted a claim to the War Department for expenses of more than $37,000 incurred during his mission to Santa Fe and his subsequent visit to Chihuahua and Durango. He was imprisoned in Chihuahua and, by his own account, expended $3,800 on bribes to recover a compromising letter from General Kearny that had fallen into Mexican hands (the letter spelled out Magoffin's services to the army and could have doomed him to execution as an enemy agent). He made no mention in his claim of any bribes offered in Santa Fe, but he did cite costs of $2,000 "for entertainments to officers military and civil and influential citizens at Santafe, Chihuahua and Durango, to accomplish the object of promoting the interests of the United States."[15] He further itemized those expenses as including bottles of claret wine at $18 a dozen and champagne at $36 per dozen.[16]

While there is no proof that Armijo literally sold out to Magoffin or Kearny, the governor was likely influenced—and indirectly compromised—by his commercial ties with American merchants in the Santa Fe trade, dealings that conditioned him to bargain with his competitors rather than do battle with them. In late June, when it appeared that an American campaign against New Mexico was imminent, he had cashed in on a recent investment by selling his goods, newly arrived by wagon train from Missouri, to trader Albert Speyer, who was bound for Chihuahua with freight that included arms and ammunition. James Webb had just reached Santa Fe with his own merchandise and decided to team up with Speyer. As Webb recollected: "Mr. Speyer had bought out General Armijo's goods; from which I infer the general, if not knowing the troops were on the way to New Mexico, thought they soon would be, and [that] his safest course would be to have as little property under his guardianship as possible. We prepared to join him [Speyer] and travel together."[17] Webb, one of numerous Americans who gladly trafficked with Mexico in wartime with the consent of their own government, was in no position to criticize either Armijo or Speyer for seeking gain while others were preparing to risk their lives in battle. These men pursued commercial interests that transcended national boundaries, and their attitude toward the obstacles that the warring parties placed in their way was perhaps best summarized by a remark attributed to Armijo during a tense moment in his negotiations with Speyer: "Damn the Americans! Damn the Mexicans!"[18]

Perhaps Armijo hoped both to pursue the war and to profit by it. On the night of August 12, after meeting with Magoffin and before Cooke left Santa Fe to rejoin the advancing American army, Armijo was still talking confidently of rallying thousands of troops to meet Kearny, a resolve that did not detract from his hospitable attentions to the visiting delegation, as Cooke related in his memoir:

> It was settled that a "commissioner" should return with me, and that we should set out at sunrise; the Governor would march next day "with six thousand men." I promised to take chocolate with him at that early hour.
>
> Accordingly on the 13th, soon after the sun rose, being all ready to mount, I paid my parting visit to Governor Armijo, when chocolate, cake and bread,—such as only Mexicans or Spaniards can make,—were served on silver plate; it is an article of my culinary creed, that only the Spanish, and their cognate tribes can make chocolate!
>
> I will not go so far in the matter of bread; but will state that notwithstanding there is not a bolting cloth in the province, their bread and cake cannot be excelled. But meanwhile the Governor is bowing me out, with a suspiciously good-humored smile, and deafening trumpets and drums seem beating to arms. I mount and ride forth, with my escort in compact order; and I pass that same guard-house, and hear the same sullen howl of the sentinel, which I still misunderstand; and rising in my stirrups I turn and with a defiant gesture, call out, in good English, "I'll call again in a week."[19]

There was a good deal of banter and bluffing on both sides, in this parting exchange between Cooke and Armijo and in the campaign as a whole. Armijo put up a brave show over the next few days, gathering forces at Apache Canyon and erecting fortifications there. In the end, however, he did not really want to fight for New Mexico any more than Kearny did. Armijo would be the one to back down, but perhaps as he showed Cooke out with that cryptic smile on his face, he was wondering if the Americans knew precisely what they were bidding for and what lay in store for them if they prevailed.

By the time Cooke left Santa Fe to rejoin Kearny, the Army of the West had made its way through Raton Pass. The journey from Bent's Fort had presented the troops with dramatic contrasts in terrain, and their mood had varied accordingly. Plodding southward from the Arkansas River to the base of Raton Pass along the dried-up Timpas Creek, they met with some of the bleakest country they had yet experienced. Buffeted by a hot, dusty wind that some likened to the Saharan sirocco, they found no grass for their mounts and water enough for man and beast only in a few murky oases such as Hole-in-the-Rock, which Marcellus Edwards's mounted company reached on August 4:

> The Hole in the Rock has been sounding upon our ears a long way off as being a place where a crystal fount, bursting from a solid rock, wended its rippling course through a beautiful and fragrant meadow. But this was a most woeful deception. We found a small, rocky branch where a few holes or deeper cuts in its channel retained a little filthy water when all the rest was dry. Our almost famished brutes rushed into these holes and soon stirred them to a thick mud, except one larger than the rest that they could not get to. Out of this last one I succeeded in watering my mare in my cap.[20]

Volunteers grew deeply attached to their mounts during the campaign, and Edwards was at first appalled when he saw a soldier shoot his faltering horse in the head. But he concluded that it was an act of mercy, far preferable to leaving the famished animal to be finished off by the wolves that followed close behind. Such conditions took a predictable toll on the morale of the volunteers, who were fast being transformed from horsemen into foot soldiers. On August 5, Kearny's adjutant, Captain Henry S. Turner, wrote to his wife from the base of Raton Pass:

> I may say we have had *no grass* for four days, and when it is remembered that our animals must be subsisted on grass, you can well conceive our embarrassment. Unless there is a change for the better in a very few days, the Army must be dismounted. . . . We are still 150 miles from Santa Fe, and expect to be there by the 16th instant. The volunteers are beginning to discover that they have made an egregious mistake and their complaints are long and loud.[21]

As the troops made their way up the pass, however, their spirits rose proportionately, despite the difficulty of the ascent and the toll it took on the army's wagons. As earlier travelers had recognized, this was a place of metamorphosis, where travelers found themselves transformed along with their surroundings. "Everything has changed—the country, game, birds, fish," noted George Gibson of the volunteer infantry battalion on August 6. "The air is cool, bracing, and pure, but pleasant." After a march of seventeen miles, he and his mates bunked down in a spot that felt as close to heaven as any pinnacle they would attain on this grueling odyssey:

> Our camp is at the base of a high peak of the Ratón, where the grass is toler-
> able and the water very fine. A small branch runs by our camp, and in a little
> while we caught in it a large mess of mountain trout, which, of course, we
> enjoyed as a luxury not met with every day. The scenery around is rich, the
> broken rocky eminences reflecting back the evening sun, and the top of the
> Ratón towering in the skies immediately over us.[22]

Henry Turner, writing to his wife that same day, was equally lyrical in describing the abrupt ascent from the desert:

> I must go on and tell you something of our route today, ascending from the
> arid plain in which for many days we had journeyed, we struck upon a fresh
> mountain stream, its limpid current presenting a stark contrast to the briny
> pools from which we have had to quench our thirst since leaving the Arkansas.
> Crossing and recrossing it clambering over rocks and jagged points at last we
> reach our camping ground, shut in on every side by mighty cliffs, a little "oasis"
> in the waste of broken surface, one green spot on which our white cotton tents,
> the grazing animals, the gurgling rivulet and the crags around, compose a pic-
> ture both grand and beautiful.[23]

Even the grumbling volunteers, Turner noted on August 9, seemed to have
profited from the change in setting and were bearing the continuing food
shortages and other hardships "much better than was expected."[24] The ninth
was a Sunday, and Kearny allowed the men a respite after a journey of only
ten miles. Turner, whose wife was a Catholic and who himself was planning
to convert to that faith, spent his free time reading through "the Mass as
devoutly, I believe, as a priest would have done and I can say more so than a
great many." Elsewhere, noted John Hughes, volunteers acknowledged the
day of rest by practicing cleanliness, if not godliness: "This was the Sabbath,
and the only Sabbath's rest we had enjoyed since our departure from Missouri. Here we shaved and dressed, not to attend church,—not to visit
friends,—not in deference to the conventional rules of society,—but in
remembrance of these privileges and requirements."[25]

For most of the troops, the descent from Raton Pass would bring them
into a land dominated by an alien faith, and Kearny may have spent some time
that Sunday considering how to appeal to Catholic New Mexico in the days
ahead. Like Cooke, he and his troops encountered no hostility from the isolated communities along New Mexico's eastern frontier. But from his own
scouts and from the Mexican spies they apprehended, he heard of resistance
brewing in Taos and Santa Fe and sensed that much depended on his ability
to quell the fears of civil and religious authorities, some of whom were said

to be plying the populace with warnings of American brutality. The first test for Kearny came at Las Vegas on August 15, where he stood atop the roof of one of the houses to address the townspeople through an interpreter and administer the oath of loyalty to the alcalde and captains of the militia. Lieutenant William H. Emory of the Topographical Engineers, who was conducting a reconnaissance of the Southwest in conjunction with the campaign, witnessed the gathering in Las Vegas that morning and recorded Kearny's remarkable address:

"Mr. Alcalde and people of New Mexico: I have come amongst you by the orders of my government, to take possession of your country, and extend over it the laws of the United States. We consider it, and have done so for some time, a part of the territory of the United States. We come amongst you as friends—not as enemies; as protectors—not as conquerors. We come among you for your benefit—not for your injury.

"Henceforth I absolve you from all allegiance to the Mexican government, and from all obedience to General Armijo. He is no longer your governor; [great sensation.] I am your governor. I shall not expect you to take up arms and follow me, to fight your own people who may oppose me; but I now tell you, that those who remain peaceably at home, attending to their crops and their herds, shall be protected by me in their property, their persons, and their religion; and not a pepper, nor an onion, shall be disturbed or taken by my troops without pay, or by the consent of the owner. But listen! he who promises to be quiet, and is found in arms against me, I will hang.

"From the Mexican government you have never received protection. The Apaches and the Navajhoes come down from the mountains and carry off your sheep, and even your women, whenever they please. My government will correct all this. It will keep off the Indians, protect you in your persons and property; and, I repeat again, will protect you in your religion. I know you are all great Catholics; that some of your priests have told you all sorts of stories—that we should ill-treat your women, and brand them on the cheek as you do your mules on the hip. It is all false. My government respects your religion as much as the Protestant religion, and allows each man to worship his Creator as his heart tells him is best. Its laws protect the Catholic as well as the Protestant; the weak as well as the strong; the poor as well as the rich. I am not a Catholic myself—I was not brought up in that faith; but at least one-third of my army are Catholics, and I respect a good Catholic as much as a good Protestant.

"There goes my army—you see but a small portion of it; there are many more behind—resistance is useless.

"Mr. Alcalde, and you two captains of militia, the laws of my country require that all men who hold office under it shall take the oath of allegiance. I do not wish for the present, until affairs become more settled, to disturb your form of government. If you are prepared to take oaths of allegiance, I shall continue you in office and support your authority."

This was a bitter pill; but it was swallowed by the discontented captain, with downcast eyes. The general remarked to him, in hearing of all the people: "Captain, look me in the face while you repeat the oath of office." The hint was understood; the oath taken, and the alcalde and the two captains pronounced to be continued in office. The citizens were enjoined to obey the alcalde, &c. &c. The people grinned, and exchanged looks of satisfaction; but seemed not to have the boldness to express what they evidently felt—that their burdens, if not relieved, were at least shifted to some ungalled part of the body.[26]

Kearny had authority from President Polk to administer the oath of allegiance to Mexican officials and to establish a temporary civil government, but other powers and responsibilities he assumed in the course of this and similar ceremonies in days to come were largely self-appointed. Intent on countering the opposition of Catholic authorities, he took on a priestly role himself by "absolving" the people of allegiance to Mexico and by asking officials to swear allegiance to the United States "in the name of the Father, Son, and Holy Ghost—Amen."[27] In seeking to reassure the populace, he made promises of protection here that would be hard to keep. His troops would sometimes requisition food and livestock from New Mexicans that they had no desire to part with, and his efforts to pacify the Navajos and other tribes in months to come would not begin to eliminate the threat of Indian raids against Mexican settlements. Many years later, correspondent Richard Elliott would look back on this speech in his memoir and remark that "the protection against Indians, so solemnly promised, and the mention of which caused the Las Vegas alcalde to grin with satisfaction, has never been realized."[28]

Kearny felt sufficiently encouraged by the results of his address in Las Vegas, however, that he repeated the procedure on Sunday the sixteenth at San Miguel, where George Kendall and other Pioneers from Texas had been detained in 1841 and two of their leaders shot to death. Some of Kearny's troops were mindful of that incident. "As we passed slowly through the Plaza in which these poor men had been executed," wrote Frank Edwards, "a moody silence pervaded the whole, save the whispered words 'Kendall,' 'Alamo,' 'Armijo'—and everyone seemed relieved when we had left San Miguel del Vada behind us."[29] Before departing, Kearny insisted that the local priest stand by while he administered the oath of allegiance to the alcalde. As one of Kearny's officers reported:

The general expressed a wish to ascend one of the houses, with the priest and Alcalde, and to address the people of the town, informing them of the object of his mission. After many evasions, delays, and useless speeches, the Padre made a speech, stating that "he was a *Mexican*, but should obey the laws that were placed over him for *the time,* but if the general should point all his cannon at his breast, he could not consent to go up there and address the people."

The general very mildly told him, through the interpreter, Mr. Robideau, that he had not come to injure him, nor did he wish him to address the people. He only wished him to go up there and hear him (the general) address them. The Padre still fought shy, and commenced a long speech which the general interrupted, and told him, he had no time to listen to "useless remarks," and repeated that he only wanted him to go up and listen to his speech. He consented.[30]

The alcalde was prevailed on to take the oath, and the priest—perhaps the same convivial padre encountered at San Miguel by James Webb in 1844—was not so offended by the proceedings that he refused to share some "refreshments" with Kearny afterward. But such rituals of compulsory allegiance left a bitter taste in the mouths of some in the army who witnessed or heard of them. Marcellus Edwards, for one, doubted if the oaths Kearny administered had any legal or moral standing, "for these poor creatures were evidently compelled to take it for fear of giving offense to our army."[31] The acerbic Captain Cooke, who had rejoined Kearny by the sixteenth, was even stronger in denouncing the administration of oaths and the imposition of American legal rights and obligations on a populace that he regarded as neither willing nor able to assume such responsibilities:

> The great boon of American citizenship thus thrust, through an interpreter, by the mailed hand, upon eighty thousand mongrels who cannot read,—who are almost heathens,—the great mass reared in real slavery, called peonism, but still imbued by nature with enough patriotism to resent this outrage of being forced to swear an alien allegiance, by an officer who had just passed their frontier. This people who have been taught more respect for a corporal than a judge, must still have been astonished at this first lesson in liberty.[32]

Most of the Americans under Kearny, however, probably agreed with Richard Elliott, who observed in a dispatch he wrote from New Mexico that the manner in which Kearny took Las Vegas and claimed the alcalde's allegiance was "a very comfortable way for both takers and taken."[33] Soldiers talked boldly of welcoming a fight when it appeared that Armijo might still make a stand in Apache Canyon, but few lamented Armijo's hasty departure for Chihuahua or deprecated Kearny's notable achievement in claiming Santa Fe without the loss of a single life in battle. "I much doubt if any officer of rank, but Stephen W. Kearny, would have undertaken the enterprise," Cooke conceded, "or, if induced to do so, would have accomplished it successfully."[34]

Part of Kearny's success could be attributed to his skill at countering Mexican charges that the invaders were out to brutalize the populace and at spreading his own tales among the opposition that made his army seem more formidable than it was. But his main strength was in gauging the weakness of his opponents and in capitalizing on that assessment. Armijo never received any substantial reinforcements from the south. He brought only 150 dragoons from the Regular Army with him when he joined his forces at Apache Canyon. Of the roughly three thousand troops assembled there, the vast majority were militiamen from the settlements and pueblos. Those recruits were poorly equipped and limited in their experience to campaigns against hostile tribes that bore little resemblance to the challenge they faced now from the well-armed Americans. Many were weary and demoralized after years of struggling to defend their communities on the frontier with scant support from a central government that they had come to regard as indifferent if not inimical to them. Rafael Chacón, a thirteen-year-old cadet at military school in Chihuahua in 1846, returned home to New Mexico that summer and, despite his father's earnest efforts to have him exempted from service as a mere boy, joined the forces at Apache Canyon as Kearny approached. He later recalled the turmoil and uncertainty that prevailed there before Armijo abandoned the field to the enemy:

> One day a disagreement arose among the militia men and in a moment such a commotion was made that they were all ready to fight one another. After the mutiny was pacified the men were put to digging trenches and building barricades of branches of pine and poplar trees. We were employed thus for three days when, all of a sudden, General Armijo issued orders that the Pueblo Indians and the militia should return to their homes, saying that he would confront the invaders with the presidial troops and with the squadron of regulars from Vera Cruz. There was a terrifying confusion when he gave this order and everyone was hastily taking whatever horse he desired most and everything he could carry.[35]

Chacón did not specify the nature of the disagreement that nearly resulted in mutiny before Armijo dismissed the militia, but one source of tension in camp may have been resentments among Pueblo recruits toward Armijo. Although Chacón referred to those Pueblos as if they were distinct from the militia, they were in fact an essential part of that force. American and New Mexican observers agreed that Pueblos were among the militia's best fighting men, and Armijo was hampered in this crisis by the fact that he had alienated those from Taos and elsewhere by suppressing the rebellion of 1837, backed by many Pueblos who feared that the central government would tax their communities beyond endurance and deprive them of autonomy.

Whatever the nature of the resentments in Armijo's camp, he plainly had to reckon with dissension in his ranks. He also quarreled with top aides, including Dámaso Salazar. If he retained any hope or intention of challenging the invaders when he arrived at Apache Canyon, that resolve soon melted away when he assessed the condition and morale of his forces. Soon after disbanding the militia, he fled New Mexico for Chihuahua, taking with him one hundred or so dragoons. Chacón, for one, was not inclined to blame Armijo for backing down:

> What could Armijo do with an undisciplined army without any military training, without commissary resources, and without leaders to direct the men? He was a dwarf against a giant. Armijo was the imaginary hero of that epoch. Had he rashly rushed to give battle, it would have been equivalent to offering his troops as victims to the invading army; the result would have been a useless effusion of blood, offering himself unnecessarily to death.[36]

Armijo, Chacón concluded, faced too much turmoil within his own camp to offer cogent opposition to the invaders. He could not contend "either with the enemy or with his own people who had already attempted a revolt."

That Armijo held a weak hand in no way diminished the credit due Kearny for calling his opponent's bluff. Jacob Robinson of Company D wrote frankly of his relief on discovering that the foe had abandoned Apache Canyon and left the road to the capital undefended:

> On the 18th day of August, we marched through the pass from which the Mexicans had fled, and on a careful survey we saw how easily five hundred good soldiers might have completely destroyed us. The rocky cliffs on each side were from two to three thousand feet high; and the fallen trees which they had cut down, hedged up our way. We all felt very well satisfied to pass without being attacked. We had all felt very brave before; but we now saw how difficult it would have been to have forced the pass, and were glad to be beyond it. After a march of 35 miles, without grass for our horses, we at length came in sight of Santa Fe. . . . The city is full of corn and wheat fields: the corn is now fit to roast, and the wheat not quite ready to harvest. The people supply themselves with water from three beautiful streams that run through the town, having their sources in a lake to the north-west. With them they also irrigate their cornfields. We entered the city just as the sun was sink-

Occupied Santa Fe under the American Flag, from J. W. Abert's report on New Mexico in 1846–47, in H.R. Ex. Doc. 41, 30th Cong., 1st sess., Serial 517. Courtesy Library of Congress, Prints and Photographs division, LC-USZ62-17606.

ing behind the distant mountain; and as its last rays gilded the hill top, the flag of our country triumphantly waved over the battlements of the holy city; minute guns fired a national salute, and the long shout of the troops spoke the universal joy that was felt at the good fortune that has attended us. But we leave the city to encamp—the men weary and hungry; no grass, no wood, and nothing to eat, as our wagons have been left behind.[37]

George Gibson's infantry battalion, preceded by the U.S. dragoons and followed by the artillery, entered Santa Fe ahead of Robinson and the other mounted volunteers, and Gibson witnessed the raising of the American flag atop the Palace vacated by Armijo:

But a few citizens showed themselves, many having fled to the mountains; and we marched into the plaza and ran up the Stars and Stripes from the top of the Palace, the artillery firing a salute of thirteen guns, when we all returned to the hill and encamped, it being dark by this time. No person came out to meet us, no troops were embodied, and there was not the least show or appearance of resistance in any way.

The appearance of [the] town was shabby, without either taste or a show of wealth—no gardens that deserved the name, the fields all unenclosed, the people poor and beggarly, and nothing to pay us for our long march.[38]

Gibson's feeling of disillusionment—of having gained rather less than he bargained for—may have been induced not just by the shabbiness of Santa Fe (Americans coming new to the town often found that it fell short of their expectations) but by the somber mood of those locals who remained in Santa Fe to witness the arrival of the occupiers. Soldiers who felt as Kearny did that the Americans were acting for the benefit of the populace were disappointed to find men in Santa Fe greeting them "with surly countenances and downcast looks," as Richard Elliott observed, and people in tears.[39] Trader Edward James Glasgow, who left his wagons behind and hurried ahead "as fast as my mule could bring me" to witness the taking of Santa Fe, found "every body frightened out of their wits, Genl Armijo with his troops run away, the citizens leaving town with their families and all in confusion."[40]

Kearny tried to allay the fears of the townspeople by sharing some refreshments at the Palace with Lieutenant Governor Juan Bautista Vigil y Alarid, who had chosen to remain in the capital and cooperate with the Americans, before delivering a proclamation the next morning in the plaza laden with assurances similar to those he had offered at Las Vegas and San Miguel. In this same speech, he referred in oddly solemn tones to a possible second coming by the departed Armijo:

I advise you to attend to your domestic pursuits, cultivate industry, be peaceable and obedient to the laws. Do not resort to violent means to correct abuses.
I do hereby proclaim that being in possession of Santa Fé, I am therefore virtually in possession of all New Mexico. Armijo is no longer your governor. His
power is departed; but he will return and be as one of you. When he shall return
you are not to molest him. You are no longer Mexican subjects; you are now
become American citizens, subject only to the laws of the United States. . . . I
am your governor—henceforth look to me for protection.[41]

Juan Bautista Vigil then swore "obedience to the Northern Republic," or the
United States, and spoke eloquently of the plight of his people: "Do not find
it strange if there has been no manifestation of joy and enthusiasm in seeing
this city occupied by your military forces. To us the power of the Mexican
Republic is dead. No matter what her condition, she was our mother. What
child will not shed abundant tears at the tomb of his parents?"[42]

Vigil's plaintive remarks went to the heart of the problem facing Kearny
and his aides. Although his campaign resembled a conquest in some respects
and an acquisition in others, its implications were not just military or economic. In effect, he had adopted the New Mexicans and their discontents—
a people bereft and bewildered at this sudden separation from their mother
country, however neglectful she may at times have been. Kearny had encouraged them in his proclamations to look to him for protection in much the
same way that dispossessed tribespeople were urged by American authorities
to rely for support on the Great Father in Washington. Yet Kearny would be
hard-pressed to make good on that sweeping personal commitment. Although
his statements were sincere to the extent that they represented his best hopes
for a peaceful and protective relationship between American authorities and
their New Mexican dependents, his job was to sell this policy, not to fulfill it.
By the time the locals began to question the terms of the deal and test the
mettle of their new overseers, Kearny would be off on the next phase of his
far-ranging campaign.

18

The Travails of Occupation

As Kearny and his troops were entering Santa Fe, Samuel and Susan Magoffin were just exiting Raton Pass, whose steep, rocky slopes wreaked havoc on the traders' wagons and caused innumerable delays. Not until August 26 did the Magoffins reach Las Vegas, where Susan was an object of great curiosity among the populace. Mothers gathered around her with babies at their breasts, puffing on tobacco wrapped in corn shucks and plying her with questions in Spanish that she barely understood. Here and at the next few settlements they passed through before reaching Santa Fe, she found the easy, country ways of the loosely clad women and their threadbare children hard to countenance. As she wrote in her diary on the twenty-seventh near San Miguel:

> We have passed through some two or three little settlements today similar to the Vegas, and I am glad to think that much is accomplished of my task. It is truly shocking to my modesty to pass such places with gentlemen.
>
> The women slap about with their arms and necks bare, perhaps their bosoms exposed (and they are none of the prettiest or whitest) if they are about to cross the little creek that is near all the villages, regardless of those about them, they pull their dresses, which in the first place but little more than cover their calves—up above their knees and paddle through the water like ducks, sloshing and spattering every thing about them. Some of them wear leather shoes, from the States, but most have buckskin mockersins, Indian style.

And it is repulsive to see the children running about perfectly naked, or if they have on a chimese it is in such ribbands it had better be off at once. I am constrained to keep my veil drawn closely over my face all the time to protect my blushes.[1]

Unlike some other visitors from the States, however, who found New Mexico hopelessly backward and felt that it had nothing to teach them, she proved to be a diligent and often appreciative student of the country, peppering her journal with snatches of Spanish and gaining insights that eluded other witnesses. To be sure, she had advantages that most other visitors did not. As the wife of a veteran trader, she had entrée to polite New Mexican society and made the most of it, getting to know a number of women who were more refined in dress and manner than those she first encountered in the countryside. At the same time, she became a favorite among the lonely American officers in Santa Fe. She thus served as a kind of intermediary between occupiers and occupied, chronicling the travails of both sides and the economic and cultural intercourse that persisted between them despite the tensions of the moment.

She received her first Mexican visitor in Santa Fe on August 31, having arrived there the evening before with her husband to be greeted at the door of their four-room adobe house by James Magoffin, who regaled them with oysters and champagne. Susan had barely settled in when she found herself playing host to one Doña Juliana, who complimented the young American on her command of Spanish and presented herself as "a great friend to the Americans and especially to the Magoffins whom she calls a *mui bien famile* [*muy buena familia*—very good family]."[2] Other Santa Feans of note spurned the Americans, but Doña Juliana was a woman of limited means and had an interest in remaining on favorable terms with this very good family, renewing her attentions the following day. Susan understood that her compliments were calculated and accepted them for what they were worth:

> Dona Juliana called again this P.M. to see *mi alma* who was out yesterday. I rather retired from the conversation, save a little which *mi alma* interpreted to her. She is a great rogue to win the respects, good wishes, and esteem of *la nina* [little child], as she flatteringly spoke of me to my good husband, who by the way took it all well. "*A que Don Manuel, la Senora es muy linda, muchachita, la nina! Y que es major, ella es muy afabla, muy placentera, muy buena.*" [Ah! Don Manuel, the lady is very pretty, only a little girl, a child: And what is more, she is very affable, very pleasing, very good.] Of course I heard none of this.[3]

Two days later, Susan received a visit from another "Senora" who professed admiration for the "foreigners," or Americans, pronounced Armijo a thief and a coward, and offered her hostess lessons on the wiles of the opposite sex in a town notorious for flirtations, prompting Susan to comment tartly in her diary: "She could lesson me to the fullest limit, I'd venture to say."[4]

This newcomer from the States was not as innocent of the world's snares as her guests suspected. She sized up these women and their ways quickly and astutely and responded to their overtures with a good-natured skepticism that befitted the circumstances. She was not easily taken in, and that suited her admirably for Santa Fe, where the locals admired those who knew how to banter and bargain. It was a trait as useful in social intercourse as it was in the marketplace. As part of her housekeeping duties, she had an instructive encounter on September 5 with a young peddler going door to door:

> I was called up to buy some vegetables from a little *muchacha* [girl], and a cunning piece she was too . . . the idea of her offering me four squashs for one real, and half a dozen ears of *mais verde* [green corn] for *un real y media* [a real and a half—7 1/2 cents]. One must look out for themselves, I find if they do not wish to be cheated though only of a few cents, and called *tonta* [stupid], into the bargain. I shall know the next time better how to deal with them.[5]

To bargain shrewdly with people here, she learned, was to show respect for them and to gain their respect in return. Within a few weeks, she was refer-ring affectionately to the salesgirl as "my little protege" and demonstrating to other youngsters in the trade that she was not to be taken lightly:

> Next is a half grown boy with mellons—here he asks me "dos reals por una" [two reals for one] believing me to be like some of my countrymen entirely young in such matters, but he found me different. I looked at him straight till he fell to *un real media* [a real and a half], when I said "*hombre*" in a long voice, as much as to say "man have you a soul to ask so much!" and without hesitation he *gladly* took *una*, the regular market price, and I dare say he will return another time since he was not able to play the cheat, and I am a pretty prompt customer.[6]

This was the spirit that had earned Americans success and a modicum of acceptance in Santa Fe—a willingness to engage the locals on their own terms and deal with them firmly but fairly. Some of the men who entered the town in triumph that August had a chance to do the same, but the common soldiers were short of cash and the officers were largely restricted in their dealings with the populace to dinners or fandangos where the social barriers between the

two sides remained palpable despite the forced air of conviviality. At one fandango that Susan Magoffin attended in September, amid clouds of tobacco
fumes emitted by the Mexican guests of both sexes, Major Thomas Swords
walked up to her "in true Mexican style," as she put it, "and with a polite,
'Madam will you have a cigarita,' drew from one pocket a *handfull of shucks
and from an other a large horn of tobacco*, at once turning the whole thing to
a burlesque."[7] It was a joke perhaps less amusing for the locals than for the
Americans, who at a similar event at the Palace in late August had placed their
seal on the occasion by displaying their flag draped around a painting of Kearny
handing a Mexican a new constitution, above the motto "*libertad*."[8]

There were other occasions and places for the occupiers to mingle with
Santa Feans and try their luck with the likes of the celebrated monte dealer
Gertrudis Barceló, described by Susan Magoffin as "a stately dame of a certain age, the possessor of a portion of that shrewd sense and fascinating manner necessary to allure the wayward, inexperienced youth to the hall of final
ruin."[9] The card game she presided over was often played at fandangos, with
those who hosted the events sharing part of the proceeds with the authorities. (Gambling establishments had once been illegal in Santa Fe, but Armijo
had since sanctioned them as a source of income.) Frank Edwards described
the setting for these mixed entertainments:

> The largest rooms are of course selected. At one end, carpets are spread, and
> all the women squat themselves on them, the men occupying the remainder
> of the room. The most common dance is the *cuna*, which resembles our
> Spanish dance. After all the couples are placed, the women begin a song, as
> dreary and monotonous as a dead march. The song keeps time with two squeak-
> ing fiddles. After each dance, your partner is allowed to find her way to her seat
> alone, where she again squats herself down, unless you have invited her to take
> a glass of brandy or wine—a stall for the sale of which is always kept in an adjoin-
> ing room—and where, also, is generally kept a monte table.[10]

Such were the means by which Santa Feans occupied the occupiers and profited by their presence. For some lonely soldiers, the chance to dance with a
woman was worth the cost of the drink and the risk of losing what little cash
they possessed at the monte table. But the contact was not very intimate, and
the men did not always find the women attractive. Gibson, who had a wife
and child back home in Missouri, was one of several witnesses who complained of their "disgusting practice, which is very common, of painting the
face like Indians," using a reddish plant extract favored for its cosmetic prop-
erties.[11] Nor was he much impressed by their dress or manner, at least when
it came to those of the less fashionable set who deigned to attend a fandango

held at an American-owned tavern on August 21, a few days after the troops claimed the town:

> The women were far from handsome or what in "the States" would be called modest, but I have since found that the most decent and respectable were not there. . . . As we could not speak Spanish nor they English, we made rather a poor showing in conversation; in fact, there was none, as it is unfashionable for men to sit amongst or talk to the women. But few women attended, some having fled to the mountains, and others not yet being willing to submit to the American yoke.[12]

Not all exchanges between American men and Mexican women were as constrained as this. One prospector heading west to California along the Santa Fe Trail in 1849 encountered a local woman in the New Mexican town of Galisteo with a two-year-old daughter fathered by an American soldier, and there were surely other such affairs.[13] Corporal William Clark Kennerly of St. Louis, who enlisted in the smartly clad volunteer artillery battalion commanded by his kinsman, Major Meriwether Lewis Clark, recalled the romantic diversions of Santa Fe nostalgically in later years:

> Our blue cloth coats faced with red and our gold-braided caps, the regulation United States Artillery uniform, proved quite attractive to the *señoritas* whom we met at the fandangos. There we danced as late as the military law allowed with these gay charmers, who kept their red-heeled slippers tapping in perfect time to their castanets. They carried on most of the conversation with their soft, dark eyes; but, knowing French, I soon picked up the Spanish language, which I had once studied, and was frequently called upon to interpret for my young companions. Many were the compliments interpolated on my own responsibility that made these gay damsels cast sidelong glances from behind their fans at the innocent ones.[14]

Kennerly pictured these flirtations in retrospect as idyllic encounters between courtly young officers and storybook señoritas, but most accounts composed during or shortly after the occupation portrayed such exchanges between the sexes in dance halls and gambling parlors as more calculated and conflicted. The officers encountered by Susan Magoffin in Santa Fe were men who seemed to prefer the company of American women and found in her a reflection of the sweethearts or sisters they left behind. General Kearny visited her early on and put himself gallantly at her disposal: "He says as he is the Gov. now I must come under his government, and at the same time he places himself at my command, to serve me when I wish will be his pleasure &c. This I am sure is quite flattering, *United States General No. 1* entirely at my disposal, ready and will feel himself flattered to be my servant."[15] Here as in her meetings with Doña Juliana, she was seemingly able to enjoy such flattery without putting too much stock in it. She understood that such compliments were soothing to Kearny's vanity as well as her own and kept in similar perspective the attentions paid to her by lower-ranking officers, one of whom visited her in a state of intoxication and unburdened himself to her in a way that she found embarrassing and led her to conclude sadly, "I do think some of my countrymen are disgracing themselves here."[16] Indeed, the town was awash in *aguardiente*—the Mexican equivalent of "firewater"—and the grogshops, as George Gibson put it, were doing "a thriving business."[17]

One time-honored antidote to dissipation was prayer and churchgoing, but here again, many occupiers found what Santa Fe had to offer less than inspiring. Unlike Protestant pastors back home, the priests here were free to imbibe on social as well as sacred occasions. Gibson described the principal priest of Santa Fe as a "fat, jolly fellow, bets high at monte, loves good liquor, and attends all the *fandangos* of the respectable people or public places."[18] Nor was this padre alone in these habits, according to Lieutenant Christian Kribben, who attended a fandango for officers hosted by "the town's elite":

> The priests, who are of the people, share all their vices and virtues. They are generally present at *fandangos* and pay their compliments to the ladies like other christians, and get disgustingly tipsy. In fact a priest present at this affair collapsed from drunkenness while dancing. They picked him up and took him to the door, where he eased his heart by a simple operation and then went home.[19]

Now as in earlier times, some Americans may have exaggerated the vices of the priests. It was not uncommon in New Mexico for a priest to have a "wife," or a woman who served as such and kept house for him. But Frank Edwards was probably overstating the case when he claimed that polygamy was common among the local priests, a conclusion perhaps based on the assumption that all the women serving in the household of a padre were necessarily on intimate terms with him:

> The priests are high in position, and always rich; but in morals and character they are, with few exceptions, even below their followers. It is not unusual for them to have three or four wives, all living in the house with them, who, as well as the other people, manifest the most servile attention to them. It really used to make my blood boil, to see these poor wretches come into the room where I might happen to be in conversation with the padre, and after kneeling down and kissing the hem of his garment, stand on one side, hat in

hand, awaiting the moment when he might condescend to speak to them; while the rascal was trying, with all his skill, to cheat me in the bargain I was making with him; not scrupling to tell the most abominable falsehoods, if they became necessary to aid his plan. Even in the street, the people will frequently kneel and kiss his robe, as he passes them, while he manifests, outwardly, no knowledge of the salute, passing on as if he had attracted no notice.[20]

Edwards, who served as a quartermaster for his outfit, did not specify the nature of his negotiations with this priest, but it may well have involved the purchase of food or livestock. Priests engaged in such deals like everyone else who had the means and inclination to do so in New Mexico, where there had long been no significant barrier between church and state, or between faith and commerce. Sunday was a market day here—a sensible practice given that many people had to travel some distance to attend church and welcomed the chance to shop or trade in town afterward. The sacred and secular seemed to have struck a bargain in New Mexico that many Americans found strange, if not offensive. Gibson reported that it was customary for those who played violin and guitar in church to tour the town afterward, "playing a lively air, and thus winding up the religious ceremonies of the Sabbath with fiddling and dancing."[21] And Lieutenant Emory described a church service in Santa Fe on August 30 attended by Kearny, who sat in the plush seat once reserved for Armijo. The ceremony and its aftermath reflected the free and easy exchange that prevailed here between the sanctuary and the plaza:

> To-day we went to church in great state. The governor's seat, a large, well-stuffed chair, covered with crimson, was occupied by the commanding officer. The church was crowded with an attentive audience of men and women, but not a word was uttered from the pulpit by the priest, who kept his back to the congregation the whole time, repeating prayers and incantations. The band, the identical one used at the fandango, and strumming the same tunes, played without intermission. Except the governor's seat and one row of benches, there were no seats in the church. Each woman dropped on her knees on the bare floor as she entered, and only exchanged this position for a seat on the ground at long intervals, announced by the tinkle of a small bell.
>
> The interior of the church was decorated with some fifty crosses, a great number of the most miserable paintings and wax figures, and looking glasses trimmed with pieces of tinsel.
>
> The priest, a very grave, respectable looking person, of fair complexion, commenced the service by sprinkling holy water over the congregation; when abreast of any high official person he extended his silver water spout and gave him a handful.

When a favorite air was struck up, the young women, whom we recognised as having figured at the fandango, counted their beads, tossed their heads, and crossed themselves to the time of the music.

All appeared to have just left their work to come to church. There was no fine dressing nor personal display that will not be seen on week days. Indeed, on returning from church, we found all the stores open, and the market women selling their melons and plums as usual.[22]

Kearny, to his credit, attended church each Sunday for as long as he remained in and around Santa Fe as part of his effort to reassure the populace. Many of those who had fled town in fear of the Americans had returned by late August and were going about their business, and Kearny confidently made plans to establish a civil government for the occupied territory. Perhaps his most enduring legacy as military governor was to instruct Colonel Doniphan and others in the army with legal training to codify the existing laws of New Mexico, making changes in those laws as necessary to conform with the Constitution of the United States. He also issued the so-called Kearny Code, a bill of rights for New Mexicans based on the American model, with certain concessions to local custom such as a clause exempting priests from military service and jury duty.[23] This decree may have exceeded his authority, but it fulfilled pledges he made to New Mexicans that they would be protected under the law.

In other respects, however, Kearny's hurried efforts to provide a secure future for the territory and its people fell short of the mark. As he prepared to depart for California with three hundred dragoons on September 25, leaving Doniphan's regiment behind, he made a singularly unfortunate appointment by naming Charles Bent civil governor of occupied New Mexico. To a commander who had spent little time there it must have seemed an obvious choice. After all, Bent knew the territory and its problems as well as any American resident and had family and friends among the New Mexicans, whose interests he would seek to protect as governor by protesting misdeeds by soldiers against the populace and by petitioning Washington for more troops to protect settlements from Indian attacks. But Bent also had vested interests in the Americanization of New Mexico and powerful local enemies. Had Kearny been headquartered in Taos, he might have gotten an inkling of the bitter feelings there toward Bent and his protégés, including twenty-five-year-old Francis P. Blair, Jr., who earlier in the year had been beaten by residents of Taos in the streets while intoxicated and was now going to preside over the courts of New Mexico as district attorney.

The only official of Spanish heritage appointed to a high position by Kearny was Donaciano Vigil, a cousin of Juan Bautista Vigil, who had welcomed

Kearny to Santa Fe. Formerly Armijo's secretary and a veteran of numerous Indian campaigns, Donaciano Vigil would now serve as territorial secretary under Bent.[24] His decision to join this American administration was consistent with public statements he had made in June 1846, in which he blamed New Mexico's most pressing problems not on American merchants, whose impact he regarded as largely beneficial, but on misrule by those who preceded Armijo as governor in Santa Fe and by higher authorities in Mexico City. He complained, for example, that Mexican officials seeking to impose a "*closed and exclusive* system" of trade had discriminated unduly against foreigners and forced Americans seeking to do business with Comanches, Utes, and other "heathen" Indians to skirt New Mexico and set up trading posts elsewhere. "Through these forts, heathens have been supplied amply with as much as they might need, in exchange for furs," Vigil wrote. "Thus, little by little, all the heathens forgot us and lost their affection for us."[25]

The participation of Donaciano Vigil did little to reconcile Mexican opponents of the American takeover to this new administration. Those in Washington who had saddled Kearny with the task of appointing a "temporary civil Government" might have done better to acknowledge the campaign for what it was—an act of war sure to provoke opposition—and to maintain outright military rule in the occupied territory for the duration of the conflict. No regime could have been more precarious at this juncture than one led by a civilian like Bent, who was seen by his Mexican foes as an instrument of oppression but who regarded himself as the legitimate representative of a new democratic order and disdained the idea of moving about the country under armed escort.

Kearny's hurried efforts to pacify New Mexico's diverse Indian population were no less problematic. Delegations from various Pueblos had paid court to him in Santa Fe and pledged their cooperation with the Americans. In early September, Kearny returned the favor by visiting the Pueblo of Santo Domingo, where he and his escort received a rousing reception, as detailed by Lieutenant Emory:

> We had not proceeded far, before we met ten or fifteen sachemic looking old Indians, well mounted, and two of them carrying gold-headed canes with tassels, the emblems of office in New Mexico.
>
> Salutations over, we jogged along, and, in the course of conversation, the alcalde, a grave and majestic old Indian, said, as if casually, "We shall meet some Indians presently, mounted, and dressed for war, but they are the young men of my town, friends come to receive you, and I wish you to caution your men not to fire upon them when they ride towards them."

When within a few miles of the town, we saw a cloud of dust rapidly advancing, and soon the air was rent with a terrible yell, resembling the Florida war-whoop. The first object that caught my eye through the column of dust, was a fierce pair of buffalo horns, overlapped with long shaggy hair. As they approached, the sturdy form of a naked Indian revealed itself beneath the horns, with shield and lance, dashing at full speed, on a white horse, which, like his own body, was painted all the colors of the rainbow; and then, one by one, his followers came on, painted to the eyes, their own heads and their horses covered with all the strange equipments that the brute creation could afford in the way of horns, skulls, tails, feathers, and claws.

As they passed us, one rank on each side, they fired a volley under our horses' bellies from the right and from the left. Our well-trained dragoons sat motionless on their horses, which went along without pricking an ear or showing any sign of excitement.

Arrived in the rear, the Indians circled round, dropped into a walk on our flanks until their horses recovered breath, when off they went at full speed, passing to our front, and when there, the opposite files met, and each man selected his adversary and kept up a running fight, with muskets, lances, and bows and arrows. Sometimes a fellow would stoop almost to the earth to shoot under his horse's belly, at full speed, or to shield himself from an impending blow. So they continued to pass and repass us all the way to the steep cliff which overhangs the town. There they filed on each side of the road, which descends through a deep cañon, and halted on the peaks of the cliffs. Their motionless forms projected against the clear blue sky above, formed studies for an artist.[26]

This militant show, staged in one form or another by Indians of many tribes when strangers entered their midst, was both a welcome and a warning. Kearny and his men met with a polite reception in town, where they were served wine and cake by the local priest, Emory noted, in a parlor "tapestried with curtains stamped with the likenesses of all the Presidents of the United States up to this time."[27] The occasion reinforced their initial impression that the Pueblo people as a whole were kindly disposed to the Americans. But as the warriors of Santo Domingo demonstrated through their forceful greeting, they were prepared to defend their pueblo against perceived threats. The Americans might yet find themselves at odds with this community or others like it if they infringed on the rights of the inhabitants or appeared weak in dealing with such traditional foes of the Pueblos as the Navajos. Deterring raids by hostile tribes was an important test of American resolve in the eyes of both the Pueblos and their Hispanic neighbors. Kearny had pledged to do as much, but he had no hope of fulfilling his other responsibilities as a commander if he waged war on the far-flung Navajos, not to mention the Utes and the Apaches. Instead, he would proceed to California and leave it to Colonel Doniphan to deal with the problem.

Doniphan's orders in regard to the Navajos were to "secure a peace and better conduct from them in future," and he did his best to comply. But if he tried to elicit "better conduct" from defiant Navajos by forcing them to quit raiding, he would not soon secure peace. Kearny instructed Doniphan to obtain the release of all prisoners and property that "may have been stolen from the inhabitants of the territory of New Mexico," and further authorized him to take Navajos hostage as "security for their future good conduct."[28] This sounded neat and businesslike, but Navajos would not submit without a fight to any deal that required them to offer such "security," nor would they voluntarily return "stolen" goods that they regarded as prizes of war. In keeping with Kearny's orders, Doniphan fostered the impression that his forces were out to whip Navajos into line. In late October, for example, he wrote Secretary of War William Marcy that he was proceeding against the Navajos and hoped to "bring the war to a close in 30 days."[29] In truth, this "war" consisted largely of seeking out remote Navajo bands and prevailing on their leaders to attend a big peace council. Doniphan could do little more than that if he and his forces hoped to play any further part in the war against Mexico. The soft deal he cut with the Navajos was among the first of many such concessions hard-pressed American authorities would make to reality in this compromising country.

Doniphan's ambiguous Navajo campaign raised questions among men in the ranks. Were they fighting men or peacekeepers? Had they gone to war to defeat Mexicans or to defend them from hostile tribes? And how could they resolve within a few months a dispute that had eluded settlement for generations? Marcellus Edwards, writing in mid-September, summed up the chronic threat posed to New Mexico's settlements by Navajo, Apache, and Ute raiders and seemed a bit skeptical of Kearny's efforts to pacify such resolute "aggressors":

> These Indians, whenever they feel themselves in need of stock of any kind, come in from their mountain retreats and drive off any stock or any quantity of stock they feel disposed, and are not often molested, though they frequently ride through the streets of their towns. In these excursions they take care to leave enough stock to enable the Spaniards to make another start. They have told the Mexicans several times that if it was not for the service they render them in raising stock, they would kill them all off. . . . General Kearny has taken the treacherous population of New Mexico under his fatherly

care and protection; and looking with an eye of pity upon the bold aggression of these adventurous savages, he has concluded to send parties out for the purpose of bringing these aggressors to justice, or to make a treaty of peace with them and seal it with hostages, if thought necessary.[30]

Edwards's company-mate, Jacob Robinson, was among a detachment of thirty men dispatched in October to summon Navajo chiefs to talk peace with Colonel Doniphan. This party was commanded by Captain John W. Reid and guided by a wealthy Navajo named Sandoval, who had served before as an agent or go-between for New Mexican authorities. As Reid's men left the western frontier of Spanish New Mexico and headed off into the rugged Navajo country, Robinson related, people harvesting corn in the fields called out to the mounted troops, "God be with you,"[31] a blessing offered with real feeling to what appeared to be a war party, out to chasten the Navajos. Robinson himself was not sure at this point whether he would end up fighting the Navajos or making peace with them.

Earlier, Robinson and others had visited Laguna Pueblo and witnessed a war dance in which four scalps claimed from "Nebajos" in battle by those "Purbelos," as he put it, were displayed on long poles as the dancers raised shouts of triumph. (The Americans were invited to join in, he added, and some of them did so.) Yet when he finally encountered those dreaded Navajos in force, after a taxing journey of several days that carried his party across the desert and up into the Chuska Mountains, near what is now the New Mexico-Arizona border, he found them more impressive than intimidating:

> At length on descending a bluff we discovered a larger party of Nebajos; as we advanced they collected into a group on a hill-top, where we met them with many compliments and much ceremony. They were about thirty warriors and eight or ten squaws; dressed in splendid Indian attire, having fine figured blankets and panther-skin caps, plumed with eagle feathers; were all well mounted, and proved to be a party of chosen Braves, who had been sent forward to invite us and guide us to the heart of their country. They are very active in all their movements, mounting and dismounting their horses in an instant.[32]

Robinson's sense of admiration grew as he delved deeper into Navajo country with these native escorts. The Americans soon found themselves greatly outnumbered, and Captain Reid feared for their safety, surrounded as they were by a people he termed "the most savage and proverbially treacherous of any on the continent."[33] But as Robinson observed, these Navajos had no designs on their vulnerable visitors other than to trade with them and admire their firearms and other wondrous possessions, charms of the sort that few in this isolated stronghold had ever laid eyes upon:

> They were very curious to examine our guns, and were astonished when shown the properties of a revolver. One of our men showed a watch, which excited great attention: on placing it to their ears they would start as from a snake. At night they hung all their bows upon the limbs of a cottonwood tree, and commenced their dance, which resembled the Purbelos, and in which some of us took part. So we danced with the Purbelos over the scalps of the Nebajos, and with the Nebajos over the Purbelos. It is astonishing how soon our confidence in each other was almost complete,—so that we mingled in their dance, and they in our camp traded for such little "notions" as our men happened to have with them, for which the Indians gave us mutton and bread.[34]

As such exchanges continued, it became increasingly difficult for Robinson to think of the Navajos as "bad Indians" in contrast to the worthy Pueblos. Indeed, he found the lines of distinction between the Navajos and the Americans blurring as each side acquired the trappings of the other and the Navajos demonstrated skills that amazed their guests:

> There was almost a continual trading going on between our men and the Indians in the way of barter; such as a cotton shirt for a hunting shirt of buckskin, a tin cup for a lasset, or a buckskin for a small piece of tobacco, or for a butcher knife, or for buckles, straps, &c., so that few of us returned with many of the clothes we wore there, but had exchanged them for buckskins and blankets, and dressed ourselves pretty nearly in the Indian style. The women of this tribe seem to have equal rights with the men, managing their own business and trading as they see fit; saddling their own horses, and letting their husbands saddle theirs. To day were exhibited several scenes of the chase, by rabbits being started from the brush; when in an instant five hundred riders at least were on the chase. No fox or steeple chase can equal it; the Arab cannot excel the Nebajo in horsemanship; and better horses can hardly be found.[35]

This enlightening exchange with the Navajos resembled those encounters of a similarly peaceful nature that occurred sporadically over the years between American envoys and Apaches, Comanches, Kiowas, and other assertive tribespeople whose genius for warfare tended to overshadow their quieter virtues in American eyes. The dominant impression such groups made on outsiders who ventured among them in good faith to trade or talk was one of power and accomplishment that transcended their strength in battle. As Robinson recognized, the pride and prosperity of the Navajos had many sources, including their skill at weaving woolen blankets or ponchos of such beauty and durability that even their confirmed enemies would offer for one such article a sum large enough to purchase "half a dozen horses."[36] At the same time, however, the Navajos owed much of their wealth in sheep and horses to their penchant for raiding their Mexican and Pueblo enemies. And their fighting men were no more inclined to abandon the assaults that brought them such glory and profit than were their American counterparts prepared to forsake conquest and relinquish their own war on Mexico. Captain Reid, who parleyed with the prominent Navajo chieftain Narbona among other tribal leaders, reported that the Navajos were far more enthusiastic about making peace with the Americans than with the Mexicans:

> We had not arrived at the place of our camp before we were met by all the head men of the nation. The chief of all, NARBONA, being very sick, was nevertheless mounted on horseback, and brought in. He slept in my camp all night. Narbona, who was probably seventy years old, being held in great reverence by his tribe for the war-like exploits of his youth and manhood, was now a mere skeleton of a man, being completely prostrated by rheumatism, the only disease, though a very common one, in this country. Conformably to a custom of the chief men of his tribe, he wore his finger nails very long, probably one and a half inches—formidable weapons! He appeared to be a mild, amiable man, and though he had been a warrior himself, was very anxious before his death to secure for his people a peace with all their old enemies, as well as with us, the "New Men," as he called us.
>
> Upon the evening after our arrival we held a grand talk, in which all the old men participated. Most of them seemed disposed for peace, but some opposed it as being contrary to the honor of the Navajos, as well as their interest, to make peace with the Mexicans; though they were willing to do so with us.[37]

Another member of Reid's party, Meredith T. Moore, recalled many years later that among the Navajos opposed to making peace was Narbona's wife, who nearly provoked violence against Reid and company by denouncing the American overture before Narbona "tapped three times on the mat with his long nails," signaling for her removal from the conclave.[38] Whatever the nature of their deliberations, Narbona and the elders ultimately agreed to meet with Doniphan and talk peace but declined to return immediately with Reid and his detachment. They would rendezvous with the Americans later, they promised. Robinson and others in his outfit feared treachery after the parley when the Navajos sat up late around their campfires, drumming and chanting, but the two sides parted peacefully the next morning.

By the time Reid and his men returned in late October to their camp, hopes for peace with the Navajos seemed like a distant dream. Navajo raiders had recently descended on the American camp and made off with forty horses, including the animal Robinson had been counting on to replace the horse he ruined during the grueling trip to the Chuskas and back. Elsewhere, Mexicans and Pueblos were suffering similar losses, and Colonel Doniphan was talking of a punitive expedition against the Navajos. In the end, however, he reasoned as Kearny had that such an effort would only divert strength from more pressing concerns—notably an emerging plan for Doniphan and much of his regiment to extend their campaign against the Mexicans by marching south from Santa Fe to Chihuahua.

Doniphan delayed that move long enough to hold council in November with Narbona and other Navajo chiefs at Ojo del Oso, or Bear Spring, near modern-day Gallup. During those talks, he assured the assembled chiefs that the United States would offer her "red children, the Navajos," the same pledge of peace and protection tendered to the defeated New Mexicans—words that must have irked the Navajos, who were perfectly capable of protecting themselves. Doniphan warned them that the United States "first offered the olive branch, and if that were rejected, then powder, bullet, and the steel." At that, John Hughes related, a keen young Navajo chief named Zarcillos Largos stood up and defended the right of his people to choose their friends and their enemies, just as the Americans did: "We cannot see why you have cause of quarrel with us for fighting the New Mexicans on the west, while you do the same thing on the east. Look how matters stand. This is *our war*. We have more right to complain of you for interfering in our war, than you have to quarrel with us for continuing a war we had begun long before you got here. If you will act justly, you will allow us to settle our own differences."[39]

This Navajo was articulating a view shared by more than a few American soldier chiefs but seldom expressed by them so frankly—war was an honor and a privilege, an opportunity for prizes and glory not to be relinquished at the insistence of a third party enthusiastically engaged in its own war. Unable to counter such logic, Doniphan tried to win the chiefs over by invoking the promise of trade, claiming that if they made peace on American terms, they could then "obtain everything they needed to eat and wear in exchange for their furs and peltries."[40] In fact, the Navajos did not deal much in pelts, and in any case they had long met their needs handsomely by alternating trading with raiding. In this region, commerce and warfare had seldom been mutually exclusive—nor were they in the ongoing conflict between the United States and Mexico.

After some deliberation, the Navajos concluded that the best way to deal with these vexing Americans was to sign their proposed treaty and simply ignore its wishful provisions, which declared in part that a "firm and lasting peace and amity shall henceforth exist between the American people and the Navajo tribe of Indians."[41] The treaty further specified that the "people of New Mexico and the Pueblo tribe of Indians are included in the term American people," an honor neither group had sought and that came as a mixed blessing, implying as it did that they were subject to American authority and liable to charges of treason if they defied the civil government Kearny had imposed. As to the efficacy of the treaty, Richard Elliott, whose Laclede Rangers had languished in and around Santa Fe since August, summed up the misgivings of the troops in a characteristically frank dispatch to his editors back in Missouri penned on December 6:

> Col. Doniphan's treaty has been much discussed. It is said to be very defective, and not likely to effect any very substantial peace. Gentlemen here, well acquainted with the Nabajoes, expect every day to hear new outrages being committed by them. The achievement of this treaty does not, therefore, seem to confer many laurels; but we ought to remember that making Indian treaties is a new business to the Col., and if he has not made a very good one on the first trial, he may do infinitely better next time.[42]

Elliott was not one to gloss over the problems facing the occupiers and their hosts. As early as September 4, when memories of the triumphant entry into Santa Fe were still fresh, he had offered a bleak assessment of the impact of the American influx on the Mexican populace:

> Our horses are all poor—some of them much exhausted. We have great difficulty in providing subsistence for them, having to move our camps every day or two. They stood the march very well, but now need better food than we can procure for them. This is a barren country, affording but scanty subsistence for man or beast. We are now consuming everything in it—flour, grass and corn. What the inhabitants are to do next season is more than any one here can tell. The truth is, the presence of our army here is a great curse to the people of New Mexico, though they are all treated as well as can be under the orders of the General. We are eating out their substance, although they are paid for all they furnish us, except the grass, which we destroy.[43]

Over time, Elliott and others had come to view the occupation as something of a curse on both sides. "There is no such thing as money in the army," reported George Gibson in his journal that September, "and the day will be celebrated when a paymaster presents himself in his official capacity."[44] In the meantime, he added, volunteers were offering brass buttons from their coats in trade. The casual dress code they adopted by necessity angered Kearny when he reviewed them on one occasion before he left for California, prompting this sharp exchange between the general and Captain Reid, as related by John Hughes:

> "Captain, have your men no jackets?" to which the captain replied, "Some of them have, and some of them have not." The general continued, "Make your men, Captain Reid, put on their jackets, or I will dismiss them from the service—the government has paid them commutation for clothing, and expects every man to dress in a manner wholesome for military discipline." The captain rejoined, "My men, sir, came here, not to dress, but to fight the enemies of their country, and they are ever ready to be of service to you and the country in that way. . . . My men have never received *one dime* since they entered the service, and what money they brought from their homes with them they have already expended for bread while on half rations, owing to the neglect of your chief commissary. As to being dismissed from the service, sir, we do not fight for wages. If there is no place for us in the army, we will furnish ourselves and fight the enemy wherever we may find him. Acting thus we shall not lose the respect of our countrymen."[45]

It seems unlikely that Reid had the nerve or presence of mind to say quite as much as this in reproval of his commanding officer. The usually reliable Marcellus Edwards, who described the same incident in his journal, made no mention of Kearny threatening to dismiss men from the service, and he encapsulated Reid's reply to Kearny in a single crisp sentence: "They have not one received a dollar from the government, and what money they could raise or clothing they could spare has been expended for bread."[46] Hughes was not above embellishing his account to drive home a point—in this case, the government's failure to honor its bargain with the volunteers. He may have overstated the case somewhat, but others in the ranks who chronicled the campaign saw the matter much as he did.

In truth, the troops were not much better off than the forlorn Mexicans they had looked upon with a mixture of pity and disdain when they entered the country. The two sides shared the same ailments, including measles, which spread from the Americans to their reluctant hosts and claimed many lives on both sides. They ate much the same food, with the soldiers compensating for their paltry rations by learning from the Mexicans how to make tortillas from cornmeal, or atole from course wheat flour mixed with ground piñon nuts and hot water or milk. And they endured similar living conditions, with the Americans stationed in Santa Fe sleeping on the dirt floors of abandoned barracks or houses amid the same vermin that plagued their Mexican neighbors.

Familiarity with the locals and their plight did not necessarily breed contempt, but neither did it foster much in the way of sympathy for New Mexicans.

Volunteers felt that they deserved better and resented being reduced to the level of the subject populace. Soldiers in Santa Fe were kept busy laboring on the construction of Fort Marcy, situated on high ground overlooking the plaza—a task that required the excavation of gravesites and did nothing to cheer troops increasingly mindful of their own mortality.[47] Hunger and frustration led some troops to take liberties with Mexicans and their property, prompting Governor Bent to warn Colonel Doniphan of serious consequences if he did not "compel the soldiers to respect the rights of the inhabitants."[48]

Amid the travails and tensions of occupation, however, there were some remarkable displays of compassion and goodwill. One of those moments occurred in October when the Mormon Battalion arrived in Santa Fe after a harrowing trek from Fort Leavenworth, during which the recruits—accompanied in some cases by their wives and children—crossed the Arkansas River well east of Bent's Fort and followed the shorter but more desolate Cimarron Route of the Santa Fe Trail to New Mexico to save time. John W. Hess, one of many Mormons who enlisted in the battalion after being driven from their homes by angry mobs at Nauvoo, Illinois, recalled their harrowing *jornada* from the Arkansas to the Cimarron, an ordeal he experienced as a teamster, or wagon driver, but which many other men endured on foot: "We passed over one desert eighty miles across; the only means of carrying water was in canteens holding two quarts each, one of which was carried by each man. A great many of the men gave out by the way and had to be helped in by others, the stronger carrying water back to their comrades."[49]

Another member of the battalion, Robert S. Bliss, described that jornada as a trek across "the most dreary desert I ever beheld," littered with the bones of dead animals and an occasional human skull.[50] The ordeal was little easier for the women, who traveled with their children in wagons, and their relief at reaching Santa Fe on October 12, two days after the vanguard of the battalion, was enhanced by the gracious welcome they received there, described by George Gibson in his journal:

> The remainder of the Mormons came up, and when the wagons containing the women stopped at the plaza, all the Mexican women near went up and shook hands with them, apparently both rejoiced and surprised to see them. The kindness and hospitality of the women throughout Mexico is proverbial, and in this instance the burst of feeling was as cordial and warm as a greeting of old friends and acquaintances after a long separation.[51]

This was not the end of the journey for the Mormons. Their mission was to continue on to California in support of Kearny—an assignment that they hoped would help them secure a homeland for the Mormons in the West with

"Fort Marcy and the Parroquia—Santa Fe," from Abert's 1846–47 report. Courtesy Library of Congress, Prints and Photographs Division, LC-USZ62-32515.

the help of grateful American authorities. But in the opinion of Captain Philip St. George Cooke, whom Kearny assigned to guide the battalion to California, the Mormons who reached Santa Fe that October were ill-prepared for the task that lay ahead:

> Every thing conspired to discourage the extraordinary undertaking of marching this battalion eleven hundred miles, for the much greater part through an unknown wilderness without road or trail, and with a wagon train.
>
> It was enlisted too much by families; some were too old,—some feeble, and some too young; it was embarrassed by many women; it was undisciplined; it was much worn by travelling on foot, and marching from Nauvoo, Illinois; their clothing was very scant;—there was no money to pay them,—or clothing to issue; their mules were utterly broken down; the Quartermaster department was without funds, and its credit bad; and mules were scarce. Those procured were very inferior, and were deteriorating every hour for lack of forage or grazing. So every preparation must be pushed,—hurried.[52]

Cooke selected out and equipped those Mormons he deemed fit to proceed and sent the others—eighty-six men who were ill or otherwise "found inefficient"—back with most of the women and children to spend the winter along the Arkansas at the trading post west of Bent's Fort called Pueblo, where some other Mormons were already encamped. Several Mormon officers were allowed to have their wives accompany them to California, but other men were ordered to proceed without their family members. Some of them balked at the idea of entrusting their loved ones to the care of men deemed unfit for service and in no condition to fight if attacked by Mexicans or Indians on their way to Pueblo. Teamster John Hess, whose wife had accompanied him to Santa Fe, refused to be separated from her, appealing first to his captain, Daniel C. Davis:

> I had been a teamster all the way and had proved that I could take good care of a team and was a careful driver, and as Captain Davis had his family with him, and also his own private team, he wanted me to drive it for him, but the intention was to send my wife back with the detachment of sick men; this I could not consent to and retain my manhood. I remonstrated with Capt. Davis, but to no purpose. I could not make any impression on him. I told him I would gladly go and drive the team if he would let my wife go along, but he said there was no room in the wagon; then I told him that I would not go and leave my wife—I would die first! This was a bold assertion for a private to make to his Captain, but the emergency seemed to demand it.[53]

Rebuffed by his captain, Hess and another man with the same complaint appealed directly to Colonel Doniphan, who at first seemed unsympathetic, remarking to them gruffly that he too had left his wife behind and implying that such sacrifices were part of a soldier's duty. But the persistent Hess would not be put off: "I thought I would venture one more remark, which was, 'Colonel, I suppose you left your wife with her friends, while we are required to leave ours in an enemy's country in care of a lot of sick, demoralized men.' This seemed to touch a sympathetic cord."[54] In the end, Hess and others were detached from the California expedition and allowed to accompany their wives to Pueblo and spend the winter with them there. Many volunteers who went west that summer as lowly privates had reason to complain of their lot, but few negotiated more boldly or successfully for better terms than John Hess.

Other soldiers in unenviable positions made the best of a bad bargain by achieving a rapport with the locals and benefiting by their courtesies. One such accommodating volunteer was William H. Richardson of the Second Missouri Mounted Volunteers under Colonel Sterling Price, whose regiment arrived in Santa Fe in October around the same time as the Mormons after a hard journey down the Cimarron Route. Richardson left the crowded capital several days later with others of his company to take up winter quarters near the small town of Abiquiu, beside the Rio Chama. Along the way, he experienced the celebrated New Mexican hospitality that George Gibson alluded to and which, at least in some areas, survived the strains of occupation:

> An old woman invited me in her house and set before me some tortillas and cornstalk molasses, which were quite a treat. I remained there several hours, but thinking I had missed my way, I was about to take leave, with many thanks for their hospitality, when, to my great surprise and embarrassment, the old lady and her daughter most affectionately embraced me. I suppose it was the custom among these simple hearted mountaineers, but of which I was quite ignorant. I was thankful for the meal my hostesses had provided for me, but the hugging was a luxury I did not anticipate, nor was I the least ambitious of having it repeated.[55]

Such embarrassment was characteristic of Richardson, a reserved and thoughtful young man from Maryland who had traveled to Missouri in early 1846 and enlisted at the town of Carrollton amid patriotic speeches on the Fourth of July. He showed little interest in fandangos, drinking bouts, and other such diversions favored by his companions, and he disapproved heartily of those who abused the Mexicans and their property, as illustrated by an incident that occurred at his camp on October 25:

> At day break this morning, a number of Mexicans came to camp; jabbering to themselves in a great rage about something. At first we could not ascertain

the cause of their trouble, there being no interpreter present, and none of the soldiers knowing enough of the Spanish language to comprehend their meaning; soon, however, it was discovered that about sundown last evening, the Captain of our company had caused the embankment of their mill and irrigating pond, to be broken, a short distance above camp on the bank of the river, so as to prevent it from overflowing the bed of his tent. The water of course rushed out with great force, tearing the embankment down and washing the earth away for a considerable distance, stopping their mill and leaving many families destitute of water; all of which serious injuries, the Captain seemed disinclined to repair. This behavior of the captain met with but little favor from his men. To their honor be it spoken.[56]

The next day, the captain set volunteers to work repairing the damage he had done. To this and other irritations, Richardson applied a thick layer of sarcasm:

The greatest *harmony* prevails in camp, especially among the officers, the Captain and first Lieutenant are the greatest *friends* imaginable, they do every thing in their power for the good of the company. They are the *bravest* and most *patriotic* officers in the regiment. In this lovely and fertile valley, encamped on the banks of the Rio Charma, we are enjoying all the *blessings* of life. We are charmed by the surpassing beauty of the polished Spanish ladies, and living in so much *harmony* with each other that we almost imagine the "garden of Eden" to have been again raised for our enjoyment; and then, Oh! heavens, what a luxury, amid these joys, to feel the delightful sensations produced by the gentle and graceful movements of a Spanish *louse*, as he journeys over one's body![57]

Such travails were at least partly redeemed by cordial relations with the local people. On the night of Sunday, November 1, after Richardson observed the Sabbath by reading aloud from his Testament to some mates, "a Spaniard came in camp with a fiddle," he related, "and played a number of tunes which so exhilarated my poor half frozen companions that they united in a dance which they kept up till a late hour."[58] He and others in his company drew up a vocabulary of Spanish words and received a lesson in the language from the local priest before attending Mass at his church. And one evening, while several of his companions accompanied a Mexican lady to a fandango, Richardson remained at her home, preparing a meal in his capacity as cook for his messmates and trying without success to get some sleep amid a household that included several fragrant donkeys, kept indoors as protection against the cold, and two crying children:

Our soldiers did not return from the fandango till 3 o'clock this morning, and I was appointed to get breakfast while they slept. I had considerable trouble in accomplishing this service, as the girls crowded around the fire, and I had frequently to pass the frying pan over the naked feet of a pretty girl who was sitting near me. In company with a young Spaniard, who was exceedingly agreeable and polite, I went out after breakfast to kill wild geese. We walked a long distance, and returned unsuccessful.[59]

At a time when many Americans and Mexicans felt they were getting a raw deal, Richardson and company engaged in amicable exchanges with their hosts that seemed to reward both sides. "Yesterday I traded off *two needles* to the Spanish girls for six ears of corn and some onions," he noted at one point, concluding that it was "a trade decidedly profitable for both parties."[60] Later, he had the good fortune to do business with a Mexican who threw in refreshments as part of his generous bargain with Richardson:

> There being no food for our horses, we chopped down some limbs of the cotton wood tree for them to eat. We then went to a Mexican village to buy corn. Having no money, I took some tobacco and buttons to trade for the corn. While here, I sold my greasy blanket for a Navihoe one, with a meal for my horse in the bargain. The man with whom I traded was very kind; he set before me some corn, mush and sausages, but being seasoned with onions, I declined eating. He then brought in some corn stalk molasses, which I drank, thanking him for his hospitality.[61]

Richardson fared better in trade with Mexicans than in his dealings with the camp sutler, who charged steep prices for articles the troops purchased on credit, with the balance to be deducted from their pay (when and if they received it). On December 1, before leaving camp, Richardson had to sign for his account:

> Paraded again soon after breakfast, and were told by our Captain, that previously to our departure, we must all march to the sutler's store, and acknowledge our indebtedness to him, so we rode up in right order and dismounted. We had a peep at our accounts, and I found mine to be $30 75. I had purchased a few articles of clothing on my route, being forced to do so from necessity. I was therefore not surprised at the amount, especially when I read the prices of some of the articles, viz. a small cotton handkerchief $1—suspenders $1—flannel shirt $3—tin coffee pot $1 50, &c. &c.[62]

The occasion for Richardson's departure was his decision to join a detachment of some one hundred men under Lieutenant Colonel David D. Mitchell, ordered to march south and open communications with Brigadier General John E. Wool, whose forces had entered Mexico from Texas and were thought to be approaching Chihuahua. As it turned out, General Wool and his men were otherwise occupied, but the drive to Chihuahua would proceed—and Mitchell's company, known as the Chihuahua Rangers, would be only a small part of it. By early December, Doniphan had concluded talks with the Navajos and was preparing to lead his regiment south to Chihuahua as ordered by Kearny, who had learned since leaving Santa Fe that much of California was already in American hands and who had decided as a result to proceed there with only one hundred or so dragoons, leaving the rest to guard New Mexico. The Chihuahua Rangers would join the remainder of Doniphan's command at Valverde, roughly midway between Santa Fe and El Paso.

The Rangers had cash to offer the populace for much-needed provisions—funds reportedly obtained from that wealthy mistress of the monte table, Gertrudis Barceló. According to a lighthearted sketch penned by Richard Elliott, she loaned $1,000 to the detachment in exchange for the honor of being escorted by David Mitchell to a theater in Santa Fe where soldiers were staging a show. Elliott added that the officer offered no further sign of appreciation to her in public other than a stiff bow as he rode from town, which she deemed "but a chilly acknowledgment of her kindness and liberality!"[63] William Clark Kennerly related in his memoir that Elliott had hoped to publish this story during the war, but that "Colonel Mitchell threatened to shoot him if he did; and he preferred giving up the scoop to giving up the ghost." In fact, the anecdote was less of an insult to Mitchell than to Barceló, implying that she was so desperate for recognition from the Americans that she had to pay for their favors. As Kennerly put it, Mitchell "walked into the room with this notorious woman on his arm, which so flattered her that she consented to make the loan."[64] The shrewd Barceló was often misrepresented and underestimated by Anglo observers, however, and she may have had a more compelling reason in this case for contributing to the American cause—a desire to protect her business interests in Santa Fe.

However the funds were secured, they proved of much use to George Gibson, who served under Mitchell as an assistant quartermaster. On December 7, three days after leaving Santa Fe, Gibson approached Albuquerque along the Rio Grande, admiring to the east the conspicuous Sandia Peak, whose crags "presented a most magnificent appearance, the snow and morning sun bringing them in bold relief."[65] In Albuquerque he purchased corn from a priest, "a close trader and shrewd man, who gave me a glass of the best Pass brandy I have found."[66] Such cordial dealings were not sufficient to meet the needs of all the Rangers and their mounts. Below Albuquerque, they

encountered some Mexicans who refused to deal with Americans on principle or who valued their crops and livestock more than money. On December
8, William Richardson, who had earlier traded amicably with the locals around
Abiquiu, felt compelled to requisition feed for the animals:

> We had six small ears of corn for our horses, and no fodder. I went to the
> Quarter Master and was informed by him that the Mexicans had refused to
> sell us any thing. I cut some buttons from a uniform jacket, and with them
> tried to purchase food for my horse, but I was refused every where. I sat down
> and made out a requisition, and with several others went to their large stacks,
> ten feet high, which we ascended, and threw down a large turn for each. We
> succeeded in coming off with our booty, and in a few minutes, we were in
> bed. We were not disturbed in conscience in the least, being fully covered by
> the axiom, "necessity knows no law."[67]

Now that he was back on the campaign trail, Richardson could no longer
afford to be quite so scrupulous in his dealings with the populace. His was a
small requisition, but the Rangers would take greater liberties with the Mexicans and their possessions in the days ahead. On the following night, December 9, Richardson related, the foraging intensified:

> Our interpreter was sent to procure forage for the horses, but he returned with
> the news that none could be had. Our Captain told the Sergeant to go up with
> a file of soldiers and *take* what was wanting. He formed a line of twenty men,
> I among them, and marched off with our Orderly at the head, and second
> Sergeant, with the bags to put the corn in. At the door of the house, we were
> ordered to halt. The lock was broken, and we entered, filled our sacks and
> packed them down to the camp. . . . After supper, we were all ordered up to
> draw fifteen rounds of cartridges. A strong guard was ordered out to-night.[68]

Gibson noted that this incident "created considerable excitement amongst
the population; but all was finally adjusted and peace restored."[69] Several days
later, as the detachment neared Valverde and their linkup with Doniphan's
command, Gibson claimed from the locals "seven fat cattle, being compelled
to press them into the service."[70] He invited the owners to come to camp for
reimbursement, which they did, but the requisition stirred up enough ill feeling that, according to Richardson, "a strong guard of twenty men was stationed around our camp."[71]

Frank Edwards, who served with the Chihuahua Rangers in a similar
capacity as Gibson, found Mexicans on the way to Valverde who were willing
to sell provisions to him, but on two occasions he felt he was being cheated—
once by a monk and later by a priest—and responded forcefully. In the first

instance, he made sure that the soldiers accompanying him filled their pockets as well as their sacks with corn and carried off from the monastery at least as much if not more than he had agreed to pay for. In the second case, he assailed the offending padre with a vehemence that betrayed his deep contempt for the priesthood:

> In the evening, while measuring the corn, a dispute about it arose between us, he trying to cheat me. At last he told me that I lied! On which, I caught him by the neckcloth, drew out my butcher's knife, told him that, in my opinion, he was a rascal, and that if he dared to repeat such words, I should use my cold steel. This brought him to his senses at once, the people, who had just before been kissing his hands and garments, stared at me as if I were a wild beast, although I could see that some were secretly well pleased at the strong hints I gave the Padre. Upon leaving the house, I read him a short sermon on the impropriety of insulting Americans, and this had such an effect on him, that he presented me with a glass of excellent brandy as a peace-offering, which I *generously* accepted.[72]

This incident was symptomatic of the nasty turn the campaign was taking—a venture that began with assurances that Americans were only interested in preserving "peace and trade," as Senator Benton put it, but which would soon be marked by bloody exchanges. Like Kearny's drive to Santa Fe, Doniphan's impending advance on Chihuahua followed a path well worn by American traders. In fact, he would serve as escort for a large party of merchants (including Samuel and Susan Magoffin) who despaired of making a profit in occupied Santa Fe and appealed to the army for safe passage to Chihuahua. But unlike Kearny, Doniphan would meet with opposition, and even some of the merchants would be caught in the fray.

Back in Santa Fe and Taos, meanwhile, resistance was building among elements of the Mexican and Pueblo population to the Americans in general and to Governor Bent in particular. Even without Bent to rally against, some in New Mexico would have found cause for revolt. As Richard Elliott reported from Santa Fe in November:

> I have no doubt that there prevails, among many of the New Mexicans, a very bitter feeling towards our Government and people; and that our presence here, as their counquerors, is but illy relished, especially by the more wealthy of them, who, of course, see that they will not figure so largely in comparison with Americans, as they have heretofore done among their own countrymen. Often in conversation I have inquired if they were well satisfied with the present condition of things—a rather impertinent question, I admit. The upper

classes invariably tell me yes—assure me they never were so happy, and that they expect to enjoy a delightful time under American rule. But the answer made me by a Mexican teamster, whom I had with me to Bent's Fort, tells the whole story. I asked him if the people generally were contented. "*Los pobres, si—los Ricos, no*"—(the poor, yes—the rich, no,)—was the answer, after which he went on to assure me, that the reason why the rich were dissatisfied was, that they could not oppress the poor as they had heretofore done—frequently requiring the laboring classes to toil from early dawn until dark, for two or three dollars per month, and giving them scarcely food sufficient to keep body and soul together.[73]

Perhaps this teamster, like the wealthy Mexicans Elliott talked to, was saying what he thought his American listener wanted to hear by portraying the campaign as a crusade against oppression (of the sort still endured by slaves in Missouri). As would soon become apparent, the potential for violent opposition to the invaders was by no means limited to the wealthier elements of the population. But that teamster was on target when he spoke of the deep divisions within Mexican society, tensions that had contributed to a rebellion less than a decade earlier and were aggravated now when Americans marched in and imposed new terms, upsetting that fragile and often unsatisfactory arrangement worked out over the generations between the *ricos* and those hard-pressed *pobres* and Pueblos on whom their prosperity and security depended. All this made the going that much tougher for Bent's unproven regime in Santa Fe. His authority would soon be tested, even as American troops were facing their baptism by fire on the trail to Chihuahua.

19

Reckoning by the Rio Grande

For Marcellus Edwards, encamped at Valverde with Company D of Doniphan's regiment and awaiting orders to head south for Chihuahua, December 10 was a milestone of sorts, and he took stock of what he and his fellow volunteers had accomplished since leaving Missouri:

> Today brings us through our six months' service, and what can we boast of having done? We volunteered to fight, but surely we have done none of it, but have always, and have now, a fight in the prospective. We have done a great deal, 'tis true, but all to no purpose. We took possession of New Mexico after a long march, and who could not have done it after it was given up? We have formed treaties with the bordering tribes of savages, which treaties will be broken by them at option as soon as we get out of sight—and it is of no interest to us whether they break or keep them. We should not be protecting our enemies, though it is a scriptural command and one of General Kearny's. Yet it is contrary to reason and common sense, and we should act more upon the principle of "an eye for an eye and a tooth for a tooth" with such people as Mexicans.[1]

Edwards's hard line reflected the mood of an army weary of seemingly profitless peacekeeping ventures and rededicating itself to the profession of war. The soldiers camped at Valverde had heard that there were 300 Mexican troops in El Paso, soon to be swelled by reinforcements from Chihuahua, but the impending arrival of the Chihuahua Rangers would give Doniphan around 850 men, and Edwards felt confident that they could "whip everything in or this side of Chihuahua."[2]

They may have been ready for battle, but their demeanor failed to impress Englishman George Frederick Ruxton, who encountered the Missourians at Valverde in early December during an extended tour of the Southwest that took him from the embattled Mexican heartland northward through Santa Fe and Taos. Ruxton, a veteran of the British army, found the manner in which Doniphan's volunteers campaigned shockingly casual:

> From appearances no one would have imagined this to be a military encampment. The tents were in a line, but there all uniformity ceased. There were no regulations in force with regard to cleanliness. The camp was strewed with bones and offal of the cattle slaughtered for its supply, and not the slightest attention was paid to keeping it clear from other accumulations of filth. The men, unwashed and unshaven, were ragged and dirty, without uniforms, and dressed as, and how, they pleased. They wandered about, listless and sickly-looking, or were sitting in groups playing at cards, and swearing and cursing, even at the officers if they interfered to stop it (as I witnessed). The greatest irregularities constantly took place. Sentries, or a guard, although in an enemy's country, were voted unnecessary; and one fine day, during the time I was here, three Navajo Indians ran off with a flock of eight hundred sheep belonging to the camp, killing the two volunteers in charge of them, and reaching the mountains in safety with their booty. Their mules and horses were straying over the country; in fact, the most total want of discipline was apparent in every thing.[3]

Despite all this, Ruxton conceded that the volunteers were "as full of fight as game-cocks" and prepared to handle anything the Mexicans might throw at them.

On December 12, Marcellus Edwards and his company prepared to move out with Doniphan's vanguard of three hundred men under Major William Gilpin. The next day they passed the camp of the traders, who were waiting for the bulk of the army to pass and preparing for possible run-ins with Mexicans or Indians. (Their wagons were arrayed in a "corral or square" that made a "most formidable fort," observed Ruxton, who saw little difference between the soldiers' camp at Valverde and this traders' bivouac, filled with "wild-looking Missourians, some cooking at the camp-fires, some cleaning their rifles or firing at targets.")[4] In the days ahead, Doniphan's advancing troops left the winding Rio Grande and followed the Chihuahua Trail due south, thus commencing the infamous Jornada across the desert. To avoid dehydration, they traveled part of the way in the dark and suffered more from chill than anything else. "We made a little fire of the stumps of the cactus and other weeds," Edwards noted after a march lasting well into the night, "and betook upon ourselves a little sleep, but 'twas quite cold."[5]

"Colonel Doniphan's Army of Missourians Marching through the Jornada del Muerto," from Richardson's *Journal*. Used by permission, State Historical Society of Missouri, Columbia, all rights reserved.

They rejoined the Rio Grande on the eighteenth, expecting to find Mexican troops awaiting them there but spotting only fresh tracks, left by suspected spies. Ahead lay the tiny settlement of Doña Ana (near present-day Las Cruces), where the soldiers were cordially greeted by the alcalde, prompting Marcellus Edwards to expound on the benefits of American rule for the downtrodden populace:

> And who is it that would not be glad when they received such kind treatment as we have showed toward the inhabitants of New Mexico? Mexico never enjoyed half the prosperity before, that she has since the American army invaded her territory. She has had protection against the savage hordes that infest her border. We have bought articles from them at the highest [price], which they heretofore could not have disposed of. We have forced nothing from them unless necessity compelled us, and for which they have always received the most liberal compensation. And instead of war being made a curse upon the nation, it is made a blessing. Never half such kind treatment did they receive from their own armies.[6]

Although these Mexicans had not yet benefited by American rule as Edwards asserted here (he knew as well as anyone that the protection offered thus far against the "savage hordes" was of little effect), they had in fact been neglected—if not misused at times—by their own authorities, which may explain the willingness of some villagers to placate these invaders. George Gibson and the Chihuahua Rangers, after enduring their own bone-chilling night marches across the desert, reached Doña Ana on December 23, to discover the vanguard ensconced there with other elements of Doniphan's command and freely enjoying the fruits of trade:

> We found the place filled with men from Major Gilpin's command, who was encamped in the bottom, all noisy and drinking. And being old acquaintances, we could scarcely find time to procure what we wanted. *Aguardiente*, dried fruit, pumpkins, corn, and a few other things are its productions. After purchasing as much of these different things as were required, we moved on to camp, and for the first time our force is together, except stragglers and the various details. From what we learn, there are troops at El Paso, and we shall have a fight. But as yet we have not been able to learn their strength or situation. Our men are in fine spirits and confidently expect to be the victors. Nor could a spectator suppose we were a war party about to measure our strength with the enemy, from the joyous and noisy crowds around camp, the little fear they possess, and the total indifference manifested.[7]

The next day, December 24, Doniphan resumed the march. It promised to be "a very dull Christmas," Marcellus Edwards observed.[8] After bivouacking at a forlorn spot they called the "Dead Man's Camp" for three corpses discovered there (victims, perhaps, of an Apache raid), the men were out early again on the twenty-fifth, marching onward not to the strains of hymns but to the tune of "Yankee Doodle" and "Hail Columbia." By late morning, Doniphan and his lead elements were approaching their intended camping place, near a small bend in the Rio Grande called Brazito ("little arm"). Guards spotted six Mexican scouts in the distance and went galloping after them but managed to retrieve only a fine-looking horse, abandoned by one of the Mexicans as he scrambled off into the bush. Deciding which of the guards would claim this prize animal was a delicate matter, Marcellus Edwards related:

> So Colonel Doniphan and staff, each personifying one of the guard, sat down at a game of loo to determine who should be the owner of the horse. Some one, seeing a dust rising below, pointed it out to the colonel. He looked up and said, "That does look rather suspicious," but threw down a card and said, "Play to that and that," until he had finished his hand.[9]

Doniphan then had another look at that growing cloud of dust in the distance and sent men on horseback to investigate, having enhanced his reputation as a gambler of poise and persistence. He promptly ordered the troops on hand to form for battle. Only about five hundred of his men were near enough to camp to respond, and many of those were distracted by various duties. "Some were engaged getting wood," wrote George Gibson, "some were after water, and all were scattered through the brush and bottom, when the alarm was given that the enemy were upon us."[10] A number of these "mounted volunteers" had already been reduced to infantry when their horses gave out along the trail, and others were too far from their browsing animals to saddle up for battle. But that suited Doniphan, for his men would be defending rather than attacking and were better off on foot.

As was customary, Doniphan and his officers mounted for the engagement, which made them prominent targets, and they were joined on horseback by a small contingent of volunteers from Company D, led by Captain Reid. Among those who followed Reid's lead was Marcellus Edwards, who described the rousing preliminaries to battle, during which trader and interpreter Thomas J. Caldwell, who had mastered Spanish in his peaceful dealings with Mexicans over the years, used that facility now to confront the opposition:

> The enemy's long bold front hove in sight and was formed a little over a half mile off, while they rid themselves of every useless and burdensome article.

Now an officer upon a foaming steed appeared from their ranks, bearing in his hand a black flag with a skull and crossbones on it, such as is used by pirates and indicates "death or victory" or "no quarters." He was met by our interpreter, Caldwell, about half way, who demanded his business of him. He replied that their commander desired an interview with ours. Caldwell told him that our commander would meet theirs half way.

"No," says the Spaniard. "He must come into our camp"—to which Caldwell replied in the negative.

"*Carajo!*" says the Mexican. "We will then come and bring him."

"Come on!" says Caldwell. "They are ready for you."

Then the Mexican shook his black flag and, pointing to it, said, "See, that is our motto. We ask no quarters and will give none. There is no mercy for you, and you will receive none."[11]

Doniphan, in his official report, wrote that if had allowed his troops to have their way, "a hundred balls would have pierced the insolent bearer of the pirate flag, but I deemed it most proper for the honor of our country to restrain them."[12] Caldwell, meanwhile, had returned from the fruitless parley and was urging the Missourians on by reminding them what that black flag meant and imploring them to fight hard for the Stars and Stripes. This preliminary exchange of challenges and insults worked to the advantage of the Americans, giving them more time to prepare their defenses and more incentive to hold the line and send these "pirates" back where they came from.

Doniphan's men could ill afford to yield any ground, for they had their backs to the river. Confronting them to the east were more than a thousand Mexicans under the command of Lieutenant Colonel Antonio Ponce de León, including seasoned dragoons from the regular army and raw militiamen from El Paso. Doniphan wisely ordered the volunteers to hold fire until the enemy was at close range—not an easy thing for inexperienced troops to do while being shot at. The oncoming Mexicans, by contrast, unleashed several volleys of musketry at long range, sending bullets flying over the heads of the Americans, but close enough to make them flinch. "Balls flew thick and fast," Edwards related, "and as they would whistle by the ear of a fellow, he would involuntarily dodge his head after the danger had passed."[13]

Mexicans later expressed astonishment that the Americans withstood these volleys without responding in kind. It was not the way men fought in this country, and it seemed unnatural and unsporting. "They asked what kind of people we are to stand up and be shot at and not return it," Gibson remarked after the battle.[14] But by refusing to engage the Mexicans on their terms, by declining to trade shots at the first opportunity, the Americans gained an enormous edge. Their delayed response, unleashed at close range, staggered the Mexicans. Among the first to endure that shock were the horsemen assailing Doniphan's left, and the effects were devastating and dramatic. As the Mexican dragoons approached, they threatened to outflank the Americans, who responded by wheeling back to form an "elbow," or ninety-degree angle, with the rest of the line—a deft maneuver of the sort drilled into them by those maligned West Pointers at Fort Leavenworth. Then they prepared to open fire, having received orders for every other man to wait until his neighbor pulled the trigger and began to reload before shooting, thus reducing the time between volleys. The prospect facing the anxious volunteers was both splendid and fearsome, Marcellus Edwards recalled:

> The Vera Cruz dragoons, the old veterans of the nation who had served in all the wars with the Texans and with Armijo as his life guard and against the Indians, were now seen advancing rapidly upon our left. This caused the colonel to order an elbow to be formed for their better reception. In doing this, the left wing fell back some distance. Seeing this and supposing our men to be retreating, they increased their speed and shouted *"Bueno! Bueno!"* (Good! Good!) so distinctly that we could hear them plainly. Their bugles sounded the charge. Their appearance was beautiful as they came abreast. Their beautiful steeds, the best of the Spanish stock, prancing and tossing their heads to the sound of the bugles, the riders erect and firm in their seats, their red coats, high brazen helmets plumed with bear skin, and each armed with a carbine, lance, holsters, and sabre, were indeed worthy of admiration.[15]

When at last the order came for the volunteers to repulse this splendid charge, they forgot their earlier instructions to reserve half their fire and unleashed a concentrated volley that sent the attackers reeling. "Now how changed the appearance of the Mexican chargers!" Edwards wrote. "Anyone who dislikes to spoil a pretty thing would have pitied them." Those who remained in the saddle tried to sweep around Doniphan's left flank and get at the supply wagons, arrayed in a defensive circle to the rear, but quartermaster Frank Edwards responded alertly to the threat by using tactics similar to those employed by trading companies on the plains when menaced by mounted warriors:

> The Mexican dragoons charged gallantly down on our left flank; but, being turned by the heavy shower of balls, swerved to their right, and, coming round the end of our line, they dashed down on the circle of wagons. Here, I had received orders to take charge; and found myself the commander of from fifteen to twenty men. I directed them to keep out of sight until the redcoats were within ten yards of us—then, we each stepped out and gave them our

"Mexican Lancer," from John Frost, *The History of Mexico and Its Wars* (1882). Courtesy Museum of New Mexico, negative no. 171107.

fire. This caused them again to swerve, and to disappear over a rising ground, whither they were hotly pursued by our little band of fifteen horsemen.[16]

Doniphan's troops to the right, meanwhile, withstood the Mexican onslaught by falling to the ground to evade the incoming volleys and create the impression that they were being shot down. Then, when the attackers were barely sixty paces away, the volunteers rose up en masse and "let fly such a galling volley," wrote John Hughes, that the Mexicans "wheeled about and fled in the utmost confusion."[17] The entire battle lasted barely thirty minutes, Hughes added, and ended with León's forces in full flight, leaving behind more than 40 Mexicans dead and 150 wounded, by Doniphan's reckoning. American casualties were negligible in comparison—only seven men wounded—and at least one of these victims recovered quickly enough to provide his comrades with both comic relief and inspiration, as Frank Edwards recollected:

> A little German amongst us, called after one of Dumas' three mousquetaires, Grimaud, attracted our attention. At the second volley, a ball entered the front of his cap, and raked the top of his skull, and, though only cutting the scalp, caused a great effusion of blood, which ran down his face. For a moment he thought himself mortally wounded; but, still, catching up his carbine, he fired away, crying out "Well! I'll have a crack before I die, any how."[18]

The victors were not so hardened to battle that they ignored its awful price for their opponents. Some of the Mexican wounded were in terrible pain and died that Christmas night, including one reluctant recruit who attracted the sympathy of Frank Edwards and others in camp:

> He was about fifteen or sixteen years of age, and said he had been forced to fight against us, although his heart was for us; and his mother and brother had advised him to join us as soon as possible, and this he had intended to do. Poor lad! That night, in his agony, he crawled a little away from the tent he had been laid in, and expired.[19]

For the victors, however, the battle was a bonanza. It cost them little and brought them rewards of the kind much appreciated by men who felt that the campaign had thus far been a losing proposition for them materially. George Gibson itemized their haul: "We found considerable spoils on the field: wine (which the men drank immediately), bread, *pinole*, trinkets, beads, crosses, clothes, etc., all of which was collected at Colonel Mitchell's tent, when it made a considerable showing, with the arms taken." The camp, he added, "was in fine spirits at the Christmas frolic."[20] Jacob Robinson, whose detachment had returned from their grueling journey to Navajo country in time to join in Doniphan's campaign, was one of many who found rich compensation that night at the expense of the enemy. "The real aguardiente rolled into camp right rapidly, and our men after all had a merry Christmas frolic," he wrote. "We ate their bread, drank their wine, and went to bed as comfortable as if no Mexicans were near."[21]

There were, in fact, no Mexicans of hostile intent nearby. León's demoralized forces retreated deep into Chihuahua, leaving the road to El Paso open. Doniphan's men, apprehensive after the battle, soon regained their high spirits when they were greeted at the outskirts of El Paso on December 27 by civilians displaying a white flag (an inviting contrast to the black flag flown at

Brazito). The volunteers gladly took possession of the town and celebrated the New Year in a place far more to their liking than Santa Fe. As George Gibson remarked: "We found El Paso different from anything in New Mexico or the United States, with its *acequias*, which are almost of the magnitude of canals, its fruit trees and shrubbery, [and] its vineyards and orchards handsomely arranged and affording arbors which must be delightful in summer." Even in winter, he added, the *placitas*, or interior courtyards, of the better houses were verdant with evergreens, flowers, and fruit trees, and their occupants were not inclined to abandon such comforts simply because a foreign army was passing through: "The great body of the population left but are daily returning, and we shall soon have all the dons and señoritas of the place to add to our society."[22]

With the return of the populace came a renewal of the trade that served the locals as a way of appeasing potentially hostile troops and engaging them profitably. Townspeople first reached out to the troops by offering them gifts of fruit, reported Jacob Robinson, who described El Paso as an "extensive vineyard."[23] Such presents gratified the Americans and drew them into exchanges for a variety of local items, including the celebrated El Paso wines and brandies. "The sale of ardent spirits to volunteers has been for some days forbidden," Robinson noted on January 6; "still many find means of getting drunk."[24] Everything looked rosy to the volunteers, flushed as they were with triumph and aguardiente, among other offerings from the accommodating townspeople. George Gibson obtained provisions for the Chihuahua Rangers from an obliging miller named Leandro Gómez and a cheerful associate named Juan Spinosa, who offered Gibson presents, danced for him to the strains of a guitar, and introduced him to several of his female relatives, who inspired the American to amend his earlier, critical assessments of Mexican women. As he wrote of Spinosa:

> The latter has taken such a fancy to me that he brought all his women up to see me, and I returned his civilities with little presents of *cigarrillos*, tobacco, and beads. His sister is a pretty girl with dark eyes, black hair, and a brunette complexion, and, like all women in the country, has a fine form and pretty hands and feet. Generally the women have small hands and tapering fingers, and altogether are superior in form to the American, probably because lacing and such things are unknown. I, of course, embraced her when she left, according to the fashion of the country, and had no objection to repeat the ceremony at another visit which she subsequently paid me.[25]

In some ways, the experience of Gibson and his fellow volunteers here was similar to that of George Kendall and company in 1841, when the courtesies of El Paso and the hospitality of Mexican women served to blunt the resentments of the Pioneers. Such gracious give-and-take could almost lull men into believing that hostile exchanges between the two sides were a thing of the past. But the war was not over. Although some of the volunteers might have been happy to rest on their laurels in El Paso, Doniphan was intent on proceeding to Chihuahua as soon as an artillery company reached him from the north to provide support. He had little doubt that his advance would be contested, for he discovered that a patriotic priest in El Paso—the same Ramón Ortiz who had befriended Kendall—was providing intelligence on American strength to Mexican forces to the south. Doniphan had Ortiz detained and vowed to bring him along under custody when the campaign resumed. Back in Santa Fe, meanwhile, Governor Bent had recently thwarted a serious plot against his administration in the capital and would soon be the target of a bloody insurrection in his hometown of Taos.

20

Uprising at Taos

On December 23, 1846, two days before the Battle of Brazito, Lieutenant J. W. Abert of the Corps of Topographical Engineers had returned from a wide-ranging survey of the New Mexico countryside to find Santa Fe up in arms. For the observant Abert, veteran of a reconnaissance that took him to Bent's Fort and beyond the previous year, the news of an attempted revolt in the New Mexican capital came as something of a surprise, for his recent dealings with the populace had been amicable. That very morning, he noted in his journal, after extricating his mule from an icy marsh, he had been warmed by an offering from a stranger he met along the road:

> I soon overtook a Spaniard on the road who had a bottle of aguardiente that he politely offered and I eagerly accepted, for my legs were wet from the mule's having sunk so deep.
>
> About 11 o'clock we reached Santa Fe, having come 23 miles since sunrise. Here we found all our friends in a high state of excitement from the discovery of an intended revolution. The guards were posted in all directions, all the guns placed in the Plaza, and everyone in a state of great vigilance.[1]

The uprising, originally scheduled for the night of December 19, had been postponed until Christmas Eve in hope of catching the Americans off guard. The plan was to purge the capital of every last invader, Abert reported: "The revolutionizers had a very well-organized plot. Detachments were to march at dead of night and surround the houses of the Governor, Col. Price, and Maj.

Clark, while another party seized the guns. The whole body of the troops were to be massacred."[2] Although this plot had been betrayed to the authorities and thwarted by them, the scheme exposed wide-ranging hostility to American rule. Back in August, Kearny had publicly sworn the alcalde of San Miguel to allegiance and required the priest there to dignify the ceremony with his presence. But such rituals evidently did little to secure the loyalty of the populace or their leaders, as Abert reported indignantly on December 24:

> We hear that San Miguel is in a state of insurrection, and the whole country seems ripe and ready for any hellish scheme to tear down the Stars and Stripes, nest of the eagle, from the rugged mountains of the west, but the noble bird looks down from his lofty position and sees through all their puerile attempts to dislodge him. Beware! beware the eagle![3]

Another place where Kearny had raised the eagle, as it were, was the pueblo of Santo Domingo. But as Abert learned on Christmas Day, there too the inhabitants proved receptive to appeals by Mexican conspirators hoping to knock the Americans from their perch. Officers learned that two plotters were recruiting a force of three hundred warriors at Santo Domingo, Abert reported, and intimidated the Pueblos into surrendering the rebels by threatening to "level the town to the ground unless those men were delivered up."[4] The threat to bombard Santo Domingo was not an idle one. As would soon be demonstrated, American forces were fully prepared to use their big guns against rebellious settlements, whether Mexican or Indian.

Governor Bent may have worried privately about the extent of the opposition he faced, but he exuded confidence in public. On the night of December 26 he threw a party at the Palace, as if to demonstrate that all was well. Lieutenant Abert, due to return east, attended the affair that evening and was duly impressed:

> We had a grand feast, and all the luxuries of an eastern table were spread before us. At the sutler's one can get oysters, fresh shad, preserves, and fine champagne. In fact, we concluded that reveling in the halls of the Armijos was far above reveling in the Halls of the Montezuma, for the latter was a poor uncivilized Indian, while [the former] boast of being descended from the nobility of Castile.[5]

Bent, for his part, was not much impressed by the stature of those involved in the recent plot, a group that reportedly included aides and associates of former governor Armijo.[6] In a letter to Secretary of State James Buchanan composed by Bent on December 26 and polished for official purposes by a hand more literate than his own, he portrayed the conspirators as men of little significance while arguing for continued vigilance against such plots by civil authorities backed by a permanent garrison of troops:

> On the 17th instant I received information from a Mexican friendly to our Government that a conspiracy was on foot among the native Mexicans, having for its object the expulsion of the United States troops and the civil authorities from the Territory. I immediately brought into requisition every means in my power to ascertain who were the movers in the rebellion, and have succeeded in securing seven of the secondary conspirators. The military and civil officers are now both in pursuit of the two leaders and prime movers of the rebellion; but as several days have elapsed, I am apprehensive that they will have made their escape from the Territory.
>
> So far as I am informed, this conspiracy is confined to the four northern counties of the Territory, and the men considered as leaders in the affair can not be said to be men of much standing.
>
> After obtaining the necessary information to designate and secure the persons of the participators in the conspiracy, I thought it advisable to turn them over to the military authorities, in order that these persons might be dealt with more summarily and expeditiously than they could have been by the civil authorities.
>
> The occurrence of this conspiracy at this early period of the occupation of the Territory will, I think, conclusively convince our Government of the necessity of maintaining here, for several years to come, an efficient military force.[7]

The conspirators may not have amounted to much in Bent's estimate, but they included several men of high standing among the New Mexicans. One of the two "leaders and prime movers" who eluded capture was Diego Archuleta, who had recently served as Armijo's top military aide and had earlier represented New Mexico in the national congress. James Magoffin, in his mission to Santa Fe earlier in the year, had deemed Archuleta a potentially formidable opponent and had reportedly appeased him by promising that Kearny would claim only that part of New Mexico east of the Rio Grande, leaving Archuleta free to rule the rest. Whether because he resented the Americans for reneging on that promise or simply because he longed to recapture his homeland for Mexico, Archuleta lent his considerable prestige to the plot. The other prime mover was Tomás Ortiz, a former alcalde of Santa Fe whose family wielded great influence. His brother, Padre Juan Felipe Ortiz, presided as vicario, or head of the church in New Mexico, which as yet had no bishop.

Charles Bent's attempt to deny the standing of Archuleta and Ortiz to Secretary of State Buchanan was characteristic of a proud man who refused to make any public concessions to his opponents or their cause. By turning over the conspirators he apprehended to military authorities, Bent not only expedited the cases but deprived the defendants of the satisfaction of challenging his authority openly in civil court. Even in military court, however, the suspected conspirators scored some points. One of the accused, Manuel Antonio Chaves, was vigorously defended against charges of treason by the same Captain Angney who had earlier antagonized the volunteer infantrymen by asking so much of them during the march to Santa Fe. Angney won acquittal for Chaves by arguing cogently that he was not a citizen of the United States, having never taken an oath, and thus could not be condemned as a traitor for actions on behalf of the nation to which he still owed allegiance.[8]

Bent's reluctance to concede anything to his foes was evidenced as well by his fateful decision in mid-January of 1847 to travel to Taos without a military escort. Although warned of the risks, he would not have it appear that he feared hostility in his hometown. Much like his superiors who installed a civil government in newly conquered territory and placed him in this precarious position, Bent failed to anticipate the breadth and depth of hostility to an American takeover that he felt to be in the best interests of the populace. Those who resisted such forceful measures on their behalf must be fools or rabble-rousers, he concluded, and he was not about to defer to them. Charles Bent was a genuinely tragic figure in that the very qualities that brought him credit and distinction during his rise to prominence contributed to his downfall. The sheer scope of his enterprise was unparalleled in the Southwest, and no man who yielded readily to opposition or adversity could have achieved half as much. In this crisis, however, a leader more cautious or accommodating might have averted disaster.

When Bent reached Taos on January 18, he was met by an angry crowd from the nearby pueblo, demanding the release of men from their community who were being held in the Taos jail on charges of theft. Some would later dismiss this complaint as a slender pretext for violence and would portray the Pueblos as pawns of Mexican dissidents. Uncle Dick Wootton, the resourceful mountain man who worked for Bent's company periodically and frequented Taos, characterized the Pueblos who joined in the uprising there as mere accessories to a scheme contracted by Mexicans:

> For a time both the Mexicans and Indians professed to be very friendly, and the Americans got along well in New Mexico. By and by, however, it was noticed that a considerable number of the Mexicans were for some reason becoming dissatisfied with the condition of affairs. . . . The Mexicans didn't seem to have much of an idea of the size of the contract they were undertaking,

and the Indians, of course, were led on entirely by the Mexicans, who promised them an easy victory and plenty of plunder.[9]

Wootton implied that Indians lacked the discipline and dedication to undertake such "contracts" on their own initiative and cared only for the spoils of war. In fact, Pueblos in general, and those at Taos in particular, had a long history of fighting not so much for plunder as for the preservation of their community and their ancestral traditions. Taos had figured prominently in the Pueblo Revolt of 1680, which claimed the lives of many of the intruding Spaniards and their priests and forced the survivors to flee New Mexico. After Spanish settlers returned and reached an accommodation with the Pueblos, those at Taos often joined with their Mexican neighbors to repulse or avenge raids by hostile Navajos, Utes, Apaches, or Comanches. The alliance took a different turn in 1837 when José Gonzales of Taos emerged as leader of that ill-fated insurrection by Pueblos and New Mexicans against the governor in Santa Fe and his superiors in Mexico City. Then in 1843, at least eighteen recruits, many of them from Taos Pueblo, lost their lives resisting an intrusion by Texans and their American confederates, a heavy loss that embittered their grieving friends and relatives toward Anglos in the area.

And yet as recently as October 1846, according to John Hughes, twenty Taos Pueblos under the leadership of one Tomás—presumably the same Tomás who would later direct his fellow Pueblos in the uprising against Governor Bent—had joined with Mexicans from the area in support of an American expedition into Navajo country commanded by Major William Gilpin.[10] In cooperating with American occupation forces, the Pueblos no doubt hoped to intimidate and pacify their principal enemies, the Navajos. Instead, the grueling campaign they endured under Gilpin turned out to be little more than a diplomatic overture to Navajo chiefs, culminating in the peace council at Ojo del Oso that yielded a toothless treaty. To make matters worse, Richard Elliott reported, Gilpin's men lost many of their mounts and pack animals to starvation during the expedition and ran short of provisions, prompting the major to impress "some pack mules and beef cattle in a Mexican settlement." The captain charged with this duty, Elliott added, found it the "most unpleasant he has yet had to perform."[11] Tomás and the Pueblos under him no doubt came away from this misadventure exasperated with the Americans and doubting their resolve.

In sum, the Pueblos of Taos had at least as much cause for concern about this new American regime as did the town's Mexican population. Both groups felt hemmed in by Governor Bent and his associates, who had bid for millions of acres of land around Taos before the war and had now asserted control over the town politically and judicially. With the governor when he returned to Taos in January were several of the men he had installed there to maintain law and order—Circuit attorney James W. Leal, Sheriff Stephen L. Lee, and Prefect Cornelio Vigil, a Mexican relative and associate of Bent's. Many in the town and the pueblo distrusted these men, much as Bent had distrusted those Mexicans who enforced the law there before the American takeover. The Pueblos jailed in Taos in January may have been guilty of theft, but this was not a trivial grievance on the part of their supporters or a convenient excuse for mayhem. Justice here was often a test of strength. Taos Pueblos feared that Americans might use the law as a weapon to deprive them of autonomy.

Bent refused their demands for release of the prisoners and forced his way through the angry crowd to his home, where his wife and children awaited him. Irate Pueblos then rallied in the night and descended on the Taos jail early the next morning, determined to free the accused thieves by force, if necessary. Richard Elliott, drawing on accounts of the uprising that reached him later in Santa Fe, described the deadly confrontation that ensued at the jail:

> On the morning of the 19th of January a large number of Pueblo Indians assembled in one of the villages of the valley of Taos, and demanded of Stephen Lee, (formerly of St. Louis,) who was sheriff of the county, the release of three Pueblo Indians, notorious thieves, who were confined in the calaboose for stealing. Lee, seeing no means of resistance, was about to comply with this demand, and, having gone to the calaboose, was in the act of taking off the irons from the prisoners, when Conrada [Cornelio] Vigil, a Mexican, and the Prefecto, came in and objected, denouncing the Indians as thieves and scoundrels. The Indians at once killed Vigil in the calaboose, and cut his body to pieces, severing all the limbs from it; and then released the prisoners.[12]

The Taos rebellion began as a struggle to free those prisoners, but it was not entirely spontaneous. Ringleaders were subsequently identified, including the Pueblo Tomás, sometimes referred to as Tomasito, and the Mexican Pablo Montoya, who had figured in the 1837 insurrection. Although they may have laid plans for a systematic uprising by Pueblos and Mexicans extending well beyond Taos, the carnage that ensued in town on the morning of January 19 bore little sign of calculation—other than the burning desire of local people to settle the score with Governor Bent and company. The slaughter of Prefect Vigil triggered a frenzy of bloodletting that claimed the lives of Sheriff Lee, Circuit attorney Leal, and Narciso Beaubien, son of the presiding district judge. The chief target of the insurgents' rage, however, was the governor himself. Many years later his daughter Teresina, who was five at the time, recalled the brutal attack that morning on their home, where her mother, Ignacia Jaramillo Bent, was hosting two other Mexican women—her sister Josefa Jaramillo Carson, the wife of Kit Carson, who was off serving as a guide for Kearny in California; and Rumalda Luna Boggs, Bent's stepdaughter and the wife of his relative and business associate, Thomas Boggs. As Teresina related in crude but compelling fashion in her original, unedited account of the assault:

> We were in bed when the Mescicans and Indians came to the house breaking the doors and some of them were on the top of the house tearing the roofs, so we got up and father step to the porch asking them what they wanted and they answered him, we want your head gringo, we do not want for any of you gringos to govern us, as we have come to kill you. Father told them what wrong have I done to you, when you come to me for help I always helped you and your familys. I have cure you people and never charged you anything. Yes, you did but you have to died now so that no American is going to govern us, then they commenced to shoot with the arrows and guns, while he was talking to them.[13]

Teresina honored her father's memory here by portraying his earlier dealings with the locals in the best possible light. In fact, some in the mob felt wronged by Bent and were trying to get even with him. But they were not just targeting the man. They were also attacking what he represented—an alien and intrusive government—and shared the conviction expressed here that whatever Bent had done to help or hinder them in the past, he had to die now "so that no American is going to govern us." What happened next is best described in an edited version of his daughter's recollections, as offered in the late 1800s to New Mexico's governor:

> While my father was parleying with the mob, Mrs. Carson and Mrs. Boggs, aided by an Indian woman who was a slave (*peon*), dug a hole through the adobe wall which separated our house from the next. They did it with only a poker and an old iron spoon; I have still the poker that they used. We children were first pushed through the hole and then the women crawled through after us. My mother kept calling to my father to come also, but for quite a while he would not. When he did try to escape he was already wounded and had been scalped alive. He crawled through the hole, holding his hand on the top of his bleeding head. But it was too late. Some of the men came after him through the hole and others came over the roof of the house and down into the yard. They broke down the doors and rushed upon my father. He was shot many times and fell dead at our feet. The pleading

and tears of my mother and the sobbing of us children had no power to soften the hearts of the enraged Indians and Mexicans.

At first they were going to take the rest of us away as prisoners, but finally decided to leave us where we were. They ordered that no one should feed us, and then left us alone with our great sorrow. We were without food and had no covering but our night-clothing, all that day and the next night. The body of our father remained on the floor in a pool of blood. We were naturally frightened, as we did not know how soon the miscreants might return to do us violence. At about three o'clock the next morning, some of our Mexican friends stole up to the house and gave us food and clothing. That day, also, they took my father to bury him. A few days later we were allowed to go to their house. Mrs. Carson and Mrs. Boggs were sheltered by a friendly old Mexican, who took them to his home, disguising them as squaws, and set them to grinding corn on metates in his kitchen.[14]

This was not the only instance in which likely targets of violence were shielded from harm. According to Richard Elliott, Padre Martínez—who had long been at odds with Bent and whom some suspected of encouraging the uprising—saved the life of Elliott Lee, the murdered sheriff's visiting brother, by first concealing him under a stash of wheat and later interceding on his behalf when he was discovered.[15]

Three other assaults on parties made up largely or entirely of Americans occurred elsewhere in the region over the next day or two. At Mora, some thirty-five miles southeast of Taos, eight traders heading east for Missouri lost their lives when they stopped at the village on January 20 and came under attack. One of the victims, Lawrence L. Waldo, had recently written a letter to his brother, Dr. David Waldo, now serving as a captain in Doniphan's regiment, in which he expressed concern about hostility toward Americans, particularly in eastern settlements such as Mora, which lay exposed to the plains and had suffered both from chronic Indian raids over the years and from the provocative assault carried out by Colonel Warfield on behalf of Texas in 1843: "It seems that a general mistake has been made by all that were acquainted with the *gente* of this Territory in regard to their willingness to be subject to the rule of the United States. It is satisfactorily ascertained that not one in ten is *agusto*, and, as far as I can judge, and I am well acquainted with the eastern side of the mountains, not one in one hundred is content."[16] Lawrence Waldo had bargained on good terms with Mexicans, but that failed to insure him and his companions against the wrath of those who felt cheated by the American takeover.

Others who fell victim soon after the attack on Governor Bent included Mark Head and William Harwood, two mountain men bound for Taos who were slain by Mexicans at the small settlement of Río Colorado. The fiercest exchange, however, occurred at Arroyo Hondo, a dozen miles northwest of Taos, where Simeon Turley, an American who had long been grinding grain and distilling liquor at Turley's Mill, was hosting a party of eight or nine trappers and traders from the United States and Canada when the uprising occurred. Turley was one of the leading producers of the brew known generically as Taos Lightning, and some moralists held that against him. Joseph Williams, a Methodist preacher in his mid-sixties who passed through Taos in 1842 on a journey that carried him back to the States along the Santa Fe Trail, commented tartly: "Mr Turley, who lives here, has a mill and distillery, and makes a great many drunkards."[17] His dealings with local Mexicans had evidently been cordial enough, however, to earn him a qualified reprieve from the insurgents, who offered to spare his life if he surrendered his guests. George Ruxton, who traveled through the area shortly before the uprising and detected widespread bitterness and hostility toward the Americans, described the confrontation at Turley's Mill as related to him afterward by a survivor. A few hours after Turley and his guests learned of the massacre of Governor Bent and associates in Taos, Ruxton related, "a large crowd of Mexicans and Pueblo Indians made their appearance, all armed with guns and bows and arrows, and, advancing with a white flag, summoned Turley to surrender his house and the Americans in it, guaranteeing that his own life should be saved, but that every other American in the valley of Taos had to be destroyed."[18]

Turley stoutly refused to turn over his guests to the insurgents and told them that if they wanted his house or its occupants, they "must take them." He then returned to his lodging, which adjoined the mill and stillhouse, while the insurgents held council:

> As soon as the attack was determined upon, the assailants broke, and, scattering, concealed themselves under the cover of the rocks and bushes which surrounded the house. From these they kept up an incessant fire upon every exposed position of the building where they saw the Americans preparing for defense.
>
> They, on their parts, were not idle; not a man but was an old mountaineer, and each had his trusty rifle, with good store of ammunition. Wherever one of the assailants exposed a hand's breadth of his person, there whistled a ball from an unerring barrel. The windows had been blockaded, loopholes being left to fire through, and through these a lively fire was maintained. Already several of the enemy had bitten the dust, and parties were constantly seen bearing the wounded up the banks of the Cañada. Darkness came on, and during

the night a continual fire was kept up on the mill, while its defenders, reserving their ammunition, kept their posts with stern and silent determination. The night was spent in running balls, cutting patches, and completing the defenses of the building.[19]

Ruxton was an author who did much to foster the legend of the mountain man, and he portrayed the defenders here in formulaic terms—stern and silent men, with trusty rifle in hand, compelling their enemies to bite the dust. Judging by their success in holding out for more than twenty-four hours against a force estimated at several hundred men, however, Turley and company lived up to frontier legend on this occasion, as did their Pueblo assailants, several of whom bravely sacrificed themselves in an effort to retrieve their leader, shot down the following morning while attempting to cross from the stable to the main building:

> The first man who attempted to cross, and who happened to be a Pueblo chief, was dropped on the instant, and fell dead in the center of the intervening space. It appeared an object to recover the body, for an Indian immediately dashed out to the fallen chief, and attempted to drag him within the cover of the wall. The rifle which covered the spot again poured forth its deadly contents, and the Indian, springing into the air, fell over the body of his chief, struck to the heart. Another and another met with a similar fate, and at last three rushed at once to the spot, and, seizing the body by the legs and head, had already lifted it from the ground, when three puffs of smoke blew from the barricaded window, followed by the sharp cracks of as many rifles, and the three daring Indians added their number to the pile of corpses which now covered the body of the dead chief. [20]

Here, as in his description of the mountain men at work, Ruxton or his informant may have embellished the tale somewhat, but the reported willingness of these warriors to die for their chief was entirely consistent with subsequent actions by Pueblos at Taos, who held together heroically and paid a terrible price for their solidarity. The sacrifice made by the warriors at Turley's Mill was not in vain, Ruxton added, for it served to inspire their confederates:

> As yet the besieged had met with no casualties; but after the fall of the seven Indians, in the manner above described, the whole body of assailants, with a shout of rage, poured in a rattling volley, and two of the defenders of the mill fell mortally wounded. One, shot through the loins, suffered great agony, and was removed to the still-house, where he was laid upon a large pile of grain, as being the softest bed to be found.

In the middle of the day the assailants renewed the attack more fiercely than before, their baffled attempts adding to their furious rage. The little garrison bravely stood to the defense of the mill, never throwing away a shot, but firing coolly, and only when a fair mark was presented to their unerring aim. Their ammunition, however, was fast failing, and, to add to the danger of their situation, the enemy set fire to the mill, which blazed fiercely, and threatened destruction to the whole building.[21]

Despite the defenders' repeated attempts to quench the flames, by nightfall they had no choice but to attempt a breakout. Several died in the effort, while Turley and a few others managed to escape. Turley was later betrayed by a Mexican "who had been a most intimate friend of the unfortunate man for many years," Ruxton wrote:

To this man Turley offered his watch (which was treble its worth) for the use of his horse, but was refused. The inhuman wretch, however, affected pity and commiseration for the fugitive, and advised him to go to a certain place, where he would bring or send him assistance; but on reaching the mill, which was now a mass of fire, he immediately informed the Mexicans of his place of concealment, whither a large party instantly proceeded and shot him to death.[22]

As Turley's ill-fated attempt to bargain with his Mexican acquaintance demonstrated, all deals were off. From now until the revolt was crushed, the rival parties would traffic only in recriminations and reprisals.

When word of the attacks in and around Taos reached Colonel Sterling Price in Santa Fe, he enlisted the help of civilians to put down the uprising. Charles Bent's business partner, Ceran St. Vrain, was in Santa Fe at the time and served as captain of a volunteer force known as St. Vrain's Avengers, which consisted mostly of American traders or mountain men along with some Mexicans opposed to the insurgency. Their opinion of the rebels was voiced by Donaciano Vigil, who succeeded Bent as civil governor and characterized those responsible for his death and related acts of violence as malcontents from the "lower order of Mexicans of the valley of Taos" and environs in league with restive Pueblos—much the same alliance that Vigil and some other New Mexicans in positions of authority blamed for fanning the "flames of the revolution" in 1837.[23] Among the Americans who joined St. Vrain's Avengers—or claimed as much—was mountain man James Beckwourth, born in Virginia to a black woman and a white slaveholder. Beckwourth narrated his memoir long after the revolt and larded his narrative with anecdotes more colorful than credible. Like James Hobbs and other imaginative mountain men who purveyed tales to the public, he may not have participated in all the actions he took credit for, but he was well informed on the efforts of St. Vrain's Avengers and offered one of the few unofficial accounts of the campaign to crush the uprising. (Price and other officers filed formal reports.) For Beckwourth as for St. Vrain and others in the Santa Fe trade and related enterprises, the revolt came as a personal affront, an attack on men they knew and admired and whose loss they felt bound to repay. Beckwourth was in Santa Fe when he learned of the uprising from an acquaintance, Charles Town, who had barely escaped becoming one of the victims himself:

> At night there came a violent rapping at my gate, and on going to open it I perceived my friend, Charles Towne, who, on being admitted, clasped me round the neck, and gave vent to uncontrolled emotion. Perceiving that something alarming had occurred, I invited him into the house, spread refreshments before him, and allowed him time to recover himself. He then informed me that he had escaped almost by a miracle from Taos, where all the American residents had been killed. He was a resident there, having married a girl of New Mexico, and his wife's father had apprised him that he had better effect his escape, if possible, for if he was caught he would be inevitably massacred. His father-in-law provided him with a good horse, and he retreated into the woods, where, after considerable risk and anxiety, he providentially eluded the assassins.[24]

Beckwourth claimed that both he and Town promptly enlisted in St. Vrain's Avengers, which left Santa Fe on January 23 with a force that included five companies of Price's Second Missouri Volunteers (others stayed behind in Santa Fe to guard against trouble in the capital), Captain Angney's volunteer infantry battalion, and a Missouri artillery outfit manning four howitzers. Dragoons of the Regular Army commanded by Captain John H. K. Burgwin would join Price en route, bringing his strength to 479 men. While Price marched on Taos, other troops stationed near Las Vegas would hurry to Mora and challenge the insurgents holed up there in an old fort. After first suffering a repulse on January 24 that cost the life of their commander, Captain Israel R. Hendley, they would return in greater force with a cannon on February 1 to drive out the remaining inhabitants and destroy the village—a reprisal that made no distinction between those residents active in the hostilities and those whose persons and property Kearny had earlier pledged to protect so long as they remained "peacefully at home."

Colonel Price had been informed that armed insurgents were advancing southward from Taos to Santa Fe, and his troops clashed twice during the march with those opposing forces, who claimed the high ground along the route and compelled the Americans literally to fight uphill battles. The first contest occurred on January 24 near the town of La Cañada (or Santa Cruz), some twenty-five miles north of Santa Fe. There Price found the enemy "in full possession of the heights commanding the road to Cañada and of three strong houses at the bases of the hills."[25] After bringing up the howitzers to bombard the houses and the heights, Price sent St. Vrain's company back to protect the wagons from an end run by the insurgents. As Beckwourth put it, he and his mates were "placed in charge of the baggage," and they did not relish the assignment: "As soon as battle was begun, however, we left the baggage and ammunition wagons to take care of themselves, and made a descent upon the foe. He fled precipitately before the charge of our lines, and we encamped upon the field of battle."[26] Thus did Beckwourth dispense with the opposition in two sentences. Price was far more detailed in his report and credited the artillery and other units for their contributions, but he confirmed that St. Vrain's company, after minding the wagons, joined in the decisive charge, which was more of an ascent than a "descent" upon the foe:

> Captain Angney with his command, supported by Lieutenant White's company, charged up one hill, while Captain St. Vrain's company turned the same in order to cut off the company in retreat. . . . In a few minutes my troops had dislodged the enemy at all points, and they were flying in every direction. The nature of the ground rendered pursuit hopeless, and it being near night I ordered the troops to take up quarters in the town.[27]

This brief but intense exchange claimed the lives of thirty-six Mexicans, by Price's reckoning, and left two Americans killed and six wounded—including five of the twenty gunners, who "with the exception of one man," reported Captain Woldemar Fischer of the Missouri artillery unit, "all had their clothes perforated by bullets."[28] This was a heavier toll than Doniphan had paid at Brazito and further proof that holding this country was proving to be a costlier proposition than seizing it.

On January 29, Price faced another challenge from insurgents occupying the slopes on either side of a narrow pass near Embudo, and again St. Vrain's men figured in the fighting, charging up the slope on the left and "doing much execution," Price noted, before their foes hastily retreated, "bounding along the steep and rugged sides of the mountain with a speed that defied pursuit."[29] The advancing Americans faced no more resistance on the road to Taos, but their struggle with the elements continued into early February, as Price reported:

> The marches of the 1st and 2d were through deep snow. Many of the men were frostbitten, and all were very much jaded with the exertions necessary to travel

over unbeaten roads, being marched in front of the artillery and wagons in order to break a road through the snow. The constancy and patience with which the troops bore these hardships deserve all commendation, and can not be excelled by the most veteran soldiers.[30]

In a sense, volunteers such as Angney's infantrymen qualified as veterans by now, at least when it came to hard marching. Having endured days of fire on the torrid plains, they slogged their way now through the snow and ice to Taos. Their approach prompted Mexicans from Taos and surrounding communities who feared retribution to flee their homes and seek refuge in a nearby canyon, according to Rafael Chacón, who earlier had been among the forces disbanded by Armijo at Apache Canyon. Despite the bitter cold, Chacón added, the refugees lit campfires only at night for fear that the smoke would betray their position and tried desperately to silence any animals that might give them away. "I remember that there was such terror instilled by the Americans that when a dog barked the people killed it," he wrote, "the burros were muzzled so they could not bray, and if the roosters crowed at daylight they killed them."[31]

Price arrived at Taos to find the town undefended and the remaining insurgents holed up within the walls of the pueblo, which he regarded in its entirety as an enemy position. As he wrote in his official report:

On the 3d I marched through Don Fernando Taos, and finding that the enemy had fortified themselves in the Pueblo de Taos, proceeded to that place. I found it a place of great strength, being surrounded by adobe walls and strong pickets. Within the inclosures and near the northern and southern walls arose two large buildings of irregular pyramidal form to the height of seven or eight stories. Each of these buildings was capable of sheltering 500 or 600 men.[32]

He might have said that each building was capable of housing five or six hundred people, but that would have drawn attention to the fact that this position he was about to attack with all the firepower at his disposal was also a village, occupied not simply by fighting men but by women, children, and elders uninvolved in the recent hostilities. By his own account, Price made no effort to parley with the Pueblos and persuade them to surrender those responsible for the attacks on Governor Bent and others, a proposal that might well have been rejected but would at least have signaled that Price was not targeting the community as a whole. For all the defenders knew, American forces meant to raze their village as they had Mora two days earlier, a prospect that could only have stiffened Pueblo resolve. As it turned out, the Pueblo warriors and the few Mexican insurgents who stayed with them to the end chose to make their stand inside the sturdy adobe church situated at the northwestern corner of the pueblo, a building that was both a strong defensive position and far enough from the multi-story residences to keep them from being exposed to fire directed at the sanctuary.

Price recognized the preparations made for defense of the church—slits, or loopholes, in the walls through which guns could be fired—and focused his assault on that structure. Wasting no time, he called up the artillery, which bombarded the western flank of the church for more than two hours on the afternoon of the third, to little effect. Captain Fischer later described in clinical fashion how adobe walls could absorb cannon fire from 6- or 12-pounders like the weapons used at Taos without crumbling: "The structure of the houses in New Mexico is such as to make the use of mortars necessary that will throw a shell of at least 50 pounds. The walls are generally 3 feet thick and built of 'adobes,' a sort of sun-dried brick of a very soft quality through which a ball of a 12-pounder will pass without doing any more damage, which in houses of brick or stone is quite different."[33] This was a chilling observation, suggesting the extent to which New Mexico had become enemy ground and the structures that sheltered its inhabitants potential targets.

In any event, Price soon concluded that it would take more than artillery to crush the opposition. On February 4, after further bombardment, he stormed the church, directing Angney's infantrymen and other troops to attack the north end of the sanctuary while Captain Burgwin and his dismounted dragoons charged the west wall, where they hacked at the adobe with axes and raised a ladder to set fire to the beams supporting the roof. Burgwin then led a small party around to the entrance at the south side of the church and tried to force the door, only to fall mortally wounded. His men fought on, however, and soon breached the west wall in several places and lobbed shells through the gaps by hand, "doing good execution," Price wrote. His gunners then capitalized on this breakthrough:

> About half past 3 o'clock the 6-pounder was run up within 60 yards of the church, and after 10 rounds one of the holes which had been cut with the axes was widened into a practicable breach. The gun was now run up within ten yards of the wall. A shell was thrown in—three rounds of grape were poured into the breach. The storming party . . . entered and took possession of the church without opposition. The interior was filled with dense smoke, but for which circumstance our storming party would have suffered great loss. A few of the enemy were seen in the gallery, where an open door admitted the air, but they retired without firing a gun. The troops left to support

the battery on the north were now ordered to charge on that side. The enemy abandoned the western part of town. Many took refuge in the large houses on the east, while others endeavored to escape toward the mountains.[34]

Many who fled the pueblo were cut down by St. Vrain's company, waiting to the east to block the anticipated flight of insurgents in that direction. James Beckwourth claimed that he and his fellow Avengers killed fifty-four of the defenders as they were trying to escape. He added a grim anecdote that, while perhaps contrived, was nonetheless revealing of American attitudes toward the Pueblos, once regarded as friendly and now condemned for treachery:

> Some of the enemy fired upon us from a position at one corner of the fort, through loop-holes; and while looking about for a covert to get a secure shot at them, we discovered a few of the enemy hidden away in the brush. One of them, an Indian, ran toward us, exclaiming, "Bueno! bueno! me like Americanos." One of our party said, "If you like the Americans, take this sword, and return to the brush, and kill all the men you find there."
>
> He took the proffered sword, and was busy in the brush for a few minutes, and then returned with his sword-blade dripping with gore, saying, "I have killed them."
>
> "Then you ought to die for killing your own people," said the American, and he shot the Indian dead.[35]

A story with a similar edge to it was told by another member of St. Vrain's company, Uncle Dick Wootton, who enlisted with the Americans the day before the battle at Taos Pueblo after learning of the uprising from a survivor of the attack at Turley's Mill and hurrying to the scene with some other trappers to join in the fight. Wootton claimed credit for saving the life of Ceran St. Vrain after an Indian who had feigned death jumped up when prodded and grappled furiously with the "colonel," as Wootton referred to St. Vrain:

> Both the Indian and the colonel were large, powerful men, and as each managed to keep the other from using a weapon, a wrestling-match followed the Indian's attack, which, it seemed to me, lasted several minutes before outside help terminated it in the colonel's favor. I sprang to his assistance as soon as I saw the struggle commence, but the Indian managed to keep the colonel between him and me, and was so active in his movements, that I found it difficult to strike a lick which would be sure to hit the right head. I managed after little, however, to deal him a blow with my tomahawk, which had the effect of causing him to relax his hold upon the colonel, and when he stretched out on the ground again, there was no doubt about his being a dead Indian.[36]

Another account credited one of the Mexicans in the company—the same Manuel Chaves who had been acquitted of treason with Angney's help—with saving St. Vrain as he grappled with an Indian that day.[37] Perhaps Wootton, as mountain men were known to do, took that exploit upon himself and shaped it to suit his own purposes. His story, like Beckwourth's, seemed tailored to confirm the hateful adage that the only "good Indians," as many occupiers classified Pueblos before the uprising, were dead Indians.

According to Price, 150 of the defenders died in the battle, most of them Pueblos, a grievous toll for a community of some 1,000 people and one that left the insurgency in shreds. "On the next morning the enemy sued for peace," Price wrote, "and thinking the severe loss they had sustained would prove a salutary lesson, I granted their supplication, on the condition that they should deliver up to me Tomas—one of their principal men, who had instigated and been actively engaged in the murder of Governor Bent and others."[38] Tomás was later shot to death by a soldier while in custody. Beckwourth amplified on Price's account of the surrender, relating that it was the Pueblo women who sued for peace, bearing a white flag and kneeling before Price "to supplicate for the lives of their surviving friends."[39]

When the news reached President Polk back in Washington, he pronounced the outcome at Taos a triumph. "The number of troops engaged was comparatively small," he wrote in his diary, "but I consider this victory one of the most signal which has been gained during the war."[40] By any standard, however, the costs of the battle were steep. Price reported seven of his men killed and forty-five wounded, many of whom later died—by far the heaviest toll for any contest waged by Price or Doniphan during the war. And the Americans suffered other consequences when they shattered the walls of the church and ousted the defenders from their sanctuary. In the bitter aftermath, hopes for a full and fruitful accommodation with the disaffected populace—the only true measure of success in a takeover bid meant not just to enlarge the nation but to enhance it—seemed more distant than ever.

In early April, two months after the battle, young Lewis Garrard reached Taos from Bent's Fort. He had been visiting among Cheyennes camped near the fort when word reached proprietor William Bent in late January of the murder of his brother Charles and others close to the family. William Bent had immediately resolved to mount an expedition to Taos and had informed Garrard and others on hand that they "could go or stay—as they choosed."[41] Not one of them withheld his services. Only an emergency could have impelled them to make such a journey in that season. En route, men slept huddled together to avoid freezing and awoke to find themselves covered with windblown snow. Garrard evoked the scene one morning as the company approached the Spanish Peaks and Raton Pass:

> What a sight greeted our eyes, on rising! The hills, ourselves, and saddles, were covered with the white drapery; bitter cold winds penetrated our clothes, while far off to the northwest, the twin mountains—*Las Cumbres Espanolas*—glittered with snow. The mules were starving; for the scanty grass was hidden early in the night with the same frigid envelop which contributed not an atom to our personal comfort; and they stood trembling over their picketpins, pricking their ears at any noise, without moving their heads.[42]

The weather had moderated by the time they reached Raton Pass, strewn with the debris of damaged wagons, and the men relaxed near the crest in the waning sun, kindled a fire, and after filling their pipes with tobacco, paid homage to the powers above in native fashion by offering to the towering peaks "the freely given homage of the first and most honorable whiff."[43]

On the far side of the pass, they learned of the defeat of the insurgents at Taos by Colonel Price and their expedition lost its urgency. Garrard spent the next several weeks on the sprawling ranchlands recently claimed by Bent, St. Vrain & Co. in northern New Mexico, corralling cattle and other livestock intended for sale to American forces but scattered by Mexicans during the uprising. By the time Garrard reached Taos, spring had arrived and the town was slowly returning to life after a winter of devastation. Troops still occupied the area and trials were being conducted for those charged with involvement in the hostilities, but he found himself entranced nonetheless by the charms of the town in general and of its women in particular, much like visitors who had arrived here in happier times. Having gone for months without female companionship before Ceran St. Vrain and his Mexican wife welcomed him to their home at Taos, Garrard proved unusually responsive to the appeals of the ladies he encountered in the street. Unlike some earlier travelers, he found their attachment to tobacco positively seductive:

> Though smoking is repugnant to many ladies, it certainly does enhance the charms of the Mexican senoritas, who, with neatly rolled up shucks between coral lips, perpetrate winning smiles, their magically brilliant eyes the meanwhile searching one's very soul. How dulcet-toned are their voices, which, siren-like, irresistibly draw the willing victim within the giddy vortex of dissipation![44]

Perhaps some of these "siren-like" temptresses hoped to sell their favors to Garrard, one form of trade that was seldom interrupted by hostilities in any war zone. But he was equally receptive to the innocent allure of the Mexican women he watched drawing water at the springs outside town:

Their peculiar style of dress displays the form to advantage; and with well-filled, antique-fashioned earthen jars—manufactured by Indians inhabiting the country between this and California—poised on the head; with arms folded, the reboza in graceful plaits on the shoulders, and erect, dignified carriage, they, indeed, formed a picturesque and pleasing sight. My thoughts were directed to the Bible descriptions of the drawers of water, and of the fair daughters of Jerusalem coming to the wells—how they lingered about the fountain to exchange salutations.[45]

Contrasting sharply to such idyllic moments that seemed to banish thoughts of war were the grim scenes Garrard witnessed in court, where the conflict was still being played out. Garrard felt as keenly as any American observer the chilling effect of imposing on the New Mexican populace alien "judges, attorneys, sheriffs, and other appurtenances and impertinences of even-handed justice."[46] This imposed legal system had helped fan the fires of revolt in Taos and was now being applied in an attempt to snuff out the last embers of resistance. Prosecuting insurgents for murder or treason was the late governor Bent's young friend and ally, Francis P. Blair, Jr. Among the judges was Charles Beaubien, whose son had been killed in the uprising. According to Garrard, one juror considering the case of six defendants charged with murder asked his Anglo foreman how he should rule, to which the man replied: "why, hang them, of course; what did you come in here for?"[47] Despite such irregularities, Garrard felt that the five Mexicans found guilty of murder in the proceedings he witnessed deserved to die. But he regarded as a gross miscarriage of justice the death sentence meted out to one of their compatriots, found guilty of treason:

It certainly did appear to be a great assumption on the part of Americans to conquer a country, and then arraign the revolting inhabitants for treason. American judges sat on the bench, New Mexicans and Americans filled the jurybox, and an American soldiery guarded the halls. Verily, a strange mixture of violence and justice—a strange middle ground between the martial and common law.

After an absence of a few minutes, the jury returned with a verdict of "guilty in the first degree"—five for murder, one for treason. Treason, indeed! What did the poor devil know about his new allegiance? But so it was; and, as the jail was overstocked with others awaiting trial, it was deemed expedient to hasten the execution, and the culprits were sentenced to be hung on the following Friday—hangman's day. When the concluding words "*muerto, muerto, muerto*"—"dead, dead, dead"—were pronounced by Judge Beaubien, in his solemn and impressive manner, the painful stillness that reigned in the

courtroom, and the subdued grief manifested by a few bystanders, were noticed
not without an inward sympathy. The poor wretches sat with unmovable features; but I fancied that, under the assumed looks of apathetic indifference,
could be read the deepest anguish. When remanded to jail till the day of execution, they drew their sarapes more closely around them, and accompanied
the armed guard. I left the room, sick at heart. Justice! out upon the word,
when its distorted meaning is the warrant for murdering those who defend to
the last their country and their homes.[48]

Another New Mexican condemned for treason in a separate trial in Santa Fe
that March, the elderly Antonio María Trujillo, was later pardoned after his
case was reviewed by Secretary of War William Marcy, who concluded that
"territory conquered by our arms does not become, by the mere act of conquest, a permanent part of the United States, and the inhabitants of such territory are not to the full extent of the term, citizens of the United States."[49]
Marcy's directive came too late, however, to spare the man found guilty of
treason as Garrard looked on.

Garrard's distaste for the proceedings in Taos did not prevent him from
playing a small part in the executions. With the adventurer's eagerness to
experience everything the West had to offer, be it good or evil, he and a companion lent their rawhide lariats to the sheriff and helped him to fashion
nooses and cover them with saddle soap so that they would fit snugly without hitching. With businesslike efficiency, the sheriff included the soap in his
bill of expenses and rewarded his assistants with aguardiente after they washed
their hands. It was not Garrard's last drink on this hangman's day. After the
execution, he proved himself one of the boys by retreating with companions
to a bar for an eggnog to mark the occasion. But the memory of the hang-
ings lingered, and he later evoked the last moments of the deceased with a
sobriety the occasion deserved. All but one of those sentenced to die for murder admitted their guilt, he noted:

> In their brief, but earnest appeals, which I could but imperfectly compre-
> hend, the words *mi padre, mi madre*—"my father, my mother"—could be dis-
> tinguished. The one sentenced for *treason* showed a spirit of martyrdom wor-
> thy of the cause for which he died—the liberty of his country; and, instead
> of the cringing, contemptible recantation of the others, his speech was firm
> asseverations of his own innocence, the unjustness of his trial, and the arbi-
> trary conduct of his murderers. With a scowl, as the cap was pulled over his
> face, the last words he uttered between his gritting teeth were, "Caraho, los
> Americanos!"[50]

Garrard's admiration for this defiant patriot seemed to come at the expense of the convicted murderers, whose "cringing, contemptible recantation" may simply have been an attempt on their part to make peace with God, the only judge with the authority to condemn or pardon the deeds they committed in defiance of the occupying forces.

Garrard perhaps came as close as any American of the day to fathoming the tragic complexities of the revolt when he walked with some companions amid the rubble of the embattled church—a monument both to the faith of the insurgents and to their fighting spirit:

> We stood on the spot where fell the gallant Burgwin, the first captain of the First Dragoons, and then passed to the west side, entering the church at the stormers' breach, through which the missiles of death were hurled. We silently paused in the center of the house of Pueblo worship. Above, between the charred and blackened rafters, which leaned from their places as if ready to fall on us, could be seen the spotless blue sky of this pure clime—on either side, the lofty walls, perforated by cannon ball and loophole, let in the long lines of uncertain gray light; and, strewed and piled about the floor, as on the day of battle, were broken, burnt beams, and heaps of adobes. Climbing and jumping over them, we made our way to the altar, now a broken platform, with scarce a sign or vestige of its former use. . . .
>
> A few half-scared Pueblos walked listlessly about, vacantly staring in a state of dejected, gloomy abstraction. And they might well be so. Their alcalde dead, their grain and cattle gone, their church in ruins, the flower of the nation slain, or under sentence of death, and the rest—with the exception of those in prison—refugees, starving in the mountains. It was truly a scene of desolation. In the strong hope of victory they made no provision for defeat; in the superstitious belief of protection afforded by the holy Church, they were astounded beyond measure that, in the hour of need, they should be forsaken by their tutelar saint—that *los diablos Americanos* should, within the limits of consecrated ground, trample triumphant, was too much to bear; and, pitiable objects, they fled as if *diablos* from *los regiones infiernos* were after them, in sooth.[51]

Garrard saw this as the end of Pueblo resistance, the death of their struggle as an autonomous people, and he paid them tribute for succumbing bravely and reluctantly to superior force:

> Much credit is due the Pueblos de Taos for their determined and manly resistance to what they considered tyranny, and for the capital manner in which their fortifications were planned; but, as a matter of course, they were defeated

Ruins of church at Taos Pueblo, ca. 1912, by Jesse L. Nusbaum. Courtesy Museum of New Mexico, negative no. 8012.

by the Americans. Who could, for a moment, expect anything else? For years the Pueblo, by reason of fierceness of disposition, has held the balance of power in this district. It was the Pueblo who first revolted, and committed the late outrages—the Pueblo who, several years since, rose in arms, to put every American to death—the Pueblo who has kept this district in a continual ferment; but at last! at last, he has met his conqueror.[52]

Yet Pueblos had met their conqueror before, in the person of the Spaniard, and had emerged intact. What Garrard could not anticipate was the ability of these defiant Pueblos—and of their Mexican counterparts—to weather defeat and to remain the masters of this country in spirit, if not in title. Northern New Mexico would remain a dangerous place for Americans for some time to come, with periodic outbreaks of violence that yielded casualties on both sides. And even when hostilities ended, the occupiers would begin to feel at home here only when they arrived at a grudging accommodation with the populace not unlike that reached by Spaniards with the Pueblos in earlier times. The true genius of these resilient New Mexicans was for dealing with *los diablos* and diverting them from the thankless task of conquest to a more rewarding exchange.

For the survivors at Taos Pueblo, one youngster in particular personified their capacity to overcome this bitter setback and restore their community. His name was Elk Heart, and it was said that his mother gave birth to him the morning after Price's troops stormed the church. Elders in later years told anthropologist Elsie Clews Parsons that dust from the shattered adobe walls shrouded the pueblo that day as Elk Heart came into the world and "blinded the new born baby."[53] He was duly compensated for the loss of his sight, however, by receiving the gift of prophecy and the rare ability to console those in mourning. He knew by heart the ritual songs of the Pueblos and the *alabanzas*, or hymns of praise, sung by Mexicans. When Pueblos died and were laid to rest amid the ruins of the church destroyed by the Americans, he raised his voice in prayer and remembrance. And his heartening presence assured all in attendance that this precious ground, defended by men dear to them at great cost on the eve of his birth, remained their inalienable sanctuary.

21

Descent to Chihuahua

News of the uprising at Taos had reached Susan and Samuel Magof-fin in late January 1847 as they were traveling southward from Santa Fe to El Paso, by then securely in the hands of Doniphan's troops. Susan herself had been trading goods from the wagons with Mexicans at stops along the way, and word of the murderous attacks on Governor Bent and other Americans caused her to view her customers in a sinister new light. As she wrote in her diary on January 28:

> My knowledge of these people has been extended very much in one day. There are among them some of the greatest villains, smooth-faced assassins in the world and some good people too. But yesterday morning while we were packing our trunks and some bales of goods, my suspicions were highly roused though perhaps unjustly; a good many men came in, some to buy goods, others merely to talk and as I suspected to see some thing of our strength, for without doubt 'tis the intention of nearly every one of them to murder without distinction every American in the country if the least thing should turn in their favour. . . . An other one made me suspicion him *from his flattering talk of the Americans* and abuse of his own people; the same was sly enough in gathering up some goods he had bought, to slip in a whole piece of calico more than belonged to him but did not succeed in carrying it off for being discovered and the piece recovered.[1]

Of course, this smooth-talking customer may have had no more nefarious a purpose than making off with a bit more cloth than he paid for. And it was characteristic of Susan Magoffin to acknowledge that her suspicions of murderous intent on the part of her Mexican clients were perhaps unjust. Her role as a merchant's wife and as a trader herself taught her to keep avenues open to the Mexicans, to give them some credit, even when she feared the worst. No harm came to the members of her party as they continued south, and by the time they reached El Paso in mid-February—a week or so after Doniphan resumed his march to Chihuahua—she had regained her faith that any obstacles the war imposed between her and her Mexican hosts and customers could be safely negotiated.

In El Paso, as in Santa Fe, she was welcomed by locals well acquainted with her husband and kindly disposed to his young wife. Among those who hosted the visiting couple were the relatives of Ramón Ortiz, the priest whom Doniphan had detained on suspicions of spying and forced to accompany the troops to Chihuahua. Maintaining the household in the priest's absence were his two sisters and his niece, who seemed intent on demonstrating to the Magoffins that the family was free of hostile intentions and deserving of trust and respect (much as Ortiz himself had demonstrated to his guest George Kendall in 1841). Their efforts were not wasted on Susan, who reveled in their hospitality:

> I am altogether pleased with our boarding house—the inmates are exceedingly kind and exert themselves so much to make me enjoy myself, 'twould be cruel if I did not attend to their solicitations. We have chocolate every morning on rising, breakfast about 10 o'k. dinner at two, chocolate again at dark, and supper at 9 o'clock, all are attentive, indeed we are so free and easy, 'tis almost a hotel, meals are served in our own room, one of the ladies always being in attendance to see and know if we are propperly attended to; the dishes are often changed, and well prepared.[2]

Such attentions may have been calculated in part to place the Magoffins in the family's debt and secure their influence in obtaining freedom for the priest. But Susan sensed that her hostesses truly cared for her, whatever their ulterior motives might be. "We are all getting quite familiar and friendly in our dealings," she noted a few days after moving in to the priest's residence; "as our acquaintance extends it is more agreeable, and to me more improving."[3] Indeed, hospitality was an article of faith for the women of the Ortiz family as it was for many of their compatriots, a good deed that improved them in spirit even as it improved their guests. While staying here Susan attended Catholic mass, as she had once or twice before in Santa Fe. On this occasion, however, she did so with a greater appreciation for the sincerity of the worshipers:

This morning I have been to mass—not led by idle curiosity, not by a blind faith, a belief in the creed there practiced, but because tis the house of God, and whether Christian or pagan, I can worship there within myself, as well as in a protestant church, or my own private chamber. If I have sinned in going there in this belief, I pray for pardon for 'twas done in ignorance. I am not an advocate for the Catholic faith. It is not for me to judge; whether it be right or wrong; judgement alone belongs to God. If they are wrong we (if alone in the right way) are not to rail at them, but in brotherly love to use our little influence to guide them into the straight path. One thing among them they are sincere in what they do. I speak of the people; of the Priests and leaders I know nothing. I am told to "judge no man but to bear the burden of my brother."[4]

This charitable suspension of judgment stood in marked contrast to the harsh assessments leveled by some of her fellow Protestants in Mexico, demonstrating that in the contest between faiths, as in that between nations, those who found ways of honoring competing values could well profit by them.

Few other traders were in a position to reach such accords with their Mexican hosts, however. Out of concern for Susan's safety, Samuel Magoffin had remained behind in tranquil El Paso while other merchants joined the advance to Chihuahua, the biggest market within reach. A few had departed for that objective in advance of the army, but the others had placed themselves at Doniphan's disposal. By mid-February his train included as many as three hundred merchant wagons—and for the first time, their owners and handlers were an integral part of the campaign.

Like most of Doniphan's men, George Gibson had had enough of El Paso by the time he received orders to head south. After a month of lolling about town, consorting with locals, and basking in the glow of the victory at Brazito, the troops were growing unruly and needed a fresh challenge. As Gibson put it:

The army was composed of men of a restless and roving disposition, and the little discipline which prevailed was totally insufficient to prevent rioting and dissipation, which endangered the health of the troops as well as their efficiency. And as a consequence they soon became wearied of any place and were urgent to be led against the enemy or any other place, so that they were in camp or on the march. . . . And all this was greatly increased by the stories we had heard of the wealth, the resources, the beauty, and the magnitude of Chihuahua, which we were determined to take before other troops could be sent against it.[5]

Much like the traders, the soldiers wanted to beat the competition to that prize. Doniphan's interests and those of the merchants under his protection were converging as never before during this conflict. According to John Hughes, the traders did good business in El Paso and shared part of the proceeds with the army:

> The merchants and sutlers, upon arriving at El Paso, hired rooms and store-houses, where they exhibited their goods and commodities for sale. Many of them sold largely to the inhabitants, whereby they considerably lightened their burdens. Certain of the merchants advanced Col. Doniphan sums of money, for the use of the commissary and quartermaster departments of the army, taking, for these accommodations, checks on the United States' treasury. To a limited extent, also, they furnished some of the soldiers with clothing, and other necessaries.[6]

Doniphan, who lacked funds, needed such loans from the merchants to pay Mexicans for supplies requisitioned from them and avoid the tensions that arose when local people felt exploited by occupation forces. One of the hazards of victory for his men was the temptation to cease bargaining and simply take what they felt entitled to by conquest. With advances from the traders, Doniphan managed to suppress this dangerous impulse for the most part, but the longer the troops remained in one place, the greater the risk that what Gibson called their "restless and roving disposition" would find destructive outlet. Three soldiers were court-martialed in El Paso for "ravishing a Mexican woman,"[7] Hughes reported in his diary in January, and Doniphan could expect further trouble—and possible reprisals by Mexicans—if he failed to resume the march and subject his men once more to the discipline of the campaign trail.

He was under no obligation to proceed to the city of Chihuahua. Although Kearny had instructed him to report to General Wool, who was then thought to be advancing toward that city, Doniphan had no firm word of Wool's whereabouts and suspected that he was far from Chihuahua. Under the circumstances, Doniphan would have been justified in remaining in El Paso or in returning to Santa Fe to protect the capital against any flare-up of the rebellion that Colonel Price was in the process of suppressing. Neither of those options would have raised the sagging morale of Doniphan's men, however, or satisfied traders who were intent on testing the market in Chihuahua and felt that Doniphan owed them protection in return for their financial support. As it turned out, they did not have to press the commander on the issue, for Doniphan and his aides saw the matter much as they did. Long before the war erupted, shrewd Missourians bound for Mexico had come to recognize

Chihuahua as a more significant and rewarding destination than Santa Fe. Doniphan shared that assessment now. He welcomed the chance to seize an asset that lay closer to the enemy's heart than the remote capital of New Mexico. And he hoped to claim at least some of Chihuahua's wealth, derived from local silver mines and stored there in a federal mint. Such a coup would earn his undercompensated forces considerable credit, financially and otherwise.

Doniphan delayed his departure from El Paso until Major Meriwether Lewis Clark arrived with an artillery unit from Santa Fe. Then on February 8, he moved south with about 1,000 men in uniform (or some semblance thereof). He soon augmented his forces by enlisting a battalion of 150 men from the trader's caravan, commanded by Samuel Owens, that respected veteran of the Santa Fe trade. Given the scandal surrounding his daughter back home in Independence, who had reportedly helped her husband escape from prison after he murdered a man for dallying with her, Owens was probably glad to be on the trail—and may even have welcomed the prospect of doing battle. He and other traders in the battalion had cultivated close ties with Mexicans, but the conflict had frayed those bonds and hardened their attitudes toward the opposition. William Henry Glasgow, the younger and more hotheaded of the two Glasgow brothers who were destined for Chihuahua on business, wrote disdainfully from El Paso in January that "as we walk the Streets here the Mexicans *take off their* hats to us. They are the most arrogant & cruel people in the world when they get once the advantage but whip them once and they are quite as servile & cringing."[8] He later conceded in another letter from El Paso that he "never was better treated in my life than I have been here," but he was happy to enlist with Doniphan to fight Mexicans and honored to be chosen by his peers as a lieutenant, remarking that he felt himself "very large while strutting about with an old sabre cracking my shins."[9]

The merchants were not the only civilians Doniphan recruited on the way south. Among the scouts he enlisted was the notorious James Kirker, a native of Ireland who had grown up in the States before migrating to Mexico, where he made his mark fighting Apaches and collecting bounties offered for their scalps by Chihuahuan authorities. One Missourian recalled that Kirker had attached himself to Doniphan's command unbidden on the way to El Paso, riding into the American camp wearing a "fringed buckskin hunting-shirt and breeches, heavy broad Mexican hat, and huge spurs, all embellished and ornamented with Mexican finery."[10] Doniphan had reason to wonder if Kirker's Mexican gear betrayed his sympathies. He was, after all, a naturalized Mexican citizen, but he had grown disenchanted with his adopted country after the Chihuahuans failed to reward him as promised for his recent assaults on Apaches. With some reluctance, Doniphan engaged the services of Kirker and several venturesome Delaware and Shawnee Indians who had accompanied the bounty hunter on his scalp raids and knew the Chihuahuans and their country intimately. For Doniphan, this was like dealing with the devil, but for all he knew of what lay ahead he and his men might be headed for hell, and he needed scouts who knew their way around.

There was, in fact, something infernal about the land the Missourians entered below El Paso—at least to the eyes of men raised amid lush fields and forests. Leaving the banks of the Rio Grande, they traversed true desert, where windblown sand stung their eyes and gathered in drifts that gripped at the wheels of their wagons. It was the worst of their jornadas, an ordeal that lasted not for a day or two but for more than a week, relieved only by stops at a few scattered oases such as Ojo Caliente, where Gibson and others bathed in the warm waters and "found ourselves considerably refreshed."[11] Even in February, the men suffered terribly from thirst, often exhausting the contents of their canteens before they reached the next water hole. Once again, Padre Ramón Ortiz transcended the hostilities of the moment, as he had with Kendall in 1841, and comforted those in need. Hughes described the priest's charity on one particularly trying day in mid-February:

> It was now still twenty-one miles to water, over a heavy sandy road, and the teams had already become feeble and broken down. Ortiz, the benevolent curate, although a prisoner, and under a strict guard, generously gave many of the soldiers a draught of water, which he had provided to be brought from the Del Norte in a water vessel. For this and other instances of kindness towards the author, he now makes his grateful acknowledgments.[12]

Hughes credited a higher authority than Ortiz for delivering the men from a similar ordeal a few days later:

> The animals were dying of thirst and fatigue. Thirty-six yoke of oxen had been turned loose. Two wagons were abandoned amidst the sand hills. . . . The trains could never have proceeded ten miles farther. But the God who made the fountain leap from the rock to quench the thirst of the Israelitish army in the desert, now sent a cloud which hung upon the summits of the mountains to the right, and such a copious shower of rain descended that the mountain-torrents came rushing and foaming down from the rocks, and spread out upon the plains in such quantities that both the men and the animals were filled. Therefore, they staid all night at this place where the God-send had blessed them, and being much refreshed, next morning passed out of the desert.[13]

Hughes introduced a note of humor and self-parody here at the end, as if aware that any serious comparison of Doniphan's profane contingent to the army of the Lord might strike some readers as sacrilegious. In truth, few on the road to Chihuahua took their mission so piously that they saw themselves as instruments of God, or Manifest Destiny. The quirks of fate on their hard journey had largely disabused them of the notion that those who prevailed in this struggle were favored by God over those who perished. They had seen too many good men go to their graves along the way while others of little faith or virtue managed to survive. But while they may not have attributed every blessing or curse that befell them to the hand of Providence, they had ample reason to feel that they were being tested on the trail, and that those who came through the ordeal intact were somehow strengthened or enhanced.

One event in particular epitomized this transforming trial—a raging wildfire touched off by careless cooks after the regiment emerged at last from the desert and camped near the grassy banks of Lake Encinillas. William Richardson of the Chihuahua Rangers evoked the terror and beauty of the spectacle in his journal entry for February 25: "Coming out of my tent, a sight appeared of such magnificence as had never before met my eyes. It was an opposite mountain on fire, and the whole prairie, as far as the eye could reach, in flames. A strange glare tinged the clouds, and all surrounding objects, and presented a scene which was fearfully grand. It consumed nearly all the grass in the country 15 miles towards Chihuahua."[14] Hughes described the wildfire as a "more terrible foe than an 'army with banners.'"[15] Men wielded their sabres to clear breaks in the grass, he added, or fought fire with fire. And in the end, they emerged unscathed. This hot scrape, following weeks of brutal conditioning on the trail, seemed to temper the troops for the battle that lay ahead.

On February 27 they learned that Mexican troops were awaiting them in force along the Sacramento River, some fifteen miles north of Chihuahua. They faced that challenge with great composure for men who were relative newcomers to battle, but then they had confronted worse prospects than warfare en route to this showdown, including the dismal thought of succumbing to disease and being buried along the roadside without honor or distinction in a shallow grave that would not long withstand the assaults of wolves. Compared to the long, grinding errand that brought them here, the trials of battle were at least brief and promised rewards for those who survived and prevailed, as the volunteers felt sure they would. George Gibson described the mood of the men as they prepared to meet the enemy on February 28:

> In the morning all was bustle about camp, and there was much said about who would be missed from the ranks on the morrow. But there was not the least hesitancy, nor the slightest evidence that fears prevailed or that we should meet with defeat. On the contrary, all appeared to have the fullest confidence

of success and were glad the time had come when the question would be settled about our capture of Chihuahua. As we left camp, Major Clark's band struck
up *Yankee Doodle*, and the scene was animating, as we shall in a few hours be
engaged with the enemy. We continued our march as speedily as possible, to
arrive at the Sacramento in time to drive the enemy from their position, as we
are cut off from the water until this is done.[16]

To disguise his strength and protect his forces from a surprise attack, Doniphan
borrowed a tactic used by caravans on the Santa Fe Trail when hostilities
appeared likely. He arranged his vehicles in four parallel columns so that they
could quickly form a square for defensive purposes, if necessary. Between the
advancing columns, made up largely of merchant wagons, he placed his foot
soldiers and artillery. The formation was neatly emblematic of the campaign
as a whole—an undertaking inspired by trading ventures but stocked with all
the matériel needed to capture the market by force.

Although Doniphan was prepared for an assault by the enemy as he
advanced toward the Sacramento River, he had received thorough reports from
Kirker and other scouts and knew that his Mexican opponents—an estimated
three thousand men under General José Heredia—were well placed to wage
a defensive battle, with their artillery entrenched on high ground overlooking
the road to Chihuahua. If Doniphan's men held to that path, they would face
withering fire from several redoubts, or fortified batteries, east of the road and
another battery on a hilltop to the southwest. A Delaware scout who surveyed
the site for Doniphan later remarked that the position of the Mexicans
"reminded him of his first efforts to trap birds when he was a little boy; that
they had constructed their fortifications on the theory that the Americans
would walk into a trap set in plain view."[17]

Doniphan had no intention of falling into that trap. While still a few miles
from the Mexican position, he conferred with his aides and ordered his
advancing columns to leave the road and ascend an unoccupied plateau to the
west from which they could sweep down on the enemy's left flank. (Heredia's
line roughly paralleled the road from north to south, and his right flank, to
the north, was more heavily fortified than his left.) Gaining that plateau was
a chore for the wagon drivers, but it was a challenge of the sort they had overcome before on the trail and they reached their goal before the Mexicans
could respond to the maneuver. Determined to knock the invaders off their
newfound perch, Heredia abandoned his defensive posture and sent his cavalry charging up the slope in a breakneck assault reminiscent of Brazito. This
time, the Mexican horsemen would face an even hotter reception. As they
approached, Doniphan rolled out his concealed battery, commanded by

Major Clark, aided by Captain Richard H. Weightman. Frank Edwards of the Chihuahua Rangers described the ensuing action:

> As we form, the enemy's artillery opens upon us, and, at that instant, Weightman's clear voice is heard—"Form battery, action front, load and fire at will;" and our pieces ring out the death-knell of the enemy; now comes the friendly struggle between our gunners, who shall pour in the deadliest and quickest fire, and beautifully are those pieces served, mowing lane after lane through the solid columns of the Mexicans. In the centre of the battery, their horses bounding at every discharge, stand Clark and his officers. As the balls fly through the opposing ranks, and the shells tear their columns, shout after shout is heard from our men.
>
> Further to our right sits Colonel Doniphan on his beautiful chestnut charger, with his leg crossed over the saddle, steadily whittling a piece of wood, but with his eye glancing proudly over the ranks of his little band. As the cannonading becomes hotter, he quietly says: "Well, they're giving us ———— now, boys!" and passes coolly to the left of our position, untouched by the copper hail that pours around him.[18]

Doniphan's remark was probably sarcastic, for the efforts of the Mexican artillerists, firing from long range and using gunpowder that may have been defective, proved no match for Clark's deadly barrage. Doniphan's men could see the blue streaks of incoming enemy cannonballs, William Richardson noted, and many literally dodged those missiles:

> When a flash would be seen from the enemy's battery, you could hear the soldiers cry out—"watch the ball boys!—here comes a ball boys," and they invariably avoided them, or the slaughter must have been very great. I saw a ball coming in the direction where I was, when immediately falling off my mule, it passed just over my saddle without injury.[19]

The charging Mexicans, for their part, had no hope of dodging the missiles that exploded in their midst. Marcellus Edwards, who was up front with Captain Reid's company of mounted infantry, described the deadly effect of Clark's first salvos:

> A thick flame and smoke arose from the muzzle. A glistening bomb whistled through the air, and leaving only a faint glimmer behind, exploded in the enemy's ranks. This was followed by another and another, until the whole six had fired. Our ranks were loud with cheers. The Mexican ranks were different; there death and the greatest consternation prevailed. They had not awaited the result of the whole round before they scampered off pell-mell toward their

"Battle of Sacramento, Feb. 28th 1847, Terrific Charge of the Mexican Lancers," Currier & Ives. Courtesy Library of Congress, Prints and Photographs Division, LC-USZ62-5222.

camp. Our first shot, as I have been told, killed or wounded seventeen men and seven horses.[20]

The battle was far from over, but the rout of the Mexican cavalry set the tone for what followed. As George Gibson put it, that opening barrage "produced a panic from which they never recovered."[21] After Clark's gunners pounded the entrenchments in the distance for a while, Doniphan capitalized on the confusion instilled in the Mexicans by their initial setback and attacked with everything he had, sending his foot soldiers forward on either flank while his artillery advanced in the center, supported by cavalry. Exposing the battery in this way was risky, but Doniphan was betting that the closer his gunners got to the enemy, the sooner the battle would be over. And his bet paid off. As William Richardson related, Clark's "flying artillery" pushed forward relentlessly, discharging five volleys a minute that raked "the enemy's redoubts and cut roads through their lines."[22] The bold maneuver demonstrated once again that Doniphan, while possessed of little military training, had a gambler's knack for recognizing the strength of his hand—in this case, the superiority of his gunners and their ordnance—and for bidding on that hand unreservedly until he cleaned out the opposition.

In the end, Doniphan's troops stormed the Mexican redoubts on foot and on horseback, ousting at sabre point defenders so shaken by the terrible barrage that, despite their strong position, they inflicted fewer than a dozen casualties on their foes. The only American to die on the field that day was Samuel Owens, commander of the traders' battalion. Most of the men in his unit spent the battle minding the wagons behind the lines, where the vehicles would serve as a bulwark of last resort if the Mexicans gained the upper hand. But Owens decided unaccountably to join in a charge against a Mexican battery, reportedly launched on a dare by James Kirker and a few other irregulars on horseback. Frank Edwards evoked the scene: "Dashing past us goes Major Owens, waving his hand in an exulting manner, and shouting out, 'Give it to them, boys! they can't withstand us'—and away he goes: falling, in two minutes a corpse, struck in the forehead by a grape-shot while storming the redoubts, and being so close to the gun that the fire actually burns his clothes."[23] Colonel Doniphan, in a letter to a friend, attributed Owens's death to "excessive bravery, or rather rashness," adding that he "rode up to the redoubt, filled with armed men, and continued to fire his pistols into it until himself and horse fell, pierced with balls, upon its very brink."[24]

There was more than a little irony to Owens's fate, for he had dealt cordially with Mexicans over the years and was sympathetic to Catholicism. Perhaps, as some of his acquaintances believed, problems back home had rendered him careless of his life. Or perhaps he was simply caught up in the heat of the battle—an enterprise that sometimes defied calculation, inspiring otherwise level-headed men to cast aside thoughts of profit or loss and act with heed-less abandon.

A few other Americans wounded during the battle died afterward, but the surprisingly light toll only heightened the elation of the victors as they gathered up the spoils left on the field. Among the fruits of victory for the hungry troops, Frank Edwards reported, were nine wagonloads of hardbread, four loads of dried meat, and an untold quantity of "sweetened flour for mak-ing atole, besides over seven hundred thousand cigaritos, several thousand head of cattle, and ten *acres* of sheep."[25] But here even more than at Brazito, the winners had to weigh their gains against the horrific price exacted from the Mexicans, including three hundred dead, by Doniphan's estimate, and at least as many wounded, many of them victims of cannon fire. The actual toll may have been less than Doniphan reckoned, but other witnesses agreed that the Mexicans suffered terribly. Gibson, for one, tallied up the earnings on one side and the dreadful losses on the other and concluded that war was not a business that anyone of conscience or good sense could promote as a way of settling accounts:

> The ten pieces of artillery which we took [and] the wagons of ammunition and provisions were all brought into camp, and there was but little sleep that night; the very fact that we had lost but two men and several badly wounded in achieving the victory being alone sufficient to create a hilarity which but seldom exists. Our transportation is greatly added to, and it takes all the extra animals we have, as well as the captured ones, to get the wagons and artillery to the city. Every man is loaded down with spoil, and the greatest difficulty is to get along with the plunder of all kinds. Many of the prisoners died, and the spectacle next morning was such that no man could help but feel that war was an evil of the worst kind and one which should be avoided if possi-ble. Had politicians who spent so carelessly in these matters been able to look upon it they would have used more precaution in their acts, and many a pri-vate and public calamity would have been averted which they brought on. Some were awfully mangled by our artillery.[26]

This sober assessment came close to summing up the entire campaign, for Sacramento was the last battle Doniphan's men fought and stood as both their proudest accomplishment and as a poignant reminder of the profitlessness of such exchanges when the claims of both parties were considered.

The volunteers still had one more triumph ahead of them, however, their grand entry on March 2 into Chihuahua, the largest and finest town they had witnessed west of St. Louis. The squat adobe houses on the outskirts were less than inspiring, Frank Edwards wrote:

> But a course which took us past the unfinished Jesuit's College, the plaza and fine cathedral, and through nicely paved streets to the Alameda or public walk, soon showed us that we had got into a city far superior to any place we had before entered. Most of the houses had white stone fronts; while the paved streets and good side walks made it somewhat home like, for we had seen no pavement before since leaving Missouri.
>
> We were quartered at the Plaza de Toros or Bull Ring. This is a fine amphitheatre, and being government property, it is built in the best manner, with several rows of white stone seats all around, and a covered gallery above and at the back of them.[27]

Chihuahua looked far better to the troops than they did to the Chihuahuans. James Webb, who had been detained for a while in town after arriving there with merchant Albert Speyer the previous September, described the panic that gripped many in Chihuahua when they learned of the outcome at Sacramento and the approach of the Americans:

> The plaza was filled with women and children (but few men) with bundles of clothes, blankets, etc., upon their backs, and those who could raise a donkey or any other animal capable of bearing the least burden, had them packed. And all were excitedly discussing what they should do or where they should go to escape violence, which the priests had told them they must expect from our soldiers.[28]

Even some of the American merchants who had remained in town found the sight of their countrymen-in-arms alarming, according to Frederick Wislizenus, who had traveled with Webb and Speyer. Wislizenus hailed the arrival of the troops, while conceding that their appearance left something to be desired:

> But, really, what a ragged set of men those brave Missouri boys were! There was not one among them in complete uniform, and not two in the whole regiment dressed alike: each one had consulted either his own fancy or necessity, in arranging the remnants of former comfort, to produce a half decent appearance. Some of the resident Americans in Chihuahua, I understood, when after the battle the first American companies entered the town and halted on the Plaza, were so thunderstruck by the savage exterior of their own countrymen, that they ran back to their houses to ascertain first to what tribe or nation they belonged. But, notwithstanding their raggedness, there was some peculiar expression in their eye, meaning that they had

seen Brazito and Sacramento, and that Mexicans could not frighten them even by ten-fold numbers.[29]

George Gibson confirmed that the troops felt superior to any challenge, noting that when they entered Chihuahua "with its churches and aqueduct and *alameda*, all were struck with astonishment that a mere handful of men should be suffered to capture such a city, and we began to think that against this people nothing was impossible."[30] That cocky attitude did not sit well with the proud Chihuahuans, who were closer to Mexico City geographically and temperamentally than were the residents of El Paso or Santa Fe and who proved less obliging to the occupiers. Friends of Samuel Owens saw to it that he was accorded a gracious funeral service in the cathedral, however, presided over by local priests.

Doniphan tried to avoid trouble with the locals by quartering his forces in the bull ring and other sites apart from the residential areas and by discouraging fraternization. As had happened before, however, the inactivity of the troops combined with ready access to aguardiente and other temptations to produce unruliness in the ranks. Susan Magoffin and her husband, trailing safely behind Doniphan's force, reached Chihuahua on April 4, and she found the place much the worse for wear after a month of occupation. "Instead of seeing it in its original beauty as I thought to have done twelve months since," she complained, "I saw it filled with Missouri volunteers who though good to fight are not careful at all how much they soil the property of a friend much less an enemy."[31] That observation, reflecting the perspective of one used to dealing peacefully with Mexicans and capable of seeing things as they did, was echoed by the man who had served as Susan Magoffin's literary guide to Mexico—Josiah Gregg, who arrived in Chihuahua in mid-April, after ending his unhappy stint as an interpreter for General Wool. Gregg was not pleased to find American troops "drinking and carousing 'with a perfect vengeance'" in the gracious streets of Chihuahua. He concluded that these "Missourians are certainly a brave and gallant, but nevertheless rather ungovernable and disorderly set of fellows."[32]

Doniphan was keenly aware of the risks of allowing such a force to remain in town much longer. He still faced the nagging problem of financing the regiment's purchases, for Mexican authorities had emptied the mint in Chihuahua before abandoning the city. Furthermore, he recognized that his men might yet encounter serious military opposition if they remained out of touch with other American forces until their terms of enlistment expired on June 1. (Americans engaged elsewhere in Mexico met with much sterner tests from opposing troops than the Missourians faced at Brazito or Sacramento.) Some

Ciudad Chihuahua, ca. 1850. Courtesy Museum of New Mexico, negative no. 171105.

officers under Doniphan, notably Major Gilpin, urged him to delve deeper into enemy territory and try for the ultimate prize—Mexico City. The colonel did consent to lead more than half his regiment southward in early April to keep the men busy and probe for opposition, but he promptly retraced his steps when he received a report that he might soon be challenged by a force of five thousand Mexican troops. Unlike some gamblers on the campaign trail, he knew better than to press his luck.

Doniphan's intention was to vacate Chihuahua as soon as he received orders to link up with the elusive General Wool, who was camped with his forces at Saltillo, several hundred miles off to the southeast, where they had supported General Zachary Taylor in a crucial victory over Mexican forces at Buena Vista in February. Doniphan had sent a dispatch to Wool in late March, making it clear that he had no desire to remain in Chihuahua simply to protect the interests of American merchants, who had ended their brief stint as soldiers and resumed their preferred trade. As Doniphan put it:

> My position here is exceedingly embarrassing. In the first place, most of the men under my command have been in service since the 1st of June, have never received one cent of pay. Their marches have been hard, especially in the Navajo country, and no forage; so that they are literally without horses, clothes, or money, having nothing but arms and a disposition to use them. They are all volunteers, officers and men, and although ready for any hardships or danger, are wholly unfit to garrison a town or city. "It is confusion worse confounded." Having performed a march of more than two thousand miles, and their term of service rapidly expiring, they are restless to join the army under your command. Still we cannot leave this point safely for some days—the American merchants here oppose it violently, and have several hundred thousand dollars at stake. . . . I am anxious and willing to protect the merchants as far as practicable; but I protest against remaining here as a mere wagon-guard, to garrison a city with troops wholly unfitted for it, and who will soon be wholly ruined by improper indulgences.[33]

This dispatch went to the core of the problem that had haunted Kearny, Doniphan, and other officers in the Army of the West since the campaign began. Warfare by its nature was a stern business that could not be conducted easily or efficiently by the same code that governed trade or other peaceful forms of exchange. Yet this campaign, more than most, was hemmed in by economic and diplomatic constraints, including the endless struggle by officers short on cash to feed and equip the men without inflaming the Mexican populace, the persistent demands from American traders for protection and access to Mexican markets, and directives from on high that impelled commanders to act as if they were engaged in a friendly takeover rather a conquest.

Doniphan had been wrestling with these often-conflicting demands for the better part of a year, and by the spring of 1847 he was fed up. When he received the reply he hoped for on April 23, ordering the regiment to Saltillo, he decamped with a speed that left some American traders in town feeling betrayed and abandoned. They had been trying to negotiate a deal with Mexican authorities that would have allowed them to remain safely in the city, but now many of them chose to leave with Doniphan rather than trust in Mexican assurances. William Glasgow, for one, hastily packed up a load of goods and followed the army. He found that he could sell none of his wares on the road to Saltillo and soon returned to take his chances in Chihuahua, where he wrote bitterly that "the only obligations we are under to anyone are to the Mexicans and not our own countrymen, who have in this matter treated us all most shamefully."[34] He never forgave Doniphan or his subordinate, Lieutenant Colonel David Mitchell, who had strongly opposed any further concessions to the traders' demands for protection. The attitude toward Mitchell among those foreigners remaining in Chihuahua was one of "universal contempt," claimed Glasgow, who later dismissed Doniphan's coup at Sacramento by insisting that the colonel deserved no more credit for the victory than "my old mule."[35]

The press and public back home were much kinder to Doniphan when he brought his regiment back to the States by ship from a port on Mexico's Gulf Coast in June of 1847. He was hailed as a homespun military hero and likened to Xenophon, an Athenian commander who had saved his forces from annihilation in 401 B.C. by leading them on a thousand-mile odyssey from Babylon to the Black Sea. The label stuck, perhaps because Athenians were renowned as citizen soldiers, a role the Missourians relished. Largely overlooked was the fact that Xenophon and his men had been mercenaries in the service of their former enemies the Persians. No one could accuse Doniphan of being a mercenary, but his obligations and accomplishments were far more complex and ambiguous than most of those who lionized him realized. Skeptics then and later would argue that his descent to Chihuahua had contributed little or nothing to the war effort, pointing out that General Taylor won the pivotal battle at Buena Vista shortly before Doniphan's victory at Sacramento. Others would contend that the drive to Chihuahua was crucial in securing the fragile hold of American forces on New Mexico and California and dealt a serious blow to the morale of the Mexicans at a time they could least afford it.

Doniphan was not running a conventional military campaign, however, and his achievement cannot be summed up in strictly military terms. From the beginning, his role resembled that of captain of a caravan in that his concerns were as much economic and diplomatic as they were military. To be sure, he welcomed a fight when the opportunity arose and showed a willingness to take big gambles that vied with his more cautious instincts—a contradiction evident in Charles Bent, Sam Owens, and other leaders of the Santa Fe trade, whose calculating disposition sometimes gave way to sheer bravado. Like his civilian predecessors who led parties safely though hostile country along the Santa Fe and Chihuahua Trails, however, Doniphan weighed the risks he took against the potential rewards to be gained and spent far more energy conserving his limited resources and seeking ways of appeasing those in occupied territory than he did maneuvering for battle. In the end, he proved better at calculating the costs and benefits of prolonging his campaign than did some of the traders in Chihuahua, who would have had the troops remain there at the risk of provoking unrest or inviting a Mexican counterattack.

Such restraint enabled Doniphan to see his men through to their goal and allowed the vast majority of those under his command who did not succumb to disease to celebrate heartening homecomings of the sort William Richardson described gratefully when he returned in July to his mother in Maryland, whom he had last seen twelve months before he enlisted in Missouri: "Let no brave soldier say he cannot shed tears of joy, when clasped in the arms of his aged widow mother, after an absence of nearly two years, in which he has encountered the perils of both land and sea—traveling nearly 6000 miles, 2,200 being through the heart of an enemy's country, and witnessing death in every shape and feature."[36] Such reunions were worth more to the troops than anything they claimed in battle from Mexicans. Doniphan's summary accomplishment was to lead them away from the fleeting fruits of conquest, which began to spoil almost as soon as they were grasped, to those lasting rewards at journey's end.

Doniphan's reluctance to expose his men to any further risks once they occupied Chihuahua can be contrasted to the actions of Sterling Price, who, after crushing the revolt at Taos in 1847 and rising to the rank of brigadier general, launched his own descent on Chihuahua early the following year. By the time he left El Paso with his troops in February 1848, he knew that there was no Mexican force to the south poised to attack American-occupied New Mexico—the only condition on which he was authorized to proceed— and yet he went ahead with his campaign, entering the city of Chihuahua unopposed in early March. The commander of Mexican forces in the area, Governor Angel Trias, assured Price that the war was over. (On February 2, negotiators had signed the Treaty of Guadalupe Hidalgo, which formally resolved the conflict and ceded New Mexico and Alta California to the United States.) Price declined to accept Trias at his word, however, and proceeded to besiege and attack his opponent's forces at Santa Cruz de Rosales, south of Chihuahua. Price claimed victory there after a brutal exchange that left more than two hundred Mexicans dead, a number of whom were killed while attempting to surrender. Four Americans lost their lives and nineteen were wounded— or roughly the same number of casualties sustained by Doniphan in two battles that may have had some bearing on the outcome of the conflict and at least had the virtue of being fought while the two sides were still officially at odds.

Price defended his actions by assuring his superiors in Washington that taking and holding Chihuahua was regarded by American citizens there as a matter of the "utmost importance," affecting "their interests to a great extent."[37] But Price's hollow victory at Santa Cruz de Rosales did nothing to improve the strained relations in Chihuahua between American traders and their Mexican clients. Even normally prudent merchants like William Glasgow's older brother, Edward, who remarked after witnessing the carnage at Santa Cruz that "war is an ugly business"[38] and had long been skeptical that fighting would settle much of anything, could not help exulting over the American victory there. As he wrote in a letter home: "The siege continued several days until the American artillery arrived when the ball opened and the Mexicans had to dance the same tune that they have practised at all other fandangoes of the kind."[39]

Glasgow's comparison of the battle to a fandango was grimly appropriate, for those dances sometimes degenerated into violent exchanges between Americans and Mexicans. George Ruxton, in *Life in the Far West*, portrayed one such clash in which mountain men brawled with Mexicans at a fandango in Taos and got the better of them, "leaving the floor strewed with wounded, many most dangerously." Afterward, the victorious Americans offered reparations of sorts by "promising to give sundry dollars to the friends of two of the Mexicans, who died during the night of their wounds, and to pay for a certain amount of masses to be sung for the repose of their souls in purgatory."[40] Ruxton, who offered this tale to the public in serialized form in 1848, made light of such mayhem, trusting that readers in these contentious times would find the killing of Mexicans amusing.

Among the casualties of this war was the measure of respect that accommodating Anglos like Edward Glasgow had paid some if not all Mexicans in writing before the conflict began. (The disparaging term "greaser," for example, seldom encountered in accounts of the Santa Fe or Chihuahua Trails before 1846, became all too common in American diaries and letters by 1848.) Mexico had been defeated, and yet Edward Glasgow, not unlike Sterling Price, maintained a hostile stance, as reflected in this bleak passage, sadly reminiscent of Charles Bent's blanket dismissal of the Mexican people two years earlier, before the war began, when he railed that the "Mexican caracter is made up of stupidity, Obstanacy, Ignorance duplicity and vanity." As Edward Glasgow put it: "I am heartily tired of the whole country. the people are cowardly in the extreme and an old adage says that without courage there can be no truth and without truth there can be no other virtue. The Mexicans have perhaps fewer redeeming traits of character than any other nation; not excepting the Comanches nor the wild Arabs."[41] This tendency to malign Mexicans and their assets, aggravated by the tensions of war, obscured the lessons learned by visitors in better days. Until the spirit of accommodation reasserted itself, Americans would derive little satisfaction from their dealings with those on either side of the artificial border they imposed here—exchanges that could never be truly fulfilling so long as one party demeaned what the other had to offer.

22

Costs and Consequences

For some Americans who followed the road to New Mexico in 1846 in pursuit of profit, glory, or sheer excitement, the war was over in a matter of months. Most of the men in Doniphan's regiment were homeward bound and counting their blessings by the time their one-year enlistments expired in June 1847. But others caught up in this sprawling conflict as soldiers or civilians still had far to travel before they could tally their gains and losses and close the books on their ventures. Three who ranked among the most perceptive witnesses of this American *entrada*—George Gibson, Lewis Garrard, and Susan Magoffin—remained in contested territory as Doniphan's regiment headed home, and their observations reveal much about the costs and consequences of this war.

In early April 1847, a month after entering Chihuahua, Lieutenant Gibson complied with orders to return to New Mexico and joined a group of thirty traders bound for Santa Fe. Gibson did not specify why his superior officer, Lieutenant Colonel Mitchell, reassigned him to New Mexico, but he welcomed the opportunity. He remained a journalist at heart, and he likely sensed that the story of Doniphan's regiment was coming to an end, whereas Santa Fe still had much to offer in the way of drama and intrigue. Departing on April 4, he reckoned that he had nearly fifteen hundred miles to cover from Chihuahua to Santa Fe and from there to Independence when his duty in New Mexico was done, yet he and his traveling companions "all were in the finest spirits when we began to retrace our steps over the long and tedious road between here and our friends in the states."[1]

Their mood turned somber the following day when they passed the battlefield at Sacramento, where signs of the recent carnage were woefully apparent. "The stench from the dead carcasses both of men and animals made our stay much shorter than it would have been," Gibson wrote, "nor was the spectacle of a kind calculated to kindle our antipathys or resentments, for the skeletons of our Enemies were strewed over the ground, having been dragged out of their graves by the wolves, great numbers of which we saw even in the day time."[2] Farther along in the journey, he saw evidence of renewal, noting that in the "Burnt District," ravaged by the wildfire sparked by Doniphan's men in February, fresh grass was already sprouting up, affording welcome nourishment for the hungry animals in his party. But the corrosive effect of war on relations between the two sides would take longer to heal. Reaching El Paso in mid-April, Gibson found the townspeople "cold and reserved" and responded in kind, looking with suspicion upon those who had shown him hospitality on the way south:

> I saw Mr. Jacques at whose Casa I boarded awhile [on the way south] and he embraced me warmly and manifested a personal friendship which I returned. But like all Mexicans he is tricky and I watched him closely without being able to discover anything. The Prefect [Sebastián Bermúdez] swindled me in some wine I bought to take home as a sample of the country, and when the highest Civil officer can do such a thing it is time to keep an eye upon every one.[3]

The next day, Gibson relented somewhat when another Mexican he knew from his earlier stay in El Paso made a characteristically magnanimous gesture, arriving in camp "loaded down with presents of vino, bread, grapes, onion seed etc which he had taken the trouble to bring 7 or 8 miles." Gibson returned the favor with gifts of sugar and tobacco, and the two parted "as good friends as ever."[4] Overall, however, Gibson's fund of tolerance for the locals had been depleted by the campaign. A day later, he wrote mockingly of an incident on the road involving "our old friend and acquaintance Don Ponce," who regained custody of two fugitive "greaser women he claimed as his servants."[5] And Gibson referred more than once to the poor people he met with in small New Mexican towns on the way north as "ignorant" and "dirty."[6]

Although Gibson and his fellow volunteers had less cause than Mexicans did to feel put-upon, the campaign had in fact been far costlier for the intruding Americans than their relatively light casualty figures in battle might indicate. At Sacramento, Gibson had confronted the fearful price paid by the losers, but on reaching Santa Fe in early May he was shocked and saddened by the costs of victory for his own side when he visited the freshly constructed Fort Marcy and counted three hundred "new made graves" in the cemetery there, most of them bearing the remains of soldiers cut down by disease and other natural hazards associated with occupying a remote and impoverished land: "Various causes brought the men to an untimely end. Some from dissipation. Some from Exposure. Some the want of attention. Some broken down constitutions. Some from fever and some from the effects of colds. The health of the army here though I found good at this time, the weak and sickly having pretty much all died off. Measles was also a fruitful disease in filling up the ground."[7]

What had been gained by exposing young men brimming with health and promise to such perils? Gibson continued to believe that this costly takeover was worthwhile, that it would benefit New Mexico as well the nation, and he set out to advance that proposition after his term of enlistment expired that summer as editor of the bilingual *Santa Fe Republican*. Although some of the assurances offered the local populace concerning American rule in that weekly were wildly optimistic, notably the promise in the inaugural edition in September that the "Savage Indians" plundering the country would "speedily be subdued by the vigor of our arms,"[8] Gibson was no mere apologist for the forces of occupation. "The People of New Mexico should have a Government of some kind which they can see and feel and understand, either military or civil," he declared in his third issue. "If the military is the only authority they should know it; if they have a Territorial Government all of the acts of which are to be observed and respected let them know it."[9]

Since the uprising in January, the civil government instituted by Kearny had come under stricter military control, with the commanding officer exercising veto power over the judicial system, the executive branch (led by Governor Donaciano Vigil, Charles Bent's successor), and the legislative assembly that would soon convene in Santa Fe. Gibson questioned this interference in a democratic process hurriedly set in motion to prove America's good intentions: "Why call together a legislative body, if its acts may be annulled and made void by the will or caprice of a commanding officer? Why frame laws, if the order of a commanding officer is paramount? Why have judges and courts if they can only act at the pleasure of the military authorities?"[10]

This tenuous civil government was further diminished in authority not long after the New Mexico legislature met for its first session in December 1847 when the commanding officer, Sterling Price, abolished the offices of U.S. district attorney and U.S. marshal and assumed full responsibility for law and order in New Mexico. At the time, the army still harbored genuine concerns about maintaining order in a territory recently convulsed by insurrection. But New Mexico would remain effectively under military rule for more than two years after the war ended, not because of any serious threat of a renewed uprising there but because of sharp quarrels within the American camp as to what to make of this acquisition. Texans, buoyed by victory in their grudge match with Mexico, promptly renewed their old claim to Santa Fe and everything else in the conquered territory east of the Rio Grande—a bid vehemently opposed not just by New Mexicans but by Americans who feared the extension of slavery to the Southwest. In the end, Congress would avert conflict along the Rio Grande by paying Texas to drop its claim and by admitting New Mexico as a territory, thus postponing the politically explosive question of its status as a free or slave state. This measure formed part of the Compromise of 1850, aimed at cooling sectional tensions aroused by the territorial gains of the Mexican War. But in the wake of that war, the deals and compromises by which Americans had long finessed their differences were no longer as durable or dependable as before. Many New Mexicans who had recently endured the trauma of conquest would live to see their territory fought over again during the American Civil War—this time by rival contingents of Confederates from Texas and Unionists from near and far.

Much of this remained well beyond the horizon when George Gibson ended his brief term as editor of the *Santa Fe Republican* in December 1847. He left unexplained his departure from that post. Perhaps he simply needed a break—his editorial stints seldom lasted long—or perhaps he felt disheartened by recent events in Santa Fe and no longer cared to play the part of interpreter for the American cause there. He had seen enough, surely, to recognize that the war effort to which he contributed had left many things unsettled, issues that went beyond the form of New Mexico's government or the question of slavery there to matters of economic and cultural control that would not easily be worked out in a society of mixed Spanish and Indian heritage dominated by an Anglo-American minority. As an admirer of that great compromiser, Henry Clay, Gibson may well have been dismayed to witness the convulsive effect on America's political landscape of developments in which he had some personal interest—including the nation's forceful westward expansion and the perpetuation of slavery. (He evidently brought two slaves with him on the campaign, for he made passing reference in his journal to the presence of "our servant, Walter" and "my servant Evans.")[11] A pattern of confrontation was developing here in New Mexico and elsewhere along the American frontier that would not eliminate peaceful give-and-take between rival parties but would render the bargains they reached more precarious.

Just how all this affected Gibson would remain something of a mystery. For a man much given to recording his thoughts in writing, he seemed strangely reluctant to share with posterity his reflections on this winter of discontent in Santa Fe. He made no entry in his journal from the time he returned there and began serving as editor of the *Santa Fe Republican* until he departed town for good on April 28, 1848, with a small party of Americans heading back to Missouri. "Against all prognostications and after saluting our friends with a parting benediction we left Santa Fe after a two years residence in Mexico," he wrote, "heartily glad that our faces were once more turned homewards and our backs to the rough adobie walls of the Country."[12]

A year or so before Gibson headed home, Lewis Garrard left Taos with a party of mountain men and made his way slowly back through Raton Pass to Bent's Fort and on to Missouri. Having arrived in New Mexico too late to witness any of the recent hostilities there other than the trial and execution of accused rebels, young Garrard was hoping for some excitement on the way home, and he would not be disappointed. Never before in the history of the Santa Fe Trail—not even in 1829, when a large force of Indians battled the first U.S. Army troops to escort traders—had there been such sharp and persistent fighting as erupted between tribal war parties and military and civilian wagon trains in late 1846 and continued into 1847. Garrard, who had dealt amicably with Plains Indians on his way west, would be caught up now in this emerging struggle between whites and Indians for control of the campsites, waterways, and hunting grounds traversed by the trail, a war that would rage on and off for the next quarter century and end with the subjugation and confinement of tribes Garrard once envied for their "free and happy life."

The early stages of Garrard's return journey offered little hint of what lay ahead. His wartime experiences had hardened him somewhat in his attitudes, leading him to remark of a rancher he encountered shortly after leaving Taos: "He was a good Mexican, if any of the nation deserve that prefixing adjective."[13] But such callousness was a kind of affectation for the susceptible Garrard, who took on some of the biases of his older traveling companions as if those prejudices were marks of maturity. All the while, he remained at heart a romantic and idealist whose fondest memories of the trail were of quiet moments of communion and contemplation, as when he and others in his party tracked a herd of deer up a mountain slope in Raton Pass on their return journey and found themselves disarmed by the beauty of the scene. "In silence we enjoyed the delectable picture of peace and innocence," he recalled, "unwilling to fright the graceful herds with deadly rifle, or even with rude, but harmless, shout."[14]

The transforming effect of Raton Pass faded as they descended into the parched terrain northeast of the mountains and encountered fresh signs of conflict in the form of a westbound company of mounted volunteers from Missouri, whose demeanor left Garrard distinctly unimpressed: "Volunteer-like,

Wagon ruts on Santa Fe Trail near Fort Union, New Mexico. Courtesy Museum of New Mexico, negative no. 12845.

they were in the rear, at the side, and in advance of their commander; they disregarding military deference, he military control. For a mile and a half, others were strung along the trace, in irregular squads, riding, sauntering carelessly, some without arms, and a few with muskets, beating the sage brushes for hares."[15] Such careless habits could get men killed at a time when tribal war parties aroused by the recent surge in military traffic were assailing vulnerable contingents like this one with a vengeance. The real danger lay not in this barren country below the mountains, however, but in the grasslands to the east, where hunter-warriors dependent on the bison that ranged there sorely resented the intrusions of soldiers and teamsters. Garrard and his party soon entered that contested territory, after stopping at Bent's Fort and nearby encampments and linking up with other eastbound travelers for protection. Garrard found himself reunited in the process with such old friends from the fort as mountain man John Simpson Smith—accompanied by his Cheyenne wife and their son—and made some new acquaintances as well, notably George Ruxton, the wide-ranging author and sportsman who did not hesitate to go stalking after buffalo at the risk of being targeted himself by Indians intent on protecting their hunting grounds.

Garrard aptly summarized tribal resentments when he wrote that Comanches and others along the trail claimed "the region over which we were journeying as their own, to be preserved inviolate from the track-leaving, wood-wasting, and game-scaring whiteman."[16] The immediate problem was not that bison were scarce, although Cheyennes and Arapahos around Bent's Fort had complained recently of poor hunting and such complaints would multiply in years to come. The more pressing concern for tribes reliant on buffalo for food and shelter was that even plentiful herds could be spooked and scattered by white hunters who discharged their firearms with raucous abandon and left carnage in their wake. Aside from scaring away game, strangers traversing this region in large parties as they had of late were gradually depleting the timber available for campfires in cottonwood groves along the Arkansas and lesser streams—a vital resource for Plains Indians, who needed the extra heat that logs provided in winter and the shade that the trees offered in summer. (East of Bent's Fort, Garrard and company met with John Smith and kindred Cheyennes ensconced in tepees pitched near one such wooded spot much favored by travelers, known as Pretty Encampment, "the loveliest on the river," Garrard wrote, "with its glossy-leaved cottonwoods.")[17] In earlier years, most attacks on travelers along the trail had been aimed at stealing animals or otherwise making intruders pay for access to Indian country. Such raids would continue, but increasingly Indians here would be reduced to fighting not for profit or advantage but for the preservation of their resources and their way of life.

Nothing symbolized the threat to tribal dominion over the plains more powerfully than the forts the U.S. Army was just beginning to erect along western pathways. Indians were quick to distinguish between those military bastions, to which they were seldom admitted, and trading centers like Bent's Fort, which readily accommodated tribal groups in the vicinity. As it happened, the army was in the process of building its first outpost along the Santa Fe Trail, Fort Mann, when Garrard arrived there with his party in May 1847. Intended as a repair station for wagons and a refuge for travelers at risk of attack, the fort was erected on the north bank of the Arkansas near one of the crossings that marked the convergence of the Cimarron Route with the Mountain Route. The fact that this was prime buffalo country, hotly contested by tribes dependent on that animal, made the fort's position all the more precarious. For an insatiably curious adventurer like Garrard, who was "out to see the elephant" and had yet to witness that elusive beast in its entirety, a sojourn at vulnerable Fort Mann promised to bring him as close as he might ever get to his quarry without being trampled. He volunteered to stay on and help complete the outpost with a dozen or so other civilian hirelings under the direction of John

Smith, who took charge after the departure of the fort's original commander, Captain Daniel P. Mann.[18]

Recent attacks by Comanches on those in and around the fort had been aimed at depriving the inmates of their lives as well as their livestock. One man had been killed and scalped while out fishing, and a number of oxen and mules had been run off. Garrard and his companions ran the risk of coming under assault every time they went outside the stockade to graze their remaining animals or gather mud by the riverside to mold into adobe bricks for construction. Their morale was not improved by the decision of their nervous captain, Smith, to abandon his post after little more than a week and head east with a wagon train belonging to Bent, St. Vrain & Co. As Garrard explained:

> Smith, who had been showing, in private conversation with me, a fear of losing his hair, gave notice of leaving with this train, which stopped while he collected his possibles. While on guard together, he often told me the utter folly, the downright madness, of staying in the fort at the mercy of the Indians, and that his pay would be nothing in comparison to the loss of his animals, and the risk of his life.[19]

After Smith's departure, the prospects for the fort's inmates seemed bleaker than ever. In late May, a band of Arapahos made up of men, women, and children approached the fort and pitched their tepees by the river. The sight of those women and children—and the fact that these were Arapahos and not dreaded Comanches or Pawnees—reassured Garrard. He still hankered for an Indian fight in some portion of his being, but the better part of him recalled the pleasures of mingling amicably with Cheyennes around Bent's Fort and felt drawn to the Arapahos in spirit as they erected their village within sight of the fort:

> Where, a short while before, lay a bare spot of turf, was now the site of eighty lodges, nearly three hundred human beings, and eleven hundred horses capering, rolling, and cropping the sweet bottom grass. The girls, from twelve years up to womanhood, waded the river for fuel; some crossing, a few returning laden with sticks, others carrying water, and all laughing, talking, and splashing. Boys played their favorite game of arrows, or, astride of ponies, ran races over the smooth prairie. This commingled scene of comfort, youth, and hilarity, brought back, with yearnings for a repetition, last winter's experience.[20]

For a while, it seemed that these hopes might be realized. Garrard and a companion visited the village, and the two sides swapped goods. But here as in

New Mexico, lasting accommodations proved hard to come by in this new era of confrontation. The crew in the fort were soon informed that these Arapahos were in league with hostile Comanches and had attacked a westbound traders' caravan a few days earlier. The Arapahos decamped before those traders reached Fort Mann and pitched their tepees at what they deemed a safer distance, a half mile or so away. The traders, for their part, were eager to avenge the recent assault and implored those manning the fort to train their cannon on the distant Arapahos and "rake the village."[21] Garrard and others fended off that rash request, pointing out that the "indiscriminate slaughter of women and children" would subject the fort's tiny garrison to venomous retribution. Advised to fight their own battles, the traders chose not to challenge the Arapahos and left for Santa Fe without causing any further trouble. Nonetheless, the incident demonstrated the increasing tendency of parties who had once settled their differences on the trail largely through exchanges of gifts or courtesies to deal in threats and reprisals.

On June 15, Garrard observed his eighteenth birthday at Fort Mann. He saw little to celebrate that morning. Having recently learned that life in the wild West could sometimes be more confining than liberating, he concluded that the "comforts of civilization will be better appreciated when regained."[22] He may have reckoned by now that he had seen the elephant, which meant encountering more in the way of an adventure than one bargained for. Late that afternoon, however, he received an unexpected reprieve when Colonel William H. Russell arrived with an eastbound government wagon train. Colonel Russell, returning from duty in California, was an old college friend of Garrard's father and was shocked to find young Lewis and others with little or no military training in such a precarious position. He prevailed on Garrard to return with him to Missouri. As it turned out, that journey with Russell and the wagon train was not without its own hazards in the form of sharp clashes with Comanches. But Garrard came through unscathed, which was more than could be said for his former bunkmates at Fort Mann. On June 19, a few days after he departed, the outpost came under withering attack by some four hundred Comanches, who killed three of the fort's occupants and lost fifteen men of their own in one of the deadliest exchanges to date between Indians and American forces along the Santa Fe Trail. The dazed survivors soon abandoned the fort, which would later be reoccupied by the army. Garrard did not dwell on that attack in his book. Perhaps he found the fate of those he left behind too painful a matter to address.

By early July, Garrard was back in Missouri, dining in the boomtown of Westport with other men of similarly savage appearance and appetites, all of them freshly returned from the far reaches of the trail and ill at ease with the implements of civilization. "Our hands unconsciously found their way to the scalpknife at the waistband," Garrard wrote of that homecoming supper, "and we laughed more than once at ourselves, for using the left-hand fingers, in lieu of the awkward two-tined fork."[23] He may have lost his manners, but in other respects he had been much enriched and enlightened by his diverse exchanges with rival cultures on the frontier—encounters that taught him new terms and endowed him with a rare capacity to appreciate the costs for all parties concerned of the hard bargain Americans were driving with the competition as they advanced westward in pursuit of their destiny.

On July 4, 1847, as Lewis Garrard prepared to travel down the Missouri River by steamboat to St. Louis and thence to his hometown of Cincinnati, Susan Magoffin found herself celebrating Independence Day in the occupied Mexican city of Saltillo, having journeyed there from Chihuahua in the wake of Doniphan's troops. Her stay in Chihuahua had not been very inspiring, marred as it was by the sight of Missourians turning gracious homes they had commandeered into stables and a public fountain into a "bathing trough."[24] But she found consolation in characteristic fashion—by repaying the courtesies of Mexicans in that city who declined to hold her and her husband liable for the excesses of their countrymen. One hospitable Chihuahuan she conversed with had visited the United States and picked up a bit of the language, drawing from her a tribute of the sort few Americans offered to Mexicans in this time of discord and disparagement: "He always spoke to me in English and I to him in Spanish and I think I learned quite as much in the few conversations I had with him, as I have with any one person in a much longer time."[25]

Unfortunately, Magoffin had few further opportunities for such easy and rewarding exchanges with Mexicans in the weeks and months ahead, for she and her husband kept close to the American forces. Turning to her diary in Saltillo on the evening of Sunday, July 4, she noted with dismay that her countrymen-in-arms had not muted their holiday festivities out of respect for the Sabbath. If General Kearny were in command here, she felt sure, he would have deferred the revelry—as well he might have, not so much for religious as for diplomatic reasons. Celebrating one's independence in the midst of foreigners who felt deprived of theirs by the act of occupation was no way to appease one's foes. Yet American forces here were emboldened by their recent victories, and they seemed less concerned with offending those under their guns than Kearny had been in Santa Fe. In late July, after an uplifting visit to a Catholic church where she admired a painting of "the Virgin Mary descending from Heaven attended by many angels, with the infant Jesus in her arms,"[26] Magoffin toured a nearby convent that American forces had transformed indecorously into an arsenal. "The officers took us through the different apartments and pointed out all the ammunition stores," she wrote. In place of vespers, the troops staged an "evening parade in the convent yard."[27]

The strains of her journey—and of reconciling her deep loyalty to her homeland with her sympathy for the people of this beleaguered nation—were beginning to tell on Susan Magoffin. She was once again pregnant and had reason to wonder if her expectations would be more happily fulfilled on this occasion than they had been at Bent's Fort a year earlier. In early August, after receiving a letter from home that told of marriages and births among friends and family, she commiserated briefly in her diary with all those in her condition: "I do think a woman *em beraso* [*embarazada*—pregnant] has a hard time of it, some sickness all the time, heart-burn, head-ache, cramp etc. after all this thing of marrying is not what it is cracked up to be."[28] She had patiently endured many such embarrassments and hardships since leaving home, but a greater trial awaited her. After she and her husband reached the Gulf Coast port of Matamoros that fall, she came down with yellow fever and gave birth in her sickbed to a boy, who died a short time later. This impending crisis brought her diary to an abrupt end in September 1847, on the road to Matamoros. Inasmuch as that diary represented her great gift to posterity, an important part of her remained here in Mexico in spirit, even as she convalesced and returned home by ship, settled down with her husband in Missouri, and started a family that grew to four children before her untimely death in 1855. Those who got to know her through her diary in later times would think of her always as she appeared in writing—a pilgrim on the trail, reckoning with its challenges and heeding its lessons. More than any other witness to these tumultuous events, she saw beyond the war and its contentious aftermath to the possibility of reconciliation, a cultural accommodation to which her gracious diary, published some seventy years after her death, made some contribution. In her next-to-last entry, on September 5, 1847, inscribed at an encampment near Matamoros, she recorded a haunting incident that summed up her rewarding exchange with this world of promise that beckoned to her at the far end of the trail:

> At this place I made a *comadre* of an old woman witch, who brought eggs and bread down to the encampment to sell; she stoped at our tent door, she looked up at me, and said, "take me with you to your country," "why," said I. "*le guerro V. los Americans*" [You are at war with the Americans]? She neither answered yes or no, but gave me a sharp pinch on my cheek, I suppose to see if the flesh and colour of it were natural—and said "*na guerro este*" [there is no war]. The pinch did not feel very comfortable, but I could but laugh at her cunning reply.[29]

This ambiguous entry, like other beguiling passages by those who entered that labyrinth called the Santa Fe Trail over the years and confronted its twists and riddles, left much to be interpreted. What possessed this old peddler to offer herself as a traveling companion to a complete stranger? Was she speaking in jest, or did she sense that this young American, so far from home and with so much yet to bear, might indeed be in need of a *comadre*, or "godmother," an older woman to look after her and see her safely to her destination? Perhaps Susan, who had become adept at Spanish by now, knew that *comadre* had an additional meaning of special relevance to the situation she found herself in—"midwife," a task for which this "old woman witch" might in fact be well qualified.

If this stranger's initial remark was enigmatic, the parting words she delivered while pinching Susan's cheek with the probing familiarity of a godmother or midwife were all the more so: "*na guerro este.*" Perhaps she meant that the war was over—which it nearly was, pending the capture of Mexico City and the resolution of treaty talks. Or perhaps this cunning woman meant exactly what she said: There is no war, a statement that made sense to Susan Magoffin. She had been in hostile Mexican territory for more than a year and had seen many signs and semblances of war, but nothing to compare with the fundamental reality governing relations between the two sides—the ceaseless cultural and commercial interplay that set the stage for this dispute, endured in spite of it, and would come to dominate this international exchange once again in good time. "Take me with you to your country," the old woman said, and Susan Magoffin did just that through her diary, smuggling this character and other riches from beyond the border back across the lines, where her gift to posterity would be treasured long after the dividends of conquest had lost currency.

Throughout the history of the American exchange with Mexico, there had been considerable confusion as to where one country ended and the other began—not just territorially but culturally. Ever since Zebulon Pike marched up the Arkansas and probed what he called the "Mexican mountains" with the professed intention of reconnoitering his own country, national and cultural boundaries in the Southwest had become increasingly blurred. For more than a quarter century, the Arkansas River had been accepted by both sides as delineating the Mexican-American frontier, and yet Anglos and Hispanics had mingled freely with one another and with Indians of various tribes in outposts on either side of the Arkansas, obscuring the distinctions that such boundary lines were supposed to sharpen. With the American conquest of New Mexico and California, the cultural frontier became even harder to define, for the conflict left tens of thousands of Hispanics firmly ensconced on the

American side of the border—and countless more would emigrate from Mexico across that line in due time to reinforce the Spanish character of the annexed territory. The situation on either side of the frontier would become a variation on that time-honored adage of hospitality, *Mi casa es su casa* ("My house is your house")—or in this case, "My country is your country."

Perhaps that old woman who confronted Susan Magoffin near Matamoros was indeed something of a witch, a fortune-teller who could see beyond the tensions of the moment to the shared future awaiting the antagonists in this curious struggle that confounded one country with another. Perhaps it took a witch to articulate what others might consider an impiety, given the earnest sacrifices made by both sides in the recent hostilities—that this war was a phantom, a fleeting distortion of that compromising give-and-take between inextricable rivals whose fortunes were forever entwined now in the Southwest, regardless of the boundaries drawn between them.

Notes

PREFACE

1. Philip St. George Cooke, *Scenes and Adventures in the Army: Or Romance of Military Life*, 239.

2. Jack D. Rittenhouse, *The Santa Fe Trail: A Historical Bibliography*, 3.

CHAPTER 1

1. Zebulon Montgomery Pike, *The Journals of Zebulon Montgomery Pike, with Letters and Related Documents*, ed. Donald Jackson, 2 vols., 1:395–96. Pike (1779–1813) led a reconnaissance up the Mississippi in 1805 to probe the headwaters of that river before embarking in July 1806 from St. Louis on the expedition that brought him to Santa Fe. Promoted from lieutenant to captain after he left St. Louis, he later commanded troops as a brigadier general during the War of 1812 and was killed in action. For more on his career and expeditions, see W. Eugene Hollon, *The Lost Pathfinder: Zebulon Montgomery Pike*.

2. Pike, *Journals*, 1:392.

3. For a discussion of this tangled territorial dispute, see David J. Weber, *The Spanish Frontier in North America*, 291–301. Not until 1819 would the United States relinquish its claim to Texas.

4. Wilkinson in Pike, *Journals*, 1:286.

5. For a summary of what Lewis and Clark accomplished, and failed to accomplish, in their dealings with tribal leaders, see James P. Ronda, *Lewis and Clark among the Indians*, 252–55.

6. Pike took with him from St. Louis a group of Osages who had been ransomed by American authorities from a rival tribe, the Potawatomis. The Osages were grateful for the favor and glad to be restored to their friends and kin, but they were not enthusiastic

about accompanying Pike to the villages of the Kansas, with whom they had their differences. Those Osages who continued with him on the journey guided him on a path that skirted the territory of the Kansas and led him instead to the Pawnees. See Jackson's note in Pike, *Journals*, 1:315 n. 58.

7. Ibid., 328.

8. Ibid., 328–29.

9. Ibid., 329.

10. Ibid., 329–30. For other accounts of Pike's dealings with this Pawnee chief—referred to variously as Characterish or Sharitarish—see the reports of Lieutenant James B. Wilkinson (Pike, *Journals*, 2:5–7), Governor Alencaster (ibid., 182–82), and George C. Sibley (ibid., 370–76).

11. Pike, *Journals*, 1:330.

12. Ibid., 338–39.

13. Ibid., 343.

14. Ibid., 344.

15. Ibid., 345.

16. Ibid., 348.

17. Ibid., 349.

18. Ibid., 352–53.

19. Ibid., 378–79.

20. James Wilkinson (1757–1825) was secretly employed as a Spanish agent while in the service of the United States and was implicated in a conspiracy hatched by former vice president Aaron Burr to seize Spanish territory in the Southwest. (The conspirators were also rumored to have designs on American territory.) Writing in the 1830s, traveler and essayist Albert Pike, a distant relative of the explorer, surmised that Zebulon Pike was indeed involved in a conspiracy against Mexico but meant no harm to his own country: "Was he not seeking a place for the army of Aaron Burr to enter and subdue Mexico? He was no traitor, I know; and neither, in my opinion, was Burr" (Albert Pike, *Prose Sketches and Poems Written in the Western Country*, ed. David J. Weber, 32). No proof has surfaced that Wilkinson's orders to Pike were part of any conspiracy, however. Despite efforts to resolve the territorial dispute between Spain and the United States, war remained a possibility and Wilkinson in his official capacity had reason to reconnoiter the approaches to New Mexico. See Francis Paul Prucha, *The Sword of the Republic: The United States Army on the Frontier, 1783–1846*, 91–94.

21. Pike, *Journals*, 1:384.

22. Ibid., 392.

23. Ibid., 393–94.

24. Ibid., 395, 396.

25. Ibid., 396.

26. Ibid., 400–401 (the term "Tetaus" here refers to Comanches). Editor Donald Jackson interjects the comment "[*not identified*]" after Pike's first reference to Ambrosio Guerra.

27. Ibid., 405.

28. Ibid., 406.

29. Ibid., 410.

30. Ibid., 413.

31. Ronda, *Lewis and Clark among the Indians,* 4.

32. Pike, *Journals,* 2:56.

33. Ibid., 58.

34. Ibid., 96–97.

35. Benton in George Winston Smith and Charles Judah, eds., *Chronicles of the Gringos: The U.S. Army in the Mexican War, 1846–1848,* 112. Thomas Hart Benton (1782–1858) worked to promote the Santa Fe trade in the U.S. Senate from the 1820s through the Mexican War.

36. Pueblos, during their revolt against Spanish colonists in 1680, employed these same symbolic terms when they met with the Spanish governor of New Mexico and tried to induce him to give up the fight. According to Josiah Gregg: "A parley was soon afterwards held with the chief leaders, who told the Spaniards that they had brought two crosses, of which they might have their choice: one was red, denoting war, the other was white and professed peace, on the condition of their immediately evacuating the province" (Gregg, *Commerce of the Prairies,* ed. Max L. Moorhead, 88).

CHAPTER 2

1. De Mun in David A. White, ed., *News of the Plains and Rockies, 1803–1865,* 2:47–48. See also Ralph Emerson Twitchell, *Old Santa Fe: The Story of New Mexico's Ancient Capital,* 171–72; and David J. Weber, *The Taos Trappers: The Fur Trade in the Far Southwest, 1540–1846,* 46–47.

2. De Mun in White, *News of the Plains and Rockies,* 2:48.

3. As David J. Weber has written in relation to Spain's tenuous claim to the Pacific Northwest: "Possession, as Spain had discovered elsewhere, did not reside in papal bulls, prior discovery, scrupulous attention to acts of possession, or the planting of wooden crosses. Sovereignty depended on occupancy, and occupancy depended on economic development" (*Spanish Frontier in North America,* 289).

4. Jules De Mun, "The Journals of Jules de Mun, Part 2: February 27–April 8, 1816," ed. Thomas Maitland Marshall, trans. Nettie H. Beauregard, 323–26. According to De Mun, the attackers included "Republican Pawnees," the same group encountered by Pike in 1806 and asked by him to remove Spanish flags from their village. See also Louise Barry, *The Beginning of the West: Annals of the Kansas Gateway to the American West, 1540–1854,* 76. Chouteau's Island has since been eroded by floodwaters and no longer exists.

5. George E. Hyde, *The Pawnee Indians,* 137. Hyde identifies the Pawnee band encountered by Pike along the Republican River in 1806 as the Kitkehahkis and notes that by 1815 "the Kitkehahkis had established a fine reputation for hostility toward the new tribe of *La-chi-kuts* or Americans" (ibid., 166).

6. William Y. Chalfant, *Dangerous Passage: The Santa Fe Trail and the Mexican War,* 23–25.

7. The Comanches were by far the largest of these three allied groups and the best known to Americans, and some early travelers on the trail may have lumped them together under the label "Comanche." Others distinguished between Comanches and Kiowas, but

the Kiowa or Plains Apaches were evidently such a small group, and so closely linked to the Kiowas, that they were seldom recognized by travelers as a distinct entity.

8. Alice Marriott, *The Ten Grandmothers*, 105, 121, 124. Marriott offers three contexts in which this death song was sung by the Kiowa chief Sitting Bear before he perished in 1871, all of them relating to the prospect of fighting or dying. "That was a hard song," Marriott comments. "You had to fight a long time and be brave and famous to have the right to sing it" (ibid., 106).

9. Don Pedro Baptista Pino, *The Exposition on the Province of New Mexico, 1812*, ed. and trans. Adrian Bustamante and Marc Simmons, 28. Pino (ca. 1752–1829) was a major landowner and rancher as well as a municipal official in Santa Fe, and he dealt cordially with the early American traders who arrived there in the 1820s. See Simmons and Bustamante's preface, xii–xiii; and James Josiah Webb, *Adventures in the Santa Fé Trade, 1844–1847*, ed. Ralph P. Bieber, 98–99.

10. Pino, *Exposition*, 8.

11. Ibid., 22.

12. Ibid., 10.

13. Ibid., 17. The figure of "33 hostile tribes" might be overstated, but some tribal groups that impinged on the Spanish settlements were made up of several distinct divisions, such as the Jicarilla and Mescalero Apaches and the Yamparika and Kotsoteka Comanches, and those divisions in turn were made up of various bands.

14. Ibid., 19. The ragged condition of New Mexican troops was often remarked upon by American observers.

15. Ibid., 52.

16. Ibid., 51.

17. Ibid., 54. The civilians guarding these caravans were often supported by regular troops, but they still came under attack periodically. See Max L. Moorhead, *New Mexico's Royal Road: Trade and Travel on the Chihuahua Trail*, 44–48.

18. Pino, *Exposition*, 40–41, 53.

CHAPTER 3

1. David Meriwether, *My Life in the Mountains and on the Plains*, ed. Robert A. Griffen, 81. Meriwether (1800–1892) served as territorial governor of New Mexico from 1853 to 1857. The Council Bluffs referred to here is not to be confused with the town of Council Bluffs, Iowa.

2. Ibid., 82.

3. Ibid., 93–94.

4. Thomas James, *Three Years among the Indians and Mexicans*, ed. Walter B. Douglas, 118. For more on the life and work of Thomas James (1782–1847), see Douglas's preface and Frederic E. Voelker, "Thomas James," in LeRoy R. Hafen, ed., *The Mountain Men and the Fur Trade of the Far West*, 10 vols., 4:153–67.

5. In a letter Thomas James wrote to President Andrew Jackson in 1834, seeking permission to negotiate a treaty with Comanches for purposes of trade, he reported that during his journey to Santa Fe in 1821 he had been "plundered by these Indians of ten thousand dollars worth of goods being the greater part of the stock he had with him."

Considering that James had already cached part of his goods and expended a sizable sum on horses before Comanches supposedly deprived him of $10,000 worth, one wonders what he had left to offer in Santa Fe. See James W. Covington, "Thomas James: Traveler to Santa Fe."

6. Thomas James, *Three Years among the Indians*, 124–25.

7. Ibid., 126, 128. This same chief had been encountered in Texas in 1808 by a Spanish officer, Captain Francisco Amangual, and had taken the name Cordero (after Antonio Cordero, the governor of Coahuila) to seal a pact he entered into with Spanish authorities. Elizabeth A. H. John, "Nurturing the Peace: Spanish and Comanche Cooperation in the Early Nineteenth Century," 354–55.

8. James in Covington, "Thomas James," 88. For a survey of reported contacts and conflicts between Comanches and Santa Fe traders from 1821 to 1834, see Thomas W. Kavanagh, *Comanche Political History: An Ethnohistorical Perspective, 1706–1875*, 210–21.

9. Glenn in Jacob Fowler, *The Journal of Jacob Fowler*, ed. Elliott Coues, 70. This entry, dated December 28, 1821, was written by Hugh Glenn (1788–1833), who took over the keeping of the journal of his partner, Fowler (1765–1850), for a few days at year's end. For more on this expedition, see Harry R. Stevens, "Hugh Glenn," in Hafen, *Mountain Men and the Fur Trade*, 2:169–73; and Weber, *Taos Trappers*, 55–56.

10. Glenn in Fowler, *Journal*, 71.

11. Merchants involved in the Santa Fe trade sold goods to trappers outfitting for expeditions in New Mexico. Weber, *Taos Trappers*, 57.

12. Larry Mahon Beachum, *William Becknell: Father of the Santa Fe Trade*, 16, 22. Becknell (ca. 1787–1856) made his third and final visit to New Mexico during a trapping expedition in 1824, returning the following year. He spent his last years in Texas.

13. Colonel Alexander Doniphan of the First Missouri Volunteers, for example, took one of his slaves with him on the campaign. Doniphan also helped draw up a legal code that fostered American democratic institutions in occupied New Mexico. See Joseph G. Dawson III, *Doniphan's Epic March: The 1st Missouri Volunteers in the Mexican War*, 17–18; and Roger D. Launius, *Alexander William Doniphan: Portrait of a Missouri Moderate*, 144.

14. Becknell in White, *News of the Plains and Rockies*, 2:63. See White's introduction, 49–50, for a discussion of Becknell's account and editor Patten's possible hand in it. Becknell's journal of his two expeditions, which originally appeared in the *Missouri Intelligencer* on April 22, 1823, can also be found in *Missouri Historical Review* 4 (January 1910): 65–84.

15. Becknell in White, *News of the Plains and Rockies*, 2:60.

16. *Missouri Intelligencer*, June 25, 1821.

17. Becknell in White, *News of the Plains and Rockies*, 2:61.

18. Ibid., 62–63.

19. Ibid., 64.

20. Ibid., 66.

21. H. H. Harris in R. L. Duffus, *The Santa Fe Trail*, 68–69.

22. Barry, *Beginning of the West*, 105; Gregg, *Commerce of the Prairies*, 14, 47.

23. Becknell in White, *News of the Plains and Rockies*, 2:66.

24. Ibid., 67.

25. *Missouri Intelligencer*, June 17, 1823; reprinted in White, *News of the Plains and Rockies*, 2:68.

26. Joel P. Walker, *A Pioneer of Pioneers: Narrative of Adventures Thro' Alabama, Florida, New Mexico, Oregon, California, & c.*, 5–6. Walker (1797–1879) was born in Virginia, fought under Andrew Jackson in the Seminole War, and moved to western Missouri in late 1819. He dictated his account late in life and recalled mistakenly that this expedition took place in 1822 rather than in 1823. He also claimed that he and Stephen Cooper, nephew of Benjamin Cooper, "raised" the company. They may have helped organize it, but Benjamin Cooper led the company. See Kenneth L.Holmes, "The Benjamin Cooper Expeditions to Santa Fe in 1822 and 1823."

27. Walker, *Pioneer of Pioneers*, 9.

28. Ibid., 10.

29. Meredith Miles Marmaduke, "Meredith Miles Marmaduke's Journal of a Tour to New Mexico, 1824–1825," ed. Harry C. Myers, 9. This article provides a full transcript of Marmaduke's journal, held by the Bancroft Library, University of California. An edited version of Marmaduke's journal first appeared in the *Missouri Intelligencer* on September 2, 1825, and can also be found in White, *News of the Plains and Rockies*, 2:71–75. Marmaduke (1791–1864) was elected lieutenant governor of Missouri in 1840 and succeeded briefly to the governorship.

30. Alphonso Wetmore to Major James H. Hook, May 6, 1824, in "Alphonso Wetmore Letters," ed. Leo E. Oliva, *Wagon Tracks* 14 (February 2000): 10. Wetmore (1793–1849) ventured down the Santa Fe Trail himself in 1828 and documented the journey in writing. For a biographical essay, see Kate L. Gregg, "Major Alphonso Wetmore."

31. Marmaduke, "Journal," 11.

32. Storrs in White, *News of the Plains and Rockies*, 2:84. Alphonso Wetmore estimated the investment for the 1824 caravan at $24,000 and the returns for that year at $130,000 (ibid., 102–4). See also Barry, *Beginning of the West*, 116. Augustus Storrs (1791–1850) was appointed the first U.S. consul to Santa Fe in 1825.

33. Wetmore in Archer Butler Hulbert, ed., *Southwest on the Turquoise Trail: The First Diaries on the Road to Santa Fe*, 176–77.

34. Benton in George Champlin Sibley, *The Road to Santa Fe: The Journal and Diaries of George Champlin Sibley*, ed. Kate L. Gregg, 6. Sibley (1782–1863) served as factor at Fort Osage from 1808 until the government ceased its involvement in trade with Indians fourteen years later.

35. Ibid., 1.

36. Ibid., 57.

37. Ibid., 184–85.

38. Ibid., 48.

39. Ibid., 5.

40. Gregg, *Commerce of the Prairies*, 331–32. According to Gregg, in 1843 "the greater portion of the traders were New Mexicans." Moorhead interprets Gregg's figures in *New Mexico's Royal Road*, 63–75.

41. Benton in Sibley, *Road to Santa Fe*, 4–5. As Kate Gregg points out, these remarks were set down not by Benton himself but by a congressional reporter, who "caught the rhetorical phrases as they fell from his lips." In the same year that Benton delivered this

enthusiastic speech, one critic described the Santa Fe Trade as "completely overdone" (Moorhead, *New Mexico's Royal Road*, 63).

42. [Alphonso Wetmore], "Book of the Muleteers," *Missouri Intelligencer*, August 19, 1825; reprinted in *Wagon Tracks* 5 (August 1991): 3; and in *New Mexico Historical Review* 17 (October 1942): 292–93. Wetmore's authorship of this piece is indicated by the fact that he composed a number of lively sketches for the *Intelligencer* over the years and by the marked similarity of the "Book of the Muleteers" to this passage from Wetmore's *Gazetteer of the State of Missouri*, describing the eviction of Mormons from the vicinity of Independence in the early 1830s: "But the Lord waxed wroth with the Mormons, for they had communed with the men-servants and the maid-servants of the people in whose land they were sojourning, seducing them from the obedience and the duty they owed to those who gave them food and raiment; and the Jacksonites, and the Old Dominionites, and the Tenneseeites, and Kentuckites, lifted up their hands and their voices with one accord, and exclaimed: 'Depart, ye cursed, to the uttermost parts of the earth, or we'll row you up Salt river!'" (97).

CHAPTER 4

1. Cooke, *Scenes and Adventures*, 59. Cooke (1809–95) served in the U.S. Army from the time he graduated from West Point as a lieutenant in 1827 until his retirement as a general in 1873. For a biography, see Otis E. Young, *The West of Philip St. George Cooke*, 1809–1895.

2. Cooke, *Scenes and Adventures*, 228.

3. Ibid., 251.

4. Ibid., 269.

5. Ibid., 229–30.

6. Ibid., 250. For a full account of the Chávez incident, see Marc Simmons, *Murder on the Santa Fe Trail: An International Incident, 1843*.

7. Philip St. George Cooke, *The Conquest of New Mexico and California, an Historical and Personal Narrative*, 7.

8. Bigelow in Richard H. Cracroft, "Josiah Gregg," 149. Cracroft notes that Gregg (1806–50) suffered periodic relapses of dyspepsia and other complaints when he returned from his western travels to the restraints of life in the States. For a biographical appraisal, see Paul Horgan, *Josiah Gregg and His Vision of the Early West*.

9. *Independence Journal*, September 19, 1844. This newspaper was edited by George Gibson, an important chronicler of the conquest of New Mexico and editor of the first newspaper published in English in Santa Fe. Gibson may well have written this unsigned review of Gregg's book.

10. Gregg in Horgan, *Josiah Gregg*, 80–81.

11. Gregg, *Commerce of the Prairies*, 251.

12. Gregg in Horgan, *Josiah Gregg*, 95–96.

13. Pike, *Prose Sketches and Poems*, 230. There were indeed white wolves on the plains, as attested by Josiah Gregg: "Although the buffalo is the largest, he has by no means the control among the prairie animals: the sceptre of authority has been lodged with the large *gray wolf*. . . . Though the color of this wolf is generally a dirty gray, it is sometimes met

with nearly white" (*Commerce of the Prairies*, 374–75). For more on the life and work of Albert Pike (1809–91), see Weber's introduction to *Prose Sketches and Poems*; Harvey L. Carter, "Albert Pike," in Hafen, *Mountain Men and the Fur Trade*, 2:265–74; and Joseph M. Flora, "Albert Pike."

14. Pike, *Prose Sketches and Poems*, 107.

15. Ibid., 102–3.

16. Ibid., 131, 132.

17. Howard Louis Conard, *"Uncle Dick" Wootton: The Pioneer Frontiersman of the Rocky Mountain Region*, 36. Wootton (1816–93) operated a toll road through Raton Pass from 1865 until 1878, when the railroad bought him out. For a biographical essay, see Harvey L. Carter, "Dick Wootton," in Hafen, *Mountain Men and the Fur Trade*, 3:397–411.

18. Conard, *"Uncle Dick" Wootton*, 40–41.

19. Ibid., 35.

20. George Frederick Ruxton, *Adventures in Mexico and the Rocky Mountains*, 206. For the life and collected writings of Ruxton (1821–48), see *Ruxton of the Rockies*, coll. Clyde and Mae Reed Porter, ed. LeRoy R. Hafen. For biographical essays, see Frederic E. Voelker, "Ruxton of the Rocky Mountains"; and Richard H. Cracroft, "George Frederick Ruxton." Shortly before Ruxton died, he wrote a note in mountain-man dialect expressing his desire to return to the region that inspired some of his best work: "this child has felt like going West for many a month, being half froze for buffler meat and mountain doins" (*Ruxton of the Rockies*, 308).

21. Conard, *"Uncle Dick" Wootton*, 96.

22. Ibid., 42.

23. Thomas J. Farnham, *Travels in the Great Western Prairies, the Anahuac and Rocky Mountains, and in the Oregon Territory*, 23–24. Farnham (1804–48) traveled extensively along the Pacific Coast after reaching Oregon and later published books on California and Mexico. Several others from the so-called Peoria party who journeyed west with Farnham in 1839 left accounts, collected by LeRoy R. Hafen and Ann W. Hafen in *To the Rockies and Oregon, 1839–1842*. Thanks to the narratives compiled and edited by the Hafens, this is among the best-documented expeditions to traverse any significant portion of the Santa Fe Trail before 1846.

24. Frederick A. Wislizenus (1810–89) immigrated to the United States in 1835. The book he wrote describing his 1839 journey was published in St. Louis in German and appeared in English posthumously in 1912 as *A Journey to the Rocky Mountains in the Year 1839*. His account of his later trip to Mexico was first published by Congress in 1848 under the title *Memoir of a Tour to Northern Mexico, Connected with Col. Doniphan's Expedition, in 1846 and 1847*.

25. Matthew C. Field, *Matt Field on the Santa Fe Trail*, coll. Clyde and Mae Reed Porter, ed. John E. Sunder, 144. Matt Field (ca. 1812–44) made another trip west by a more northerly route in 1843, documented in his *Prairie and Mountain Sketches*, coll. Clyde and Mae Reed Porter, ed. Kate L. Gregg and John Francis McDermott. For Field's reflections on life in St. Louis shortly before his journey to New Mexico, see "The Diary of Matt Field," ed. William G. B. Carson.

26. Field, *Matt Field on the Santa Fe Trail*, 228–29.

27. George Wilkins Kendall, *Narrative of the Texan Santa Fé Expedition*, 2 vols., 1:16. For a biography of Kendall (1809–67), see Fayette Copeland, *Kendall of the Picayune*.

28. Texas president Mirabeau Lamar in Noel M. Loomis, *The Texan–Santa Fé Pioneers*, 169.

29. Kendall, *Narrative*, 1:289. Kendall's note defines *pobrecitos* as "poor fellows."

30. Ibid., 352.

31. Ibid., 319.

32. Webb, *Adventures in the Santa Fé Trade*, 62. Webb (1818–89) began writing this account in 1888, when he was seventy, and died before he could complete the work. Although his narrative ends in 1847, he remained a prominent figure in the Santa Fe trade until 1861. See Jane Lenz Elder and David J. Weber, eds., *Trading in Santa Fe: John M. Kingsbury's Correspondence with James Josiah Webb, 1853–61*.

33. Webb, *Adventures in the Santa Fé Trade*, 87–88.

34. Janet Lecompte, "Manuel Armijo's Family History."

35. Edward James Glasgow in Mark L. Gardner, ed., *Brothers on the Santa Fe and Chihuahua Trails: Edward James Glasgow and William Henry Glasgow, 1846–1848*, 79. Edward James Glasgow (1820–1908) and William Henry Glasgow (1822–97) remained active in trade with New Mexico and old Mexico until the late 1870s.

36. Francis Parkman, *The Oregon Trail*, ed. E. N. Feltskog. Parkman (1823–93) based his narrative, first published in book form in 1849 under the title *The California and Oregon Trail*, on a journal he kept during the trip. See *The Journals of Francis Parkman*, ed. Mason Wade, vol. 2.

37. Alfred S. Waugh, *Travels in Search of the Elephant: The Wanderings of Alfred S. Waugh, Artist, in Louisiana, Missouri, and Santa Fe, in 1845–1846*, ed. John Francis McDermott, 122. Waugh (ca. 1800–1856) won little recognition either as an artist or writer during his lifetime and left the manuscript describing his western travels unpublished at the time of his death.

38. Frank S. Edwards, *A Campaign in New Mexico with Colonel Doniphan*, 4. See Mark L. Gardner's foreword to this 1996 edition for what little is known about Edwards before and after the Mexican War.

39. Ibid., 5.

40. [John D. Stevenson], "Invasion of New Mexico, 1846," ed. Harry C. Myers, *Wagon Tracks* 7 (August 1993): 19. Myers notes that this letter, dated August 23, 1846, and held in the Getty Collection, New Mexico State Records Center and Archives, Santa Fe, was written "by an officer of Company E, most likely Captain John D. Stevenson."

41. Edwards, *Campaign in New Mexico*, 47.

42. Richard Smith Elliott, *The Mexican War Correspondence of Richard Smith Elliott*, ed. Mark L. Gardner and Marc Simmons, 74–76. Elliott (1817–90) summed up his restless and varied career in his 1883 memoir, *Notes Taken in Sixty Years*.

43. Elliott, *Mexican War Correspondence*, 94.

44. Ibid., 106.

45. Ibid., 160.

46. George Rutledge Gibson, *Journal of a Soldier under Kearny and Doniphan, 1846–1847*, ed. Ralph P. Bieber, 316. Gibson (ca. 1810–85) left behind at his death an unpublished journal of epic proportions covering the New Mexico campaign as he experienced it

from 1846 to 1848. Bieber's edition, enhanced with a lengthy introduction that offers a concise history of the campaign Gibson took part in, encompasses the first four parts of that journal, which is held by the Missouri Historical Society. The last two parts appear in *Over the Chihuahua and Santa Fe Trails, 1847–1848*, ed. Robert W. Frazer.

47. Gibson, *Journal of a Soldier*, 350.

48. Gibson in Susan Shelby Magoffin, *Down the Santa Fe Trail and into Mexico: The Diary of Susan Shelby Magoffin, 1846–1847*, ed. Stella M. Drumm, 217 n. 90.

49. *Santa Fe Republican*, September 10, 1847.

50. Magoffin, *Down the Santa Fe Trail*, 20, 102. Susan Shelby Magoffin (1827–55) claimed only that she was the "first American lady" to reach Santa Fe under the "Star-spangled banner," adding that "some of our company seem disposed to make me the first under any circumstances that ever crossed the Plains" (ibid., 102–3). For accounts of women who preceded her on the Santa Fe Trail, see Gregg, Commerce of the Prairies, 32–33; and Marian Meyer, *Mary Donoho: New First Lady of the Santa Fe Trail*, 26–33, 117–18. A black cook named Charlotte and her husband, Dick Green, traveled the Santa Fe Trail as slaves and were working at Bent's Fort by the early 1840s.

51. Magoffin, *Down the Santa Fe Trail*, 34.

52. Ibid., 22.

53. Ibid., 67.

54. Ibid., 95.

55. Ibid., 209.

56. Lewis H. Garrard, *Wah-to-yah and the Taos Trail*, ed. Ralph P. Bieber, 256. Garrard (1829–87), who was christened Hector Lewis but gave his name as Lewis H. Garrard for publication, wrote little of interest after *Wah-to-yah* and lived out his days as a physician, farmer, and politician in Minnesota. For more on his life and travels, see Bieber's introduction and Richard H. Cracroft, "Lewis H. Garrard."

57. Bieber, introduction to Garrard, *Wah-to-yah*, 35.

58. Garrard, *Wah-to-yah*, 83.

59. Ibid., 332.

60. Richard F. Townsend, *The Aztecs*, 186–88.

61. Although the term "Montezumians" was used humorously by Americans to link contemporary Mexicans to the ancient Aztecs, Mexicans themselves proudly referred to their culture as Neo-Aztec. Neo-Aztecism was venturesome in spirit—amounting to the Mexican equivalent of Manifest Destiny—and those two expansive impulses collided in New Mexico. See Thomas E. Chávez, "Up from Mexico and Beyond the Ruts: Some Commemorative Thoughts on the Santa Fe Trail," 5–8.

62. *St. Louis Morning Missouri Republican*, June 1, 1846.

63. W. W. H. Davis, *El Gringo: New Mexico and Her People*, 14. For the identity of Captain Reynolds, see Barry, *Beginning of the West*, 1187. Marc Simmons, in quoting this same verse, comments: "By crossing the Jordan, American merchants, wagon masters, and teamsters entered the Promised Land and continued on to the new Jerusalem at Santa Fe." The fact that, for many of these pilgrims, "reality failed to live up to the dream and the promise" did not prevent others from following faithfully in their path. Simmons, *Along the Santa Fe Trail*, with photographs by Joan Myers, 10.

CHAPTER 5

1. Field, *Matt Field on the Santa Fe Trail*, 60.

2. Ibid., 60.

3. George Catlin, *Letters and Notes on the Manners, Customs, and Conditions of the North American Indians*, 2 vols., 2:29. Catlin (1796–1872), after returning to St. Louis from the upper Missouri River in 1832, attached himself in 1834 to a peacekeeping expedition on the southern plains commanded by Colonels Henry Leavenworth and Henry Dodge and made sketches and observations of the Comanches and Kiowas, among other tribes of the region.

4. Ibid., 30.

5. Field, *Matt Field on the Santa Fe Trail*, 61.

6. *Missouri Intelligencer and Boon's Lick Advertiser*, September 18, 1829.

7. Ibid., June 26, 1829.

8. Captain Frederick Marryat, *Diary in America*, ed. Jules Zanger, 254. Marryat (1792–1848), not content with his own observations of the West, later concocted a narrative entitled *Travels and Adventures of Monsieur Violet among the Snake Indians and Wild Tribes of the Great Western Prairies* (1843), which borrowed from the work of George Kendall and Josiah Gregg and exposed Marryat to charges of plagiarism.

9. Charles van Ravenswaay, *Saint Louis: An Informal History of the City and Its People, 1764–1865*, ed. Candace O'Connor, 337.

10. Benjamin F. Taylor, *Short Ravelings from a Long Yarn, or Camp March Sketches of the Santa Fe Trail*, from the notes of Richard L. Wilson, 9. Taylor (1819–87), a newspaper editor in Chicago, used Wilson's account of a journey to Santa Fe in 1841 to craft this flowery narrative, resembling a work of fiction in places. For details on the caravan Wilson joined in 1841, see Barry, *Beginning of the West*, 426–31.

11. Field, "Diary of Matt Field," 95.

12. Field wed Cornelia Ludlow in February 1841. He was already much attached to her when he left St. Louis for Santa Fe in June 1839, for he described himself in verse in his journal, "Musing upon a dear friends Daughter, / Of whom he thinks both night and day" (*Matt Field on the Santa Fe Trail*, 15–16).

13. Gregg, *Commerce of the Prairies*, 23–24.

14. Barclay in George P. Hammond, *The Adventures of Alexander Barclay, Mountain Man*, 23.

15. William Fairholme, *Journal of an Expedition to the Grand Prairies of the Missouri, 1840*, ed. Jack B. Tykal, 41–42. Fairholme (1819–68), born in Scotland and serving as a lieutenant in Canada when he took leave of his regiment for this hunting expedition, traveled to St. Louis down the Illinois and Mississippi Rivers by steamboat and offered a fine description of conditions aboard the paddle wheeler. "None of our fellow passengers could understand our motives in leaving our comfortable homes to go on such an expedition as we were engaged in," he wrote, "and what puzzled them most was our disclaiming any idea of profit accruing to us therefrom" (ibid., 46).

16. Ibid., 48.

17. Ibid., 64.

18. Cooke, *Scenes and Adventures*, 16–17.

19. Warren Angus Ferris, *Life in the Rocky Mountains*, ed. Leroy R. Hafen, 46.

20. William Clark Kennerly, *Persimmon Hill: A Narrative of Old St. Louis and the Far West*, as told to Elizabeth Russell, 44–45. Kennerly (1824–1912), who took part in the occupation of New Mexico in 1846, dictated this memoir to his daughter late in life.

21. Fairholme, *Journal of an Expedition*, 47–48.

22. Kennerly, *Persimmon Hill*, 51.

23. Ravenswaay, *St. Louis*, 329.

24. *Daily Missouri Republican*, May 19, 1841. A number of merchants traveling back and forth between the United States and Mexico made at least part of the journey by water. Some traveled overland from Missouri to Santa Fe and on to Chihuahua before heading for the Gulf Coast and returning by ship to New Orleans and on up the Mississippi to St. Louis.

25. Kennerly, *Persimmon Hill*, 34.

26. Victor Tixier, *Tixier's Travels on the Osage Prairies*, ed. John Francis McDermott, trans. Albert J. Salvan, 97–98. Tixier (1815–85), who trained as a physician in his native France, traveled up the Missouri by steamboat from St. Louis to Lexington and then overland to Independence before heading for Osage country.

27. Emily Ann O'Neil Bott, "Joseph Murphy's Contribution to the Development of the West," 22. Mark L. Gardner critiques the legend of the Murphy "monster" wagon in *Wagons for the Santa Fe Trade: Wheeled Vehicles and Their Makers, 1822–1880*, 35–39.

28. Gregg, *Commerce of the Prairies*, 80.

29. Ralph P. Bieber, ed., "Letters of James and Robert Aull," 280. See also Lewis E. Atherton, "James and Robert Aull—A Frontier Missouri Mercantile Firm," 18. Atherton comments that the goods James Aull offered to Santa Fe traders "were purchased in the East in January on credit and were sold on credit to the caravans in May. Some return was made in the autumn, but twenty-four months would elapse before all the money could be collected." For more on James Aull (1805–47) and the credit problems plaguing the Santa Fe trade, see Moorhead, *New Mexico's Royal Road*, 79–80.

30. Webb, *Adventures in the Santa Fé Trade*, 41–42.

31. Parkman, *Oregon Trail*, 1.

32. Ibid., 2.

33. Parkman, *Journals*, 2:416. Curiously, this entry is dated "April 31st."

34. Ibid.

35. Ibid., 417. Speyer (d. 1880), born in Prussia, entered the Santa Fe Trade around 1843. He later became involved in an even riskier business, assisting financier Jay Gould in an effort to corner the gold market in New York in 1869.

36. Parkman, *Oregon Trail*, 2–3.

CHAPTER 6

1. Gregg, *Commerce of the Prairies*, 22.

2. Edwin James, *Account of an Expedition from Pittsburgh to the Rocky Mountains*, 2 vols., 1:11–12.

3. Jonas Viles, "Old Franklin: A Frontier Town of the Twenties," 275–77. Viles notes that many who settled in Franklin were Kentuckians "of some means who brought slaves,

blooded stock, and considerable cash with them." For a more recent look at Franklin and its role in the development of the Santa Fe trade, see Simmons, *Along the Santa Fe Trail*, 3–15.

4. *Missouri Intelligencer*, August 14, 1821.

5. Ibid., June 25, 1821. Becknell's article is reprinted in *Wagon Tracks* 7 (November 1992): 22.

6. Larry Mahon Beachum, "To the Westward: William Becknell and the Beginning of the Santa Fe Trade," 6. See also Beachum, *William Becknell*, 21–24.

7. *Missouri Intelligencer*, May 13, 1823. This reference to Colonel Cooper indicates that Benjamin Cooper, rather than his nephew Stephen Cooper, was captain of this beleaguered company, which went west in May, lost most of its horses and mules to an Indian raid in early June, and later suffered terribly from thirst before reaching Santa Fe, as recounted by Joel Walker.

8. *Missouri Intelligencer*, June 2, 1826: "It has the air of romance to see splendid carriages, with elegant horses, journeying to the Republic of Mexico; yet it is sober reality."

9. [Alphonso Wetmore], "Book of the Muleteers," Chapter One, *Missouri Intelligencer*, August 5, 1825; reprinted in *Wagon Tracks* 5 (August 1991): 1–2; and *New Mexico Historical Review* 17 (October 1942): 288–90. Wetmore may have been inspired here by reports concerning Benjamin Cooper's troubled 1823 expedition, whose members suffered so from thirst. After the "men and brethren of the tribe of Benjamin" reached the "great desert," Wetmore quipped in this same article, "their tongues were parched and cleaved unto the roofs of their mouths." Each man "went his own way in search of a fountain," until Benjamin rallied them and led them to water.

10. [Alphonso Wetmore], "Book of the Muleteers," Chapter Two, *Missouri Intelligencer*, August 19, 1825; reprinted in *Wagon Tracks* 5 (August 1991): 3; and *New Mexico Historical Review* 17 (October 1942): 291–93.

11. *Missouri Intelligencer*, October 12, 1826; reprinted in Edwin L. Sabin, *Kit Carson Days: 1809–1868*, 2 vols., 1:12. Kit Carson (1809–68), born in Kentucky, came to Missouri as an infant in 1811 when his family immigrated to Howard County. He had brothers in the Santa Fe trade and may have joined one or more of them in the 1826 caravan after fleeing his apprenticeship.

12. *Missouri Intelligencer*, June 9, 1826. See the account of this trip by José Agustín Escudero in *Three New Mexico Chronicles*, ed. and trans. H. Bailey Carroll and J. Villasana Haggard, 114–15. As explained there, Manuel Simón Escudero had traveled from Mexico to Missouri and on to Washington, D.C., in 1825 after accepting a commission from the Mexican government "to go to the United States of North America . . . in an effort to obtain the necessary protection for caravans traveling across the vast unoccupied spaces, and also to protect our frontiers from the Indians who were perpetrating depredations on both frontiers." Manuel Simón Escudero completed his diplomatic mission in early 1826 and evidently tried to recoup some of the costs of his long journey by purchasing trade goods and conducting them back to New Mexico that summer. As José Agustín Escudero wrote: "He made the trip from Mexico to the United States at his own expense and, in a grievous journey, sustained a great financial loss." For background on the Escuderos and their role in the Santa Fe trade, see Susan Calafate Boyle, *Los Capitalistas: Hispano Merchants and the Santa Fe Trade*, 58–59.

13. William Workman, "A Letter from Taos, 1826," ed. David J. Weber, 158–59. For more on William Workman (1800–1876) and his brother David (1798–1855), see David J. Weber, "William Workman," in Hafen, *Mountain Men and the Fur Trade*, 7:381–92.

14. Workman, "Letter from Taos," 159.

15. Barry, *Beginning of the West*, 142. David Workman resided in Missouri as late as 1838, when he played host at his home in New Franklin to the unfortunate Sarah Ann Horn, a Texan abducted by Comanches in 1836 who was later ransomed in New Mexico and aided by William Workman and other sympathizers, who saw her safely back east along the Santa Fe Trail.

16. Edwin James, *Account of an Expedition*, 89. For an account of the slow death of Old Franklin at the hands of the encroaching Missouri, see H. Denny Davis, "Franklin: Cradle of the Trade." The worst in a series of floods struck the town in June 1844, Davis notes, when the *Boon's Lick Times* reported that the water was "deep enough in the streets of Old Franklin . . . to make them navigable for the largest class of steam boats" (16).

17. Gregg, *Commerce of the Prairies*, 23.

18. *Missouri Intelligencer*, June 4, 1825.

CHAPTER 7

1. Gregg, *Commerce of the Prairies*, 23.

2. Charles Joseph Latrobe, *The Rambler in North America: 1832–1833*, 2 vols., 1:128. Latrobe (1801–75) had more to say about Independence than did his traveling companion Washington Irving, who made only passing reference to the town in his journal; see *The Western Journals of Washington Irving*, ed. John Francis McDermott, 20, 89.

3. John Kirk Townsend, *Narrative of a Journey across the Rocky Mountains to the Columbia River*, ed. Ruben Gold Thwaites, intro. Donald Jackson, 25–26. See Jackson's introduction for more on Townsend (1809–51), a well-educated Philadelphian who made the journey with his fellow naturalist Thomas Nuttall (1786–1859), from Harvard. In St. Louis the two men purchased clothing of the sort that made greenhorns from back East stick out like sore thumbs on western trails, including "enormous overcoats, made of green blankets, and white wool hats, with round crowns, fitting tightly to the head, brims five inches wide, and almost hard enough to resist a rifle ball" (ibid., 11–12).

4. Barry, *Beginning of the West*, 266.

5. *Missouri Intelligencer and Boon's Lick Advertiser* (Fayette, Mo.), July 17, 1829.

6. Conard, *"Uncle Dick" Wootton*, 35–36. As pointed out by Conard, Wootton was born on "the sixth day of May, 1816" (ibid., 28). He was thus twenty years old in the summer of 1836.

7. Pike, *Prose Sketches and Poems*, 227–28.

8. Farnham, *Travels in the Great Western Prairies*, 11.

9. Garrard, *Wah-to-yah*, 55.

10. Gregg, *Commerce of the Prairies*, 26.

11. Field, *Matt Field on the Santa Fe Trail*, 64–65.

12. Taylor, *Short Ravelings*, 2.

13. George Frederick Ruxton, *Life in the Far West*, ed. Leroy R. Hafen, 11. Loosely translated, Maurice's reply means that the one hundred or so Indians he saw by the creek were a war party because they were on foot rather than on horseback and carried lariats to rope horses or mules (which they would then ride or lead back to their camp).

14. Ibid., 55–56.

15. Ibid., 53.

16. Ibid., 56–57.

17. Letter of John McCoy to his brother Samuel dated July 5, 1838, in an unpaginated booklet entitled *Pioneering on the Plains*. Storekeeper John McCoy—not to be confused with merchant John Calvin McCoy, who helped found the town of Westport in the mid-1830s—was referring specifically here to mountain men, but he observed in the same letter that men from the Santa Fe companies appeared much the same when they came in, "bearing more the resemblance of savages than civilized beings. They look like tenants indeed of other regions from this." In another letter written later in 1838, he complained that those arriving from the East to settle in the area were rather untidy as well: "These folks clean their feet a little too much upon the front plate and deposit a superabundance of snow and mud. This we have to bear patiently hoping that a few removals westward, or Platte-wards, may clear us from this present population." All this was good for business, however, and McCoy had little cause to regret his move to Independence. "This is a great place," he wrote, "depend upon it."

18. Tixier, *Travels on the Osage Prairies*, 103.

19. Ibid., 104.

20. *Weston Journal*, January 18, 1845. Editor George Gibson started up the *Weston Journal* in January 1845 as the successor to his short-lived *Independence Journal*.

21. Ruxton, *Life in the Far West*, 11.

22. Webb, *Adventures in the Santa Fé Trade*, 45.

23. Wislizenus, *Memoir of a Tour to Northern Mexico*, 14. Speyer told Wislizenus that the mules "crowded all around a little fire which he had kindled, but the cold was so intense that most of them died the same night; and others, in a state of starvation, commenced eating the ears of the dead ones." Their bones become relics on the road to New Mexico, witnessed by many a pilgrim and rearranged in bizarre formations by some of the more irreverent of them.

24. Moorhead, *New Mexico's Royal Road*, 89–90; Webb, *Adventures in the Santa Fé Trade*, 107.

25. *Independence Journal*, October 24, 1844. Samuel C. Owens (1800–1847), born in Kentucky, was one of the founders of Independence. See Bieber's biographical note in Webb, *Adventures in the Santa Fé Trade*, 42 n. 53.

26. Rufus B. Sage, *Rufus B. Sage: His Letters and Papers, 1836–1847*, ed. LeRoy R. Hafen and Ann W. Hafen, 2 vols., 2:45. This edition includes a reprint of Sage's travel narrative, published in 1846 under the title *Scenes in the Rocky Mountains, and in Oregon, California, New Mexico, Texas, and the Grand Prairies*. Sage (1817–93), born in Connecticut and trained as a printer, began his three-year western odyssey at Independence in 1841 with the avowed intention of collecting materials "for a *book*, which I intend publishing upon my return" (ibid., 1:84).

27. Ibid., 134–35.

28. Field, *Matt Field on the Santa Fe Trail*, 278–79.

29. *Independence Journal*, September 19, 1844.

30. Waugh, *Travels in Search of the Elephant*, 91–92. Waugh, in notes supplemented by editor McDermott, identifies many of those in town during the spring of 1846.

31. Ibid., 95.

32. Edwin Bryant, *What I Saw in California*, 15. Bryant (1805–69), a native of Massachusetts, was a seasoned journalist by the time he set out for California in 1846.

33. W. Z. Hickman, *History of Jackson County, Missouri*, 176.

34. Parkman, *Journals*, 2:415.

35. Hickman, *History of Jackson County*, 175–76.

36. Waugh, *Travels in Search of the Elephant*, 109.

37. Ibid., 110.

38. Ibid., 108.

39. Ibid., 93.

40. Ibid., 93–94.

41. Ibid., 94 n. 119.

42. Ibid., 129.

43. Parkman, *Oregon Trail*, 3–4.

44. Parkman, *Journals*, 2:417.

45. Wislizenus, *Memoir of a Tour to Northern Mexico*, 5.

46. Ibid.

CHAPTER 8

1. Farnham, *Travels in the Great Western Prairies*, 12. Obadiah Oakley, a member of Farnham's company, agreed that the prairie just west of the Missouri border was "one of the finest countries the eye of man ever gazed upon" (Oakley in Hafen and Hafen, *To the Rockies and Oregon*, 28).

2. Bryant, *What I Saw in California*, 22.

3. Ibid., 24.

4. Wislizenus, *Memoir of a Tour to Northern Mexico*, 5.

5. Bryant, *What I Saw in California*, 15.

6. Ibid., 34. Bryant observed that these traders returning from Santa Fe were driving before them about a thousand mules, so lean that their ribs were showing, "and the bones of some of them appeared to have worn through the flesh. I never saw a more ghostly collection of animals. The operative men composing these companies were principally New-Mexicans; the chiefs of the parties, however, were Americans. They all presented a most fagged and worn appearance."

7. Wislizenus, *Memoir of a Tour to Northern Mexico*, 6. As Wislizenus feared, that surviving tree at Lone Elm did not last long. W. W. H. Davis, passing through in 1853, wrote its obituary: "Travelers came to look upon it as an old friend—they felt an attachment for the tree that had so often sheltered and shaded them from storm and sun, and no inducement could have made them cut it down. But in the course of time some modern Vandal came along, and laid low this last of its race; and when we passed, it was all gone but

a small portion of the stump, and part of that cooked our breakfast" (Davis, *El Gringo*, 19).

8. Gregg, *Commerce of the Prairies*, 27.

9. Garrard, *Wah-to-yah*, 56.

10. Gregg, *Commerce of the Prairies*, 28.

11. Wislizenus, *Memoir of a Tour to Northern Mexico*, 6.

12. Gregg, *Commerce of the Prairies*, 29.

13. Ibid., 28.

14. Ibid., 29.

15. Sibley, *Road to Santa Fe*, 57.

16. Ibid., 253 n. 40.

17. Ibid., 57–58.

18. Richard Peters, ed., *The Public Statutes at Large of the United States of America*, 7:240.

19. Ibid., 269.

20. Ibid.

21. Sibley, *Road to Santa Fe*, 58–59.

22. William E. Unrau, *The Kansa Indians: A History of the Wind People, 1673–1873*, 160.

23. Taylor, *Short Ravelings*, 24.

24. Gregg, *Commerce of the Prairies* 29–30. The letter Gregg refers to here was first published anonymously in the *Evansville Journal* and reprinted in *Niles' National Register* on December 4, 1841. The author, perhaps John McClure of Indiana, joined up that summer with a westbound caravan that included Richard Wilson, whose account formed the basis for Taylor's *Short Ravelings*. See White, *News of the Plains and Rockies*, 2:135–43.

25. Farnham, *Travels in the Great Western Prairies*, 15–16.

26. Another who later expressed similar fears was Susan Shelby Magoffin, who, while visiting Big John's Spring near Council Grove, had visions of "some wily savage or hungry wolf . . . lurking in the thick grape vines" (Magoffin, *Down the Santa Fe Trail*, 18).

27. Farnham, *Travels in the Great Western Prairies*, 18.

28. Wislizenus, *Memoir of a Tour to Northern Mexico*, 7.

29. Gregg, *Commerce of the Prairies*, 30–31.

30. Ibid., 32–33; Barry, *Beginning of the West*, 204.

31. Gregg, *Commerce of the Prairies*, 33–34.

32. Field, *Matt Field on the Santa Fe Trail*, 79.

33. Fairholme, *Journal of an Expedition*, 89–91.

34. Ibid., 90.

35. Cooke, *Scenes and Adventures*, 240.

36. Webb, *Adventures in the Santa Fé Trade*, 46.

37. Ibid., 47.

38. Field, *Matt Field on the Santa Fe Trail*, 79–80.

39. Garrard, *Wah-to-yah*, 61.

40. Frank Doster, "Eleventh Indiana Cavalry in Kansas in 1865," 524.

41. Gregg, *Commerce of the Prairies*, 35–36.

CHAPTER 9

1. Sibley, *Road to Santa Fe*, 60.
2. Cooke, *Scenes and Adventures*, 241–42.
3. Webb, *Adventures in the Santa Fé Trade*, 47–48.
4. Gregg, *Commerce of the Prairies*, 37.
5. Wetmore in Hulbert, *Southwest on the Turquoise Trail*, 184–85.
6. Farnham, *Travels in the Great Western Prairies*, 22.
7. Sibley, *Road to Santa Fe*, 60.
8. Farnham, *Travels in the Great Western Prairies*, 18.
9. Ibid., 23.
10. Oakley in Hafen and Hafen, *To the Rockies and Oregon*, 37. These catfish were caught by Oakley and other members of a hunting party who set out in advance of the others. Farnham related that the hunters roasted and ate part of the catch fresh and left the rest for their trailing comrades, who found the fish the next day "in an unwholesome state of decomposition" but devoured them anyway (Farnham, *Travels in the Great Western Prairies*, 22). Obadiah Oakley (1815–50) first offered accounts of his journey to the press in 1839, two years before Farnham's book was published. By and large, the two men agreed in their interpretation of events, while differing sharply with some others in their party (see chapter 12).
11. Field, *Matt Field on the Santa Fe Trail*, 83–84.
12. Ibid., 88–89.
13. Ibid., 89.
14. Ibid., 111–12.
15. Fairholme, *Journal of an Expedition*, 98–99.
16. Webb, *Adventures in the Santa Fé Trade*, 51.
17. Garrard, *Wah-to-yah*, 74.
18. Oakley in Hafen and Hafen, *To the Rockies and Oregon*, 42.
19. Cooke, *Scenes and Adventures*, 43.
20. Webb, *Adventures in the Santa Fé Trade*, 60, 72.
21. Ibid., 62.
22. William Henry Glasgow in Gardner, *Brothers on the Santa Fe and Chihuahua Trails*, 84.
23. Ibid., 85.
24. Cooke, *Scenes and Adventures*, 274–75.
25. Ibid., 275–76.
26. Garrard, *Wah-to-yah*, 66.
27. Plains Indians sometimes killed more buffalo than they could make use of by driving the animals off cliffs or into traps, but most bands were efficient in their hunting techniques. William Boggs, who visited Bent's Fort in the mid-1840s at a time when Cheyennes in that area were surrounding and killing large numbers of buffalo for the fur trade, observed that they packed away much of the meat—enough to feed an encampment for several weeks—and took measures to preserve the herds: "They never hunted or killed the buffalo in the springtime of the year when the cows were dropping their calves." William M. Boggs, "The W. M. Boggs Manuscript about Bent's Fort, Kit Carson, the Far West, and Life among the Indians," ed. LeRoy R. Hafen, 66.

28. Philip St. George Cooke, "The Journal of Captain Philip St. George Cooke, First U.S. Dragoons, on an Escort of Santa Fe Traders in the Year of 1843," ed. Harry C. Myers, 55–56. For a briefer account of this same episode, see Cooke, *Scenes and Adventures*, 260–61.

29. Milo Milton Quaife, ed., *Kit Carson's Autobiography*, 5–6. This same operation is described by Gregg in *Commerce of the Prairies*, 41–42. The amateur surgeon who performed the amputation has been identified as Richard Gentry of Columbia, Missouri, who ventured three times to Santa Fe between 1826 and 1830. See Richard R. Forry, "Richard Gentry: Trader and Patriot." For another account of an amputation on the Santa Fe Trail, see Alphonso Wetmore's 1828 diary: "The whole operation was concluded by the application of a dressing from the nearest tar bucket. Not a groan nor a sigh was uttered during the operation, and the patient recovered" (Wetmore in Hulbert, *Southwest on the Turquoise Trail*, 197).

30. Conard, *"Uncle Dick" Wootton*, 90–91.

31. Ibid., 92.

32. Ibid., 90.

33. Ibid., 42.

CHAPTER 10

1. Gregg, *Commerce of the Prairies*, 16.

2. Becknell in White, *News of the Plains and Rockies*, 2:61–62.

3. Gregg, *Commerce of the Prairies*, 417.

4. Benjamin R. Kracht, "The Kiowa and the Santa Fe Trail," 27.

5. Gregg, *Commerce of the Prairies*, 413.

6. Field, *Matt Field on the Santa Fe Trail*, 124–25.

7. Conard, *"Uncle Dick" Wootton*, 41.

8. Storrs in White, *News of the Plains and Rockies*, 2:91.

9. Gregg, *Commerce of the Prairies*, 19. For more on these hostilities in 1828 and the calls for protection that led to Major Riley's 1829 escort, see Otis E. Young, *The First Military Escort on the Santa Fe Trail, 1829*, 15–45; Leo E. Oliva, "The 1829 Escorts," in *Confrontation on the Santa Trail*, 17–19; and David Dary, *The Santa Fe Trail: Its History, Legends, and Lore*, 111–16.

10. Cooke, *Scenes and Adventures*, 42.

11. Ibid., 46.

12. Riley in White, *News of the Plains and Rockies*, 2:116–17. Otis Young argues that Cooke wrote this report "at Riley's instance" (*First Military Escort*, 59).

13. Cooke, *Scenes and Adventures*, 47–48.

14. William Waldo, "Recollections of a Septuagenarian," 73. William Waldo (1812–81), born in Virginia and raised in Missouri, died in Texas, shortly after writing this memoir and a few months shy of his seventieth birthday.

15. Cooke, *Scenes and Adventures*, 60.

16. *Missouri Intelligencer*, May 8, 1829; in Young, *First Military Escort*, 42.

17. Cooke, *Scenes and Adventures*, 48–49.

18. David Waldo in Young, *First Military Escort*, 186. David Waldo's authorship of this letter is indicated by the fact that he was first to sign the document, which bears little resemblance stylistically to Bent's correspondence.

19. Cooke, *Scenes and Adventures*, 49.

20. Riley in White, *News of the Plains and Rockies*, 2:118.

21. Cooke, *Scenes and Adventures*, 60.

22. Ibid., 52–53.

23. Ibid., 54.

24. Ibid., 53.

25. Ibid., 53–54.

26. Riley in White, *News of the Plains and Rockies*, 2:119.

27. Cooke, *Scenes and Adventures*, 59.

28. Ibid., 56.

29. Waldo, "Recollections of a Septuagenarian," 69. Although Waldo erred in stating that Comanches had been at war with whites since 1828, he testified graciously to many kindnesses done him by Indians over the years: "I have been found exhausted and starving, and have been hospitably entertained by them" (ibid., 76).

30. For a discussion of the half-dozen or so escorts conducted by American troops between 1829 and the outbreak of the Mexican War, see Leo E. Oliva, *Soldiers on the Santa Fe Trail*, 25–54.

31. Wharton in Fred S. Perrine, "Military Escorts on the Santa Fe Trail," *New Mexico Historical Review* 2 (July 1927): 273–76.

32. Ibid., 278.

33. Gregg in ibid., 304. In this letter to Wharton, dated June 27, 1834, Gregg did not specify why he considered himself unworthy of continuing as captain of the caravan. But he seemed torn between cooperating with Wharton (whom he thanked here for his "sincere & unceasing desire to lend us every possible aid") and satisfying the more militant traders in his company, who wanted the Comanches driven away. It was not Gregg's finest hour, and he made no mention of this tangled episode in his book.

34. Wharton in ibid., 284.

35. Gregg later identified the Indians encountered by Vizcarra as Gros Ventres in *Commerce of the Prairies*, 60. But Cooke, who was closer to the event than Gregg, referred to them as "Ar-ra-pa-hoes and Camanches (our old friends)" in *Scenes and Adventures*, 84. If there were indeed Comanches among this party, then they were most likely accompanied not by Arapahos but by allied Kiowas. The incident occurred in an area dominated by Kiowas and Comanches, and both tribes had been at odds with Mexicans in recent years.

36. Cooke, *Scenes and Adventures*, 84–85.

37. Austin Smith to his father, September 24, 1831, in Barry, *Beginning of the West*, 202. For a discussion of the circumstances surrounding the death of Jedediah Smith (1798–1831), see Harrison Clifford Dale, ed., *The Explorations of William H. Ashley and Jedediah Smith, 1822–1829*, 300–310.

38. Gregg, *Commerce of the Prairies*, 65.

39. Wetmore in Hulbert, *Southwest on the Turquoise Trail*, 190–91. This entry from Wetmore's diary, dated July 16, 1828, evidently refers to the two traders, McNees and Monroe, who were attacked while asleep by Comanches while returning from New Mexico that year, setting off the disturbances that peaked in 1829. Wetmore could not have seen their gravesites on his way west in July 1828, for they were not attacked until later in

the year. Apparently, he added this description of the burial place to his diary before submitting it to Secretary of War Lewis Cass in 1831.

40. In 1839, long after the truce between New Mexicans and Comanches ended, Josiah Gregg met along the upper Canadian River with a band of Comancheros who were returning to New Mexico after a trading venture. He reported that they seemed eager to have the protection of Gregg's party "against the savages, who, after selling their animals to the Mexicans, very frequently take forcible possession of them again, before the purchasers have been able to reach their homes" (*Commerce of the Prairies*, 257). One wonders just how frequently the Comancheros suffered such losses, inasmuch as they still found the trip worth making. This vulnerable trade could not long have survived any concerted hostility on the part of Comanches.

41. Mexico later lifted the ban on residents of Spanish birth, and some of these women returned with family members to Santa Fe in 1831 with the same caravan that Josiah Gregg joined on his inaugural journey to New Mexico. See *Commerce of the Prairies*, 33; and Marc Simmons, "New Mexico's Spanish Exiles."

42. Cooke, *Scenes and Adventures*, 86–87.

CHAPTER 11

1. Wetmore in Hulbert, *Southwest on the Turquoise Trail*, 176–77.

2. Gregg, *Commerce of the Prairies*, 47.

3. Ibid., 50.

4. Pike, *Prose Sketches and Poems*, 231.

5. Gregg, *Commerce of the Prairies*, 51–52.

6. Ibid., 52.

7. Ibid., 53.

8. Ibid., 55. Editor Moorhead identifies the oasis Gregg refers to here as the Lower Cimarron Spring.

9. Ibid., 57.

10. Pike, *Prose Sketches and Poems*, 232–33. That animals could be scorched by fires fueled only by buffalo chips was confirmed by Gregg, who reported that buffalo dung when dry gave off more heat than a wood fire (*Commerce of the Prairies*, 237).

11. Pike, *Prose Sketches and Poems*, 232.

12. Gregg, *Commerce of the Prairies*, 68.

13. Wetmore in Hulbert, *Southwest on the Turquoise Trail*, 192.

14. Ibid.

15. Gregg, *Commerce of the Prairies*, 71.

16. Pike, *Prose Sketches and Poems*, 235–36.

17. Wetmore in Hulbert, *Southwest on the Turquoise Trail*, 193 (*amor de la patria*: "love of country"; *mi alma* means "my soul," but often serves as an endearment for loved ones).

18. Gregg, *Commerce of the Prairies*, 63.

19. Lieutenant John G. Bourke in Marc Simmons, *Coronado's Land: Essays on Daily Life in Colonial New Mexico*, 81. This same quote accompanies a *carreta* on display at the Palace of the Governors in Santa Fe.

CHAPTER 12

1. Farnham, *Travels in the Great Western Prairies*, 21. Although Farnham identifies the "partner" he encountered only as Mr. Bent, the man in question was Charles Bent. See Barry, *Beginning of the West*, 371–73; and Hafen and Hafen, *To the Rockies and Oregon*, 36 n. 18, 99.

2. Farnham, *Travels in the Great Western Prairies*, 21. Oakley noted that they were later rewarded for retrieving many of the lost animals and delivering them to Bent's Fort, receiving "two of the mules and 200 lbs. of flour for their trouble" (Oakley in Hafen and Hafen, *To the Rockies and Oregon*, 40).

3. Farnham, *Travels in the Great Western Prairies*, 22–23.

4. Ibid., 24.

5. Ibid., 27.

6. Oakley in Hafen and Hafen, *To the Rockies and Oregon*, 40.

7. Farnham, *Travels in the Great Western Prairies*, 27.

8. Ibid., 28.

9. Ibid., 30.

10. Ibid., 31.

11. Ibid. The doctor referred to by Farnham as "Walworth," or David Waldo, was one of the leaders of the spring caravan in 1839 along with the Spanish-born Manuel Alvarez, who was on his way to Santa Fe to become U.S. consul there. See Hafen and Hafen, *To the Rockies and Oregon*, 41 n. 27; Barry, *Beginning of the West*, 369–70; and Moorhead, *New Mexico's Royal Road*, 123 n. 1.

12. Farnham, *Travels in the Great Western Prairies*, 34–35.

13. Oakley in Hafen and Hafen, *To the Rockies and Oregon*, 45.

14. Farnham, *Travels in the Great Western Prairies*, 35.

15. Shortess in Hafen and Hafen, *To the Rockies and Oregon*, 297. Unlike the restless Farnham, Robert Shortess (ca. 1800–1878) remained in Oregon and played a part in its organization as an American territory.

16. Ibid., 97.

17. Holman in Hafen and Hafen, *To the Rockies and Oregon*, 127. Joseph Holman (1815–80), born in England, settled in Oregon at the end of this journey and helped found the town of Salem.

18. W. H. Gray in Hafen and Hafen, *To the Rockies and Oregon*, 95.

19. Farnham, *Travels in the Great Western Prairies*, 39.

20. Ibid.

21. Ibid., 70. William Bent, as manager of the outpost—often referred to by Farnham and others as Fort William—was almost certainly present; and Matt Field noted when he passed through a month after Farnham that Robert Bent was there as well (*Matt Field on the Santa Fe Trail*, 144). For more on the history of this outpost and the careers of Charles Bent (1799–1847) and William Bent (1809–69), see David Lavender, *Bent's Fort*; and Harold H. Dunham, "Charles Bent," in Hafen, *Mountain Men and the Fur Trade*, 2:27–48.

22. Farnham, *Travels in the Great Western Prairies*, 65. Bent's Fort has been meticulously reconstructed. For an account of the original fort by one who contributed to that

reconstruction, see Enid Thompson, "Life in an Adobe Castle, 1833–1849." For eyewitness accounts of the outpost, see Nolie Mumey, *Old Forts and Trading Posts of the West: Bent's Old Fort and Bent's New Fort on the Arkansas River.*

23. Farnham, *Travels in the Great Western Prairies,* 70.

24. Ibid., 66.

25. Ibid., 66–67.

26. Oakley in Hafen and Hafen, *To the Rockies and Oregon,* 49–50.

27. Field, *Matt Field on the Santa Fe Trail,* 127.

28. Ibid., 128. Field also memorialized Bernardo in verse: "None but the wolves shall visit thee, / Their howl thy requiem shall be" (ibid., 37).

29. Ibid., 128.

30. Ibid., 144.

31. Ibid., 145.

32. Ibid., 146.

33. Another traveler, E. Willard Smith, who passed Bent's Fort in early September 1839, wrote that "Mr Bent had seventy horses stolen from the fort this summer by a party of Comanchee Indians, nine in number," according to the version of his journal found in the *Quarterly of the Oregon Historical Society* 14 (September 1913): 258; also found in Hafen and Hafen, *To the Rockies and Oregon,* 163. Still another account of the losses at Bent's Fort in the summer of 1839 was offered by Frederick Wislizenus, who stopped there in September. "At the time they had no superfluity of horses at the fort," he wrote, "because only a short time before a band of Indians with incredible audacity had driven away a hundred head of horses" (*Journey to the Rocky Mountains,* 141).

34. Field, *Matt Field on the Santa Fe Trail,* 157, 160.

35. Ibid., 149.

36. Conard, *"Uncle Dick" Wootton,* 111–12.

37. James Hobbs, *Wild Life in the Far West: Personal Adventures of a Border Mountain Man,* 34. Hobbs recalled that he went west with Charles Bent and company in 1835, but David Lavender argues that the year was 1836 (*Bent's Fort,* 422 n. 1).

38. One of Hobbs's more blatant errors or fabrications was his assertion that Colonel Alexander Doniphan, after occupying Chihuahua in March 1847, dispatched him to Santa Fe, where he supposedly conferred with Governor Charles Bent—who had in fact been assassinated in January. Hobbs, *Wild Life in the Far West,* 137–39.

39. Ibid., 24.

40. Ibid., 29.

41. Conard, *"Uncle Dick" Wootton,* 96.

42. Catlin, *Letters and Notes,* 2:67–69.

43. Hobbs, *Wild Life in the Far West,* 47. David Lavender includes the ransoming of Hobbs in his account of the 1840 peace talks (*Bent's Fort,* 202).

44. Hobbs, *Wild Life in the Far West,* 48–49.

45. Conard, *"Uncle Dick" Wootton,* 108.

46. Hobbs, *Wild Life in the Far West,* 19.

47. As David Lavender remarks of Bent, St. Vrain and Co., "they unquestionably resorted to liquor when circumstances demanded" (*Bent's Fort,* 160).

48. Sarah M. Olson, "Furnishing a Frontier Outpost," 162–63.

49. Barclay in Hammond, *Adventures of Alexander Barclay*, 26.

50. Boggs, "The W. M. Boggs Manuscript about Bent's Fort," 48–49. Boggs added that the Cheyenne chief Cinemo, or Old Tobacco, "a great friend of the white traders of Bent's Company," was shot to death by an American soldier or teamster in 1846 after mistaking a hand gesture meaning "Go back" for an Indian sign meaning "come quick." Cinemo "lived but a few hours or days," Boggs related, "and warned his tribe not to go to war with the whites, as they threatened revenge for his death" (ibid., 52).

51. Ibid., 49.

52. Ibid., 50.

53. Ibid., 69.

54. J. W. Abert, *Gúadal P'a: The Journal of Lieutenant J. W. Abert, from Bent's Fort to St. Louis in 1845*, intro. and notes by H. Bailey Carroll, 10. James W. Abert (1820–97) graduated from West Point in 1842 and followed this tour in 1845 by serving as a topographical engineer during the American occupation of New Mexico in 1846.

55. Ibid., 11–12.

56. Ibid., 13.

57. Ibid., 15.

58. Sublette in Mumey, *Old Forts and Trading Posts*, 64.

59. Garrard, *Wah-to-yah*, 75.

60. Ibid., 165.

61. Ibid., 83.

62. Ibid., 120.

63. Ibid., 132. Garrard followed this disdainful passage by detailing his own contribution to the liquor traffic: "We began to trade briskly in robes—owing to the cold weather, plenty of buffalo, and liquor, which last seemed to open the Indians' hearts."

64. Ibid., 114.

65. Ibid., 145.

66. Ibid., 129–30.

67. Barclay in Hammond, *Adventures of Alexander Barclay*, 25.

68. *St. Louis Weekly Reveille*, May 18, 1846; reprinted in Edgeley W. Todd, "Bent's Fort in 1846," 210.

69. Janet Lecompte calculates that "between 1832 and 1858 there were more than a dozen distinct trading posts and settlements along a hundred-mile stretch of the Arkansas River and its tributaries in the present state of Colorado" (*Pueblo, Hardscrabble, Greenhorn: Society on the High Plains, 1832–1856*, xi). Most of those establishments were west of the Timpas Creek turnoff that led travelers heading for New Mexico on the Mountain Route through Raton Pass. The two trading posts dealt with here—Bent's Fort and Pueblo de Leche—were east of Timpas Creek and thus served as noteworthy stops for some on the Santa Fe Trail.

70. Field, *Matt Field on the Santa Fe Trail*, 151.

71. Ibid., 152.

72. Ibid., 153. Thomas Farnham, who reached Pueblo de Leche shortly before Field, was little impressed with the place, perhaps because trappers had recently arrived there with whiskey to trade: "The proprietors are poor, and when the keg is on tap, dream away their existence under its dangerous fascinations" (*Travels in the Great Western Prairies*, 71).

73. Abert, *Gúadal P'a*, 31.

74. Conard, *"Uncle Dick" Wootton*, 157–58.

75. Field, *Matt Field on the Santa Fe Trail*, 156–57.

76. Ibid., 162–63.

CHAPTER 13

1. Becknell in White, *News of the Plains and Rockies*, 2:64–65.

2. Pedro Ignacio Gallego, "The Diary of Pedro Ignacio Gallego," ed. Michael L. Olsen and Harry C. Myers, 18.

3. Becknell in White, *News of the Plains and Rockies*, 2:65.

4. Antonio Barreiro, "Ojeada sobre Nuevo Mexico," ed. and trans. Lansing B. Bloom, 96. Barreiro's "Ojeada" ("glance" or "quick look" over New Mexico), composed in 1832, is also incorporated in Carroll and Haggard, *Three New Mexico Chronicles*.

5. Becknell in White, *News of the Plains and Rockies*, 2:67.

6. Thomas James, *Three Years among the Indians*, 134.

7. Ibid., 139.

8. Ibid., 141–43.

9. Facundo Melgares, "An Unforgettable Day: Facundo Melgares on Independence," ed. David J. Weber, 41–42.

10. Thomas James, *Three Years among the Indians*, 143–44.

11. Ibid., 138.

12. Ibid., 146–47.

13. Ibid., 148–49.

14. Ibid., 157–58.

15. Ibid., 160.

16. For more on the problems facing the young Mexican republic and its northernmost territories, see David J. Weber, *The Mexican Frontier, 1821–1846: The American Southwest under Mexico*, 1–42. At the time of independence, New Mexico, formerly a province of New Spain, became a Mexican territory. In the 1830s it would be designated a department of Mexico before reverting to territorial status under American control.

17. Marmaduke, "Journal," 14.

18. Ibid.

19. Barreiro, "Ojeada," 160.

20. Marmaduke, "Journal," 14–15.

21. Ibid., 15.

22. Sibley, *Road to Santa Fe*, 111. The valley of Taos contained several ranches and settlements, the largest of which was the one known simply as Taos or more elaborately as Don Fernando de Taos (for a prominent early settler), or San Fernández de Taos (for the saint). In some accounts, the town of Taos was referred to as Fernando or Fernández.

23. David J. Weber, *On the Edge of Empire: The Taos Hacienda of Los Martínez*, 60–61. Weber notes that an alcalde "had judicial and legislative as well as executive duties, his responsibilities exceeding those of an Anglo-American mayor" (ibid., 50). Santa Fe had a principal alcalde and several subsidiary ones.

24. Sibley, *Road to Santa Fe*, 113. See also pp. 130–31 for an account of this same meeting in his diary, which served as the basis for his more fully developed journal. Sibley often closed his journal entries with observations on the weather, but this day may have been especially fine for him, given the barriers he overcame.

25. Ibid., 38. In the words of editor Kate Gregg, Sibley "waited with something of the patience of oaks and glaciers." It could take many months for written inquiries and replies to travel back and forth between Santa Fe and Mexico City.

26. Ibid., 134.

27. Ibid., 135.

28. See, for example, Josiah Gregg, who concludes that "the little procession is nothing but glee and merriment" (*Commerce of the Prairies*, 185).

29. Sibley, *Road to Santa Fe*, 140–41.

30. Ibid., 154–55.

31. Marmaduke, "Journal," 15.

32. James O. Pattie, *The Personal Narrative of James O. Pattie of Kentucky*, ed. Timothy Flint, 54–55. Pattie (ca. 1804–ca. 1833) traveled widely throughout the Far West between the time he reached New Mexico in late 1825 and returned east from California through Mexico in 1830. For more on his travels and tales, see Richard Batman, *American Ecclesiastes: The Stories of James Pattie*.

33. Pattie, *Personal Narrative*, 55.

34. Ibid., 55–56.

35. Official efforts to restrict beaver trapping to licensed Mexicans were not successful. As noted by José Agustín Escudero in 1849: "The North Americans began to corrupt the New Mexicans by purchasing their licenses from them" (Carroll and Haggard, *Three New Mexico Chronicles*, 105).

36. Pattie, *Personal Narrative*, 59. The governor referred to here would have been Antonio Narbona, who took office in September 1825. But whether Narbona actually considered such a proposal from the Americans is an open question, given the possibility that this entire episode was distorted or contrived by Pattie. See Weber, *On the Edge of Empire*, 50, and *Taos Trappers*, 95–96.

37. Pattie, *Personal Narrative*, 69–70.

38. Batman (*American Ecclesiastes*, 114–19) suggests that Pattie and Albert Pike were working from the same tale here.

39. Pike, *Prose Sketches and Poems*, 147–49.

40. Ibid., 150–51.

41. Ibid., 152. Americans were not alone in acknowledging the bravery of the fighting men from Taos Pueblo. As Antonio Barreiro observed: "Their occupants are reputed to be the most valiant in New Mexico and they have given repeated proofs of this in the continuous campaigns which they wage with the barbarous nations to the north" ("Ojeada," 86).

42. Pike, *Prose Sketches and Poems*, 162.

43. Ibid., 157.

44. Ibid., 104–6. Among the Spanish words and phrases Pike does not translate here are *Mira!* ("look!"), *pelayo* (a variant of *pelado*, "pauper"), "*Valgamo Dios y La Virgen!*" ("Good God and the Virgin!" per Weber), *picaros* ("rogues"), and *Tata Dios!* (something like "God the Father," per Weber).

45. Ibid., 127.

46. Ibid., 132–33.

47. Field, *Matt Field on the Santa Fe Trail*, 253. Like other Anglo visitors to New Mexico, Field was taken aback by the instrumental accompaniment to mass: "In a recess at one side of the altar, stood two men, one playing a fiddle and the other a guitar, and on these instruments the musicians seemed to be studying what kind of an extravagant and fantastic discord they could make."

48. Ibid., 179.

49. Ibid., 226.

50. Ibid., 228.

51. Ibid., 228–29.

52. Ibid., 226.

CHAPTER 14

1. For a critique of Gregg's literary treatment of New Mexicans, see Horgan, *Josiah Gregg*, 62–69. Gregg's portrait of the New Mexican people was "failing in sympathy, however keen and accurate it might have been," writes Horgan, who adds that "very few of the early Anglo-Saxon travelers to New Mexico showed any more perception than Gregg in appreciating the valuable qualities of the inhabitants." Indeed, many early Anglo-American visitors showed less appreciation than Gregg did for New Mexicans and their culture. After echoing the complaints of other visitors about the "dreadful state of ignorance" in New Mexico, for example, Gregg qualified that indictment by praising "the correctness with which the common people speak their mother tongue, the Spanish. . . . They have also adopted many significant Indian words from their aboriginal predecessors and neighbors, which serve to embellish and amplify this already beautiful and copious language" (*Commerce of the Prairies*, 142). Such charms were lost on visitors who lacked Gregg's mastery of the language.

2. Gregg, *Commerce of the Prairies*, 77. The town of Las Vegas, situated northeast of San Miguel, sprouted up a few years after Gregg first traveled the trail and promptly supplanted San Miguel as "the first settlement of any note" encountered by those bound for Santa Fe. By 1844, Las Vegas had "three or four hundred inhabitants," according to Webb, *Adventures in the Santa Fé Trade*, 76.

3. Webb, *Adventures in the Santa Fé Trade*, 79.

4. Gregg, *Commerce of the Prairies*, 77.

5. Ibid., 78. The Spanish phrases here refer to "The Americans!—The wagons!—The entry of the caravan!" *Léperos* means literally "lepers," and by extension, any undesirables.

6. Webb, *Adventures in the Santa Fé Trade*, 80.

7. Gregg, *Commerce of the Prairies*, 79.

8. Ibid., 79–80.

9. Janet Lecompte, *Rebellion in Río Arriba, 1837*, 59–64 (*Río Arriba*, or "upriver," was the country north of Santa Fe, as opposed to *Río Abajo*, or "downriver," the country below Santa Fe).

10. William Henry Glasgow in Gardner, *Brothers on the Santa Fe and Chihuahua Trails*, 20–21.

11. Webb, *Adventures in the Santa Fé Trade*, 87.

12. Ibid., 138.

13. Field, *Matt Field on the Santa Fe Trail*, 221 (*douceur*: French for a "softener" or "sweetener"). Field was describing commerce in the plaza in Santa Fe as he witnessed it in 1839. James Webb related that in 1844 Governor Mariano Martínez issued an order that "Americans would not be permitted to retail goods in Santa Fé" (*Adventures in the Santa Fé Trade*, 82). Although this order was in keeping with a new Mexican law that restricted the involvement of foreigners in the retail trade, two American merchants on good terms with Martínez were exempted from the ban, and Americans continued to sell goods from shops in Santa Fe in later years. See Moorhead, *New Mexico's Royal Road*, 137–44.

14. Field, *Matt Field on the Santa Fe Trail*, 213.

15. Ibid.

16. Ibid., 214.

17. Ibid., 215.

18. Waugh, *Travels in Search of the Elephant*, 132.

19. Deena J. González, *Refusing the Favor: The Spanish-Mexican Women of Santa Fe, 1820–1880*, 17–19.

20. Field, *Matt Field on the Santa Fe Trail*, 216.

21. Barreiro, "Ojeada," 146.

22. Lewis E. Atherton, "Business Techniques in the Santa Fe Trade," 335–37.

23. Edwards, *Campaign in New Mexico*, 35–36.

24. Gregg, *Commerce of the Prairies*, 168–69.

25. Janet Lecompte, "La Tules and the Americans," 218–20. See also González, *Refusing the Favor*, 39–78. González observes of Barceló that "Euro-American men called her everything but what she was: a businesswoman" (ibid., 39).

26. Field, *Matt Field on the Santa Fe Trail*, 208.

27. Ibid., 211.

28. Lopes in González, *Refusing the Favor*, 28.

29. Gregg, *Commerce of the Prairies*, 182. Commenting on Gregg's assertion that most marriages were "forced," Janet Lecompte notes that "betrothals arranged by parents were investigated by the priest to ensure that the bride was acquainted with the groom and wished to marry him" ("The Independent Women of Hispanic New Mexico, 1821–1846," 23).

30. Gregg, *Commerce of the Prairies*, 185.

31. Webb, *Adventures in the Santa Fé Trade*, 96–97.

32. Ibid., 76.

33. Barreiro, "Ojeada," 164.

34. Ibid., 163.

35. For more on the troubles of the Catholic Church in New Mexico and environs, see Weber, *The Mexican Frontier*, 43–82. "Just when the Anglo-Americans began to surge across the continent," Weber observes, "the Church on the Mexican frontier became a paper tiger, its temporal and ecclesiastical power greatly diminished" (ibid., 81).

36. Gregg, *Commerce of the Prairies*, 190.

37. Ibid., 189. For discussions of Pecos Pueblo and the Montezuma legend as described by travelers on the Santa Fe Trail, see Marc Simmons, *The Old Trail to Santa*

Fe: Collected Essays, 90–97; John L. Kessell, *Kiva, Cross, and Crown: The Pecos Indians and New Mexico, 1540–1840*, 459–63; and Frances Levine, *Our Prayers Are in This Place: Pecos Pueblo Identity over the Centuries*, 26–31.

38. Elsie Clews Parsons, *Pueblo Indian Religion*, 2 vols., 1:499; 2:1078–79. Some Pueblos likened the anticipated return of Montezuma to the resurrection of Christ and kindled bonfires on hilltops to summon Montezuma and hasten the dawn of a new day for their people. These legends may derive in part from an older Aztec myth concerning the god Quetzalcoatl, who had once ruled on earth and was prophesied to return from the east and reclaim his throne. Montezuma reportedly saw the coming of conquistador Hernán Cortés as fulfillment of this prophecy. See R. F. Townsend, *The Aztecs*, 18.

39. Webb, *Adventures in the Santa Fé Trade*, 78–79.

40. Field, *Matt Field on the Santa Fe Trail*, 251.

41. Gregg, *Commerce of the Prairies*, 199.

42. Ibid., 200.

43. Ibid., 203.

44. Ibid., 268–69.

45. Ibid., 273.

46. Ibid., 303. Other Americans were similarly impressed by Chihuahua. Trader William Henry Glasgow, who stopped here in February 1843, described the large church, or cathedral, that dominated the city plaza as a "magnificent building in any Country," and observed that "the Commerce of this place is generally in the hands of the Americans and a few German & French merchants" (in Gardner, *Brothers on the Santa Fe and Chihuahua Trails*, 18).

CHAPTER 15

1. Loomis, *Texan–Santa Fé Pioneers*, 6.

2. Lamar in William Campbell Binkley, "New Mexico and the Texan Santa Fé Expedition," 95. Lamar wrote this letter in April 1840, more than a year before the Texan Santa Fe expedition was organized.

3. Lamar in Loomis, *Texan–Santa Fé Pioneers*, 169.

4. Kendall, *Narrative*, 1:16.

5. Ibid., 265–66.

6. Ibid., 269.

7. Ibid., 272.

8. Ibid., 270.

9. Ibid.

10. Ibid., 289. Kendall's note offers this definition of *pobrecitos*: "Poor fellows! I believe, is a literal translation, although it means much more. Nothing can be more touchingly sweet than the pronunciation of this word by a Spanish or Mexican woman. The tones come fresh and warm from the heart when an object worthy of compassion presents itself."

11. Ibid., 293.

12. Ibid., 290, 401.

13. Ibid., 335–36.

14. Ibid., 336.

15. Ibid., 318–19.

16. Ibid., 292. George Ruxton later expanded on this theme of Anglo-Saxon superiority in *Life in the Far West*. New Mexican women, Ruxton insisted, "do not hesitate to leave the paternal abodes, and eternal tortilla-making, to share the perils and privations of the American mountaineers in the distant wilderness. Utterly despising their own countrymen, whom they are used to contrast with the dashing white hunters who swagger in all the pride of fringe and leather through their towns—they, as is but natural, gladly accept husbands from the latter class; preferring the stranger, who possesses the heart and strong right arm to defend them, to the miserable cowardly '*peládos,*' who hold what little they have on sufferance of savage Indians, but one degree superior to themselves" (182).

17. Kendall, *Narrative*, 1:352.

18. Ibid., 301–2.

19. Armijo had been expecting an incursion by Texans since early 1840 and had written letters to his superiors over that period expressing concern that restive New Mexicans might make common cause with the intruders, insisting in one dispatch to the minister of war that the "people will not defend themselves because they have expressed a desire to join the Texans" (Binkley, "New Mexico and the Texan Santa Fé Expedition," 93).

20. Manuel Alvarez, *Conflict and Acculturation: Manuel Alvarez's 1842 Memorial,* ed. Thomas E. Chávez, 49–51. See also Thomas E. Chávez, *Manuel Alvarez, 1794–1856: A Southwestern Biography,* 71–86.

21. Alvarez, *Conflict and Acculturation,* 52–53.

22. Ibid., 58–59.

23. Kendall, *Narrative,* 1:315.

24. Ibid., 346–48. Kendall identifies "Old Chavez" as "a wealthy *haciendero,* or large plantation owner, in the vicinity of Albuquerque, named Francisco Chavez." This, presumably, would be Francisco Xavier Chávez, a prominent landholder who succeeded Facundo Melgares as governor of New Mexico in 1822. His son, Antonio José Chávez, wed a niece of Manuel Armijo and was murdered in 1843 while traveling to Missouri on the Santa Fe Trail to engage in trade. See Simmons, *Murder on the Santa Fe Trail,* 1–3.

25. Ruxton in Janet Lecompte, "Manuel Armijo's Family History," 252. Lecompte concludes that Armijo (1790–1853) was not "of low and disreputable parents, and if he stole sheep, it must have been as a prank, certainly not to provide the foundation of his fortune" (256).

26. Kendall, *Narrative,* 1:358–59 (*La gobernadora* and *La comandante generala*: the feminine forms of Manuel Armijo's twin titles—governor and commandant general; *alcahueta*: "procuress").

27. Ibid., 359.

28. Ibid., 298.

29. Ibid., 364.

30. Ibid., 371.

31. Ibid., 391–92. For more on Ernest, Fitzgerald, and others mentioned in Kendall's account, see Loomis's roster of the expedition in *Texan–Santa Fé Pioneers,* 202–55.

32. Kendall. *Narrative,* 1:393–94.

33. Thomas Falconer, *Letters and Notes on the Texan Santa Fe Expedition, 1841–1842,* intro. and notes by F. W. Hodge, 26, 55.

34. Ibid., 57. "San Dia" here refers to Sandia, situated between Santa Fe and Albuquerque.

35. Kendall, *Narrative*, 2:12.

36. Ibid., 28. Kendall's note defines *ladrones* and *picaros*: "Loafers, scoundrels, thieves—the terms mean anything and everything opprobrious." Thomas Falconer reported that in El Paso the commandant, Colonel José María Elías González, "gave assurances of the personal safety of all, and strongly expressed his disapprobation of the outrageous cruelty of Capt. Salazar. He took several of us into his house and acted in a courteous and generous manner" (*Letters and Notes*, 57–58).

37. Kendall, *Narrative*, 2:36.

38. Ibid., 38–39.

39. Rafael Chacón, *Legacy of Honor: The Life of Rafael Chacón, a Nineteenth-Century New Mexican*, ed. Jacqueline Dorgan Meketa, 19.

40. Gregg, *Commerce of the Prairies*, 340–41. For more on Antonio José Chávez and his family, see Simmons, *Murder on the Santa Fe Trail*, 1–11.

41. *St. Louis New Era*, May 3, 1843; in Simmons, *Murder on the Santa Fe Trail*, 52.

42. Sage, *Rufus B. Sage*, 242–43. For more on the hostilities of 1843, see Seymour V. Connor and Jimmy M. Skaggs, *Broadcloth and Britches: The Santa Fe Trade*, 107–14; and Simmons, *Murder on the Santa Fe Trail*, 13–23, 65–74. Shortly after the attack at Mora, Sage related, Warfield's company lost all but a few of their horses to pursuing Mexican troops.

43. Hockley in Simmons, *Murder on the Santa Fe Trail*, 16.

44. Gregg, *Commerce of the Prairies*, 341.

45. Ibid., 341–42. Here as in his account of the attack on Mora, Gregg claimed that the victims had previously been partial to Texans. "These people had not only remained embittered against Gov. Armijo since the revolution of 1837," he wrote of the Taos Pueblos, "but had always been notably in favor of Texas." Perhaps Gregg's statements derived in part from Armijo's questionable assertions that those in his department who resented or opposed him—including Pueblos at Taos and elsewhere who had backed the revolt he put down in 1837—were sympathetic to the Texans and their takeover scheme. In any case, Gregg deserves credit for recognizing the disruptive nature of the raids by Warfield and Snively a few years before Taos and Mora emerged as trouble spots for American troops occupying New Mexico.

46. Cooke, "The Journal of Captain Philip St. George Cooke," 59. For a retrospective account of this incident by Cooke, see his article "One Day's Work of a Captain of Dragoons." "These rude Texans," recalled Cooke, "evidently with no discipline, and uncontrolled, were very clamorous, made many demands; they submitted with a very bad grace to my exhibition of force, which had been in no degree too stern and threatening" (40). Cooke proved correct in his assertion that Snively and company were on the American side of the border, east of the one hundredth meridian.

47. Charles Bent, "The Charles Bent Papers," ed. Frank D. Reeve, *New Mexico Historical Review* 30 (July 1955): 254; transcribed from a document in the Benjamin M. Read Collection, folder F-66, New Mexico State Records and Archives, Santa Fe. (All quotes here from the letters of Charles Bent conform to the transcriptions in the *New Mexico Historical Review* and have been checked against the originals in the Read Collection. As noted

by Frank D. Reeve in his introduction to the "Charles Bent Papers," Bent's letters are at times "hard to read and some errors may have crept into the printing." But the transcriptions reproduced here are accurate in all essentials.)

48. Martínez in William A. Keleher, *Turmoil in New Mexico*, 67. For discussions of the conflict between Padre Antonio José Martínez (1793–1867) and Charles Bent, see Weber, *On the Edge of Empire*, 73–76; and two works by David Lavender: *Bent's Fort*, 244–46, 266–69, and *The Southwest*, 127–33.

49. Bent, "Charles Bent Papers," *New Mexico Historical Review* 29 (October 1954): 314; Read Collection, F-46.

50. Lavender, *Bent's Fort*, 210–11; Chávez, *Manuel Alvarez*, 72–74.

51. Bent, "Charles Bent Papers," *New Mexico Historical Review* 29 (October 1954): 315; Read Collection, F-47.

52. Bent, "Charles Bent Papers," *New Mexico Historical Review* 29 (October 1954): 316; Read Collection, F-48.

53. Bent, "Charles Bent Papers," *New Mexico Historical Review* 30 (April 1955): 155–56; Read Collection, F-50.

54. Bent, "Charles Bent Papers," *New Mexico Historical Review* 30 (April 1955): 157; Read Collection, F-51.

55. Weber, *On the Edge of Empire*, 36–39.

56. Bent, "Charles Bent Papers," *New Mexico Historical Review* 31 (January 1956): 159; Read Collection, F-84.

57. Bent, "Charles Bent Papers," *New Mexico Historical Review* 31 (January 1956): 160; Read Collection, F-86.

58. Bent, "Charles Bent Papers," *New Mexico Historical Review* 30 (July 1955): 254; Read Collection, F-66. Although this document is contained in the same folder as a letter Bent wrote to Alvarez in 1845, it refers to the victory of the "Parrades party," news of which reached Santa Fe in early 1846. David Lavender concludes that "internal evidence indicates late March 1846" as the date of composition (*Bent's Fort*, 435 n. 3).

CHAPTER 16

1. Magoffin, *Down the Santa Fe Trail*, 53. Editor Stella M. Drumm notes that the physician who treated Susan Magoffin on this journey was Dr. Philippe Auguste Masure from Belgium, who had placed a notice in a St. Louis newspaper offering his "professional services in different branches of physic, surgery and midwifery."

2. Ibid., 61.

3. Ibid.

4. Ibid., 62.

5. Ibid., 63–64.

6. Ibid., 67.

7. Benton in Smith and Judah, *Chronicles of the Gringos*, 112. Smith and Judah state that this letter, published on May 22, 1846, in the *Daily Missouri Republican*, was "written apparently by Thomas Hart Benton." Other sources also describe the letter as Benton's. See, for example, Bieber's introduction to Gibson, *Journal of a Soldier*, 27.

8. Polk in Smith and Judah, *Chronicles of the Gringos*, 113.

9. Edwards, *Campaign in New Mexico*, 4.

10. Ibid., 5.

11. Doniphan in Launius, *Alexander William Doniphan*, 89–90. For more on Doniphan (1808–87) and his dealings with Kearny (1794–1848), see Dawson, *Doniphan's Epic March*, 61–62; and Dwight L. Clarke, *Stephen Watts Kearny: Soldier of the West*, 148–49.

12. Gibson, *Journal of a Soldier*, 124.

13. Hughes in William Elsey Connelley, *War with Mexico, 1846–1847: Doniphan's Expedition and the Conquest of New Mexico and California*, 137–38. Connelley's edition contains a reprint of John T. Hughes's history of the campaign, *Doniphan's Expedition: Containing an Account of the Conquest of New Mexico*, published in 1848, along with his wartime diary and much additional material. For a biographical sketch of Hughes (1817–62), born in Kentucky and raised in Missouri near Franklin, see Connelley, *War with Mexico*, 46–59.

14. Dawson, *Doniphan's Epic March*, 36–37.

15. Hughes in Connelley, *War with Mexico*, 141. The lasting influence of Hughes's account is reflected by the fact that this and many other passages from his narrative are reproduced without attribution in a 1903 memoir by Isaac George, *Heroes and Incidents of the Mexican War*.

16. Launius, *Alexander William Doniphan*, 144–45, 150. For more on Doniphan's views on slavery and the presence of slaves in his regiment, see Dawson, *Doniphan's Epic March*, 18, 44.

17. Abraham Robinson Johnston, Marcellus Ball Edwards, and Philip Gooch Ferguson, *Marching with the Army of the West, 1846–1848*, ed. Ralph P. Bieber, 112–13. For biographical details on Marcellus Edwards (1828–49), see Bieber's introduction, 21, 56.

18. Elliott, *Mexican War Correspondence*, 34.

19. Glasgow in Gardner, *Brothers on the Santa Fe and Chihuahua Trails*, 79.

20. Jacob S. Robinson, *Sketches of the Great West: A Journal of the Santa-Fe Expedition, under Colonel Doniphan*, 5.

21. Wislizenus, *Memoir of a Tour to Northern Mexico*, 16.

22. Robinson, *Sketches of the Great West*, 6.

23. Ibid., 6–7.

24. Ibid., 10.

25. Ibid., 12.

26. Johnston et al., *Marching with the Army of the West*, 129.

27. Hughes in Connelley, *War with Mexico*, 158–59.

28. Edwards, *Campaign in New Mexico*, 16. The "servant" who performed this dangerous operation for the major was most likely a slave.

29. Ibid., 9, 11, 12, 14.

30. Ibid., 14–15.

31. Ibid., 15.

32. Johnston et al., *Marching with the Army of the West*, 142–43.

33. Gibson, *Journal of a Soldier*, 153.

34. Ibid., 128–29. Angney was the senior of the two company captains in the battalion and became commander by default when Kearny declined to authorize an election. See Bieber's introduction to Gibson, ibid., 121.

35. Ibid., 130.

36. Ibid., 145.

37. Ibid., 156.

38. O'Sullivan in Dawson, *Doniphan's Epic March*, 11.

39. Gibson, *Journal of a Soldier*, 164.

40. Ibid., 168.

41. Ibid., 173.

42. Magoffin, *Down the Santa Fe Trail*, 68 (*mi alma*, or "my soul," was Susan Magoffin's term of endearment for her husband).

43. When Francis Parkman reached Bent's Fort in late August on his way back east, he found "a few invalid officers and soldiers" sauntering about and noted that the area had been picked clean: "It seemed as if a swarm of locusts had invaded the country. The grass for miles around was cropped close by the horses of General Kearney's soldiery" (*Oregon Trail*, 334).

44. Magoffin, *Down the Santa Fe Trail*, 71.

45. Ibid., 72.

CHAPTER 17

1. Kearny in Henry Smith Turner, *The Original Journals of Henry Smith Turner: With Stephen Watts Kearny to New Mexico and California, 1846–1847*, ed. Dwight L. Clarke, 66.

2. Clarke, *Stephen Watts Kearny*, 109, 114; Lavender, *Bent's Fort*, 273.

3. Johnston et al., *Marching with the Army of the West*, 91.

4. Young, *The West of Philip St. George Cooke*, 174. Young comments that Kearny chose Cooke for the assignment because his actions in 1843 made him "*persona grata* to the Mexicans."

5. Cooke, *Conquest of New Mexico and California*, 7–8.

6. Ibid., 10.

7. Ibid., 14–15.

8. Ibid., 18–19.

9. Ibid., 20–21.

10. Ibid., 25.

11. Hughes in Connelley, *War with Mexico*, 194. Hughes, citing reports by a captured Mexican spy, claimed in his diary entry for August 17, 1846, that Pueblos were refusing to fight against Americans "in consequence of an ancient tradition that at a certain period of time succor would come from the east to deliver them from the Spanish oppression & restore the kingdom of Montezuma. They regard the Americans as the long expected succor" (ibid., 60).

12. Cooke, *Conquest of New Mexico and California*, 27–29.

13. James Magoffin to Secretary of War George W. Crawford, April 4, 1849, in William Elsey Connelley, *A Standard History of Kansas and Kansans*, 1:125. For more testimony from James Magoffin on his meeting with Armijo and Archuleta, see Keleher, *Turmoil in New Mexico*, 18–19.

14. Thomas Hart Benton, *Thirty Years' View; or, a History of the Working of the American Government for Thirty Years, from 1820 to 1850*, 2 vols., 2:683.

15. Connelley, *Standard History of Kansas*, 1:126–27.

16. Secretary of War Crawford, in recommending that Magoffin be allowed the reduced sum of $30,000 for his claim, questioned the entertainment expenses as they related to Durango and Chihuahua but conceded that Magoffin's outlays in New Mexico may have been well worth it: "If this item had been confined to entertainments given in Santa Fe, it would have been better understood, and perhaps might not be deemed too high a charge, considering the importance of the object obtained by them" (ibid., 129).

17. Webb, *Adventures in the Santa Fé Trade*, 186–87.

18. Armijo in Bieber's introduction to Gibson, *Journal of a Soldier*, 65. Armijo's refusal to let the war disrupt his commercial ties to Americans is evidenced by a letter he wrote to Samuel C. Owens on July 15, 1846, in which he announced that he was sending payment of "six thousand eagle dollars, & nineteen ounces of gold" to the New York firm of "P. Harmony & Co.," which imported goods for the Santa Fe trade. The bill was not due until October, Armijo added, "but I have advanced the money as the circumstances of the commerce of this country and that one are not very agreeable, according to what you tell me." Bieber, "Letters of James and Robert Aull," 293.

19. Cooke, *Conquest of New Mexico and California*, 31–32.

20. Johnston et al., *Marching with the Army of the West*, 145–46.

21. Turner, *Original Journals*, 136–37. Turner (1811–81), a West Point graduate from Virginia, served prior to the war as an officer of dragoons under Kearny before becoming acting assistant adjutant general of the Army of the West.

22. Gibson, *Journal of a Soldier*, 182.

23. Turner, *Original Journals*, 138.

24. Ibid., 139.

25. Hughes in Connelley, *War with Mexico*, 186.

26. Kearny in W. H. Emory, *Notes of a Military Reconnoissance, from Fort Leavenworth, in Missouri, to San Diego, in California*, 27–28. Emory (1811–87) served during the campaign as both a cartographer and a reporter, compiling information on the people and places encountered by Kearny's army and seeking in his report to "give the government some idea of the regions traversed." See Ross Calvin's introduction to *Lieutenant Emory Reports: A Reprint of Lieutenant W. H. Emory's Notes of a Military Reconnoissance*, 9.

27. Kearny in Smith and Judah, *Chronicles of the Gringos*, 116.

28. Elliott, *Notes Taken in Sixty Years*, 233.

29. Edwards, *Campaign in New Mexico*, 22. The massacre of rebellious Texans by Mexican forces at the Alamo in 1836 had no direct relationship to George Kendall, Manuel Armijo, and the Texan Santa Fe expedition of 1841, but the fact that some within Edwards's hearing made that connection suggests the extent to which the mistreatment of the Pioneers had become a pretext for conquest.

30. Anonymous correspondent in Smith and Judah, *Chronicles of the Gringos*, 115. Kearny's interpreter was Antoine Robidoux.

31. Johnston et al., *Marching with the Army of the West*, 155.

32. Cooke, *Conquest of New Mexico and California*, 34–35.

33. Elliott, *Mexican War Correspondence*, 64.

34. Cooke, *Conquest of New Mexico and California*, 40.

35. Chacón, *Legacy of Honor*, 64–65. For details on the forces at Armijo's disposal at Apache Canyon, see Keleher, *Turmoil in New Mexico*, 19.

36. Ibid., 63.

37. Robinson, *Sketches of the Great West*, 20–21.

38. Gibson, *Journal of a Soldier*, 205–6.

39. Elliott, *Mexican War Correspondence*, 74–75.

40. Edward James Glasgow in Gardner, *Brothers on the Santa Fe and Chihuahua Trails*, 86–87.

41. Kearny in Ralph Emerson Twitchell, *The History of the Military Occupation of the Territory of New Mexico from 1846 to 1851 by the Government of the United States*, 73–74.

42. Vigil in Twitchell, ibid., 75. Once one of the most powerful men in New Mexico, Juan Bautista Vigil had been suspended in 1825 as treasurer and customs inspector for alleged abuses that included taking money under the table (Weber, *On the Edge of Empire*, 61–63). He later returned to office under Armijo, but he may have resented Mexican authorities for upholding against him charges of the sort that could have been leveled at others in financially responsible positions in Santa Fe over the years.

CHAPTER 18

1. Magoffin, *Down the Santa Fe Trail*, 95.

2. Ibid., 107.

3. Ibid., 108.

4. Ibid., 110.

5. Ibid., 112.

6. Ibid., 132.

7. Ibid., 119.

8. Gibson, *Journal of a Soldier*, 225.

9. Magoffin, *Down the Santa Fe Trail*, 120–21.

10. Edwards, *Campaign in New Mexico*, 39.

11. Gibson, *Journal of a Soldier*, 223.

12. Ibid., 216.

13. John P. Bloom, "New Mexico Viewed by Anglo-Americans, 1846–1849," 191.

14. Kennerly, *Persimmon Hill*, 191.

15. Magoffin, *Down the Santa Fe Trail*, 106–7.

16. Ibid., 149.

17. Gibson, *Journal of a Soldier*, 213.

18. Ibid., 214–15.

19. Kribben in ibid., 216–17 n. 355.

20. Edwards, *Campaign in New Mexico*, 37–38.

21. Gibson, *Journal of a Soldier*, 218.

22. Emory, *Notes of a Military Reconnoissance*, 34.

23. Clarke, *Stephen Watts Kearny*, 149.

24. Kearny also appointed Antonio José Otero as one of the justices in the newly established court system. See Launius, *Alexander William Doniphan*, 116. Launius comments

that all the appointees "had much to gain from the American conquest of New Mexico, and their appointments set off the ire of both Mexicans and Indians alike."

25. Donaciano Vigil, *Arms, Indians, and the Mismanagement of New Mexico: Donaciano Vigil, 1846*, ed. and trans. David J. Weber, 5. Donaciano Vigil (1802–77) succeeded Charles Bent as civil governor of occupied New Mexico after Bent's death in January 1847 and served in that position until October 1848.

26. Emory, *Notes of a Military Reconnoissance*, 37–38.

27. Ibid., 38.

28. Kearny in Connelley, *War with Mexico*, 266.

29. Doniphan in Launius, *Alexander William Doniphan*, 125. For more on Doniphan's Navajo campaign, see ibid., 118–33; Dawson, *Doniphan's Epic March*, 96–102; and Frank McNitt, *Navajo Wars: Military Campaigns, Slave Raids, and Reprisals*, 95–123.

30. Johnston et al., *Marching with the Army of the West*, 176–77.

31. Robinson, *Sketches of the Great West*, 32.

32. Ibid., 34–35.

33. Reid in Connelley, *War with Mexico*, 291.

34. Robinson, *Sketches of the Great West*, 35–36.

35. Ibid., 37.

36. Ibid., 39.

37. Reid in Connelley, *War with Mexico*, 292.

38. Moore in ibid., 295 n. 68.

39. Hughes in ibid., 305–6.

40. Ibid., 307.

41. Ibid.

42. Elliott, *Mexican War Correspondence*, 121–22.

43. Ibid., 80.

44. Gibson, *Journal of a Soldier*, 238.

45. Hughes in Connelley, *War with Mexico*, 224–25.

46. Johnston et al., *Marching with the Army of the West*, 166–67.

47. Gibson, *Journal of a Soldier*, 237: "In excavating for the magazine at the fort, they dug up a great many coffins and bones. It is said to have been the American graveyard."

48. Bent in Lavender, *Bent's Fort*, 292.

49. John W. Hess, "John W. Hess, with the Mormon Battalion," ed. Wanda Wood, 50.

50. Robert S. Bliss, "The Journal of Robert S. Bliss, with the Mormon Battalion," 72–73.

51. Gibson, *Journal of a Soldier*, 252.

52. Cooke, *Conquest of New Mexico and California*, 91.

53. Hess, "John W. Hess," 50. The wife and son of Captain Daniel C. Davis were among the family members who accompanied the battalion to California, as listed by Sergeant Daniel Tyler in *A Concise History of the Mormon Battalion in the Mexican War, 1846–1847*, 125.

54. Hess, "John W. Hess," 51.

55. William H. Richardson, *Journal of William H. Richardson, a Private Soldier in the Campaign of New and Old Mexico, under the Command of Colonel Doniphan*, 24.

56. Ibid., 27.
57. Ibid., 28.
58. Ibid., 30.
59. Ibid., 33–34.
60. Ibid., 29.
61. Ibid., 40.
62. Ibid., 39.
63. Elliott, *Mexican War Correspondence*, 215.
64. Kennerly, *Persimmon Hill*, 192.
65. Gibson, *Journal of a Soldier*, 283.
66. Ibid., 287. "Pass brandy" was from El Paso, renowned for its vintages.
67. Richardson, *Journal*, 41.
68. Ibid., 41–42.
69. Gibson, *Journal of a Soldier*, 288.
70. Ibid., 291.
71. Richardson, *Journal*, 43.
72. Edwards, *Campaign in New Mexico*, 47.
73. Elliott, *Mexican War Correspondence*, 106.

CHAPTER 19

1. Johnston et al., *Marching with the Army of the West*, 215.
2. Ibid., 214.
3. Ruxton, *Adventures in Mexico*, 178. The two soldiers killed by the Navajos in this incident were sent out on their own to retrieve the stolen sheep and went after them unarmed. The Navajos responsible were probably not aware of the recent treaty and may have been avenging the deaths of three Navajos at the hands of soldiers who were part of Kearny's expedition to California. See McNitt, *Navajo Wars*, 122; and Connelley, *War with Mexico*, 275.
4. Ruxton, *Adventures in Mexico*, 177. Among the traders in the camp Ruxton observed was William Henry Glasgow, who boasted in a letter home that they had "formed a Fort of our waggons 100 in number which 1000 Mexicans could not have taken" (Gardner, *Brothers on the Santa Fe and Chihuahua Trails*, 95).
5. Johnston et al., *Marching with the Army of the West*, 216.
6. Ibid., 222–23.
7. Gibson, *Journal of a Soldier*, 298.
8. Johnston et al., *Marching with the Army of the West*, 228.
9. Ibid., 229.
10. Gibson, *Journal of a Soldier*, 300.
11. Johnston et al., *Marching with the Army of the West*, 230. (*Carajo!*: one of several variant spellings of this versatile Spanish curse word, laden with contempt and sometimes translated as "Damn!")
12. Doniphan in Launius, *Alexander William Doniphan*, 146.
13. Johnston et al., *Marching with the Army of the West*, 231.
14. Gibson, *Journal of a Soldier*, 311.

15. Johnston et al., *Marching with the Army of the West*, 232–33.
16. Edwards, *Campaign in New Mexico*, 55.
17. Hughes in Connelley, *War with Mexico*, 374.
18. Edwards, *Campaign in New Mexico*, 56.
19. Ibid., 55–56.
20. Gibson, *Journal of a Soldier*, 308.
21. Robinson, *Sketches of the Great West*, 52.
22. Gibson, *Journal of a Soldier*, 312–13.
23. Robinson, *Sketches of the Great West*, 54.
24. Ibid., 53.
25. Gibson, *Journal of a Soldier*, 316.

CHAPTER 20

1. J. W. Abert, *Western America in 1846–1847: The Original Travel Diary of Lieutenant J. W. Abert*, ed. John Galvin, 73–74. Galvin's edition is drawn directly from Abert's field notebook and differs appreciably from Abert's official report of the campaign, published by Congress in 1848. For a reprint of that version, with a foreword by William A. Keleher, see *Abert's New Mexico Report: 1846–'47*.
2. Abert, *Western America in 1846–1847*, 74.
3. Ibid.
4. Ibid., 75.
5. Ibid.
6. Twitchell, *History of the Military Occupation*, 313–14. Twitchell's roster of those "cognizant of this plan to overthrow the government" suggests that the backers of the December plot in Santa Fe were men of means and social prominence. By contrast, the Taos revolt in January 1847 was more of a popular uprising. Some who supported the insurrection in Santa Fe later opposed the rebels in Taos, while others in the capital frowned on any attempt to oust the Americans. According to Twitchell, the December plot was betrayed to Donaciano Vigil by one "Tules Barcelona," or Gertrudis Barceló, whose warnings were then relayed by Vigil to Colonel Price.
7. Charles Bent to James Buchanan, December 26, 1846, in U.S. Senate, *Insurrection against the Military Government in New Mexico and California, 1847 and 1848*, 6. Bent's letter to Buchanan and other testimony pertaining to the revolt can also be found in Michael McNierny, ed., *Taos 1847: The Revolt in Contemporary Accounts*.
8. Twitchell, *History of the Military Occupation*, 299–300.
9. Conard, *"Uncle Dick" Wootton*, 174.
10. Hughes in Connelley, *War with Mexico*, 299. Hughes states here in a note to his narrative that this "allied force consisted of twenty Taos Mexicans, commanded by Lieut. Vigil; twenty Pueblos under Tomas; and twenty-five *peones* in charge of the pack-mules." Although there may have been more than one Tomás in Taos Pueblo at that time, the man in charge of this contingent was plainly a figure of some importance in the community and most likely the same Tomás who led the uprising against Governor Bent a few months later.
11. Elliott, *Mexican War Correspondence*, 121.
12. Ibid., 139.

13. Statement of Teresina Bent Scheurich, furnished by Governor Bent House Museum, Taos, New Mexico.

14. Scheurich in Ralph Emerson Twitchell, *The Leading Facts of New Mexican History*, 2 vols., 2:235 n. 170.

15. Elliott, *Mexican War Correspondence*, 139–40.

16. Waldo in Twitchell, *History of the Military Occupation*, 330–31 (*gente*: "people"; *agusto*: "pleased"). For more on the attack on the traders at Mora and the ensuing reprisals by American troops, see James W. Goodrich, "Revolt at Mora, 1847."

17. Joseph Williams, *Narrative of a Tour from the State of Indiana to the Oregon Territory in the Years 1841–2*, intro. James C. Bell, Jr., 55. The indefatigable Williams later preached to the heathen at Bent's Fort. "These people were wicked, and would play cards and billiards on the Sabbath," he wrote. "But they were very civil, friendly, and kind to me. There was not as much swearing and drunkenness as at other places I had passed" (ibid., 56).

18. Ruxton, *Adventures in Mexico*, 228.

19. Ibid., 228–29.

20. Ibid., 229.

21. Ibid., 229–30.

22. Ibid., 230.

23. Vigil in U.S. Senate, *Insurrection*, 6, 29. Donaciano Vigil cited as further evidence of the maliciousness of this cabal of Pueblos and lower-class Mexicans in Taos the attacks carried out there in 1843 against foreigners after a number of Taos Pueblos lost their lives opposing the incursion by Texans and their American recruits.

24. James P. Beckwourth, *The Life and Adventures of James P. Beckwourth*, as told to Thomas D. Bonner, intro. and notes by Delmont R. Oswald, 484. See the roster of St. Vrain's company in Twitchell, *Old Santa Fe*, 282. Twitchell does not list Beckwourth (1798–1866) among St. Vrain's Avengers, but he does list Charles Town. Perhaps Beckwourth went along with the company as a freelance. His narrative displays a familiarity with the campaign that could have come from conversations with those who took part but most likely reflected his personal involvement.

25. Price in U.S. Senate, *Insurrection*, 9.

26. Beckwourth, *Life and Adventures*, 485.

27. Price in U.S. Senate, *Insurrection*, 9.

28. Fischer in ibid., 13.

29. Price in ibid., 10.

30. Ibid., 11.

31. Chacón, *Legacy of Honor*, 67.

32. Price in U.S. Senate, *Insurrection*, 11.

33. Fischer in ibid., 13–14.

34. Price in ibid., 12.

35. Beckwourth, *Life and Adventures*, 487–88.

36. Conard, *"Uncle Dick" Wootton*, 183–84.

37. Twitchell, *Old Santa Fe*, 282–83.

38. Price in U.S. Senate, *Insurrection*, 12.

39. Beckwourth, *Life and Adventures*, 488.

40. James K. Polk, *Polk: The Diary of a President, 1845–1849*, ed. Allan Nevins, 218–19.

41. Garrard, *Wah-to-yah*, 183.

42. Ibid., 187.

43. Ibid., 205.

44. Ibid., 238.

45. Ibid., 247–48.

46. Ibid., 252.

47. Ibid., 249.

48. Ibid., 239–40.

49. Marcy in Sister Mary Loyola, *The American Occupation of New Mexico, 1821–1852*, 71. See also Twitchell, *Old Santa Fe*, 301–5.

50. Garrard, *Wah-to-yah*, 266.

51. Ibid., 255–56.

52. Ibid., 257.

53. Elsie Clews Parsons, *Taos Pueblo*, 14, 69. According to Parsons, Elk Heart died in 1920, a decade or so before she visited the pueblo to conduct her research. That people there remained reluctant to open their community to outsiders and divulge their secrets is evidenced by Parsons's dedication: "To my best friend in Taos, the most scrupulous Pueblo Indian of my acquaintance, who told me nothing about the pueblo and who never will tell any white person anything his people would not have him tell, which is nothing."

CHAPTER 21

1. Magoffin, *Down the Santa Fe Trail*, 192–93.

2. Ibid., 208–9.

3. Ibid., 209.

4. Ibid., 209–10.

5. Gibson, *Journal of a Soldier*, 323–24.

6. Hughes in Connelley, *War with Mexico*, 386.

7. Ibid., 92. This tendency of the troops to become disorderly and provocative the longer they stayed in one town was evidenced earlier in Santa Fe and later in Chihuahua. George Ruxton, who passed through Santa Fe in December 1846, complained that "crowds of drunken volunteers filled the streets, brawling and boasting. . . . Every other house was a grocery, as they call a gin or whisky shop, continually disgorging, reeling, drunken men, and every where filth and dirt reigned triumphant" (*Adventures in Mexico*, 190). Admittedly, Ruxton tended to portray the volunteers in the worst possible light, but such intemperate behavior by troops at loose ends, combined with what Ruxton called their "overbearing demeanor" toward the populace, may in fact have contributed to the "determined hostility" toward Americans that he detected on the eve of the revolt (ibid., 197).

8. William Henry Glasgow in Gardner, *Brothers on the Santa Fe and Chihuahua Trails*, 102.

9. Ibid., 108, 167.

10. Connelley, *War with Mexico*, 388 n. 99. For more on James Kirker and his dealings with Doniphan, see Ralph Adam Smith, *Borderlander: The Life of James Kirker, 1793–1852*, 176–81.

11. Gibson, *Journal of a Soldier*, 338.

12. Hughes in Connelley, *War with Mexico*, 400.

13. Ibid., 401.

14. Richardson, *Journal*, 60.

15. Hughes in Connelley, *War with Mexico*, 404.

16. Gibson, *Journal of a Soldier*, 343–44.

17. Connelley, *War with Mexico*, 388 n. 99.

18. Edwards, *Campaign in New Mexico*, 76–77.

19. Richardson, *Journal*, 63–64.

20. Johnston et al., *Marching with the Army of the West*, 262.

21. Gibson, *Journal of a Soldier*, 346.

22. Richardson, *Journal*, 64.

23. Edwards, *Campaign in New Mexico*, 77–78.

24. Doniphan in Magoffin, *Down the Santa Fe Trail*, 221 n. 91.

25. Edwards, *Campaign in New Mexico*, 80.

26. Gibson, *Journal of a Soldier*, 350.

27. Edwards, *Campaign in New Mexico*, 83.

28. Webb, *Adventures in the Santa Fé Trade*, 272–73.

29. Wislizenus, *Memoir of a Tour to Northern Mexico*, 54.

30. Gibson, *Journal of a Soldier*, 353.

31. Magoffin, *Down the Santa Fe Trail*, 228–29.

32. Josiah Gregg, *Diary and Letters of Josiah Gregg*, ed. Maurice Garland Fulton, 2 vols., 2:100–101.

33. Doniphan in Connelley, *War with Mexico*, 455.

34. William Henry Glasgow in Gardner, *Brothers on the Santa Fe and Chihuahua Trails*, 120.

35. Ibid., 120, 170. William's older brother Edward was just as hard on Doniphan, characterizing him as a "perfect zero—a weather cock turned about by the breath of any man supposed to have any *political* influence" (ibid., 131).

36. Richardson, *Journal*, 100.

37. Price in Gardner, *Brothers on the Santa Fe and Chihuahua Trails*, 161 n. 135. For more on Price's Chihuahua campaign, see Robert E. Shalhope, *Sterling Price: Portrait of a Southerner*, 70–75. Moorhead concludes that the "only effect of the renewal of hostilities in Chihuahua was the further anxiety of the remaining American merchants" (*New Mexico's Royal Road*, 183).

38. Edward James Glasgow in Gardner, *Brothers on the Santa Fe and Chihuahua Trails*, 137.

39. Ibid., 135.

40. Ruxton, *Life in the Far West*, 189–90.

41. Edward James Glasgow in Gardner, *Brothers on the Santa Fe and Chihuahua Trails*, 137.

CHAPTER 22

1. Gibson, *Over the Chihuahua and Santa Fe Trails*, 10.

2. Ibid., 11.

3. Ibid., 21.

4. Ibid., 22, 23.

5. Ibid., 24.

6. Ibid., 34.

7. Ibid., 39.

8. *Santa Fe Republican*, September 10, 1847.

9. Ibid., September 24, 1847.

10. Ibid., October 30, 1847.

11. Gibson, *Journal of a Soldier*, 153, 330. See Dawson, *Doniphan's Epic March*, 245 n. 35, for references to slaves or "servants" in Gibson's journal and other accounts of the campaign.

12. Gibson, *Over the Chihuahua and Santa Fe Trails*, 62.

13. Garrard, *Wah-to-yah*, 305.

14. Ibid., 314.

15. Ibid., 321.

16. Ibid., 330.

17. Ibid., 326.

18. For more on the building of Fort Mann and Garrard's stay there, see Chalfant, *Dangerous Passage*, 48–63.

19. Garrard, *Wah-to-yah*, 339.

20. Ibid., 347–48.

21. Ibid., 350.

22. Ibid., 355.

23. Ibid., 376.

24. Magoffin, *Down the Santa Fe Trail*, 229.

25. Ibid.

26. Ibid., 241–42.

27. Ibid., 243.

28. Ibid., 245.

29. Ibid., 259.

Bibliography

PRIMARY SOURCES

Abert, J. W. *Abert's New Mexico Report: 1846–'47*. 1848. Facsimile reprint, with foreword by William A. Keleher. Albuquerque: Horn & Wallace, 1962.

———. *Gúadal P'a: The Journal of Lieutenant J. W. Abert, from Bent's Fort to St. Louis in 1845*. 1846. Reprint edition, with introduction and notes by H. Bailey Carroll. Canyon, Tex.: Panhandle-Plains Historical Society, 1941.

———. *Western America in 1846–1847: The Original Travel Diary of Lieutenant J. W. Abert*. Edited by John Galvin. San Francisco: John Howell Books, 1966.

Allison, W. H. H. "Santa Fe as It Appeared during the Winter of the Years 1837 and 1838." *Old Santa Fe* 2 (October 1914): 170–83.

———. "Santa Fe in 1846 (Recollections of Col. Francisco Perea)." *Old Santa Fe* 2 (April 1915): 392–406.

Alvarez, Manuel. *Conflict and Acculturation: Manuel Alvarez's 1842 Memorial*. Edited by Thomas E. Chávez. Santa Fe: Museum of New Mexico Press, 1989.

Barreiro, Antonio. "Ojeada sobre Nuevo Mexico." Edited and translated by Lansing B. Bloom. 2 parts. *New Mexico Historical Review* 3 (January, April 1828): 73–96, 145–78.

Becknell, William. "The Journals of Capt. Thomas Becknell from Boone's Lick to Santa Fe and from Santa Cruz to Green River." *Missouri Historical Review* 4 (January 1910): 65–84.

Beckwourth, James P. *The Life and Adventures of James P. Beckwourth*, as told to Thomas D. Bonner. 1856. Reprint edition, with introduction and notes by Delmont R. Oswald. Lincoln: University of Nebraska Press, 1972.

Bent, Charles. "The Charles Bent Papers." Edited by Frank D. Reeve. 8 parts. *New Mexico Historical Review* 29 (July, October 1954): 234–39, 311–17; 30 (April, July,

October 1955): 154–67, 252–54, 340–52; 31 (January, April, July 1956): 75–77, 157–64, 251–53.

Benton, Thomas Hart. *Thirty Years' View; or, a History of the Working of the American Government for Thirty Years, from 1820 to 1850.* 2 vols. New York: D. Appleton, 1879.

Bieber, Ralph P., ed. "Letters of James and Robert Aull." *Missouri Historical Society Collections* 5 (1927–28): 267–310.

Bliss, Robert S. "The Journal of Robert S. Bliss, with the Mormon Battalion." 2 parts. *Utah Historical Quarterly* 4 (July, October 1931): 67–96, 110–28.

Boggs, William M. "The W. M. Boggs Manuscript about Bent's Fort, Kit Carson, the Far West, and Life among the Indians." Edited by LeRoy R. Hafen. *Colorado Magazine* 7 (March 1930): 45–69.

Bryant, Edwin. *What I Saw in California.* 1848. Facsimile reprint, with introduction by Thomas D. Clark. Lincoln: University of Nebraska Press, 1985.

Carroll, H. Bailey, and J. Villasana Haggard, eds. and trans. *Three New Mexico Chronicles.* Albuquerque: Quivira Society, 1942.

Catlin, George. *Letters and Notes on the Manners, Customs, and Conditions of the North American Indians.* 2 vols. 1844. Facsimile reprint, with introduction by Marjorie Halpin. New York: Dover, 1973.

Chacón, Rafael. *Legacy of Honor: The Life of Rafael Chacón, a Nineteenth-Century New Mexican.* Edited by Jacqueline Dorgan Meketa. Albuquerque: University of New Mexico Press, 1986.

Conard, Howard Louis, *"Uncle Dick" Wootton: The Pioneer Frontiersman of the Rocky Mountain Region.* 1890. Facsimile reprint. Alexandria,Va.: Time-Life Books, 1980.

Connelley, William Elsey. *War with Mexico, 1846–1847: Doniphan's Expedition and the Conquest of New Mexico and California.* Topeka, 1907.

Cooke, Philip St. George. *The Conquest of New Mexico and California, an Historical and Personal Narrative.* New York: Putnam, 1878.

———. "The Journal of Captain Philip St. George Cooke, First U.S. Dragoons, on an Escort of Santa Fe Traders in the Year of 1843." Edited by Harry C. Myers. In Leo E. Oliva, ed., *Confrontation on the Santa Fe Trail*, 41–75. Woodston, Kans.: Santa Fe Trail Association, 1996.

———. "One Day's Work of a Captain of Dragoons." *Magazine of American History* 18 (July 1887): 35–44.

———. *Scenes and Adventures in the Army: Or Romance of Military Life.* Philadelphia: Lindsay & Blakiston, 1857.

Davis, W. W. H. *El Gringo: New Mexico and Her People.* 1857. Facsimile reprint. Lincoln: University of Nebraska Press, 1982.

De Mun, Jules. "The Journals of Jules de Mun, Part 2: February 27–April 8, 1816." Edited by Thomas Maitland Marshall, translated by Nettie H. Beauregard. *Missouri Historical Society Collections* 5 (1927–28): 311–26.

Doster, Frank. "Eleventh Indiana Cavalry in Kansas in 1865." *Collections of the Kansas State Historical Society* 15 (1919–22): 524–29.

Edwards, Frank S. *A Campaign in New Mexico with Colonel Doniphan.* 1847. Reprint edition, with foreword by Mark L. Gardner. Albuquerque: University of New Mexico Press, 1996.

Elder, Jane Lenz, and David J. Weber, eds. *Trading in Santa Fe: John M. Kingsbury's Correspondence with James Josiah Webb, 1853–1861*. Dallas: Southern Methodist University Press, 1996.

Elliott, Richard Smith. *The Mexican War Correspondence of Richard Smith Elliott*. Edited by Mark L. Gardner and Marc Simmons. Norman: University of Oklahoma Press, 1997.

———. *Notes Taken in Sixty Years*. St. Louis: R. P. Studley & Co., 1883.

Emory, W. H. *Lieutenant Emory Reports: A Reprint of Lieutenant W. H. Emory's Notes of a Military Reconnoissance*. 1848. Reprint edition, with introduction and notes by Ross Calvin. Albuquerque: University of New Mexico Press, 1951.

———. *Notes of a Military Reconnoissance, from Fort Leavenworth, in Missouri, to San Diego, in California*. Washington: Wendell and Van Benthuysen, 1848.

Fairholme, William. *Journal of an Expedition to the Grand Prairies of the Missouri, 1840*. Edited by Jack B. Tykal. Spokane: Arthur H. Clark, 1996.

Falconer, Thomas. *Letters and Notes on the Texan Santa Fe Expedition, 1841–1842*. Introduction and notes by F. W. Hodge. 1930. Facsimile reprint. Chicago: Rio Grande Press, 1963.

Farnham, Thomas J. *Travels in the Great Western Prairies, the Anahuac and Rocky Mountains, and in the Oregon Territory*. Poughkeepsie, N.Y.: Killey and Lossing, 1841.

Ferris, Warren Angus. *Life in the Rocky Mountains*. Reprint edition, edited by LeRoy R. Hafen. Denver: Old West Publishing Company, 1983.

Field, Matthew C. "The Diary of Mat Field." Edited by William G. B. Carson. 2 parts. *Bulletin of the Missouri Historical Society* 5 (January, April 1949): 91–108, 157–84.

———. *Matt Field on the Santa Fe Trail*. Collected by Clyde and Mae Reed Porter, edited by John E. Sunder. Norman: University of Oklahoma Press, 1960.

———. *Prairie and Mountain Sketches*. Collected by Clyde and Mae Reed Porter, edited by Kate L. Gregg and John Francis McDermott. Norman: University of Oklahoma Press, 1957.

Fowler, Jacob. *The Journal of Jacob Fowler*. Edited by Elliott Coues. 1898. Facsimile reprint. Minneapolis: Ross & Haines, 1965.

Gallego, Pedro Ignacio. "The Diary of Pedro Ignacio Gallego." Edited by Michael A. Olsen and Harry C. Myers. *Wagon Tracks* 7 (November 1992): 1, 15–20.

Gardner, Mark L., ed. *Brothers on the Santa Fe and Chihuahua Trails: Edward James Glasgow and William Henry Glasgow, 1846–1848*. Niwot: University Press of Colorado, 1993.

Garrard, Lewis H. *Wah-to-yah and the Taos Trail*. 1850. Reprint edition, edited by Ralph P. Bieber. Glendale, Calif.: Arthur H. Clark, 1938.

Gibson, George Rutledge. *Journal of a Soldier under Kearny and Doniphan, 1846–1847*. Edited by Ralph. P. Bieber. Glendale, Calif.: Arthur H. Clark, 1935.

———. *Over the Chihuahua and Santa Fe Trails, 1847–1848*. Edited by Robert W. Frazer. Albuquerque: University of New Mexico Press, 1981.

Gregg, Josiah. *Commerce of the Prairies*. 1844. Reprint edition, edited by Max L. Moorhead. Norman: University of Oklahoma Press, 1954.

———. *Diary and Letters of Josiah Gregg*. Edited by Maurice Garland Fulton. 2 vols. Norman: University of Oklahoma Press, 1941–44.

Hafen, Le Roy R., and Ann W. Hafen, eds. *To the Rockies and Oregon, 1839–1842*. Glendale, Calif.: Arthur H. Clark, 1955.

Hess, John W. "John W. Hess, with the Mormon Battalion." Edited by Wanda Wood. *Utah Historical Quarterly* 4 (April 1931): 47–55.

Hobbs, James. *Wild Life in the Far West: Personal Adventures of a Border Mountain Man*. 1872. Facsimile reprint. Alexandria, Va.: Time-Life Books, 1980.

Hughes, John T. *Doniphan's Expedition: Containing an Account of the Conquest of New Mexico*. 1848. Facsimile reprint. New York: Arno Press, 1973. [See also Connelley, William Elsey.]

Hulbert, Archer Butler, ed. *Southwest on the Turquoise Trail: The First Diaries on the Road to Santa Fe*. Stewart Commission of Colorado College and Denver Public Library, 1933.

Irving, Washington. *The Western Journals of Washington Irving*. Edited by John Francis McDermott. Norman: University of Oklahoma Press, 1944.

James, Edwin. *Account of an Expedition from Pittsburgh to the Rocky Mountains*. 2 vols. 1823. Facsimile reprint. Ann Arbor: University Microfilms, 1966.

James, Thomas. *Three Years among the Indians and Mexicans*. Edited by Walter B. Douglas. Saint Louis: Missouri Historical Society, 1916.

Johnston, Abraham Robinson, Marcellus Ball Edwards, and Philip Gooch Ferguson. *Marching with the Army of the West, 1846–1848*. Edited by Ralph P. Bieber. Glendale, Calif.: Arthur H. Clark, 1936.

Kendall, George Wilkins, *Narrative of the Texan Santa Fé Expedition*. 2 vols. New York: Harper and Brothers, 1844.

Kennerly, Willam Clark. *Persimmon Hill: A Narrative of Old St. Louis and the Far West*, as told to Elizabeth Russell. Norman: University of Oklahoma Press, 1948.

Latrobe, Charles Joseph. *The Rambler in North America: 1832–1833*. 2 vols. 1836. Facsimile reprint. New York: Johnson Reprint Corporation, 1970.

Magoffin, Susan Shelby. *Down the Santa Fe Trail and into Mexico: The Diary of Susan Shelby Magoffin, 1846–1847*. Edited by Stella M. Drumm. 1926. Reprint edition, with foreword by Howard R. Lamar. New Haven: Yale University Press, 1962.

Marmaduke, Meredith Miles. "Meredith Miles Marmaduke's Journal of a Tour to New Mexico, 1824–1825." Edited by Harry C. Myers. *Wagon Tracks* 12 (November 1997): 8–16.

———. "Santa Fe Trail: M. M. Marmaduke Journal." Edited by Francis A. Sampson. *Missouri Historical Review* 6 (October 1911): 1–10.

Marryat, Captain Frederick. *Diary in America*. 1839. Reprint edition, edited by Jules Zanger. Bloomington: Indiana University Press, 1960.

McCoy, John. *Pioneering on the Plains; Journey to Mexico in 1848; the Overland Trip to California*. Kaukauna, Wisc.: 1924.

McNierney, Michael, ed. *Taos 1847: The Revolt in Contemporary Accounts*. Boulder: Johnson Publishing Company, 1980.

Melgares, Facundo. "An Unforgettable Day: Facundo Melgares on Independence," ed. David J. Weber. *New Mexico Historical Review* 48 (January 1973): 27–44.

Meriwether, David. *My Life in the Mountains and on the Plains*. Edited by Robert A. Griffen. Norman: University of Oklahoma Press, 1965.

Parkman, Francis. *The Journals of Francis Parkman*. Edited by Mason Wade. Vol. 2. New York: Harper & Brothers, 1947.

———. *The Oregon Trail*. 1849. Reprint of 1892 edition, edited by E. N. Feltskog. Lincoln: University of Nebraska Press, 1994.

Pattie, James O. *The Personal Narrative of James O. Pattie of Kentucky*. Edited by Timothy Flint. 1831. Reprint edition, with introduction and notes by Milo Milton Quaife. Chicago: Lakeside Press, 1930.

Perrine, Fred S. "Military Escorts on the Santa Fe Trail." 3 parts. *New Mexico Historical Review* 2 (April 1927, July 1927): 175–93, 269–304; 3 (July 1928): 265–300.

Peters, Richard, ed. *The Public Statutes at Large of the United States of America*. Vol. 7. Boston: Little, Brown, 1856.

Pike, Albert. *Prose Sketches and Poems Written in the Western Country (with Additional Stories)*. Reprint edition, edited by David J. Weber. College Station: Texas A&M University Press, 1987.

Pike, Zebulon Montgomery. *The Expeditions of Zebulon Montgomery Pike*. Edited by Elliott Coues. 2 vols. 1895. Facsimile reprint. Mineola, N.Y.: Dover, 1986.

———. *The Journals of Zebulon Montgomery Pike, with Letters and Related Documents*. Edited by Donald Jackson. 2 vols. Norman: University of Oklahoma Press, 1966.

Pino, Don Pedro Baptista. *The Exposition on the Province of New Mexico, 1812*. Edited and translated by Adrian Bustamante and Marc Simmons. Santa Fe and Albuquerque: El Rancho de las Golondrinas and the University of New Mexico Press, 1995.

Polk, James K. *Polk: The Diary of a President, 1845–1849*. Edited by Allan Nevins. London: Longmans, Green and Co., 1929.

Quaife, Milo Milton, ed. *Kit Carson's Autobiography*. 1935. Facsimile reprint. Lincoln: University of Nebraska Press, 1996.

Richardson, William H. *Journal of William H. Richardson, a Private Soldier in the Campaign of New and Old Mexico, under the Command of Colonel Doniphan of Missouri*. Baltimore: John W. Woods, 1848.

———. *William H. Richardson's Journal of Doniphan's Expedition*. 1850. Reprint edition, with introduction by William B. McGroarty. Columbia: State Historical Society of Missouri, 1928.

Robinson, Jacob S. *A Journal of the Santa Fe Expedition under Colonel Doniphan*. 1848. Reprint edition, with introduction and notes by Carl L. Cannon. Princeton: Princeton University Press, 1932.

———. *Sketches of the Great West: A Journal of the Santa-Fe Expedition, under Colonel Doniphan*. Portsmouth, N.H.: Portsmouth Journal Press, 1848.

Ruxton, George Frederick. *Adventures in Mexico and the Rocky Mountains*. New York: Harper & Brothers, 1848.

———. *Life in the Far West*. 1849. Reprint edition, edited by LeRoy R. Hafen. Norman: University of Oklahoma Press, 1951.

———. *Ruxton of the Rockies*. Collected by Clyde and Mae Reed Porter, edited by LeRoy R. Hafen. Norman: University of Oklahoma Press, 1950.

Sage, Rufus B. *Rufus B. Sage: His Letters and Papers, 1836–1847, with an Annotated Reprint of "Scenes in the Rocky Mountains, and in Oregon, California, New Mexico,*

Texas, and the Grand Prairies." Edited by LeRoy R. Hafen and Ann W. Hafen. 2 vols. Glendale, Calif.: Arthur H. Clark, 1956.

Sibley, George Champlin. *The Road to Santa Fe: The Journal and Diaries of George Champlin Sibley.* Edited by Kate L. Gregg. Albuquerque: University of New Mexico Press, 1952.

Smith, E. Willard. "Journal of E. Willard Smith while with the Fur Traders, Vasquez and Sublette, in the Rocky Mountain Region, 1839–1840." *Quarterly of the Oregon Historical Society* 14 (September 1913): 250–58.

Smith, George Winston, and Charles Judah, eds. *Chronicles of the Gringos: The U.S. Army in the Mexican War, 1846–1848.* Albuquerque: University of New Mexico Press, 1968.

[Stephenson, John D.] "Invasion of New Mexico, 1846." Edited by Harry C. Myers. *Wagon Tracks* 7 (August 1993): 18–20.

Storrs, Augustus, and Alphonso Wetmore. *Santa Fé Trail, First Reports: 1825.* 1825. Facsimile reprint. Houston: Stagecoach Press, 1960.

Taylor, Benjamin F. *Short Ravelings from a Long Yarn, or Camp March Sketches of the Santa Fe Trail,* from the notes of Richard L. Wilson. 1847. Reprint edition, with foreword by Henry R. Wagner. Santa Ana: Fine Arts Press, 1936.

Tixier, Victor. *Tixier's Travels on the Osage Prairies.* Edited by John Francis McDermott, translated by Albert J. Salvan. Norman: University of Oklahoma Press, 1940.

Todd, Edgeley W., ed. "Bent's Fort in 1846." *Colorado Magazine* 34 (July 1957): 206–10.

Townsend, John Kirk. *Narrative of a Journey across the Rocky Mountains to the Columbia River.* 1839. Reprint of 1905 edition, edited by Reuben Gold Thwaites, with an introduction by Donald Jackson. Lincoln: University of Nebraska Press, 1978.

Turner, Henry Smith. *The Original Journals of Henry Smith Turner: With Stephen Watts Kearny to New Mexico and California, 1846–1847.* Edited by Dwight L. Clarke. Norman: University of Oklahoma Press, 1966.

U.S. Senate. *Executive Documents.* Vol. 1. 30th Cong., 1st sess., 1847. Serial 503.

———. *Insurrection against the Military Government in New Mexico and California, 1847 and 1848.* 56th Cong., 1st sess., 1900, S. Doc. 442.

Vigil, Donaciano. *Arms, Indians, and the Mismanagement of New Mexico: Donaciano Vigil, 1846.* Edited and translated by David J. Weber. El Paso: Texas Western Press, 1986.

Waldo, William. "Recollections of a Septuagenarian." Edited by Stella M. Drumm. *Missouri Historical Society: Glimpses of the Past* 5 (April–June 1938): 59–94.

Walker, Joel P. *A Pioneer of Pioneers: Narrative of Adventures Thro' Alabama, Florida, New Mexico, Oregon, California, & c.* Los Angeles: Glen Dawson, 1953.

Waugh, Alfred S. *Travels in Search of the Elephant: The Wanderings of Alfred S. Waugh, Artist, in Louisiana, Missouri, and Santa Fe, in 1845–1846.* Edited by John Francis McDermott. St. Louis: Missouri Historical Society, 1951.

Webb, James Josiah. *Adventures in the Santa Fé Trade, 1844–1847.* Edited by Ralph. P. Bieber. Glendale, Calif.: Arthur H. Clark, 1931.

Weber, David J., ed. and trans. *The Extranjeros: Selected Documents from the Mexican Side of the Santa Fe Trail, 1825–1828.* Santa Fe: Stagecoach Press, 1967.

[Wetmore, Alphonso.] "The Book of the Muleteers." *Wagon Tracks* 5 (August 1991): 1–3.

Wetmore, Alphonso. "Alphonso Wetmore Letters." Edited by Leo E. Oliva. *Wagon Tracks* 14 (February 2000): 10.

————. *Gazetteer of the State of Missouri.* 1837. Facsimile reprint. New York: Arno Press, 1975.

White, David A., ed. *News of the Plains and Rockies, 1803–1865.* Vol. 2. Spokane: Arthur H. Clark, 1996.

Williams, Joseph. *Narrative of a Tour from the State of Indiana to the Oregon Territory in the Years 1841–2.* 1843. Reprint of 1921 edition, with introduction by James C. Bell, Jr. Fairfield, Wash.: Ye Galleon Press, 1977.

Wislizenus, Frederick A. *A Journey to the Rocky Mountains in the Year 1839.* 1912. Facsimile reprint. Glorieta, N.M.: Rio Grande Press, 1969.

————. *Memoir of a Tour to Northern Mexico, Connected with Col. Doniphan's Expedition, in 1846 and 1847.* 1848. Facsimile reprint. Glorieta, N.M.: Rio Grande Press, 1969.

Workman, William. "A Letter from Taos, 1826." Edited by David J. Weber. *New Mexico Historical Review* 41 (April 1966): 155–64.

SECONDARY SOURCES

Anderson, Hattie M. "Frontier Economic Problems in Missouri, 1815–1828." 2 parts. *Missouri Historical Review* 34 (October 1939, January 1940): 38–70, 182–203.

Atherton, Lewis E. "Business Techniques in the Santa Fe Trade." *Missouri Historical Review* 34 (April 1940): 335–41.

————. "James and Robert Aull—A Frontier Missouri Mercantile Firm." *Missouri Historical Review* 30 (October 1935): 3–27.

————. "The Santa Fe Trader as Mercantile Capitalist." *Missouri Historical Review* 77 (October 1982): 1–12.

Ball, Larry D. "Federal Justice on the Santa Fe Trail: The Murder of Antonio José Chavez." *Missouri Historical Review* 81 (October 1986): 1–17.

Bancroft, Hubert Howe. *History of Arizona and New Mexico.* Works of Hubert Howe Bancroft, vol. 17. San Francisco: History Company, 1889.

Barbour, Barton H. "Westward to Health: Gentlemen Health-Seekers on the Santa Fe Trail." In Mark L. Gardner, ed., *The Mexican Road: Trade, Travel, and Confrontation on the Santa Fe Trail,* 39–43. Manhattan, Kans.: Sunflower University Press, 1989.

Barry, Louise. *The Beginning of the West: Annals of the Kansas Gateway to the American West, 1540–1854.* Topeka: Kansas State Historical Society, 1972.

Batman, Richard. *American Ecclesiastes: The Stories of James Pattie.* New York: Harcourt Brace Jovanovich, 1984.

Beachum, Larry Mahon. "To the Westward: William Becknell and the Beginning of the Santa Fe Trade." In Mark L. Gardner, ed., *The Mexican Road: Trade, Travel, and Confrontation on the Santa Fe Trail,* 6–12. Manhattan, Kans.: Sunflower University Press, 1989.

————. *William Becknell: Father of the Santa Fe Trade.* El Paso: Texas Western Press, 1982.

Berthrong, Donald J. *The Southern Cheyennes.* Norman: University of Oklahoma Press, 1963.

Binkley, William Campbell. "New Mexico and the Texan Santa Fé Expedition." *Southwestern Historical Quarterly* 27 (October 1923): 87–107.

Bloom, John P. "New Mexico Viewed by Anglo-Americans, 1846–1849." *New Mexico Historical Review* 34 (July 1959): 165–98.

Bloom, Lansing B. "New Mexico under Mexican Administration." 4 parts. *Old Santa Fe* 2 (July 1914, October 1914, January 1915, April 1915): 3–56, 119–69, 223–77, 351–80.

Bott, Emily Ann O'Neil. "Joseph Murphy's Contribution to the Development of the West." *Missouri Historical Review* 47 (October 1952): 18–28.

Boyle, Susan Calafate. *Los Capitalistas: Hispano Merchants and the Santa Fe Trade*. Albuquerque: University of New Mexico Press, 1997.

Chalfant, William Y. *Dangerous Passage: The Santa Fe Trail and the Mexican War*. Norman: University of Oklahoma Press, 1994.

Chávez, Thomas E. *Manuel Alvarez, 1794–1856: A Southwestern Biography*. Niwot: University Press of Colorado, 1990.

———. *Quest for Quivira: Spanish Explorers on the Great Plains, 1540–1821*. Tucson: Southwest Parks and Monuments Association, 1992.

———. "Up from Mexico and beyond the Ruts: Some Commemorative Thoughts on the Santa Fe Trail." In Leo E. Oliva, ed., *Confrontation on the Santa Fe Trail*, 1–8. Woodston, Kans.: Santa Fe Trail Association, 1996.

Chittenden, Hiram Martin. *The American Fur Trade of the Far West*. 2 vols. 1902. Reprint. Stanford, Calif.: Academic Reprints, 1954.

Clarke, Dwight L. *Stephen Watts Kearny: Soldier of the West*. Norman: University of Oklahoma Press, 1961.

Comer, Douglas C. *Ritual Ground: Bent's Old Fort, World Formation, and the Annexation of the Southwest*. Berkeley: University of California Press, 1996.

Connelley, William Elsey. *A Standard History of Kansas and Kansans*. Vol. 1. Chicago: Lewis Publishing Company, 1918.

Connor, Seymour V., and Jimmy M. Skaggs. *Broadcloth and Britches: The Santa Fe Trade*. College Station: Texas A&M University Press, 1977.

Copeland, Fayette. *Kendall of the Picayune*. Norman: University of Oklahoma Press, 1943.

Covington, James W. "Correspondence between Mexican Officials at Santa Fe and Officials in Missouri, 1823–1825." *Bulletin of the Missouri Historical Society* 16 (October 1959): 20–32.

———. "Thomas James: Traveler to Santa Fe." *Bulletin of the Missouri Historical Society* 10 (October 1953): 86–89.

Cracroft, Richard H. "George Frederick Ruxton." *Dictionary of Literary Biography*, 186:327–35.

———. "Josiah Gregg." *Dictionary of Literary Biography*, 186:145–53.

———. "Lewis H. Garrard." *Dictionary of Literary Biography*, 186:137–43.

Crutchfield, James A. *Tragedy at Taos: The Revolt of 1847*. Plano, Tex.: Republic of Texas Press, 1995.

Dale, Harrison Clifford, ed. *The Explorations of William H. Ashley and Jedediah Smith, 1822–1829*. 1941. Reprint. Lincoln: University of Nebraska Press, 1991.

Dary, David. *The Santa Fe Trail: Its History, Legends, and Lore*. New York: Knopf, 2000.

Davis, H. Denny. "Franklin: Cradle of the Trade." *Wagon Tracks* 7 (May 1993): 11–17.

Dawson, Joseph G., III. *Doniphan's Epic March: The 1st Missouri Volunteers in the Mexican War.* Lawrence: University Press of Kansas, 1999.

DeVoto, Bernard. *The Year of Decision.* Boston: Little, Brown, 1943.

Dorsey, Dorothy B. "The Panic and Depression of 1837–43 in Missouri." *Missouri Historical Review* 30 (January 1936): 132–61.

Duffus, R. L. *The Santa Fe Trail.* 1930. Reprint. Albuquerque: University of New Mexico Press, 1972.

Flora, Joseph M. "Albert Pike." *Dictionary of Literary Biography,* 74:297–302.

Forry, Richard R. "Richard Gentry: Trader and Patriot." *Wagon Tracks* 1 (August 1987): 7–8.

Franzwa, Gregory M. *The Santa Fe Trail Revisited.* St. Louis: Patrice Press, 1989.

Gardner, Mark L. *Wagons for the Santa Fe Trade: Wheeled Vehicles and their Makers, 1822–1880.* Albuquerque: University of New Mexico Press, 2000.

———, ed. *The Mexican Road: Trade, Travel, and Confrontation on the Santa Fe Trail.* Manhattan, Kans.: Sunflower University Press, 1989.

González, Deena J. *Refusing the Favor: The Spanish-Mexican Women of Santa Fe, 1820–1880.* New York: Oxford University Press, 1999.

Goodrich, James W. "Revolt at Mora, 1847." *New Mexico Historical Review* 47 (January 1972): 49–60.

Gregg, Kate L. "The History of Fort Osage." *Missouri Historical Review* 34 (July 1940): 439–88.

———. "Major Alphonso Wetmore." *Missouri Historical Review* 35 (April 1941): 385–93.

Hafen, LeRoy R., ed. *The Mountain Men and the Fur Trade of the Far West.* 10 vols. Glendale, Calif.: Arthur H. Clark, 1965–72.

Hammond, George P. *The Adventures of Alexander Barclay, Mountain Man.* Denver: Old West Publishing Company, 1976.

Hickman, W. Z., *History of Jackson County, Missouri.* Topeka: Historical Publishing Company, 1920.

Hoig, Stan. *The Peace Chiefs of the Cheyennes.* Norman: University of Oklahoma Press, 1980.

Hollon, W. Eugene. *The Lost Pathfinder: Zebulon Montgomery Pike.* Norman: University of Oklahoma Press, 1949.

Holmes, Kenneth L. "The Benjamin Cooper Expeditions to Santa Fe in 1822 and 1823." *New Mexico Historical Review* 38 (April 1963): 139–50.

Horgan, Paul. *Josiah Gregg and His Vision of the Early West.* New York: Farrar Straus Giroux, 1979.

———. *Great River: The Rio Grande in North American History.* Hanover, N.H.: University Press of New England, 1984.

Hyde, George E. *The Pawnee Indians.* Norman: University of Oklahoma Press, 1974.

Inman, Colonel Henry. *The Old Santa Fe Trail: The Story of a Great Highway.* New York: Macmillan, 1897.

Johannsen, Robert W. *To the Halls of the Montezumas: The Mexican War in the American Imagination.* New York: Oxford University Press, 1985.

John, Elizabeth A. H. "Nurturing the Peace: Spanish and Comanche Cooperation in the Early Nineteenth Century." *New Mexico Historical Review* 59 (October 1984): 345–69.

Jones, Oakah L., Jr. *Pueblo Warriors and Spanish Conquest.* Norman: University of Oklahoma Press, 1966.

Kavanagh, Thomas W. *Comanche Political History: An Ethnohistorical Perspective, 1706–1875.* Lincoln: University of Nebraska Press, 1996.

Keleher, William A. *Turmoil in New Mexico.* Albuquerque: University of New Mexico Press, 1982.

Kessell, John L. *Kiva, Cross, and Crown: The Pecos Indians and New Mexico, 1540–1840.* Tucson: Southwest Parks and Monuments Association, 1986.

Kracht, Benjamin R. "The Kiowa and the Santa Fe Trail." In Leo E. Oliva, ed., *Confrontation on the Santa Fe Trail,* 25–40. Woodston, Kans.: Santa Fe Trail Association, 1996.

Launius, Roger D. *Alexander William Doniphan: Portrait of a Missouri Moderate.* Columbia: University of Missouri Press, 1997.

Lavender, David. *Bent's Fort.* 1954. Reprint. Lincoln: University of Nebraska Press, 1972.

———. "Bent's Fort: Outpost of Manifest Destiny." In *The Santa Fe Trail: New Perspectives,* 11–25. Niwot: University Press of Colorado, 1992.

———. *The Southwest.* New York: Harper & Row, 1980.

Lecompte, Janet. "The Independent Women of Hispanic New Mexico, 1821–1846." *Western Historical Quarterly* 12 (January 1981): 17–35.

———. "Manuel Armijo, George Wilkins Kendall, and the Baca-Caballero Conspiracy." *New Mexico Historical Review* 59 (January 1984): 49–65.

———. "Manuel Armijo's Family History." *New Mexico Historical Review* 48 (July 1973): 252–56.

———. *Pueblo, Hardscrabble, Greenhorn: Society on the High Plains, 1832–1856.* Norman: University of Oklahoma Press, 1978.

———. *Rebellion in Río Arriba, 1837.* Albuquerque: University of New Mexico Press, 1985.

———. "La Tules and the Americans." *Arizona and the West* 20 (Autumn 1978): 215–30.

Levine, Frances. *Our Prayers Are in This Place: Pecos Pueblo Identity over the Centuries.* Albuquerque: University of New Mexico Press, 1999.

Loomis, Noel M. *The Texan–Santa Fé Pioneers.* Norman: University of Oklahoma Press, 1958.

Loomis, Noel M., and Abraham P. Nasatir. *Pedro Vial and the Roads to Santa Fe.* Norman: University of Oklahoma Press, 1967.

Loyola, Sister Mary. *The American Occupation of New Mexico, 1821–1852.* 1939. Reprint. New York: Arno Press, 1976.

Marriott, Alice. *The Ten Grandmothers.* Norman: University of Oklahoma Press, 1945.

McCaffrey, James M. *Army of Manifest Destiny: The American Soldier in the Mexican War, 1846–1848.* New York: New York University Press, 1992.

McNitt, Frank. "Navajo Campaigns and the Occupation of New Mexico, 1847–1848." *New Mexico Historical Review* 43 (July 1968): 173–94.

———. *Navajo Wars: Military Campaigns, Slave Raids, and Reprisals.* Albuquerque: University of New Mexico Press, 1972.

Meyer, Marian. *Mary Donoho: New First Lady of the Santa Fe Trail.* Santa Fe: Ancient City Press, 1991.

Moorhead, Max L. *New Mexico's Royal Road: Trade and Travel on the Chihuahua Trail.* Norman: University of Oklahoma Press, 1958.

Mumey, Nolie. *Old Forts and Trading Posts of the West: Bent's Old Fort and Bent's New Fort on the Arkansas River*. Denver: Artcraft Press, 1956.

Myres, Sandra L. "Women on the Santa Fe Trail." In *The Santa Fe Trail: New Perspectives*. Niwot: University Press of Colorado, 1992.

Oliva, Leo E. "The Santa Fe Trail in Wartime: Expansion and Preservation of the Union." In Mark L. Gardner, ed., *The Mexican Road: Trade, Travel, and Confrontation on the Santa Fe Trail*, 53–58. Manhattan, Kans.: Sunflower University Press, 1989.

———. *Soldiers on the Santa Fe Trail*. Norman: University of Oklahoma Press, 1967.

———, ed. *Adventure on the Santa Fe Trail*. Topeka: Kansas State Historical Society, 1988.

———. *Confrontation on the Santa Fe Trail*. Woodston, Kans.: Santa Fe Trail Association, 1996.

Olson, Sarah M. "Furnishing a Frontier Outpost." In *Bent's Old Fort*, 139–68. State Historical Society of Colorado, 1979.

Parkison, Jami. *Path to Glory: A Pictorial Celebration of the Santa Fe Trail*. Kansas City: Highwater Editions, 1996.

Parsons, Elsie Clews. *Pueblo Indian Religion*. 2 vols. Lincoln: University of Nebraska Press, 1996.

———. *Taos Pueblo*. 1936. Reprint. New York: Johnson Reprint Corporation, 1970.

Prucha, Francis Paul. *The Sword of the Republic: The United States Army on the Frontier, 1783–1846*. Lincoln: University of Nebraska Press, 1986.

Ravenswaay, Charles van. *Saint Louis: An Informal History of the City and Its People, 1764–1865*. Edited by Candace O'Connor. St. Louis: Missouri Historical Society Press, 1991.

Rittenhouse, Jack D. *The Santa Fe Trail: A Historical Bibliography*. Albuquerque: University of New Mexico Press, 1971.

Ronda, James P. *Lewis and Clark among the Indians*. Lincoln: University of Nebraska Press, 1984.

Sabin, Edwin L. *Kit Carson Days, 1809–1868*. 2 vols. 1935. Reprint, with introduction by Marc Simmons. Lincoln: University of Nebraska Press, 1995.

Sandoval, David A. "Gnats, Goods, and Greasers: Mexican Merchants on the Santa Fe Trail." In Mark L. Gardner, ed., *The Mexican Road: Trade, Travel, and Confrontation on the Santa Fe Trail*, 22–31. Manhattan, Kans.: Sunflower University Press, 1989.

———. "Montezuma's Merchants: Mexican Traders on the Santa Fe Trail." In Leo E. Oliva, ed., *Adventure on the Santa Fe Trail*, 37–60. Topeka: Kansas State Historical Society, 1988.

———. "Who Is Riding the Burro Now? A Bibliographical Critique of Scholarship on the New Mexican Trade." In *The Santa Fe Trail: New Perspectives*, 75–92. Niwot: University Press of Colorado, 1992.

Shalhope, Robert E. *Sterling Price: Portrait of a Southerner*. Columbia: University of Missouri Press, 1971.

Simmons, Marc. *Coronado's Land: Essays on Daily Life in Colonial New Mexico*. Albuquerque: University of New Mexico Press, 1991.

———. *Following the Santa Fe Trail: A Guide for Modern Travelers*. Santa Fe: Ancient City Press, 1984.

———. *Murder on the Santa Fe Trail: An International Incident, 1843*. El Paso: Texas Western Press, 1987.

———. *New Mexico: An Interpretive History.* Albuquerque: University of New Mexico Press, 1988.

———. "New Mexico's Spanish Exiles." *New Mexico Historical Review* 59 (January 1984): 67–79.

———. *The Old Trail to Santa Fe: Collected Essays.* Albuquerque: University of New Mexico Press, 1996.

———. "The Santa Fe Trail as High Adventure." In Leo E. Oliva, ed., *Adventure on the Santa Fe Trail,* 1–9. Topeka: Kansas State Historical Society, 1988.

Simmons, Marc, with photographs by Joan Myers. *Along the Santa Fe Trail.* Albuquerque: University of New Mexico Press, 1986.

Smith, Ralph Adam. *Borderlander: The Life of James Kirker, 1793–1852.* Norman: University of Oklahoma Press, 1999.

———. "The 'King of New Mexico' and the Doniphan Expedition." *New Mexico Historical Review* 38 (January 1963): 29–55.

Stocking, Hobart E. *The Road to Santa Fe.* New York: Hastings House, 1971.

Thompson, Enid. "Life in an Adobe Castle, 1833–1849." In *Bent's Old Fort,* 7–27. State Historical Society of Colorado, 1979.

Townsend, Richard F. *The Aztecs.* London: Thames and Hudson, 1992.

Twitchell, Ralph Emerson. *The History of the Military Occupation of the Territory of New Mexico from 1846 to 1851 by the Government of the United States.* 1909. Reprint. Chicago: Rio Grande Press, 1963.

———. *The Leading Facts of New Mexican History.* 2 vols. Cedar Rapids, Iowa: Torch Press, 1912.

———. *Old Santa Fe: The Story of New Mexico's Ancient Capital.* 1925. Reprint. Chicago: Rio Grande Press, 1963.

Tyler, Daniel. "Gringo Views of Governor Manuel Armijo." *New Mexico Historical Review* 45 (January 1970): 23–46.

———. "Mexican Indian Policy in New Mexico." *New Mexico Historical Review* 55 (April 1980): 101–20.

Tyler, Sergeant Daniel. *A Concise History of the Mormon Battalion in the Mexican War, 1846–1847.* 1881. Reprint. Glorieta, N.M.: Rio Grande Press, 1969.

Unrau, William E. *The Kansa Indians: A History of the Wind People, 1673–1873.* Norman: University of Oklahoma Press, 1971.

Vestal, Stanley. *The Old Santa Fe Trail.* 1939. Reprint. Lincoln: University of Nebraska Press, 1996.

Vigil, Ralph H., Frances W. Kaye, and John R. Wunder, eds. *Spain and the Plains: Myths and Realities of Spanish Exploration and Settlement on the Great Plains.* Niwot: University Press of Colorado, 1994.

Viles, Jonas. "Old Franklin: A Frontier Town of the Twenties." *Mississippi Valley Historical Review* 9 (March 1923): 269–82.

Voelker, Frederic E. "Ruxton of the Rocky Mountains." *Bulletin of the Missouri Historical Society* 5 (January 1949): 79–89.

Wagner, Henry R., and Charles L. Camp. *The Plains and the Rockies: A Critical Bibliography of Exploration, Adventure and Travel in the American West, 1800–1865.* San Francisco: John Howell Books, 1982.

Weber, David J. *The Mexican Frontier, 1821–1846: The American Southwest under Mexico*. Albuquerque: University of New Mexico Press, 1982.

———. *On the Edge of Empire: The Taos Hacienda of Los Martínez*. Santa Fe: Museum of New Mexico Press, 1996.

———. *The Spanish Frontier in North America*. New Haven: Yale University Press, 1992.

———. *The Taos Trappers: The Fur Trade in the Far Southwest, 1540–1846*. Norman: University of Oklahoma Press, 1971.

———, ed. *New Spain's Far Northern Frontier: Essays on Spain in the American West, 1540–1821*. Albuquerque: University of New Mexico Press, 1979.

Wells, Eugene T. "The Growth of Independence, Missouri, 1827–1850." *Bulletin of the Missouri Historical Society* 16 (October 1959): 33–46.

Wolferman, Kristie C. *The Osage in Missouri*. Columbia: University of Missouri Press, 1997.

Young, Otis E. *The First Military Escort on the Santa Fe Trail, 1829*. Glendale, Calif.: Arthur H. Clark, 1952.

———. "Military Protection of the Santa Fé Trail and Trade." *Missouri Historical Review* 49 (October 1954): 19–32.

———. *The West of Philip St. George Cooke, 1809–1895*. Glendale, Calif.: Arthur H. Clark, 1955.

Index